Chichester Excavations V

The late Dr. Francis Steer
(from a drawing by Nigel Purchase, 1965, reproduced by permission of Philip Harris, Esq.)

Chichester Excavations V

by

Alec Down

with specialist contributions by
Marion Archibald, M.A., F.M.A., F.S.A. F. G. Aldsworth, B.A., F.S.A.
Helena Barnes, M.B., M.R.C.P. Sarnia Butcher, B.A., F.S.A.
Robert Charleston, B.A., F.S.A. Dorothy Charlesworth, M.A., F.S.A.
G. B. Dannell, F.S.A. Brenda Dickinson, B.A. Brian Hartley, M.A., F.S.A.
Mark Hassall, F.S.A. Dr. Martin Henig, M.A., D.Phil., F.S.A. Roger Lintott
D. F. Mackreth, B.A., F.S.A. Sheila Morgan R. R. Morgan Julian Munby, M.A.
Dr. D. P. S. Peacock, Ph.D., F.S.A. Valery Rigby, B.A.
Anthony Streeten, B.A. Dr. Graham Webster, M.A., Ph.D., F.S.A.
Dr. C. J. Young, M.A., D.Phil., F.S.A.

Published for
Chichester Excavations Committee

by

Phillimore

Acknowledgements

The Committee wish to record their thanks to the undermentioned bodies whose generous donations have made this publication possible:

H.M. Department of the Environment
West Sussex County Council
Chichester District Council
Chichester City Council
C. Howard & Sons Ltd.
Geoffrey Osborne Ltd.
A. Olby & Sons Ltd.
John Wiley Ltd.
Marks & Spencer Ltd.
Whiteheads Ltd.
Thomas Eggar & Co.

ISBN 0 85033 415 2

Published by
PHILLIMORE & CO. LTD.,
Shopwyke Hall, Chichester, Sussex

Printed and bound in England by
PLYMOUTH WEB OFFSET LTD.
Plymouth, Devon

Foreword

This fifth volume of the Chichester excavation reports is dedicated to the memory of Francis Steer, who died in September 1978, Maltravers Herald Extraordinary, historian and scholar, and a great friend of Sussex archaeology.

Born at Ashington in Essex in 1912, he began his career as a historian as Assistant Archivist to the Essex County Record Office, a post he was to hold from 1946 to 1953. His elevation to Sussex came in 1953, when he was appointed County Archivist of both the East and West of the county. Six years later, in 1959, he moved to Chichester, as County Archivist for West Sussex, when the arduous dual post was eventually split. For the next decade he became deeply involved with the history and archaeology of the city, serving on the Chichester Excavations Committee, editing a highly successful series of Chichester Papers to which he regularly contributed and acting as archivist to the Bishop and Dean and Chapter.

In 1969 he retired from his post as County Archivist to give more time to his other impressive range of activities, foremost among which was his curatorship of the Archives and Library of the Duke of Norfolk at Arundel Castle. This was to be an energetic period in his already busy life. He could list among his many activities Archivist to New College, Oxford, and to the College of Arms, editor of the Sussex Archaeological Collections and honorary secretary to the Marc Fitch Fund. Failing health, however, required him to give up much of this work in 1977, only a year before he died.

A mere catalogue of activities and achievements gives little impression of the man. I remember him particularly as a friendly man with a quiet jollity, a man who could easily be approached and would encourage, but who would not tolerate the second best. His love of scholarship, thoroughness and quiet determination made him a great strength to those of us who worked in Chichester in the sixties and seventies. We are among the many who gained reassurance from his unassuming confidence, and understanding from his wisdom.

BARRY CUNLIFFE

Author's Note

This volume follows on from Volume 3, published in 1978, and is the record of a series of excavations carried out within the historic core of the city and outside the walls. The work spans almost the complete life of the town, from A.D. 43 until the 17th century.

There has been a shift of emphasis during the last few years; as many of the available prime development sites within the walls have been built on, the rescue threat is now towards sites outside the walls and wherever possible these are being investigated in advance. As will be seen, the policy of excavating the extra mural areas where Roman and medieval suburbs are likely to be has paid handsome dividends in terms of new knowledge and this will be extended in Volume 6, due out in about three years' time, when the results of the vast Roman excavation on the Cattlemarket site outside the south-east walls will be published. The excavations in the north-west quadrant have filled in a number of gaps between the sites dug along Chapel Street and Crane Street and reported on in Volume 3 and this has resulted in fresh dating evidence for the final phase of the large Roman house on the north side of the Chapel Street cross roads and a reconsideration of the dating of some of the 1st-century timber buildings. One of the most exciting and demanding projects reported in the following pages has been the recording of the work by contractors within the new pedestrian precinct and this has produced a rich harvest of discoveries which at present can only be imperfectly understood. The work started in 1977 and has not quite finished as this note goes to press. It has been a triumph of co-operation on the part of the County and District Councils; the contractors, Geoffrey Osborne Ltd., J. Doyle Ltd. and O. C. Summers Ltd.; the Portsmouth Water Co. Ltd., Southerngas and the Post Office. We are also indebted to Messrs. Marks & Spencer, who gave us every facility to observe the contractors' work on their site, and who made a generous contribution towards the cost of publishing the results.

On other sites, the help given to us by the landowners and their architects is acknowledged in the introductions to the relevant sections of the reports. The Supervisors were Helen Porter, John Piper, Ann Leyland, Aiden Cooper, Alison Macaulay and Fred Aldsworth and the site assistants, Frank Greenaway, Wilf Shannon, Jane Russell and Jack Eschbaecher. Max Wholey drew the samian wares illustrated in the report, together with most of the small finds. Diane Dixon of the Department of the Environment drew the gladius from Chapel Street; Jenny Stringer was responsible for the illustrations of the medieval glass and Ann Leyland, John Piper, F. G. Aldsworth and the Writer drew the pottery, plans and sections. The bulk of the small finds were conserved in our laboratory by Ron Maskelyne and Carol Edwards, but we owe considerable thanks to John

Musty and the staff of the Ancient Monuments Laboratory of the D.O.E., especially Leo Biek, John Price, Justine Bayley, Maureen Girling, Alison Locker, Glynis Edwards and Carole Keepax for their co-operation, and for their forbearance in dealing, often at short notice, with problems of conservation and analysis. The bulk of the excavation work on the north-west quadrant sites was carried out by young people employed on the first of a number of Job Creation schemes financed by the Manpower Services Commission and augmented at weekends and holiday times by our regular team of volunteers.

Professor Barry Cunliffe kindly read the reports in draft and made a number of helpful comments. However, I must reserve to myself full responsibility for any errors which persist.

Finally, the assembly of the many parts of this volume into a coherent document would not have been possible without Beryl Bray, who typed most of the manuscripts; John Piper and Carol Edwards, who spent many hours checking the drawings and typescript, and to Betty and Christopher Down who assisted with the proof reading and uncomplainingly put up with the disruption of their home life for over a year.

ALEC DOWN

Abbreviations

ANT. J.	*Antiquaries Journal*
ARCH. J.	*Archaeological Journal*
ARCH. AEL.	*Archaeologia Aeliana*
B.A.R.	*British Archaeological Reports, Oxford*
C I L	*Corpus Inscriptione Latinorum*
RIB	*Roman Inscriptions of Britain, Vol. I (Oxford)*
S.R. (with date)	*Chichester Excavations Committee Annual Summary Reports*
S.A.C.	*Sussex Archaeological Collections*
VCH Sx.	*Victoria County History, Sussex*

Contents

Reports published at Level III (in archive)

a) *Various specialist reports from the Ancient Monuments Laboratory of the Department of the Environment.*

i) Roman fish bones from Chapel Street by Alison Locker.
ii) The conservation of the Roman gladius from Chapel Street by Maureen Robson.
iii) Examination of tesserae from Chapel Street by F. W. Anderson.
iv) Examination of replaced organic material from Chapel Street by Carole Keepax.
v) Report on the seed impressions on straw-tempered Saxon loomweights by P. Paradine.

b) *Other reports*

vi) Detailed report on the late-Saxon loomweights from Chapel Street by Carol Edwards.
vii) The Roman mortaria by K. Hartley.
viii) The post-Flavian Roman fine wares from the sites (Part II) by C. J. Young.
ix) The human skeletal remains from Eastgate (Part II) by Helena Barnes.
x) The figured samian ware (Part II) by G. B. Dannell.

Note: All the Level III Reports listed above have been deposited with the Chichester District Museum, together with the finds and the schedules. Excavation records and working drawings will be deposited in the West Sussex Record Office and eventually micro-film copies will be held in the National Monuments Record.

List of Subscribers 299

List of Plates

(between pages 228 and 229)

ACKNOWLEDGEMENTS TO PLATES

Robert Wilkins, Plates 19 a and 19 b; John Adams, Plate 13; Alec Down, remainder.

Sites location plan.

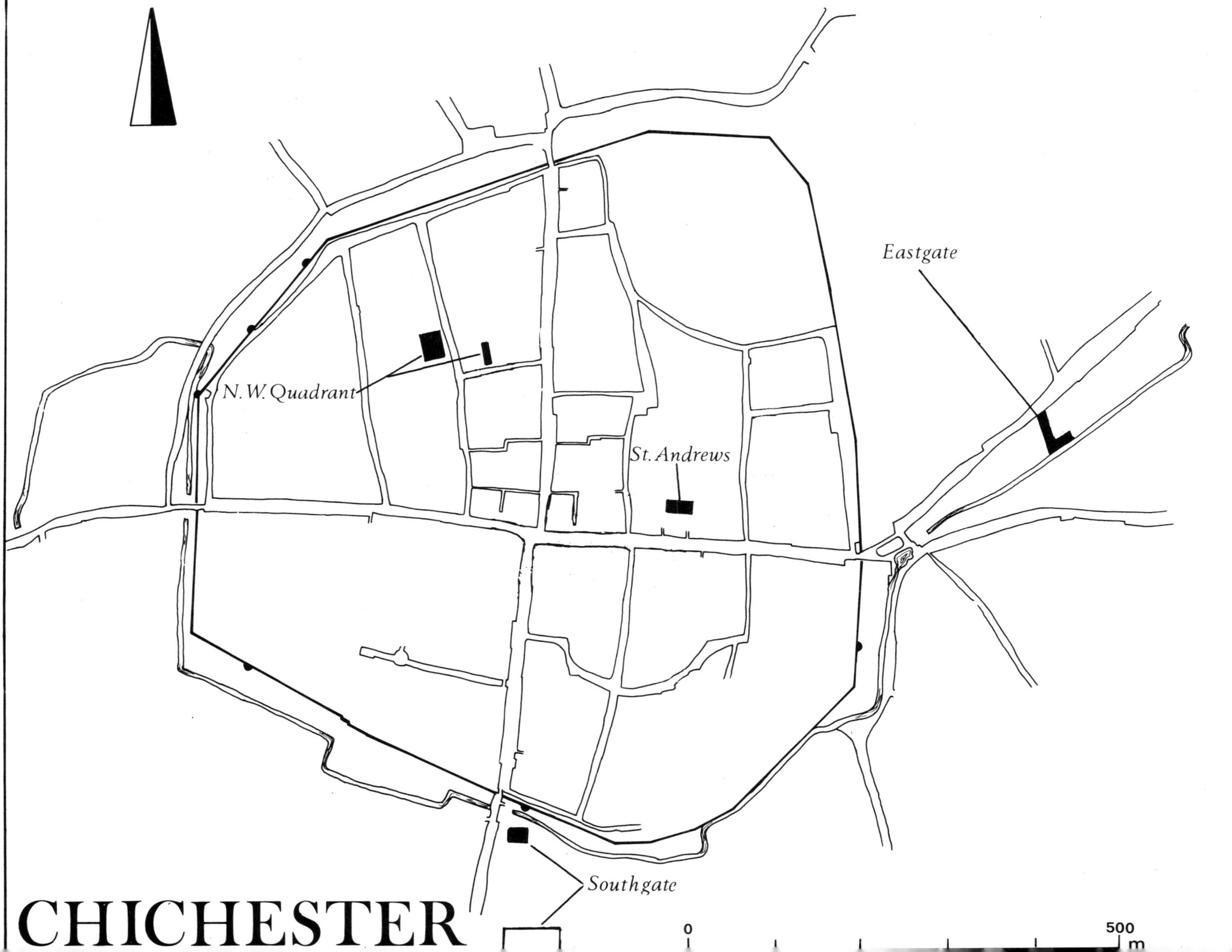

1

The Church of St. Andrew-in-the-Oxmarket, Chichester

This church became redundant in 1953 following upon the reorganisation of the urban parishes within the city. It had been disused since 1943, as a result of bomb damage and after the furniture and fittings had been removed in 1959, the building was leased to the Trustees of the Chichester Arts Centre in 1972. The money for the first phase of the Arts Centre project having been raised in 1975, work was planned to commence at the end of January 1976. The Committee for the Trustees readily gave permission for limited excavation to take place inside the east end of the church in advance of building works, and we are grateful to Mrs. Doris Wilson, the Chairman of the Committee and to Mr. John Dixon, the Architect, for their help. The work was funded by a small grant from the Department of the Environment.

The intention was to study where possible the construction of the building, to try to establish its date and whether a Saxon church lay below. It was known that part of a Roman tessellated floor had been located below the floor of the church (*Chichester 1*, p. 10, No. 15) and it was hoped to be able to relate this to other fragments of Roman building in the vicinity (*Chichester 2*, pp. 104–113). Two weeks were allowed for this work, which took place in late December to early January 1976. The excavation was supervised for the greater part of the time by Fred Aldsworth, who also carried out a survey of the building and drew the plans and section which accompany this report.

The excavations

The original intention had been to open up three areas within the church, but the presence of post-medieval burials necessitated a change of plan and eventually six trenches were dug (Fig. 1.2).

Roman (Fig. 1.3)

Roman. It was found that the east wall of the church was built upon a tessellated pavement. A wall (Wall 1), running north–south bounded this floor on the west side, about 3 metres from the east end of the church. It was 0.57 metre thick and constructed of flints in buff mortar and there was a 9 cm offset on the west side. It stood to a height of 0.60 metre up to the offset and there was a band of red-painted wall plaster on the west side above it, which suggests that it was an outside wall. The practice of plastering and painting exterior flint wall surfaces down to just below ground level to weatherproof them has been noted at one of the Chilgrove Roman villas (*Chichester 4*, 88).

The north–south wall was joined by a second wall (Wall 2) of similar construction, coming in at right-angles from the east side. On the west side of Wall 1 was a series of layers of mortar, crushed chalk and loam which butted up against the wall (Fig. 1.5). These layers thinned out and sloped westwards but, owing to the limitations of the excavation and disturbance by later grave digging, it was not possible to establish whether they represented earlier destruction debris re-laid

ST. ANDREW'S CHURCH

INTERNAL ELEVATIONS & GROUND PLAN

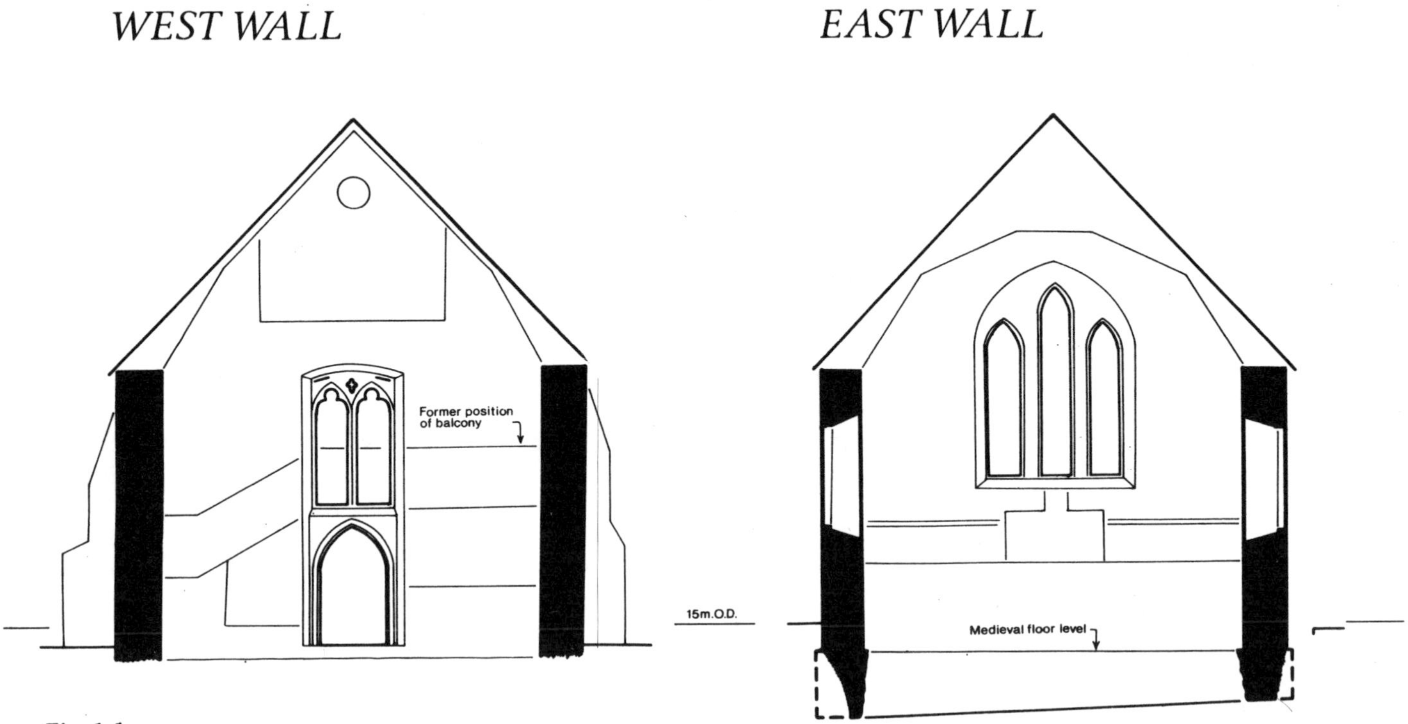

Fig. 1.1

as a base for a floor or a courtyard. Amongst the debris were numbers of red tile tesserae and some smaller ones from a destroyed mosaic, together with amounts of wall plaster painted pink. The dateable pottery from the layers (D49–D52), consisted of samian sherds of Antonine date and a sherd of Rhenish ware and all that can be said is that the deposition post-dated the end of the second century.

Discussion

The Roman house of which the features excavated were a part must face on to East Street. Other parts of this building have been noted previously. The mosaic found below the rear of David Greig's shop in 1959 and the fragmentary remains of a tessellated pavement and a hypocaust found during excavations in Sadler's garden from 1959–63 must belong to the same house (*Chichester 2*, 110–113 and Pl. 14). There the evidence for the final phase of the house suggests a 4th-century date and there is nothing in the destruction debris re-laid as a floor base on the west side of Wall 1 to disagree with this.

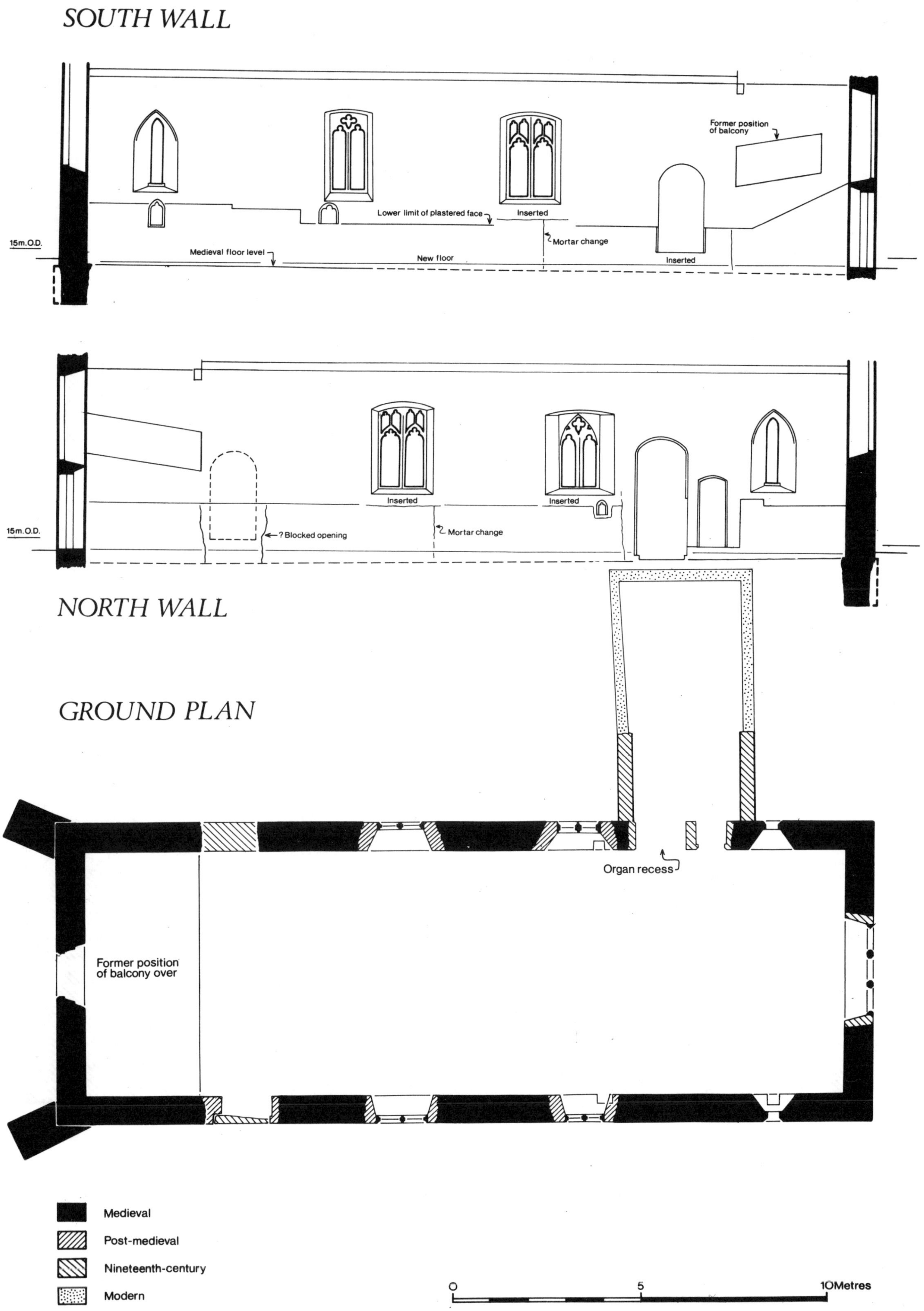
SOUTH WALL
Former position of balcony
Lower limit of plastered face
Inserted
Mortar change
15m. O.D.
Medieval floor level
New floor
Inserted
15m. O.D.
Inserted
Inserted
? Blocked opening
Mortar change
NORTH WALL
GROUND PLAN
Organ recess
Former position of balcony over
Medieval
Post-medieval
Nineteenth-century
Modern
0
5
10Metres

ST. ANDREW'S CHURCH
MEDIEVAL & LATER FEATURES

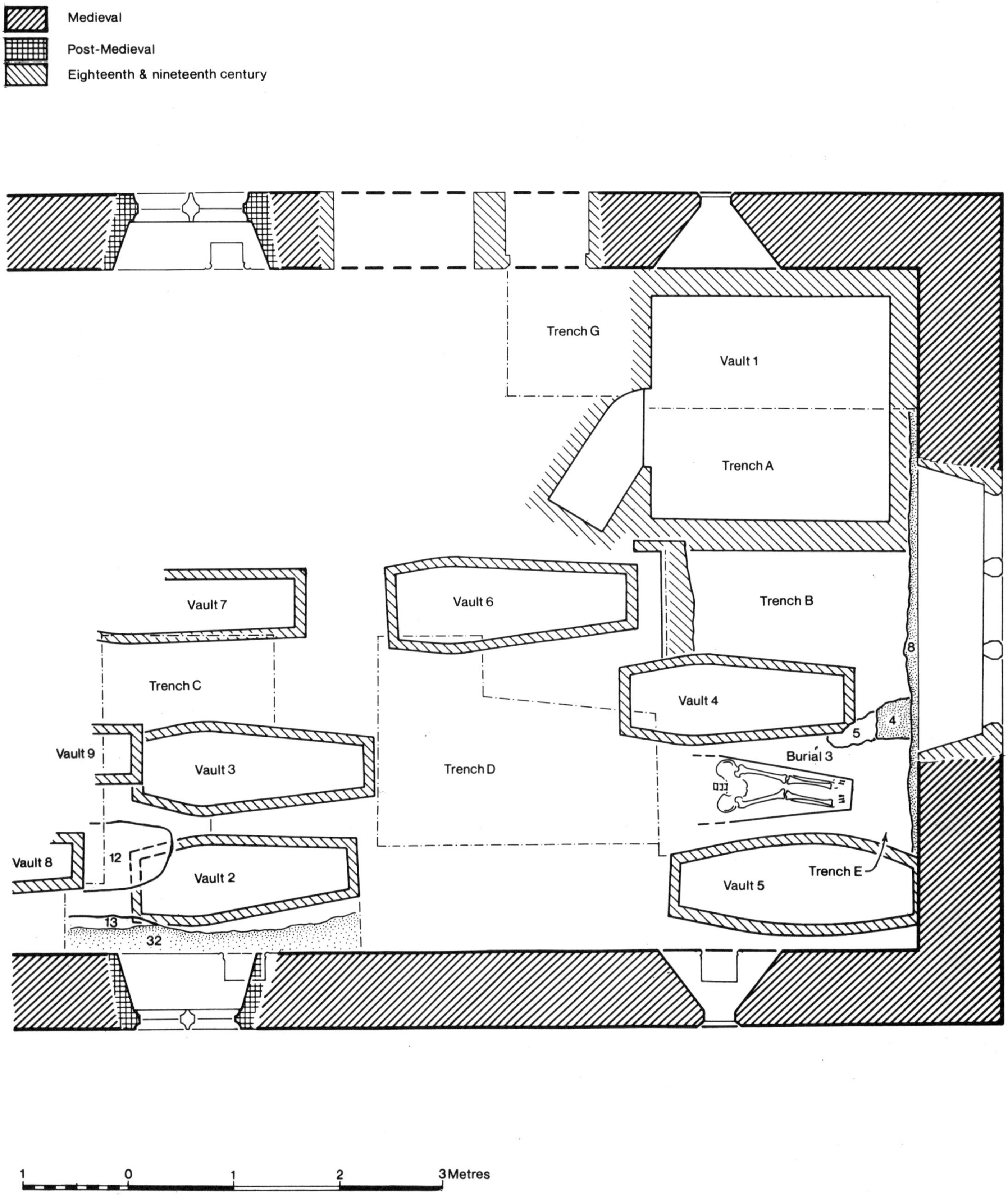

Fig. 1.2

ST. ANDREW'S CHURCH
ROMAN FEATURES

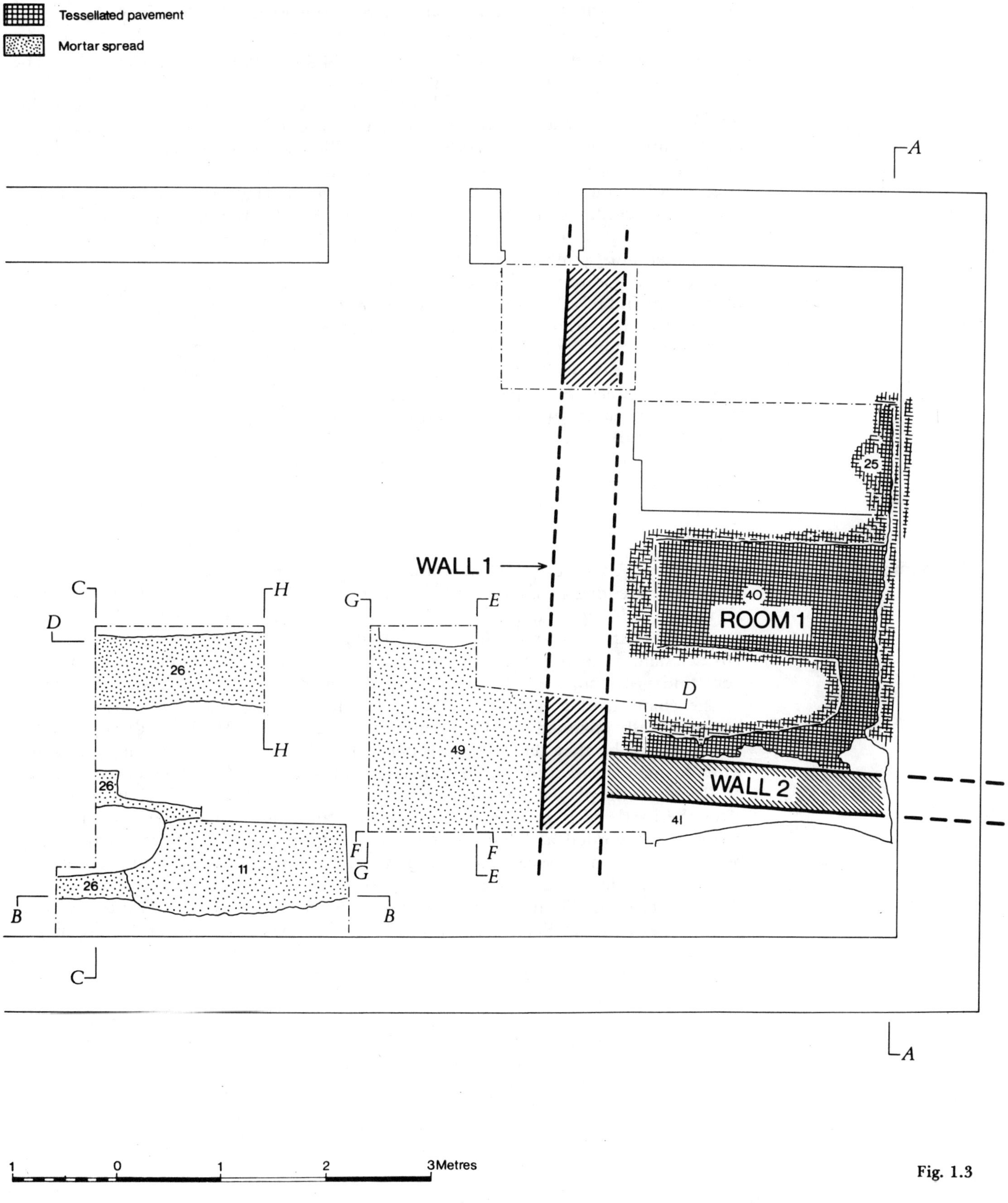

Fig. 1.3

Medieval and later features

Within the area investigated there was no evidence to suggest that an earlier church with a different ground plan ever existed on the site.

The footings of the standing structure were investigated under the east wall (Trenches A, B and E—Section A) and under the south wall (Trench C—Section B). Under the east wall they comprised alternate layers of loam and buff-mortared rubble (Layers 17 and 24 inclusive), standing directly upon the Roman pavement (Layers 25 and 40). Any evidence for a foundation trench had been completely destroyed by the brick vaults, although a fragment of what may have been foundation trench fill was seen in Trench E (Layer 5).

Under the south wall, in Trench C, the situation appeared more complex. The upper consolidation layers were cut by a loam-filled feature (Layer 13), which appears to continue westwards. This was overlaid by mortared rubble (Layer 35) which appears to be a wall foundation. This was cut by a pit or trench (Layer 34), which appears to have been subsequently filled with rubble (Layer 33). These layers (33 to 35) were overlaid by the mortared rubble foundation of the south wall of the church (Layer 32). The pit or trench (Layers 33 and 34) did not appear to continue northwards into the church. Within the limited space available the precise form and function of these features could not be determined, and must remain in doubt.

The Roman consolidation levels were cut, in Trench C, by what appears to be the eastern end of a Medieval or post-Medieval grave with a loam fill (Layer 12).

The floor levels contemporary with the Medieval church had been completely destroyed within the area investigated, except for a narrow lip of mortar (Layer 8) along the east wall of the church at 14.5 metres OD and, in Trench E, this was accompanied by a patch of mortar (Layer 4) overlying rubble (Layer 5), which appeared to be the foundation trench fill of the east wall of the church. Part of a coffin burial (Burial 3) was located in Trench E, which had been partially cut into the top of Wall 2, but both this and the nine brick vaults appear to be of eighteenth- or nineteenth-century date.

The memorials

A survey of the surviving memorials within the church was carried out and this was later extended to include the copying of the inscriptions on the tombstones in the churchyard and those set in the paved area. Those in the church were compared with those recorded by the late Mr. Lindsay Fleming (*Fleming* 1957, 16–22), and it is not thought necessary to repeat them here. One important new find not recorded by him, was the discovery, lying loose among the rubble in the chancel, of a memorial tablet (Pl. 1), recording Thomas Gounter whose life practically spanned the 17th century, being born in 1611 and dying in 1696. It might well be that the tablet was below the altar and thus not seen by Fleming when he made his record. Thomas Gounter was cousin to Colonel George Gounter of Racton who played an important part in getting Charles II safely to France after the battle of Worcester in 1651. A Captain Thomas Gounter, cousin to the colonel, is recorded as having helped in the attempt to get a boat for the King, but this is not necessarily the same man as the one recorded on the tablet as it appears that there was at least one other Thomas Gounter who was cousin to the colonel.[1] Our Thomas was the son of Richard Gounter or Gunter, who is recorded as living in East Street in 1621. He was a younger member of the family from Racton.[2] The stone is now in the care of the Chichester District Museum.

Notes

1. Information from Mrs. Alison McCann, WSRO.
2. Information from Mr. R. R. Morgan, Documentary Research Group.

The Structure of St. Andrew's Church[1]

by F. G. Aldsworth, B.A., F.S.A.

The church is generally assigned, on architectural grounds, to the thirteenth century and a documentary source infers that it was mentioned "slightly earlier than 1248".[2]

The roofed church survived, in January 1976, as a rectangular shell measuring internally 20.08 metres by 6.47 metres, with a vestry on the east end of the north side which appears to have been added between 1852 and 1873[3] to accommodate an organ recess. The vestry appears to have been extended northwards in recent years. The walls of the church are between 0.70 and 0.75 metre thick. They are straight and have been externally rendered with pebbledash, preventing any detailed study of the relationship between the architectural features and the walls on the outer faces, apart from the lower portion of the north-east quoin. Internally the walls are plastered though several areas of stone coursing were visible where the panelling and balcony had been removed. The west doorway is through a two-centred arch with continuous chamfered jambs of thirteenth- or fourteenth-century date. Above this is a fairly recently inserted window of two trefoil lights with a quatrefoil and tracery under a segmental head. In the gable is a small circular opening and over the gable is a weather-boarded turret with shingled pinnacle which is shown on a drawing of 1852.[4] At the north-west and south-west corners are diagonal buttresses with sloping offsets. These are not centrally placed on the corners suggesting that they are additions.

On the interior elevation of the west wall and to the north of the west door, which had been inserted in an earlier wall, the lower 1.10 metres of the regular rubble courses on the wall were visible and were of stone and flint in yellow mortar which is not dissimilar in character to that found in the footings of the east and south walls during excavation. This wall contained one course of flint and stone laid at an angle but not in true "herring-bone" style. The lower 1.30 metres of the north wall was stripped of plaster and the fabric of the west wall was seen to continue along this wall, though interrupted by a blocked opening, for a distance of 9.20 metres (see Fig. 1.1), at which point there was a distinct change in the fabric above the foundation level. The foundation appeared to continue in yellow mortar but the wall above was built of very irregular courses of knapped and nodular flint in a white mortar, which contained small lumps of yellow mortar, presumably re-used during rebuilding. This rebuild continued eastward at least as far as the nineteenth-century organ recess and doorway and, although the old plaster had not been completely removed, the white mortar containing lumps of yellow mortar appeared to continue and probably dates from the addition of the probably thirteenth-century north-east quoin.

ST. ANDREW'S CHURCH
SECTIONS

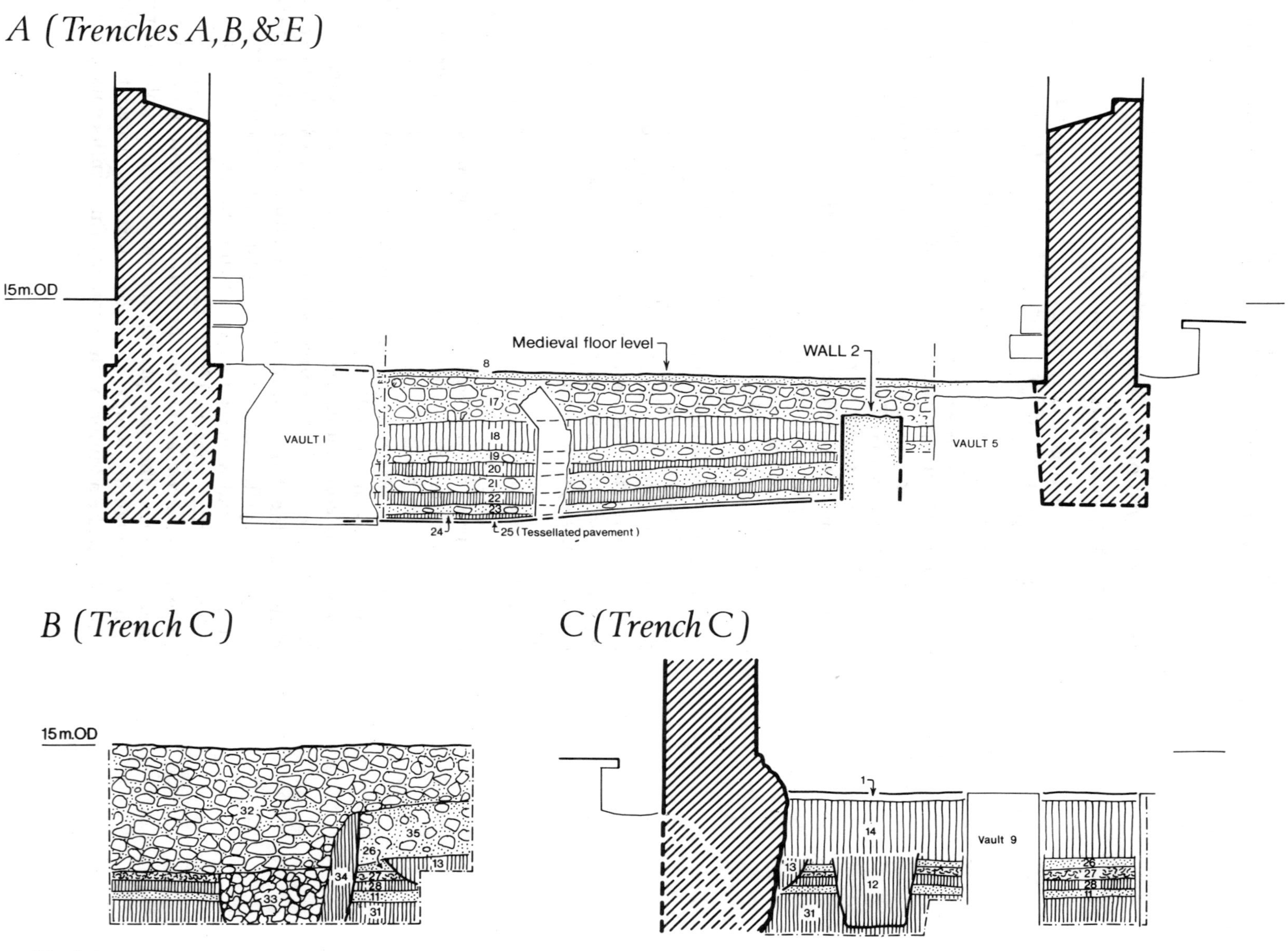

Fig. 1.4

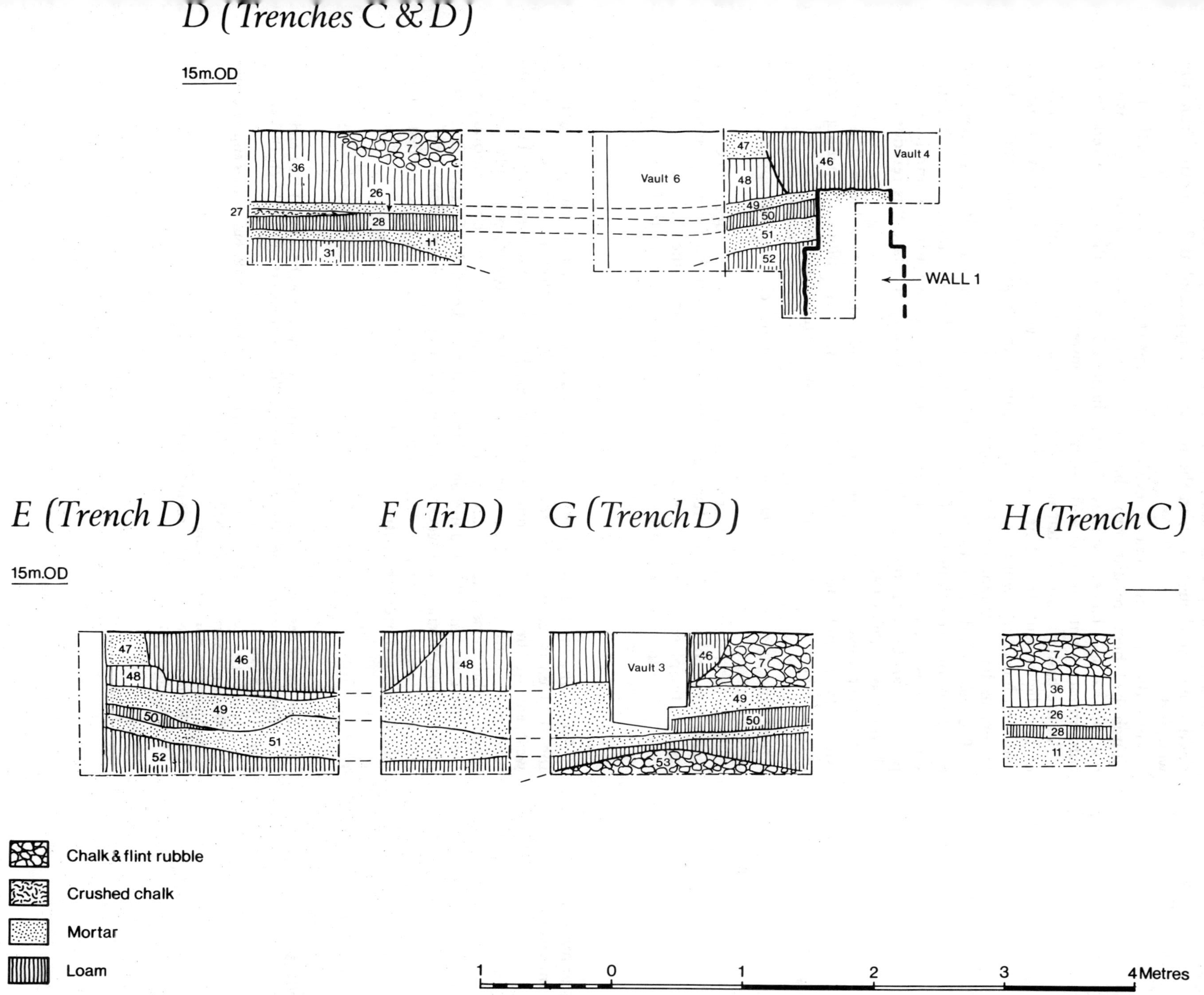
D (Trenches C & D)
15m.OD
36
7
26
27
28
11
31
Vault 6
47
48
46
49
50
51
52
Vault 4
WALL 1
E (Trench D)
F (Tr.D)
G (Trench D)
H (Trench C)
15m.OD
47
46
48
49
50
51
52
48
Vault 3
46
7
49
50
53
7
36
26
28
11
Chalk & flint rubble
Crushed chalk
Mortar
Loam
1
0
1
2
3
4 Metres

Fig. 1.5

The evidence seen in the south wall differed little from that seen in the north wall although the plaster had not been so extensively removed. The very distinctive mortar change, seen in the north wall, appeared at 8.0 metres from the west end.

Thus there is considerable evidence to suggest that the eastern half of the church had been rebuilt, probably in the thirteenth-century when the pair of opposed single lancet windows were included, since these appeared to be contemporary with the wall and had not been inserted.

At the eastern end of what was the nave, a pair of fourteenth-century windows of two lights with trefoil heads and tracery above and, further west, a pair of fourteenth-century windows of two lights with cinquefoil heads and vertical tracery under a segmental arch had been inserted.

The east window, a triple lancet under a two-centred arch, is modern and post-dates Borrer's drawing of 1852 on which a fourteenth-century window is shown. A wooden reredos once stood beneath the east window and its former position can be seen on the plaster face. A faculty to place this reredos in the church was made in 1901.[5]

Near the west end of the south wall is an inserted, but now blocked, doorway with curved head and opposite, in the north wall, is a blocked opening which may also have been a doorway. At the eastern end of the nave are two trefoil-headed piscinas, one on each side, indicating the former position of the rood screen, and there is another in the south wall of the chancel. All appear to have been inserted.

Fleming[6] refers to the western gallery, which may have been erected in the eighteenth-century, but this has been removed although its former position was seen on the plaster face of the walls at the western end of the church.

At no point was any earlier plaster face seen other than that which appears to be of nineteenth-century date.

Summary and conclusion

Although, on the evidence of the east end, the church should be assigned to the thirteenth-century, the footings and at least the lower 1.30 metres of the west end of the standing church are earlier, but how much earlier? The north-west and south-west quoins are not visible internally or externally, and the diagonal buttresses, which are probably additions, may be contemporary with the west door and the rebuilding of the east end, i.e. *c.* 1300. Thus there is, at present, no evidence to suggest a date for the original construction of the church either on archaeological or architectural grounds, although it was substantially rebuilt in the thirteenth century.

Notes

1. For earlier descriptions, see *Victoria County History (Sussex)* 3; (1935), 161 and Lindsay Fleming, *The Little Churches of Chichester*, Chichester Papers No. 5 (1957), 16–22.
2. *VCH* 3 (1935), 165.
3. It is not shown on Borrer's drawing of the 27th August 1852, but it does appear on the Ordnance Survey map of 1873.
4. Shown on Borrer's drawing.
5. Document No. 5325 in Diocesan Office.
6. *Fleming, op. cit.* p. 17.

2

Addendum to Roman Gazetteer (Fig. 2.1)

Note:—Figure numbers run on from *Chichester 3*, see pp. 17–21, that volume. More detailed notes on the finds resulting from works within the pedestrian precinct are given in "Chichester Below the Streets", this volume, pp. 22-57, and in the various annual summary reports (*SR* with date), available from the Chichester District Museum.

North-East Quadrant includes both sides of North and East Streets

107. *Northgate*

Gas main trench in 1977 cut through part of a masonry wall at Northgate. This may have been part of the west guard-tower of Northgate.

108. *North Street*

At junction with Crane Street; excavations for a manhole in 1977 cut through a layer of gravel which might be the junction of the east-west Roman street and Roman North Street.

109. *North Street*

In front of No. 23; excavations for a sewer interceptor in 1978 showed a layer of gravel which might be part of the large gravel spread seen in the north-west quadrant excavations (*Chichester 3*. 97).

110. *North Street*

Sewer interceptor holes dug through North Street in 1977 and 1978 showed walls and floors belonging to at least one large building running east-west across North Street, with a hypocaust in front of the Buttermarket.

111. *East Street*

In front of the Midland Bank; a line of massive sandstone blocks were found in 1979. They were aligned north-south and might be the remains of a stylobate. Another wall joined it at right-angles from the east.

112. *East Street*

On the north side of the street in front of Hardy and Co., a layer of mortar and gravel at a depth of 1.38 metre. Possibly the remains of a hardstanding. This was seen again further east.

113. *East Street*

Outside No. 5 (National Westminster Bank), Roman destruction levels with ashlar masonry and flue tiles, which had been cut by a later pit.

114. *East Street*

No. 5 (National Westminster Bank); (*SR* 1978). Building work in the basement showed the following features:

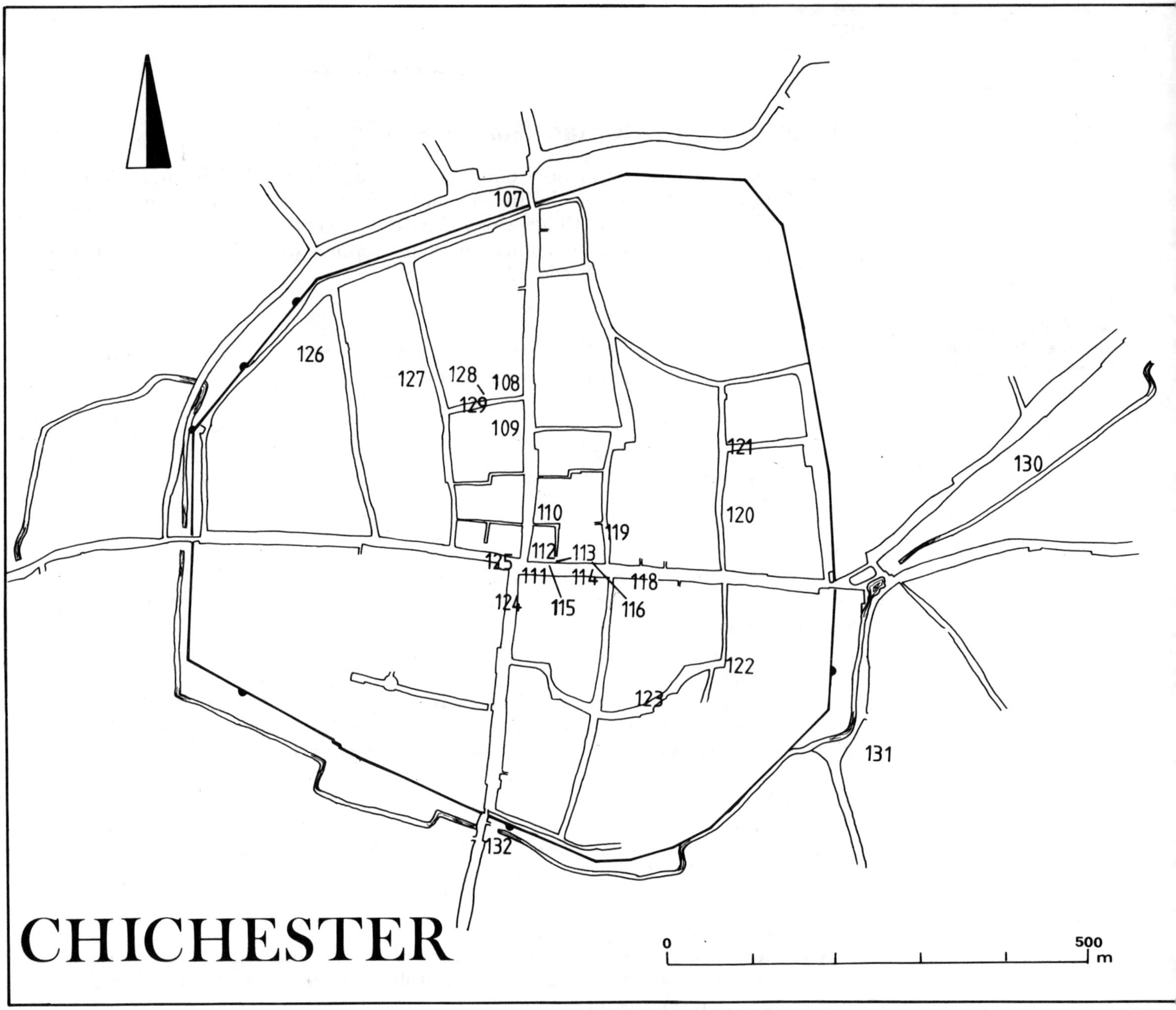

Fig. 2.1. Roman Gazetteer.

(i) A Roman wall running north–south with a spread of demolition debris on the east side.

(ii) A second wall aligned east–west joining the first wall on the east side. It was approximately 6.45 metres from the north kerb of East Street.

115. *East Street*

In 1977 in front of Tesco and Lloyds Bank. A large sandstone block set into compacted gravel. Possibly a column base.

116. *East Street*

In front of Lloyds Bank in 1979. Excavations revealed the south face of an east–west wall resting upon a layer of gravel. The remains of a gutter were seen running alongside and a layer of dirty compacted gravel abutted the gutter. This was cambered and might be the north edge of the Roman street.

117. *East Street*

Surface water drainage trench in 1977 cut through Roman and medieval street levels in the centre of the road, with some evidence for medieval robbing or pit digging.

118. *East Street*

A series of excavations for sewer interceptors in 1979 along the south edge of East Street cut through compacted gravel lying above earlier occupation layers. The gravel had a layer of silt above and probably represents the edge of Roman East Street.

119. *St. Martin's Street* (*SR*. 1979) (Fig. 5.24)

(i) North–south Roman wall found during laying of new sewer west of Marks and Spencer's. This was joined by an east–west wall coming in from the east.

(ii) The same sewer trench struck a deep feature running east–west, probably a Roman timber-lined sewer. This was confirmed by later excavations within Marks and Spencer's. (This volume, p. 39).

(iii) North of (ii) above, and behind Marks and Spencer's. Building works struck a layer of compacted gravel aligned east–west, almost certainly a Roman Street (Fig. 5.24).

120. *Little London* (*SR* 1979)

A Roman north–south wall was found in 1980 when the Water Company laid a new main. Later on in the same year, part of a hypocaust belonging to the same building was found when alterations were carried out in the cellar of No. 35. The hypocaust had gone out of use, the flue blocked and a mortar floor laid over the top.

121. *East Row* (*SR* 1979)

East-west Roman wall found (this volume, p. 48, and Fig. 5.23).

South-East Quadrant

122. *Newtown* (*SR* 1977)

Roman north–south street confirmed during street works in 1977.

123. *East Pallant*

A north-south Roman wall discovered outside Thomas Eggars in a gas main trench in 1979.

124. *South Street* (*SR* 1977)

(i) East-west Roman walls recorded in 1977 when surface water drain laid.

(ii) North-south Roman wall found in 1980 when sewer interceptors dug on the east side of South Street. This is the eastern wall of the building noted in (i) above and this building is seen to run across the north end of South Street.

North-West Quadrant

125. *West Street*

In 1977, the surface water drainage trench cut through a layer of compacted gravel. Below this was a spread of Roman building debris sealing a layer of dirty clay. This appears to be from a destroyed building below the "Dolphin and Anchor".

126. *County Hall.* Excavation site; (*SR* 1978)

Excavations north of the Council Chamber in 1978 showed a number of phases of timber buildings with cesspits and two wells. The earliest occupation on the site was mid 1st century, with timber revetted drains below. The contemporary ground surface yielded two ballistae bolt heads and two legionary belt buckles.

127. *Chapel Street.* Excavation site 1977. (*SR* 1977 and this vol., p. 119)

(i) Part of Roman House 2 (*Chichester 3*, Fig. 7.3), alongside Roman street.

(ii) An earlier timber-framed building below House 2.

(iii) A series of timber-framed buildings below, the earliest of which were military.

128. *Crane Street.* Excavation site; (*SR* 1978 and this volume, p. 147)

An east-west Roman street (Street 3), noted in 1972 excavations (*Chichester 3*, Fig. 7.20), found at the south end of the site, with a gravel courtyard to the north. Below the courtyard and street were timber buildings aligned north-south with timber-lined drains below. The earliest were of Flavian date.

129. *Crane Street* (*SR* 1977)

Part of a Roman tile-bonded wall was found during street works in 1977, probably relating to a building on the south side of Street 3 (see No. 128 above).

Outside Eastgate

130. *Needlemakers 1978.* (This volume, p. 77)

(i) More inhumations belonging to the late Roman cemetery first noted in 1976 were found.

(ii) A military ditch aligned north-east-south-west found at the south end of the site. This may be another "leg" of the ditch found below the Roman cremation cemetery on the north side of St. Pancras in 1965 (*Chichester 1*, 53). It was cut by the River Lavant, which in its present course must post-date the 1st century A.D.

131. *Cattlemarket 1978–80*, (*SR* 1979)

Excavations since 1978 have recorded the following sequence of Roman occupation:

(i) A defensive ditch aligned north-east–south-west, probably of late 1st century date. It may represent an earlier defensive system for the civitas capital.
(ii) A series of timber buildings east of the ditch, some of which may be of mid 1st century date.
(iii) Continuous occupation from the 1st to the late 4th century, the later phases being associated with iron working.

Outside Southgate

132. *Southgate* (This volume, p. 59)

Roman pits recorded in 1979 during building works.

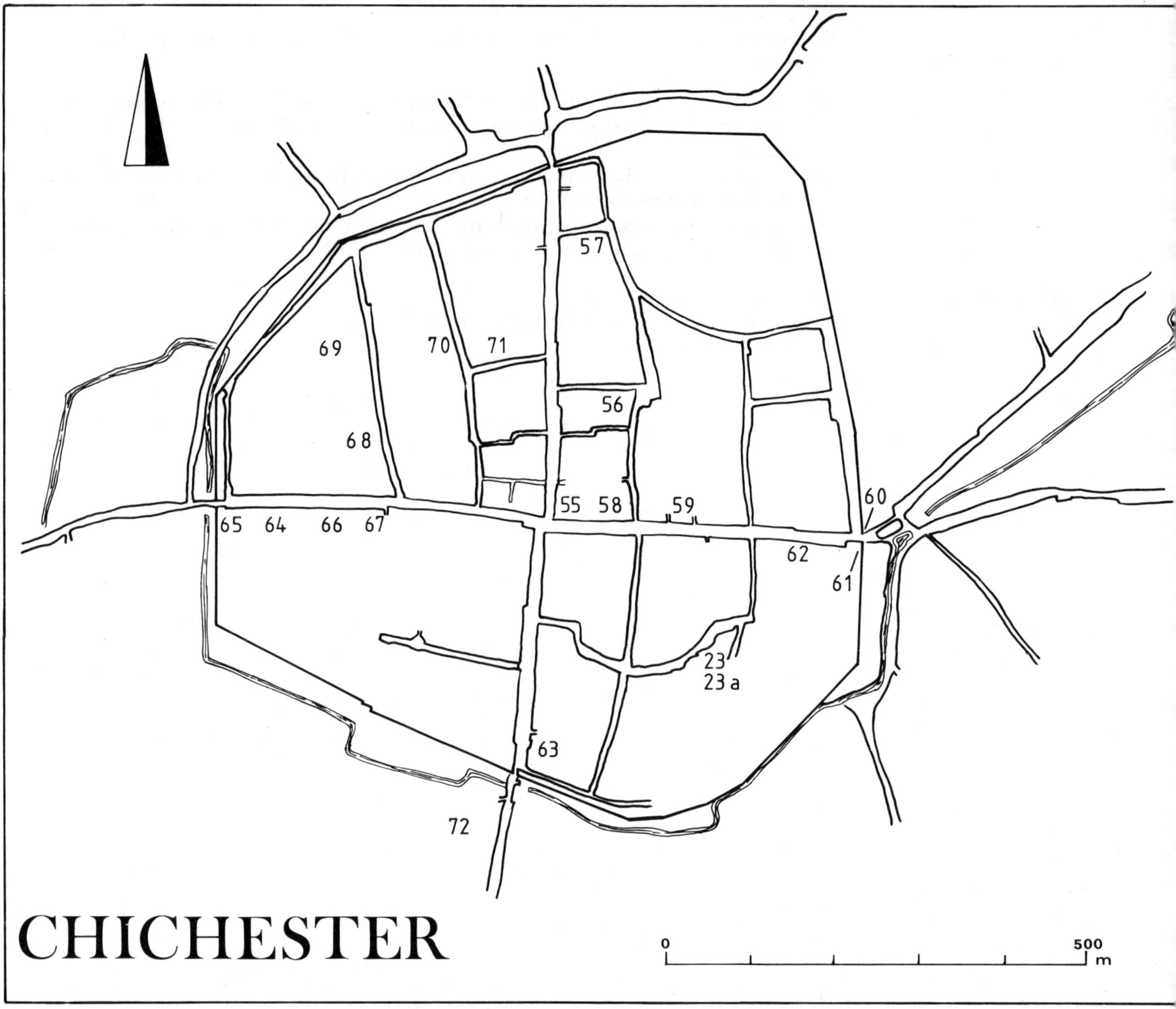

Fig. 3.1. Saxon and Medieval Gazetteer.

3, 4

Addenda to the Gazetteers of Saxon, Medieval and Post-medieval Sites in Chichester

by R. R. Morgan

General Note

Since the Gazetteers in *Chichester 2* and *Chichester 3* were published, continuing documentary research has extended our knowledge of sites. In particular, a transcription by Alison McCann, B.A. (of the West Sussex Record Office), has produced a rental of Dean and Chapter Properties for 1402–14, and Mr. W. E. Thumwood has completed a transcription of a similar rental and records of repairs to Dean and Chapter properties for 1534. Additional information from these sources (both in WSRO CAP 1/23/1) and other new material follows. In the two previous Gazetteers references to properties were assigned numbers, which were repeated on location maps. These numbers ranged from 1–54 (Saxon and Medieval) and 1–167 (Post-Medieval). New information for these sites is assigned the same number in the following addenda; completely new entries take numbers 55 onwards, and 168 onwards, respectively.

List of Abbreviations

CC	Cathedral Chartulary (SRS 46).
Ch	Chapter Acts (SRS 52).
CL	City Leases.
CW	Chichester Wills (in WSRO; SAC 87).
DCL	Dean and Chapter Leases.
PS	Parliamentary Survey (WSRO CAP 1/30).
R (with date)	Earliest documentary record seen in WSRO.
Rp	Raper MSS (WSRO).
SAC	Sussex Archaeological Collections.
SM	St. Mary's Hospital Chartulary (see SAC 24, 51).
SRS	Sussex Record Society.
WSRO	West Sussex Record Office.
VCL	Vicars Choral Leases.
SR (and date)	Chichester Excavations Summary Annual Reports.

Acknowledgements

The continuing support and guidance of the County Archivist and her staff (especially Alison and Tim McCann), is gratefully acknowledged.

Addendum to Saxon and Medieval Gazetteer (Fig 3.1)

North-East Quadrant

55. Market Place (north-east). SM.
Tenements 13th century with land to north and east.

St. Martin's Lane

56. Nos. 1–2 St. Martin's Square: WSRO CAP 1/23/1: CC: R 1254.

Guildhall Street (*SR* 1978)

57. Medieval pottery of 13th century date found at No. 4 during building operations.

East Street (north side)

58. Westminster Bank site: WSRO CAP 1/23/1, three shops and a tenement, R 1402.

59. No. 21: DCL: WSRO CAP 1/23/1, tenement R 1402.

60. *At Eastgate* (north side) WSRO CAP 1/23/1. Messuage adjoining gate R 1402.

South-East Quadrant

61. *Eastgate and City Gaol:* CC. R 1363. *East Pallant* (see *Chichester 2*, p. 11).

23. Car Park east side of East Pallant House: WSRO EP V1/1/3. Croft and pigeon house 1379.

23a. South end of same car park: WSRO EP V1/1/3. "Sickleases"—1379. "3 crofts enclosed within the grounds of the Friars".

St. John's Street (*SR* 1977)

62. Skeletal remains of Blackfriars found during street works.

South Street (east side)

63. No. 47: WSRO CAP 1/23/1. Chantry property of St. Augustine and Holy Cross. R 1402.

South-West Quadrant

West Street (south side)

63. (*SR* 1979). Medieval pottery found and a kiln or clamp, during building works in 1979, at No. 44/45.

65. Castle Inn: CC. House in 1227.

66. No. 54: WSRO CAP 1/23/1. "Subsean's Place". R 1402

67. Nos. 55-56: WSRO CAP 1/23/. Tenement R 1402.

North-West Quadrant

Tower Street (west side)

68. No. 9: WSRO CAP 1/23/1. "St Richard's house'. Tenement R 1402.

69. *County Hall* (*SR* 1978). Excavation site. Shallow postholes belonging to a barn or barns, possibly part of the medieval Common Barns.

Chapel Street: Excavation site (this volume, p. 138)

70. Late Saxon pottery clamps found in 1977; Middle-late Saxon cesspits and wells.

Crane Street: Excavation site (this volume, p. 153)

71. Saxon and medieval pits, 1978.

Outside Southgate

72. Medieval kilns found during construction of new supermarket in 1979 (*SR* 1979).

Fig. 4.1. Post-Medieval sites, 1450-1750.

Addendum to Post-medieval Gazetteer (Fig. 4.1)

North-East Quadrant

North Street (east side)

168. North of "Ship": DCL: PS. Three tenements and garden. R 1521.
3. Site of Old Town Hall (Guildhall): SAC 89 "By the Town Pound".
9. St. Olav's Rectory: PS: Ch.

Guildhall Street

169. Corner of Friars Lane (south side): CW: WSRO Add. Mss. 19648. Described as "the Rose" in 1676. R 1491.

170. Site of Nos. 3-4: WSRO Add. Mss. 19648. New messuage 1676 described.

St. Martin's Street (west side)

18. Trumpet (siting corrected).

171. Nos. 1-2 St. Martin's Square: DCL: Ch. D and C properties Nos. 217-8. Ownership in 13th century from Ralph de Montfort to Abbot and Convent of Jumieges; bought by John de Reigate who granted to Dean and Chapter (in return for recognitions of his anniversary). R 1254.

St. Martin's Street (east side)

172. Marks and Spencer: WSRO Add. Mss. 5999. Black Horse Inn disused by 1780.

Priory Lane

173. North of Park tavern: VCL, PS. House described 1649.

East Street (north side)

174. At Eastgate: WSRO Add. Mss. 16668-747: CW: House and garden adjoining gate (now footway). R 1474.

Little London (east side) and *East Row* (south side)

175. Lands of St. John of Jerusalem, became Crown lands at Dissolution then to City: SRS 36: CL.

176. *East Row.* WSRO Add. Mss. 2254. Stable and garden 1598.

177. *Militia Depot;* CW. Carthouse, barn, gateroom, malthouse and stable, up to 1750.

178. *East Walls* (west side). Rp. Stable, barn and malthouse 1718.

Little London (east side). Rp.

179. No. 38 Timber yard, early 18th century then Court with five dwellings.

South-East Quadrant

East Street (south side)

45. Bell Inn (nos. 58-9) DCL (abuttal). Lands of Thomas West, dean 1581.

East Pallant (south side)
61. Car park, east side of East Pallant House: SML.
Culverhouse Close next to Blackfriars Wall. R 1529.

South Pallant
62. WSRO Add. Mss. 6846, 12516: Rp; Messuage R 1587. "Plough" R 1661.
63. Corner, *West Pallant*, Houses. R 1587.

South Street (east side)
180. No. 47. WSRO CAP 1/26.
To City upon Dissolution, then freehold "Great house" 1563.
181. *Cooper Street* (between Nos. 63 and 64). WSRO Add. Mss. 7177. Two freehold houses. R 1544.

South-West Quadrant

South Street (west side)
81. Cross to Vicar's Hall. WSRO CAP 1/23/1. Tenement and gardens. R 1402.
85. Canongate to No. 33. WSRO CAP 1/23/1. Tenement and gardens. R 1402.

North-West Quadrant

West Street (north side): HT
121. Nos. 29–30. Six hearths 1670.

Tower Street (west side)
126. Library (No. 9) WSRO CAP 1/23/1. St. Richard's house; tenement R 1402.
182. Rear of Library: WSRO CAP 1/23/1 (abuttal). Land of Bishop Arundel's Chantry 1534.

North Street (west side)
183. Nos. 16–17: WSRO CAP 1/23/1; CL; SAC 89.
Guild of St. George, tenement 1534; then City property.
184. No. 15: WSRO CAP 1/23. Tenement of Bishop Arundel's Chantry.

Crane Street (north side): Excavation site (this volume, p. 196)
185. Mid-17th century pottery kiln found adjacent to No. 6.

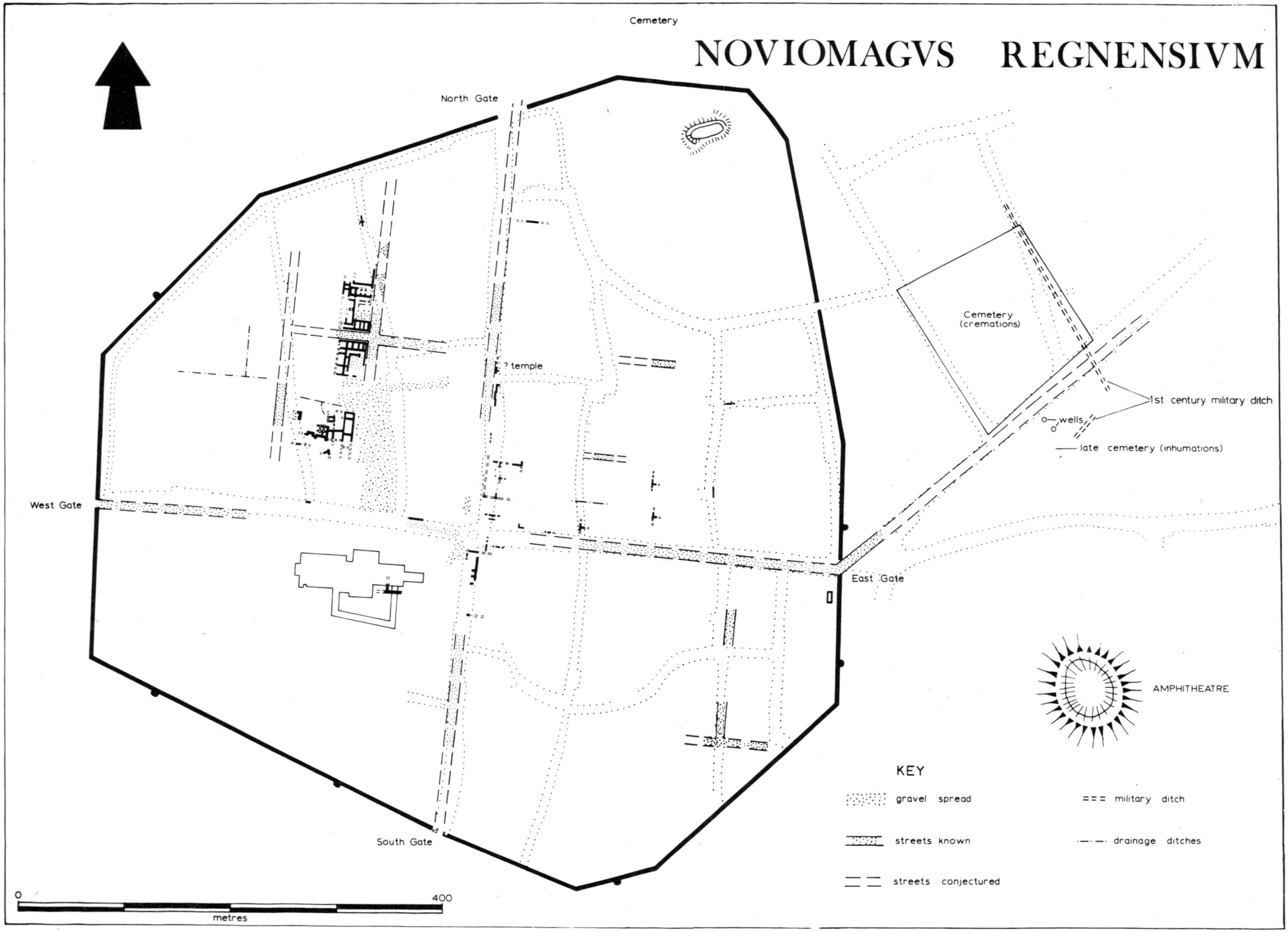
NOVIOMAGVS REGNENSIVM
Cemetery
North Gate
? temple
Cemetery
(cremations)
1st century military ditch
wells
late cemetery (inhumations)
West Gate
East Gate
South Gate
AMPHITHEATRE
KEY
gravel spread
streets known
streets conjectured
military ditch
drainage ditches
0
400
metres

Fig. 5.1

5

Chichester below the Streets (Fig. 5.1)

From 1976 onwards the main streets within the historic core of the City have been torn up by contractors laying new surface water drains, new gas and water mains, telephone cables and renewing sections of the foul sewer. In addition, all the sewer interceptors along the main streets have had to be lowered, making a total of 80 deep holes throughout East, North, West and South streets for this purpose alone. All of this work has been carried out in advance of the paving of the pedestrian precinct.

This vast disturbance of areas normally inaccessible to the archaeologist has been closely monitored and it is greatly to the credit of the Chichester District Council and their contractors, Geoffrey Osborne Ltd. and E. Doyle Ltd., that every facility has been made available to us to record the features revealed by their activities. Southerngas went out of their way to be of help by siting their trial trenches to locate the old gas main in North Street in areas most likely to pick up features located elsewhere by other contractors and have readily halted their work whenever archaeological features have been located. Similarly, the Post Office and the Portsmouth Water Co. Ltd. have maintained liaison with us when laying new services.

Most of the discoveries made during these operations were of Roman features; only rarely could a medieval layer be identified, but wherever possible, sections through the streets were recorded and these are published in the following pages. Some are capable of interpretation now, others may yet be in the light of future discoveries. Some of the finds have been noted in the Addenda to the Roman Gazetteer in Volume 3, but are treated more fully in this paper.

Many people were involved in the recording, but special mention must be made of Frank Greenaway, Ann Leyland and John Piper, who assisted the Writer, and bore the brunt of the emergency work in North and East streets, often in bad weather and sometimes at risk to themselves.

The finds are dealt with on a street by street basis, with the Gazetteer numbers in brackets alongside.

North Street (Figs. 5.2-5.7)

1. (107). At the north end of North Street in 1977, the gas main trench cut through part of a masonry wall constructed of squared limestone blocks. This may have been part of the west guard tower of Roman North Gate, but there was so much disturbance by modern services that it was not possible to come to any firm conclusions. The masonry was identical to that noted by Dr. Wilson on the east side of the road (*Wilson* 1962, 75-77; *Chichester* 1, 7 (1)).

At a point 5.8 metres north of the south wall of No. 3 Northgate and 3.2 metres east of the west kerb, the back face of a large block of squared limestone was seen, resting upon a layer of soft black silt. Immediately north of it was a large greensand slab which extended across the gas main trench. Other slabs of masonry were traced in the east section of the trench, northwards for a distance of 3.7 metres. Thereafter the wall was cut away by a brick culvert and a manhole.

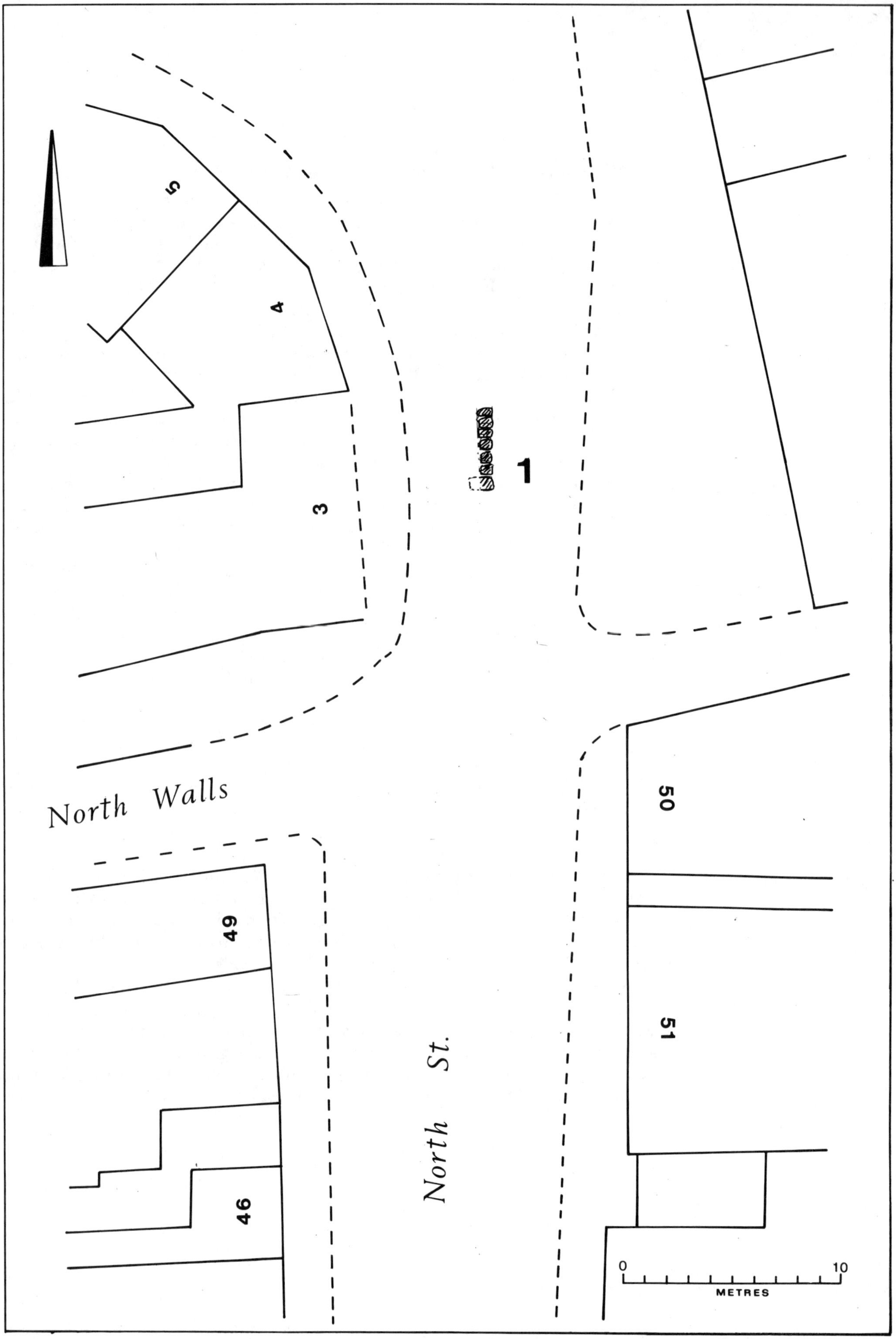

Fig. 5.2

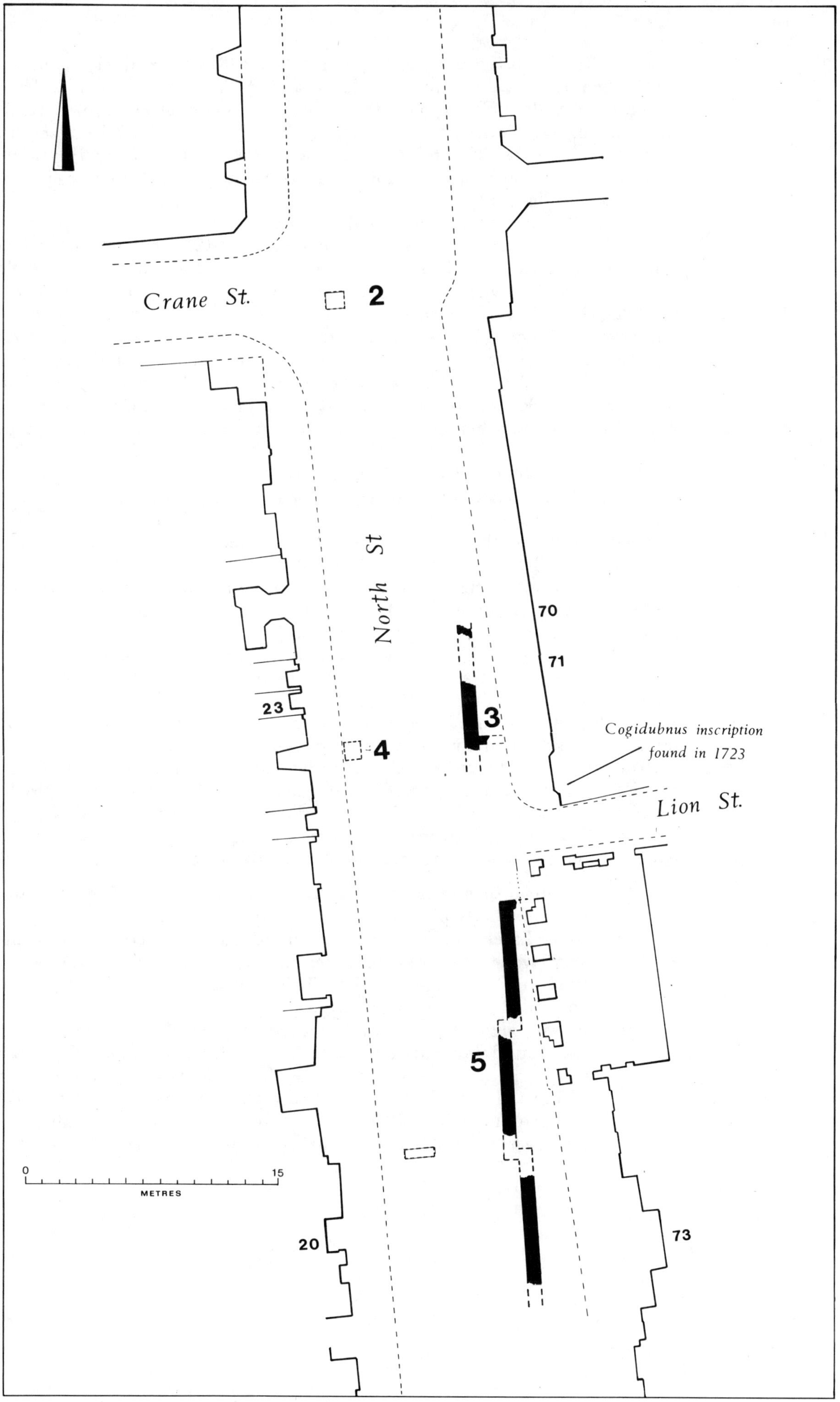

Crane St.
2
North St
70
71
23
3
Cogidubnus inscription found in 1723
4
Lion St.
5
0
15
METRES
20
73

Fig. 5.3

2. (108). Opposite the junction with Crane Street, a thick layer of gravel seen when the manhole for a surface-water drain was constructed. The gravel rested upon yellow clay at a depth of 1.4 metres below street level. Several layers of metalling were noted and it is likely that this could have been the junction between the Roman North street and the east-west street (Street 3) connecting it to the north-south street below Chapel Street (see this volume, p. 151, and *Chichester 3*, Fig. 7.14).

3. (91 (i)). On the east side of the street and just north of its junction with Lion Street, the surface-water drainage trench in 1977 cut through a length of wall *c.* 0.85 metre wide, built of flints in white mortar and tile bonded along its western face. The wall was aligned north-south (Fig. 5.3), and was joined at right-angles on the east side by a narrower wall *c.* 0.5 metre wide. A layer of burning 20–25 cm thick lay above the foundations seen in the east section of the trench and this burning was covered by 25 cm of dirty clay and then a well-compacted 30 cm of dirty flints and gravel. It looked like an ancient road surface, possibly a later Roman feature, laid out after demolition of the building, possibly when the town was being re-planned after the death of Cogidubnus, or perhaps later still.

The position of this wall is 4 metres west of No. 72 North Street, the shop below which the Cogidubnus inscription was found in 1723 (*Chichester 1*, 9 (9)). The wall was traced for a distance of 4.7 metres north of the junction with the east-west wall and this is the same feature noted by Mrs. Rule in 1967 as "a tile bonded wall seen in a service trench at a depth of 0.58 metre", (*Chichester 1*, 9 (7)). It is possible that the structure of which the wall forms the western side is the temple of Neptune and Minerva, and that the famous inscription was in or near its primary position when it was found (*VCH* Sx, 3; 3, 13).

The position of the wall further south at the junction of Lion Street and North Street could not be traced due to the presence of a large manhole which had completely destroyed the stratigraphy.

4. (109). A hole for a new sewer interceptor in front of No. 23 North Street on the west side of the road, revealed a layer of gravel at a depth of 0.77 metre, with a top layer of oyster shells and grey rubble 0.16 metre thick on the west side of it. Possibly part of the large gravel spread seen in the Chapel Street excavations (*Chichester 3*, Fig. 7.3), or perhaps the Roman North Street.

5. (91 (ii)). The surface water drain trench dug in 1977 in front of the Council House on the east side of the road showed the following features:

(a) A spread of mortar, possibly from a destroyed building, in front of the most northerly pier of the Council House colonnade.

(b) Immediately south of this and in front of the second pier, a spread of very well-compacted flint pebbles 0.55 metre below modern street level and 0.30 metre thick. This sealed a layer of dirty clay which contained greensand and chippings.

(c) A wall, aligned north-south and comprising flints set in creamy mortar was found immediately south of the flint metalling. One course of greensand ashlar survived above the footings along the western edge of the wall, which appeared to turn eastwards below the Council House at the point where it was first noted (Fig. 5.3). The wall was traced southwards for 23 metres and was seen to have an offset on the west side. It was 1.5 metres below street level and measured 0.77 metre in width.

Note: Due to the hiatus at the west end of Lion Street, it is not possible to be sure whether this wall is part of the same building noted in Note 3. On balance it seems unlikely, as the alignment seems to be slightly different and the wall of the northern fragment of building is thicker. Also, the compacted pebbles noted in (b) above might have been a hardstanding or street between the two structures. Nevertheless, the wall, with its offset, is reminiscent of the 4th century temple at Lydney, Glos. (*Lewis* 1966, Fig. 94), and it is just possible that *this* represents part of the temple of Neptune and Minerva, and not the building to the north.

6. (110). In front of W. H. Smith's, below the pavement on the west side of the road, a wall, aligned north–south, constructed of flints in mortar with a white mortar floor on the east side of it. The top of the wall was 1 metre below street level; was at least 1 metre wide and the footings were 1 metre deep. The wall and floor were noted again in front of Sainsbury's (No. 15 North Street) and here the thickness of the floor was seen to be *c.* 15 cm.

7. (110). Further south on the west side of the road and in front of Acres the Bakers, traces of the base of the mortar floor were found. This was only seen in the north section and it was cut away by what might have been a pit or an east-west robber trench. Below the floor was *c.* 0.15 metre of dirty clay make-up with oyster shells. Further south, in front of Rediffusion (No. 13 North Street), the floor was again noted and here it was seen to have a screeded surface.

8. (91 (iii)). In 1977 the surface water drainage trench in front (west), of No. 82 cut through an east–west wall, the top of which was 0.75 metre below street level. It was 0.6 metre wide and constructed of greensand, flint and tile and was 2.9 metres south of the south-west corner of St. Olaf's Church. South of the wall was an ancient metalled surface consisting of dirty pebbles, mortar and tile, 0.65 metre below street level. This was sealed by a layer of compacted gravel 0.30 metre thick and this in turn sealed a layer of greenish silt (Fig. 5.4). The wall either cut the metalling or the latter was laid up against it. South of the metalled surface, in front of the Buttermarket, was a compacted surface comprising flints, greensand and chalk set in mortar. This was 0.5 metre below street level and had been covered with compacted gravel and re-used building debris. It is possible that this metalled surface may have been the medieval or post-medieval market paving. Below it was a thick layer of sticky black soil 0.61 metre thick in places which lay above a spread of Roman building rubble, including tegulae, pilae tiles and mortar. Two piers of a hypocaust survived, the one in the pipe trench had the medieval paving laid directly on to it, but the other, in the manhole south of the pipe trench, was only four courses high (Fig. 5.5). The pilae were constructed of greensand ashlar and only small amounts of charcoal were present below the rubble, which may indicate that the destroyed room was not subjected to excessive heat. A large hole dug for a manhole just south of the Buttermarket on the line of the foul sewer revealed much disturbed Roman building material and the remains of a destroyed hypocaust. The base of the hypocaust was approximately 1.80 metres from street level.

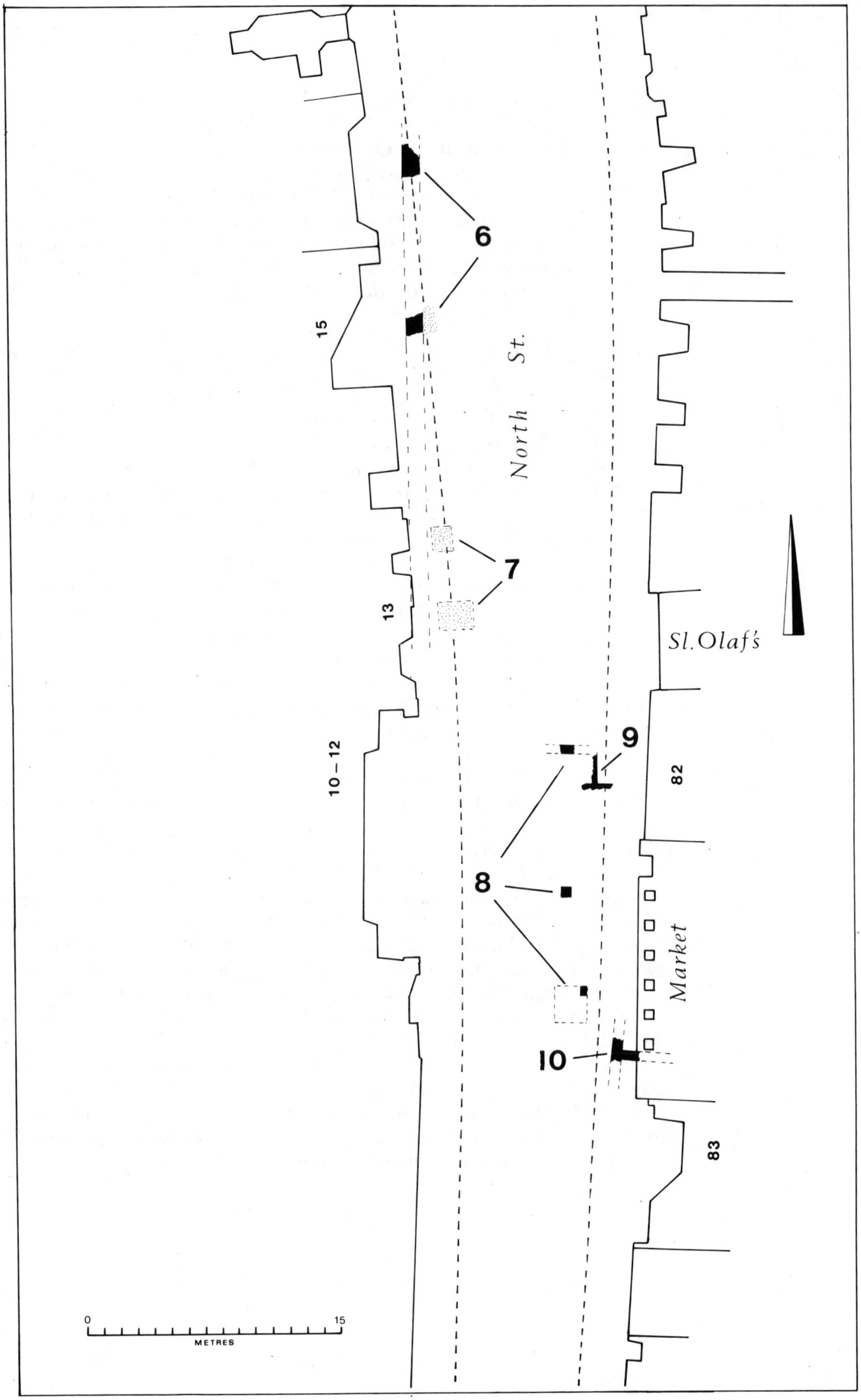

Fig. 5.4

NORTH ST. 1977; SITE 8

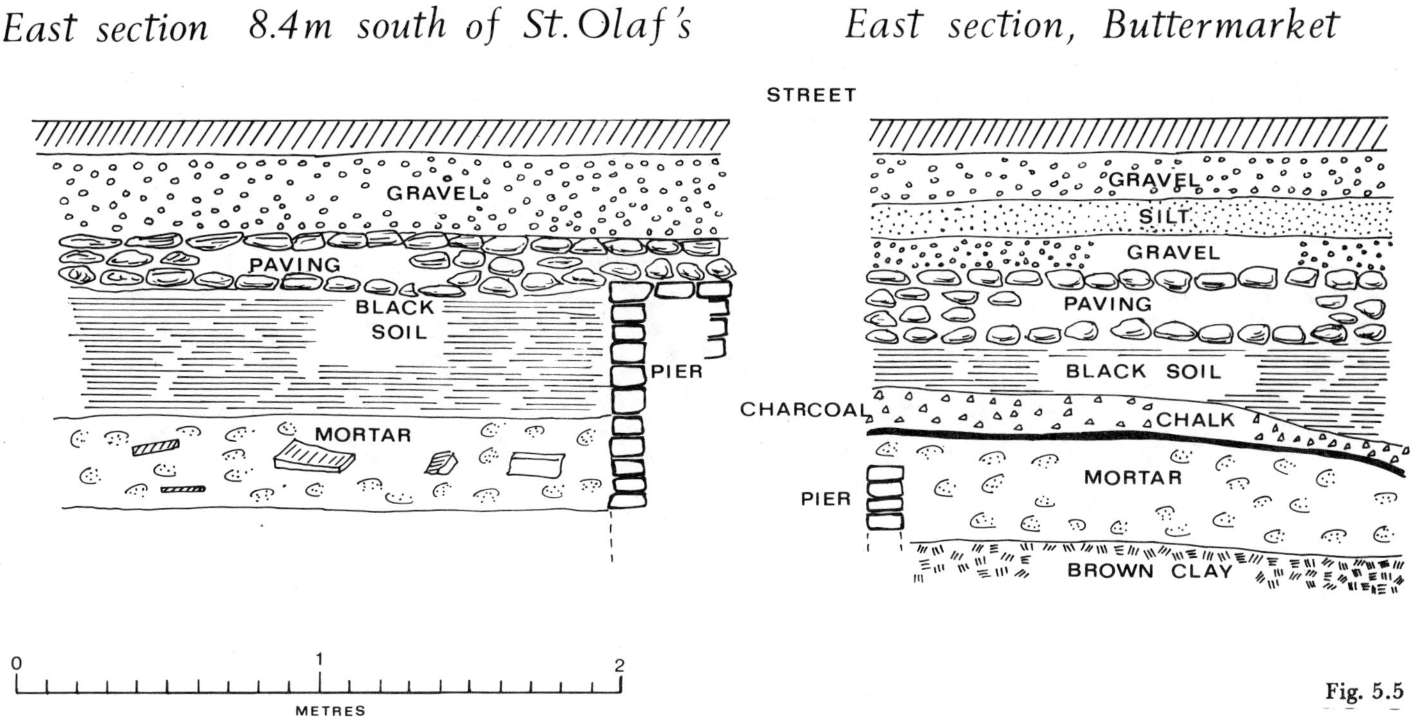

Fig. 5.5

Pl.2

9. (110). In 1979, a sewer interceptor dug in front of No. 82 showed a deep Roman wall in the south section, running east-west and constructed of greensand ashlar (Fig. 5.4). This might well be the north wall of the hypocaust seen in 1976 in front of the Buttermarket (No. 8). The wall footing was in excess of 2 metres deep. A north-south wall joined it at a point 2.9 metres west of the building line outside No. 82 (Plumbs). This was robbed in the upper layers and was keyed into the east-west wall. Further probing by the workmen on our behalf showed that the east-west wall ended or turned at the point where the north-south wall joined it. Within the angle formed by the junction of the two walls was a layer of dirty clay with a thin spread of mortar at a higher level.

10. (110). Below the east pavement of North Street outside the Buttermarket. In 1977 the Council workmen cut a deep sewer connection to the new foul sewer. This cut through the same compacted surface recorded in Note 8 as possibly being the medieval market paving. Below it were traces of a north-south Roman wall 0.55 metre wide which had a spread of Roman building debris. This wall was joined on the east side by another wall coming in at right angles from below the Buttermarket. There was a slight gap between the two walls, both of which were constructed of flints in mortar, faced with greensand ashlar.

LENNARDS, NORTH STREET.
East section across sewer trench

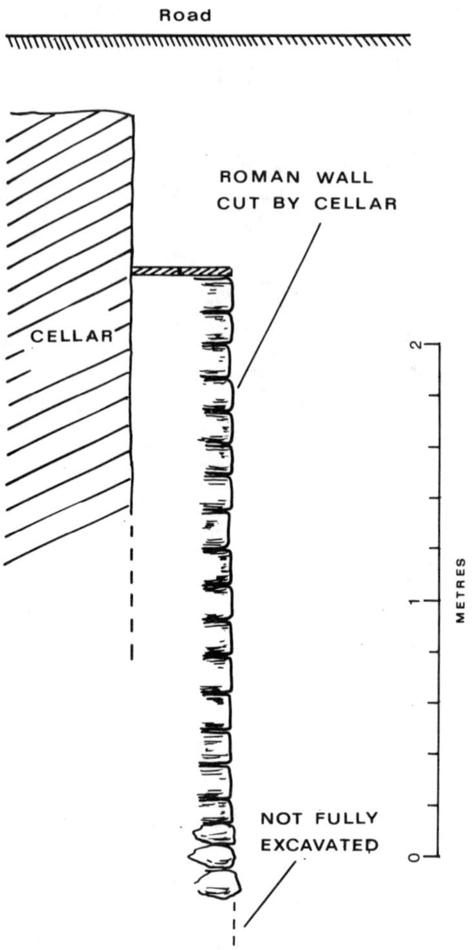

Fig. 5.6

11. (110). In front of No. 84. A north-south wall partly below the east pavement. This had a column fragment of fine-grained sandstone built into it. The wall joined another one running east-west, which measured 0.90 metre in width. Both walls were well constructed of flint and greensand ashlar with tile bonding. Within the angle of the wall were the remains of a destroyed hypocaust with large amounts of charcoal and destroyed pilae tile and tegulae. The latter were quite thin in section and are probably late in date, i.e. 4th century. The column drum, which had a dowel hole at each end, had had a long life before it was built into the wall. Considerable wear on one side and around the edges at each end suggests that it may have been used as a sharpening stone after having been demolished, possibly from an earlier classical building.

12. (110). In front of 85 North Street (H. Turner & Sons), the sewer interceptor cut through the core of a very thick tile bonded wall. No finished exterior surfaces were found, but the size of the remains suggest that it might be part of a destroyed apse. The foundations were in excess of 3.5 metres deep.

13. (110). The gas main trench along the west side of North Street in 1977 struck an east-west Roman wall at a point 21 metres north from the north kerb of West Street and 1.9 metres east of the west kerb of North Street. The wall was 0.4 metre wide and constructed of greensand and flint. It was recorded at a depth of 0.55 metre.

14. (110). In front of Hart's on the east side of the road; an east-west wall constructed of flints and greensand, 0.9 metre below street level. The base of the wall was at least 3.40 metres below the street level.

15. (110). In front of Lennards on the east side of North Street. A brick cellar runs out westwards from below the shop and this had partly cut away an east-west Roman wall. The footings could not be traced to the full depth but were in excess of 3.40 metres below street level (Fig. 5.6).

East Street (Figs. 5.7-5.15)

16. (111). In front of the doorway of the Midland Bank in East Street at a depth of 1.30 metre from street level, a line of massive sandstone blocks set above a layer of clay and flints. Three blocks were seen in line in the hole dug for the foul sewer interceptor (Pls. 3 & 4, and Fig. 5.7). The centre one was recovered by the workmen and measured 1.25 metre by 0.85 metre by 0.50 metre deep. Reading clay was packed between the stones, which were covered by a layer of sticky yellow clay and gravel. It is possible that these stones represented the remains of a stylobate running from below the Midland Bank northwards up the west side of North Street. On the west side of the blocks the soil consisted of black sticky pit fill with oyster shells and re-deposited greensand fragments.

17. (111). In front of "Lindy Lou" (93 East Street), a wall running east-west at a depth of 0.9 metre. The wall was constructed of flints and mortar and was capped by flat sandstone slabs measuring 0.61 metre square by 0.16 metre thick. One stone was recovered; this had four rectangular holes cut into the top of it. The wall was 0.50 metre wide.

18. (112). In front of Hardy and Co. on the north side of East Street. At a depth of 1.32 metres a layer of mortar and gravel 0.38 metre thick, laid upon natural gravel. The layer was well compacted and had a spread of mud in it *c.* 4 cm thick, 0.30 metre down from the top. It extended southwards outside the limits of the hole and might represent a hardstanding, re-surfaced on one occasion, rather than a floor within a building.

19. (112). In front of Finlays (No. 4 East Street). A similar layer of mortar and gravel to that noted in 18 above, but here the top of the layer was 0.90 metre below street level and the bottom of the layer rested upon 0.22 metre of hoggin which in turn lay above 10 cm of organic green silt.

20. (118). A sewer interceptor excavation in front of Boots on the south side of East Street showed a layer of gravel metalling cambering from north to south, probably the edge of the Roman east-west street. It had a layer of silt 0.20 metre thick above and sealed a dark occupation layer below (Fig. 5.11). See also No. 24 and Fig. 5.14.

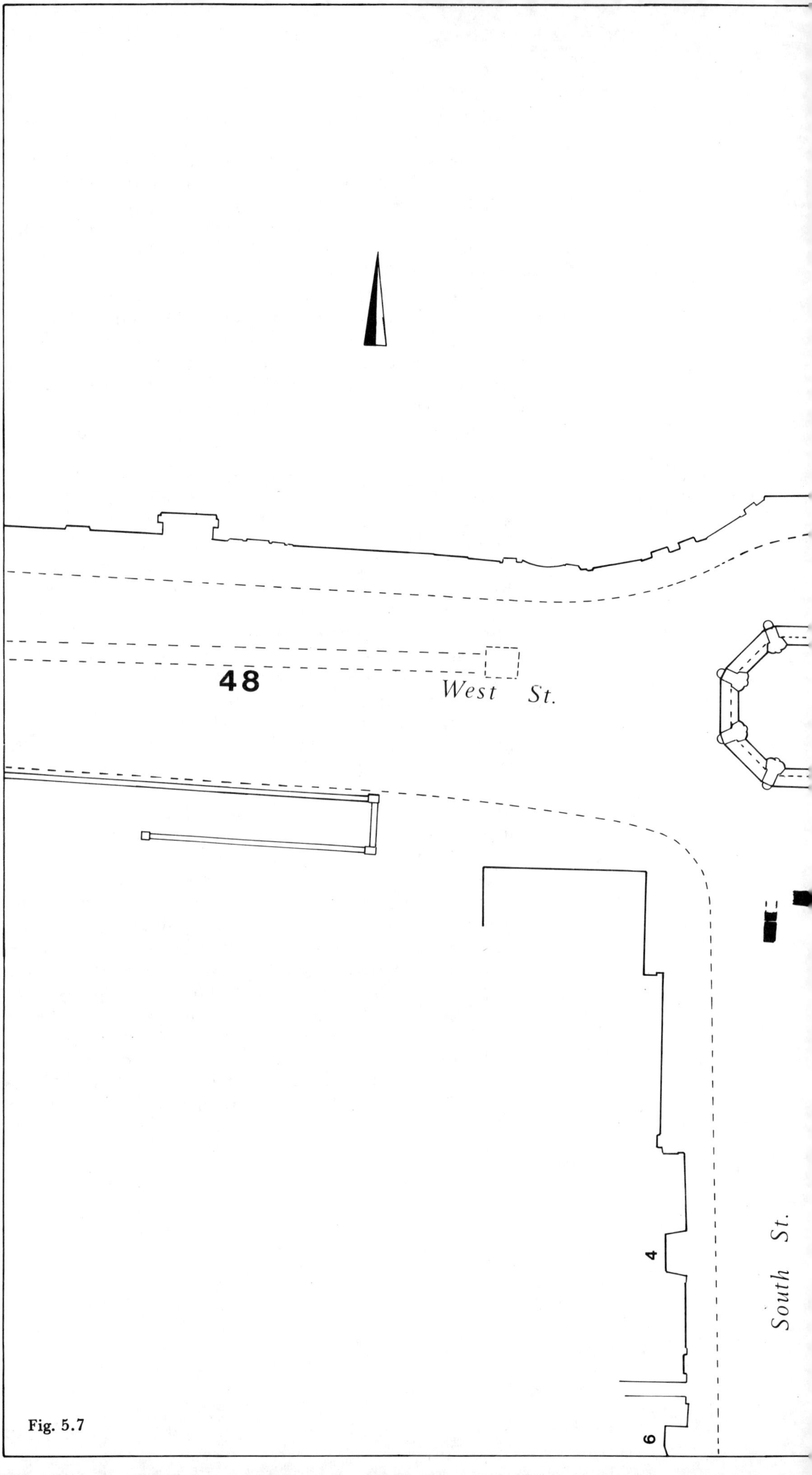

Fig. 5.7

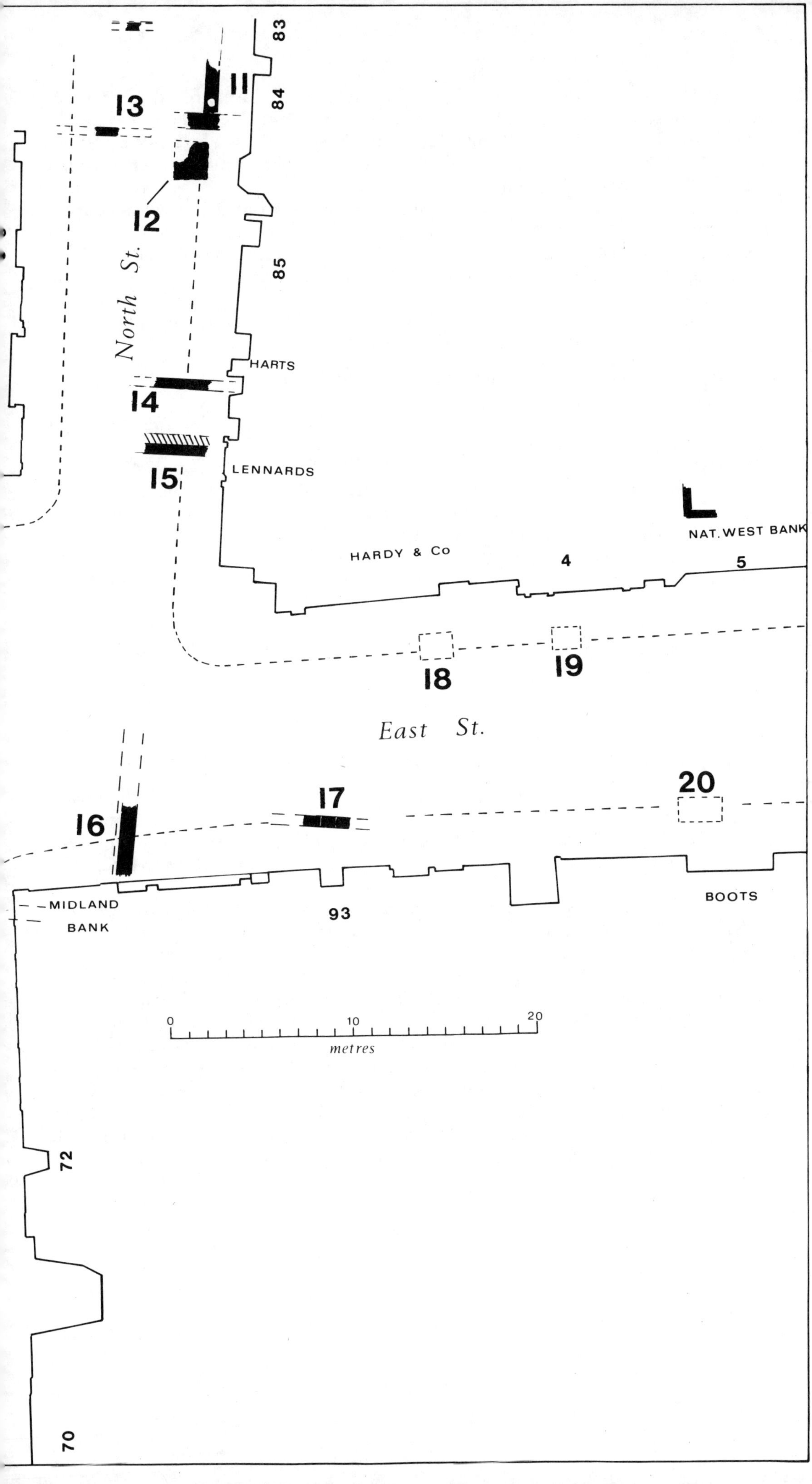

83
84
11
13
12
North St.
85
HARTS
14
15
LENNARDS
HARDY & Co
4
NAT. WEST BANK
5
18
19
East St.
20
17
16
MIDLAND
BANK
93
BOOTS
0
10
20
metres
72
70

21. (113). Outside the National Westminster Bank (5 East Street), the excavation for the sewer interceptor showed a layer of ash and charcoal approximately 0.20 metre thick. The upper Roman layers had been destroyed by a pit, but there were a large number of greensand blocks and flue tiles present in the fill, which might indicate a destroyed hypocaust (Fig. 5.10).

22. (117). (Fig. 5.8). The presence of cellars running out into the street from the south side made it necessary for the contractors to construct a large junction box in 1977 so that the surface water pipe could avoid them. The resulting excavation produced an interesting section through the later street levels and the earlier Roman ones, with evidence for pit digging and/or robbing in late Saxon or early medieval times. The key to the sections published in Fig. 5.9 is given below, recorded from the lowest level upwards:

(A). Roman gravel with lumps of pink mortar in it.
(B). Greenish clayey silt resting on A.
(C). A destruction layer of soft white mortar with tile and greensand chippings.
(D). A pit, cutting C and sealed by E. The fill was black soil. No dating evidence recovered, but a similar pit to the south of the trench had three sherds of coarse unglazed Saxo-Norman ware. The stratification was disturbed by the pipe trench and the cellar, but it is possible that the pit might in fact be a robber trench.
(E). Layer of dirty metalling sealing C and D, possibly the earliest medieval street.
(F). Clean gravel sealing E.
(G). Layer of mud on F.
(H). Gravel.
(J). Layer of mud on H.
(K). Gravel.
(L). Gravel and large stones, probably the base for the modern street.
(M). Pit or robber trench filled with dark soil, cutting E and sealed by F.

23. (115). In the north section of the surface water trench in 1977, opposite the boundary between Tesco's and Lloyds Bank. At a depth of 0.65 metre a large sandstone block 0.6 metre wide and at least 0.5 metre deep. Only the south face of the stone was seen, set into a layer of compacted gravel. It may have been a column base.

24. (118). Four excavations for sewer interceptors in 1979 in front of Nos. 85–81 East Street, over a distance of 25 metres showed the following stratification (see Fig. 5.14).

At a depth of 0.80 metre, a layer of clayey silt 0.20 metre thick. This rested upon a compacted layer of oyster shells 0.25 metre thick, which in turn lay upon 0.70 of compacted gravel which is probably the edge of the Roman street. Below this was 0.15 metre of charcoal and oyster shells above natural gravel.

Pl.5 25. (116). In front of Lloyds Bank in 1979, excavations for a sewer interceptor revealed an east-west wall of which only the south face was visible. It had a deeper foundation incorporated into it (see Figs. 5.12-5.13). The wall comprised greensand ashlar and flints set in white mortar and resting upon a layer of gravel. Set in the wall and resting upon a platform of mortared flints was an arrangement

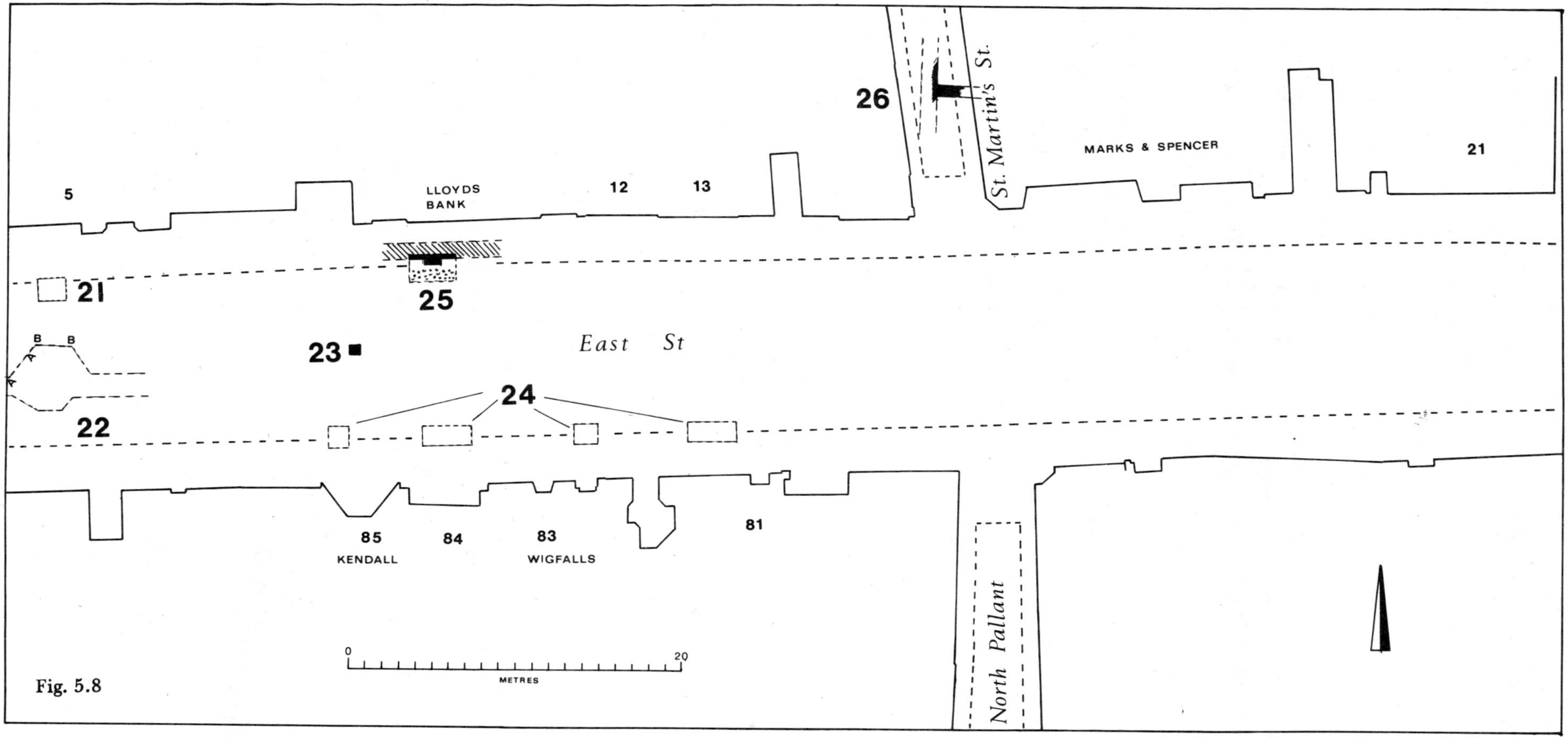
26
St. Martin's St.
MARKS & SPENCER
21
5
LLOYDS
BANK
12
13
21
25
B
B
A
A
23
East St
24
22
85
KENDALL
84
83
WIGFALLS
81
North Pallant
0
20
METRES

Fig. 5.8

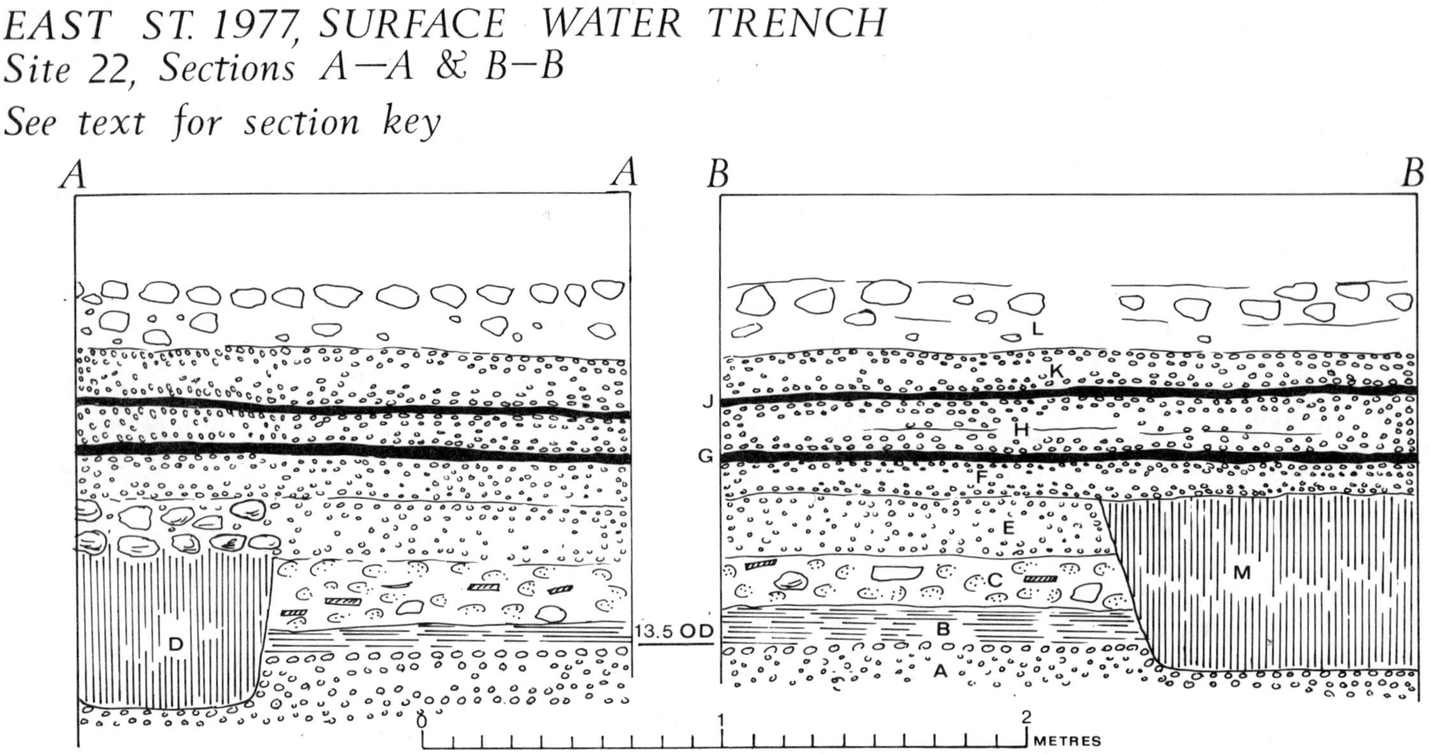

Fig. 5.9

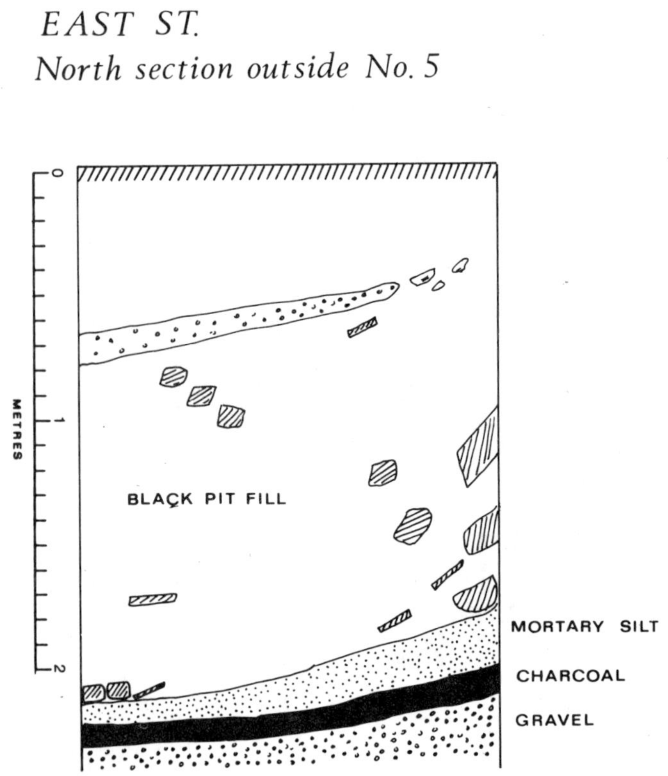

Fig. 5.10

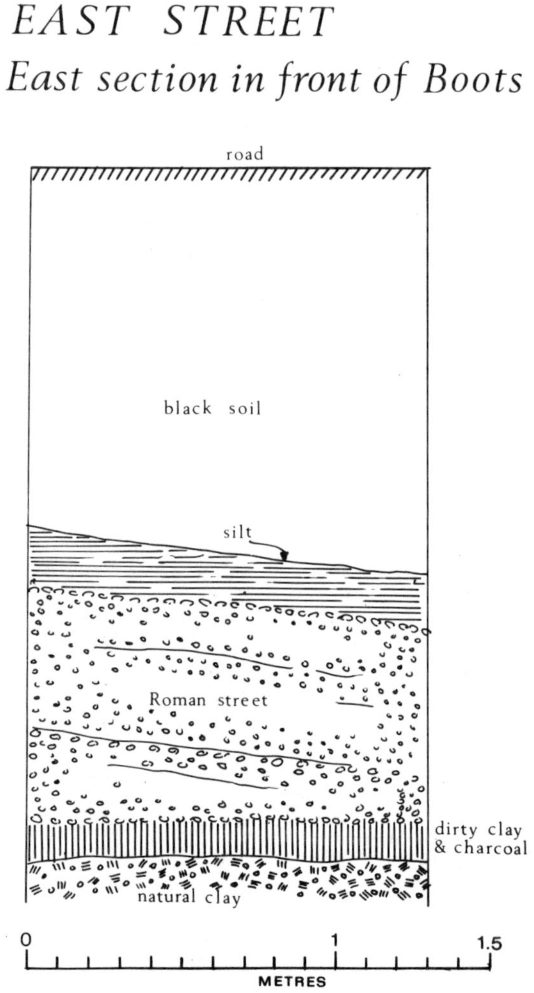

Fig. 5.11

EAST ST, LLOYD'S BANK
East & West sections

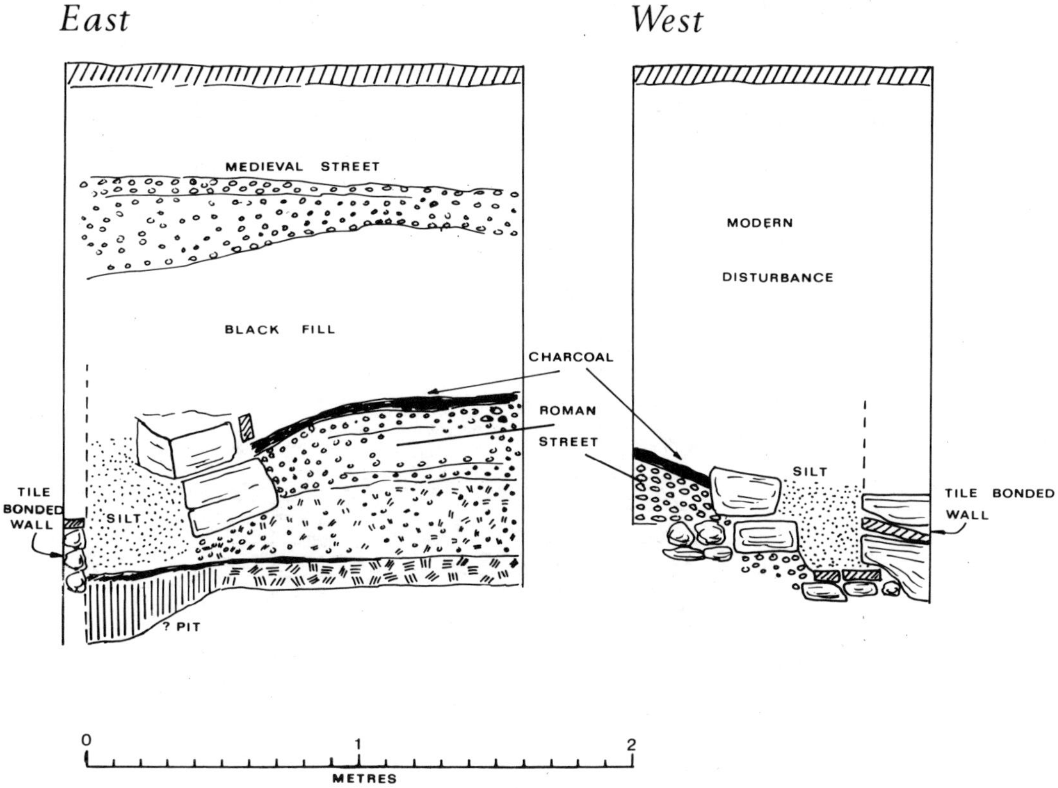

Fig. 5.12

EAST ST, LLOYD'S BANK.
North section

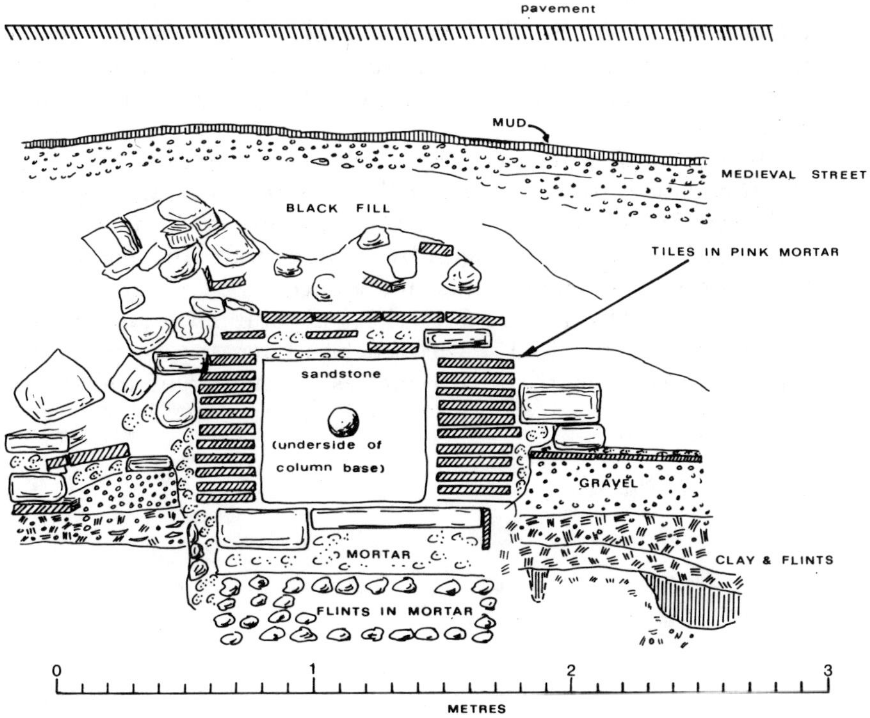

Fig. 5.13

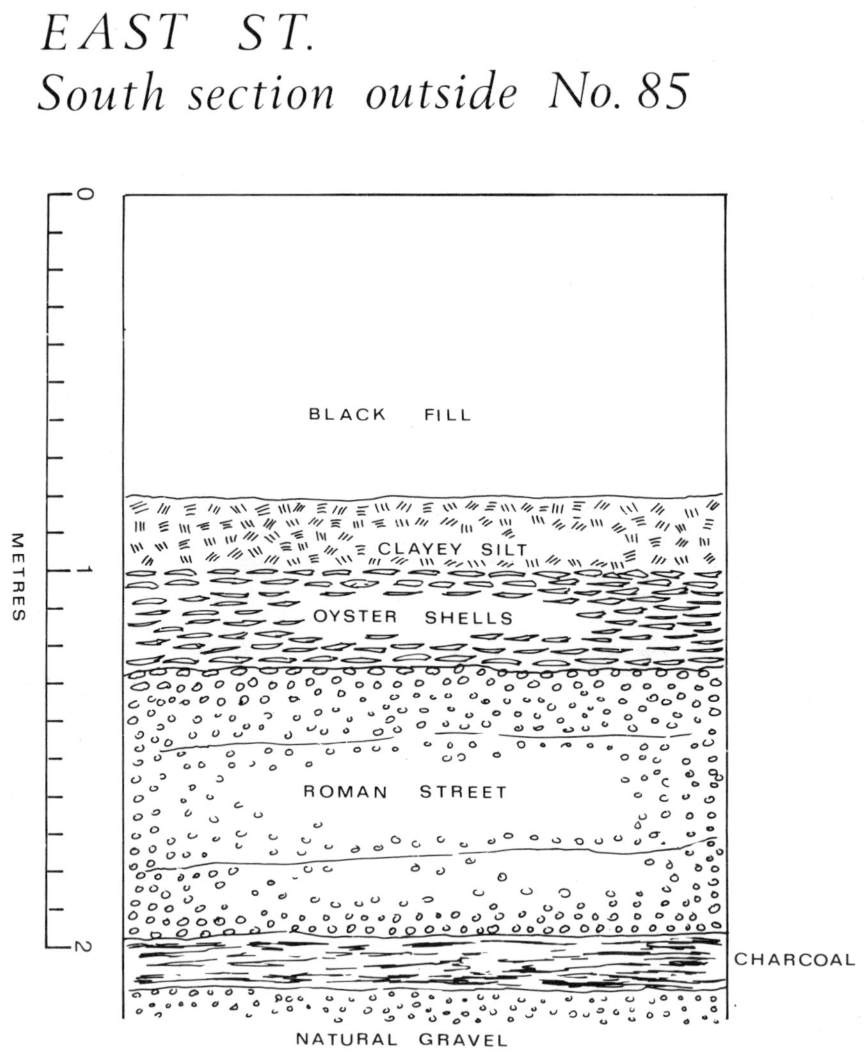

Fig. 5.14

of pilae tiles set in pink mortar with the base of a column set on edge and laid against the core of the wall (Fig. 5.13). On the south side of the wall was the remains of a ? gutter filled with fine black silt, with a compacted layer of dirty gravel laid up against it on the south side. It had a layer of charcoal above it and it might be the remains of an earlier Roman street surface as it cambered northwards.

26. (119). A new sewer trench dug along St. Martin's Street in 1979 struck the foundations of a massive wall consisting of unmortared blocks of greensand and large flints. The bottom of the footings was 2 metres from street level. The wall was joined at right-angles by another wall 0.62 metre wide coming in from the east side, just below Marks and Spencer.

27. (119). St. Martin's Street. At a point 25.4 metres from the north kerb of East Street, the foul sewer trench cut across a deep feature filled with black silty soil. At a depth of 2.5 metres a number of fourth-century sherds were

recovered, including a complete New Forest flagon. The bottom of this feature was not reached at a depth of 3.5 metres, where the pipe was laid.

A month later, excavations inside Marks and Spencer's for a new elevator foundation showed a deep feature, 3.4 metres in depth, with waterborne silts in the bottom. This was approximately the same distance north of East Street and it seems fairly certain that it is part of the same linear feature (Fig. 5.24). It may well be an east-west Roman sewer, similar to the one found in the north-west quadrant (*Chichester 3*, Fig. 7.3).

28. (118). In front of Finlay's, No. 72 East Street, excavations for a sewer interceptor showed a typical section through the Roman street gravel (see Fig. 5.14 for example).

29. (118). In front of Elphick's (No. 71). A large block of sandstone 0.50 metre wide and 0.20 metre thick was noted in the south section at a depth of 0.90 metre. This was set into the top of a layer of gravel which was probably the Roman street. Further sewer interceptor holes dug in East Street in 1979, east of No. 71 all provided similar sections through the Roman street, viz.: layers of compacted gravel with a band of dirty clayey silt below. The sites are numbered Nos. 30-38 (see Fig. 5.15), and are set out below:

30. Zales (25 East Street).
31. Morelli's (66 East Street).
32. 29 East Street.
33. Token House (65 East Street).
34. 30 East Street.
35. Hamels (31-32 East Street).
36. Clarks (60 East Street).
37. The Fleece.
38. Wyatt's (57 East Street).

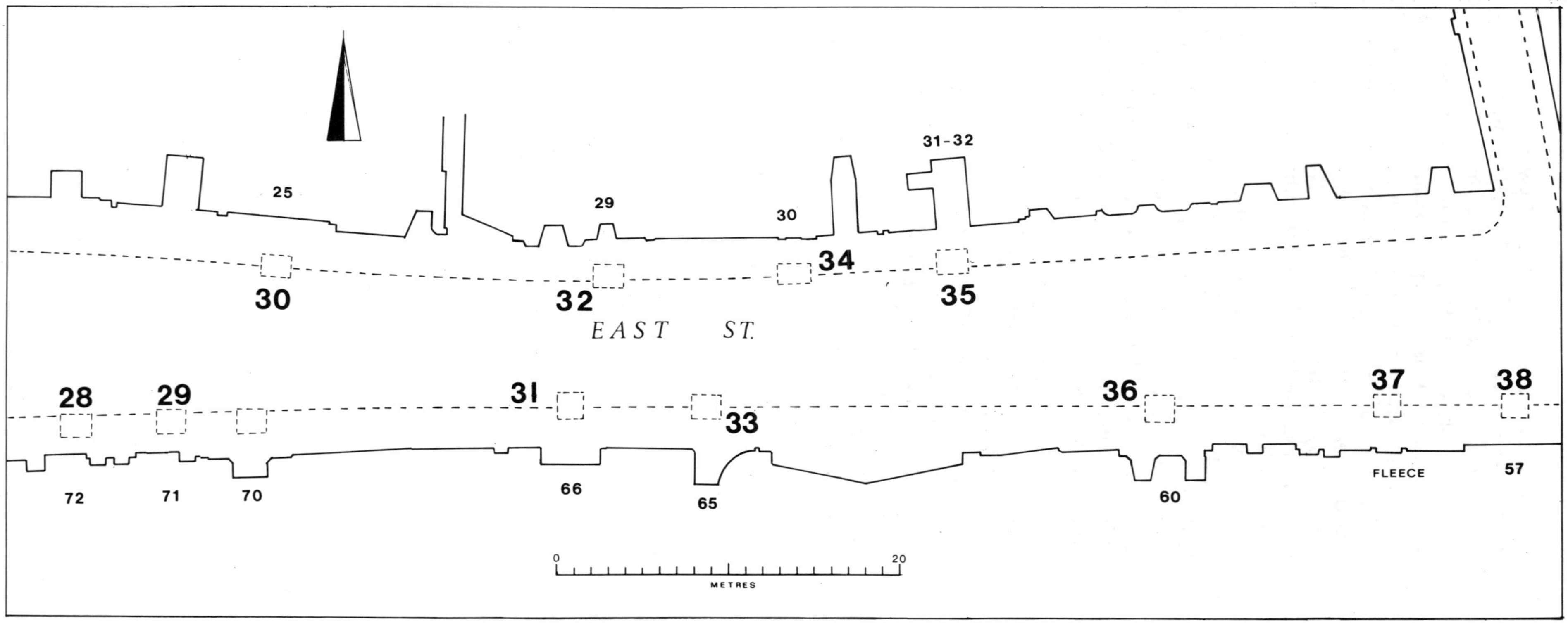

31-32
25
29
30
34
30
32
35
EAST ST.
28
29
31
33
36
37
38
72
71
70
66
65
60
FLEECE
57
0
20
METRES

Fig. 5.15

South Street (Figs. 5.16-5.21)

39. (99). *Southgate* (Figs. 5.16-5.21).

In 1979 the surface water drainage trench sectioned the Roman wall at Southgate. A pipe trench (Fig. 5.17), had been dug up against it on the south side without disturbing the face of the wall, which was constructed of sandstone blocks mortared together. This was slightly south of Rumbelows on the corner of Southgate and Market Avenue. At 1.25 metre from ground level there was some sign that the foundations may have been stepped outwards, or alternatively, that it was the rough mortared footings of the gate. The back face of the wall was made up with clay and rubble tapering upwards as it spread northwards. Above this, in the east section was a well-constructed floor of bricks in mortar. In the west section the situation was a little more complex as the wall appeared to return northwards at the point where the trench cut it. The north-south wall was shallower and may have been the west wall footing of the east guard-room of the Southgate, if two guardrooms are postulated.

Trial excavations on the site of Rumbelow's shop in 1959 showed attenuated fragments of the town wall on the line with this latest find (*Holmes*, unpublished). No trace of the gate was found and it was assumed that it must lie beneath the modern street. This now seems to have been proved, but what is not yet known is the size of the gate and whether it had two guardrooms as suggested in Fig. 5.18, or one, as suggested for the East and West gates (*Chichester 1*, 146 and Pl. II; *Chichester* 2, 72–3 and Pl. 10).

40. Just north of Theatre Lane and in front of "Sussex Homes" (43 South Street). At a depth of 0.5 metre the remains of a kerb built of sandstone blocks with a layer of large flint cobbles set against it on the west side. The cobbles and the kerb were laid upon dirty clay 0.35 metre thick. This had a thin layer of charcoal below it, apparently resting upon natural clay.

41. In front of Nos. 44 and 49, a layer of compacted gravel above a layer of oyster shells, probably the edge of Roman South Street.

42. In front of the "White Horse" (No. 61), the lower levels of the Roman street were seen at a depth of 1.5 metre, the upper levels having been destroyed by an earlier service trench.

43. (124). Outside the north-west corner of No. 63, by the junction with Cooper Street, the base of an east-west Roman wall constructed of greensand and flints. It was 0.9 metre wide and the bottom of it was 1.9 metre below street level. Only the bottom 0.45 metre of wall survived, the upper part having been previously destroyed by street works.

44. In a manhole at the west end of Cooper Street and in front of No. 64, a layer of gravel 0.35 metre thick, 1.5 metre below street level. Below the gravel was a layer of grey clay, but in front of No. 64, slightly to the north, the gravel sealed a layer of Roman building debris.

45. (124). In front of No. 68 at a depth of 0.8 metre, a large east-west Roman wall constructed of greensand ashlar and mortared flints, 0.83 metre wide. The wall stood on footings of flint to a height of 0.7 metre.

46. (124). In front of No. 69 and 4.7 metres north of the wall noted above was an east-west wall of similar size and construction.

Sewer interceptors dug along the east kerb of South Street during 1980 showed a north-south Roman wall running from a point outside No. 68 northwards, at least as far as No. 74. The footings were in excess of 2.90 metres below pavement

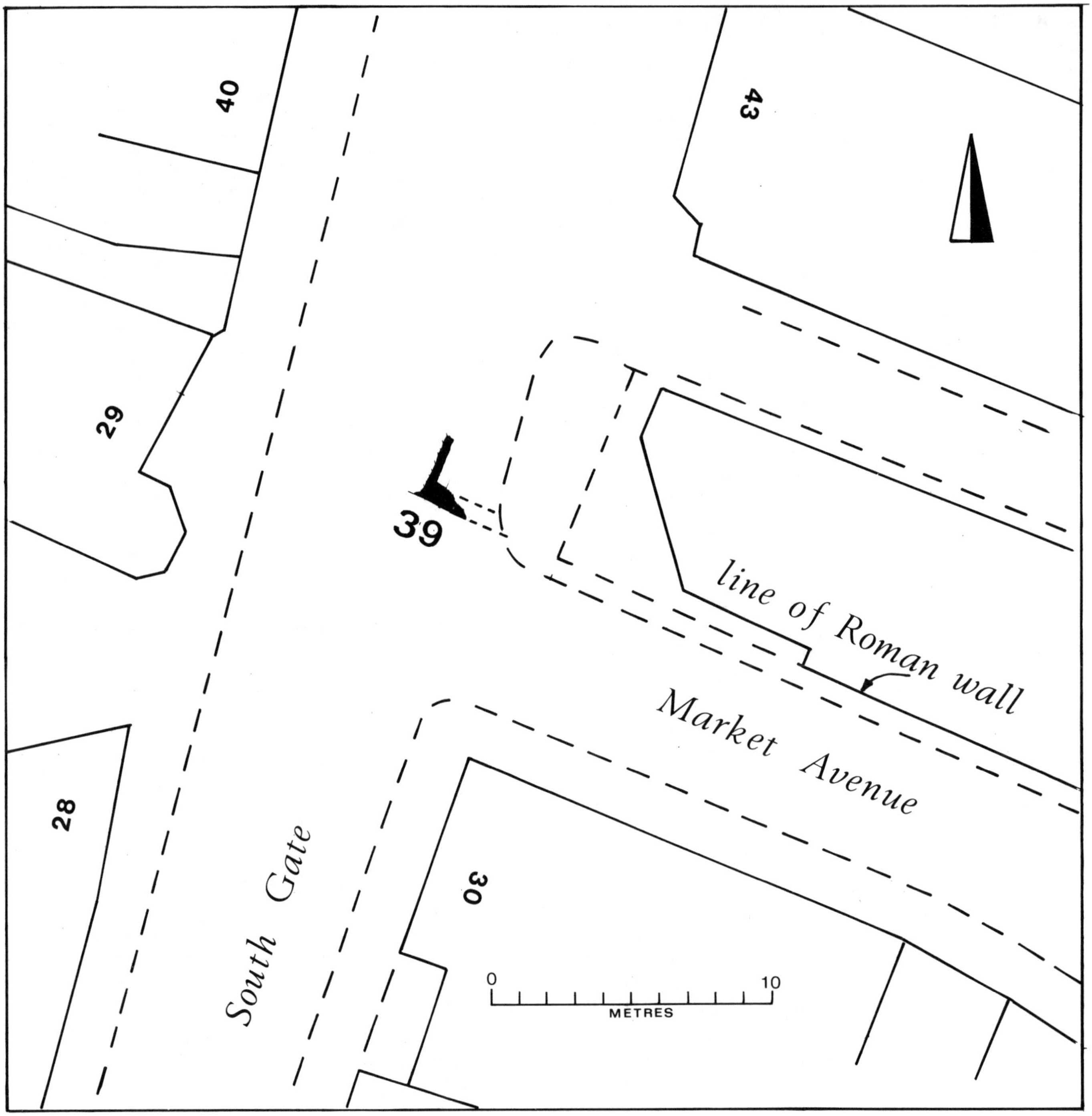
40
43
29
39
28
30
line of Roman wall
Market Avenue
South Gate
0
10
METRES

Fig. 5.16

SOUTHGATE 1977

Sections through service trench

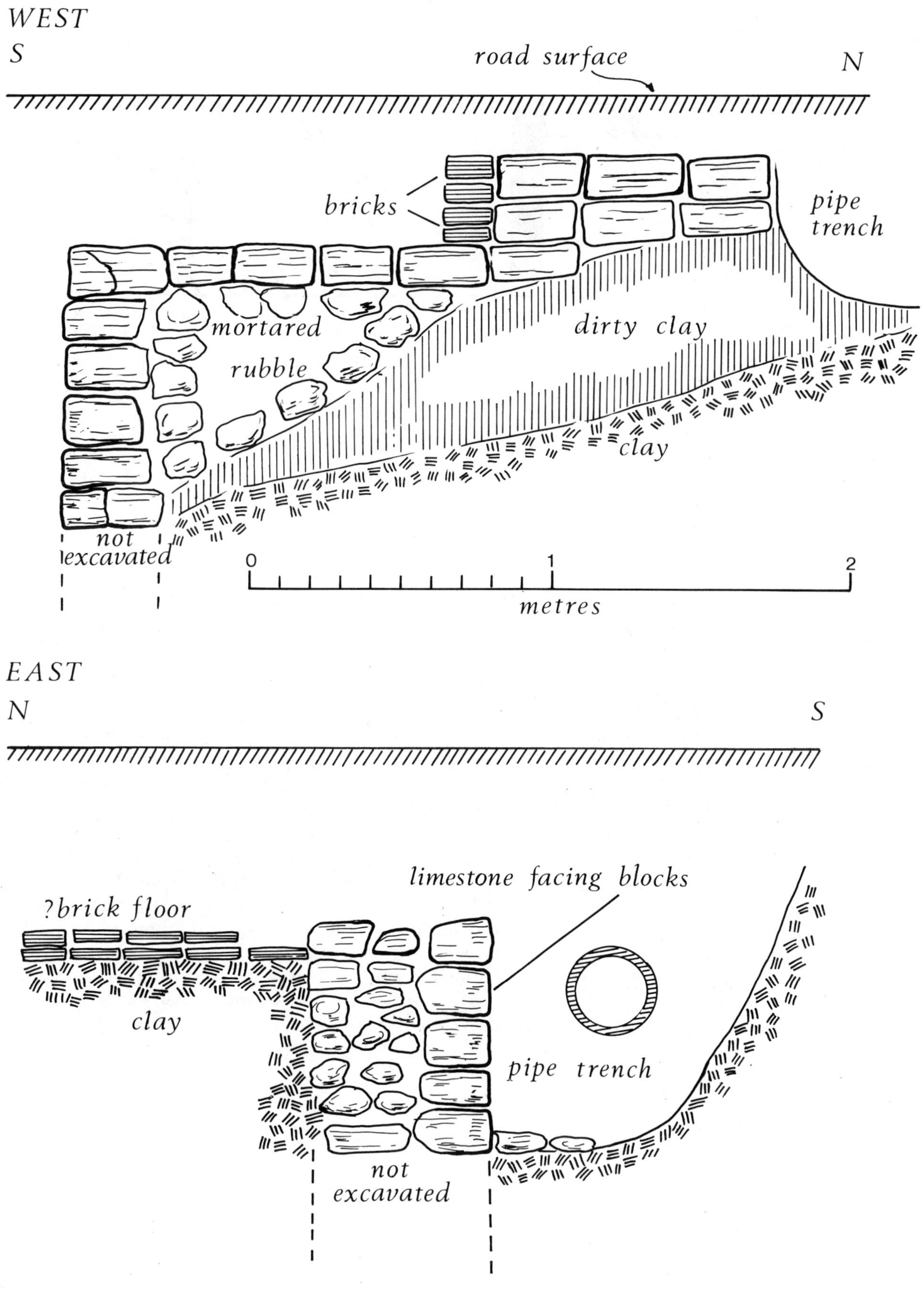

Fig. 5.17

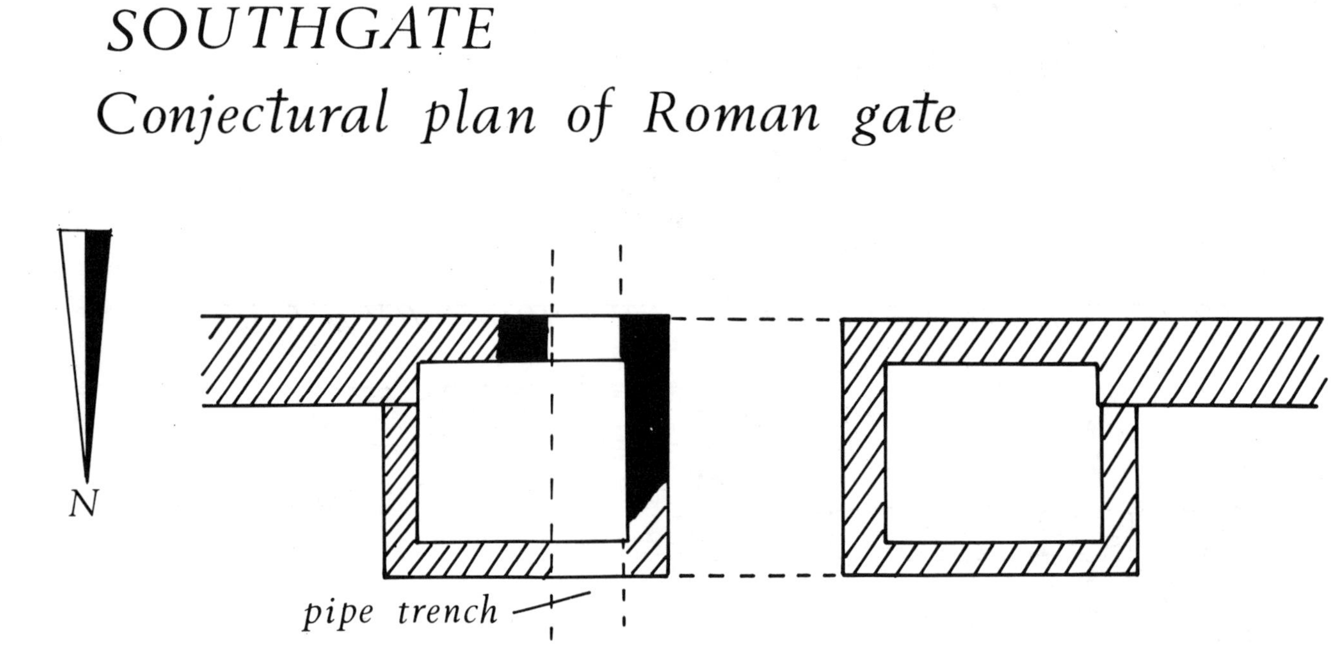

Fig. 5.18

level and were 1 metre wide. The wall was constructed of greensand ashlar on mortared flint footings and it must join the east-west wall running below the Midland Bank (see No. 47), while at the south end it must turn westwards between Nos. 66 and 65. On the east side of the wall the ground was made up with soft brown clay which had a spread of greensand chippings 0.30 metre thick in it (Fig. 5.21). At no point where the interceptor holes were dug was a cross wall seen coming in from the east and it seems likely that this north-south wall forms the eastern boundary of a large building running westwards below the north end of South Street towards the Cathedral. It might relate to the Roman building noted by Mrs. Rule (*Chichester 1*, 127-137 and Fig. 6.3). It measures approximately 49 metres from north to south.

47. (124). (Fig. 5.7). At a point 2.8 metres south from the south kerb in East Street and 0.6 metre south of the north-west corner of the Midland Bank, a large east-west wall, 0.9 metre wide. The top of the foundation was 1.1 metre below street level and the observed depth of the foundations was 0.75 metre. In January 1980 the wall was again seen when the Water Company laid a new main in South Street. The same trench sectioned a wall built of large sandstone blocks set into white mortar and aligned north-south. The blocks were 1.10 metre long, 0.52 metre wide and at a depth of 0.70 metre below modern pavement level.

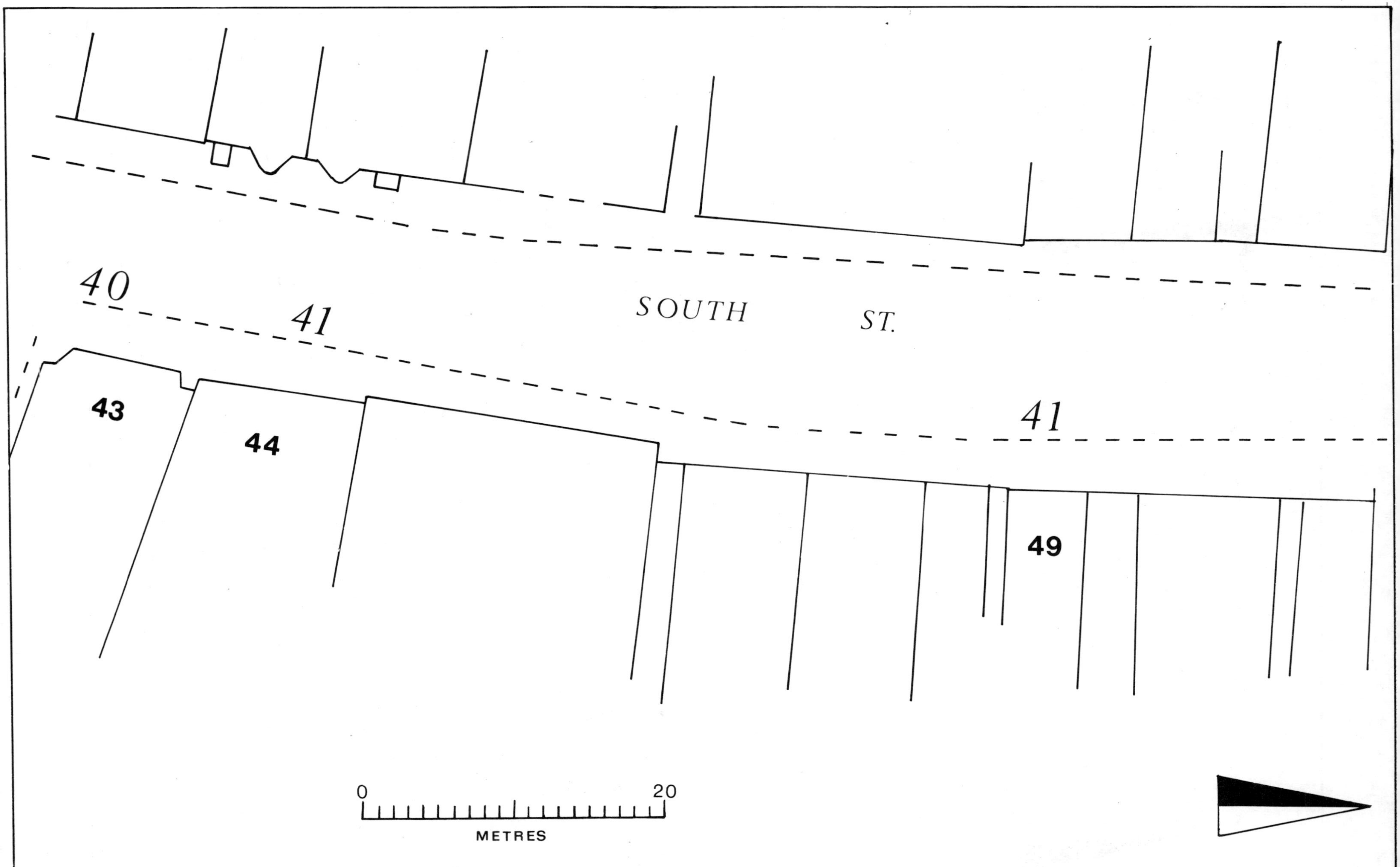

Fig. 5.19

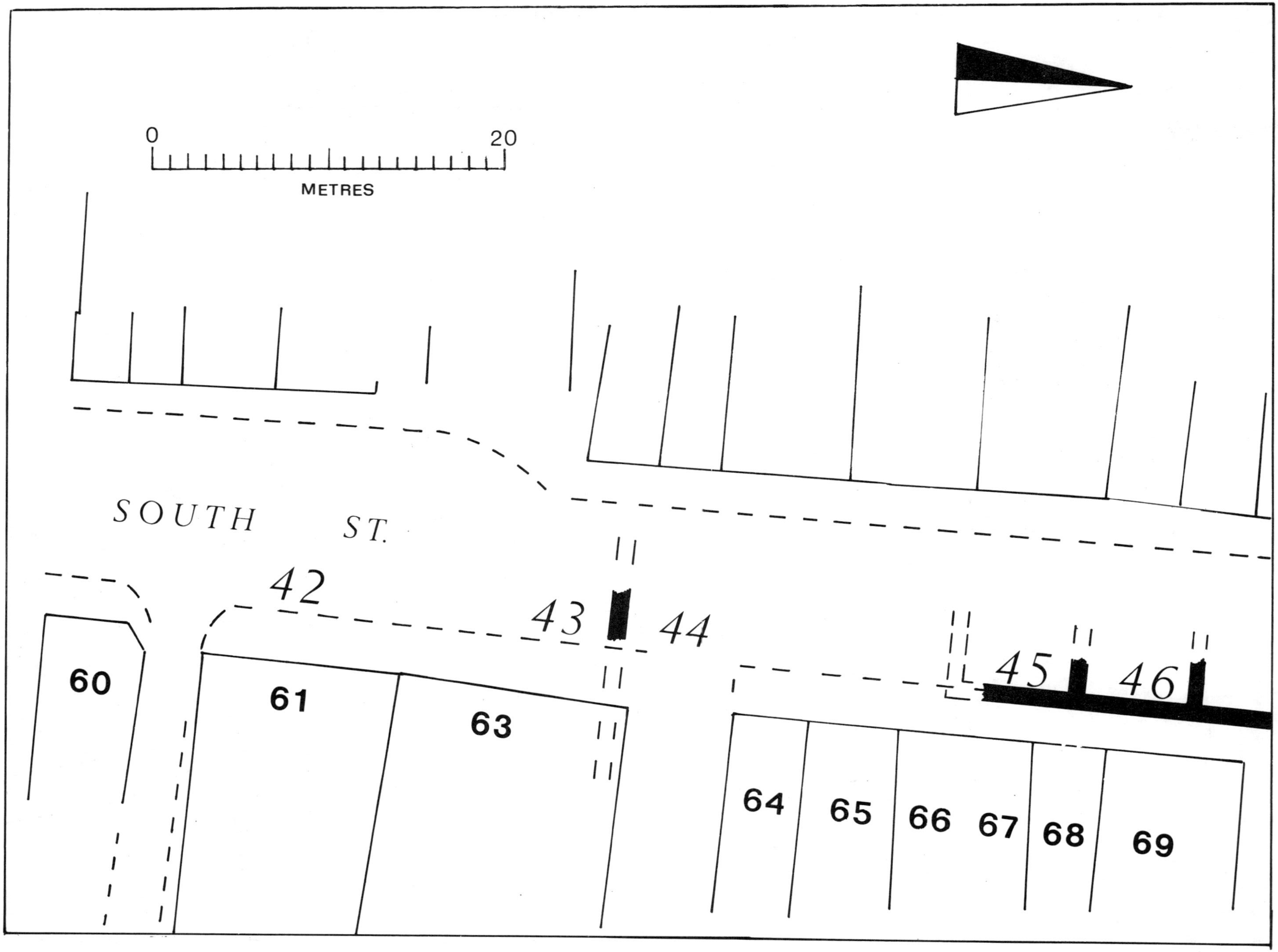

Fig. 5.20

SOUTH ST.

North section outside No.66

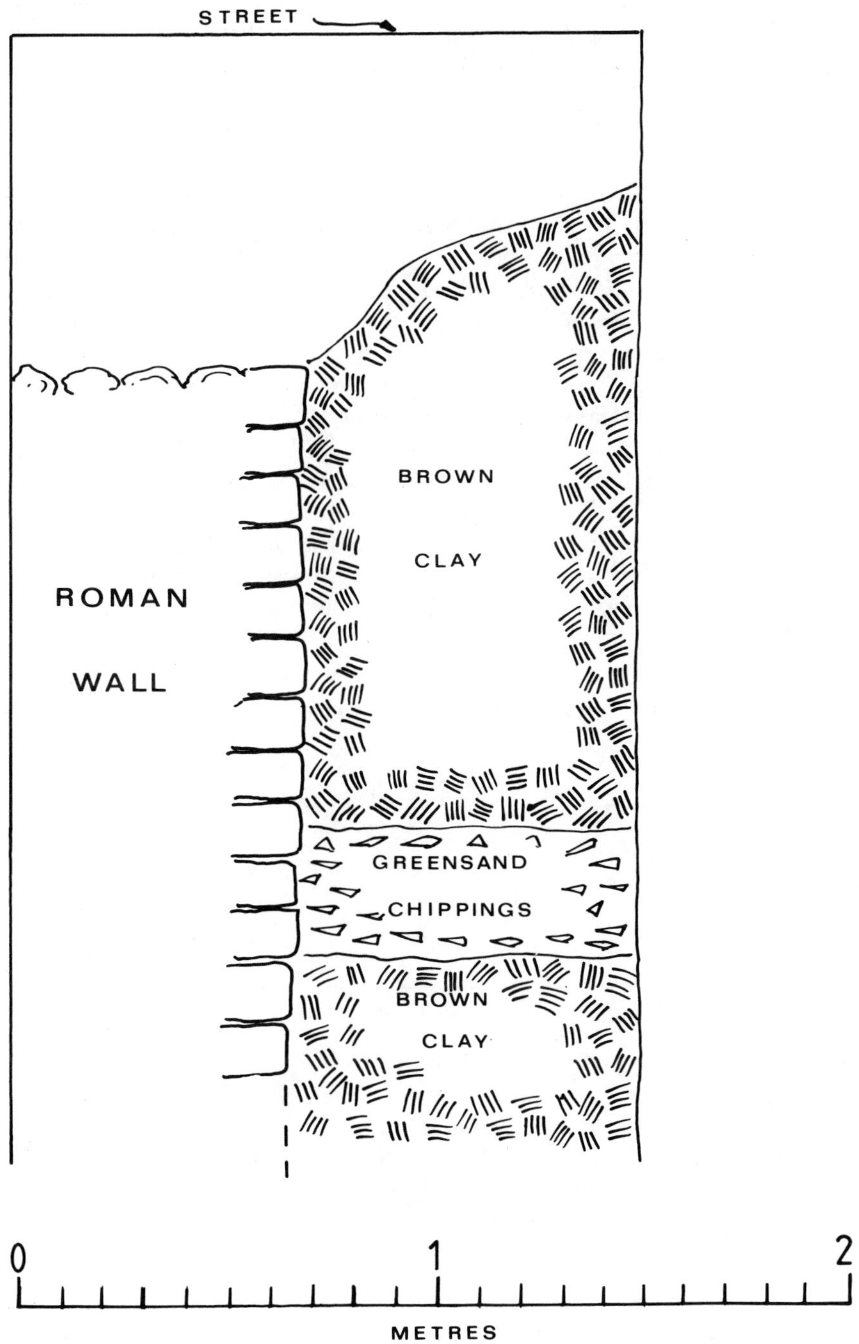

Fig. 5.21

West Street

48. (125). The surface water drainage trench dug in 1977 cut through a layer of flints, greensand and creamy mortar which extended across the bottom of the trench at a depth of 1.1 metre. This layer was above a spread of dirty clay, charcoal and wall plaster in which a sherd from a Dr. 33 samian cup of Antonine date was found. The layer of building material contained a number of dressed limestone fragments, one measuring 25 by 15 by 7 cm. Above the rubble, which was evidently from a destroyed building below the "Dolphin and Anchor", was a layer of compacted gravel 0.40 metre thick and above this was a spread of compacted gritty soil 0.20 metre thick. This section was observed over a distance of 8.8 metres. At the manhole, 4.35 metres west of the City Cross (Fig. 5.7), the section was different, with the gravel lying above a dark sticky fill which may have been a pit.

Little London and East Row (Fig. 5.23)

49. (120). During the laying of a new water main in 1980, the machine cut along the top of a tile bonded flint and limestone wall aligned north–south. The top was 0.75 metre below kerb level and the width was in excess of 0.65 metre. Further north, opposite No. 34, a layer of burnt clay and tile was noted in the bottom of the trench at a depth of 1.10 metre. This extended across an area of *c.* 1.7 metre and was covered by 0.4 metre of brown soil with flints. Building developments in the cellar below No. 35 later in the same year revealed that the 17th century house was built upon foundations of part of a Roman house and traces of a hypocaust (later converted to a cold room), were found.

50. (121). A water main trench dug eastwards from the junction of Little London and East Row cut along the south face of a tile-bonded wall aligned east–west. The top of the foundation was 0.75 metre below road level. The south section along the pipe trench consisted of gravel and clay. At the west end of the wall was what appeared to be a gutter, but this was not seen in section on the south side, nor did it appear to run along the south side of the wall (see Fig. 5.22).

Fig. 5.22

EAST ROW 1980

North section in pipe trench

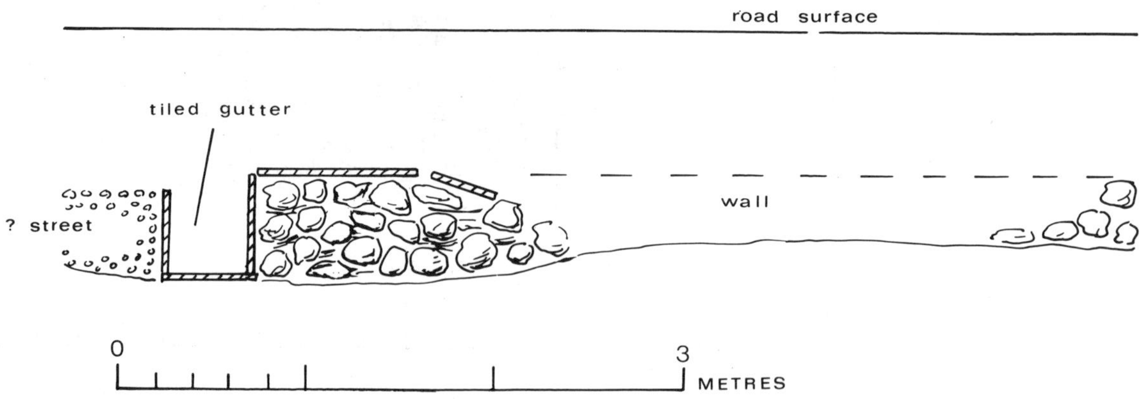

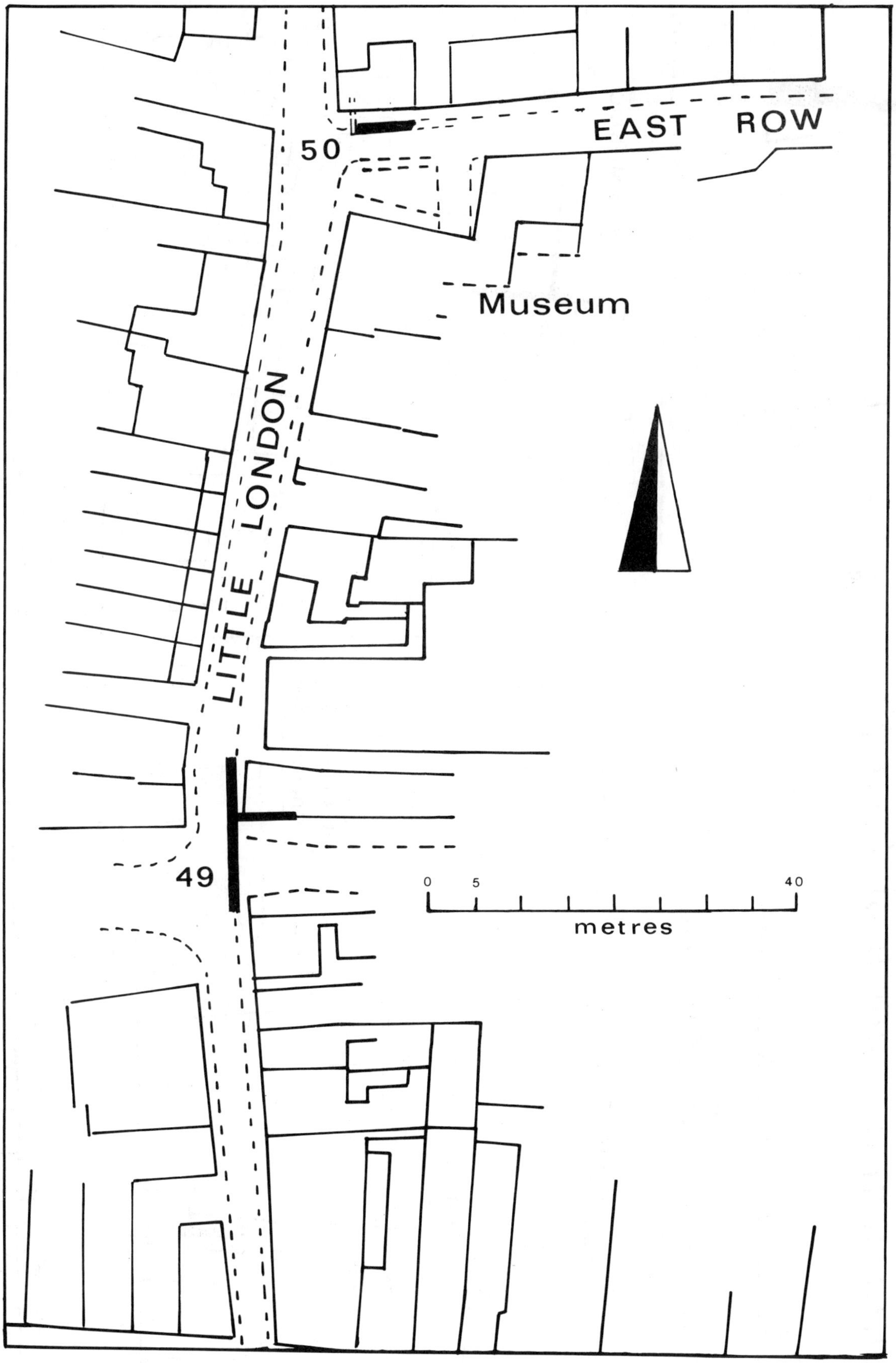

Fig. 5.23

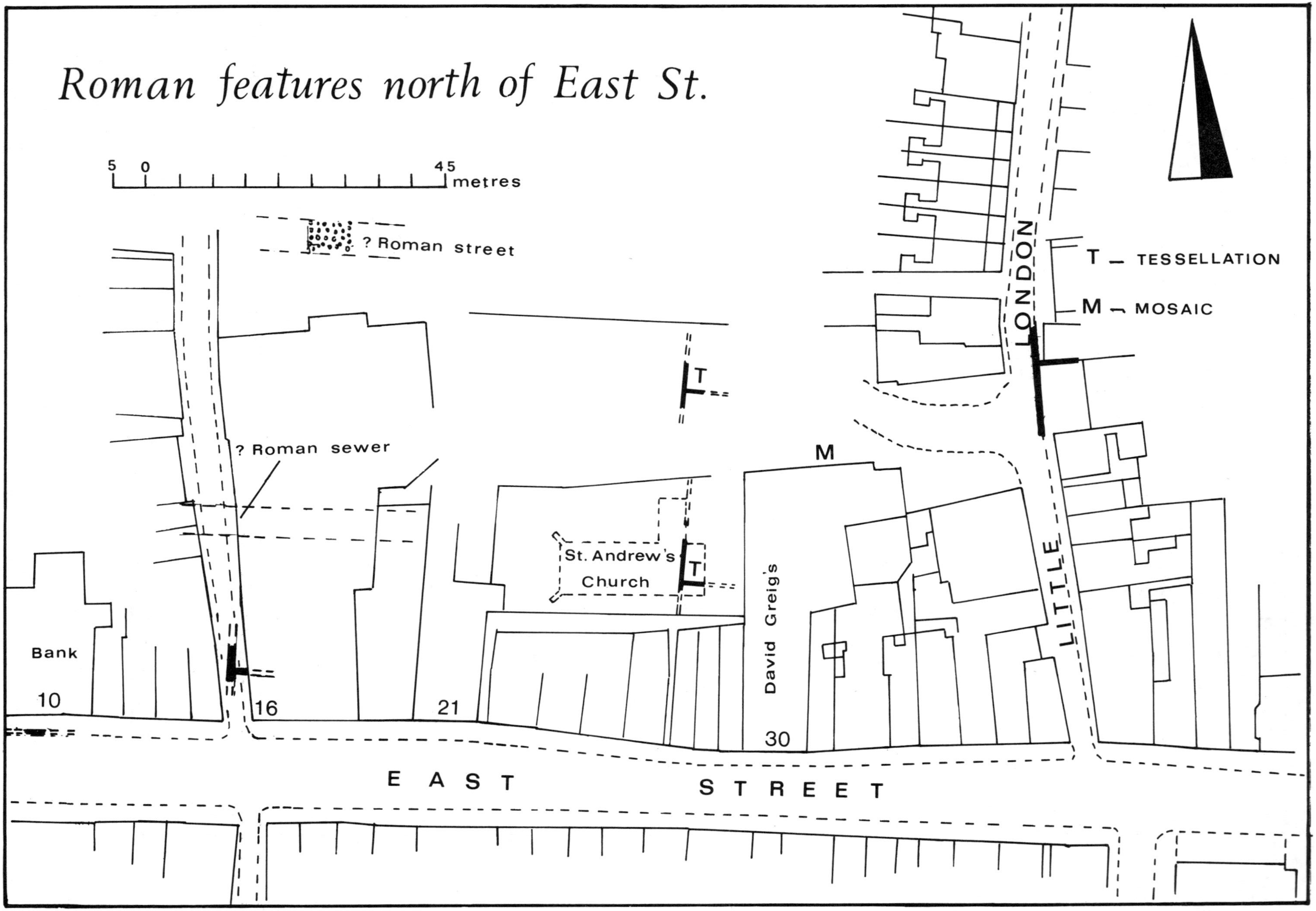

Roman features north of East St.
5 0 45 metres
? Roman street
T — TESSELLATION
M — MOSAIC
LONDON
LITTLE
T
M
? Roman sewer
St. Andrew's Church
T
David Greig's
Bank
10
16
21
30
EAST STREET

Fig. 5.24

Addendum

In late September 1980, Southerngas commenced to lay a new gas main along the north side of West Street and at about the same time the Portsmouth Water Company laid further new sections of water main in the north end of South Street. Although by that time this report was ready for the press, it has been thought useful to include the discoveries made as an addendum to the main report. These are listed below, and the find spots shown on a plan on the central area of the town, which also shows earlier finds below the streets which may be relevant to the area around the site of the Forum (Fig. 5.25).

West Street

Note:—All measurements quoted in reference to finds are along an east–west line, the zero point of which rests upon the east kerb of Tower Street at its junction with West Street.

51. At a depth of 1.10 metres in the gas main trench along the north side of West Street, extending from zero to 53.5 metres, a layer of pink mortar on top of compacted gravel. This is south of a large east–west wall found along the south end of Tower Street (*Chichester 3*, p. 21, 106 (iv); this volume, p. 48) and seen again on this occasion. The pink mortar might well be the base for a tiled ambulatory south of the assumed stylobate. Four tiles, measuring 38 cm by 29 cm by 4 cm thick, were found in position just west of the robber trench (see No. 52 below), at zero plus 50 metres. The tiles were butted against one another and there were a number of broken fragments which had been destroyed by the machine. Between 47 and 49 metres from datum were a number of fragments of flat sandstone lying along the bottom of the trench at 1.10 metre depth, which might have been the remains of a paved area.

52. A possible north–south robber trench 53.5 metres east of datum. The trench was 1.6 metres wide and on the west boundary it cut the layer of pink mortar noted above, while outside the eastern boundary there was a distinct change of stratification, with large amounts of food bones and other debris resting upon dirty brown soil.

53. Between 72 and 74 metres east of datum, a layer of tiles at least four high, set in pink mortar. This appeared to be a plinth, probably two metres square, of which the southern face was inside the trench. At 78 metres, a column drum 0.40 metre in diameter and 0.40 metre high was found, together with a fragment of marble frame moulding.

54. At 79 metres from datum, at a depth of 1.7 metres below street level, a large stone gutter aligned east-west (Fig. 5.26 A & B). Two blocks laid end to end were seen and one was recovered (Pl. 6). It measured 0.74 metre wide overall, 0.84 metre long and the gutter was 0.43 metre wide and 0.21 deep. It was covered by a fill of sticky black earth from which two 4th-century coins were recovered, together with some 4th-century colour coated wares. The gutter blocks rested upon a thin layer of compacted gravel which in turn lay above silty yellow clay (not natural). Immediately north of the gutter was a line of large sandstone blocks, also aligned east-west, with the bottom of the block level with the top of the gutter (Fig. 5.26A). The blocks rested upon a substantial foundation of flints and tile in mortar, to a depth of 0.9 metre, with natural clay below. North of these blocks, which were probably the remains of a stylobate, was an area of mortar, greensand and flint, 1.13 metre wide which had evidently been disturbed

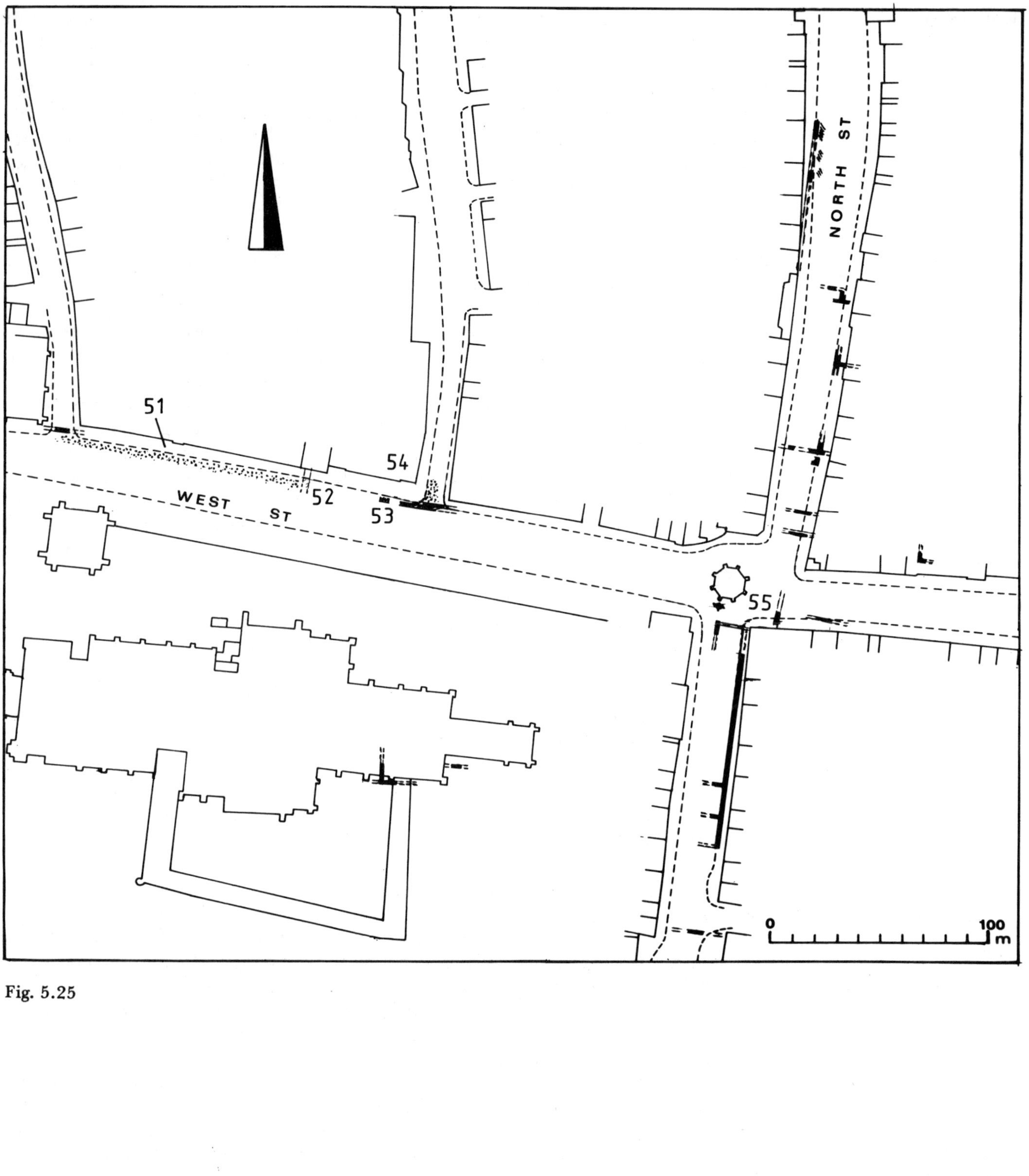

Fig. 5.25

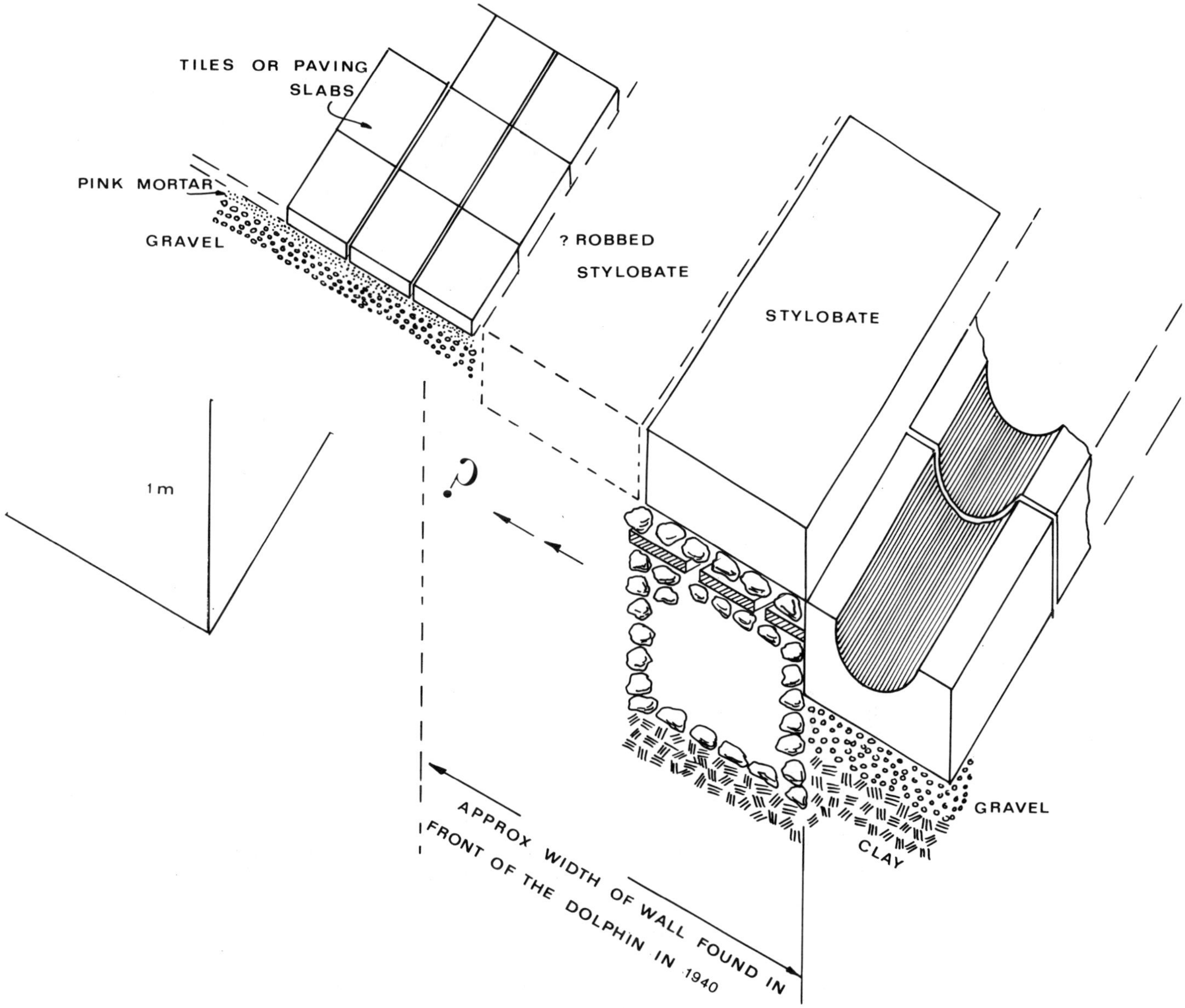
TILES OR PAVING SLABS
PINK MORTAR
GRAVEL
? ROBBED STYLOBATE
STYLOBATE
1 m
?
APPROX WIDTH OF WALL FOUND IN FRONT OF THE DOLPHIN IN 1940
GRAVEL
CLAY

Fig. 5.26A

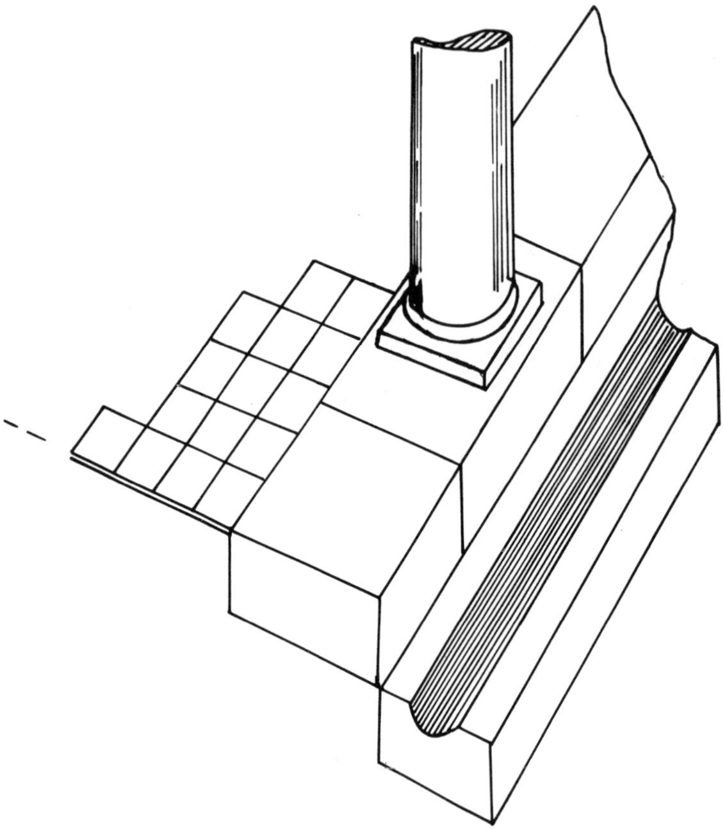

Fig. 5.26B

by the Post Office cable trench. It might represent the backfilled robber trench of a second line of sandstone blocks alongside the first line, but this point could not be established due to the extreme complexity of the various service trenches and pipes which criss-crossed the trench. The measurement of the sandstone block seen in position was 1.30 metre long by 0.8 metre wide by 0.30 metre deep. Another one was seen butted up against it on the east side, but the Post Office cable chamber dug many years ago had destroyed the one on the south, although the foundations could be seen going below the cable chamber.

The possible robber trench cut through a layer of compacted gravel on the north side and this extended northwards up Chapel Street for at least 4 metres. The gravel had a layer of pink mortar on top, very similar to that seen in West Street (see No. 51 above). The mortar was approximately 2–3 cm thick and could well be the bedding either for a tiled or paved area (see reconstruction, Fig. 5.27).[1]

Discussion

In 1940, the construction of an air raid shelter in the cellars of the "Dolphin and Anchor" Hotel on the north side of West Street revealed massive flint walling "at least six feet thick", running along the West Street frontage of the hotel

(*Chichester 1*, p. 16, No. 72). This is now no longer visible in the cellars, which have been lined with bricks, but the direction of the stylobate found in the gas main trench indicates that it is part of the same feature. The reported width of the wall in front of the hotel (nearly 2 metres), suggests perhaps either a very wide stylobate consisting of two lines of sandstone blocks each *c.* 0.8 metre wide, giving a total width of *c.* 1.6 metres plus, or a wide wall foundation supporting a single line of stylobate blocks. The width of the foundation wall below the blocks could not be determined due to the large number of service pipes all constricted within the narrow entrance of Chapel Street.

At all events, the evidence points to a large east-west building below the "Dolphin and Anchor" of which we have the south facing aspect in the gas main trench. Whether this is the basilica is a matter for conjecture (see Fig. 5.27). The southern limits of the building appear to align with the southern limits of the public baths and it is possible that the eastern boundary of the baths marks the western boundary of the area in which the Forum lies. There is a large building below North Street which may have its western boundary running north-south below the west pavement of North Street and this would give us three sides of a rectangle, with the north side still in doubt. More discoveries are needed below the buildings north of the "Dolphin and Anchor" and south of Crane Street before the problem can be resolved.
before the problem can be resolved.

South Street (Figs. 5.25 and 5.28)

55. In October, work by the Portsmouth Water Company revealed more of a line of sandstone blocks previously noted (No. 47 above). Two large stones were found in position. They were angled roughly north-east-south-west and they abutted a large chalk block to the north. The blocks were set in a hard creamy pink mortar and had been cut through by an earlier service trench. They are not on the same alignment as those found earlier and might perhaps be part of a large stone base, perhaps for a statue.

1. On January 29th, 1981, a few days before this paper went to the press, Southerngas opened a wider trench at the south end of Chapel Street. Two slabs of sandstone measuring 61 by 75 cm, and 22 cm thick, were found side by side. They were bedded upon a screed of pink/white mortar laid upon compacted gravel and appear to be the surviving fragments of a flagged pavement along the west side of the building below the "Dolphin and Anchor". The depth at which the slabs were found (1.3 metres below road level), agrees well with the earlier discoveries in 1980 and if the suggestion that this is an ambulatory along the west side of a public building is correct, then the north–south stylobate and gutter must be within a few feet on the west side, either below the pavement or just below the Post Office.

References

CHICHESTER 1 — Down, A. and Rule, M., *Chichester Excavations 1*, 1971.

CHICHESTER 2 — Down, A., *Chichester Excavations 2*, 1974.

CHICHESTER 3 — Down, A., *Chichester Excavations 3*, 1978.

LEWIS 1966 — Lewis, M. J. T., *Temples in Roman Britain*, Cambridge, 1966.

VCH SX. 3 — *Victoria County History of Sussex*, Vol. 3.

WILSON 1962 — Wilson, A. E., "North Wall and Northgate", *S.A.C.* 100 (1962).

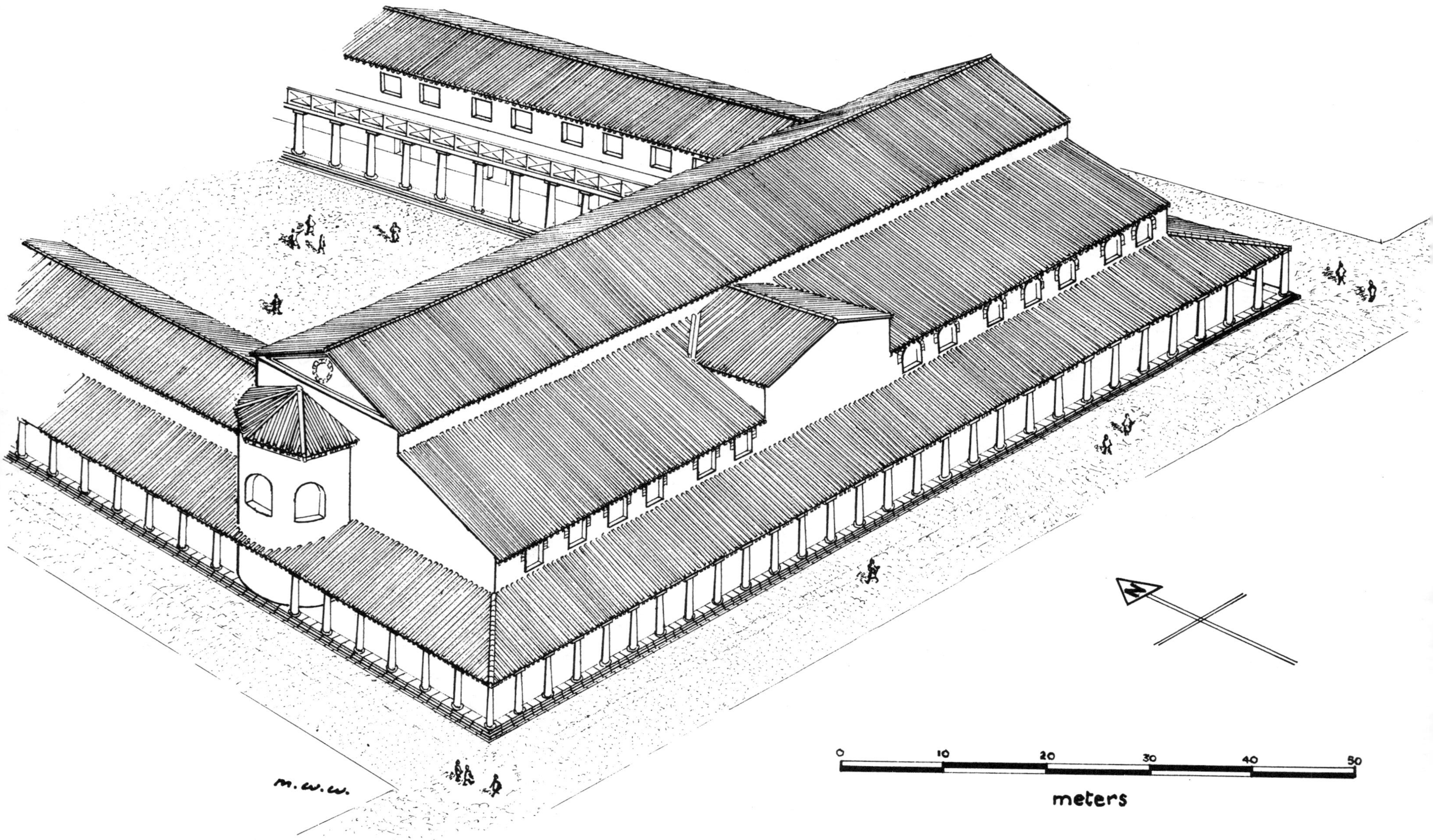

Fig. 5.27. Imaginative reconstruction of the building below the Dolphin & Anchor, possibly the Basilica (after Boon, Roman Silchester). Drawn by Max Wholey.

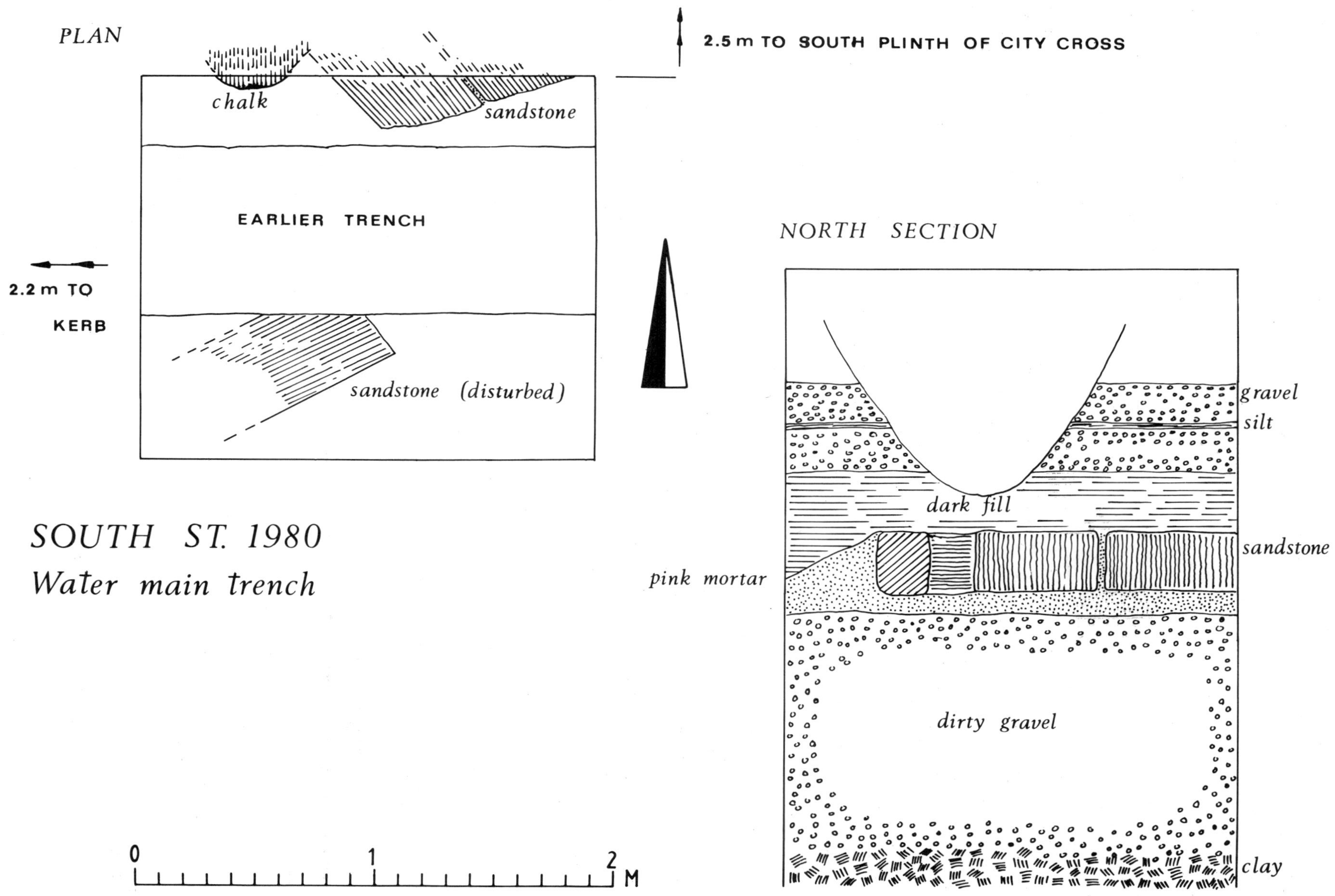
PLAN
chalk
sandstone
2.5 m TO SOUTH PLINTH OF CITY CROSS
EARLIER TRENCH
2.2 m TO
KERB
sandstone (disturbed)
NORTH SECTION
gravel
silt
dark fill
sandstone
pink mortar
dirty gravel
clay
SOUTH ST. 1980
Water main trench
0
1
2
M

Fig. 5.28

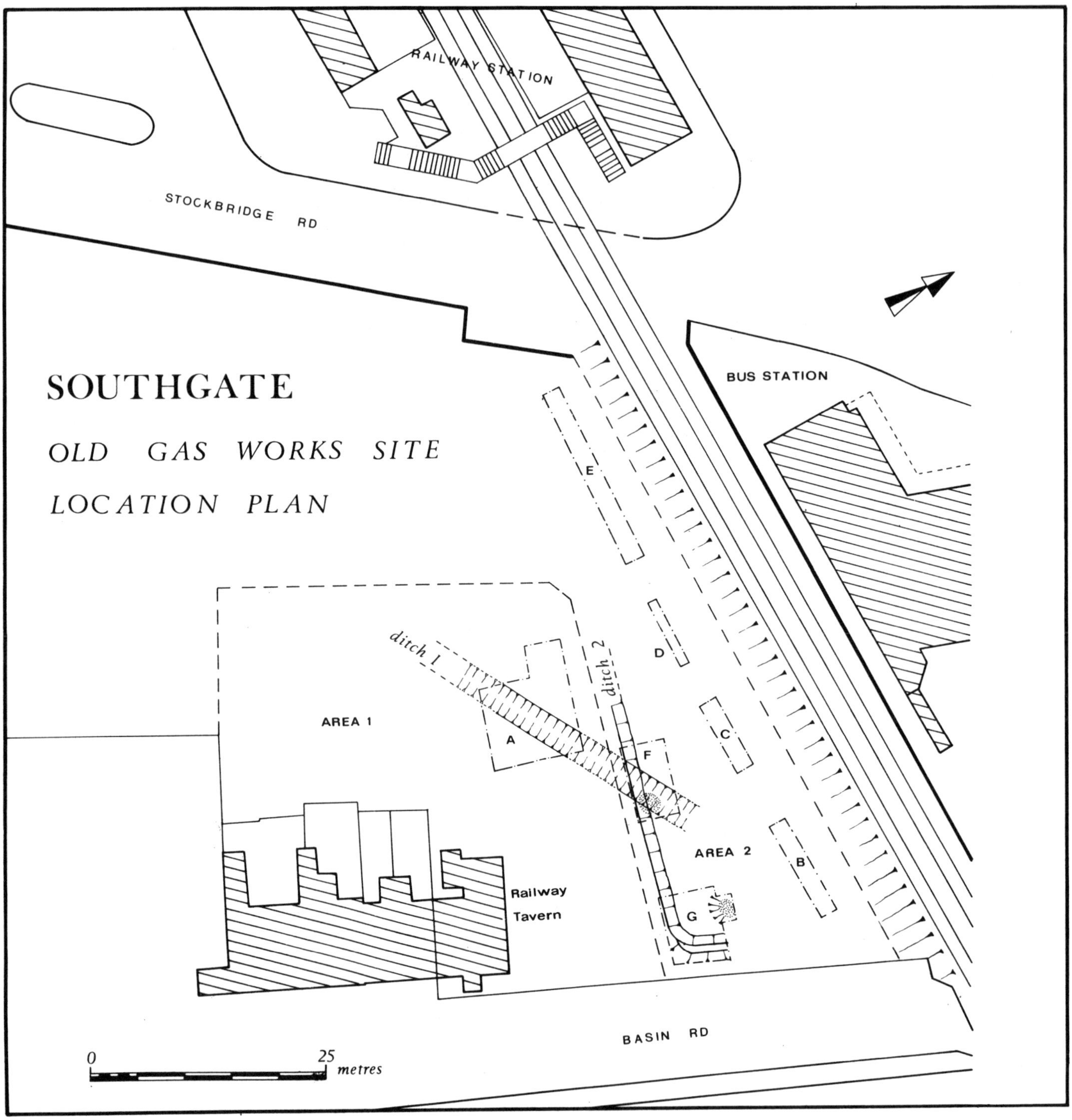

RAILWAY STATION
STOCKBRIDGE RD
BUS STATION
SOUTHGATE
OLD GAS WORKS SITE
LOCATION PLAN
E
ditch 1
ditch 2
D
AREA 1
A
C
F
AREA 2
B
Railway
Tavern
G
BASIN RD
0
25
metres

Fig. 6.1

6

Excavations outside Southgate 1975-76

Introduction

SITE 1

In 1975, trial excavations were carried out on the site of the north of the old Gas Works, and just south of the railway line (Fig. 6.1). The site and the land to the north of it, formerly belonging to British Rail, had been acquired by Marler Estates Developments Ltd., and we are grateful to Mr. Clifford Tippett for permission to excavate, and to his Architect, Mr. Richard Leggatt, for his co-operation. The object was to examine the ground for signs of any Roman or medieval suburban development and in particular to try and locate the Roman cemetery thought to exist outside the Southgate and also to find the Roman road to the settlement at Selsey. In the event, the proposed development has not yet taken place at the time of writing (1980), and pressure of other rescue work both inside and outside the city led to the postponement of further excavation on the Gas Works site. It has been thought best to publish the results of the trial excavations in view of the lapse of time, and not wait until the opportunity arises to follow-up the discoveries reported here.

In addition to these trial excavations, cuts were made alongside the Canal Basin (Site 3), and at the east end of the Littlemead School site (now Lacey House), further south in Stockbridge Road, where the District Council were carrying out a building programme (Site 2). While this work was going on, the opportunity arose to dig a trial hole on a site just south of Southgate and north of the Magistrates Court, where in 1974, medieval kilns were found. On this occasion, the object was to try and find other kilns, and later on, in 1979-80, when the site was finally developed, a watching brief was maintained on the groundworks.

Acknowledgements are due to Beadle Property Holdings and their Architects, E. G. Nash and Partners for permission to excavate in 1967, and to Geoffrey Osborne Ltd., the contractors, for facilities for observation in 1979-80. The three operations were funded by small grants from the Department of the Environment.

Site history

Sites 1 and 3

(a) Roman

In September 1819, workmen digging the Canal Basin in Palace Field, discovered Roman pottery, querns, a square glass bottle enclosed in lead and containing "ashes" and a pot containing 700 Roman silver coins, with a skeleton nearby. The coins ranged from A.D. 69 to 180 (*Gentlemen's Magazine*, 1830, Part 2). These finds and the discovery of two late 1st century tombstones near Southgate in 1833 (*S.A.C.* 95, 130), suggest that a Roman cemetery exists somewhere outside the gate.

(b) Post-Roman (see Fig. 6.1)

The following notes have been compiled by Mr. R. R. Morgan:

The site has been curiously affected by the transport and industrial expansion of the last 200 years. First the line of the old lane to Stockbridge was lost when the turnpike road was built in the 19th century;[1] next the Canal Company cut through down the east side;[2] then the railway on the north side[3] and finally, the gas works was built on the south.[4]

The area covered by trenches B, C, D, F and G was freehold land used for agriculture. In the early 18th century the site contained a cottage, greenhouses, pigsty, nursery and garden, with buildings specifically at B and D.[5]

Trench E was Vicars' Choral land and as such was leased to a succession of tenants as garden plots.[6] There were two cottages on the road frontage at the west end of Trench E. They are shown on the Gardner map (1769). The Parliamentary Survey of 1649[7] describes the area of E, and to the north and a little to the south as "2 orchards and 2 tenements, lately demolished when the city was a garrison, and a little low house of one room at the west end of the orchards",

Trench A was part of the meadowland of the Prebend of Bracklesham[8] which was leased to farmers until Basin Road drove through it, whereupon it became a garden and orchard briefly,[9] and then being leased severally to various domestic and commercial occupiers. Specifically a house, pigsty and garden are recorded in 1843.[10] Thus the only early domestic occupation might be found at the Stockbridge Road frontage.

Notes

1. WSRO Raper Deeds;
2. WSRO QDP/W38.
3. WSRO QDP/W85.
4. WSRO CAP 1/29/37.
5. WSRO QDP/W85.
6. WSRO Vicars' Choral Lease Books.
7. WSRO Cap III/4/1.
8. WSRO Cap II/23/1.
9. WSRO Cap I/29/28.
10. WSRO QDP/W85.

SITE 2 Area 4; (New Market Avenue, north side). (Fig. 6.8).

This site was part of a one-acre plot of the Dean and Chapter which stretched south along the east side of the Southgate road, from the Lavant southwards. History has repeated itself, because the dig adjoins the new road cut through from Southgate, and this road is almost on the line of "an ancient road which led into the meadows of the prebend of Bracklesham".

The earliest documentary source traced is 1534[1] when the site was cultivated ground as it still was in 1649[2] (described then as "a garden").

In the 18th century[3] it was still basically a garden, but a shop had now been built on the Southgate road frontage. This can be seen on the Gardner Map (1769). During the 19th century the whole site was intensively developed and with the opening of Basin Road in 1821 the "ancient road" was no longer required and was partially built over. The two properties still standing as Nos. 31–32 Southgate show clear signs of timber framing and are probably the original shop. Building continued behind the properties—primarily commercial and industrial, e.g. cordwaining, carpentry, upholstery, brewing; with stables, cart-houses and workshops. The business of Gatehouse, a brewer extended over the excavation site.

Notes

1. WSRO Cap I/23/1 and SRS 58, No. 487.
2. WSRO Cap I/30/1.
3. WSRO Cap I/27/20/1774.

The excavations

Site 1 (Figs. 6.1-6.7)

Four trial trenches (B, C, D and E, Area 2). were dug by machine along the south side of the railway line to search for the line of the Roman road to Selsey and to examine the ground for signs of Roman burials. Trench A (Area 1), was dug to the rear of the disused Railway Inn and trenches F and G (Area 2), were dug to the north-east of it to follow up features discovered. Area 3, the Gas Works site, has so far not been dug.

Trial trenches B, C and D (Figs. 6.1-6.2)

As the stratification is identical, these three trenches are discussed together. Below the cultivated topsoil, formerly the gardens of the railway cottages on the site, was a layer of brown loam containing 19th–20th century pottery in addition to earlier wares. This layer was very compacted and dry and might well represent make-up over the natural brick-earth, brought from within the city. Trench C was cut by four pits and Trench B by three. Of these, Pits C1 to C3 and Pit B1 contained nothing later than medieval glazed and unglazed pottery, together with residual Roman wares, while Pit B2 had nothing later than abraded Roman sherds in it. The other pits (C4 and B3), had modern material. Layer 3 in all three trenches was yellow clay which was the top of natural brick-earth. One sherd of medieval ware was found in the top of B.3. Unstratified wares from all three trenches showed that in fact 16th and 17th century pottery was present, giving a total post-Roman date range of *c.* 13th–20th century.

As a result of these three cuttings, which indicated the presence of Roman, medieval and post-medieval occupation, further trenches were cut (see below).

Trial trench E

This was cut to the west of D, as near as possible to the Stockbridge Road, to see if the Roman road ran just to the east of it. Here a deep feature (see Fig. 6.2), was sectioned. It is likely that a large pit, possibly for gravel, was dug at some time in the medieval period as pottery and tile of 14th–15th century date was found in the bottom, together with some fragments of slate roofing tile which are probably contemporary. The area must have remained as a flooded pit for some time, but later on, loose gravel was dumped back into the hole and thereafter the eastern end silted up slowly. At the west end, what appears to be a narrow drainage channel was later dug, draining from north to south. Finally, at some time during the 17th century, the hole was filled in and the ground made up at intervals as it subsided.

The western end of the trial trench could not be further explored towards the road due to the presence of the cellar behind the house which formerly fronted on to Stockbridge Road.

Trench A (for location see Fig. 6.1)

This was dug on the south side of the wall dividing the old builders' yard from the railway property and was excavated by hand after the top 0.5 metre of garden soil had been removed by machine.

Period 1, ? Roman

The earliest feature found was a ditch (Ditch 1), running north-east to south-west across the site. It was seen again in Trench F to the north. The dimensions

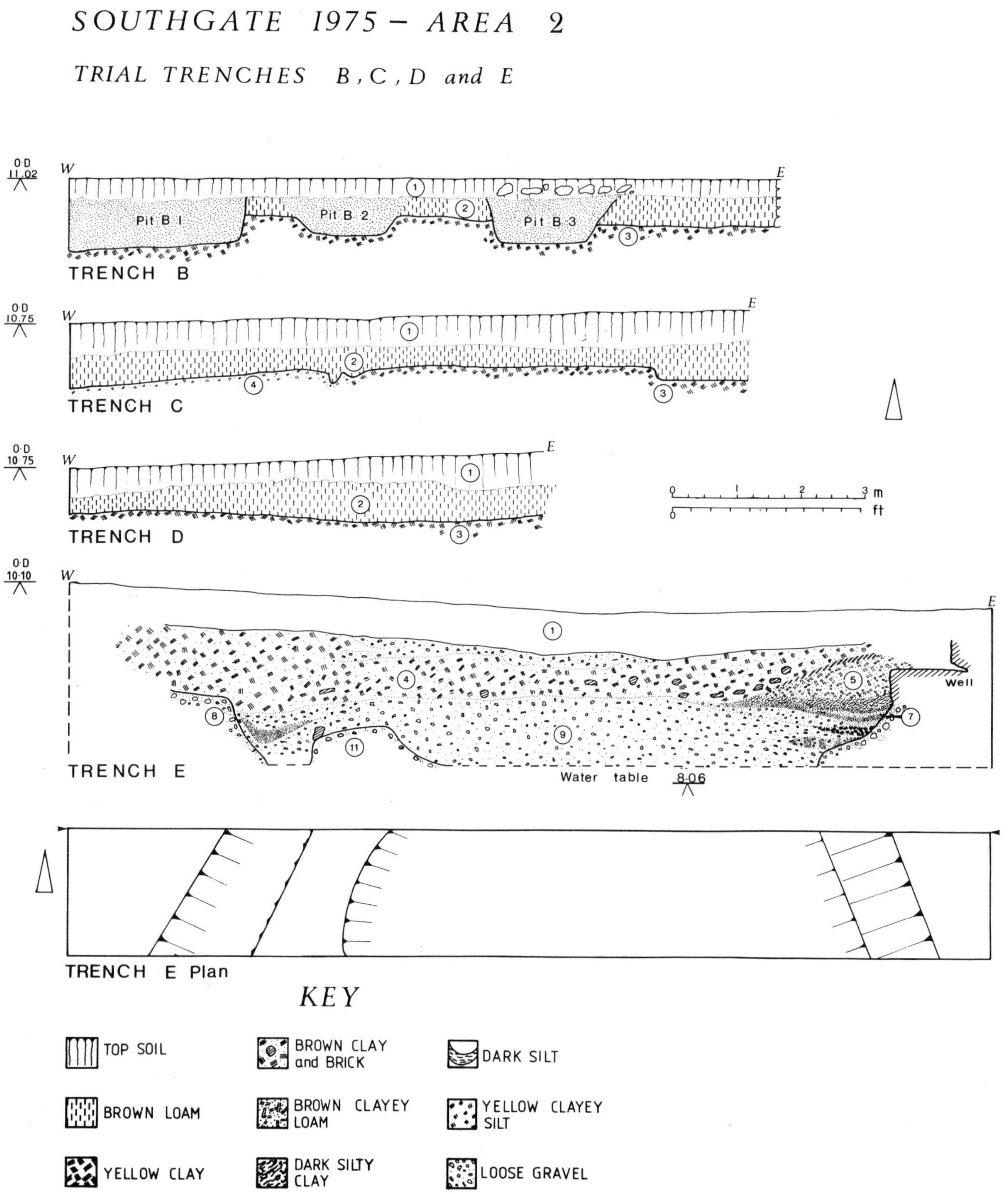
SOUTHGATE 1975 – AREA 2
TRIAL TRENCHES B, C, D and E
O·D 11.02
W
E
Pit B 1
Pit B 2
Pit B 3
TRENCH B
O·D 10.75
TRENCH C
O·D 10.75
TRENCH D
0 1 2 3 m
0 ft
O·D 10·10
Well
Water table 8·06
TRENCH E
TRENCH E Plan
KEY
TOP SOIL
BROWN LOAM
YELLOW CLAY
BROWN CLAY and BRICK
BROWN CLAYEY LOAM
DARK SILTY CLAY
DARK SILT
YELLOW CLAYEY SILT
LOOSE GRAVEL

Fig. 6.2

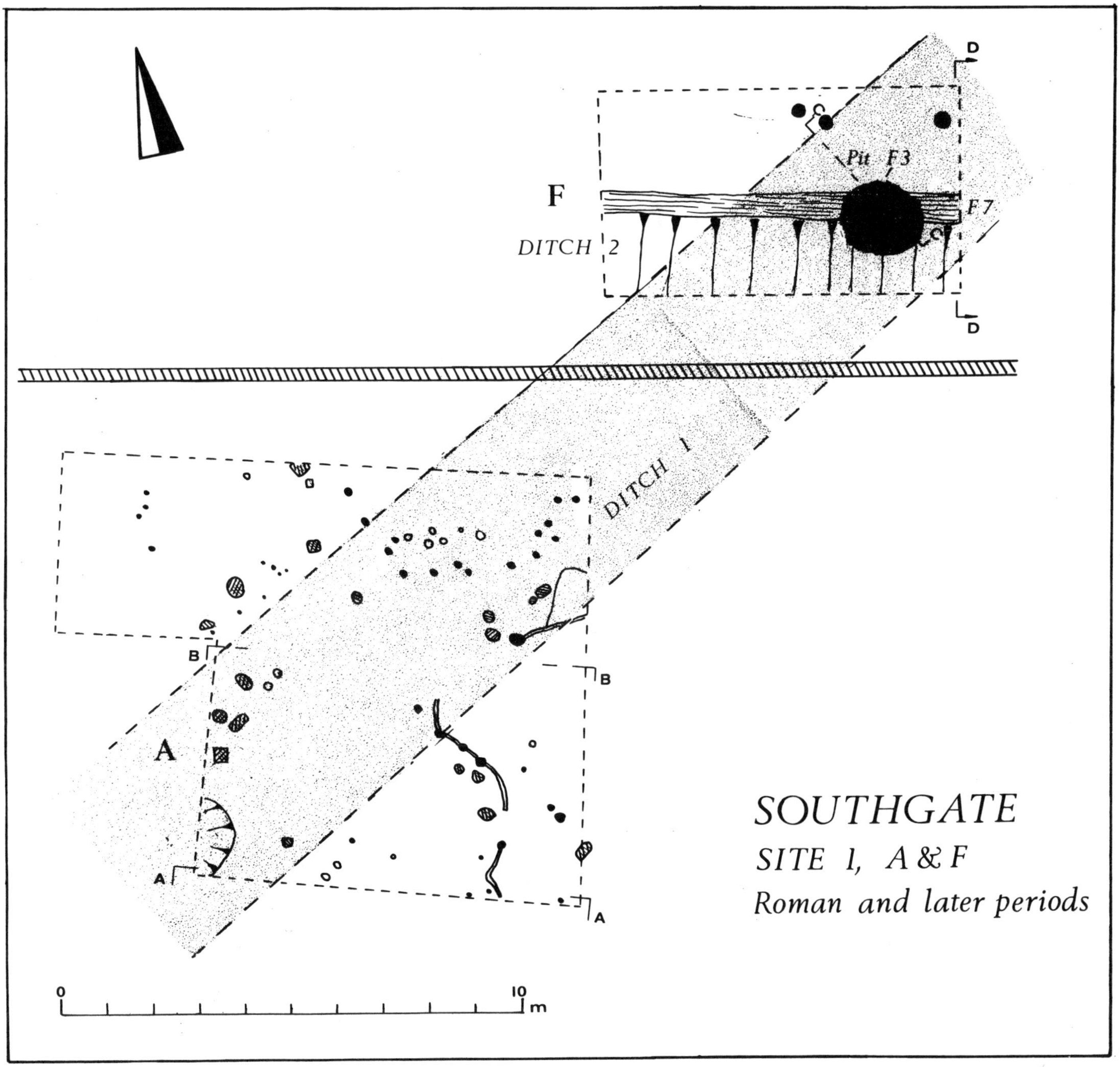

D
Pit F3
F
F7
C
DITCH 2
D
DITCH 1
B
B
A
A
A
0
10
m
SOUTHGATE
SITE 1, A & F
Roman and later periods

Fig. 6.3

SOUTHGATE 1975–6 AREA 1

TRENCH A, SECTION A – A

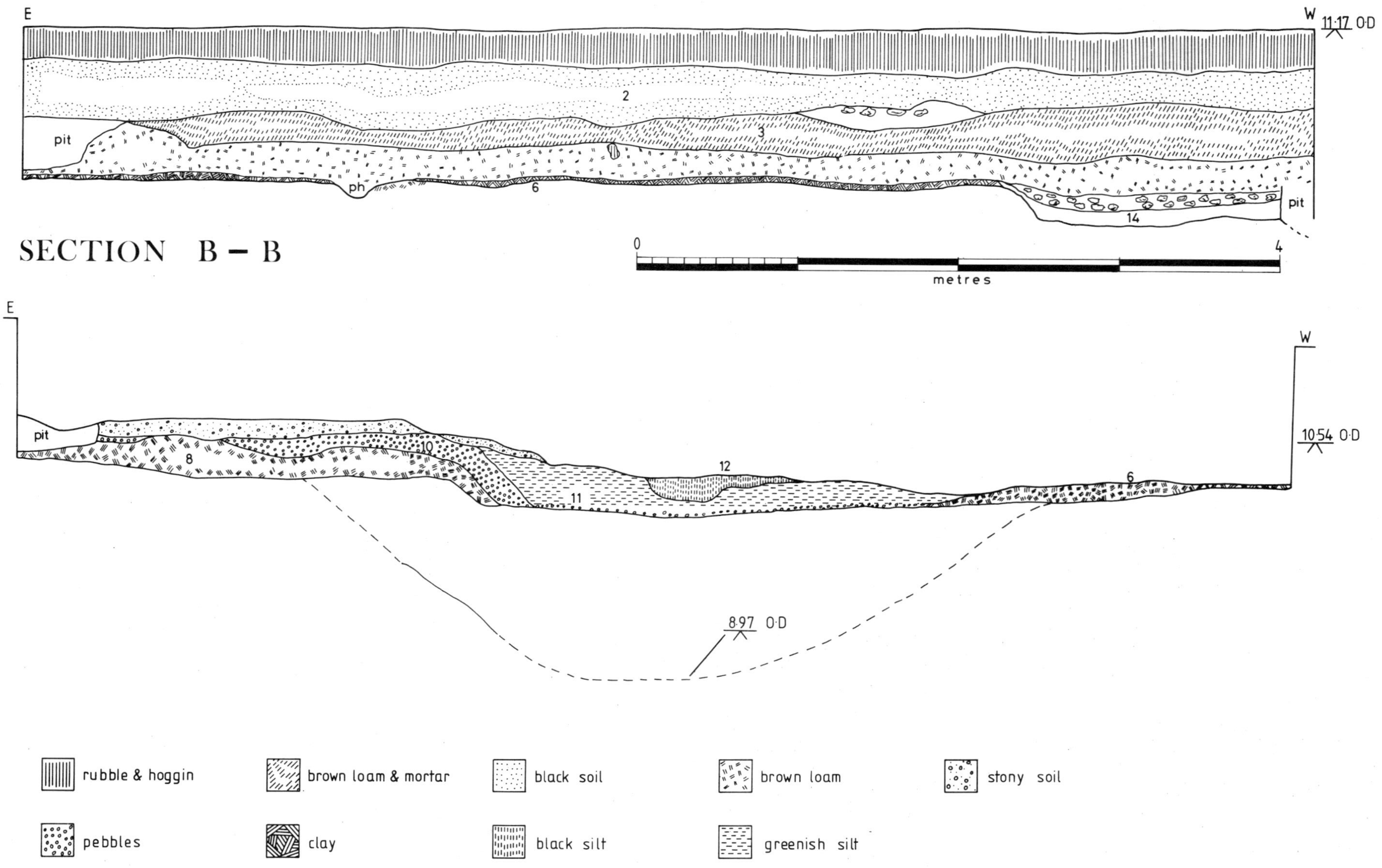

Fig. 6.4

(see Fig. 6.4) were *c.* 4.5 metres wide and *c.* 1.5 metre deep. It drained to the south-west and presumably discharged into a creek running up from the harbour. No artifacts were found and it appears to have silted up slowly and eventually became no more than a shallow depression. It was round-bottomed in profile and probably functioned as a boundary/drainage ditch. It was probably Roman but could be earlier.

Period 2, Phase 1 (Fig. 6.3 and Pl. 7)

At some time after the ditch had silted up, slight timber buildings were erected on both sides of the shallow depression that remained. The full scope of the structures could not be determined within the limits of the excavation and no hearths or occupation spreads could be seen. The silt into which the postholes were cut (Layer A.11), contained Antonine samian as the latest artifacts and the residual samian in the post-Roman levels above was of the same date. A pit (A.14) which cut the silt in the south-west corner of the trench produced an amount of Roman building material, Antonine samian and two coins, one of Domitian and one of Hadrian. The earliest residual Roman wares in the upper layers were of mid-late 1st century date.

Period 2, Phase 2

At some time later, a circular structure was erected at the north end of the site. Only a part of it was within the excavation and the postholes were dug from a higher level than the Phase 1 structures as they cut A.6, a layer of yellow clay which contained only a few scraps of Roman grey ware.

Trench F (Fig. 6.3)

This was excavated on the north side of the boundary wall from Trench A with with a view to tracing the Period 1 ditch. Two periods of Roman occupation were found:

Period 1, Ditch 1 (see above)

This had been partly destroyed by another ditch cutting across it from the east (see below).

Period 2, Phase 3

Phase 3 was represented by a deep pit (Pit F.3, Fig. 6.5), which cut through Ditch 1 and which might have been a shallow well. It was filled with burnt daub, charcoal and Roman pottery and tile. The pottery had a date range from *c.* early 2nd to 4th century.

Period 3, Phase 1, late or post-medieval

At some time after Pit F.3 was filled in, a shallow gulley (F.7) was dug from east to west across the site. It petered out towards the western boundary of the trench and contained a few abraded sherds of unglazed medieval coarse ware.

Phase 2 (Pl. 8)

An east-west ditch (Ditch 2), cut away the south side of the Phase 2 gulley. It was cut into the natural coombe deposits and only the northern half was in the trench. It destroyed all but the last few centimetres of Ditch 1 and the pottery recovered from the bottom comprised three fragments of medieval roofing tile and some thin-sectioned dish rims in a fine pale fabric very similar to the painted wares of the late 15th century. These were the latest fabrics in an assemblage which contained earlier abraded medieval wares, giving a maximum date range for the finds of *c.* 13th to 15th century.

SOUTHGATE

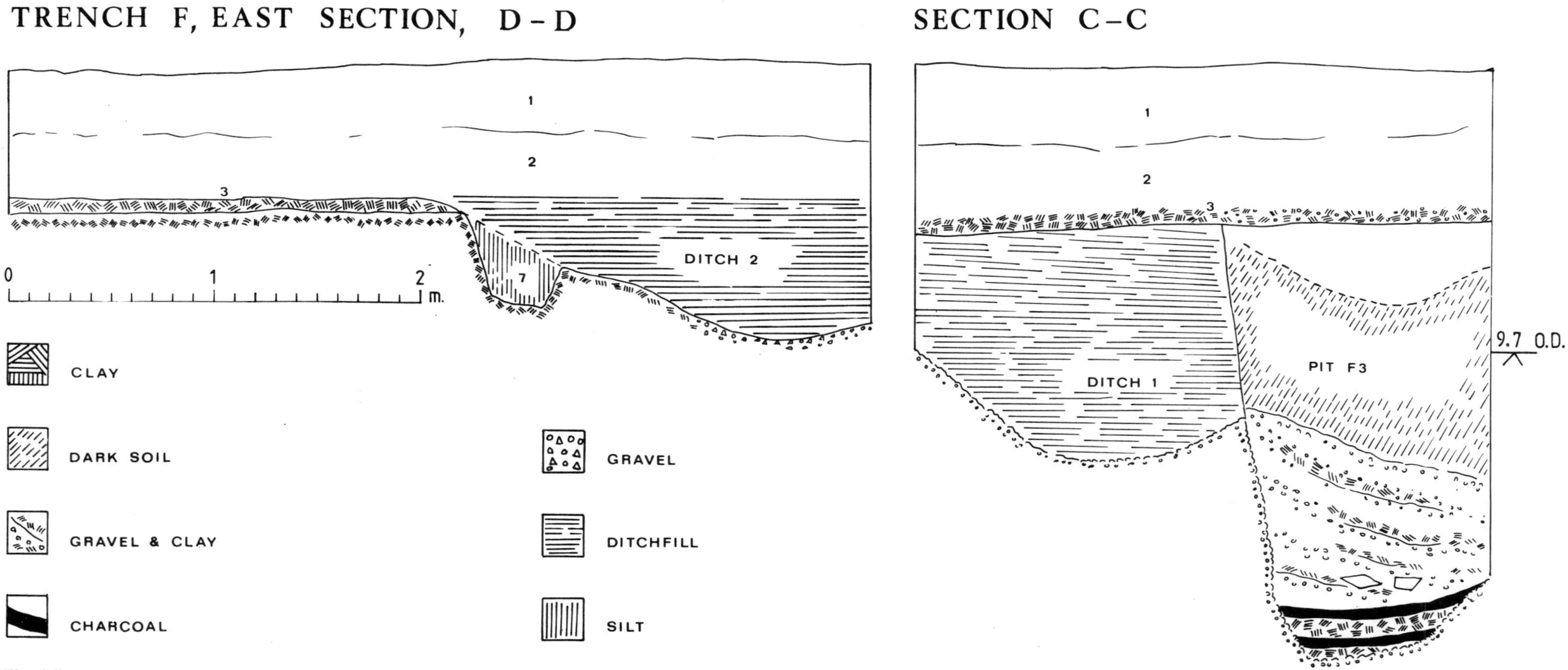

Fig. 6.5

Trench G (Fig. 6.7)

This was dug to the east of F to trace the course of Ditch 2. Two periods of occupation were noted:

Period 2, Roman

The Roman ground level was represented by layer G.8, yellow brick-earth resting on natural. Part of a slot for a timber building (G.9) was cut into this. It ran roughly north-east, but the rest of it was destroyed by Ditch 2 (see below). It was not possible to date the remains of the structure, but it might have been contemporary with Pit G.3, a deep pit on the north side which contained large amounts of ash and charcoal, with pilae and tegulae and wall plaster from a destroyed building. The date range for the pottery from the pit was from the 2nd to the 4th century. None of the samian was earlier than Antonine and most was late Antonine. At the other end of the range were New Forest purple and red wares which can go to the early 5th century.

Period 3, Phase 2, post-medieval

It was found that Ditch 2 ran north-south and turned within the limits of the excavation to run westwards, thus destroying most of the Roman levels. The bottom level of the ditch (dug as Pit G.2), contained medieval glazed and unglazed wares of the 13th–14th century, together with tiles which are post-medieval in date, possibly Tudor or later. There was also one fragment of 19th century stoneware, but this might be contamination from the layer above (G.5) which represented the top filling and which had pottery dating from the 13th to 19th century in it.

Discussion

(i) The Roman road to Selsey

Trial trenches B–E failed to locate the road, which must either lie on the course of Stockbridge Road at this point or further west below the area now occupied by the Railway Station. On balance, the former seems the most likely in view of the gravel layer located outside the Courthouse in 1972 (SR 1972), which was probably the Roman road.

(ii) The cemetery

The location of the Southgate cemetery, if one exists, has so far eluded discovery. It is possible that the burials found in 1819 when the Canal Basin was dug might belong to an estate outside the city rather than to a town cemetery. More work needs to be carried out before this can be proved, but it is worthy of note that with the exception of the 1819 discoveries, there has been no record of finds suggesting burials from outside the Southgate in spite of considerable development.

(iii) Roman occupation

The evidence from the three trenches A, F and G clearly shows occupation dating at least from the 2nd century to the 4th and possibly earlier, as in Trench A the residual material included a 1st century imported flagon and a mortarium of the same date. The occupation appears to have been slight and probably not continuous and it extended across land which had previously been drained by a ditch which had silted up by the 2nd century. It is not possible to say whether this ditch belonged to an earlier Iron Age settlement, or not.

SOUTHGATE

TRENCH G, SECTION E – E

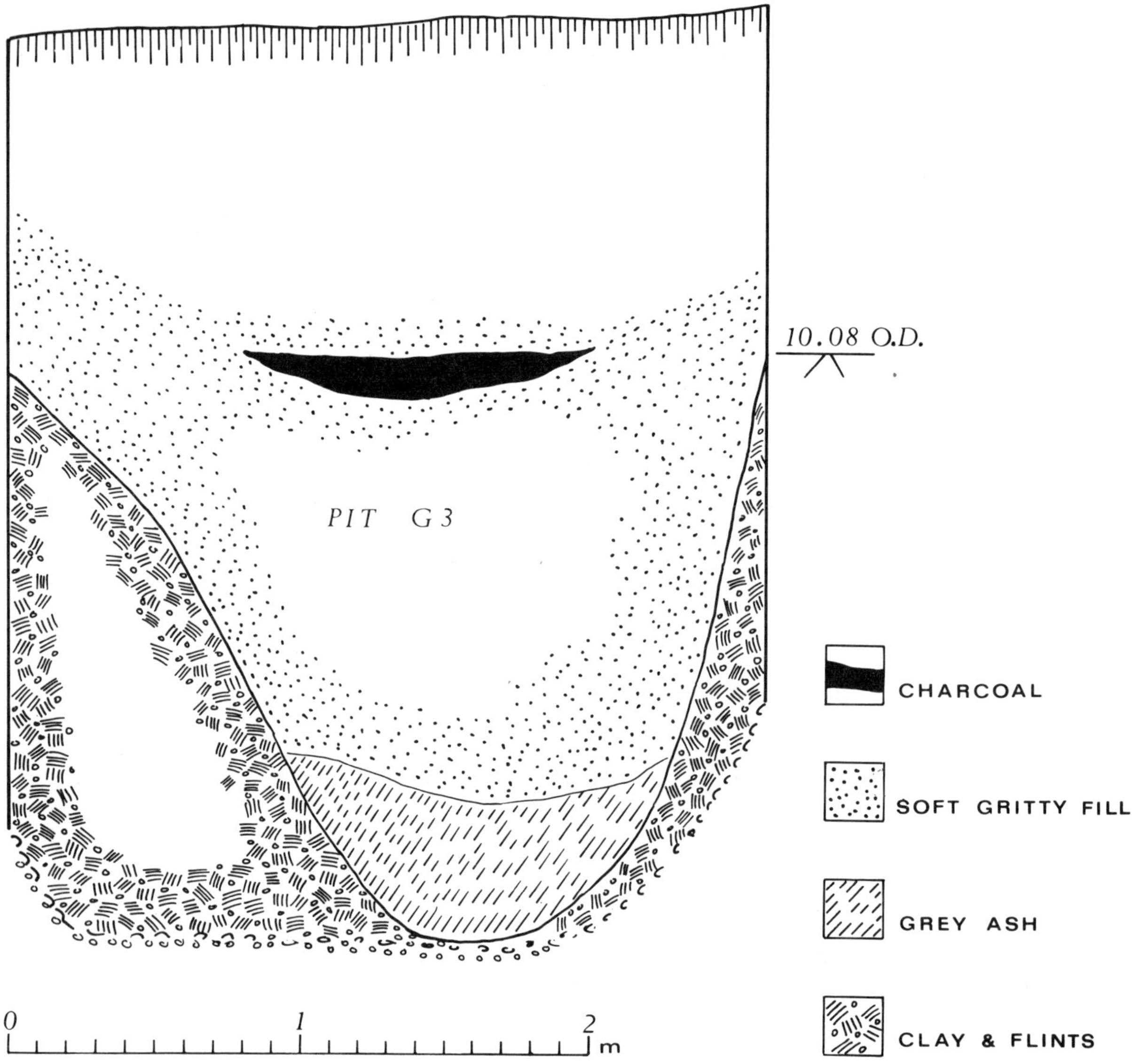

Fig. 6.6

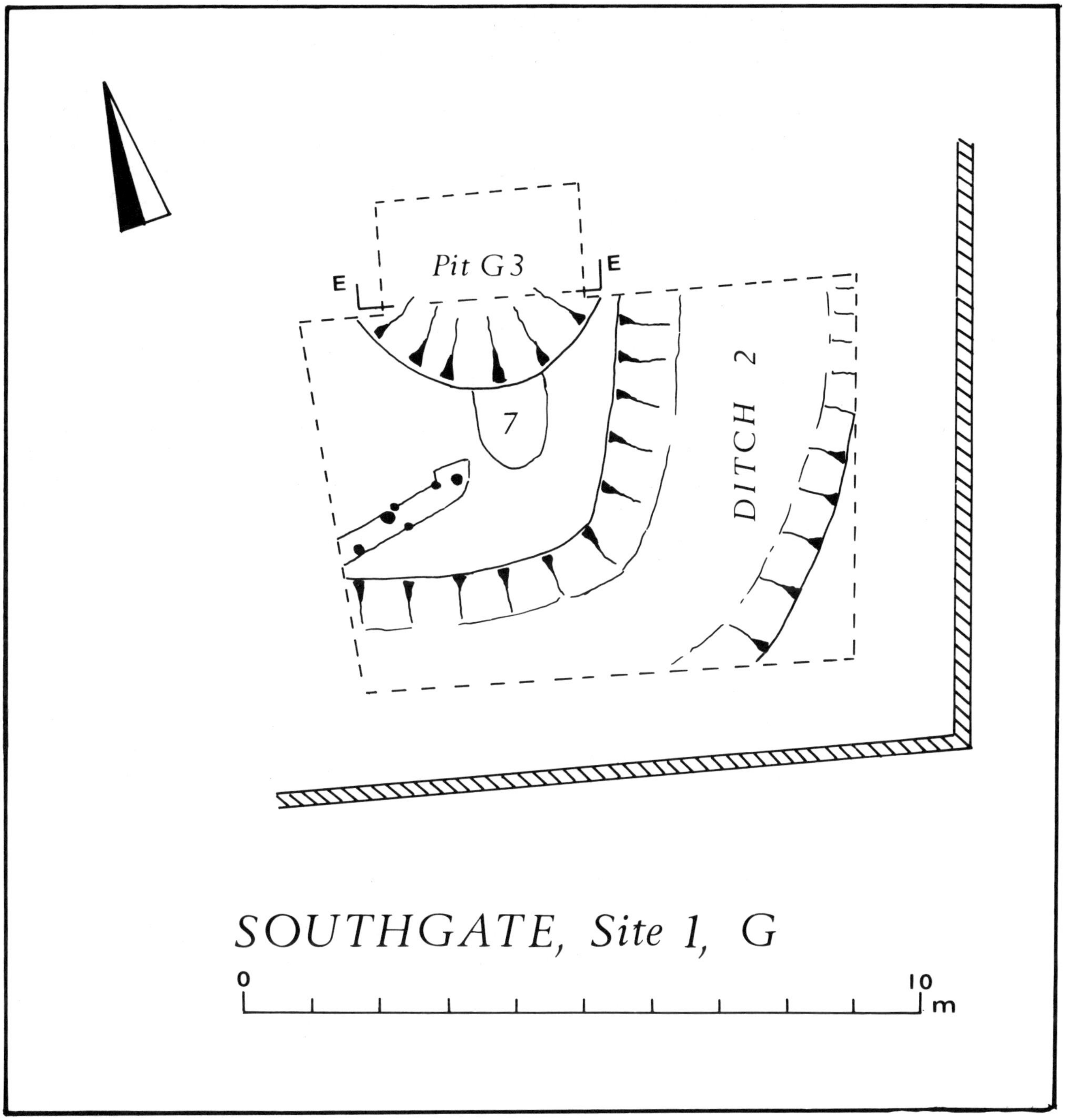

Fig. 6.7

(iv) Late-post medieval activity

Considerable amounts of medieval wares were found in Ditch 2 and in the topsoil and pits in trial trenches B–E. Some of this pottery may have derived from the manuring of fields with the contents of cesspits from within the city, while the pits behind the tenements fronting on to Stockbridge Road might account for the rest. It is not possible to date Ditch 2 with certainty as the material in the bottom represents what went in after it was last cleaned out, if it ever was. If it is assumed that it was never cleaned out, then on the evidence of the pottery and tile it must be post-medieval in date and not earlier than, say, the 16th century.

The feature in Trial Trench E

The deep feature sectioned in Trial Trench E is approximately 245 metres from the Southgate and it was thought at the time that it might have been a pit dug for gravel and then left open for some time. Reference to the Gardner Map of 1769 (Fig. 7.5), shows a series of large ponds around the city, from the north-east corner (The Dell Hole, now filled in), to the two large ones out in Westgate Fields which are still there although very overgrown. They could well have been gravel pits, dug during the late or post-medieval period, and the Gardner Map shows the ones which were still open in the late 18th century. The feature in Trench E is on a line with the ponds along the south side of the city and could quite well be contemporary.

Site 2, North of New Market Avenue

Trench A (Figs. 6.8-6.9)

This trial trench was dug in 1976 to the east of buildings at the rear of No. 33 Southgate. The object was to examine the ground for more of the medieval kilns first found in 1974 below the New Magistrates Court, to the south of the present site.

Layer 2, below the make-up for the modern car park surface consisted of sticky yellow clay which contained Roman and medieval pottery. Two fragments of vitrified brick were found which looked as if they might have been used either in a kiln or a smithy.

Below Layer 2 in the south-west corner, was a large pit of which only one quarter was within the excavation.The fill was entirely Roman and contained much charcoal, burnt clay and iron slag from forging activities, with a particularly large accretion of iron at the bottom of the pit.

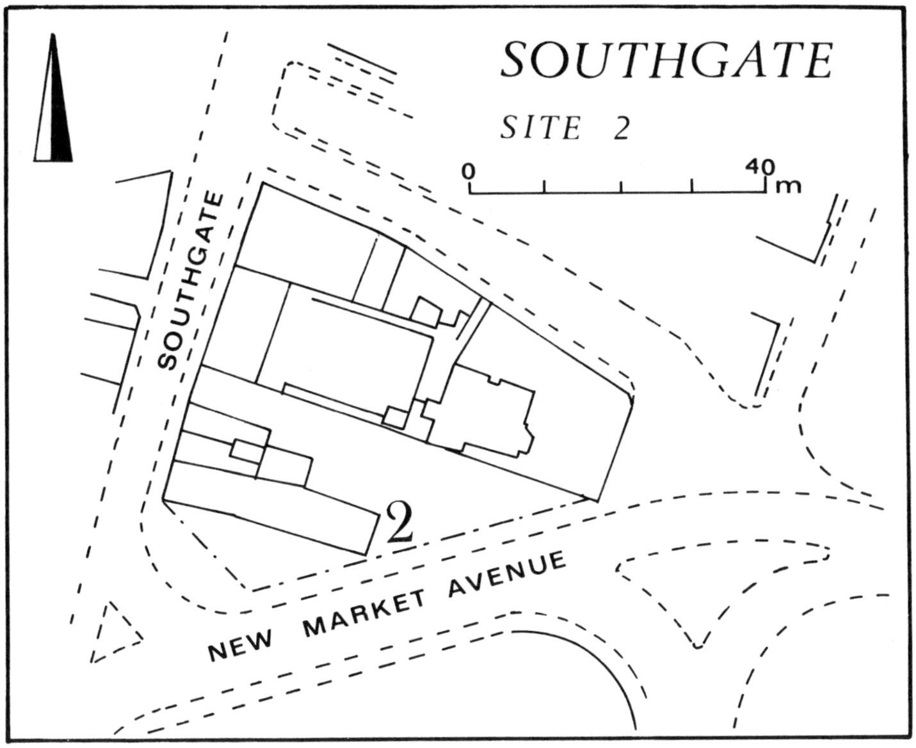

Fig. 6.8. Southgate, location plan, Site 2.

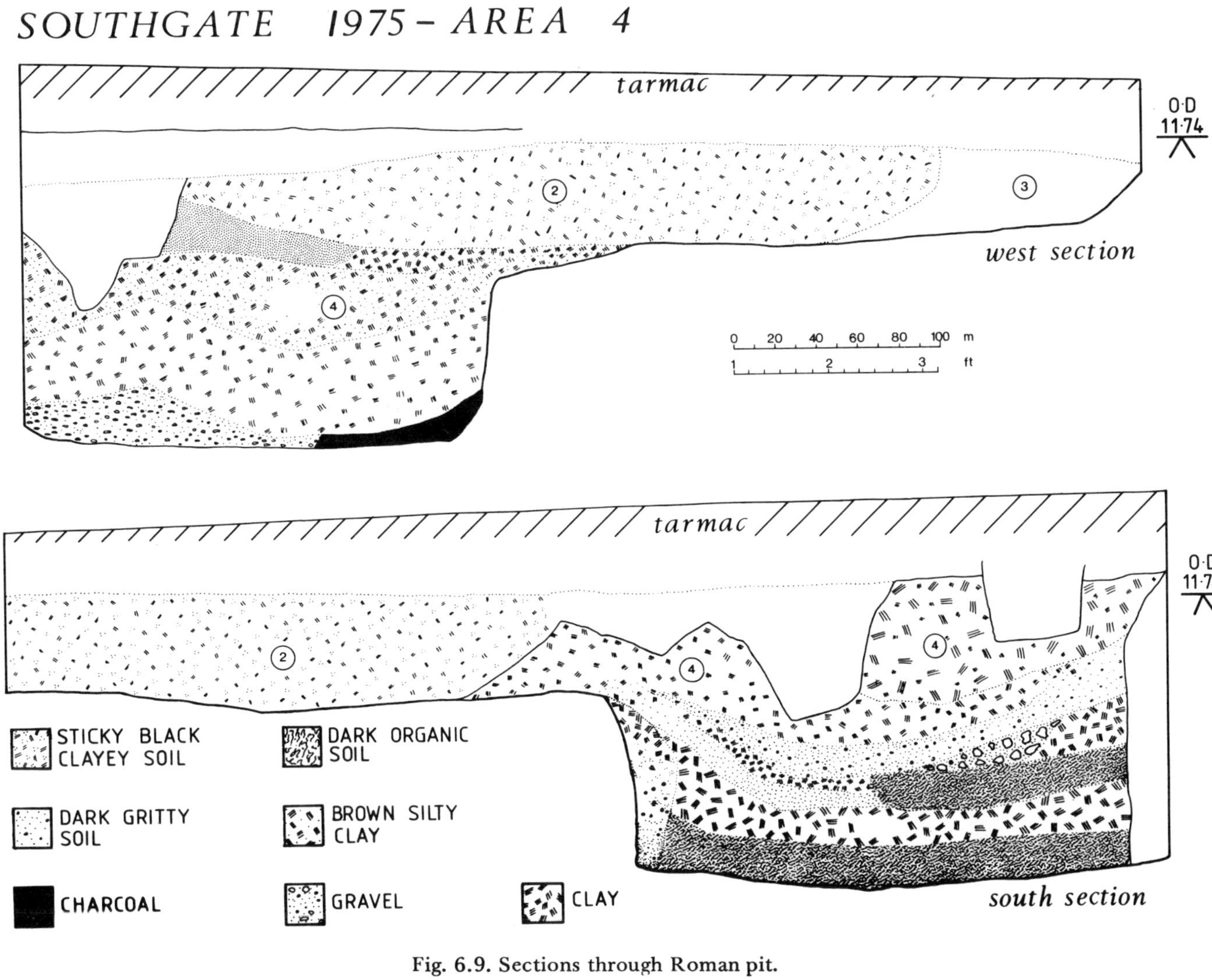

Fig. 6.9. Sections through Roman pit.

Note

In 1980, the remainder of the site was observed by Mark Bowden during building operations. No sign of any medieval kilns were seen, although small amounts of medieval pottery were found. A number of Roman pits, some containing iron slag, were found and several almost complete vessels, but there was nothing with them to suggest that they might have been cremation deposits. The presence of iron slag in quantity outside the Southgate points to the existence of a forge, or forges, outside the gate in Roman times. Similar evidence, but not on such a large scale, was found at Westgate in 1964 (*Chichester 1*, pp. 143-147). The intense heat needed to vitrify the brick found in A.2 could well have been caused by either the Roman forging processes or as a result of being used in a medieval pottery kiln.

Fig. 6.10. Southgate.

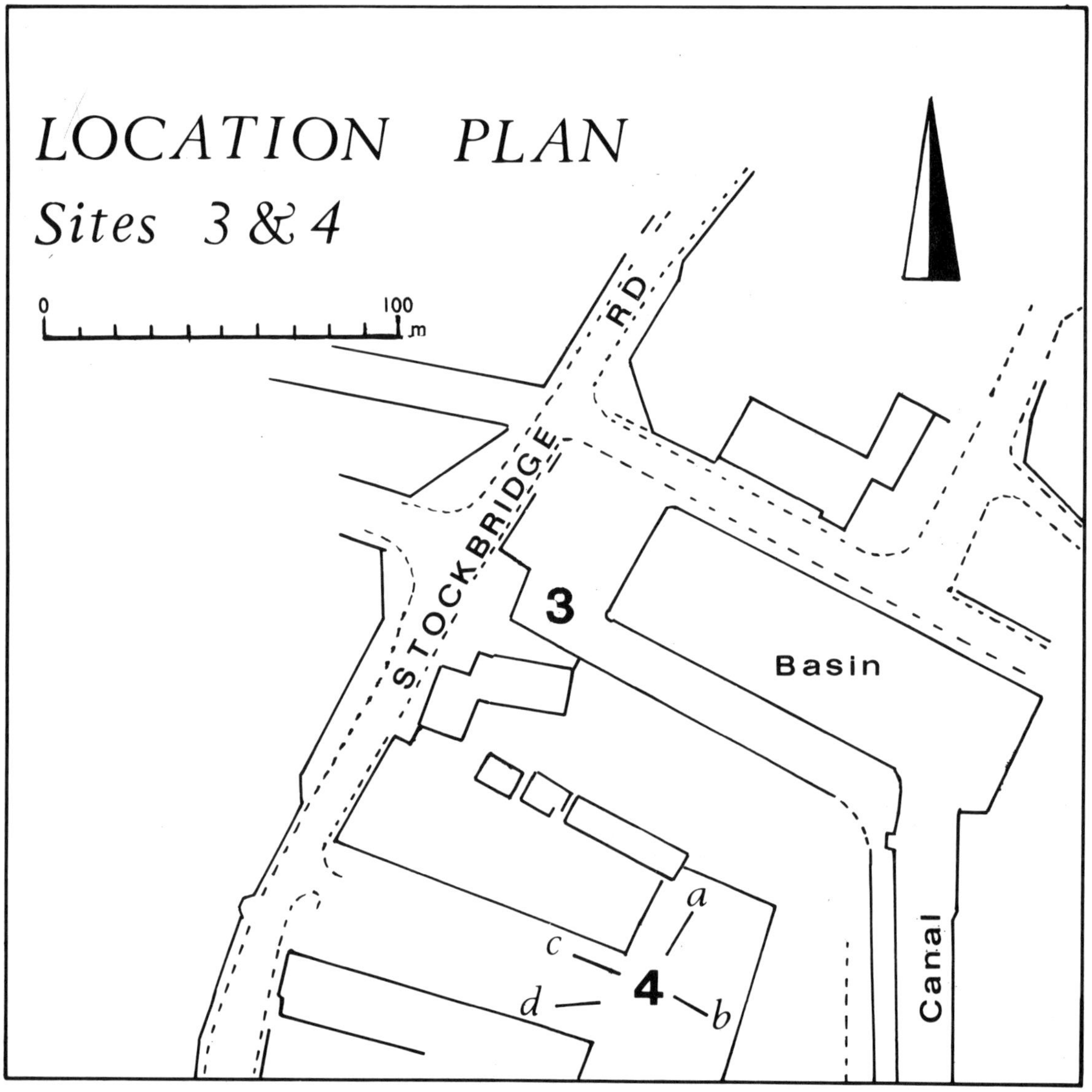

Site 3, Canal Basin (Fig. 6.10)

In view of the discoveries made when the Canal and Basin was dug in 1819, a small trial trench was dug close to the west end of the Basin, just north of the boundary with the S.E.B. property. Natural gravel was found at a depth of 0.6 metre, with 0.15 metre of grey silt above. Above this again was approximately 0.20 metre of brick-earth, with 0.26 metre of black topsoil above it. No finds were made below the topsoil and the grey silt above the gravel suggests that it might be estuarine in origin and that the basin was dug along the line of a meander from the harbour. Certainly, the fall of the ground southwards from Basin Road and eastwards from Stockbridge Road would tend to confirm this.

Site 4, Littlemead School (now Lacey House)

With the kind co-operation of the Chichester District Council, a series of trial cuts (A, B, C and D) were made by machine in advance of the new building programme. They were cut from east to west from the Canal bank (Fig. 6.10). No traces of Roman burials were found, but Roman tiles and pottery were found in the top of a thick layer of silty clay at a depth of 2 metres from modern ground level. Above this layer was the material dumped on the side of the canal when it was dug. This consisted of gravel and clay.

The Small Finds from Southgate (Fig. 6.11)

Note: Figures in brackets are small find numbers.

(a) Bronze

1. (13). Two fragments of brass strip with chisel and punch-dot decoration. Roman; Pit G.3.
2. (16). Bronze wire with a loop at one end. Roman; Pit G.3.
3. (6). Fragment of bronze sheet with holes punches in the edge, probably for stitching to leather. Roman; A.14.
4. (4). Object of cast bronze; function unknown. Roman; posthole A.56.
5. (10). Small brass wire hook, probably from a garment.
6. (34). Ring and intaglio; see note by Dr. Henig below. From Pit G.3 (B).

(b) Marble

7. (24). Fragment of marble inlay, 85 cm wide by 13 cm thick by 11 cm long. *Not illustrated.*

A Romano-British Intaglio Ring from Southgate

by Martin Henig

Bronze ring with simple ribbon hoop, ornamented with groups of transverse grooves and prominent expanded shoulders. It has a raised ovoid bezel surrounded by a rilled flange and contained an intaglio of sky-blue glass. The "gem" having become loose, it was possible to ascertain that the seating for it is cup-shaped.

The intaglio (*Henig* 1978, 310, No. App. 166) is of uneven shape and it is now difficult to replace in the bezel, which consequently must be slightly distorted. It portrays a cross-like figure, probably intended to represent a man.

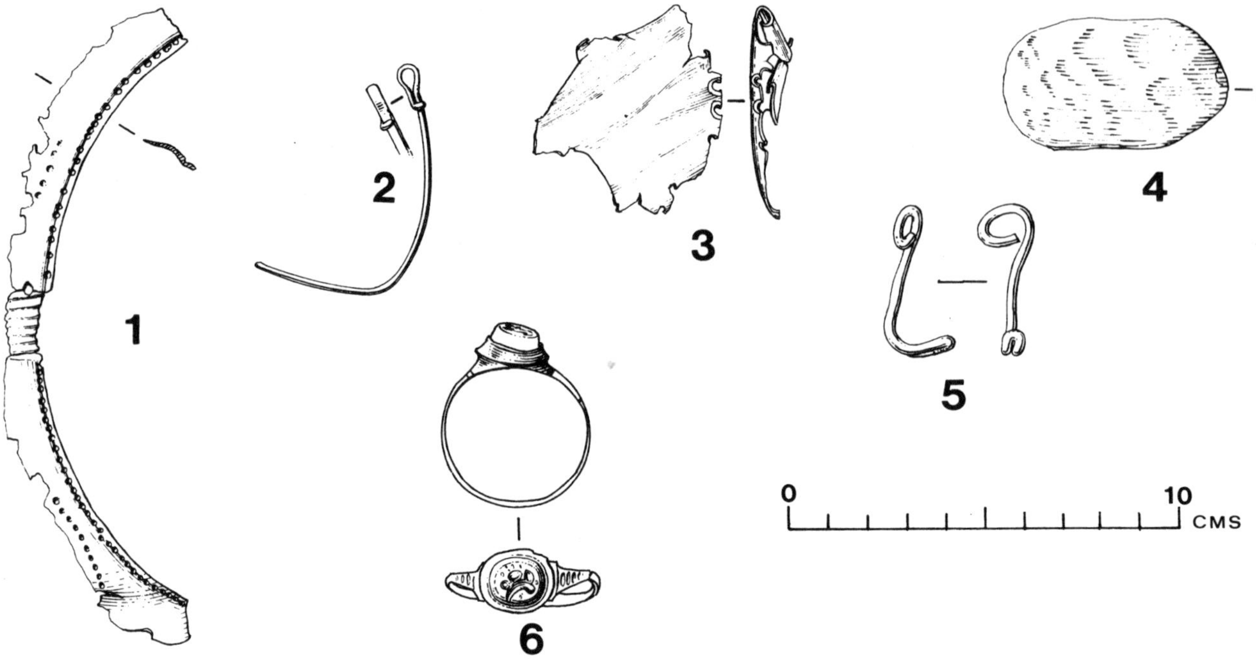

Fig. 6.11. Small finds from Southgate, (½).

Dimensions of ring

External diameter of hoop 19 mm, internal diameter 18 mm. Width of hoop, 1.5 mm; length of bezel, 11 mm; width of bezel, 9 mm; height of bezel above hoop. 3 mm.

Dimensions of intaglio

Length 7 mm; width 5 mm; thickness 3 mm. Both ring and glass setting have analogies with an earlier find from Chichester (*Down* 1974, p; 141 and Fig. 8.16, No. 35; *Henig* 1978, p. 310, No. App. 165) and another from Upmarden (*Henig* 1978, p. 310, No. App. 164: *Down* 1979, p. 149 and Fig. 44.10). The expanded shoulders and the flange around the bezel are basically third-century features (*Henig* 1978, Pls. LII, LIII, Nos. 729 and 741), although Henkel ascribes a ring from Avenches with rilling (1913, p. 124 and Pl. LII, No. 1355), to the following century. Furthermore, as I have already stated (*Henig* 1978, p. 132 ff.), it is probable that debased moulded devices on glass settings from Britain are contemporaneous with the barbarous radiate coinage. However, there is no reason why it need have been lost until the 4th century, and indeed, one of the examples of the class was excavated in the Anglo-Saxon cemetery at Highdown (*Henig* 1978, p. 256, No. 555).

A large number of "Romano-British imitations" have been found throughout Southern England (*Henig* 1978, pp. 255-7, Nos. 539-576, Pls. XVII, XVIII), but although rather more specimens are known from Gloucestershire than from any other county, the centres of manufacture are not yet known.

References

DOWN 1974 — *Chichester Excavations* 2, 1974.
DOWN 1979 — *Chichester Excavations* 4, 1979.
HENIG 1978 — Henig, M., *A Corpus of Roman engraved Gemstones from British Sites;* BAR 8, Second Edition 1978.

THE COINS FROM SOUTHGATE—compiled by **Roger Lintott**. (For list of abbreviations see p. 183)

No.	S.F.No.	Denomination	Emperor and date	Reverse type	Mint mark	Date of coin	Ref. No.	Notes
1	5	Dupondius	Domitian, A.D. 81–96	illegible		A.D. 86		Coin is a brockage. The obv. is in reverse and incuse on the reverse. A14
2	1	Dupondius	Domitian, A.D. 81–96	illegible		A.D. 81–96		Unstratified
3	3	Dupondius or As	Trajan, A.D. 98–117					A6
4	21	Ae Ant.	Claudius II, A.D. 268–270	Consecratio (eagle)				Pit G3
5	33	Ae Ant.	Claudius II, A.D. 268–270					Pit G3
6	28	Ae Ant.	Tetricus type Br. 12 mm.	Spes				G5
7	27	Ae Ant.	Br. 15 mm.					Pit G3
8	25	Fol	Constantine I, A.D. 307–337	Sol	F/T over PLG Lugdunum	A.D. 309–10	RIC 308	Unworn. Pit G3
9	15	Fol	Constantine I, A.D. 307–337	Beat a Tranquillitas	1 over PTR Trier	A.D. 321	RIC 309	Pit G3
10	31	Fol	Constantine I, A.D. 307–337	Geno Pop Rom	London			Pit G3(C)
11	30	Small Fol	Constantine I, A.D. 307–337	Sol	S/F over PLN London	A.D. 313–4	RIC 10	Pit G3(B)
12								
13		illegible Roman coins						Pit G3
14								
15	8	illegible 18th-century coin						F1
16	7	Token		Wilcox & Abraham		19th century		"Clothe your boys". F1

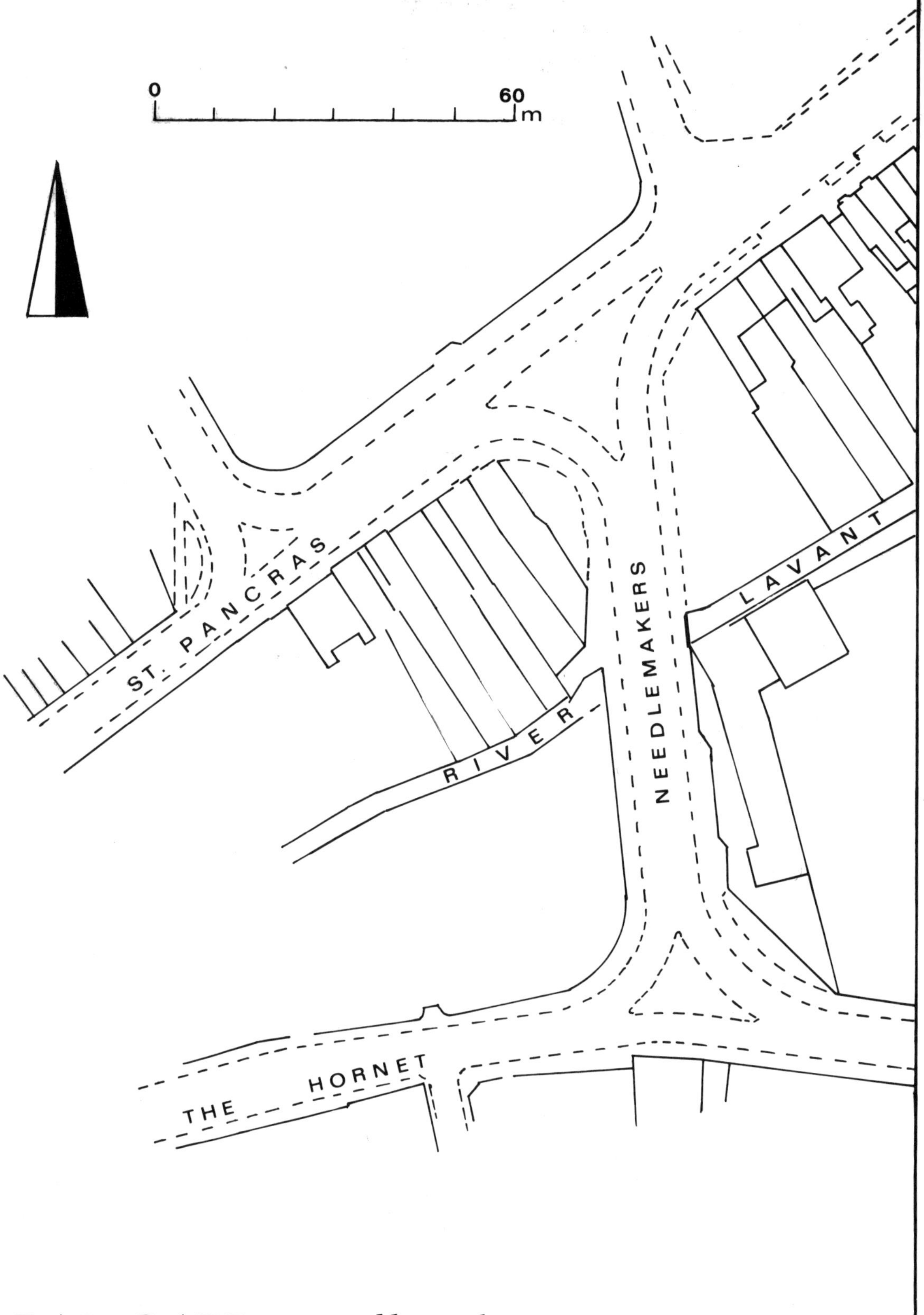

EASTGATE; Needlemakers
Location plan

Fig. 7.1

7

Excavations at Eastgate Needlemakers Site, 1976 and 1978

Introduction

In 1976, the West Sussex County Council in the teeth of bitter opposition from one of the local amenity groups, decided to link St. Pancras with the Hornet by means of a new road across the River Lavant (Fig. 7.1). The work involved the demolition of six cottages fronting on to St. Pancras and the uprooting of some large trees along the north bank of the stream together with the partial demolition of some barns to the south of the Lavant. As a result of prior consultation with the County Council, who gave us every facility to carry out the work, an excavation on the line of the road was planned for the early summer. In the event, as a result of delays imposed by the opposition to the scheme, work did not start until July 1976 and we were forced to vacate the site in September to allow the Highways Department to proceed.

The objects of the excavation were threefold:

(i) To examine the ground for traces of a Roman cementery. The cremation cemetery on the north side of the road had been extensively excavated in 1965-68 (*Chichester 1*, pp. 53-126), but no burials had ever been reported from the south side of Stane Street.

(ii) To establish whether the military ditch found below the cemetery on the north side (*op. cit.* Pl. 4) and seen to be running southwards, turned westwards through the site.

(iii) To excavate below the floors of the demolished houses along St. Pancras to look for traces of the late or post-medieval needle industry and to evaluate the extent of medieval development in the area.

In 1978, by kind permission of Mr. Robert Pine, the landowner, further excavations were carried out on the east side of the new road in advance of development. The work was restricted to the south end of the plot and was intended to further examine the inhumation cemetery found in 1976.

Site history

(Compiled from notes provided by Mr. R. R. Morgan).

Property is recorded outside the Eastgate in St. Pancras as early as the 13th century. It all relates to St. Mary's Hospital and the Dean and Chapter, neither of whom have owned the site which was excavated.

When the Civil War reached Chichester on 21st December 1642, St. Pancras was a suburb where many needlemakers worked. The defenders cleared an area outside the Eastgate by burning "with wildfire" certain houses near to it. There is documentary evidence for the burning of houses beyond the church on the north and south sides. The church tower was used by the attacking forces as a gun platform. If the garrison had not surrendered on the sixth day of the siege the Parliamentary forces would have attacked through the east and west gates.[1]

Poverty was endemic in St. Pancras in normal times and after the devastation of the siege the suburb became a slum, with twice as many poor as previously.

The Justices of the Peace attempted to relieve the poverty by levying a special rate on seventeen nearby parishes; in every case the parishes made excuses to be let off the levy and ten years later the situation was still unresolved.[2]

The earliest record of a building on the site is in 1617 when the western part was occupied by the Chichester House of Correction.[3] These bridewells were depositories for the poor, the vagrant, the wrong-doers and the unmarried mothers who were a nuisance to society. The House was closed in 1650.[4] It is therefore unlikely that cottages were burnt on the site in the Civil War.

Cottage property is recorded from the 18th century onwards including a malthouse in 1737.[5]

Trades recorded on the site are: gingerbread maker; needlemakers (18th century); bricklayer; chairmaker; carpenter; shoemaker; constable.

Sources

1 *Sussex in the Great Civil War* (Thomas-Stanford)
2 Quarter Sessions Rolls (SRS 54)
3 WSRO Add. Mss. 12513
4 Quarter Sessions Rolls (SRS 54)
5 WSRO Add. Mss. 18277–9, 23313; Goodwood E 1857 and 3433: Parish Rates; Land Tax: 1851 Census.

A Note on the Chichester Needle Industry

by R. R. Morgan

Despite comments to the contrary by Hay in his *History of Chichester*, later writers are now convinced that the Chichester needle industry commenced in the 16th century.

John Stow[1] says that the manufacture of needles was not introduced into England before the reign of Queen Elizabeth I. It was first brought to London by a German (Elias Crowse), although there is one previous record of manufacture on "Chepeside". The *Encyclopaedia Brittannica* (7th ed.) says that needle making was brought to Long Crendon in Bucks by Christopher Greening about 1560. Surnames usually had great significance in the 14th century; Richard le Needler[2] is recorded in 1308; also the name "le Aguiller" but these are isolated references and are considered as referring to vendors rather than makers in Chichester.

By the beginning of the 17th century, needle making was concentrated in the parish of St. Pancras and Chichester had much of the manufacturing trade in England.[3] The decline in Chichester occurred after the Civil War and this coincides with the obtaining of a Charter by the Worshipful Company of Needlemakers of the City of London in 1656.[4] By 1669 the importation of foreign needles was prohibited,[4] but this was too late to save the Chichester industry which had been devastated and which had soon to compete with the manufacturers of Birmingham, Sheffield and Long Crendon, Studley, Alcester and Redditch, which produced inferior but very much cheaper needles.[4,3] They were, in fact, one third of the price.

The cause of the disaster can be indirectly attributed to the very forces which the ordinary people of Chichester supported. The Parliamentary army under Waller found nearly every house in St. Pancras occupied by needle manufacturers.

St. Pancras Church became the base for firing into the city.[3] The defenders burned the houses to the ground so as to give no shelter to the besiegers;[3] doubtless the besiegers were also responsible for some destruction. There had been a large population in the parish: there was now a hiatus and the rebuilding of the houses was slow. The needle trade never recovered, but lingered for some considerable time. By 1725 instead of many master needlemakers, journeymen and apprentices, there was only one.[6]

One reason the trade had flourished in St. Pancras was to supply the retailers who frequented the St. James Fairs and who distributed the needles throughout the adjoining counties.[2]

Names of Chichester Needlemakers
(with dates of Documentary References)
N: needlemaker; P: pinmaker

1635	John Mounslow	All Saints	N
1640	William (or Robert) Luckes	St. Bart	P
1640	John Mounsloue	St. P. G.	N
1682	Joel Farndon	St. Pa.	N
1685/6	Thomas Belchamber	St. O.	N
1686	Edward Dolman		N
1687	Abraham Collicke	St. Pa.	N
1704/5 1721	Joseph Smith	St. Pa.	N
1707	Stephen Vicars	St. Pa.	N
1709 1717/8	Isaac Hammond	St. Pa.	N
1715/6	John Blackwell	East Street	N
1716	Thomas Raymond		N
1716	William Vicars		N
1717/8	John Newsam (or Newcombe)	St. Pa.	N
1718 1728	John Farrenden	St. Pa. N	
1725	Magdalen Roell		N
1727	Abraham Collicke	St. Pa.	N
1732 1738	Thomas Dollman		N
1774	William Powell	St. P. G.	N
1788	James Dollman	St. Pa.	N

There is a detailed inventory of Isaac Hammond's will.[5]

There is a description of the history of needlemakers (Morrall)[5]—wire drawing, cutting to length, flattening, softening, piercing, eyeing, filing, tempering, scouring, polishing.

The industry was a cottage one.

Trade tokens were issued by Robert Hitchcock (Needlemakers' Arms) in 1667.[8]

The exact location of most of the needlemakers has not yet been established.

References

1. John Stow's "Annals, or a General Chronicle of England", 1632.
2. Dalloway.
3. S.A.C. 22, p. 223.
4. *Chamber's Encyclopaedia.*
5. Chichester Papers (Steer).
6. Spershot "Memoirs of Chichester".
7 Wyndham Hulme, S.N.Q.
8 S.A.C. 24, p. 126.

The excavations (Figs. 7.2-7.13)

In 1976, due to the pressure of events, the topsoil along the line of the new road was removed by machine down to the subsoil, in this case to the top of the brickearth. At the north end of the site (Trench A), the demolition of the houses and removal of the foundations and rubble by the demolition team left the ground surface below the floorboards of the houses reduced by approximately 25 cms. At the south end (Trench C), the ground was very deeply disturbed by the roots of several large trees along the north bank of the Lavant. These had been felled and the roots grubbed out in preparation for the road works.

The trenches dug in 1978 (Trench B) were excavated by hand and were intended to follow up the discovery of the inhumation cemetery during the 1976 season. The work was carried out in advance of development along the east side of the new road and was confined to the south end of the plot.

Period 1; Roman: Phase 1, c. Nero-Flavian

Trench A.—A ditch (Ditch 2), was found cut into the natural brickearth and running roughly east-west; parallel with Stane Street. It was a shallow feature containing a large amount of Roman pottery and had been considerably disturbed by later pit digging. Only the bottom levels in the ditch (A.19/25/122) are considered for dating purposes and these contained mainly Flavian samian, but with a few sherds of pre-Flavian samian, Terra Nigra and some imported pale wares. A slightly pre-Flavian date for the ditch digging is therefore likely. Other wares in the filling include a small quantity of 1st-century wares from Alice Holt, and two sherds of 2nd-century samian, the latest of Antonine date. The size of the feature suggests that it was no more than a shallow drain connected with occupation somewhere near at hand. It appears to have gone out of use and become a tip for rubbish by the middle of the 2nd century, and a well was cut through it (see below).

Phase 2, c. mid 1st century

Trench B. (Pl. 9). A large ditch (Ditch 1) was found along the southern edge of the site, aligned roughly N.E.-S.W. This was the earliest feature in Trench B and only a small length of the ditch was within the area available for excavation. Because of this, and the requirements of the developer, only two half sections could be obtained (Fig. 7.4). Due to later pit digging through the upper levels, the true depth and width could only be estimated, but the depth is not likely to have been less than 2 metres and the width is conjectured as *c.* 5.2 metres. The two half sections show different rates of silting, the northern half section having about 0.5 metre of silt washed down into the bottom, while the southern half was slightly over 0.3 metres. This silt was barren of artifacts, and in the layer of clay and gravel above it were three fragments of samian, two of Flavian

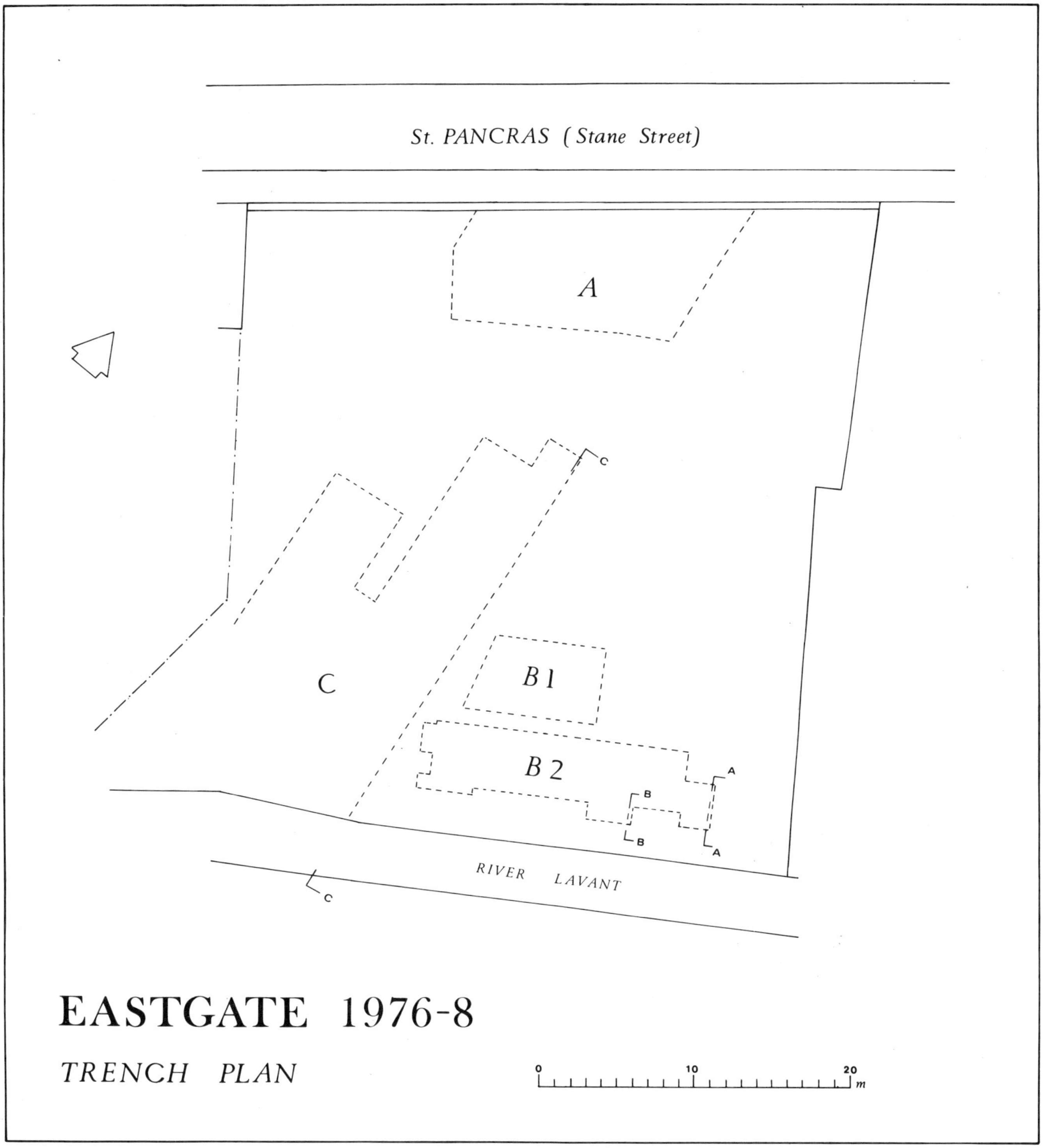

Fig. 7.2

date, and a third of pre-Flavian. These went in at a time when the ditch was going out of use and the small sample is not reliable as an indication of date.

The ditch was cut away on the south side by the River Lavant (Figs. 7.7 and 7.8), which in its present course must post-date the 1st century A.D.

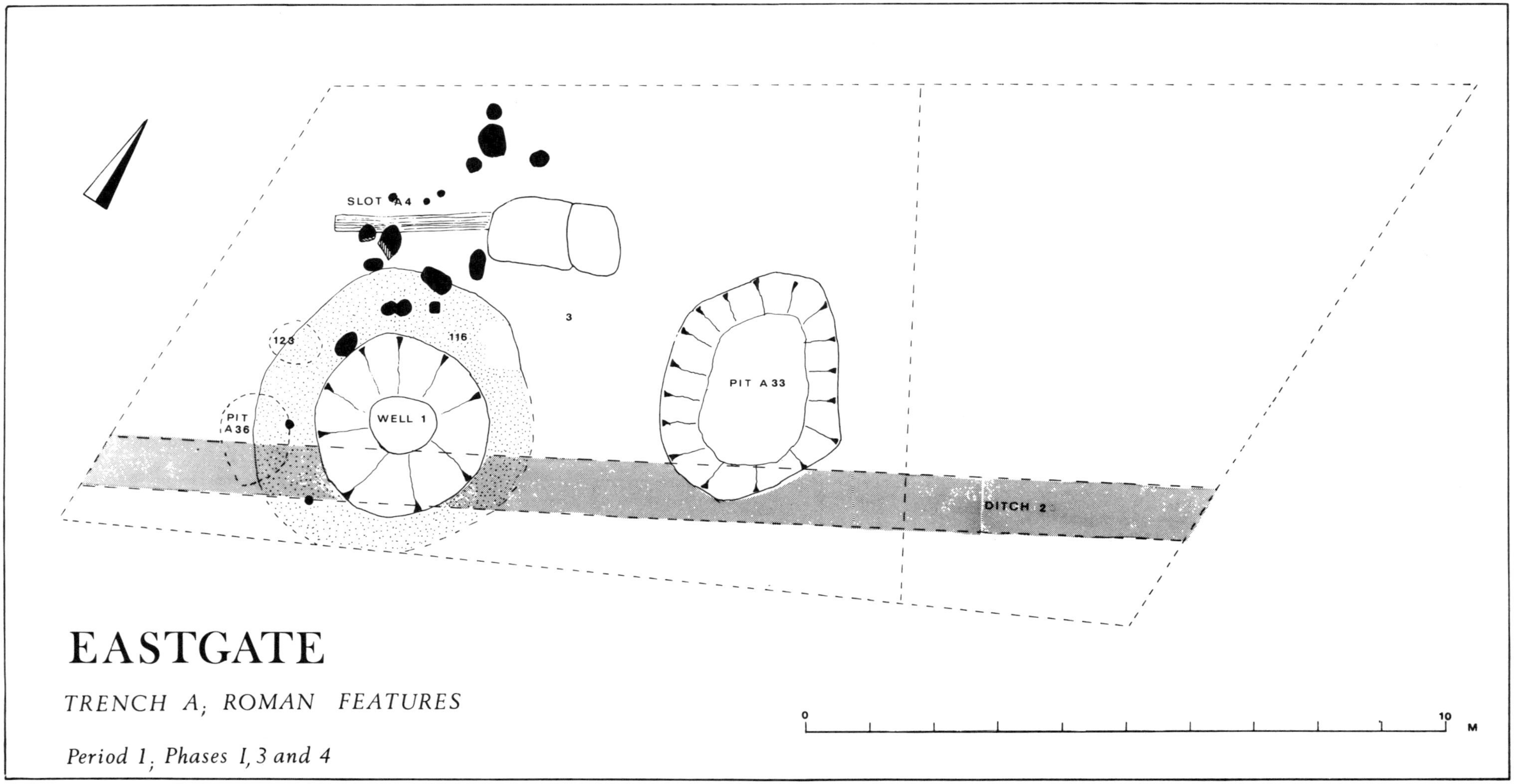
SLOT A4
3
116
123
PIT A36
WELL 1
PIT A33
DITCH 2
EASTGATE
TRENCH A; ROMAN FEATURES
Period 1; Phases 1, 3 and 4
0
10
M

Fig. 7.3

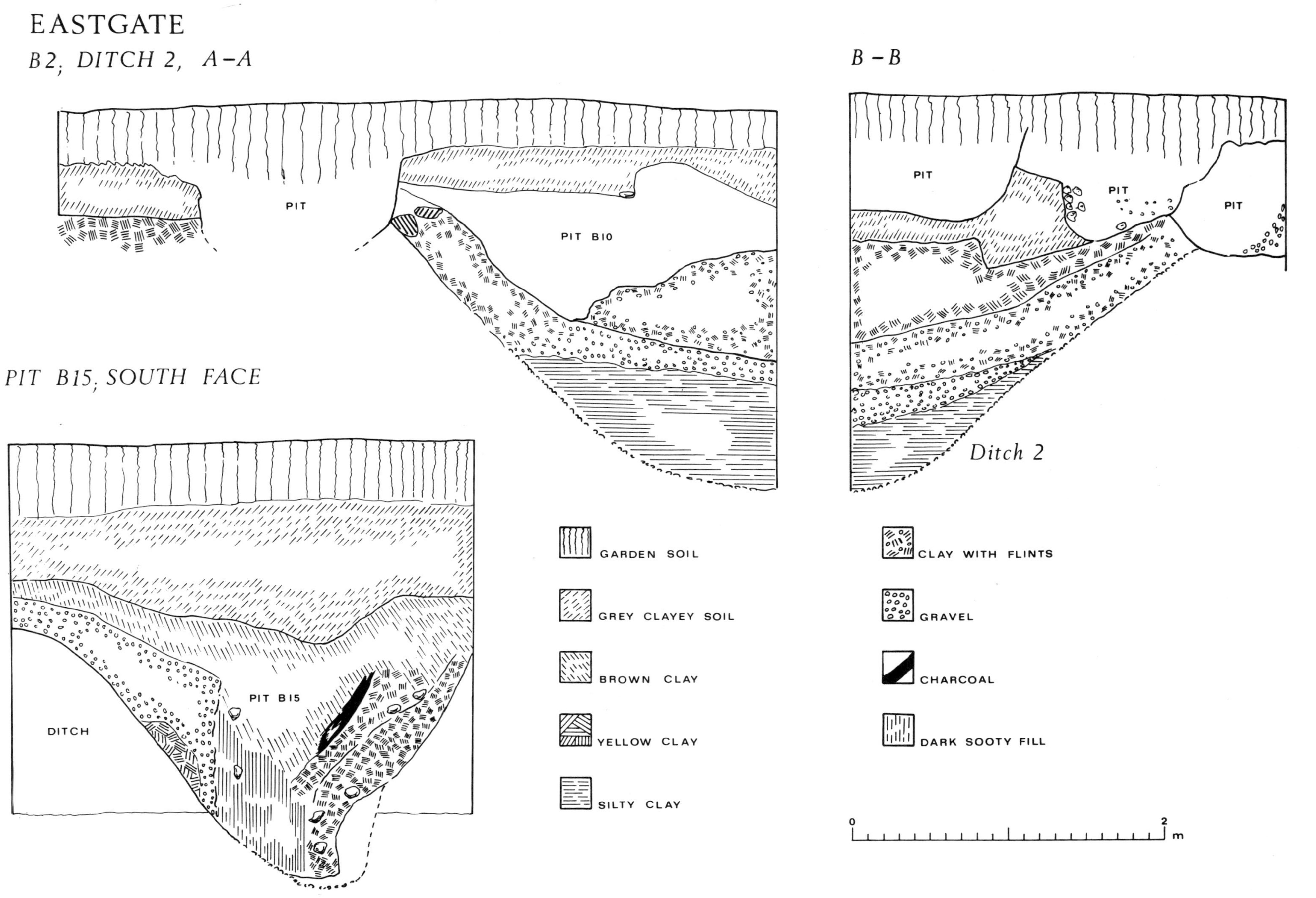
EASTGATE
B2; DITCH 2, A–A
PIT
PIT B10
B – B
PIT
PIT
PIT
Ditch 2
PIT B15; SOUTH FACE
DITCH
PIT B15
GARDEN SOIL
GREY CLAYEY SOIL
BROWN CLAY
YELLOW CLAY
SILTY CLAY
CLAY WITH FLINTS
GRAVEL
CHARCOAL
DARK SOOTY FILL
0
2
m

Fig. 7.4

Discussion

In 1965, during excavations on the site of the Roman cremation cemetery on the north side of St. Pancras (*Chichester 1,* 53, 67) a military-style ditch was found below the cemetery. This was aligned north–south, and the lips of the ditch had been quarried away by subsequent excavations for gravel, possibly to construct (or repair) Stane Street. There were a number of puzzling features about this ditch. It was outside the city limits and could not be reconciled with what is known of the early military occupation of the area. It also had what appeared to be a small palisade trench on the east side for which a satisfactory explanation cannot be offered.

At the time, the ditch was assigned to the mid–1st century on the basis of the pottery from the rapid silt, which was all pre-Flavian. and on the dating of vessels from burials cut into the ditch. These contained Flavian samian, although, of course, the possibility of these vessels being "heirloom survivals" must be taken into account.

It can be assumed that the Needlemakers ditch *is* the same feature as the ditch below the cemetery, and if the lines of the two ditches are projected, one southwards and the other north-eastwards, they meet below Briants, the builders, on the south side of St. Pancras. The relationship of the two ditches suggests an early defensive enclosure on the east side of the later town, perhaps the earliest marching camp of Legio II Augusta.

One of the most important results of the 1978 excavation was the discovery that the River Lavant post-dates the defensive ditch. There seem to be three occasions when it is likely that the river could have been diverted from its natural course to run in towards the Eastgate and then around the south and west sides of the town. The first possibility is during the 4th century, when bastions were built against the walls and a flat-bottomed ditch dug, replacing the two 2nd century ditches which had silted up (*Holmes*, 1962, 81). The second occasion might have been when the town was re-fortified as a *burgh* against the Danes, in the late 9th–early 10th century by Alfred the Great. The town at that time was assessed at 1500 hides, thought to provide insufficient force to man the walls (*Hill*, 1978), and it might well be that the addition of a water defence around the vulnerable south-west quarter was designed to augment the small force of defenders.

The third possibility and in this writer's view, the most feasible is that the diversion took place in 1378 when the town defences were replanned and a new ditch, 50 ft. wide was dug. The Lavant runs in the course of the great medieval ditch along the south-west side of the town and before it was diverted through Westgate fields it used to run northwards along the west side of the walls to Squitry Bridge, where it turned off to the west. (Gardner Map, p. 85).

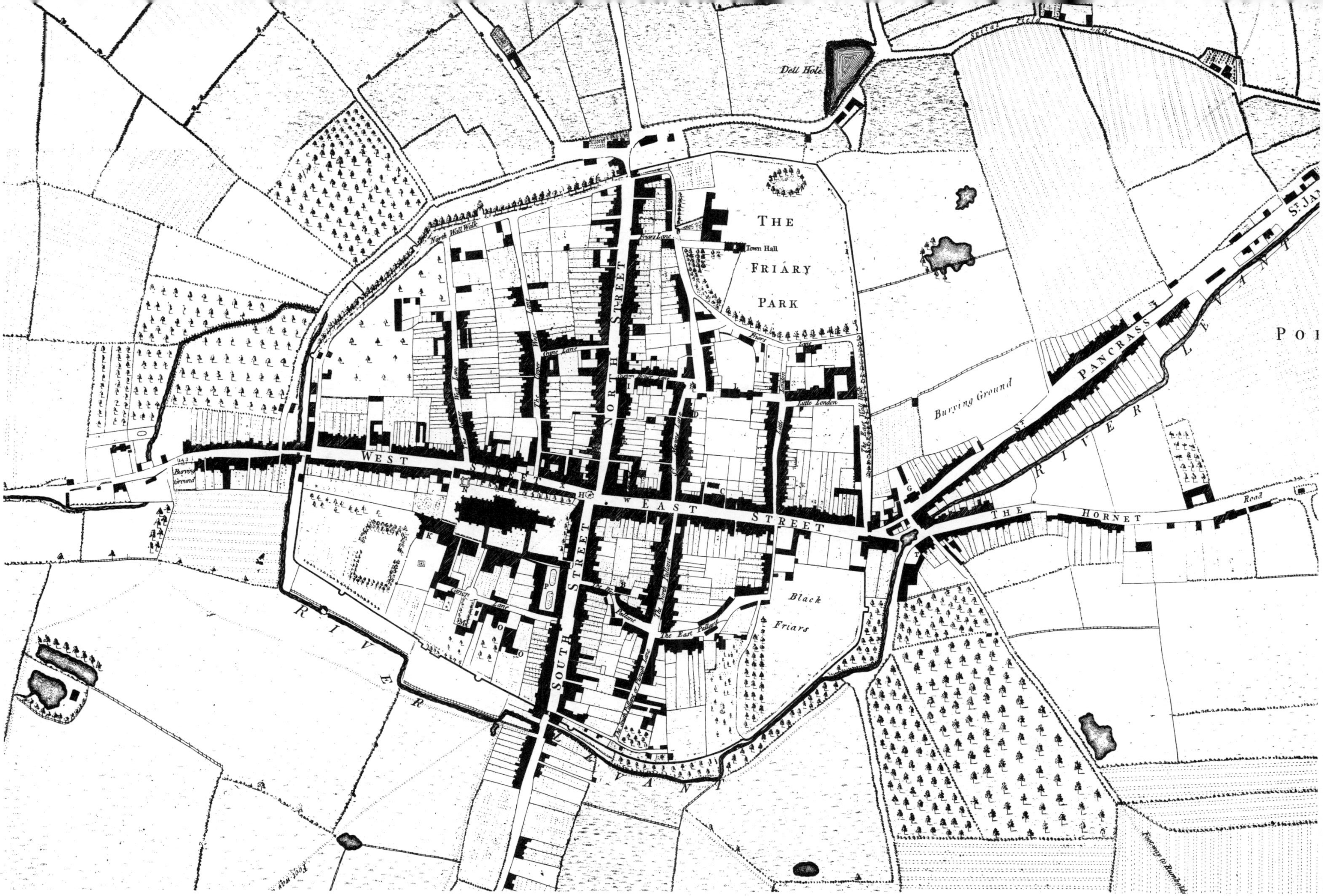

Fig. 7.5. Extract from a map of Chichester by William Gardner, 1769.

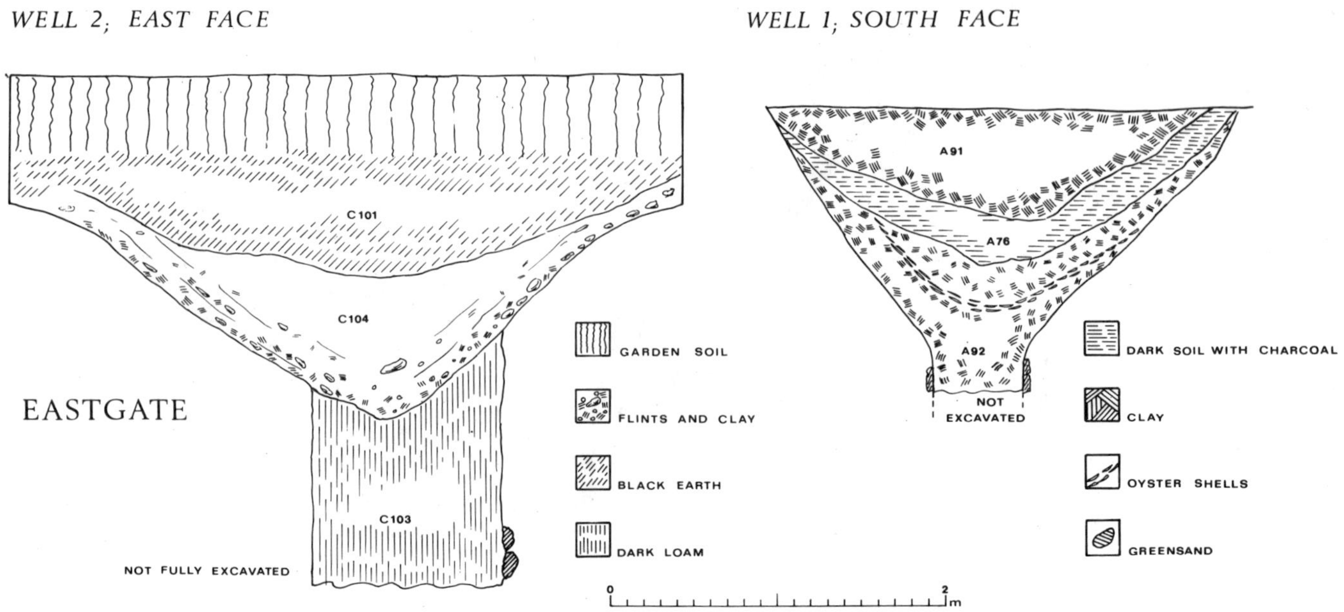

Fig. 7.6

Phase 3, c. 2nd century

Trench A. (Fig. 7.3). A well (Well 1), was dug through the Phase 1, Ditch 2. There were traces of a well house around the top of the cone. Originally designated Pit A.29, the upper layers within the cone were layers 91, 76 and 92. Large amounts of fine and coarse pottery were recovered, but due to the extremely narrow diameter of the well shaft and the unstable nature of the ground into which it was dug, it was not possible to reach the bottom without adopting special precautions which time did not permit us to do. The same limitations were imposed upon us when we came to excavate Well 2 (see below).

The date range of the samian was from pre-Flavian to Antonine, and the coarse wares span roughly the same period.

Two pits, A.123 and Pit A.36, pre-dated the well and both had pre-Flavian pottery as the only dateable wares. On the evidence of the pottery, the well cannot have been dug much more before the early-mid 2nd century and seems to have had a relatively short life in view of the fact that the backfill has nothing later than late 2nd century wares in it. Around the lip of the well was a layer of dark brown dirty clay (A.116) which was concentric with the well and probably represents the trodden area within a wellhouse. No trace of this remained, and it is likely that it would have been no more than a slight timber structure. The well was badly constructed, being only 1.05 metre in diameter and lined with soft greensand which had virtually disintegrated. It had to be abandoned at a depth of 3.32 metres from ground level.

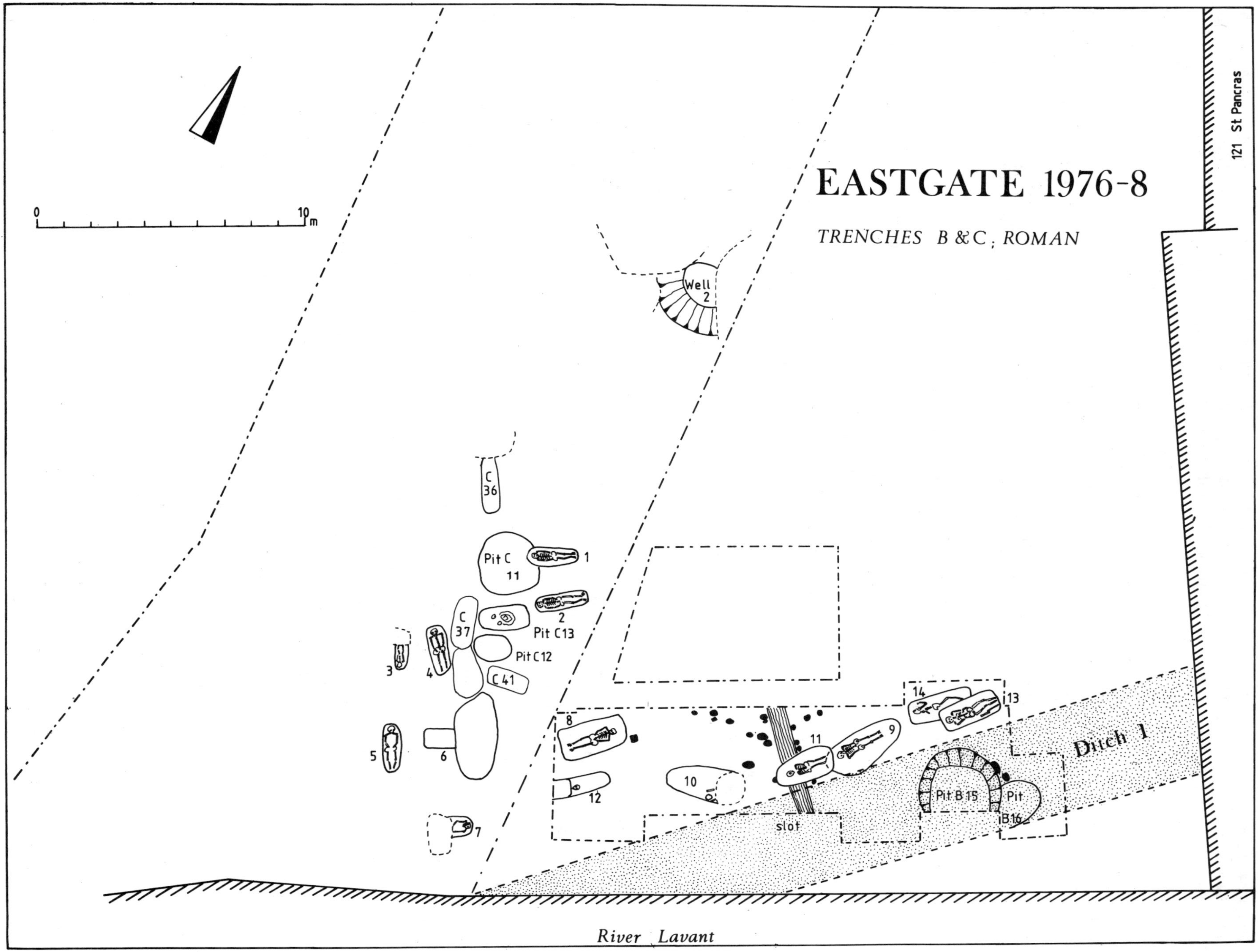
EASTGATE 1976-8
TRENCHES B &C ; ROMAN
121 St Pancras
0
10 m
Well 2
C 36
Pit C 11
1
2
Pit C13
Pit C12
C 37
C 41
3
4
5
6
7
8
9
10
11
12
13
14
slot
Pit B 15
Pit B16
Ditch 1
River Lavant

Fig. 7.7

Phase 4, late 2nd-3rd century

Trench A.—A cesspit, Pit A.33 was dug to the east of Well 1, and on the evidence of the pottery is slightly later in date. The latest dated samian is late Antonine from East Gaul, and the pit also contained Rhenish ware which is likely to be 3rd century in date together with Alice Holt wares which Mr. Lyne dates to late 3rd century. The pit, which in addition to samian and fine wares contained large amounts of coarse wares, together with window glass, nails and food bones, indicates substantial domestic occupation near at hand.

Uncertain

Trench A.—Two groups of post-holes, some packed with tiles, ran for a short distance across the trench in a northerly alignment. The most easterly line cut through A.116, the tread around the well head, and must post-date the well. The other group cut an east–west timber slot (Slot A.4). Neither the slot or the postholes contained any dateable pottery, nor were they seen above the latest Roman horizon (A.3) and no coherent plan can be offered.

Trench B. (Fig. 7.7). A slot, aligned north-south and a number of postholes belonging to one or more timber buildings were found cut into Layer 3. At its south end the slot cut into the fill of Ditch 1 and was itself cut by Burial 11. The slot was shallow and probably housed a cill beam. It was barren of finds as were the post-holes, which were all shallow. The closest date that can be offered for these features is between *c.* 2nd century and the late 4th. If the ? well, Pit B.10/15 relates to these structures then they could be assigned to Phase 5, but in the absence of any satisfactory evidence it is not possible to be certain.

Phase 5, late 3rd to late 4th — early 5th century

No structures survived that could be identified and the only evidence for continued occupation is provided by a pit in Trench C cut by Burial 1 and Pit B.10/15 which was probably a well, cutting through Ditch 1 at the south end of the site.

The pit or well contained late Roman grogged wares and burnt black sandy wares (see below and Fig. 7.4) together with a few sherds of New Forest purple ware and the base of a red colour coated bowl, probably of local manufacture. The distribution of the later wares was fairly even from top to bottom and implies that it was back-filled at some time in the 4th century. Even so, the absence of Oxford wares similar to those found in Well 2 (C.103) may suggest that the two wells were functioning at different times and Pit B.10/15 is the earlier of the two. The top fill of the pit contained part of a Roman inscription (see p. 101 and Pl. 13). Pit C.11 which was cut by Burial 1 had similar wares to those found in Pit B.10/15.

Well 2. (Figs. 7.6-7.7). Only half of the feature was within the area available for excavation and this, plus the unstable nature of the soil and the time limit to which we were working, made it difficult and dangerous to attempt to reach the bottom. The top part of the well below the cone had been robbed of masonry and eventually we had to abandon the excavation.

The fill of the robbed out well shaft (C.103) contained large amounts of late Roman coarse wares, including Alice Holt and local grogged wares, plus substantial quantities of New Forest and Oxford colour coated wares (Fig. 14.1). The coins found in the well range in date from late 3rd century to Valens (A.D. 364–378) which is as late in date as the Chichester late Roman bronze coinage goes, and a date in the late 4th century or later still for the back-filling of the well, is implied.

EASTGATE; TRENCH C, SECTION C — C

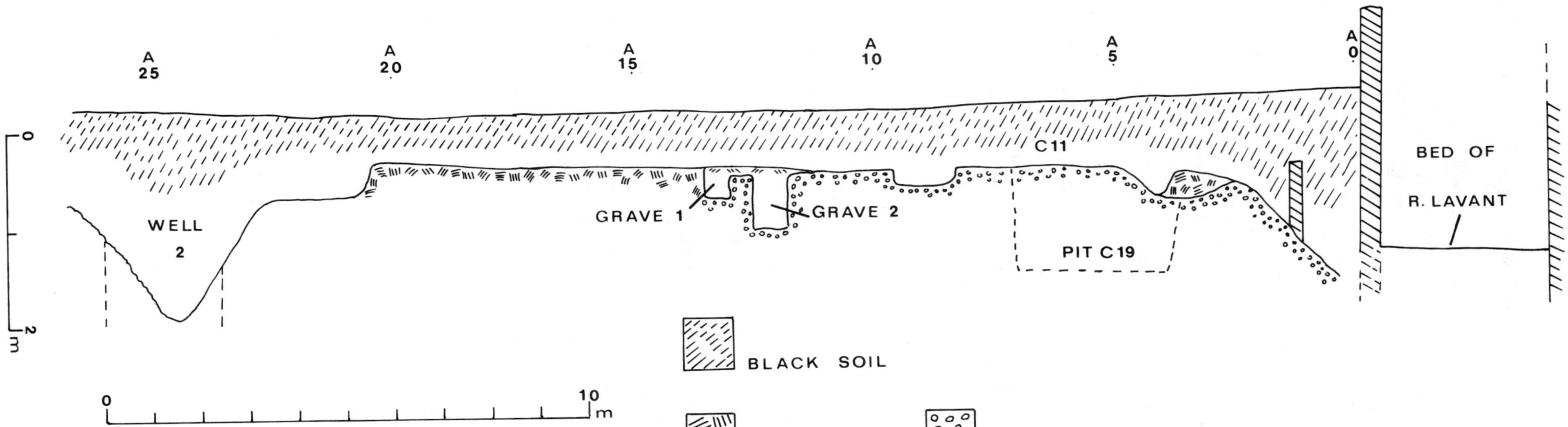

Fig. 7.8

Discussion

Well 2 has an important group of late Roman pottery in it which consists of fine grey wares from the Alice Holt kilns; 4th century grey wares from an unknown source and a small group of coarse wares, some of which are in a black burnt sandy fabric and others in a dark brown to black fabric grogged with coarse sand and some chalk. These wares were first recognised at Chilgrove (*Chichester 4*, p. 192 and Fig. 72) and are present in Chichester in late Roman contexts. They usually have an external lumpy finish and are likely to be of local manufacture and it may not be stretching the evidence too far to suggest that they replaced coarse wares which had been coming in to the district from other production sources at a time when the money supply was drying up. With the coarse wares were large amounts of late Roman fine wares from the New Forest and Oxford on which Dr. Young has reported (pp. 286-293). The external dating evidence consists of a number of late Roman coins of which the latest date to the last quarter of the 4th century, which, on present evidence, seems to be the time when the last coin issues reach the town.The big question-mark hanging over the Chichester coinage is "how long did the money continue to circulate before the inhabitants reverted to a barter economy". The bronze coins could well have continued in use in a limited way for perhaps another twenty years and by then the fine table wares from New Forest, Oxford and Alice Holt would have ceased to be traded and local wares, still wheel made, but in coarser fabric and with a limited distribution would have succeeded them. The fill of Well 2 must represent the end of an era. At the time when the well was abandoned it may have been advisable for people living in the suburbs to find safer shelter within the walls and the spread of domestic occupation from the 1st to the late 4th–early 5th century which is apparent from the pottery sequence, ended. We shall never know who backfilled the well, but the upper masonry appears to have been robbed and all the surface rubbish nearby was pushed into it. No finds of later periods were noted so it is possible that it was backfilled because it was a danger to people using the site for other purposes.

Phase 6, The cemetery c. late 4th century-5th century (Figs. 7.7, 7.9 and 7.10 and Pl. 10)

A total of fourteen inhumations were identified and excavated. These were located towards the south end of the site and most of them were placed in shallow graves dug into the natural gravel, randomly orientated. In addition to the fourteen graves excavated there were numbers of human bone fragments present in later pits.

The burials are discussed below, and a summary of Dr. Barnes' report on the skeletons is attached. Her detailed report is placed in the Level III archive.

The burials (Figs. 7.9-7.10)
(See also pp. 117-118)

Burial 1.—Supine, with head to west, arms fully extended with hands on pelvis. The grave was dug into the gravel from an unknown level to a depth of 0.32 m. It cut the eastern edge of Pit C.11 (Fig. 7.7) which was a Roman cesspit containing late colour coated wares from the New Forest. This body may have been buried in quicklime as traces of a greyish-white deposit were found around the bones and below the skeleton, very similar to that found with the 17th-century burials below St. Andrew's Church, where it certainly was quicklime. The pH of the soil below the pelvis was 8.2.

Burial 2.—To the south of Burial 1 and parallel with it. Supine, head to west, arms fully extended with hands at the side of the body. This body was also probably buried in quicklime and there were much larger amounts of the deposit present. The grave fill contained a sherd from a New Forest rusticated beaker (Fulford type 47), mid 3rd to 4th century in date, together with a rim in a cream fabric with traces of a red-brown slip.

Burial 3.—This was the grave of a young child and was incomplete. It was aligned north-south, with the head to the south. It had been disturbed by a modern pit containing the remains of a large dog. Part of a beaker in a white fabric was found near where the feet would have been and four nails were found around the skeleton in positions which suggest that it was encoffined.

Burial 4.—Supine, head to the north. No traces of coffin nails. Fragments of a grey-ware vessel were found above the body and a long bone, probably from an earlier burial, was beside the left elbow.

Burial 5.—Supine; head to the north. Lower left arm across middle; lower right arm bent with hand on pelvis. Probably encoffined as 3 nails were found along the bottom and west side of the grave. The ribs and upper vertebrae had been destroyed by a later pit. One abraded sherd of cream ware with red-brown slip was found in the grave fill, identical in fabric to the one in Burial 2.

Burial 6.—This was badly disturbed by Pit C.19 and only fragments of the upper jaw, hip joint and femur, together with a number of vertebrae, were present. The position of the vertebrae suggests that the body was aligned east-west. A brooch (Fig. 10.1, No. 12), found in Pit C.19 might have originally been with the burial.

Burial 7.—Cut by Pit C.6 and had only the skull, very crushed, part of the pelvis, the left femur and lower right arm still in position. The body was supine with head to the east.

Burial 8.—Supine, head to east, arms extended; left hand folded across pelvis; right hand behind pelvis. The bottom of the grave was 1.27 metre below the top of B.2 which was the yellow clay below the cultivated top soil. The grave fill contained New Forest beaker sherds which have a date range of *c.* late 3rd-early 5th century, a red ware sherd, probably late 4th century, and the rim of a vessel in black sand tempered ware (see above, p. 106).

Burial 9.—Supine; head to east; partly overlaid by a 19th-century culvert which caused some damage to the skeleton. The grave was much larger than the body it accommodated. In the fill above the feet of the skeleton were a number of bronze coins dating to the late 3rd to 4th centuries. More were found below the body, together with the fragments of an indented New Forest beaker. It seems likely that the coins were originally placed within

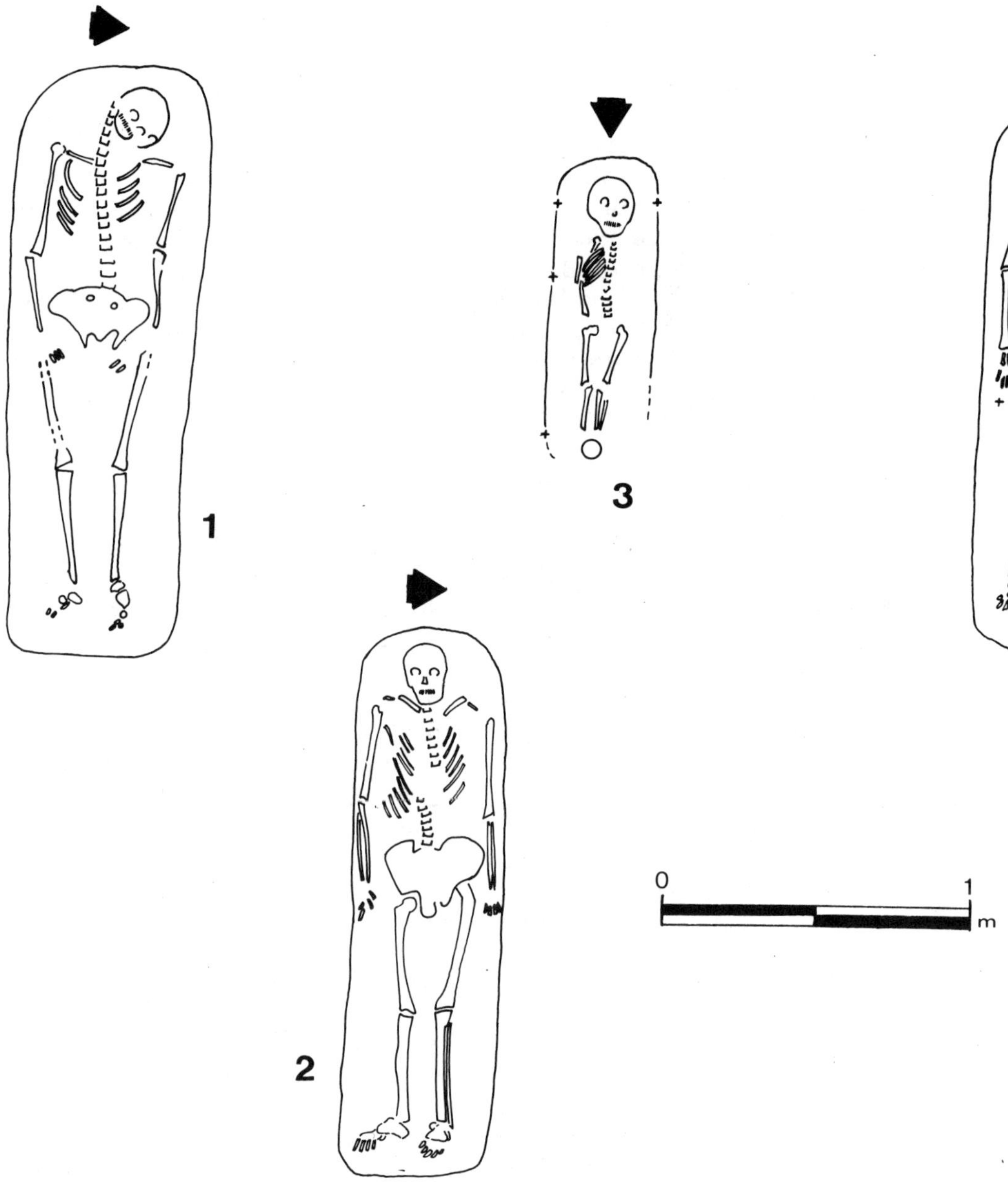

Fig. 7.9. Eastgate Needlemakers, Roman burials.

this vessel and buried as a hoard before the cemetery extended across the site and that it was broken when the grave was dug and the contents scattered. The fact that they were not recovered for use might suggest perhaps that money had ceased to be used. The presence of nails around the edge of the grave indicates that the body was encoffined.

Burial 10.—First identified as Pit B.12, this was a shallow pit which had been cut through by a modern pit (Pit B.13). Part of a skull was found in Pit B.12 with most of the remainder of it being in Pit B.13. Two complete indented New Forest beakers (*Fulford* 1975, Fig. 12, 27.3), were found side by side at the west end of the "grave", and it seems from the total absence of other bones that only the head was buried with the pots, both of which were empty.

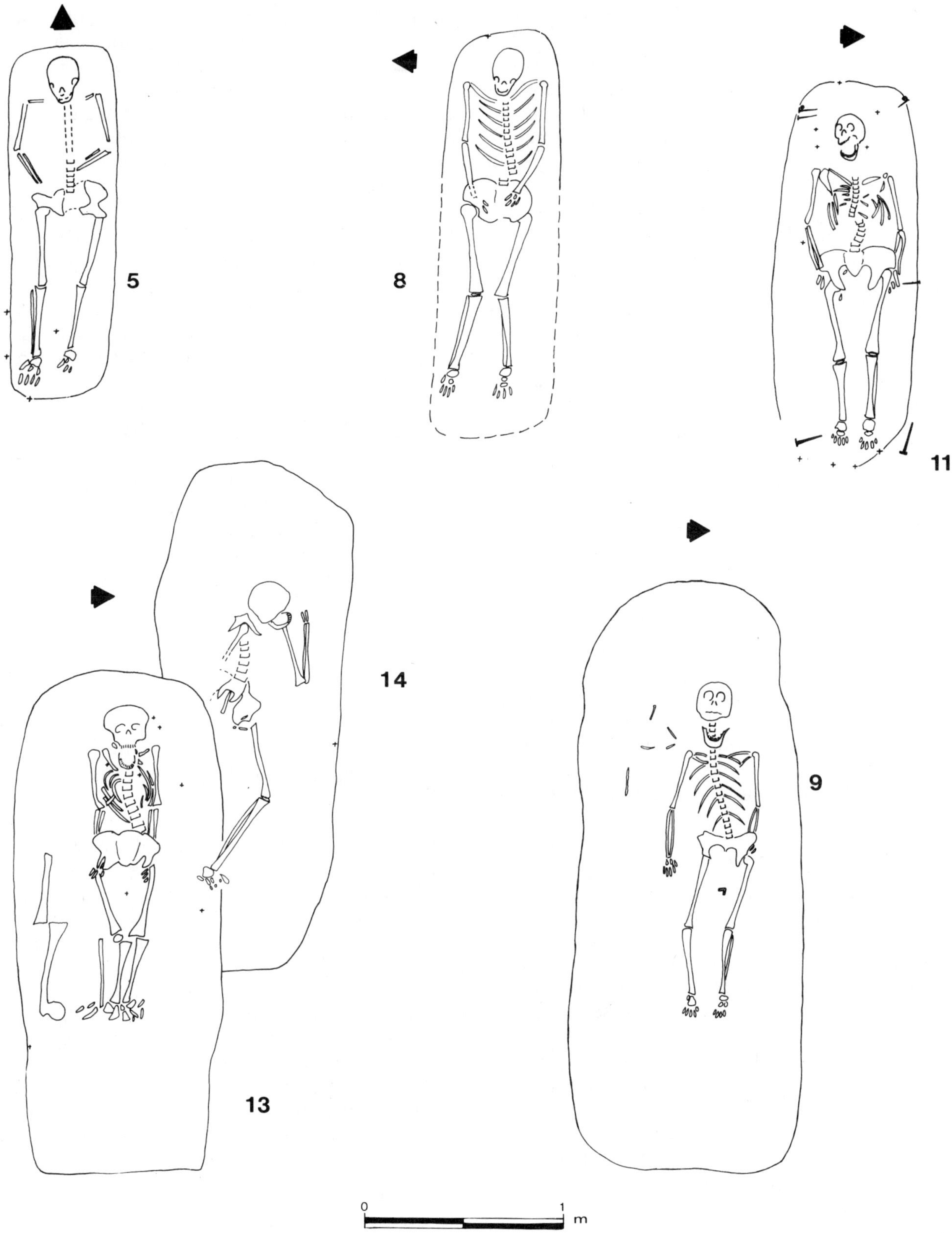

Fig. 7.10. Eastgate Needlemakers, Roman burials

Burial 11.—The grave just clipped the western end of Burial 9, and was on the same alignment. Head to west; upper jaw and cranium damaged in antiquity and all the cervical vertebrae missing. The body was encoffined, with exceptionally large spikes in the corners and midway down the sides (Fig. 7.10). Two spikes were found in each corner, one pointing up and one down. The absence of the neck vertebrae is puzzling and could not be accounted for by the soil conditions. The body might have been decapitated, but this would scarcely have resulted in the loss of the vertebrae. Five coins were found in the upper fill, probably from the same source as those in Burial 9, which it cuts, and one of these could be identified as 4th century in date. The grave fill also contained a cooking pot base in a grogged fabric (see above p. 106).

Burial 12.—Grave 12 had only part of a cranium belonging to a small child. This was placed at the eastern end of the grave, which cut an earlier grave-shaped feature to the east. This feature had nails around the sides and a few small bones, probably from an infant.

Burial 13.—Supine; head to west, encoffined. Coin of Constantine in skull. This grave cut Burial 14 and the partially articulated right leg of the earlier burial was deposited in Grave 13 when it was backfilled. There was also one of the long bones from another burial in the grave fill (Fig. 7.10 and Pl. 10). Two sherds from a New Forest beaker were found above the body. A radio carbon date was obtained for the skeleton which gave a date bracket of A.D. 320 ± 65.

Burial 14.—Cut by Burial 13; skeleton very damaged, lying on left side with head to the west and facing north. Right leg missing (see above, Burial 13), left leg flexed, left arm bent upwards with hand level with jawbone. Probably encoffined, as two nails found along the sides of the grave.

Other features

Three shallow, grave-shaped features were excavated: C.36, C.37 and C.41. None had human remains, but the shape suggests that they might have been dug as graves. C.41 was barren, but the other two contained only Roman wares, none of which were closely dateable.

Discussion

The northern limits of the cemetery appear to be indicated by the position of Burial 1, or perhaps C.36 if it is accepted that this was a grave. The south-western end of the site was heavily disturbed by the grubbing out of large tree roots and modern pits, but here the presence of a number of skeleton fragments indicates that burials had been placed there. The southern limits cannot be fixed at present as although a watch was kept when the County Council completed their road works south of the Lavant, they did not go deep enough to strike burials. It is possible that the cemetery might extend as far south as the Hornet (Fig. 7.1). While this road has not been proved to be Roman in origin, it seems likely that it was the start of a road coming out of East Gate and leading to the coastal settlements to the east of the civitas capital. Similarly, neither the eastern or western boundaries can be fixed. They must lie beneath the gardens of the houses on to the south side of St. Pancras and there is a need to watch all future development along the north side of the Hornet to provide answers to these questions.

The date of the cemetery is likely to be late in the Roman period. In considering this, the relationship between the cemetery and the latest domestic occupation on the site must be assessed. The disturbed hoard found in Burial 9 could not have been deposited much before *c.* mid 4th century and could well have been very much later. The coin found in the skull of Burial 13 was well worn and again, could have been deposited as the fee for the ferryman a long time after it was minted. Similarly, the two New Forest beakers are of a type that has a long life, which Dr. Fulford estimates to be from *c.* late 3rd to possibly as late as early 5th century (*Fulford*, 1975) and the pottery from the graves and from pits cut by graves does not sharpen the dating any more.

Samples were taken for carbon 14 dating from Burial 13. The results (320+65), would on the face of it indicate a date of somewhere between mid to late 4th century for the likely deposition of the body and if, as is likely, the latest end of the date bracket is the correct one, then it might well be about the turn of the century. Unfortunately, the reliability of C.14 dates is uncertain in a late Roman context and really, all the dating provides is an exclusion of a later, pagan Saxon, date.

If the cemetery came later than the domestic occupation a few metres to the north, then on the evidence from Well 2, it would be at least no earlier than the time at which the coins of Valens were lost, which cannot be any earlier than A.D. 384, and might well be up to several decades later. Some of the fine wares from Oxford and New Forest were produced after A.D. 350, with the possibility, and it is no more than that, that the grogged wares might go on later still. Putting it all together, a date between, say, A.D. 395 and *c.* A.D. 425 could be postulated for the abandonment of the well and its backfilling, with the extension of the inhumation cemetery across the area immediately to the south coming along later still. By this time there is some evidence that proper records were not being kept and that graves were being dug through earlier ones, in one case a not very much earlier one. The indication of quicklime in two of the graves suggest that they were plague victims and the dearth of grave goods—poverty. There is no clear evidence for de-capitation. Where this has been identified as a burial rite elsewhere the heads are usually placed with the body, either at the feet or between the knees. All we have is a burial (No. 11), where the head is a little further from the rest of the body than perhaps it should be, with all the cervical vertebrae missing and a grave pit (Burial 10) with the remains of a skull only, with two New Forest vessels.

Until a larger number of burials from this cemetery are available for study, it would be fruitless to speculate too far on the burial customs and it can only be said that this sample indicates a late or perhaps sub-Roman graveyard and that the inhabitants appeared to be poor. Such a graveyard might fit well into the picture of a society where the quality of life (and death) was declining; where plague and poverty were facts of life that had to be coped with alongside the need to maintain a defence against the Saxon raiders, at the same time as cultivating the soil on a subsistence basis.

Period 2, Medieval: c. 13th-15th centuries

During the 13th-15th centuries there was a spread of occupation out from Eastgate along the south side of St. Pancras and, to a limited extent, along the north side also, although this was inhibited by the medieval cemetery of St.

Michael (St. Michael's Lighten or Litten), which extended almost from the city walls up to what is now Alexandra Road. At some time, probably early in the 18th century, St. Pancras was widened and provided with paved sidewalks and as a result of this, only the rear part of the tenements fronting onto the road could be excavated.

Trench A. (Fig. 7.11)

Three possible phases of building and occupation are detectable. The earliest phase, on the evidence of the small sample of pottery found is not likely to date much before the beginning of the 14th century. Nowhere could 13th century wares be recognised with any certainty although it is possible that some of the coarse flint gritted wares found as residual material in A.2 might be of that date.

Phase 1 This is represented by a number of shallow pits (A.37, A.38, A.47 and A.59), which were probably dug for clay, possibly to provide daub for the walls of structures nearby. They were backfilled and consolidated with gravel and the postholes of a building were later dug through them.

Phase 2A A line of postholes ran east-west across the trench, marking the back of the property fronting on to the road. Two patches of yellow clay with flecks of chalk in it were found on this alignment and these probably represent the vestiges of a "cob" wall. Two burnt patches representing hearths probably also belong to this phase.

Phase 2B A double line of postholes suggest the remains of a north-south wall which cuts across the ? cob wall footing of Phase 2A. To the east of it, a hearth (A.113) was constructed above an earlier Roman pit. It was roughly oval in shape and had the remains of a burnt beam lying on the north-east side of it. The oven base was laid across the line of the cob wall and must therefore postdate it. There had been considerable subsidence of the hearth into the pit.

Uncertain On the east side of the trench was a deep stone-packed posthole and three others (A.23, 56 and 57), which appear to be of the same period, but which probably belong to another building.

Phase 3 The Phase 2B wall on the west side of the hearth appears to have been superseded by a rectangular structure of which only a right-angle representing the south-west corner can be seen on the plan. On the ground it was no more than the impression of a beam against which darker soil had accumulated on the outside (south) and suggests a timber-framed building. This was butted up against a layer of gravel aligned north-south, into which had been inserted a number of posts rectangular in section (hatched on plan). Five of these were placed close together and formed the south-east corner of a structure, but nothing more of the building survived.

Trenches B and C (Fig. 7.12)

Seven pits were identified as being of probable medieval date and these produced a range of wares dating from 14th to 15th century.

Discussion

Although the suburb outside the Eastgate dates from the 13th century, the fragmentary structures on the site do not appear to pre-date the 14th century. The insubstantial nature of the structural remains and the small amounts of pottery recovered suggest that the occupation was slight and possibly sporadic and reflects the poverty for which St. Pancras was apparently well known.

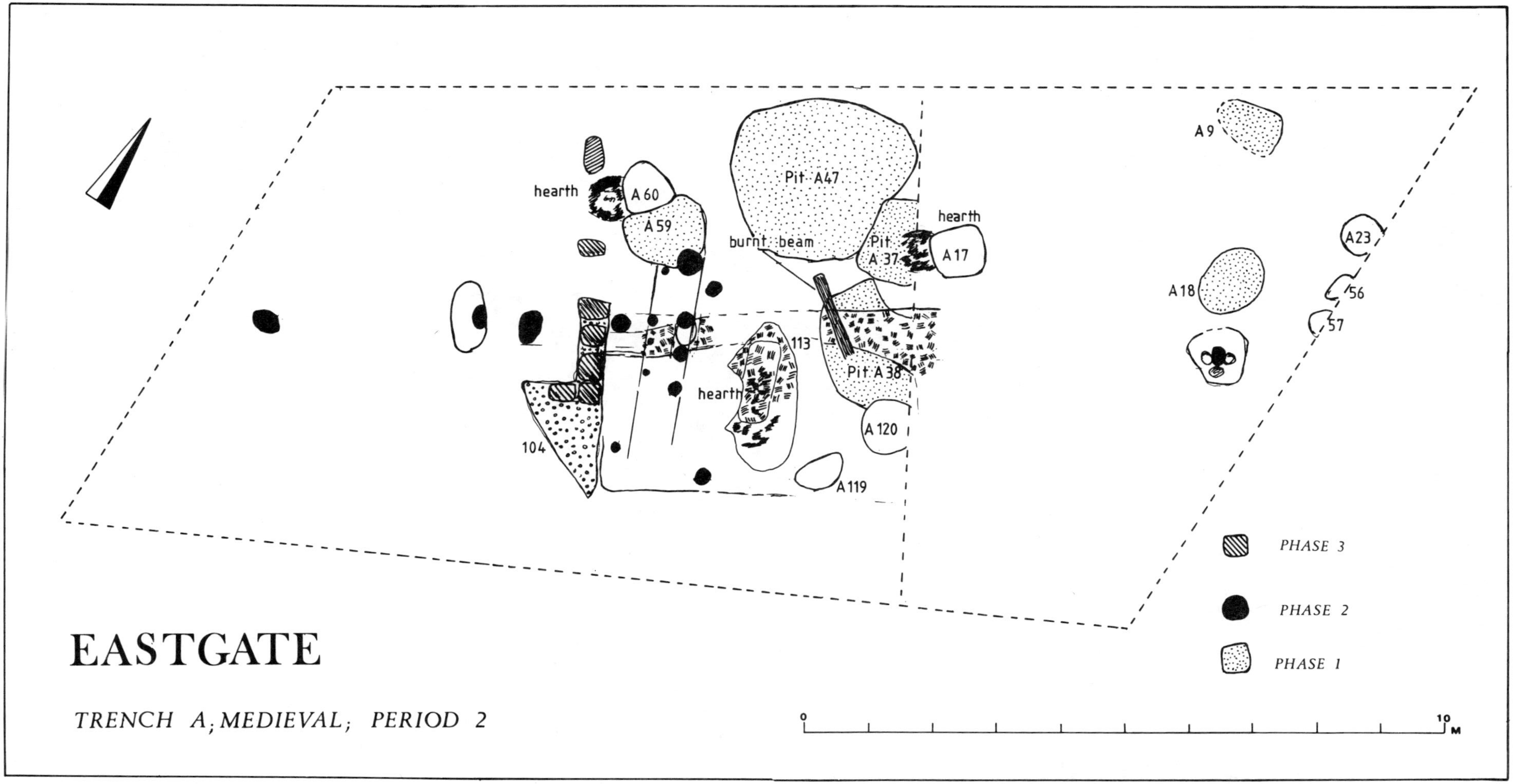
hearth
A 60
A 59
Pit A47
burnt beam
Pit
A 37
hearth
A 17
113
hearth
Pit A 38
A 120
A 119
104
A 9
A23
A18
56
57
PHASE 3
PHASE 2
PHASE 1
EASTGATE
TRENCH A; MEDIEVAL; PERIOD 2
0
10
M

Fig. 7.11

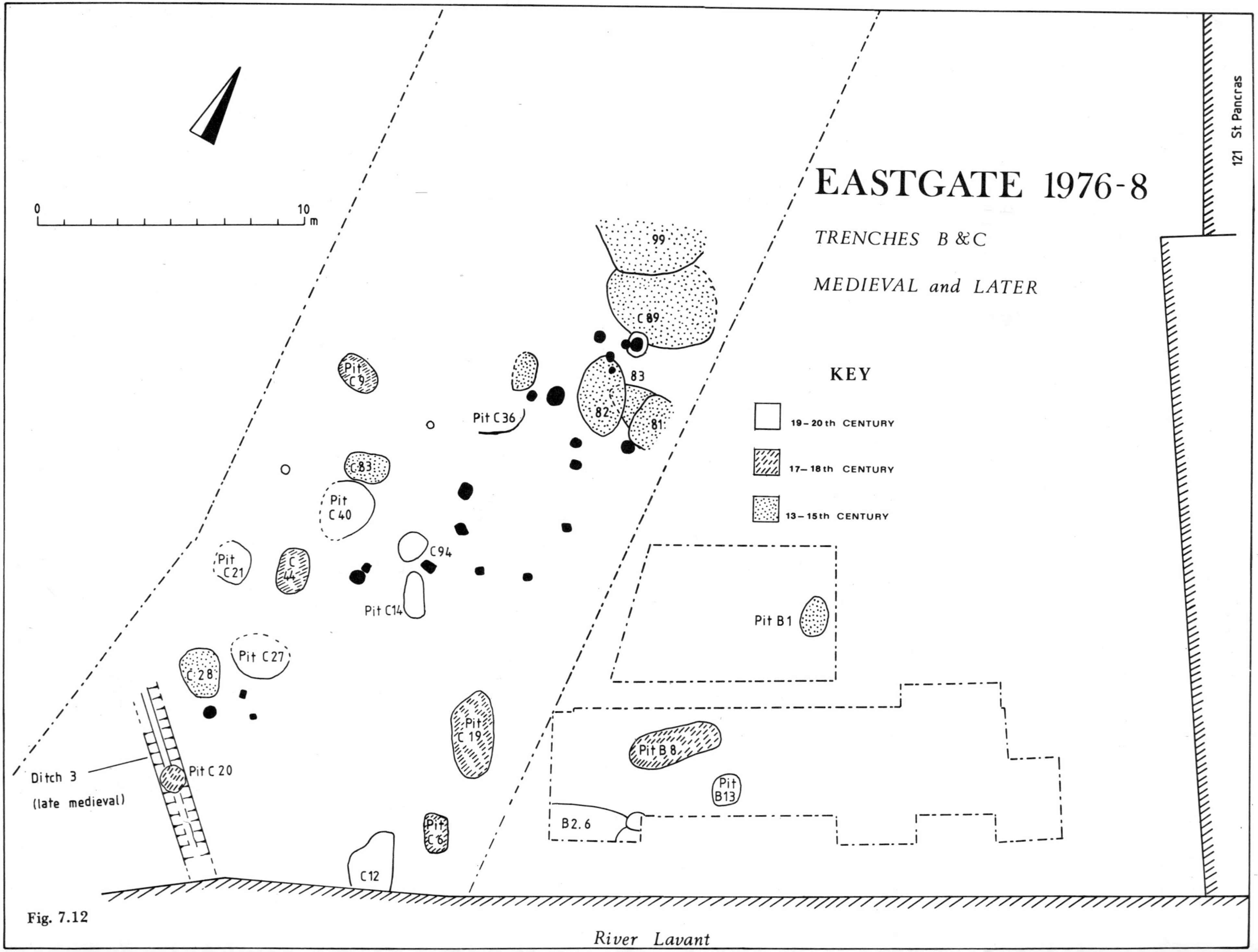
EASTGATE 1976-8
TRENCHES B &C
MEDIEVAL and LATER
KEY
19–20th CENTURY
17–18th CENTURY
13–15th CENTURY
0
10 m
121 St Pancras
99
C 89
83
82
81
Pit C 9
Pit C 36
C 83
Pit C 40
C 94
Pit C 21
C 44
Pit C 14
C 28
Pit C 27
Pit C 19
Pit C 20
Ditch 3
(late medieval)
Pit C 6
C 12
Pit B1
Pit B 8
Pit B13
B2.6
River Lavant

Fig. 7.12

Period 3, Post-medieval: c. early 16th-17th century

Trench A (Fig. 7.13)

By the 16th century the suburb of St. Pancras had extended further eastwards from the Eastgate and by the mid 18th century the extent of the development had reached nearly half a mile outside the walls (see Gardner Map, p. 85).

In Trench A, the postholes (Pl. 12) of a building or buildings in excess of 15 metres long was found. Some of the buildings cut a series of shallow pits (A.2, A.4, A.5, A.7, A.9 and A.13), which, as in Period 2, appear to have been dug for clay as they were not deep enough for cesspits. The earliest pits, A.7 and A.13 produced a few sherds of late 16th–early 17th-century wares, and that part of the structure cannot therefore be any earlier. Only the back rooms of the tenement could be excavated; these measured 4 metres from north to south and allowing the front half of the building below the pavement to be of the same dimensions, then the true width of the building must have been in the region of 8 metres.

At the rear end of the house was a rough cobbled area comprising brick and flints set in sticky clay, and cut through this was a shallow gulley or drain (A.75) which drained to the east. This in turn was cut by a well, which may be contemporary with the latest phase of the building or possibly the 18th-century house which replaced it. Although the latest pottery in Pits A.7 and A.13 gives a late 16th–17th-century date for that part of the building there is a significant amount of earlier painted wares which date from the mid 15th to early 16th century, present in the pits and as surface debris, which suggests that either part of the building may be earlier, or that the slight Period 2 building overlapped into the 16th century.

Trench C (Fig. 7.12)

Five pits, C.6, C.19, C.20, C.44 and B.8 are assigned to Period 3 on the evidence of the contents.

Ditch 3

A small ditch drained from the north-west into the Lavant (Pl. 11). This was cut square at the bottom and had evidently been lined with timber to prevent the gravel silting into it. The pottery from the fill (C.42) contained Surrey white wares ("Tudor" Green), 16th/17th century stonewares and residual painted wares.

Discussion

It is unlikely that the building in Trench A is part of the House of Correction mentioned by Mr. Morgan (p. 78), although the location of that institution could not have been far away and was almost certainly immediately west of the excavation.The Bridewell survived the destruction of the siege of 1642 as there is a record of it being closed down in 1650, and it seems certain that other buildings to the east of it would also have escaped damage by fire. Certainly, there is no evidence from the site to suggest a large scale conflagration.

No trace was found of the needlemaking industry, but as this was a cottage industry involving only small amounts of material and small hearths, the absence of evidence is inconclusive. One small bronze ingot was found in Pit C.20 which cut the top of the ditch, but it is impossible to connect this to the manufacture of pins or needles.

The ditch might well be earlier than the 17th century. Being a box drain it would have been cleaned out at intervals and the latest wares found in C.42 may only indicate the last date it was dug out.

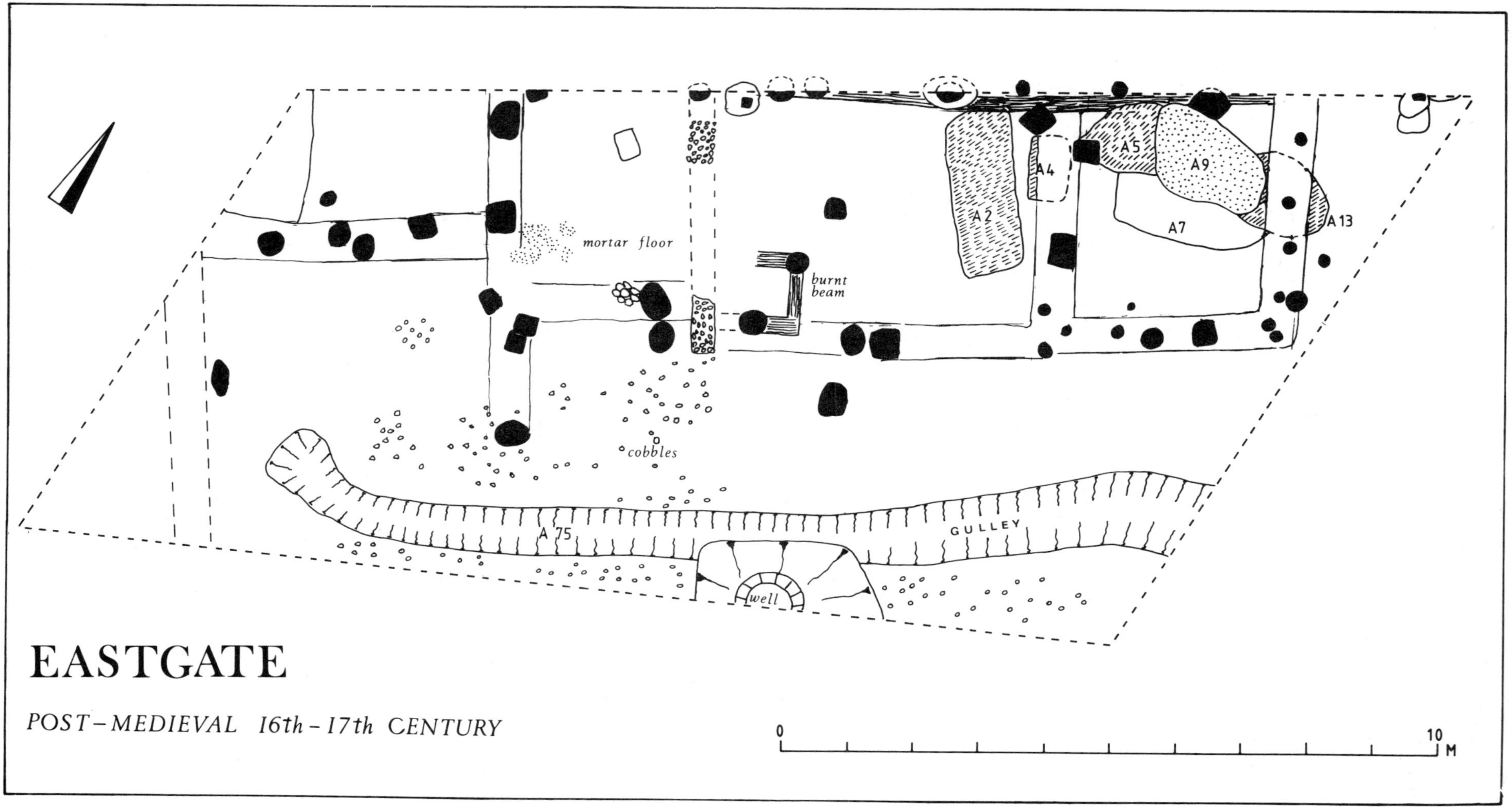
A 13
A9
A5
A4
A7
A2
burnt
beam
mortar floor
cobbles
GULLEY
A 75
well
EASTGATE
POST–MEDIEVAL 16th–17th CENTURY
0
10
M

Fig. 7.13

Period 4, c. 18th-19th centuries (Gardner Map, Fig. 7.5)

By the mid 18th century the building line along the south side of St. Pancras had been established on the same frontage that exists today. This is shown on the Gardner Map and some of the houses seen there are still standing. Many were replaced in the 19th century, including the six cottages demolished to make way for the roads, which were built *c.* 1920.

The Purbeck Marble Inscription from Eastgate Needlemakers (Plate 13 and Fig. 7.14)

by M. W. C. Hassall

Fragments of inscribed Purbeck marble together measuring 0.48 metre wide by 0.39 metre high and *c.* 28 mm thick found in 1978 in a pit dug into the top of a military type ditch on the site of the late Roman cemetery outside the Eastgate.[1] The fragments come from the right-hand edge of a six-sided slab originally 0.825 metre wide and 0.39 metre high. The surface of the stone is slightly concave, while the back is roughly dressed with the exception of smooth rebates 45 mm wide and 15 mm deep running the full width of the stone at top and bottom. It was probably originally capped by a second triangular piece of Purbeck marble and flanked by two more to form a pediment *c.* 1.8 metre (6 feet) wide, and 0.65 metre (just over 2 feet) high.[2] Sections of its moulded cornice were also found (Fig. 7.20), and an uninscribed corner fragment which could come either from the main central slab or one of the three subsidiary pieces. The apex will have formed a right-angle unlike the obtuse angle normal for a pediment of classical proportions.[3] The central slab carried the following inscription:

MATRI] BVS DOMEST / [. . . . .] VS ARK[4] / [D S] P.

Matri] bus Domesticvs / [. . . . .] us ark(arius) / [d (e) s (uo)] p(osuit).

"To the Mother Goddess of the Homeland[5] — the treasurer set this up at his own expense".

The *Matres Domesticae* are attested on three British inscriptions (*RIB* 652, 2025 and 2050), but the main centre of their cult was at Bonn where they were associated with the *Matronae Aufaniae.*[6] Carved reliefs show the *Aufaniae* with large hats or head-dresses seated in niches surmounted by pediments.[7] The Chichester pediment presumably came from a larger shrine in which were placed seated statues of the *Matres Domesticae* carved in the round. The *arcarivs* who built the shrine could have been a municipal official, attached to a guild or even attached to the household of a great man such as King Cogidubnus. All are possible at Chichester.[8]

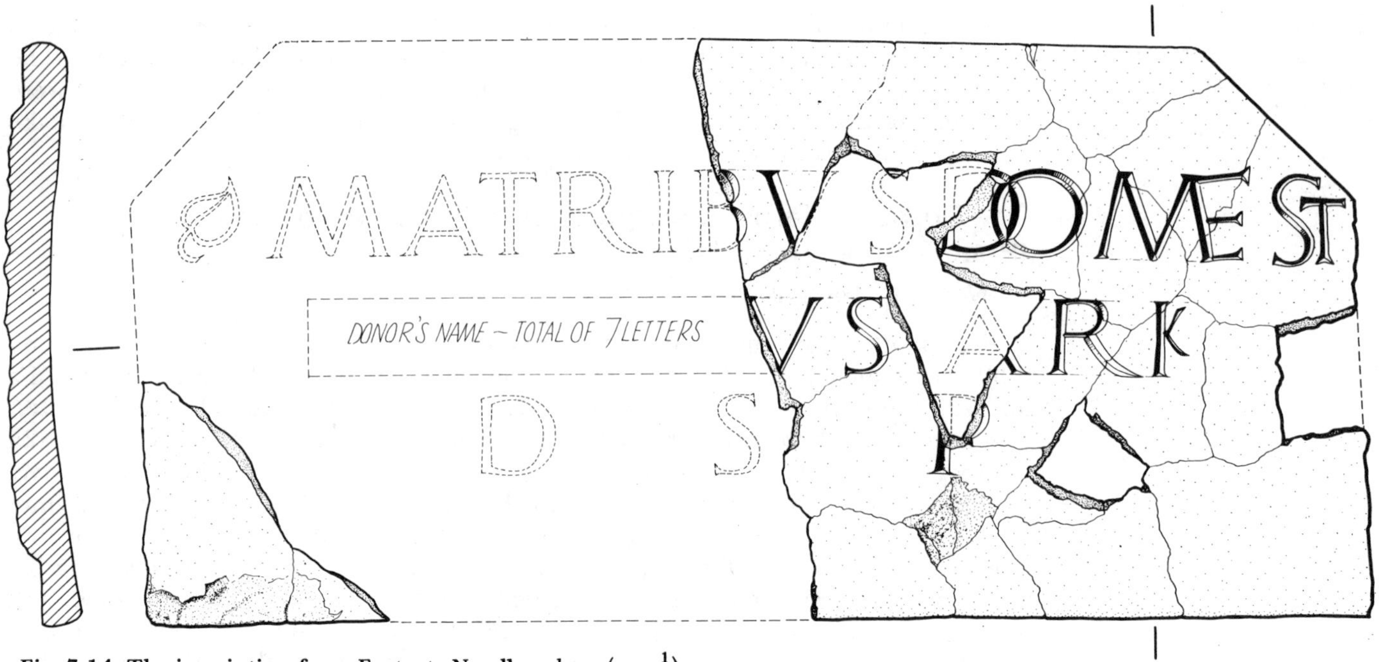

Fig. 7.14. The inscription from Eastgate Needlemakers (app.$\frac{1}{6}$)

Notes

1. The ditch lies to the south of St. Pancras (Stane Street).
2. Compare the pediment of the Wolf and Twins at Corbridge which measures 1.8 metre (6 feet) wide and 0.6 metre high. *Arch. Ael.* 4th Ser. XXI (1943), 173, Pl. XE.
3. The use of a right-angle would mean that all three subidiary pieces of pediment could have been cut from a single slab.
4. For the form of the K see e.g. *RIB* 882 and 883. The E, S and T in 1.2 appear to be additions. They could have been balanced by cutting a leaf stop at the beginning of the line. Five letters are missing at the beginning of 1.2.
5. Ihm translates *Domesticae* as "of the homeland" (*RE* V 1. 1296 article "Domesticae") comparing the description of the *Matres* as *suae* (as *RIB* 654, 2055) and *patriae* (as *RIB* 1318). Wright translates "of the household" in *RIB* 652, 2025 and 2050. The restoration of *Matribus* here is virtually certain, the only other possibility being LARI]BVS DOMEST(ICIS), but such a dedication is apparently only attested once CIL III 4160=ILS 3607 (Savaria).
6. CIL XIII 8021 appears to identify the two groups: *Matribus sive Matronis Aufaniabus domesticis,* AE 31 No. 15 on the other hand distinguishes between them: *Aufanis et Matribus Domesticis.* For the evidence from Bonn see H. Lehner, "Römisches Steindenkmäler von der Bonner Miiunsterkirche", *Bonner Jahrbucher* 135 (1930), 1–48 and H. Lehner and W. Bader, "Baugeschichtliche Untersuchungen am Bonner Münster" in *ibid.* 136/7 (1932), 3–216.
7. See Lehner, *op. cit.*, Pls. VIII, X, XI, XV, XVI, XIX.
8. See ILS index, Vol. III, 2, p. 699, municipal *arcarii, ibid.* 721, *curatores arcae* of *collegia* and *ibid.* 726 *arcarii* attached to great households. For the presence of a *collegium fabrorum* and of Cogidubnus at Chichester, see *RIB* 91.

The Roman Pottery from Eastgate (Fig. 7.15)

Pit A.29 (Fig. 7.15)—Well 1. The fill comprises A.76, A.91 and A.92.
Note; All in a sandy grey fabric unless otherwise stated.

1. Bowl, *c.* 21 centimetres diameter in a fine grey ware oxidised buff. Exterior burnished with vertical combed decoration.
2. Dish, imitation Camulodunum, 16 Ac with functionless footring, micaceous grey fabric reduced black, smooth surfaces.
3. Bowl, imitation Camulodunum 16B. Fine grey core, exterior oxidised buff and mica dusted.
4. Flagon with conical neck; cf. *Chichester 1,* Fig. 5.21, 59 c.
5. Lid.
6. Carinated bowl, reduced black outside.

7-8. Cooking pots with everted rims.
9-13. Cooking pots with everted rims, similar in fabric and form to 7 and 8.
Not illustrated.
14. Lid-seated bowl in reddish sandy ware.
15. Carinated bowl (A.91).
16. Lid-seated cooking pot (A.92).
17. Necked bowl with grooved decoration above shoulder (A.92).
18-19. Cooking pots with everted rims (A.92).
20. Small beaker, fine grey ware; burnished exterior and over lip (A.92).
Alice Holt wares. (cf. *Lyne & Jeffries 1*).
21. Necked jar, ? Trajanic (1–12).
22. Lid-seated bowl, late 1st century (5–1).

Fig. 7.15

A.19 (Fill of Ditch 2)
23. Necked jar.
24. Necked jar, grooved on shoulder, laminated grey fabric.
25. Necked jar, lightly burnished exterior.
26–29. Cooking pots, oxidised reddish buff.
30. Jar in fine dark grey fabric; lightly burnished above groove.
31. Narrow necked jar.
32. Cooking pot; fine light-grey sandy ware; exterior reduced slate-grey.
33. Necked jar.
34. Narrow mouthed jar.
35. Jar with slightly hooked rim, similar fabric to 32.
36. Jar in black sandy fabric.
37. Jar with everted rim, similar fabric to 32.
38. Necked jar with shoulder groove. Similar ware to 32.
39. Body sherd from cordoned jar.
40. Dish in a similar fabric to 32.
41. Double-handled flagon from Alice Holt; late 1st–2nd century (8–1).

Fig. 7.16

Pit A.33
41-43, Flagons with traces of an exterior black slip.
44. Bowl; burnished inside.
45. Shallow dish.
46-47. Flanged bowls.

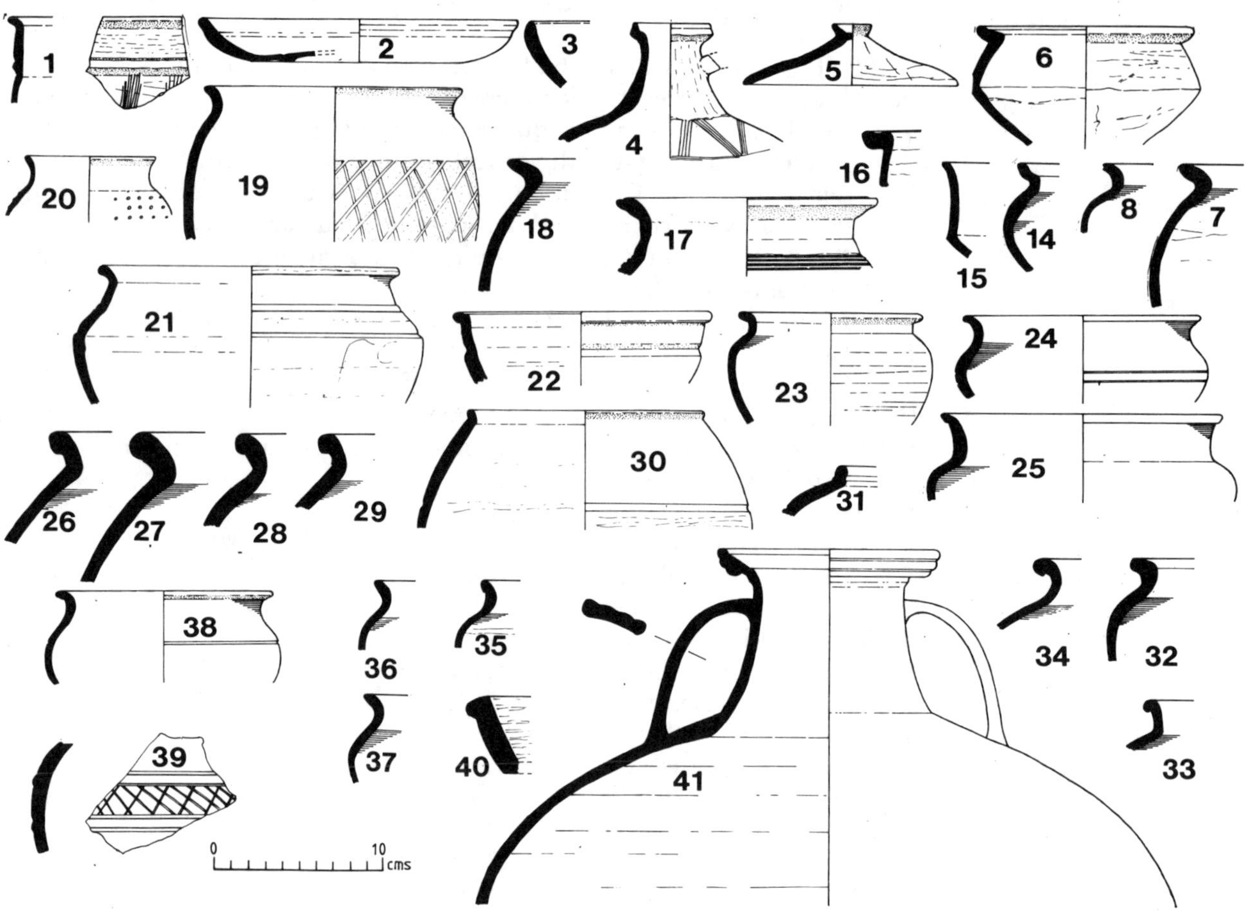

Fig. 7.15. Eastgate Needlemakers, Roman coarse wares.
Nos. 1-22, Well 1; Nos. 23-41, A.19 (¼)

48. Carinated bowl, burnished over lip.
49. Cooking pot, grey fabric, oxidised reddish-buff on exterior surfaces.
50. Necked vessel, probably cooking pot; similar fabric to 49.
51-52. Necked jars.
53. Small jar in a fine greyish-white fabric with slate-grey exterior slip.
54. Beaker; fine sandy fabric, burnished over lip, exterior black slip.
55. Jar with everted rim.
56. Small cooking pot, burnished on shoulder and over rim, fire blackened inside and out.

Alice Holt wares

57. Narrow-necked storage jar, late 3rd century (1A–11).
58. Flat-rimmed jar, early 3rd century (3A–19 variant).
59. Dish, 3rd century (GA–2).

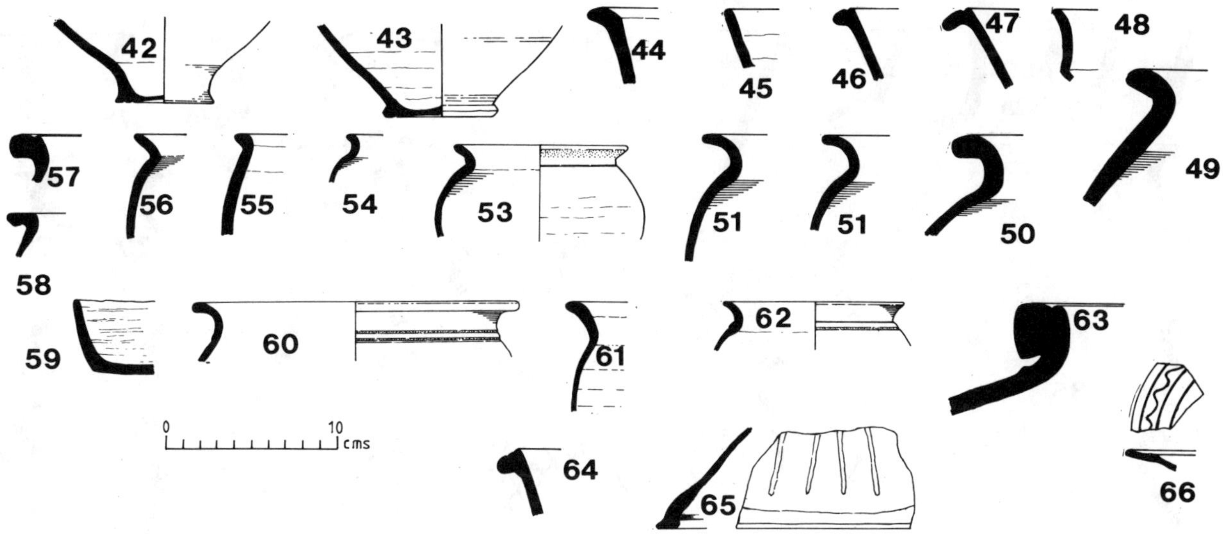

Fig. 7.16. Eastgate Needlemakers, Roman coarse wares. Nos. 42-62, Pit A.33, Nos. 63-66, miscellaneous. (¼)

60. Necked and cordoned jar, early 3rd century (1-31).
61. Cooking pot; late 3rd century (3B-10).
62. Cordoned jar; 3rd century (2-3).
63. Storage jar, 3rd century, post A.D. 220 (1C-4). Pit C,12.
64. Buff flanged bowl, post A.D. 330, could be late 4th-early 5th century. Layer C.101.

Miscellaneous.

65. Lid in a sandy grey ware with traces of white slip striped decoration on the outside.
66. Shallow plate in a red fabric with white slip coating and sgraffito decoration.

The Pottery from Well 2. (all in a hard sandy fabric unless otherwise stated.)[2]

67-69. Dishes, burnished inside, black surfaces.
70-71. Dishes in a grey fabric. From a different source than 67-69.
72. Flanged bowl.
73. Lid seated bowl.
74. Necked jar with pecked rim.
75. Necked jar; fabric oxidised reddish-buff.
76. Jar with hooked rim.
77. Necked jar.
78. Jar with everted rim; traces of white slip inside rim.
79. Necked jar, burnished over rim.
80. Jar with everted rim.
81. Jar with everted rim.
82. Jar with everted rim; fine grey fabric with slate grey exterior slip above burnished shoulder.
83. Small jar.

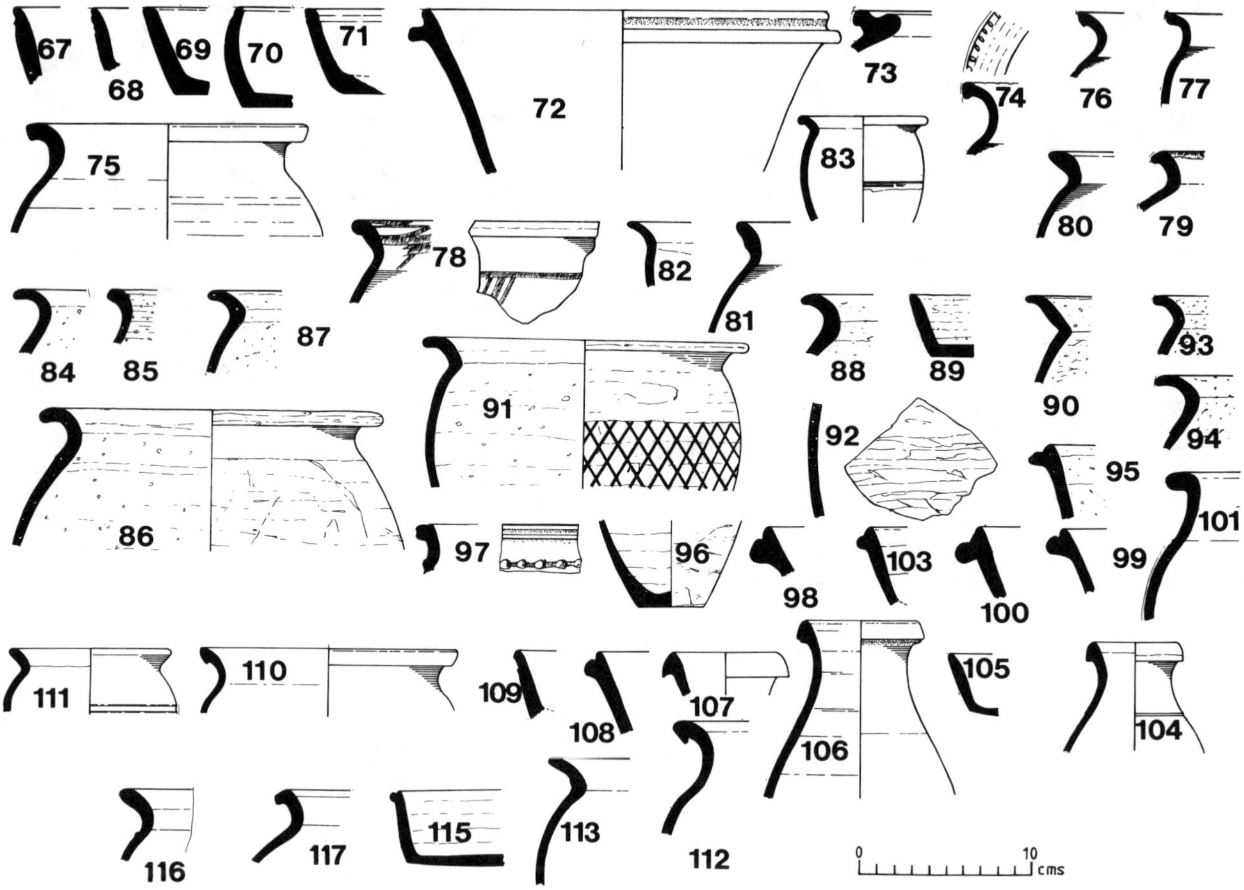

Fig. 7.17. Eastgate Needlemakers, Roman coarse wares.
Nos. 67-83, greywares, Nos. 84-96, black grogged wares, Nos. 97-117, Alice Holt wares. (¼)

Black sandy wares

These wares were first noted at Chilgrove (*Chichester 4,* 192 and Fig. 72), where they were seen in a late 4th-century context. The colour is black to dark brown (sepia), and the blacker sherds appear to have been burnt. There is a lot of coarse sand and some flint in the fabric, with occasional chalk grog. The exterior finish is usually uneven but has been smoothed, especially on the shoulder and rim of the vessels. The firing varies from fairly soft to hard.

84–85. Jars in a soft black fabric, grogged with chalk and flint.
86–88. Similar fabric to 84.
89. Similar fabric but with some organic tempering.
90–91. Similar fabric to 84.
92. Body sherd from a cooking pot. Similar ware to 84, lumpy exterior which has been roughly tooled.

93-94. Similar fabric to 84.
95. Flanged bowl.
96. Base of small jar or beaker.

Fig. 7.17

The Alice Holt wares

97. Necked jar with finger-impressed cordon, mid-late 4th century.
98. Flanged bowl, late 4th century (5B-9).
99. As 98 (5B-8).
100. As 98 (5B-5 variant).
101. Necked jar; 4th century (1-33 variant).
102. Body sherd from a storage jar, cf. *Chichester 4*; Fig. 72.81). *Not illustrated.*
103. Flanged dish, mid-late 4th century (6C-1).
104. Flagon, 4th century (8-11).
105. Dish, mid 4th century (6A-1/4 variant).
106. Flagon, 4th century (8-11).
107. Flagon, 4th century (8-14).
108. Flanged bowl (5B variant).
109. Dish with wide groove below the rim.
110. Hook-rimmed jar (3C-7).
111. Small jar (3B-11).
112. Hooked rimmed jar, 3rd or 4th century (3C-7).
113. Jar (3B-10/12).
114. Club rimmed strainer (5C-2), cf. *Chichester 4,* Fig. 70.11. *Not illustrated.*
115. Flanged dish, ? late 4th century (6C-1).
116. Cordoned jar, 4th century (33-10/22).
117. Necked jar (1-33 variant).

Notes

1. Identification by Mr. Malcolm Lyne, to whom thanks are due.
2. See p. 285 and Fig. 14.1 for the post-Flavian fine wares.

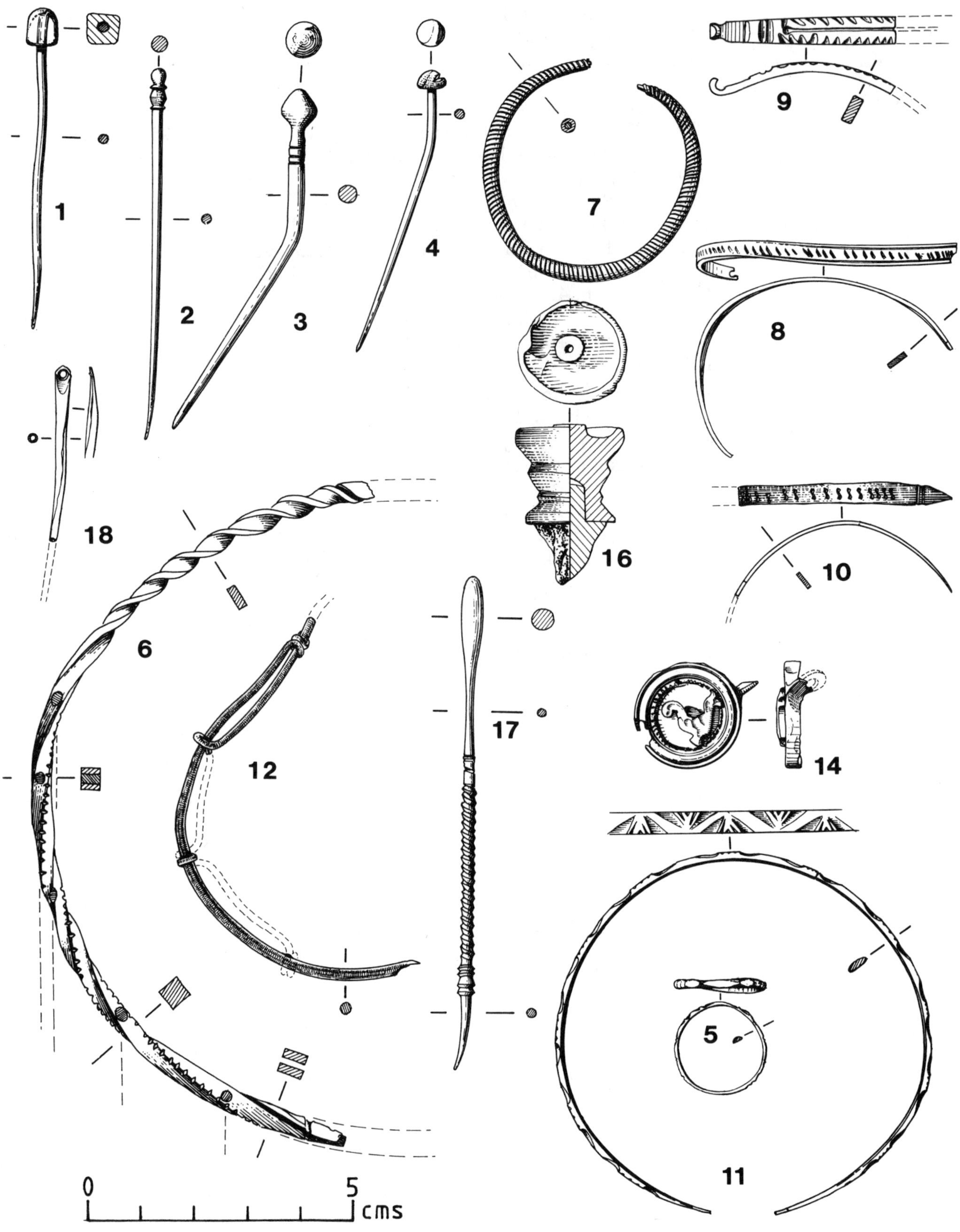

Fig. 7.18. Eastgate Needlemakers, Roman small finds.
Nos. 1-18, Bronze ($\frac{1}{1}$)

Small Finds from Eastgate Needlemakers

Roman

Fig. 7.18

A. Objects of bronze

1. Hairpin with blue glass head. C. 103 (70).
2. Hairpin with a grooved head which may have provided a "key" for a glass knob, now lost. C.104 (73).
3. Hairpin. C.104 (74).
4. Hairpin with blue glass head. Unstratified. (67).
5. Ring. Pit C.13 (17).
6. Necklace, with copper anchor pins for pendants. A.19 (11).
7. Bracelet. C.103 (80).
8. Bracelet. C.103 (48).
9. Fragment of a bracelet. C.103 (58).
10. Bracelet. C.103 (86).
11. Bracelet. C.103 (98).
12. Part of an expanding bracelet. C.103 (87).
13. Part of a toilet set (cf. *Chichester 3,* Fig. 10.37, 93), Pit B.10 (B). *Not illustrated.* (218).
14. Lid of a seal box with a device in the form of a bird, probably a cockerel. A.19 (13).
15. Part of a seal box (cf. *Chichester 3,* Fig. 10.38, 118). *Not illustrated.* Pit B.10 (E), (227).
16. Handle, with the remains of an iron shank. A.108 (90).
17. Ligula. Pit B.10 (B), (220).
18. Needle. C.83 (33).

Fig. 7.19

B. Objects of bone

19. Handle of a toilet instrument with a bulbous end. C.103 (63). *Not illustrated.*
20. Bone point with graffiti cut into it. C.11 (19).
21. Pin, probably a hairpin, cut from horn. C.103 (79).

C. Objects of iron

22. Carpenter's bit. (Cf. *Chichester 4,* Fig. 46, 5). C.103 (84). *Not illustrated.*
23. Latch lifter. Pit B.10 (188).

D. Objects of clay

24. Bead. *c.* 12 mm. diameter. A.2 (4). *Not illustrated.*

E. Objects of lead

25. Disc or plug. Pit A.29 (42).
26. Lead plug with T A I and T L cut into the convex face. A.15 (10).

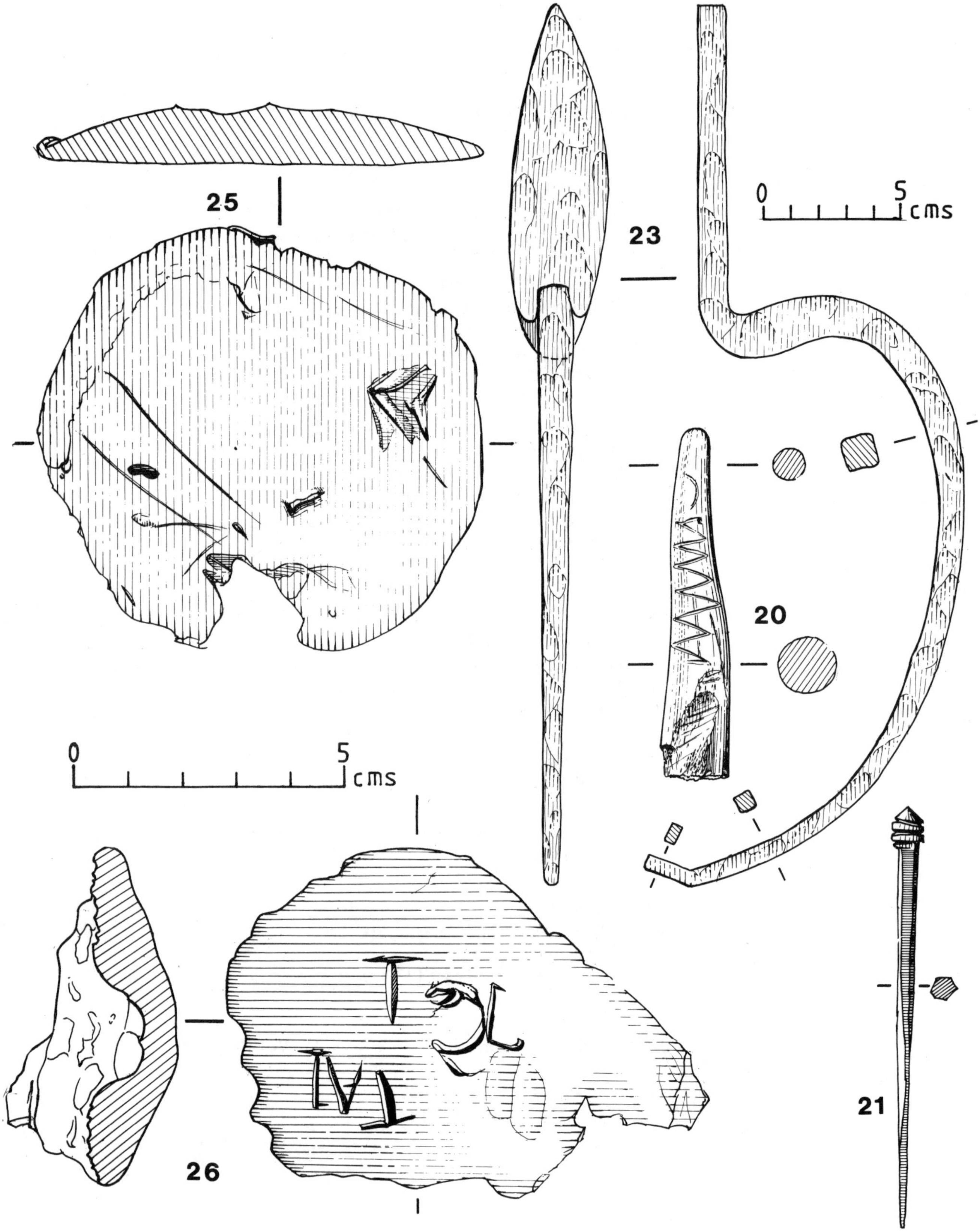

Fig. 7.19. Eastgate Needlemakers, Roman small finds.
Nos. 19-21, bone; No. 23; iron; Nos. 26-26, lead. No. 23 (½), remainder ($\frac{1}{1}$)

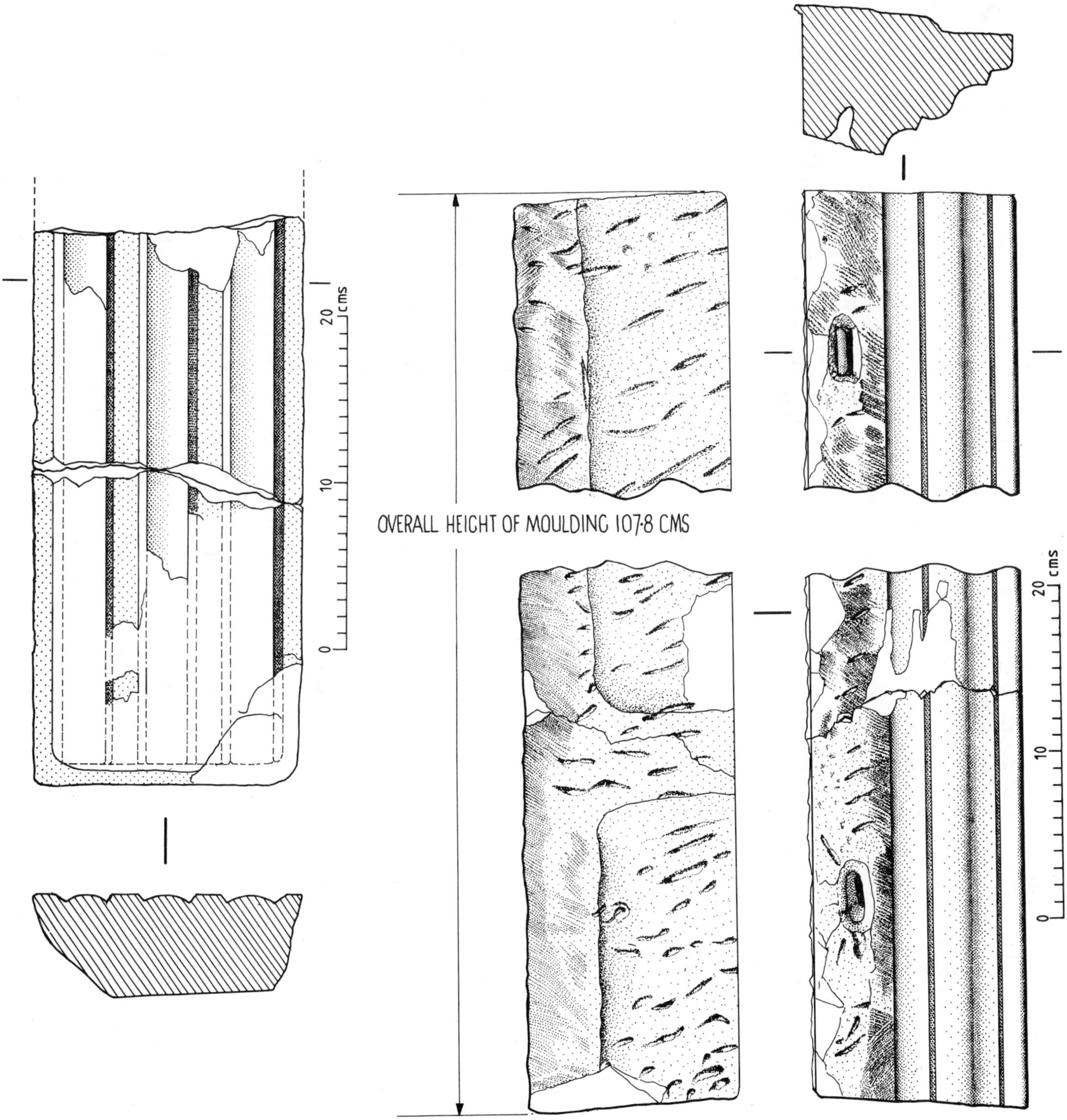

Fig. 7.20. Eastgate Needlemakers, fragments of moulded cornice, ($\frac{1}{3}$)

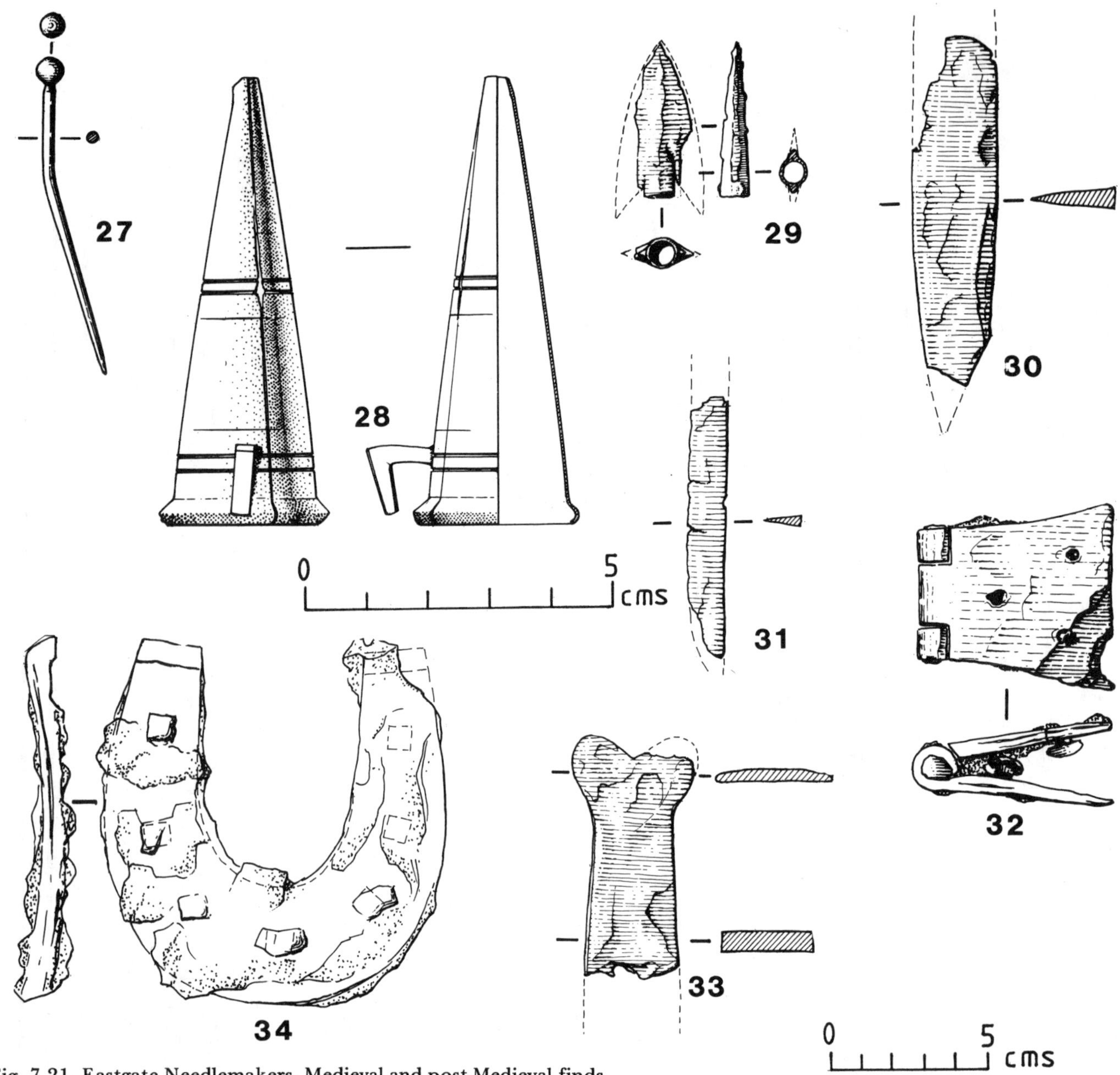

Fig. 7.21. Eastgate Needlemakers, Medieval and post-Medieval finds.
Nos. 27-28, bronze; Nos. 29-34, iron; Nos. 27-28 ($\frac{1}{1}$), remainder (½)

Fig. 7.21

Medieval and post-Medieval

F. Objects of bronze

27. Pin, probably made locally, *c.* 16th–17th century. A.2 (3).
28. Candle snuffer; probably 19th century. Pit C.16 (129).

G. Objects of iron

29. Arrow head. A.48 (22).
30. Knife blade from the fill of a late or post-medieval hearth. A.113 (69).
31. Knife blade. A.15 (15).
32. Hinge, probably from a door. Posthole A.44 (24).
33. Fragment of iron strapping, either from a door hinge or a chest. A.15 (9).
34. Late or post-medieval horseshoe. Pit C.20 (26).

THE COINS FROM EASTGATE—compiled by Roger Lintott. (For list of abbreviations, see p. 183).

Small find No.	Denomination	Emperor and date	Reverse type	Mint mark	Date of coin	Ref. No.	Notes
110	Ae As	Nero, 54–68 A.D.	Nero as Apollo		54–68 A.D.	RIC 364	ph A94
50	Ae Ant	Salonina w. of Gallianus, 260–268 A.D.	Felicitas	Rome	266 A.D.		Layer C99
68	Ae Ant	Claudius II, 268–270 A.D.	Equity				Layer C103
117	Ae Ant	Divo Claudio	Eagle		*c.* 270		Layer B2, I
118	Ae Ant	Tetricus I, 270–273 A.D.					Layer B2, I
138	Ae Ant	Tetricus I, 270–273 A.D.	Victory				Pit B9
81	Ae Ant	Tetricus I, 270–273 A.D. (fragment)					Layer C103
189	Ae Ant	illegible					Pit B9 (B)
210	Ae Ant	illegible					Layer B2.8
230	Ae Br	Tetricus 1 type (2 coins)					Burial 14
91	Ae Br 10mm.						Layer C103
1	Ae Br 12mm.						Layer A2
2	Ae Br 10mm.						Layer A2
127	Ae Br 9mm.						Layer B2, 2
3 coins		Tetricus 1 type					from B2
1 coin		Tetricus 11 type					Layer 8
10 coins		illegible					
43 coins		1 Claudius II 6 Tetricus 1 types 1 Tetricus II type 35 illegible	Large altar type				from Pit B9
75	Ae Fol	Constantine 1, 307–337 A.D.	Sol	SP/MSL London	316 A.D.	RIC 68	Layer C104
78	Ae 3	Constantine I, 307–337 A.D.	Camp gate	I/PLG Lyons	324–5 A.D.	RIC 225	Layer C103
103	Ae Fol	Constantine I, 307–337 A.D.	Camp gate	S F/Q Const. Arles	328 A.D.	RIC 323	Layer C103
213	Ae 3	Constantine I, 307–337 A.D.	Gloria exercitvs 2 stds		330–6 A.D.		Layer B2, 2
104	Ae 4	Constantine II, 317–340	Gloria exercitvs 2 stds	I/TR. P Trier	332–3 A.D.	RIC 540	Layer C103
76	Ae 4	Constantine II, 317–340	Gloria exercitvs 1 std		336–341 A.D.		Layer C104

THE COINS FROM EASTGATE—*continued*

Small find No.	Denomination	Emperor and date	Reverse Type	Mint mark	Date of coin	Ref. No.	Notes
85	Ae 3	Constans 333–350 A.D.	2 Victories	$\overline{\text{TRS}}$ Trier	341–346 A.D.	LRBC 162–4	Layer C103
106	Ae 4	Constans 333–350 A.D.	2 Victories	D/TRP Trier	341–346 A.D.	LBRC 146–7	Layer C103
53	Ae ½ cent	Constans 333–350 A.D.	Phoenix on globe		343–349 A.D.		Layer C99
116	Ae 4	Constantius II, 324–361 A.D.	Gloria exercitvs 1 std	I/TRS Trier	337 A.D.	LRBC 124	Layer B2, 1
201	Ae 3	Constantius, II, 324–361 A.D.	Gloria exercitvs 1 std		336–341 A.D.		Layer B2, 8
96	Ae 4	House of Constantine	Gloria exercitvs 2 stds		330–336 A.D.		Layer C103
108	Ae 4	House of Constantine	Gloria exercitvs 2 stds		330–336 A.D.		Layer C103
38	Ae 4	House of Constantine	Gloria exercitvs 1 std		336–341 A.D.		Layer A53
88	Ae 4	House of Constantine	Gloria exercitvs 1 std		336–341 A.D.		Pit A33
181	Ae 4	House of Constantine	Gloria exercitvs 1 std		336–341 A.D.		Pit B9
77	Ae 3	Urbs Roma	Wolf and twins	TRP Trier	333–334 A.D.	RIC 561	Layer C104
72	Ae 4	Urbs Roma	Wolf and twins	P X/P Const Arles	336	RIC 400	Layer C104
101	Ae 3	Urbs Roma	Wolf and twins		330–335 A.D.		Layer C103
97	Ae 3	Constantinopolis	Victory on prow	I/TRS Trier	330–331	RIC 523	Layer C103
102	Ae 4	Constantinopolis	Victory on prow		330–337		Layer C103
107	Ae 3	Constantinopolis	Victory on prow		330–337		Layer C103
114	Ae 4	Constantinopolis	Victory on prow		330–337		Layer B2, 1
231	Ae 3	Constantinopolis	Victory on prow		330–337		Burial 13 (in skull)
105	Ae 4	Theodora, 2nd w. of Constantine	Pietas		337–341 A.D.		Layer C103
60	Ae Ant	Magnentius 350–3 A.D.	Barb. copy				Layer C103
47	Ae 3	Valentinian I, 364–375 A.D.	G R		364–375 A.D.		Layer C103
34	Ae 3	Valens 364–378 A.D.	S R		364–378 A.D.		Layer C89
57	Ae 3	Valens 364–378 A.D.	S R		364–378 A.D		Layer C103
39	Ae 3	Valens 364–378 A.D.	G R		364–378 A.D.		Pit C28
41	Ae 3	Valentinian or Valens	G R		364–378 A.D.		Layer C101
223	Ae 3	Valentinian or Valens	S R		364–378 A.D.		Pit B2
Post-Roman coins							
8	halfpenny	Geo. III, 1760–1820	Britannia		1806		Layer B2
115	halfpenny	Geo. III, 1760–1820	Britannia		1806		Layer A16

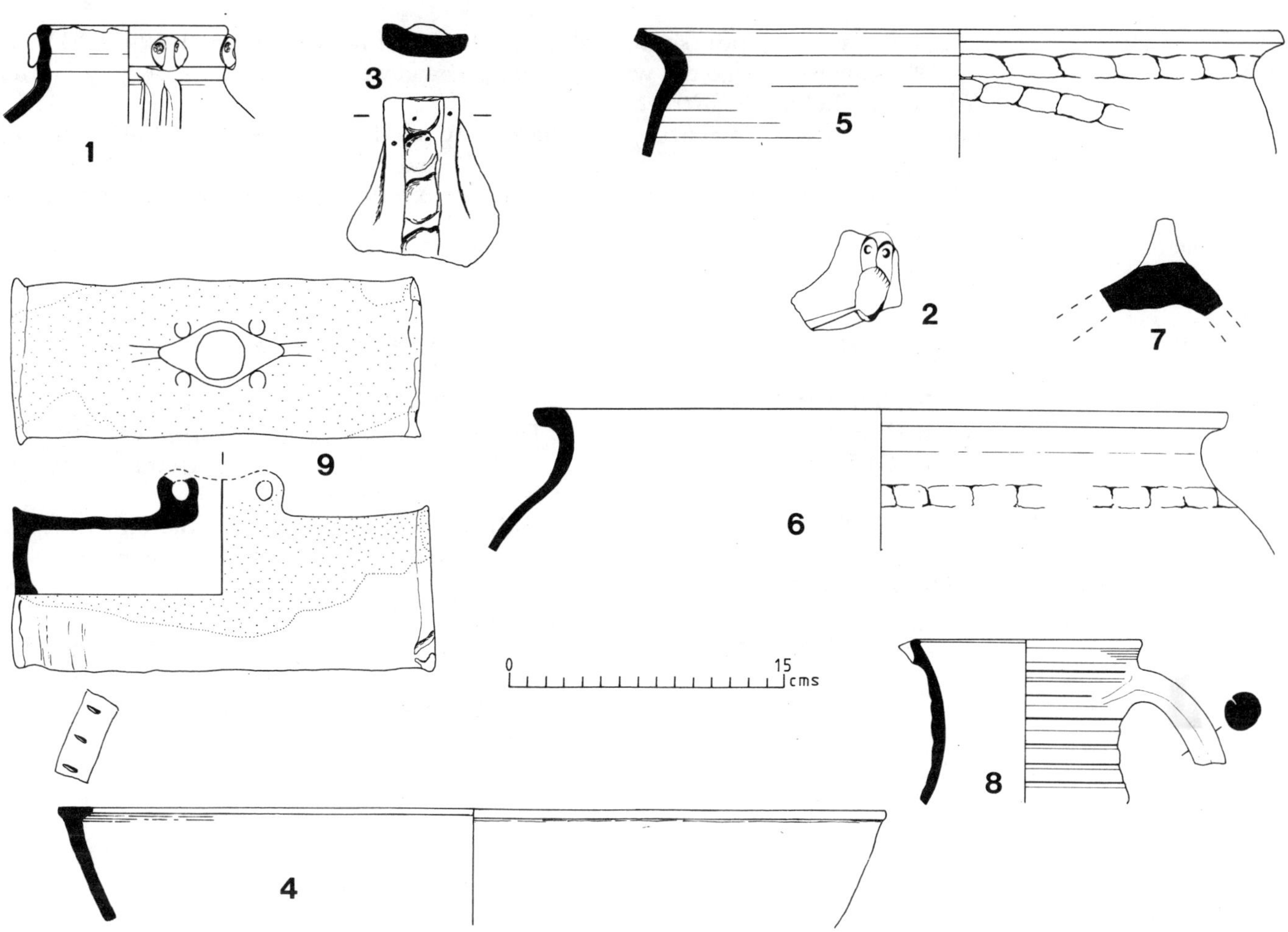

Fig. 7.22. Medieval pottery. Nos. 1-7, Needlemakers; Nos. 8 & 9, Guildhall St. (¼)

Medieval Pottery

Fig. 7.22

(*a*) *From Needlemakers*

1. Two fragments from the rim of a jug with anthropomorphic decoration. Sandy-grey fabric oxydised pinky buff and with an olive-green exterior glaze. (A.15). 14th century.
2. Body sherd from a second anthropomorphic jug. Similar fabric but the sherd is oxydised to a paler pink and the glaze is a paler green. (A.15).
3. Strap handle from a jug. Grey fabric with some sparse flint temper and a patchy green glaze with traces of white painted decoration below. (Pit B.1).
4. Steep walled bowl with flattened rim. Buff fabric, flint tempered. (C.89).
5. Cooking pot; similar fabric to No. 4. (C.89).

6. Large cooking pot; similar fabric to No. 5 but heavily abraded. (Pit A.31).
7. Fragment of ridge tile with exterior green glaze. Hard, sandy pale grey fabric.

(*b*) *From 4 Guildhall Street*

8. Neck of a 14th-century jug; hard grey sandy ware oxydised buff, with an exterior green glaze and a band of white paint inside rim.
9. Costrel in a pale buff fabric with an exterior green glaze over the upper part.

References

CHICHESTER 1	Down, A. and Rule, M., *Chichester Excavations* 1, 1971.
CHICHESTER 3	Down, A., *Chichester Excavations* 3, 1978.
CHICHESTER 4	Down, A., *Chichester Excavations* 4, 1979.
FULFORD 1975	Fulford, M., "New Forest Roman Pottery", *B.A.R.* 17, Oxford, 1975.
HILL 1978	Hill, D., "The origins of the Saxon towns", in P. Brandon (Ed.), *The South Saxons*, 1978.
HOLMES 1962	Holmes, J., "The Defences of Roman Chichester", *S.A.C.* 100 (1962).
LYNE & JEFFRIES	Lyne, M. A. B. and Jeffries, R. S., "The Alice Holt/Farnham Roman Pottery Industry", *C.B.A. Research Report*, No. 30.

The Human Skeletal Remains from Eastgate Needlemakers

by Helena M. Barnes, M.B., M.R.C.P.

This Report is in two sections. Part 1 (below), summarises the results of the examination of the skeletons, while Part 2 (in the Level III archive), gives a more detailed account of each burial together with such measurements as it was possible to take.

Fourteen skeletons were found, 4 adult male, 5 adult female, 2 children and 3 other adults in whom the sexing was impossible due to the fragmentary nature of the bones. The age at death of the adults varied between 18 and the mid 60s, most of them dying probably in their early 30s; The heights ranged from 155 cms. (5 feet 1 inch) to 176 cms. (5 feet 9 inches).

The determination of sex is based upon examination of those bones which emphasise sexual dimorphism. The pelvis is probably the most helpful. The male pelvis has an acute angled greater sciatic notch, with deep acetabulum, the female pelvis has a wider sciatic notch and shallow acetabulum. The sub-pubic angle is also more acute in the male skeleton. The male bones are generally larger, heavier and have marked muscle attachments. Some morphological overlap obviously occurs which can make sexing difficult particularly where the skeleton is incomplete.

The age at death of the skeletons may be rather inexact. It depends partly on fusion of the epiphyses, both of the long bones and the skull, and also the degree of wear and caries of the teeth (*Brothwell*, 1963). Pathological changes, particularly osteoarthritis, are also helpful, although comparisons between the age of onset of osteoarthritis in modern man and in Roman times may be misleading. These people died on average at a very much earlier age than present-day man, and even in their early 30s showed quite marked osteoarthritis, whereas this would be very unusual in modern man.

Estimates of stature in this Report have been calculated from the regression equation formulae of *Trotter and Gleser* (1952, 1958). These equations were computed from measurements of long bones of North American whites, the femur having the smallest standard error. It would appear that the people from Eastgate were shorter than present day man.

The commonest pathological process found in these skeletons was osteo-arthritis. Four of the 14 showed varying degrees of osteoarthritis, though Burial 4 had very gross changes throughout the skeleton. There was fusion of the bodies of the thoracic vertebrae by calcification of the spinal ligaments, and gross distortion of the bodies. The shoulder joints were also flattened and distorted. Many other bones were severely affected. Ageing this skeleton on the wear of the teeth and fusion of the epiphyses would make it 45 or more. The degree of osteoarthritis, by present day terms would put it into the 60s.

Burial 11 had a fracture of the radius and ulna which showed callus formation and marked displacement with overlap of the broken ends. This skeleton also showed complete loss of the cervical and two thoracic vertebrae, whilst all the other vertebrae were present. The skull was in line with the body in the grave, but possibly slighly further away from it than one would expect. It is impossible to explain this situation by examination of the bones.

Probably the most interesting pathology was the finding of a Brodie's abscess in Burial 2. This was seen as a smooth deformity on the left tibia. On X-ray this was shown to be a circular cavity surrounded by a zone of thickened bone. This is diagnostic of a Brodie's abscess, a form of chronic osteomyelitis which arises insidiously without a preceding acute attack. This skeleton could be accurately aged owing to the degree of fusion of the epiphyses of the long bones and died between the ages of 18 and 20. The abscess had presumably been present for some time since the changes in the bone were quite pronounced, possibly since childhood.

The dental disease in these skeletons was not too severe.. The most common finding was the wear on the grinding surfaces with loss of enamel, thought to be caused by an abrasive substance in the food from the grit from the lava and sandstone querns. Fibrous foods may have also played a part. Only 4 of the 14 skeletons showed evidence of caries and none of these was severe.

In summary, 14 skeletons were examined, most being fragmentary in nature. These people died on average in their early 30s and were shorter than modern man. Pathology was not marked, osteoarthritis being the commonest finding. Dental disease was not severe and there was little evidence of caries.

References

BROTHWELL, D. R. "Digging up bones". In "The Excavation, Treatment and Study of Human Skeletal Remains". 1963. London. p. 192.

TROTTER, M. and GLESER, G. C. "Estimation of stature from long bones of American Whites and Negroes", *Amer. J. Phys. Anthrop.* 1952, 10, 463–514.

TROTTER, M. and GLESER, G. C. "A re-evaluation of estimation of stature based on measurements of stature taken during life and long bones after death". *Amer. J. Phys. Anthrop.* 1958, 16, 79–123.

8

Excavations in the North-West Quadrant, 1977-78

Introduction

From 1968–75 the Excavations Committee carried out a programme of work in advance of development in the Tower Street and Chapel Street areas of the north-west quadrant under the direction of the present writer. The results were published in *Chichester Excavations*, Volume 3, in 1978.

In 1977, following the proposal by the Chichester District Council to acquire land from the Post Office on the west side of Chapel Street and develop it as a housing complex, the Post Office and the Council agreed to make the land available for excavation in advance. This was an important and most welcome demonstration of co-operation from both bodies and was greatly appreciated by the Committee. The plot in question, approximately 750 sq. metres in area, linked our excavations below the Central Girls School (Area 2) with those beneath Gospel Hall (Area 5) and comprised the site previously occupied by Bell House, Coronation Hall and Nos. 4, 5 and 6 Chapel Street (see *Chichester 3*, Fig. 7.1 and this volume, Fig. 8.1).

A year later, the Council gave us another opportunity to excavate a strip of land alongside No. 6 Crane Street in order to answer a number of questions arising from the earlier trial excavations carried out by machine in 1974 (*op. cit.* Fig. 7.51).

The excavations (Figs. 8.1-8.23)

The site on the west side of Chapel Street was designated Area 8 in line with the site classification adopted in the earlier excavations, and that alongside No. 6 Crane Street, Area 9 (see Fig. 8.1). Wherever possible, the occupation periods have been equated to those recognised in the earlier series of excavations.

SUMMARY (see also *Chichester* 3, pp. 43–47).

Pre-Roman occupation

No additional evidence for a pre-Roman oppidum on or near the present site has been discovered in Areas 8 and 9. Where imported pre-invasion wares were found they were always associated with Claudian wares or were residual. The same can be said for the scraps of identifiable Iron Age ware present on the sites.

Roman — the military occupation

Further evidence for a military presence was found in Area 8 but not in Area 9. Three slight buildings in Area 8 preceded a fourth phase of building which could be equated with the 'barrack'-like buildings first seen in Area 2.

Industrial activity

Area 8 seems to have been peripheral to the pottery kilns found in Area 2 to the south. Some traces of wasters and puddling clay were found, together with two timber-lined pits which may have been settling tanks.

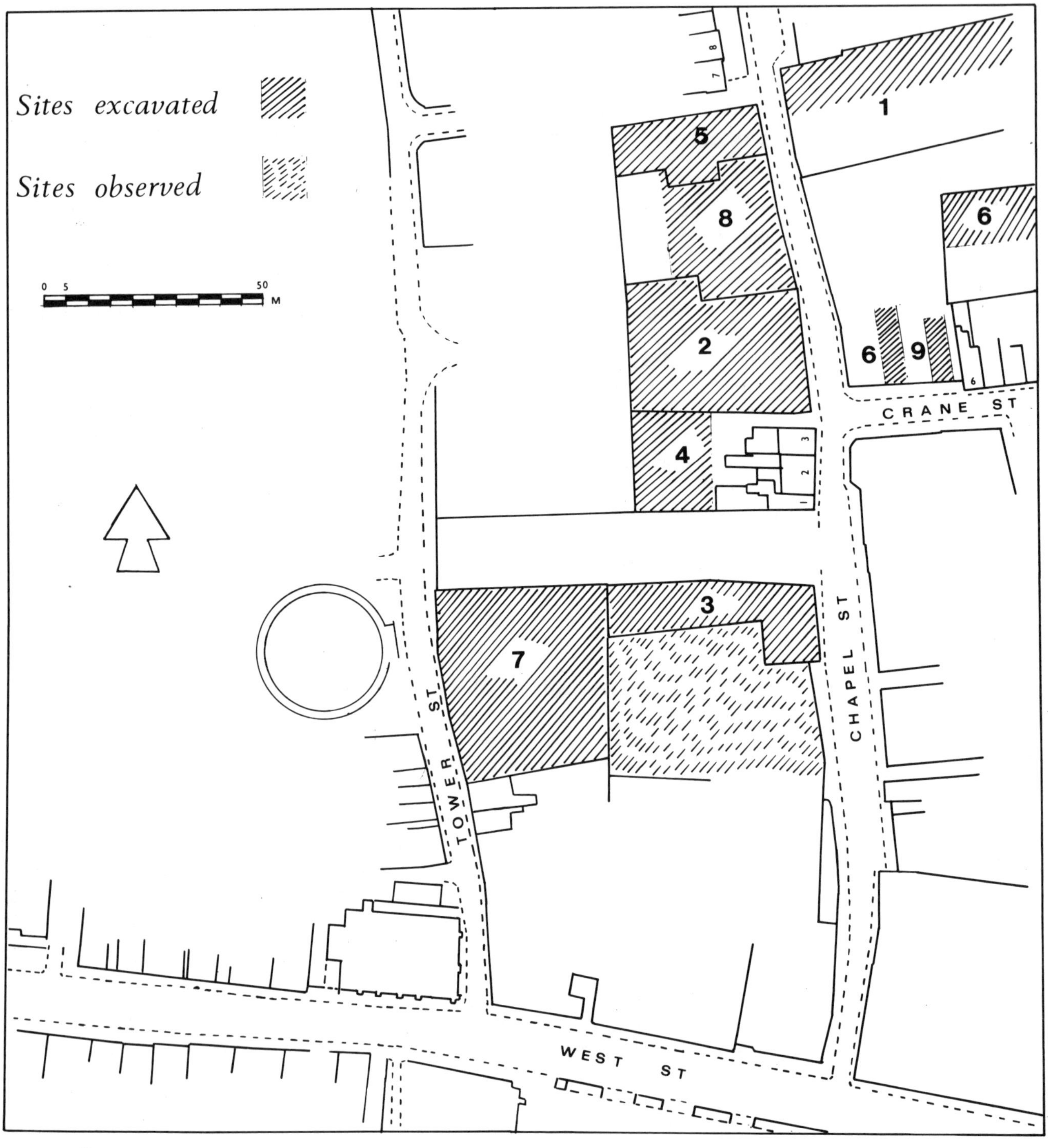

Fig. 8.1. N.W. Quadrant, Site location plan.

The development of the native town and the civitas capital

The early Flavian period saw the erection of a large timber house on the east side of the earlier (?) barrack block, and this probably had a narrow street running northwards alongside it. Later on, towards the end of the century, the street was widened, and early in the second century the Flavian building had been replaced by another timber building. The street widening probably coincides with the re-planning of the town after the death of Cogidubnus.

4th and 5th centuries

In Area 8, more of the Roman house (House 2) on the north side of the cross-roads was excavated, and a detailed study indicates that the dating for the first timber phase and the second masonry phase requires revision. The coin evidence now clearly shows that the first phase of the house was not constructed until about the middle of the 4th century and that the fourth phase, when the house was largely rebuilt in masonry on a much larger ground plan, must come a good deal later, possibly as late as *c.* A.D. 360–370.

Middle to late Saxon

Middle Saxon occupation on the ground was sparse, but the evidence for a large increase in population in the north-west quadrant during the 10th–11th centuries is implicit in the number and size of the cess pits, although no structures could be identified. This reinforces the impression gained from Areas 2 and 4.

At some time towards the mid-11th century a number of pottery clamps were producing domestic coarse wares, and the size of the operation suggests that this activity was on a commercial scale.

Medieval and post-medieval, 12th-18th centuries

After the Norman Conquest the land seems to have reverted to agricultural use with few traces of occupation other than slight timber buildings during the 16th and 17th centuries and the occasional sub-division of the land by fences. The late Saxon levels show signs of having been heavily ploughed, and in the 18th and 19th centuries, much of the area excavated had been cottage gardens.

Area 9, Crane Street

Earliest periods

From the pottery evidence it seems clear that occupation on the east side of the boundary line formed by the later north-south Roman street was slight before Period 3 (Flavian) and this confirms the earlier work in Areas 1 and 6. It appears from the absence of regularly aligned "barrack-type" buildings and the absence of early imported wares as if the eastern boundary for the military occupation was on the line of the later north–south street and that the main extent of the barracks is below Lancastrian Grange and County Hall. Throughout the rest of the Roman occupation the excavation site was peripheral to property fronting on to the west side of North Street and the latest evidence for occupation is a timber-lined well which was backfilled late in the 4th century.

Period 8, Saxon

As in Area 8, no structures survive, but the presence of mid-late Saxon wares in great quantity in the cess pits testifies to the same fairly dense occupation as the rest of the north-west quadrant.

Medieval

Medieval

During the 13th–14th centuries, the land was held by the Sancta Cruce family and there is documentary evidence for the existence of tenements (probably agricultural buildings). This is confirmed by the presence of a number of medieval pits of that date on the site.

NORTH WEST QUADRANT

ROMAN: PERIODS 1–3; 43AD – FLAVIAN

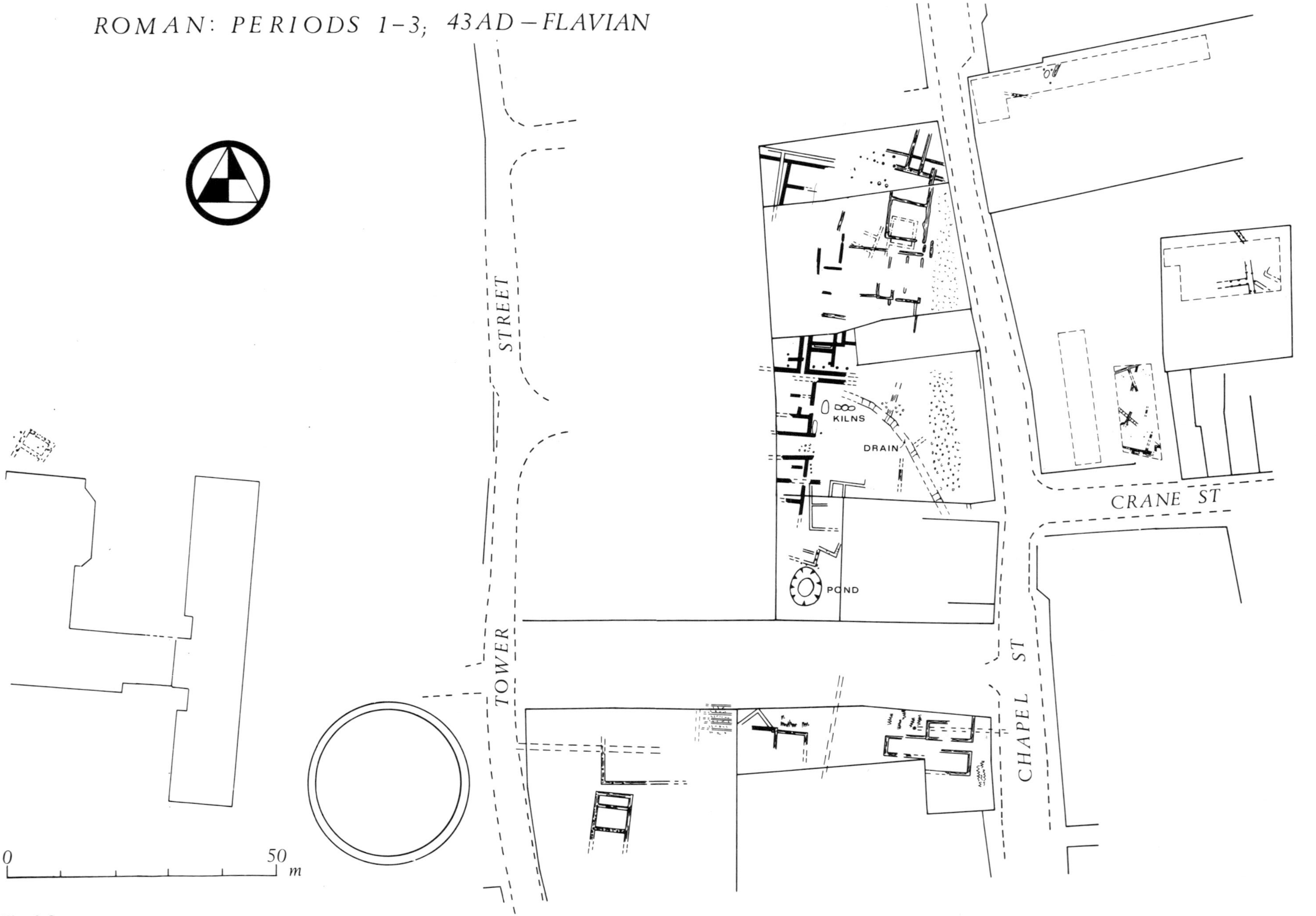

Fig. 8.2

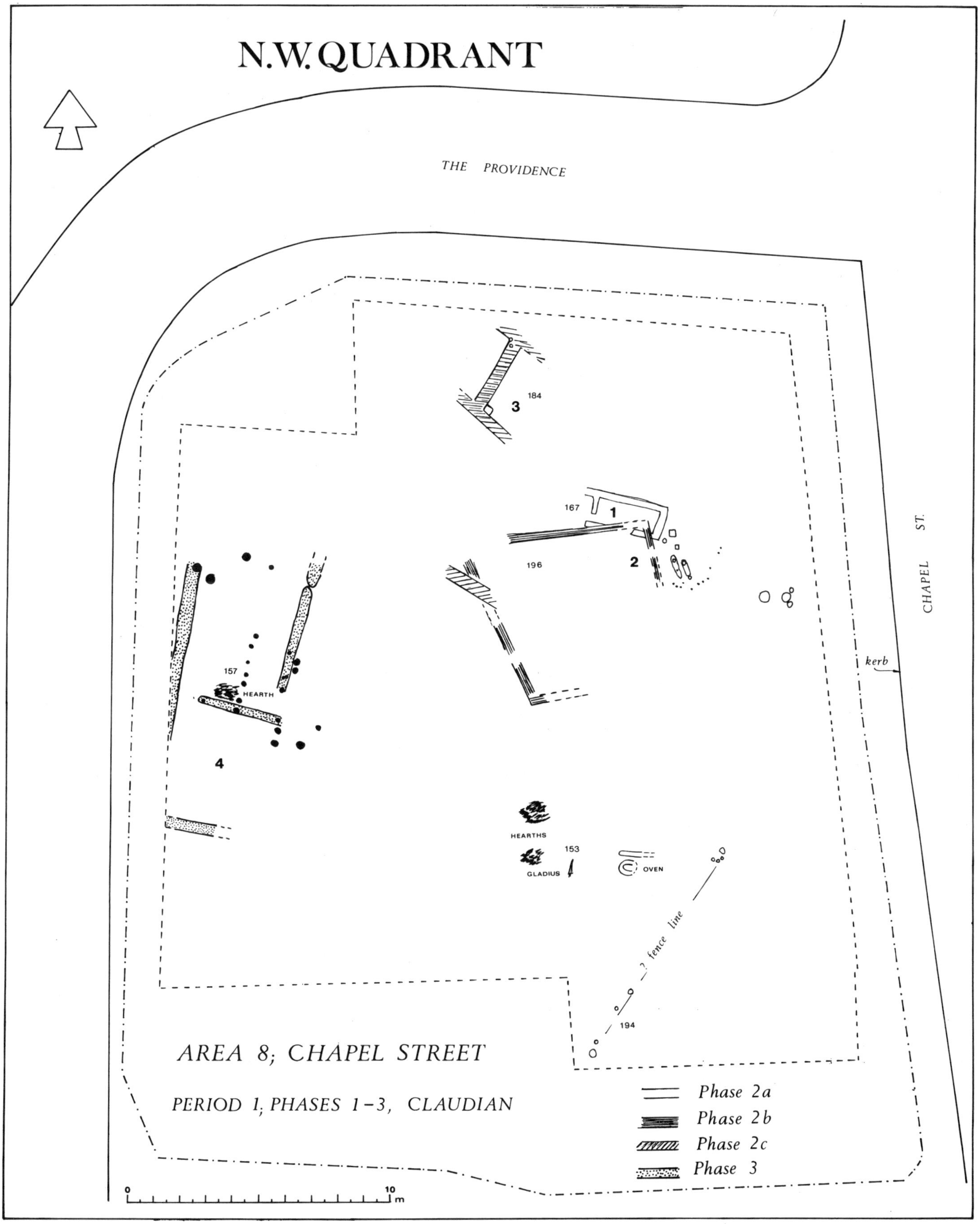
N.W. QUADRANT
THE PROVIDENCE
CHAPEL ST.
kerb
184
3
167
1
196
2
157
HEARTH
4
HEARTHS
153
GLADIUS
OVEN
? fence line
194
AREA 8; CHAPEL STREET
PERIOD 1, PHASES 1–3, CLAUDIAN
Phase 2a
Phase 2b
Phase 2c
Phase 3
0
10
m

Fig. 8.3

Post-medieval, 16th-19th centuries

Continuous occupation is recorded from early 17th century onwards and the area was devoted to malting and pottery manufacture up to the early 18th century. Wasters from a kiln making slipped wares similar to those produced in Staffordshire were found, dating to mid-late 17th century. Later still, a large timber building, possibly a barn was erected on the site.

Area 8; Trench X (Figs. 8.3-8.17)

Period 1, Claudian; Phase 1 (Layer X194/196, X97, X184, X168, X172) (Pl. 14)

The earliest layers on site comprised yellow or brown clay resting upon natural gravel. X194/196 had several burnt areas which might have been hearths, but finds were sparse and the only fragment of samian was a Dr. 18 from South Gaul dated "1st century". The lateral replacement for X194 at the north end of the trench was X184. This had a number of fragments of iron, some possibly of military origin, together with window and vessel glass and an early mortarium and one fragment of white imported ware. One sherd of early Iron Age ware was found in association with a few fragments of Roman grey ware in X168.

Phase 2 (Layers 144/172, 148, 153, 155, 157, 167, 185)

Three phases of timber buildings were identified as cut from the layers above the Phase 1 levels, but only a few fragments remained.

Phase 2a, Structure 1 (Slots X53 and 54)

This was a small longhouse 2.5 metres wide and of unknown length. It was cut from X167 but had been truncated by the later slots X34 and 46. The level from which it was cut contained Iron Age wares, Arretine and Claudian samian.

Phase 2b, Structure 2 (Slot X46)

This structure or structures comprised two lengths of narrow slot which together seem to make up the plan of a roughly rectangular building, the northern part of which cuts across the south wall of Structure 1.

Phase 2c, Structure 3 (Slot X43)

Two sections of slot dug for a cill beam were found cut into X184, together with another section further south on a similar alignment. This latter section could be seen to postdate the Phase 2b, Structure 2.

Phase 3, Structure 4

This is represented by the slots of a more substantial timber building along the west side of the excavation, which had been partially destroyed by the foundations of House 2.

In Area 2, the range of buildings of which this is the northern part was identified as Period 1, Phase 2 (*Chichester 3*, Fig. 7.6 and p. 54). The latest dated pottery from the slots was Claudian samian. Probably contemporary with the building was a small slot alongside an oven, both dug into Layer X153; a horizon of dark stained clay with much charcoal which lay above X196. X153 had a complete gladius lying upon the surface (Pl. 15 and Fig. 8.28). The latest wares from this level were fragments of Claudian samian, Gallo-Belgic and Arretine wares of Augustan/Tiberian date. To the east of the site was a line of small post and stakeholes aligned north-east, roughly on the same line as the later Roman street. It might possibly represent a fence line set up by the military planners and if it was, it gave an alignment around which all future planning pivoted.

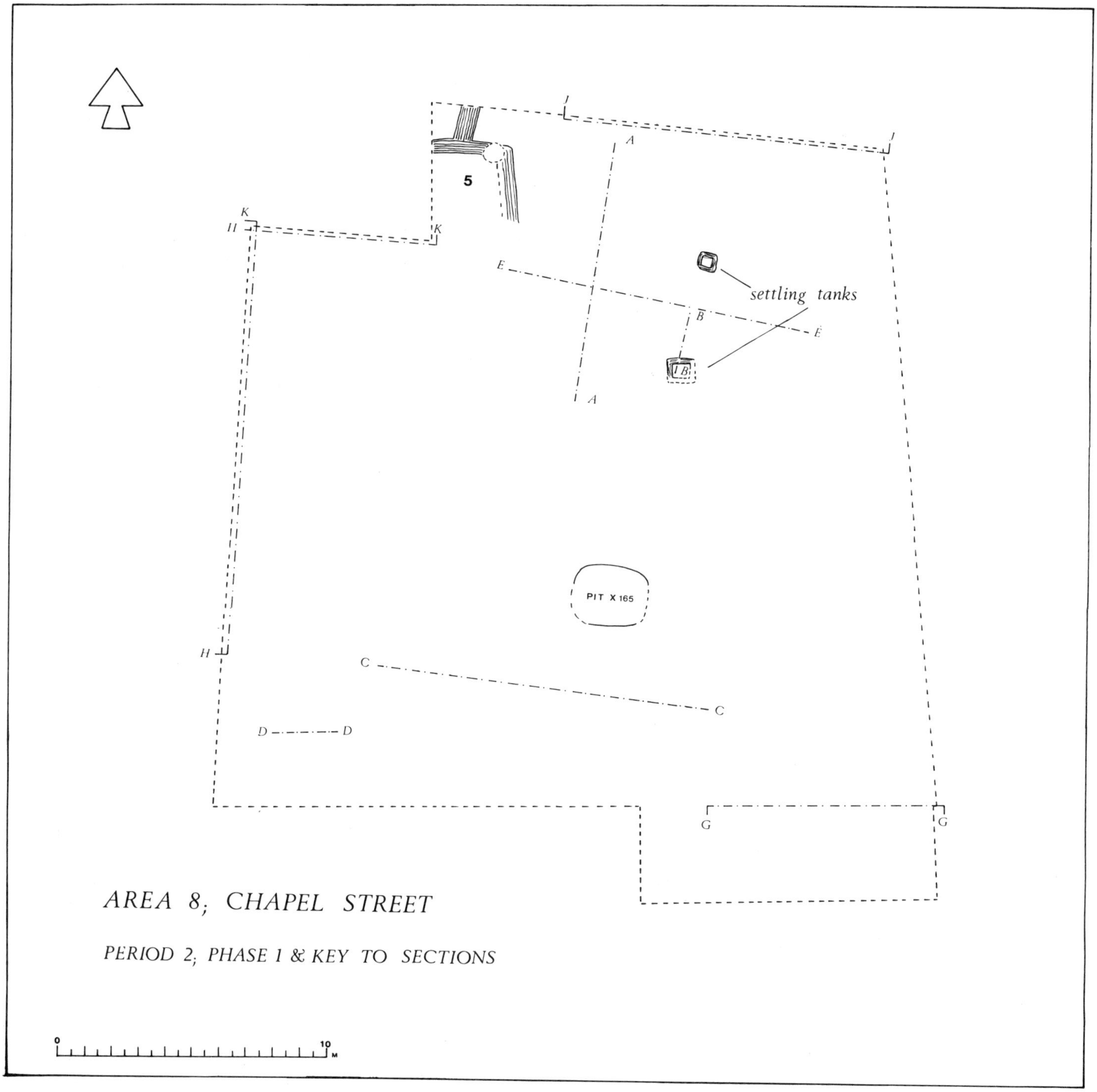

5
K
H
K
E
A
B
E
settling tanks
B
A
PIT X 165
H
C
C
D
D
G
G
AREA 8; CHAPEL STREET
PERIOD 2; PHASE 1 & KEY TO SECTIONS
0
10
M

Fig. 8.4

Period 2; Phase 1; c. Claudius-Nero (Fig. 8.4)

In Area 2 (*Chichester 3*, pp. 56–57), Phase 1 was identified as an industrial phase which consisted initially of pottery kilns manufacturing fine imitation Gallo-Belgic wares and coarser grey wares in the local Atrebatic tradition. No kilns were found in Area 8, but there is likely to be one in the small part remaining undug at the south-east end of the site, where wasters associated with waste Reading clay were found in a small pit (X171). Wares from the kilns found in 1971 were also found in the timber-lined drains (Slot X22 and X38). At the north end of the trench were two timber-lined pits or tanks (X42 and X55). These were filled with a fine clay silt in which were layers of fine white clay which had settled out by sedimentation (see Fig. 8.4). It is likely that these two features, both badly truncated by later building activity, may represent the remains of small settling tanks where the fine white clay was washed before being used as a slip.

Pit X165 also belongs to this phase. It cut away one of the Period 1 hearths and contained a large amount of early fine wares. None of the *sigillata* can be dated later than A.D. 43 (*Dannell*, this volume, p. 265), except for a stamp which has a date bracket of *c*. A.D. 35–60 (*Hartley and Dickinson*, this volume, p. 271, No. 21), and a T.N. stamp (*Rigby*, this volume, p. 282, GB29), with a date range of *c*. A.D. 50–85). Within the same pit was a small amount of Atrebatic "overlap" wares and butt-breaker fragments from the Chapel Street Kilns, which together places the pit within Period 2.

Structure 5

Slot X37 at the north end of the site is part of a building which is probably contemporary with Phase 1, since it post-dates Period 1 and is earlier than the Period 3 Flavian building (see below and Fig. 8.5). It was seen when X144 was removed and only a small part could be traced. Neither the slot or X144 above it contained any pottery later than pre-Flavian samian.The finds from X144 included one fragment from a crucible similar to those found in Areas 2 and 4 (*op. cit.* 57, 58), together with a bronze hinge from the *lorica*.

Period 3 Early Flavian — late 1st-early 2nd century Phase 1 (Fig. 8.5)

Phase 1

This is represented by X155, a shallow pit containing a number of fragments of legionary equipment and many residual fine wares of pre-Flavian date. However, the latest samian ware was a Curle 11 of Flavian date and as this pit is earlier than the timber building then both are later than the date it was discarded.

Also possibly belonging to this phase is the slot (X38/49) which may be a timber-lined drain and which runs northwards from below the Phase 2 building.

Phase 2 (Fig. 8.2 and Pl. 16)

A large timber building (Building 6), was erected on the site, only part of it being within the excavation. Reference to the general plan (Fig. 8.2) which shows the excavation in relation to previous work, indicates that this building is part of the one found below Gospel Hall (Area 5) in 1973 (*Chichester Excavations 3*, 114 and Fig. 7.37). It was there designated Building 0.1 and assigned to Period 2. The dating evidence was sparse and the foundations were truncated by later

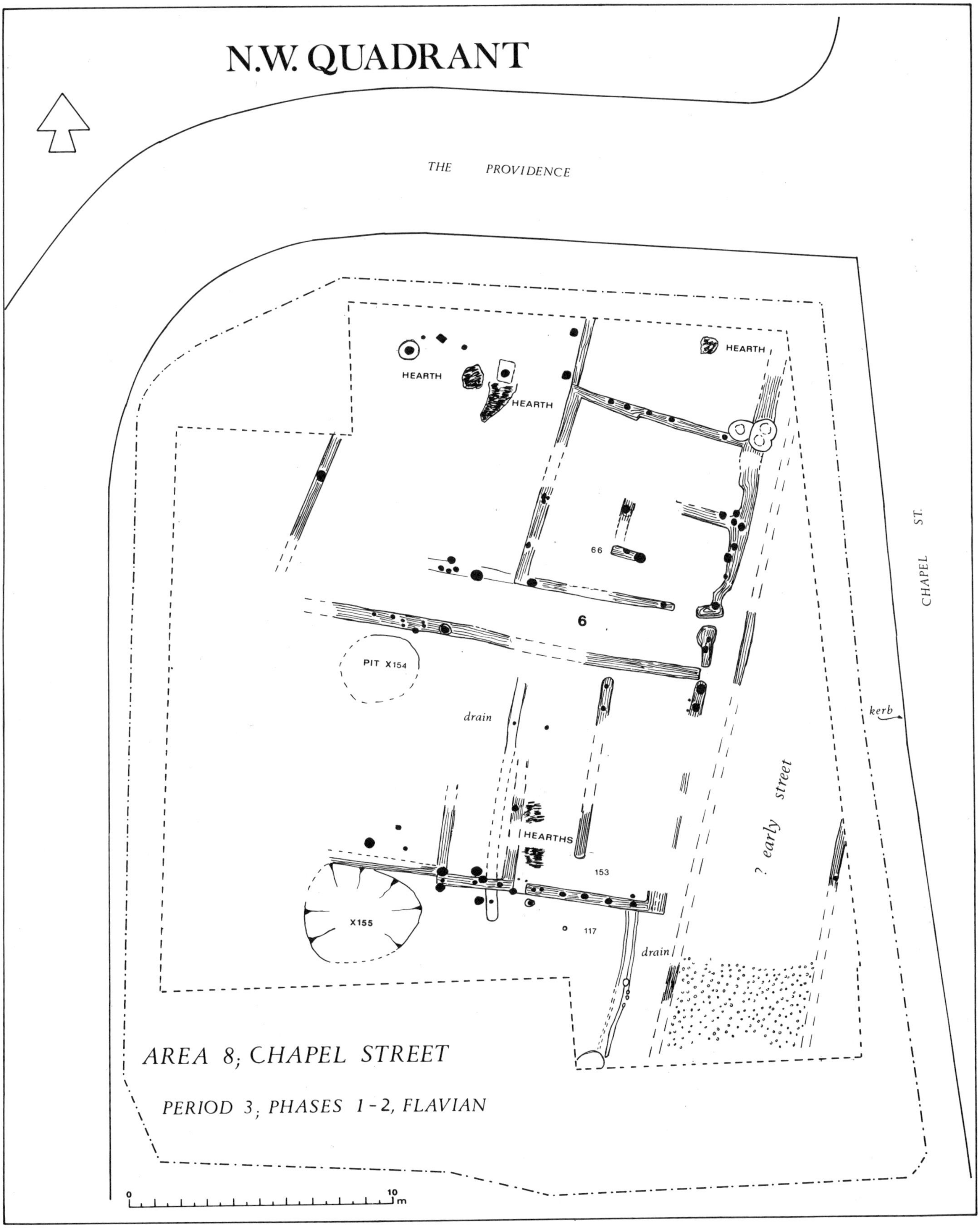
N.W. QUADRANT
THE PROVIDENCE
HEARTH
HEARTH
HEARTH
66
6
PIT X154
drain
HEARTHS
153
X155
117
drain
? early street
kerb
CHAPEL ST.
AREA 8; CHAPEL STREET
PERIOD 3; PHASES 1-2, FLAVIAN
0
10
m

Fig. 8.5

cultivation. The date can now be revised in the light of additional evidence. In Area 8, the post trenches were dug through X66 and X117. These were layers of brown clay which contained nothing later than Flavian samian. The pattern was repeated within the fill of the slots, two sherds of Flavian samian being found in Slot X21 which formed the south wall of the building.

The eastern side of the structure was partly eroded by the cellars below Bell House and Nos. 4, 5 and 6 Chapel Street, but sufficient remained to see that there was a gap of 5 metres between the two short lengths of slot seen on the east side of the plan. The building itself is slightly out of line with the earlier, Phase 2, Structure 4 which was erected on the west side of the site and which is probably part of the military barrack building, and it seems as if we are looking at a replacement of the earlier military buildings by later ones built to the east of them.

The gap on the east side might be accounted for by a street, initially no more than 5 metres wide. All the later street levels had been removed by the cellars except at the south end, where a study of the section (Fig. 8.16, section G—G) shows that an earlier layer of street metalling (X3g) exists, cut on the west side by a shallow slot which could well be the remains of a small box drain. The dating evidence for the metalling is consistently Flavian and the slot on the west side is exactly in alignment with the short stretch of slot (X25), to the east of the building.

Period 4, 2nd century

The Period 3 building (Building 6), was demolished, probably by the end of the 1st century or soon after, and by the early 2nd century another structure, (Building 7), had replaced it. By then, it is likely that the narrow Flavian street had been widened, partly sealing one of the late 1st-century pits. Only a small part of Building 7 was recognisable and there was no close dating evidence from the postholes, but the layer into which they were cut (X147), had nothing later than Antonine samian in it. A number of pits can be assigned to this period (see Fig. 8.6).

Period 5 Early-mid 4th century; House 2 Phases 1 and 2 (Fig. 8.7)

House 2 was first recognised in Areas 2 and 5 in the earlier excavations and two phases of building construction were seen. In Area 8, Phase 1 was seen as a range of rooms with sleeper walls of gravel, upon which timber cills had been placed. In Area 5 (*op. cit.* p. 116, and Pl. 10), clay partition walls were found together with two fragments of tessellated floors. At that time a date of *c.* late 3rd to early 4th century was suggested, but this now requires revision in the light of new evidence. One of the gravel wall footings (X80) had a coin of Constantine (A.D. 330–335) in it, which means that this part of House 2 at least must date from the second quarter of the 4th century at the earliest. The foundations were cut into X79, a layer of dark organic clay which may well have been cultivated during an earlier phase. All the pottery was small and abraded and it contained an infant burial. Layer X57 above it was a deposit of brown clay with mortar flecks and it must have been the contemporary ground level for the first phase of House 2. The latest dated pottery from it was a red-ware base which Dr. Young dates to post-270 A.D., but five coins were found in this layer, four of which were of Constantine, the latest being A.D. 341–6. This evidence fits well with the coin in the wall foundation.

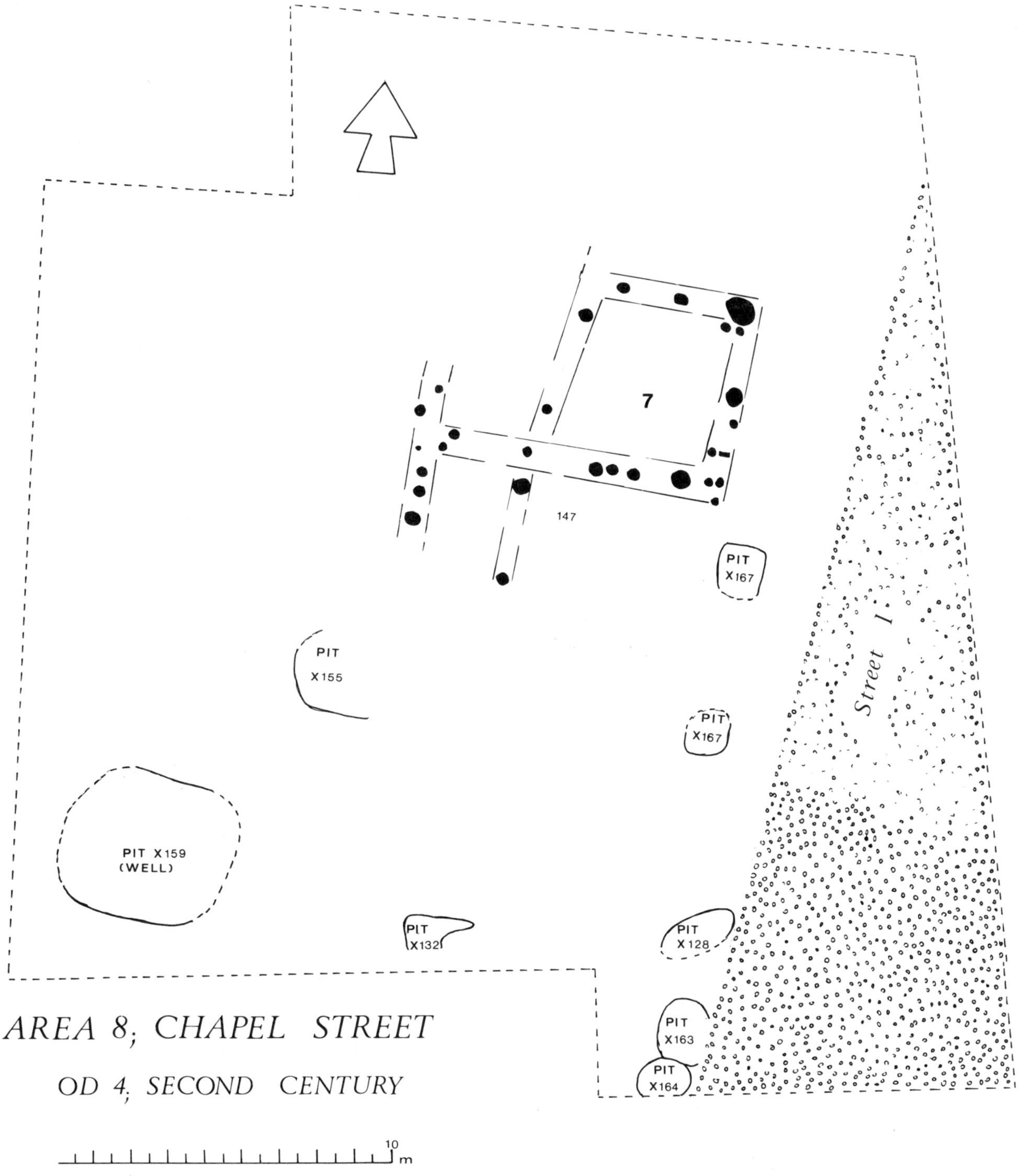

AREA 8; CHAPEL STREET

OD 4, SECOND CENTURY

Fig. 8.6

Three groups of domestic ovens belong to Period 5. They are not all contemporary, nor can it be certain whether or not they were within the building as only fragments of three rooms remain of what might have been an east-west range. To the north, a fragment of east-west wall footing with a spread of pink mortar (X88), making an east-west line to the north of it, and a small fragment of tesselated floor abutting it on the south side are all that remains of what might have been another range of rooms.

The well belongs to Phase 1. It was constructed of limestone and sandstone blocks set in clay and it survived on into the late Saxon period. The well pit produced no later wares than late 2nd century, but it could be clearly seen to post-date the earlier structures on the site.

Phase 2

This is represented by three flint and mortar bases which were laid out on a north-south axis, one being built half on and half off the edge of the well pit; one being placed across one of the east-west gravel foundations and the third being built over two of the Phase 1 domestic ovens. The three bases may be compared with the one found in Area 5 to the north in 1973 *op. cit.* Fig. 7.40 and p. 121), although that one was probably later (Period 6, Phase 2). The construction of the three bases, possibly as foundations for statues or other garden "furniture", implies a re-planning of the house, with part of it being demolished and with the area to the east being laid out as a formal courtyard facing on the street. This courtyard, first seen in Trench J in Area 2 (*op. cit.* Fig. 7.20), was constructed of dirty gravel (X65) which had been used elsewhere before being laid here. It contained nothing later than 2nd-century pottery. Through it was cut two pits; one of these, Slot X10 was a timber lined latrine which was probably cut by a deeper pit (Pit X97). The correct relationship could not be established without doubt owing to a late Saxon pit which cut both of the Roman pits away at their juntion, but Pit X97 might have been the sump for the latrine.

The latest pottery from both pits was colour coated ware which Dr. Young dates to *post* A.D. 270.

Period 6
Late 4th century onwards: House 2
Phases 3 and 4
(Fig. 8.8)

On the evidence of the coins from layer X57 and the Period 5, Phase 1 wall foundation, the earlier house could not have been built before A.D. 341-6. Two further building phases are assigned to Period 6, as it is during this time that the house was expanded and re-built on much more substantial lines.

Phase 3

This is seen only as two lengths of east-west walling running off the north-south wall along the west side of the excavation. Both walls had been robbed of flints, but the chalk foundations remained and these had been cut by the Phase 4 north-south wall. It seems therefore that in Phase 3, the range of rooms represented by rooms 5, 6 and 7 did not extend quite so far to the north.

Phase 4

At some time later the whole house appears to have been re-structured with more substantial foundations and on a larger plan. This was seen in Area 2 where the building was extended southwards and eastwards to the cross-roads (*Chichester 3*, Fig 7.20) and again in Area 5, where a range of rooms was extended to Street 1 (Fig. 8.9, this volume). The full extent of the house may

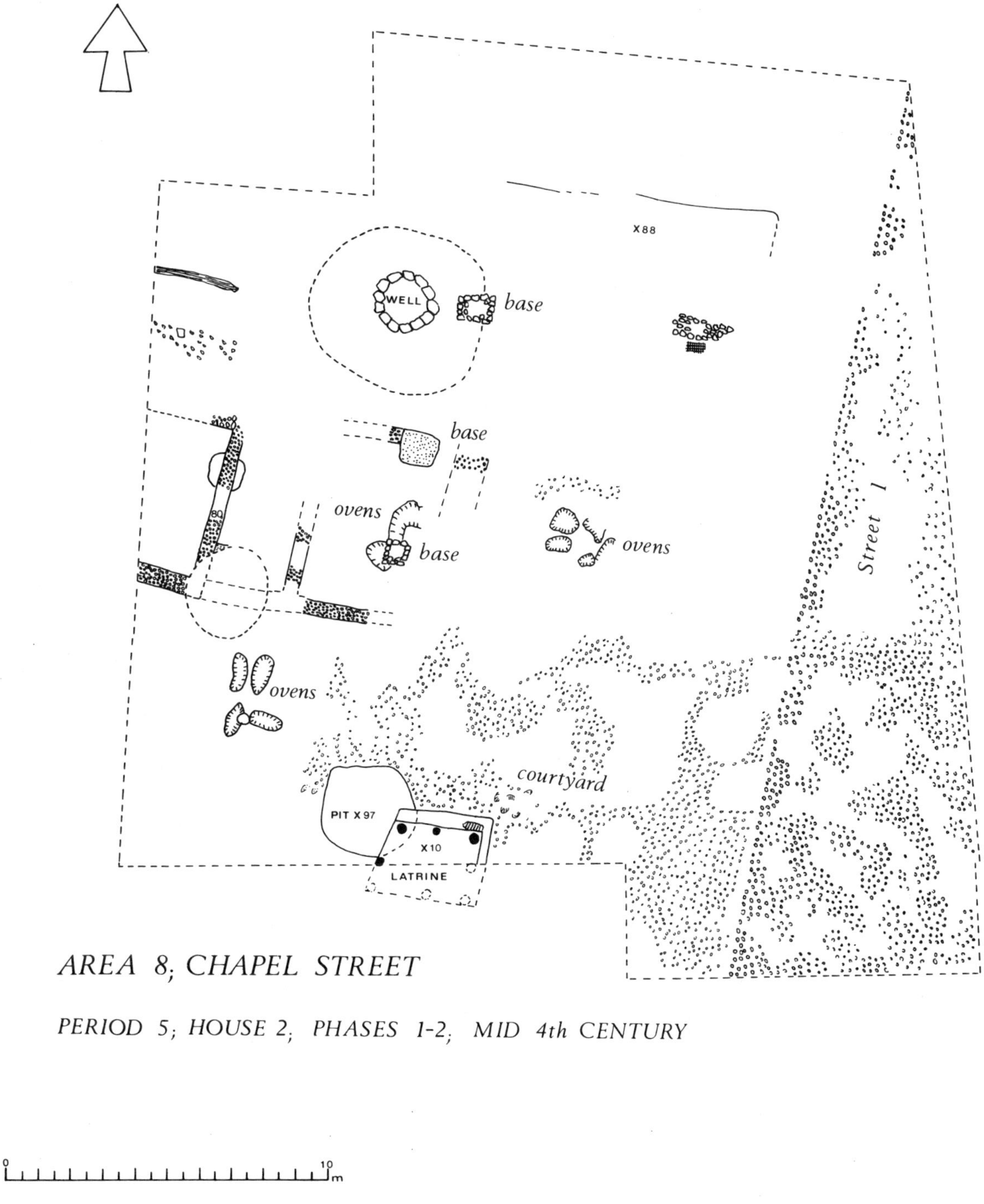

AREA 8; CHAPEL STREET

PERIOD 5; HOUSE 2; PHASES 1-2; MID 4th CENTURY

Fig. 8.7

never be known. Certainly, it extends westwards below Lancastrian Grange and traces of it have been seen in service trenches in Chapel Street as far north as the Providence Chapel, giving it a length, north to south, of approximately 105 metres (*op. cit.* 121).

Rooms 5, 6 and 7

In Phase 4, the westerly range of rooms seen on the plan (Fig. 8.8) was extended northwards slightly and the sizes of the rooms were altered. Room 8, the corridor along the east side of this range had no floor levels surviving, but it is likely that it was present in Phase 3.

Room 1

Later on, Room 1, an east-west corridor, was built across the north end of Room 8 and as part of the coving around the edges of the floor survived it suggests that access from Room 8 to Room 1 was by a door, although no trace of a sill remained. Room 1 was built partly over the earlier well pit and the floor had slumped badly into it. It was constructed of red tile tesserae and there was part of a geometric design in greensand tesserae surviving at the west end (Fig. 8.13). At the east end it was completely destroyed by pits and cellars, but it seems certain that it extended to meet the east wall of the house which is shown projected southwards (Fig. 8.8). Thus Rooms 1 and 8 would form the north and west sides of a courtyard or service area opening on to the street, with the southern boundary being formed by the range of rooms in Area 2 (see Fig. 8.9 for the final plan).

Immediately to the north of Room 1 was a flint wall with post sockets in it, with a small slot alongside which might have been a timber box drain. A passageway ran east-west between Room 1 and the range of rooms to the north. This was 3.5 metres wide and was probably intended as a service area giving access to the well. It may have been roofed over.

Rooms 2, 3 and 4

The northern range of rooms belong to the part of the house excavated in Area 5, and Room 2 = Room 10 in the 1973 excavations. There, two phases of alteration were detected. In the latest phase, Room 2/10 had under-floor heating and a very fine polychrome mosaic was laid above. This was later robbed and many fragments were found in 1973 and again in 1977 in the room and in pits dug through it. Several fragments were found in the bottom of the hypocaust flue which ran alongside Wall 1 (*Chichester 3*, Fig. 7.10). Part of a destroyed flue, aligned east-west, was found in Room 2. This is roughly at right-angles to the other one and may well be another fragment of what was a cross-flue hypocaust, possibly fired with charcoal, since there is no trace of any stoking chamber. In Room 2 there were traces of the mortar base for a floor, and Rooms 3 and 4 had remains of tessellated floors.

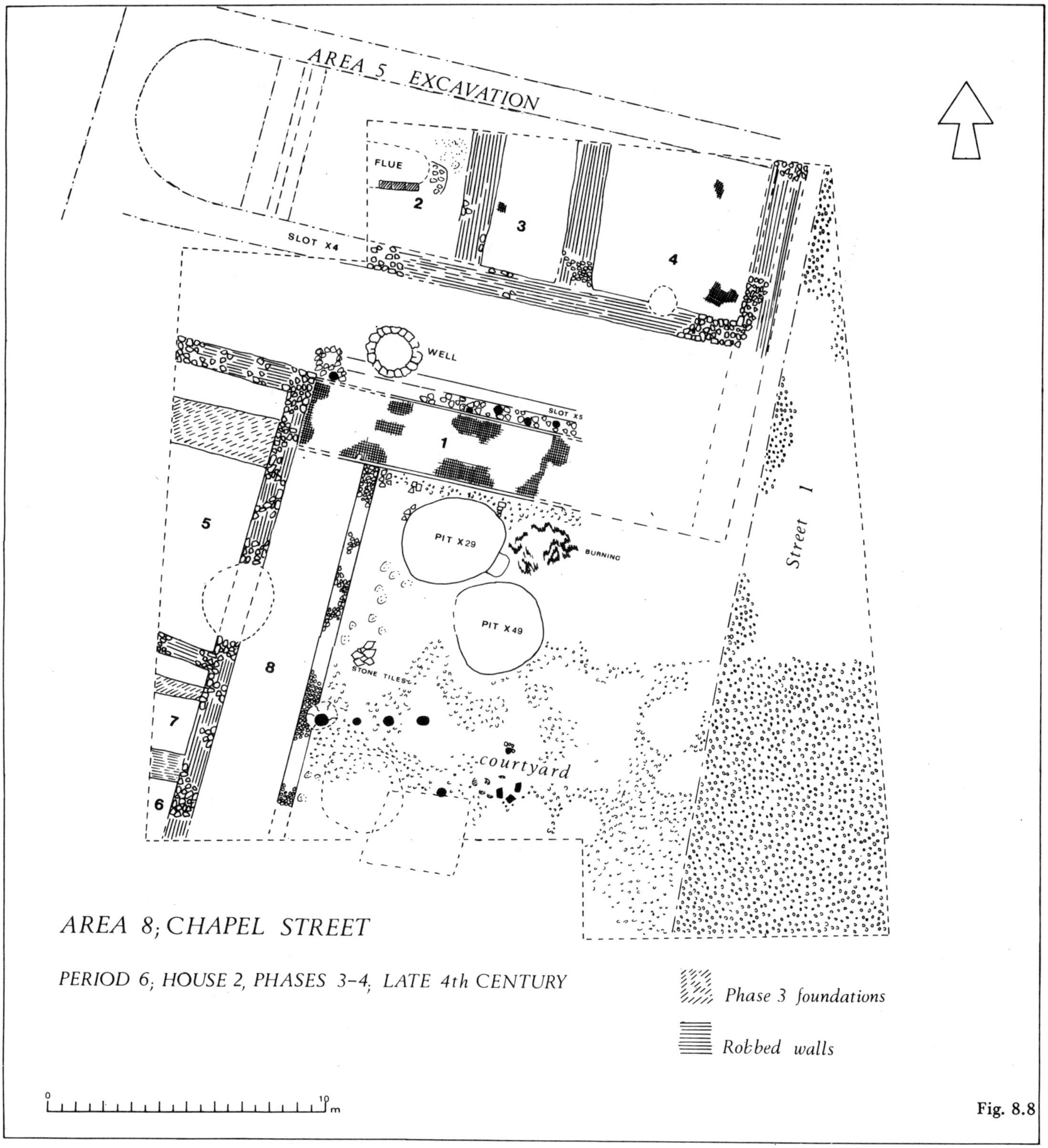

AREA 8; CHAPEL STREET

PERIOD 6, HOUSE 2, PHASES 3–4, LATE 4th CENTURY

Fig. 8.8

The Courtyard

By the time that House 2 had been rebuilt for the last time, the latrine and sump at the south end had probably ceased to function and had been backfilled. Two other pits (X29 and X49), were dug inside the courtyard, and these in turn served to take the nightsoil from the house. This was probably removed at intervals and spread on the gardens and fields belonging to the owners, on a fairly regular basis, and the pits were situated in a service area adjacent to the street to facilitate the process. The final filling of the pits can therefore be seen as representing the time when for one reason or another, the nightsoil was not being collected any more. The whole of the service area at this time must have been quite malodorous, especially in summer. Much of the domestic food debris, including thousands of oyster shells, had accumulated on top of the gravel surface of the courtyard and combined with the smell from the cesspits would have created a stink quite unacceptable to 20th-century nostrils, although it might have passed unnoticed in medieval and Saxon times.

In Pit X29, the latest dated pottery is colour-coated ware which is post 345 A.D., and the latest coin is of Valens (367–375 A.D.), whilst Pit X49 also had a coin of Valens and coarse ware which dates to mid-late 4th century. The upper layer of dirty gravel (X19), which represents the final re-metalling, was much contaminated by later occupation, but the latest Roman artifact was a late 4th-century coin.

Discussion

The revision of the dating of House 2, Phases 1 and 2, as the result of the latest coin evidence means that the date for the expansion of the house in Phase 4 must be pushed further towards the end of the 4th century. If, say, 10 years is allowed between the construction of Phase 1 and the final rebuilding, then a date between *c.* 353–356 A.D. could be suggested for Phase 4. This may well prove to be a conservative estimate.

House 2 in its final form appears to be an ambitious and well-executed project, carried out by someone who could command considerable resources. If the estimated length (105 metres) is equalled by the same dimensions east-west, then a town property of the order of 10,000 square metres is possible.

NORTH WEST QUADRANT

ROMAN; c.4TH CENTURY A.D.

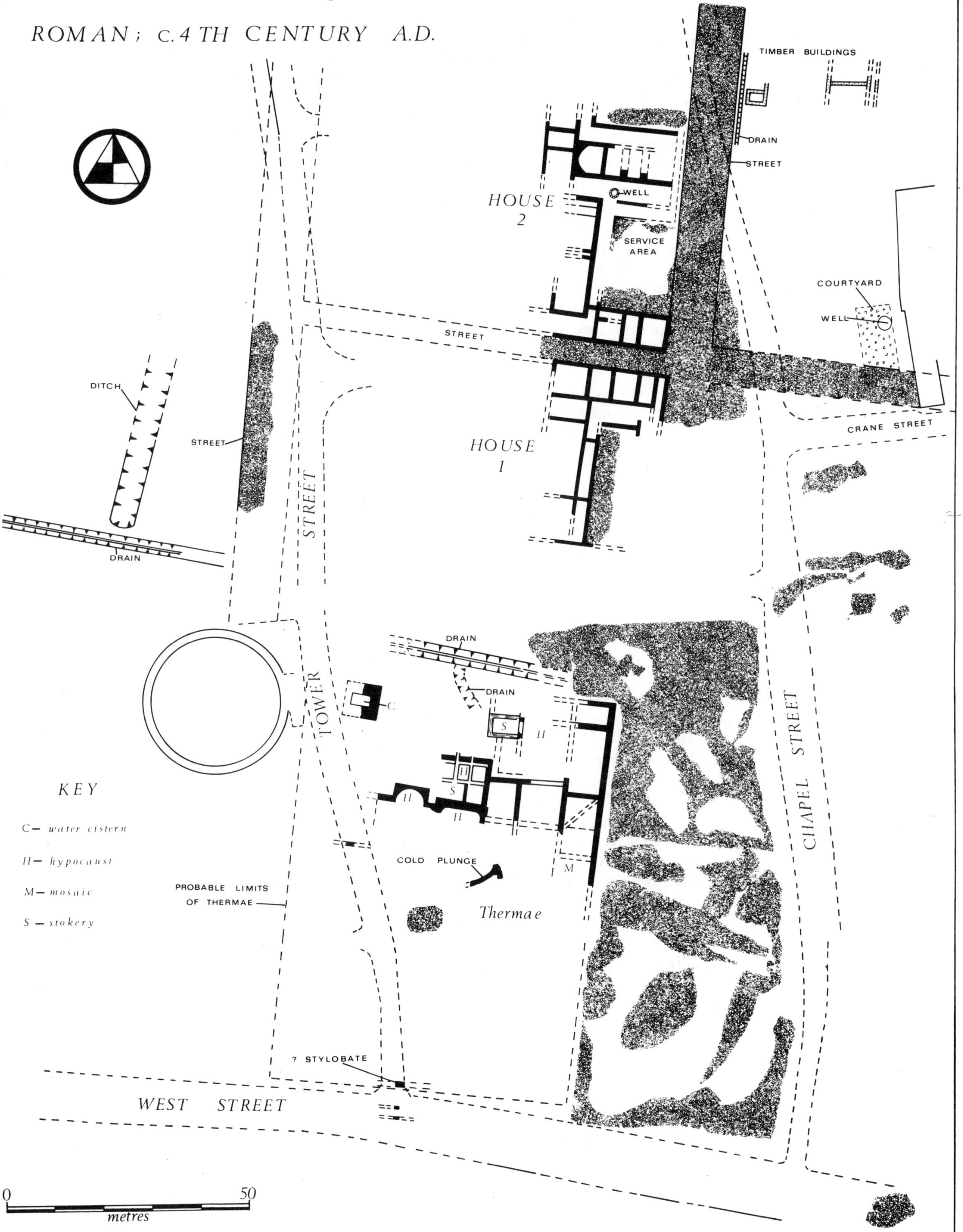

Fig. 8.9

Period 7
c. 5th century onwards

In Volume 3, Period 7 was defined as the period when the town was in decay and properly organised town life was breaking down. It was recognised in the sub-division of rooms in House 1 and in rough hearths being built upon floors in House 2, with hurdles being driven through floors; the accumulation of silt upon the streets and the silting-up of the town sewers. The approximate date for the commencement of what must have been a very gradual process was then suggested as *c.* late 4th–early 5th century (*op. cit.*, pp. 81–83).

No evidence was found in Trench X for any late or sub-Roman activity which could be equated with that seen in Areas 2 and 4, but this is not surprising in view of the tremendous amount of later disturbance, especially the robbing of the wall footings. In view of the later date suggested for House 2, Phase 4 it is apparent that town life was still expanding nearer to the end of the 4th century than we have previously thought. The latest bronze Roman coins hitherto found in Chichester have been of Valens or Gratian, but the recent excavations have produced a coin of Valentinian II (388–393 A.D.), which pushes the date when the last bronze issues were reaching Chichester almost to the end of the 4th century.

Period 8
Saxon; 9th-11th centuries (Fig. 8.10)

In Area 2, Saxon occupation was noted only in the form of cesspits and slight timber buildings, mainly cut into the Roman street levels at the cross-roads south of Area 8. The pattern was repeated in Trench X and only three phases could be detected in terms of features.

Phase 1;
c. 9th-early 10th centuries

Two pits (X52 and 137) contained closed groups of earlier Saxon pottery with parts of two loom weights. The wares probably date to the late 9th century or perhaps slightly later (see below p. 184 and Fig. 8.38). Earlier hand-made wares were also found in later Saxon and medieval pits, similar to those classified as Group 1 (A), (*Chichester 3*; Fig. 11.1). No buildings could be identified, but part of a slight flint wall was found which predates a later Saxon pit (X51), and might relate to a structure. The late Roman destruction level (X4) which was an accumulation of black soil and mortar from destroyed Roman buildings produced a coin of Charles the Bald, A.D. 840-877.

Phase 2; 10th-11th centuries

During this phase the use of the site intensified and a large number of cess pits were dug through the Roman levels. Two wells were in use during this phase. One was the old Roman well which had been re-built in the top courses. Late Saxon pottery was found behind and between the top stones and several complete and near complete cooking pots were found in the water at the bottom. A second well (Pit X32), had been timber-lined and this is seen to pre-date one of the pottery clamps. The wares from the pits do not permit of close dating, but the latest fabrics fit into Group 2 (*c.* mid/late 10th–early 11th century). It is likely that some robbing of the foundations took place during Phase 2. The Phase 3 clamps were built across the partially robbed wall foundations, and the east-west wall of the northern range of rooms belonging to House 2 (Slot X4), which had been completely robbed, had only unglazed late Saxon wares in the backfill. It is tempting to see in this activity the need for masonry to repair the old Roman defences and perhaps to build a Minster.

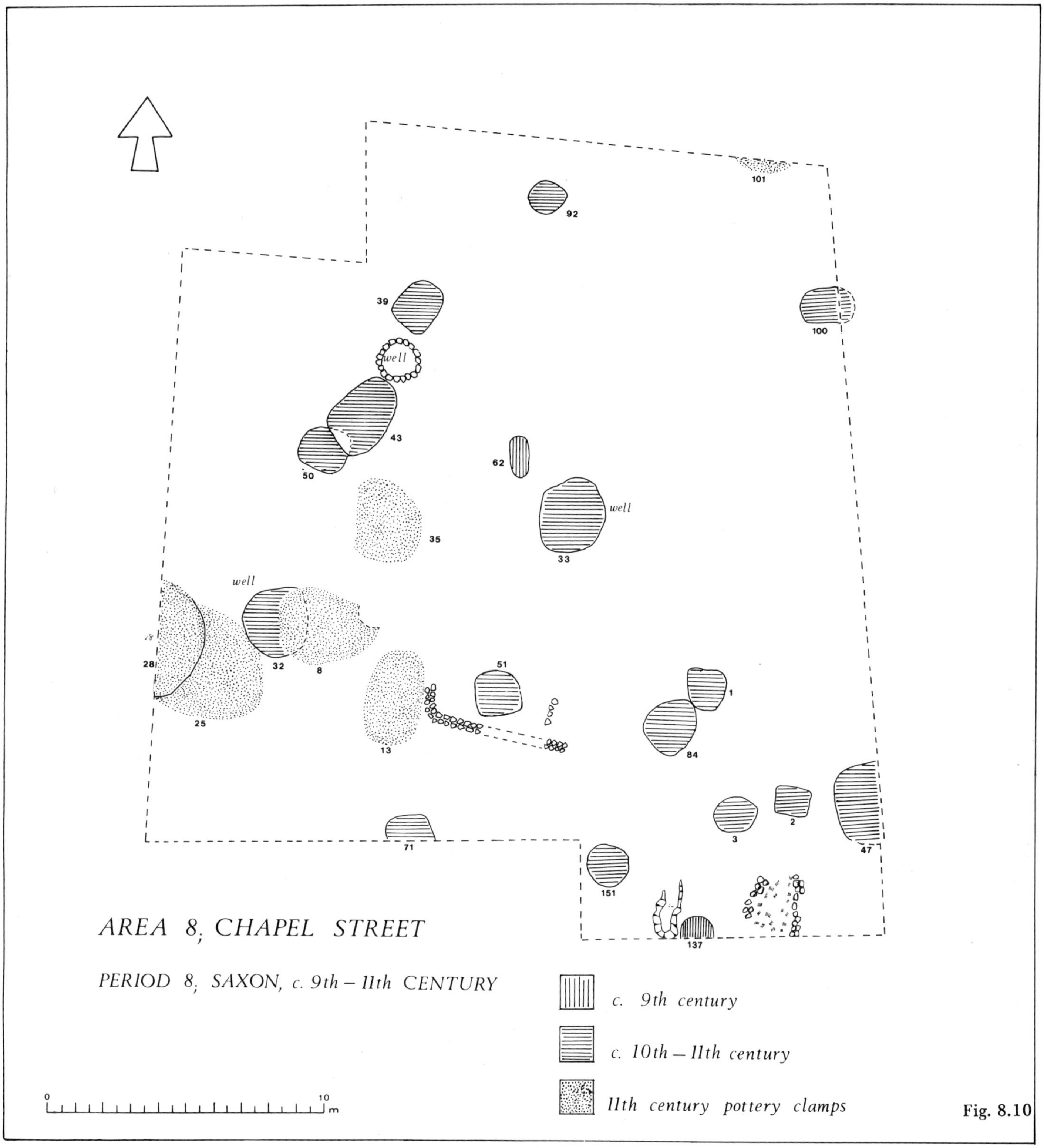
101
92
39
100
well
43
62
50
well
35
33
well
28
32
8
51
1
25
13
84
2
3
71
47
151
137
AREA 8, CHAPEL STREET
PERIOD 8, SAXON, c. 9th – 11th CENTURY
c. 9th century
c. 10th – 11th century
11th century pottery clamps
0
10
m

Fig. 8.10

The size of the pits, as well as the number, considerably increased during Phase 2. It is noticeable that the pits which have so far produced closed groups of hand-made wares *c.* 7th–9th century are small and few and far between, whereas the pits producing the wares dating from *c.* 10th to late 11th century are often of great size, very numerous and contain large amounts of coarse wares, many nearly complete. This implies a considerable increase in the population using the land from the 10th century onwards, which was probably the result of the increased urban settlement encouraged by Alfred the Great when the town was re-fortified as a *fluchtburh* in the late 9th–early 10th century.

Phase 3; c. mid 11th century (Figs. 8.10 and 8.12, Pl. 17)

At this time the area was used for pottery production. Six clamps were identified, five of which were dug into the partially robbed foundations and floors of the Roman house. The fill of the clamps consisted of dark soil with a lot of charcoal and the pottery found in them was mostly oxidised Group 3 material (*op. cit.* Fig. 11 and this volume, p. 190). The top of the clamps had been ploughed away and little survived of the walls, except in one instance (Fig. 8.12). The number of clamps and the fact that they were concentrated in one area may indicate that this was a commercial enterprise producing wares for a local market rather than domestic production by individual family units. Other evidence for Saxon clamps was found in 1974 (*op. cit.* p. 158) in Area 7, although there they had been destroyed by the subsequent robbing of the Roman public baths and the remains backfilled into the hole.

Archeomagnetic samples were taken from the floors of the clamps by Dr. A. J. Clark of the Ancient Monuments Laboratory of the Department of the Environment and these indicate a mean date of *c.* A.D. 1030+40. In this writer's view a slightly pre-Conquest date is likely, as the scarcity of 12th-century activity on the site (see below) may be an indication that the land changed hands after A.D. 1066.

Other activity

Weaving was also carried out on or near to the site, as the presence of 39 loom weights in Pit X84 testifies. These are briefly reported on below (p. 192), and in more detail in the Level III archive (Carol Edwards).

Period 9 Medieval; c. 12th-15th centuries

In Area 2 (*op. cit.* p. 88), it was noted that activity during the greater part of period 9 was minimal. Slightly more activity can be recorded for Area 8, but here again, it seems that the land was not occupied by domestic tenements and was farmland or small-holdings.

Phase 1; c. 12th century (Fig. 8.11)

Only five pits could be tentatively assigned to Phase 1 on the basis of the pottery. The assessment was difficult to make and was based partly on the absence of recognisable 13th-century wares and the presence of "early" coarsewares with the residual Saxo-Norman pottery.

Phase 2; c. 13th-14th centuries

Fourteen pits had wares dating to the 13th–14th century as the latest dateable artifacts, but glazed wares were few in number. During this period, two lines of fence-posts were erected across the southern part of the site. The most easterly posts were driven in along the edge of the old Roman street and it almost seems

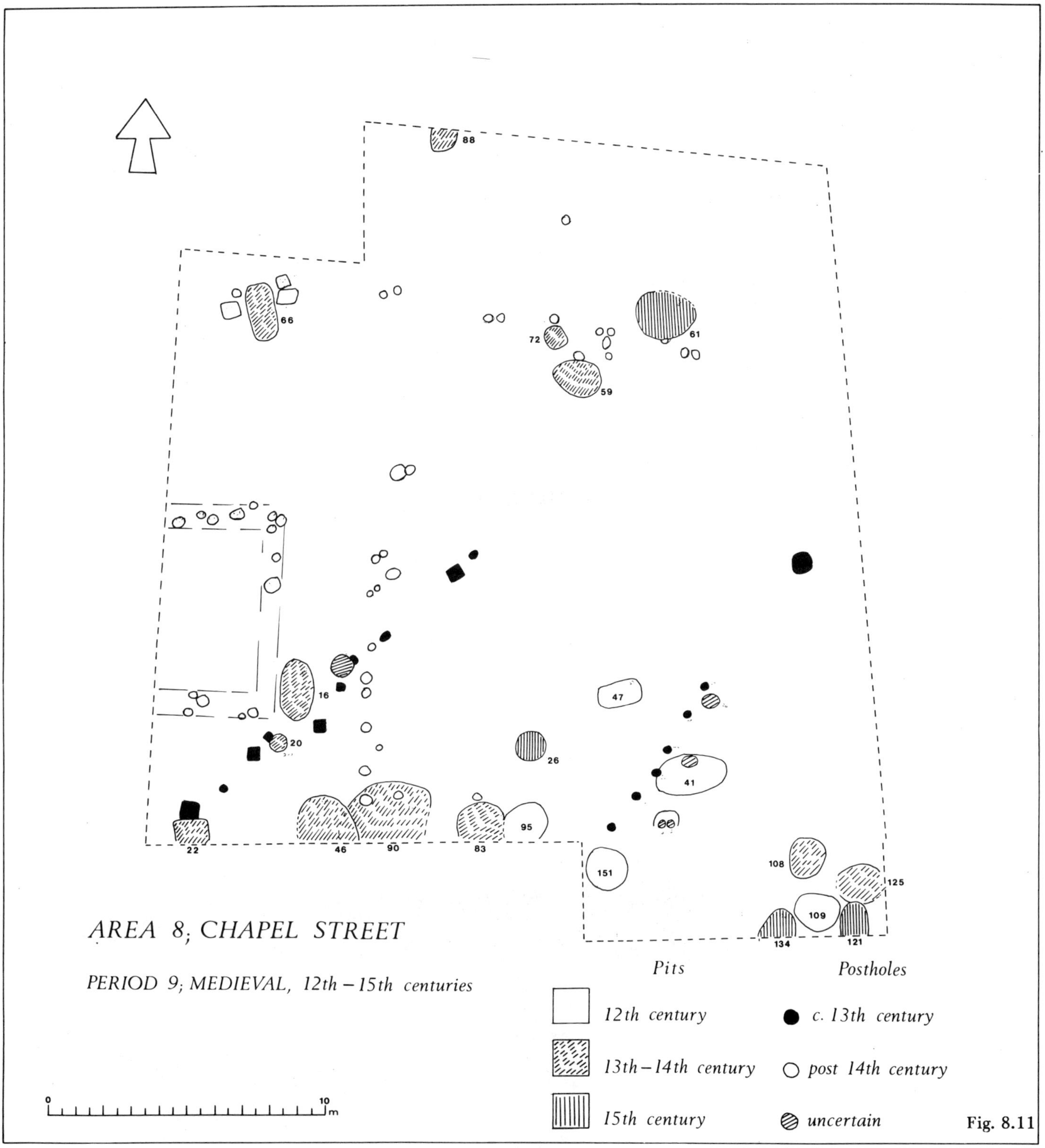
AREA 8; CHAPEL STREET
PERIOD 9; MEDIEVAL, 12th – 15th centuries
Pits
Postholes
12th century
13th–14th century
15th century
c. 13th century
post 14th century
uncertain
0
10
m
88
66
72
61
59
16
20
47
26
41
22
46
90
83
95
151
108
125
109
134
121

Fig. 8.11

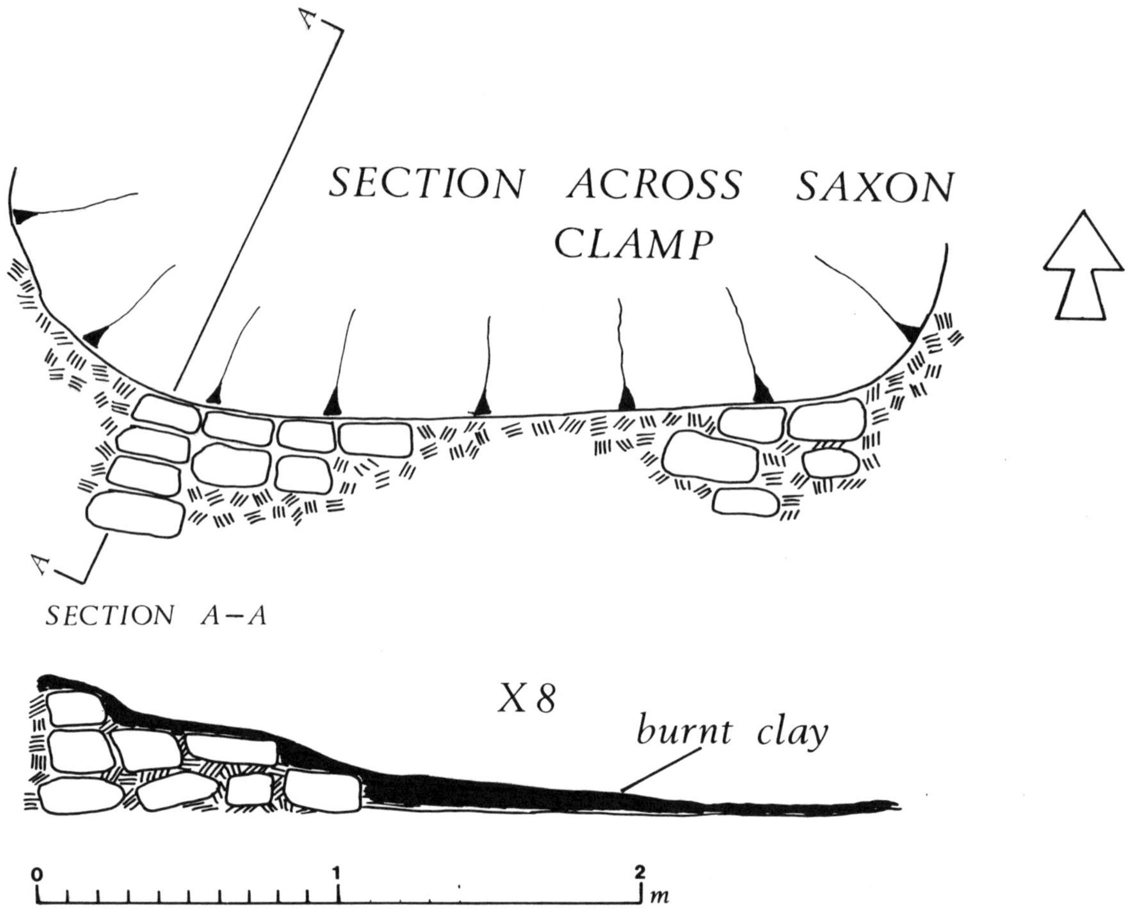

Fig. 8.12

ROOM X1, HOUSE 2, DESIGN ON PAVEMENT

Fig. 8.13

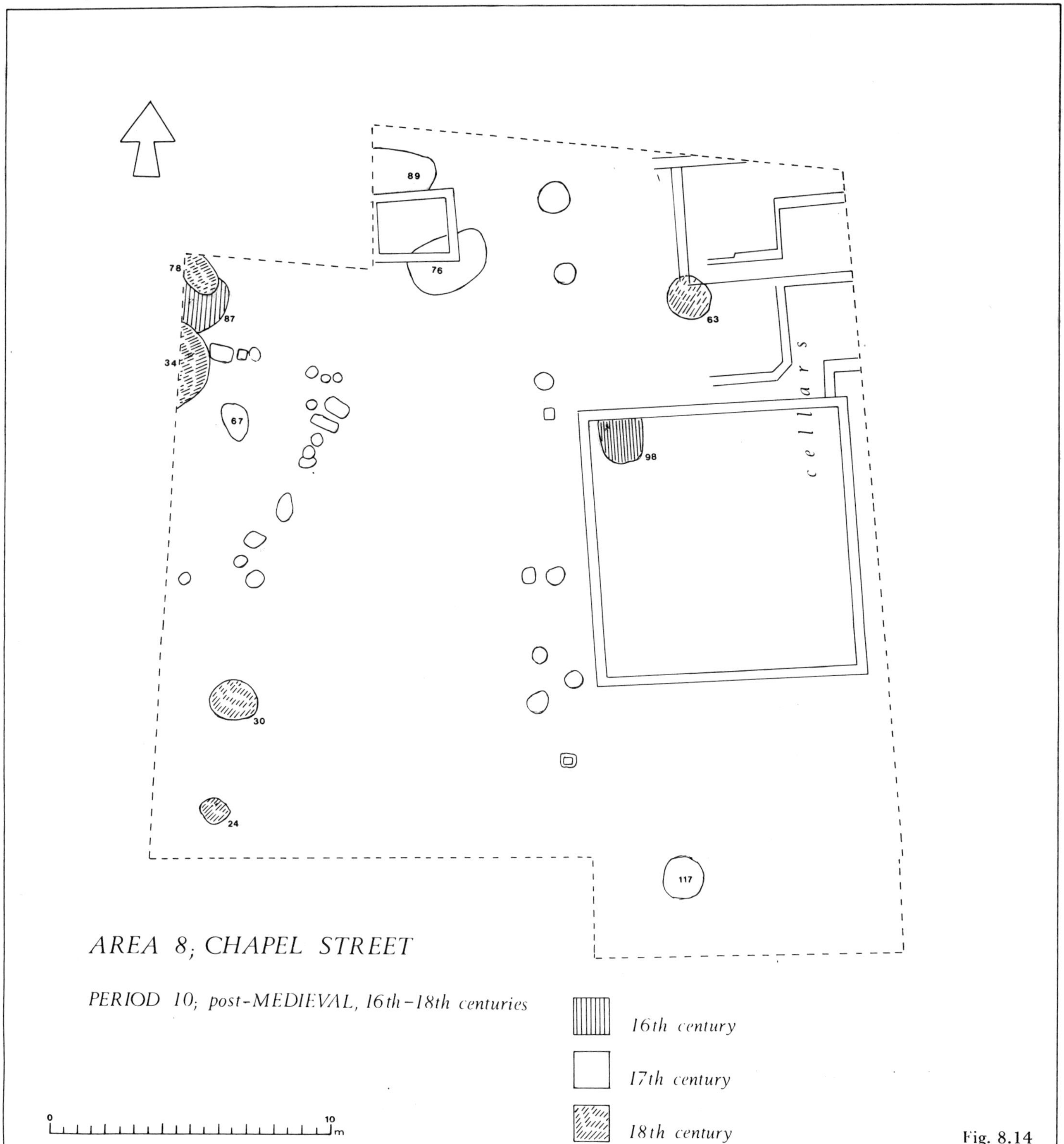
89
76
78
87
34
67
63
98
cellars
30
24
117
AREA 8; CHAPEL STREET
PERIOD 10; post-MEDIEVAL, 16th–18th centuries
16th century
17th century
18th century
0
10
m

Fig. 8.14

as if this might still have been in use, in part at least, as a property boundary. The second line of posts, which may be contemporary, was roughly parallel and about 10 metres to the west. The full extent northwards could not be traced due to the presence of the large basement below the properties fronting on to Chapel Street.

None of the postholes produced any closely dateable material. All the latest wares were coarse medieval sherds from cooking pots. The eastern fence-line cuts one of the 12th-century pits.

Phase 3; c. 15th century

Only four pits had 15th-century pottery as the latest artifacts. A line of postholes, some cutting the Phase 2 pits, was found in the western part of the trench. The postholes ran almost due north, in contrast to the earlier fence lines. Another line of posts ran roughly east–west across the north end, and at the south end, two more postholes aligned east–west suggest that the fence turned eastwards towards the street. This would give an enclosure of about 18 metres by 17, assuming that the present day Chapel Street was on the same line in the 15th century, which is very likely. To the west of the north-south fence was another enclosure with the postholes of a structure, probably a small barn, 7.5 metres wide.

Period 10
Post-medieval; c. 16th-18th centuries (Fig. 8.14)

Three phases of occupation could be distinguished.

Phase 1

Phase 1; c. 16th century is attested by two pits (X87 and 98).

Phase 2; c. 17th century

Phase 2; c. 17th century. A line of substantial postholes, most of them stone-packed, ran northwards across the site. They had been truncated by later agricultural activity and seem to be too substantial for a fence. However, they cannot be related to a building although it is possible that the cellars along the frontage of Chapel Street has destroyed the evidence. Along the western boundary was part of a timber building which may well have been the replacement for the Period 9, Phase 3 structure. Again, the postholes were very truncated, but the evidence from two of them suggests a 17th-century date, and an 18th-century pit (X34), cuts it away on the western boundary.

Phase 3; c. 18th century

Phase 3; c. 18th century. Only five pits can be assigned to this phase. Most of them were dug in the back gardens of the earlier properties fronting on to Chapel Street.

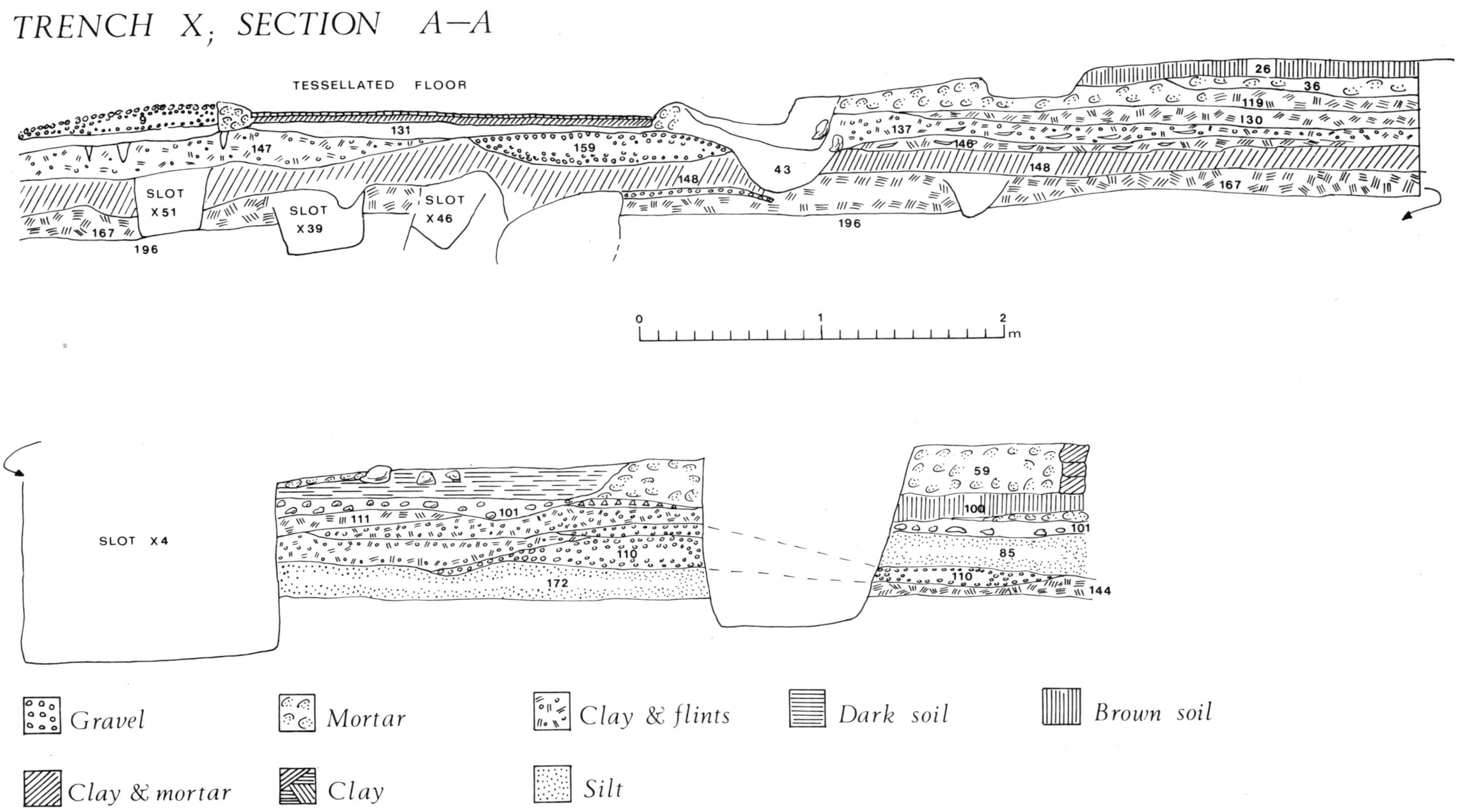
TRENCH X; SECTION A–A
TESSELLATED FLOOR
9
131
147
159
148
43
137
146
130
119
26
36
167
196
SLOT X51
SLOT X39
SLOT X46
0
1
2
m
SLOT X4
111
101
110
172
59
100
85
144
Gravel
Mortar
Clay & flints
Dark soil
Brown soil
Clay & mortar
Clay
Silt

Fig. 8.15

TRENCH X, SECTION G–G

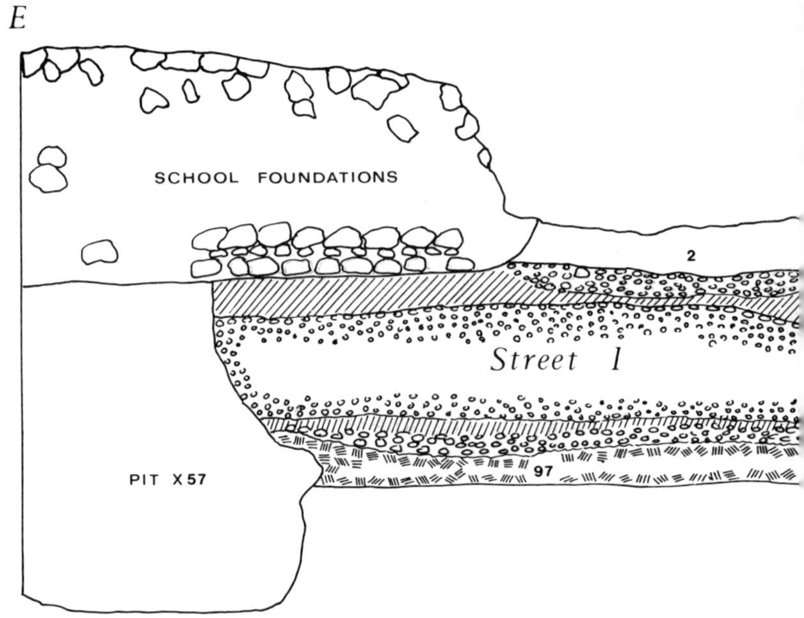

SECTION C—C

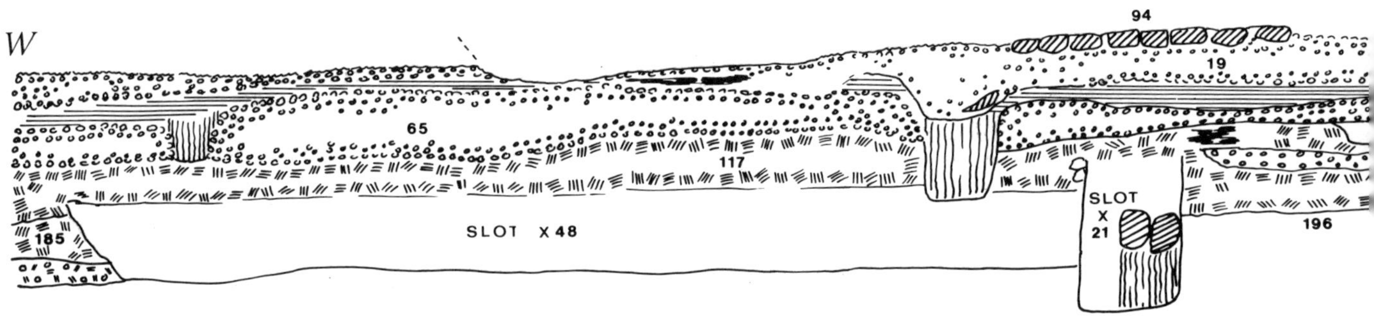

Fig. 8.16

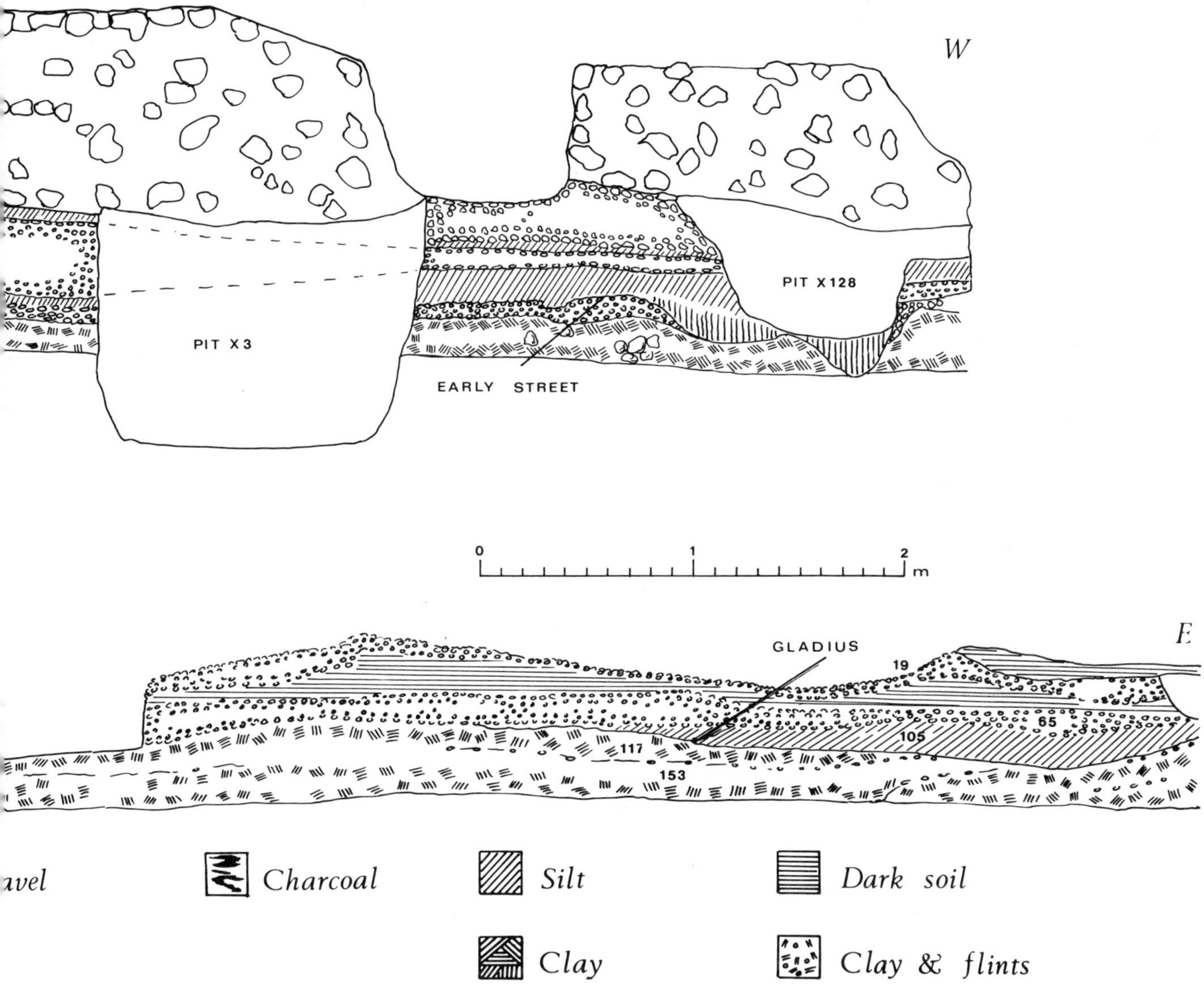
W
PIT X 3
PIT X 128
EARLY STREET
0
1
2
m
E
GLADIUS
19
65
105
117
153
Charcoal
Silt
Dark soil
Clay
Clay & flints

TRENCH X, WEST SECTION, H–H

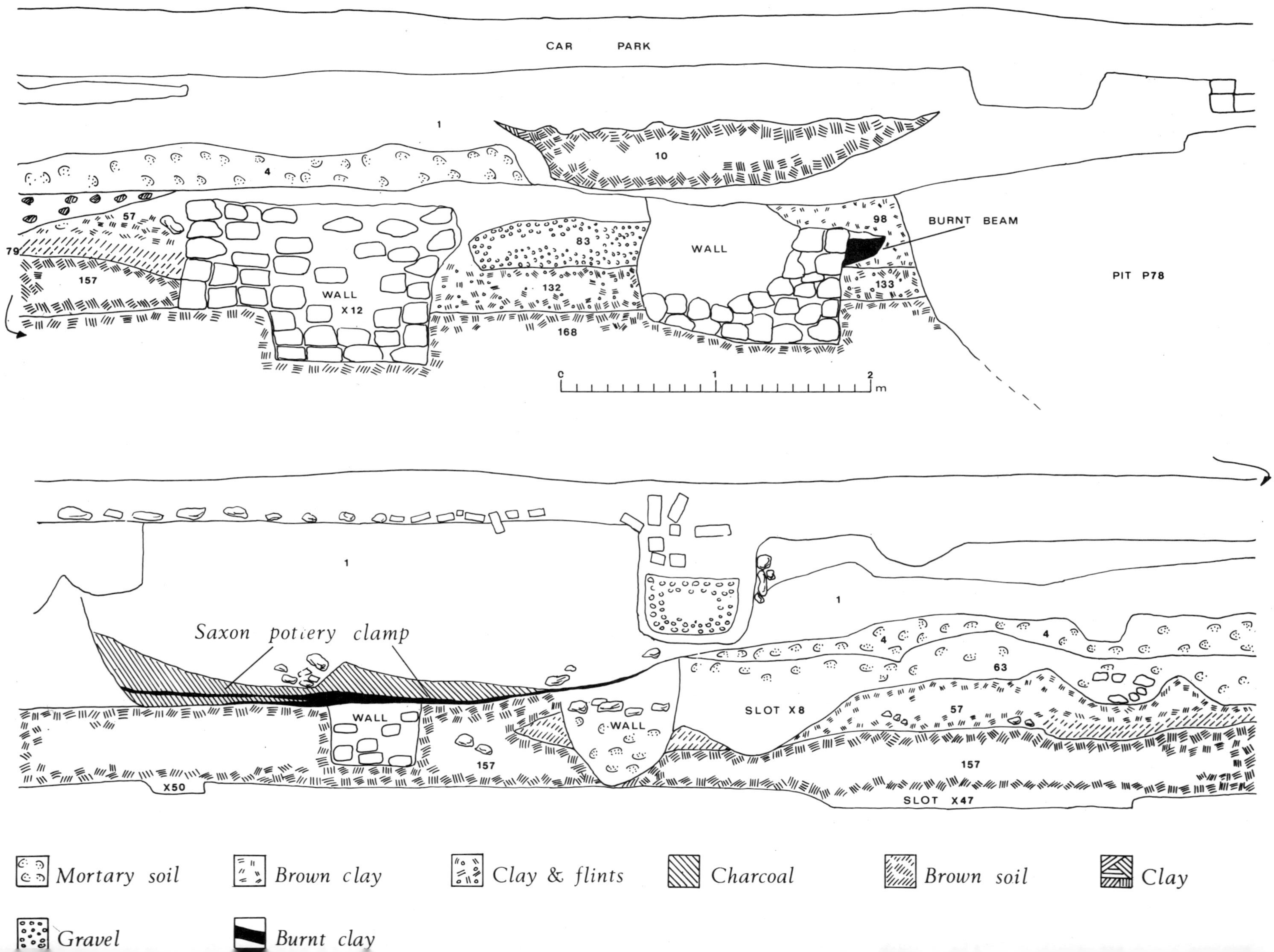

Area 9; Crane Street; Trench P

Site history (compiled from notes provided by R. R. Morgan)

13th century (see also, Chichester Excavations 3; *Fig. 5.2)*

All of the area north of Crane Lane and east of Chapel Street (Parislane), was one plot. In July 1277 and February 1283, John de Sancta Cruce received it from Simon Curte and Geoffrey de Bebitone (WSRO Add. Mss. 2594; City deeds AY4). The site had a house, curtilage and barn. There was a gate in Crane Lane leading northwards to the barn. Other owners include John Lude.

14th century

The property was still in the ownership of the Sancta Cruce family. It was described as a "tenement" in 1335 when John de Sancta Cruce left it to Isabel his wife, and John and Richard, his sons. (WSRO CAP 1/37/1).

16th century

The corner site is recorded as a garden in 1534 (WSRO CAP 1/23/1) and also in 1558 and 1597 (WSRO CAP 1/26). The Norden Map of 1595 shows buildings fronting on to the north side of Crane Street and the east side of Chapel Street.

17th century

In 1616 a corner garden is recorded (WSRO CAP 1/26). A house was "converted from a garden and a stable" by 1665 (WSRO CAP 1/27/4), confirmed as small (Hearth Tax; 1 hearth in 1676). Tax records of 1609/20 shows that the family of Chatfield owned the wite (WSRO PAR 44/6/2). Frances Chatfield who was buried in 1627 was described as a "gentleman" (WSRO Burials, St. Peter the Great). There was a malthouse on the site from 1700 and possibly earlier.

18th century

The land from No. 6 Crane Street westwards, supported a series of malthouses (WSRO Rate Returns EPI/16/2: 1755 and Wills STD 1/7, 1754 onwards), which survived into the 19th century. One malthouse was in the occupation of John Taplin, whose family were pipemakers in Chapel Street on a site about 200 feet north of Crane Street in the 18th century.

Two wills are known (i) Dated 1730, relates to John Chatfield, Brewer, who owned a messuage or tenement with backside, garden, malthouse. (WSRO STD/1/9, p. 18).

(ii) Dated 1795, relating to John Gates, Bricklayer. He owned a freehold dwellinghouse, malthouse (heretofore Chatfield's).WSRO STD/1/9, p. 18).

Discussion

It can be seen that the excavation site was part of a plot which was continuously occupied from the early 17th century and that for much of the time, up to the late 18th century at least, it was used for industrial purposes. Malting was a major industry in Chichester; there were no fewer than eight malthouses recorded in the parish of St. Peter the Less in 1709. The dangers inherent in the drying process were such that the Town Council forbade the burning of straw for this purpose. In addition to malting, we now know that a small pottery

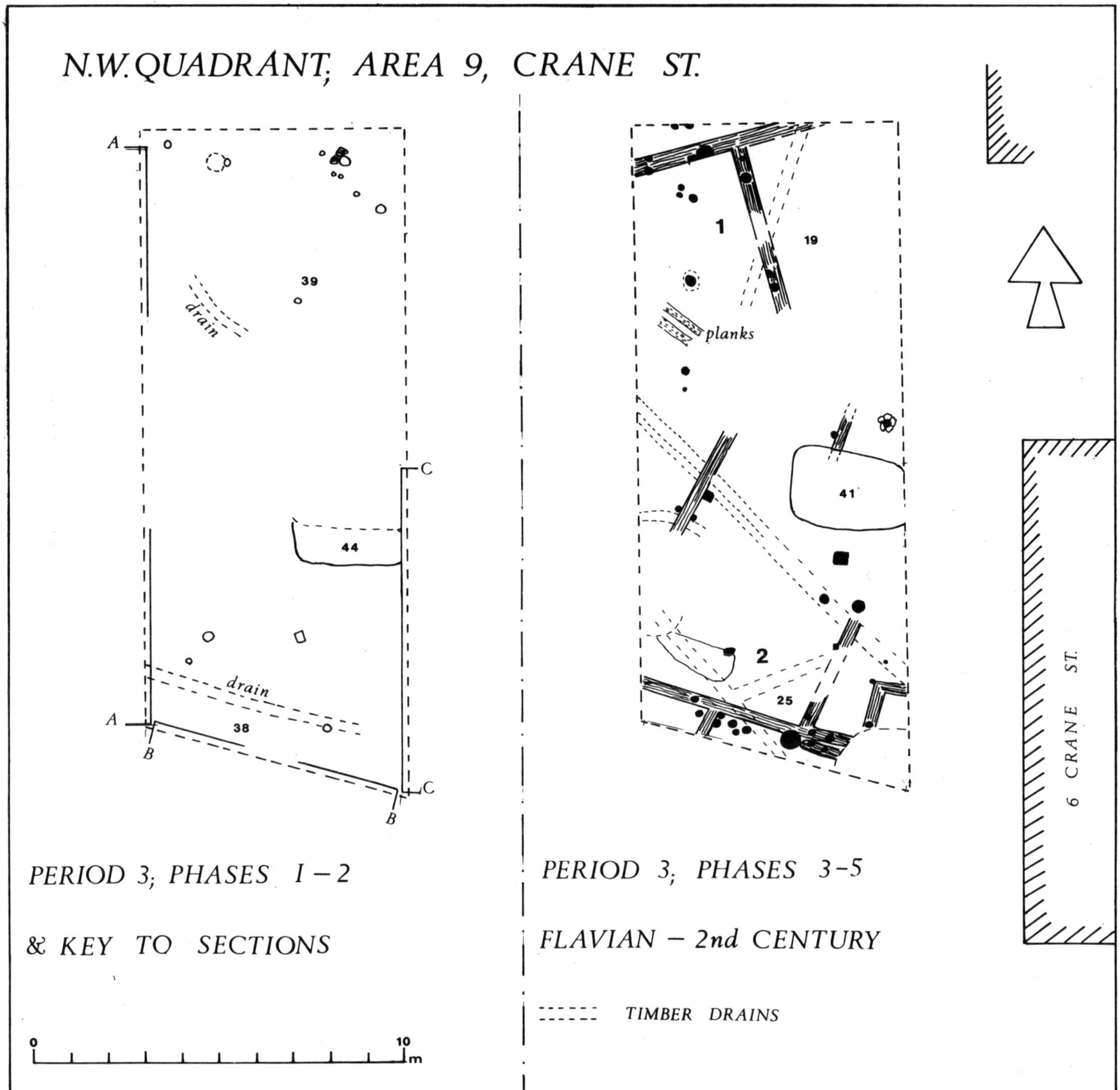
N.W. QUADRANT, AREA 9, CRANE ST.
A
A
B
B
C
C
39
drain
44
drain
38
1
19
planks
41
2
25
6 CRANE ST.
PERIOD 3; PHASES 1 – 2
& KEY TO SECTIONS
PERIOD 3; PHASES 3–5
FLAVIAN – 2nd CENTURY
TIMBER DRAINS
0
10
m

Fig. 8.18

industry was functioning on or near the site of No, 6 Crane Street in the mid-17th century (p. 153), another "hot" process which would require the use of fuel (either wood or sea coal). For a time at least, the kiln or kilns must have functioned contemporaneously with the malthouses and it might well be that they were complementary seasonal activities.

The excavation (Figs. 8.18-8.23)

Earliest periods

Neither Period 0 (pre-Conquest) or Period 1 (Claudian) were recognisable in this excavation and this reinforces the impression gained during the earlier excavations in Areas 1 and 6 (*op. cit.* pp. 47 and 128), that pre-Flavian occupation on the east side of the north–south Roman street was minimal.

Trench P yielded only one fragment of Arretine ware and very few sherds of Claudian samian, all as residual material, together with two sherds as possible Atrebatic ware which were also in later deposits.

Period 2 Claudius-Nero

At the south end of the trench a layer of yellow-brown clay (P.38), heavily stained by charcoal, rested upon natural brickearth. A charred beam lay across it. Only native coarse grey wares were found and the occupation spread cannot be closely dated, but a fragment of crucible, similar to those found in Area 2 (*op. cit.* 57–58), may indicate that the site was on the fringe of the Period 2 industrial activity. Layer P.38 was below the area covered by the later street. Further north, and separated from it by a number of large pits, was a layer of greenish clay above natural brickearth (P.39), which was probably contemporary with P.38. This had a sherd of samian dated to Nero–Vespasian in it, which suggests that these ephemeral traces of occupation should perhaps be towards the end of Period 2.

Period 3 c. Flavian-early 2nd century (Fig. 8.18, Pl. 18)

Phase 1; early Flavian. The earliest features comprised a timber lined drain (Slot P.14) which was cut into P.38 at the south end of the trench and ran east–west. Four postholes were also cut from the same horizon. At the north end a short length of curved slot (P.40) was cut into P.39 and a number of post and stakeholes indicate the presence of a slight structure of which only a small part was within the excavation.

Phase 2(a) and (b) A layer of clay ((P.19), was laid down over P.39 at the north end. This contained a number of sherds of Flavian samian as the latest dated pottery. Phase 2 (b) is represented by a pit (P.41) which also contained nothing later than Flavian wares and which was cut from the P.19 horizon (Fig. 8.23, section C—C).

Phase 3. At some time later the slots of a timber structure (House 1), were cut through P.19. This had a timber-lined drain below and may well have had a planked floor as traces of two planks were found where they had rotted in the top of P.19. The south end of the building had been destroyed by pits, one of which was of early 2nd-century date.

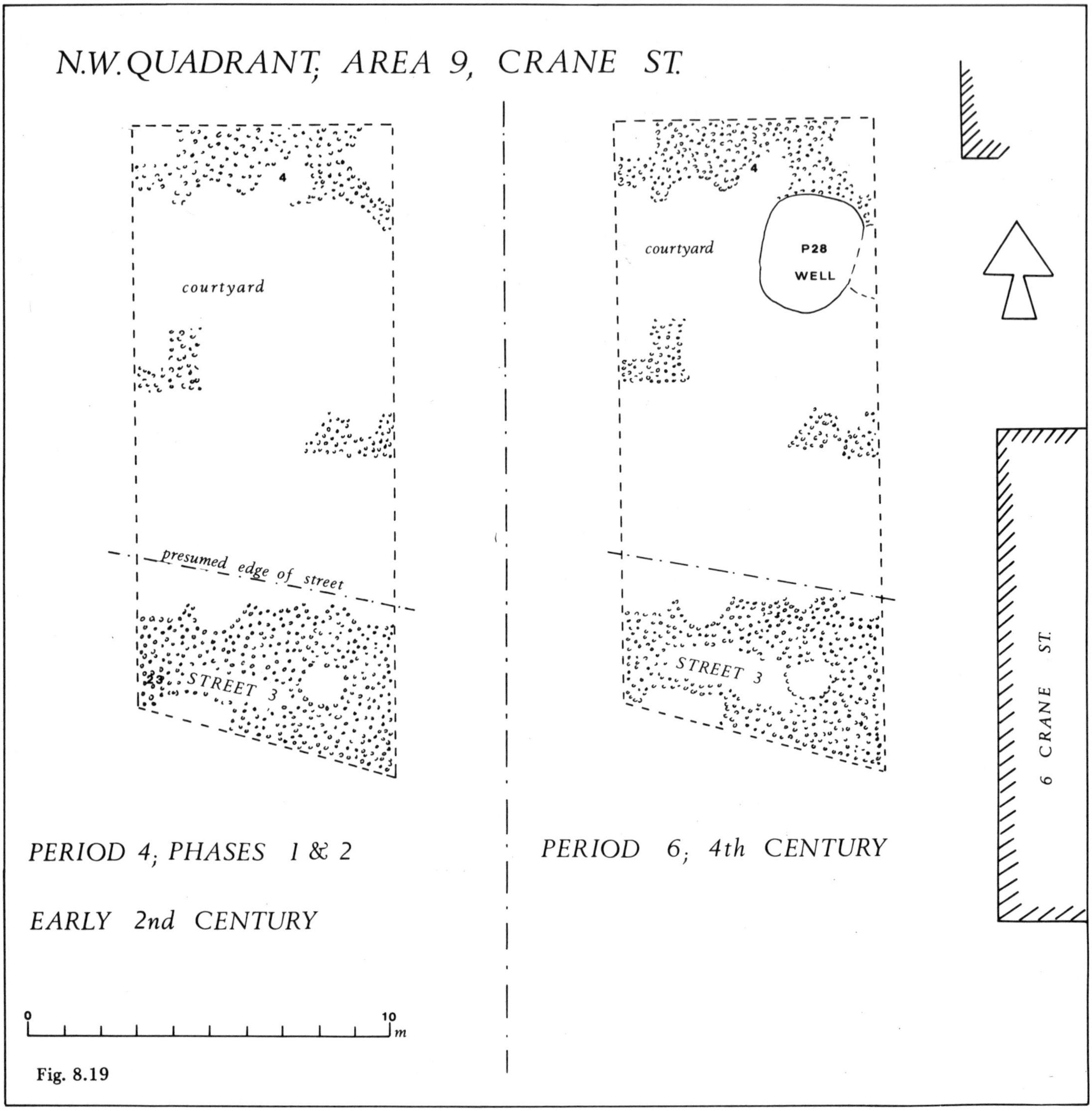
N.W. QUADRANT; AREA 9, CRANE ST.
4
courtyard
presumed edge of street
23
STREET 3
PERIOD 4; PHASES 1 & 2
EARLY 2nd CENTURY
0
10
m
4
courtyard
P28
WELL
STREET 3
PERIOD 6; 4th CENTURY
6 CRANE ST.

Fig. 8.19

Phase 4. At the south end of the site, a layer of yellow clay (P.25), was deposited over P.38. It was cut by the slots of a timber building (House 2), which had a system of timber-lined drains below. The northern end of the structure was destroyed by pits, but it is clear that House 2 is of a different date to House 1, and in support of this, although there was no evidence from the slots, P.25 had a sherd from a Dr. 42 dating to *c.* 2nd century.

Phase 5; c. early second century. A pit (P.41) was dug through Layer 19 near the east section. It cut away Pit P.44 and part of House 2 and probably destroyed part of the earlier House 1. The fill from the pit and from the layer above it is consistently Flavian. Most of the wares may derive from the earlier pit P.44 and it also contained amounts of building material (tegulae, imbrices, etc.), either from Houses 1 and 2 or from a more substantial building nearby.

Period 4
c. early 2nd century
(Fig. 8.19)

Phase 1. At the south end of the site, a layer of street metalling (P.23) was laid down. Only the northern edge of the street was within the excavation and the true boundary could only be conjectured, due to erosion by later pits, but the gravel could be seen to be cambering northwards. Only four fragments of 1st-century samian were found in the metalling, but the presence of a sherd of 2nd-century samian in P.25 below the street, together with the evidence from Area 2 (*op. cit.* p. 66), suggests that a date fairly early on in the 2nd century is probably right. North of the street, a layer of dark soil (P.21/22) accumulated or was dumped above the Period 3 horizon P.19. This contained only 1st-century samian, together with a large number of black and white mosaic tesserae. These were of small enough size to have been intended for a fine mosaic, but they showed no signs of ever having been mortared into a floor, and it might well be that they were surplus stock thrown out from a temporary mosaic workshop in the vicinity.

Phase 2. A layer of dirty gravel was laid down above 21/22, probably as a hardstanding belonging to a building outside the area of the excavation. Only a few patches remained between the later pits, but it could be seen to extend across the trench north of the street and probably formed a boundary with it. The gravel had been re-used from elsewhere and only one sherd of Flavian samian was found, the remainder being earlier.

Period 5
c. mid 3rd-early 4th century

No evidence was found for any activity during this period.

Periods 6 and 7; early-late 4th-5th centuries
(Fig. 8.19)

At some time during the 4th century, and probably quite late, a deep pit (P.28) was dug through the gravel courtyard north of the street. It appeared to have been lined with charred timbers and shows a close similarity to timber-lined wells of this period and probably is one, although it is quite shallow. It was backfilled at some time in Period 7. Large quantities of pottery were thrown in, all of it late in date, and some of the Oxford wares (Fig. 14.1) date after A.D. 380. Many hundreds of iron studs and a number of iron tools were found in the fill, together with 14 coins. The latest of these was a coin of Valens (A.D. 364–378).

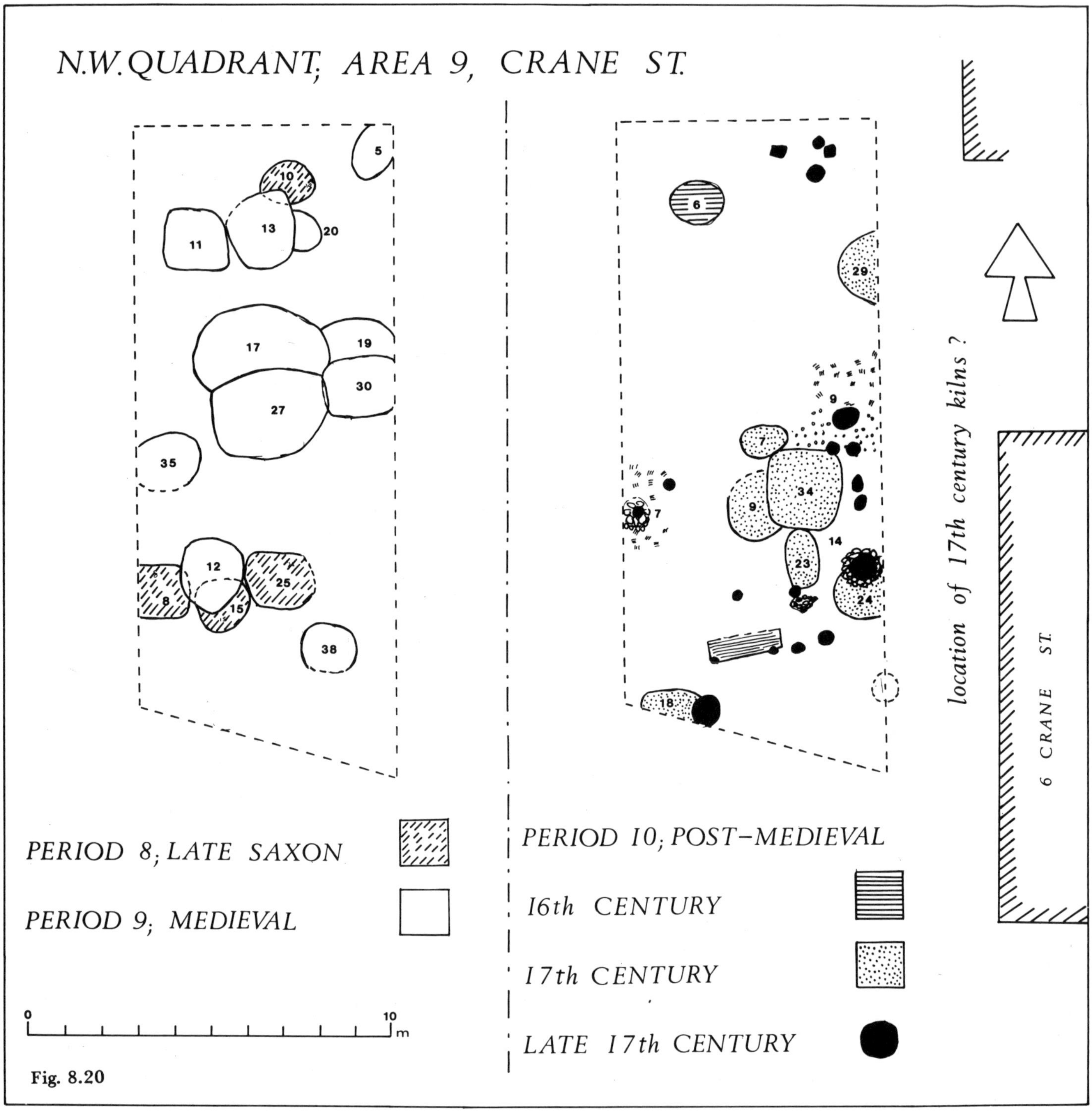
N.W. QUADRANT; AREA 9, CRANE ST.
5
10
11
13
20
17
19
30
27
35
12
25
8
15
38
6
29
9
7
34
9
7
14
23
24
18
location of 17th century kilns ?
6 CRANE ST
PERIOD 8; LATE SAXON
PERIOD 9; MEDIEVAL
PERIOD 10; POST–MEDIEVAL
16th CENTURY
17th CENTURY
LATE 17th CENTURY
0
10
m

Fig. 8.20

Discussion

This excavation, linked with the earlier trial trench to the west (Trench S), and the excavations in Purchase's garden to the north (Area 6), further confirms the impression that the main area of development in the Roman period was along the North Street frontage and that the pits and slight timber buildings noted are at the rear (west) of the houses. Similarly, Street 3, which connected Street 1 below Chapel Street to the north-south street below North Street, showed little signs of wear and did not appear to have been re-metalled at all, which suggests that it was a minor thoroughfare.

Period 8
Saxon; c. 9th-11th centuries
(Fig. 8.20)

Four pits were recognised as Saxon in date. Of these, Pit P.10 had five sherds of Group 2 ware, being handmade, soft and gritty and probably dating to *c.* mid to late 10th century (pp. 184-189 and Fig. 8.37). The other three pits (P.8, 15 and 25) had nothing but late Saxon–Saxo-Norman wares. The tremendous degree of disturbance made it impossible for any structures of this period to survive.

Period 9;
Medieval, c. 12th-15th century
(Fig. 8.20)

Eleven pits could be assigned to Period 9 and it is possible to sub-divide them, into three phases on the basis of their contents:

Phase 1; Early medieval, c. *12th–13th century.* Pit P. 35.

Phase 2; 13th/14th century. Pits P.7, 11, 12, 17, 19, 26, 27 and 38. Of these, Pit P.11 was rectangular in section and showed traces of having been lined with timber. It might have been a timber-lined well, albeit a shallow one.

Phase 3. c. *15th century.* Pits P.5, 27 and 30. As in the Saxon period, no structures could be recognised.

Period 10;
c. 16th-17th century
(Fig. 8.20)

Phase 1; c. *16th century.* Only one pit could be isolated as having no later wares than *c.* 16th century.

Phase 2. A total of seven pits were found with 17th-century wares as the latest artifacts, although they were present in large amounts in later pits. The most common wares were the green glazed wares previously identified as likely to have been made at Graffham, but now seen to have been made on or near the site.

These are discussed in detail below (pp. 196-211). The small industry seems to have functioned during the Civil War period if the presumed date of 1644 on the imitation Bellarmine jug (Fig. 8.49, 19) is any guide. The location of the kiln is likely to be below the path beside No. 6 Crane Street or actually under the house.

Phase 3. At some time after the Phase 2 pits had been filled in, a substantial building was erected of which only part can be seen on the plan. Two of the post-holes cut through the Phase 2 pits and the building might well have survived into the 18th century. Most of the postholes were large and stone-packed and the structure was probably a large barn or storehouse. The floor may have been of trampled earth and clay, represented by layers P.8 and P.14, but this only survived in patches.

Period 11
18th-19th centuries
(Fig. 8.21)

During the 19th century the "Butcher's Arms" Beerhouse fronted on to Chapel Street. Pit P.3 was dug through the 17th-century layers and contained large amounts of broken beer-bottles which could have derived from the beer-house, which suggests that at that time the excavation site was in the back garden

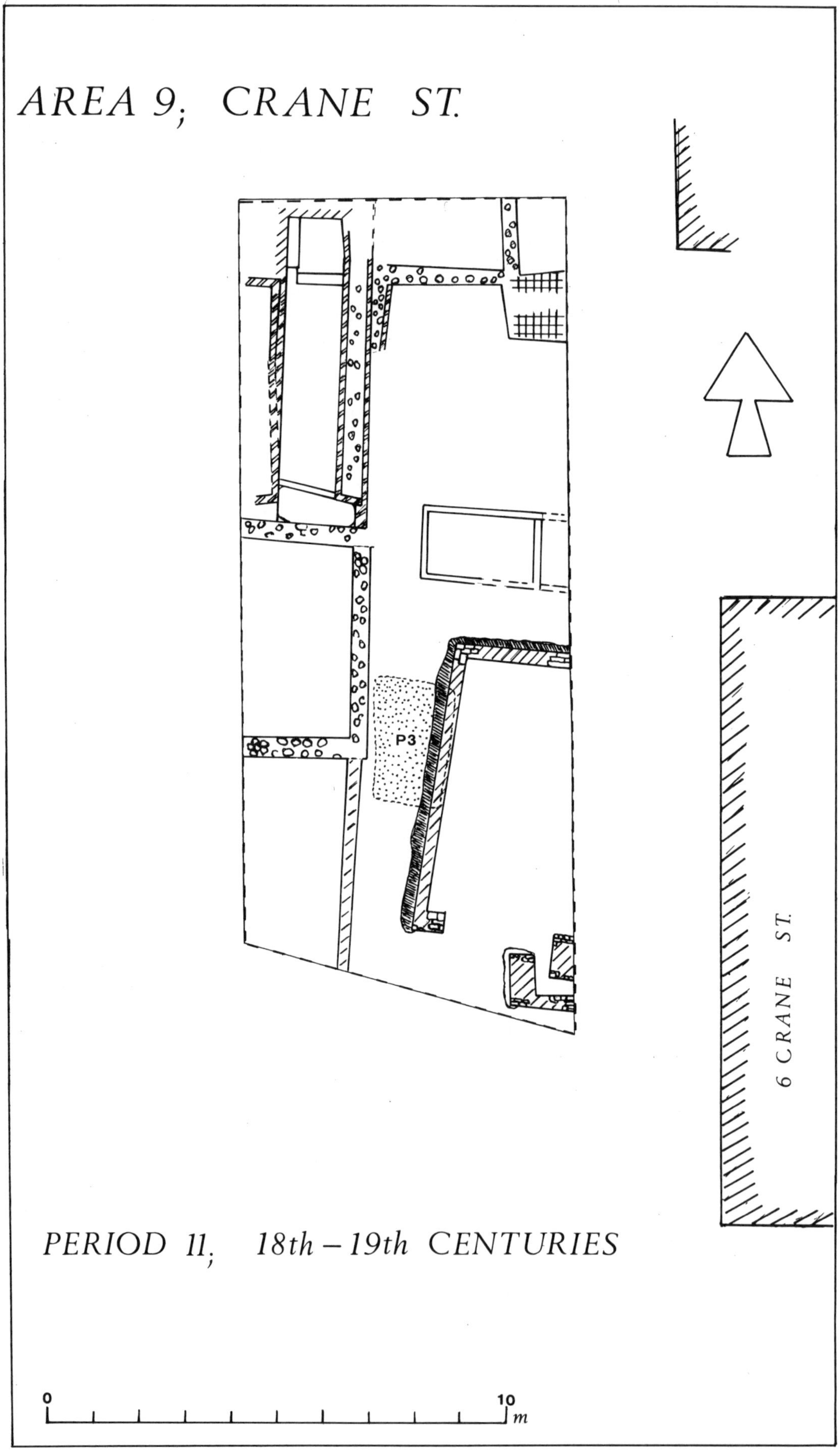
AREA 9; CRANE ST.
P3
6 CRANE ST.
PERIOD 11; 18th – 19th CENTURIES
0
10
m

Fig. 8.21

TRENCH P; WEST SECTION, A–A

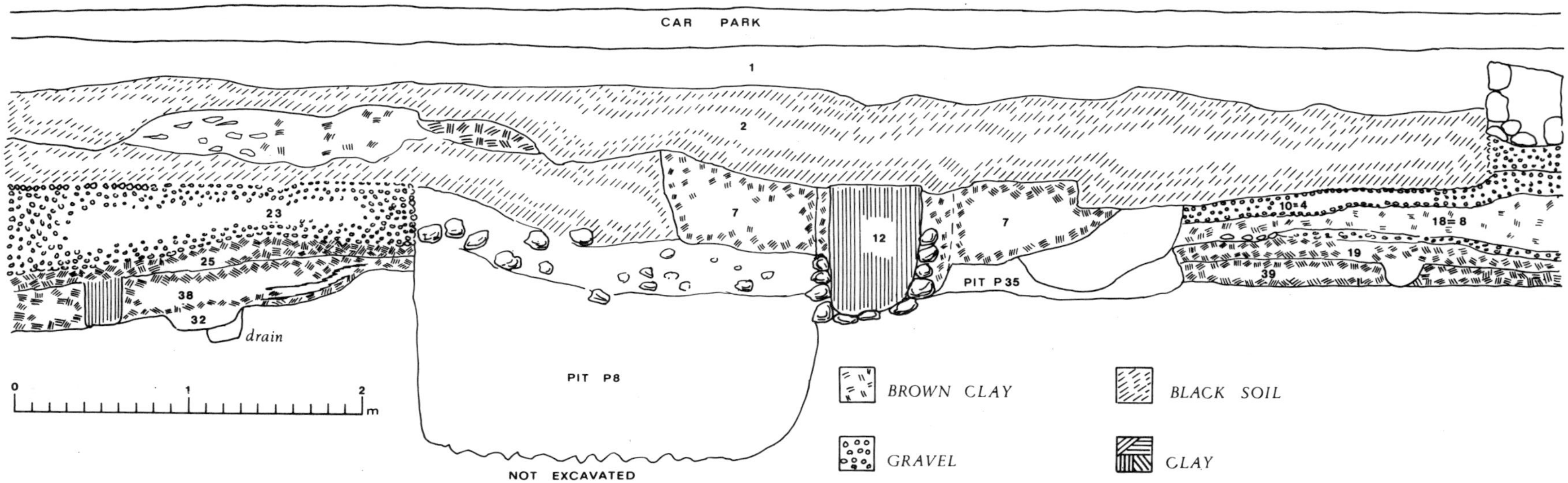

Fig. 8.22

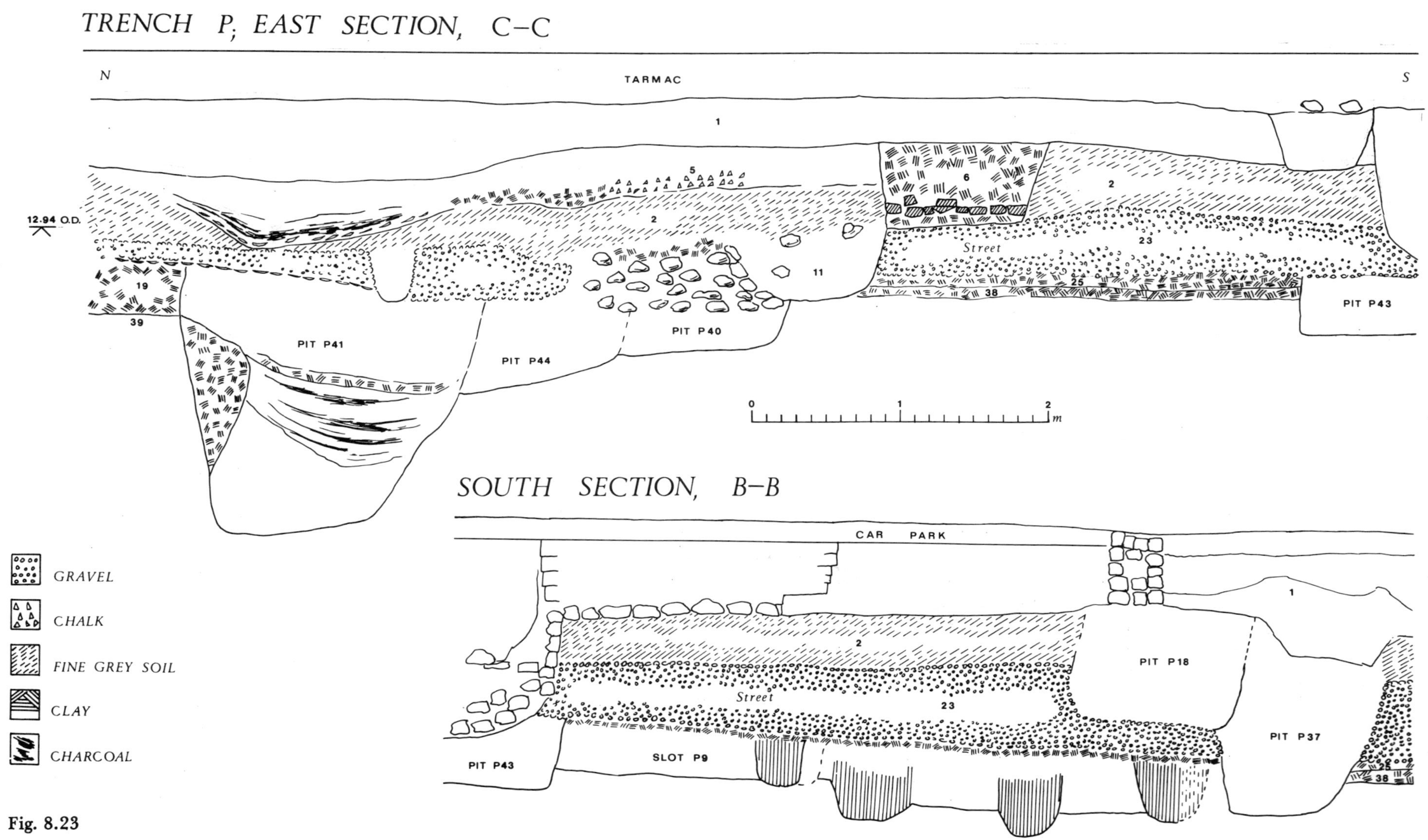
TRENCH P; EAST SECTION, C–C
N
TARMAC
S
1
5
6
2
12.94 O.D.
23
Street
11
19
38
25
39
PIT P43
PIT P41
PIT P44
PIT P40
0
1
2
m
SOUTH SECTION, B–B
CAR PARK
1
2
PIT P18
Street
23
PIT P37
PIT P43
SLOT P9
38
GRAVEL
CHALK
FINE GREY SOIL
CLAY
CHARCOAL

Fig. 8.23

of the Chapel Street property. Thereafter, until recent times, the alignment remained the same. After Pit P.3 was backfilled a series of brick-built structures were erected, the foundations of which are seen in Fig. 8.21. These in turn were covered by garden soil in the present century.

The Finds from the North-West Quadrant (Areas 8 & 9)

Note. All are Roman unless otherwise stated; numbers in brackets are small finds numbers.

Fig. 8.24

Objects of stone.

(a) Hones.[1]

1. (129). Indurated fine-grained quartz sandstone, probably a pebble. (Pit X 97).
2. (630). Slate whetstone; not a local slate, probably imported. (Pit P.25).
3. (422). Micaceous slate whetstone. Not local; probably imported. (X 155, in a Flavian context).
4. (32). Glauconitic sandy limestone, cf. *Fishbourne*, Part 11, pp. 153–5. (Pit X 41, residual in an early medieval context).
5. (441). As No. 4. (X 151, Roman well pit). *Not illustrated.*
6. (597). As No. 4. (Pit X 1, Saxon context).

Fig. 8.24

(b) Miscellaneous.

7. (262). Spindle whorl of sandstone (unstratified).
8. (240). Spindle whorl of chalk (X 68).
9. – Fragment from an alabaster bowl (Pit X 107).
10. (28) Fragment of frame moulding in Carrara marble. (Pit X 46).
11. (429) As No. 10. (X 147). *Not illustrated.*
12. (750). Roughly trimmed disc of slate with central hole, probably used as a spindle whorl. (P.15).
13. – Fragment of slate beading. (X 131).

1. I am indebted to Dr. D. P. S. Peacock of Southampton University who kindly identified the hones.

Fig. 8.25

Objects of jet.

14. (197). Melon bead. (X 84).
15. (49). Bangle. (Pit X 29b).
16. (684). Part of a hairpin. (Pit P.28d).
17. (100). Fragment of a bangle (cf. *Chichester 4*, Fig. 55.5), but unpolished. (X 20).

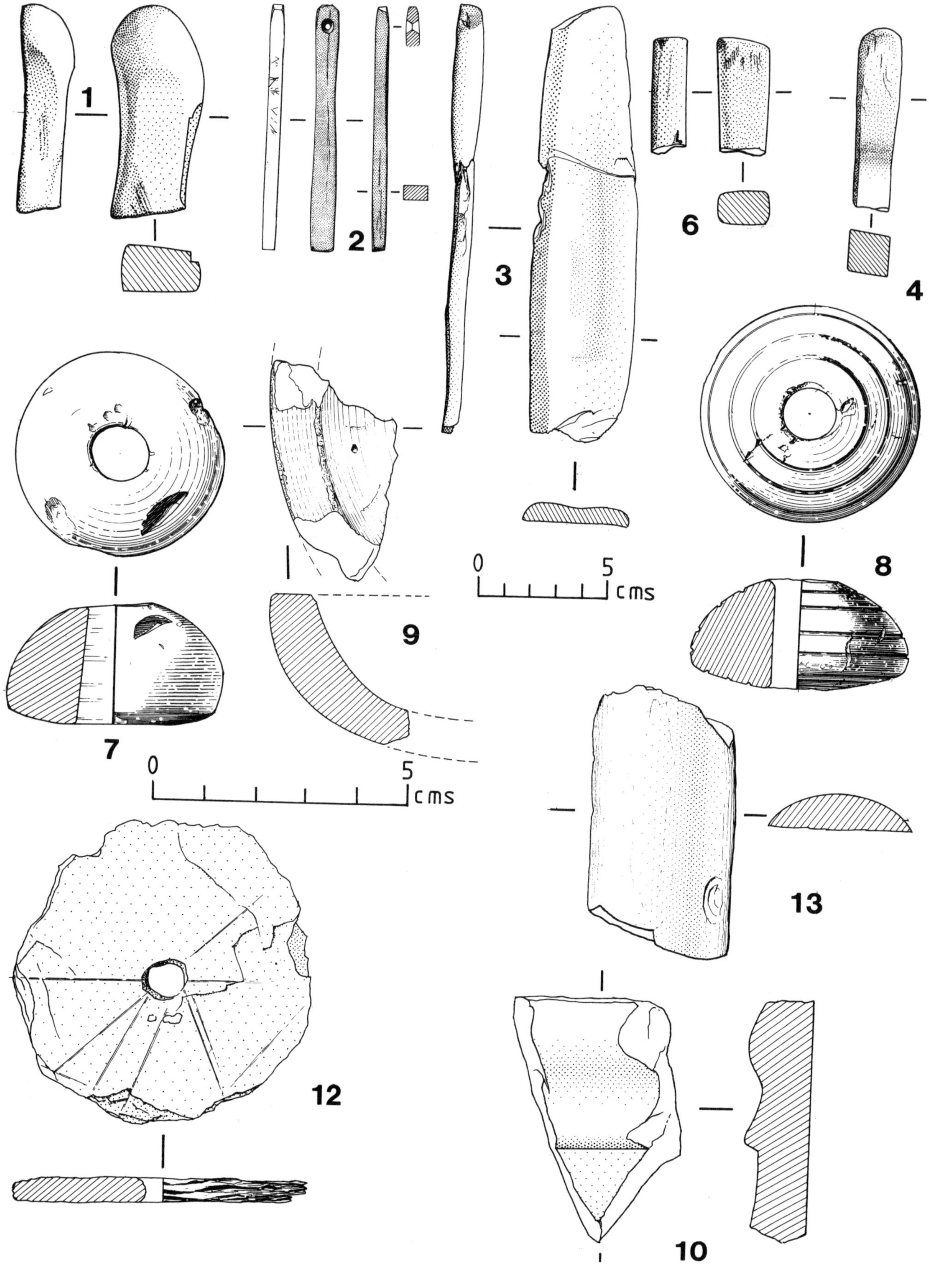

Fig. 8.24. Small finds from Chapel Street. Stone and slate. Nos. 1-6 & 10 (½), Remainder ($\frac{1}{1}$)

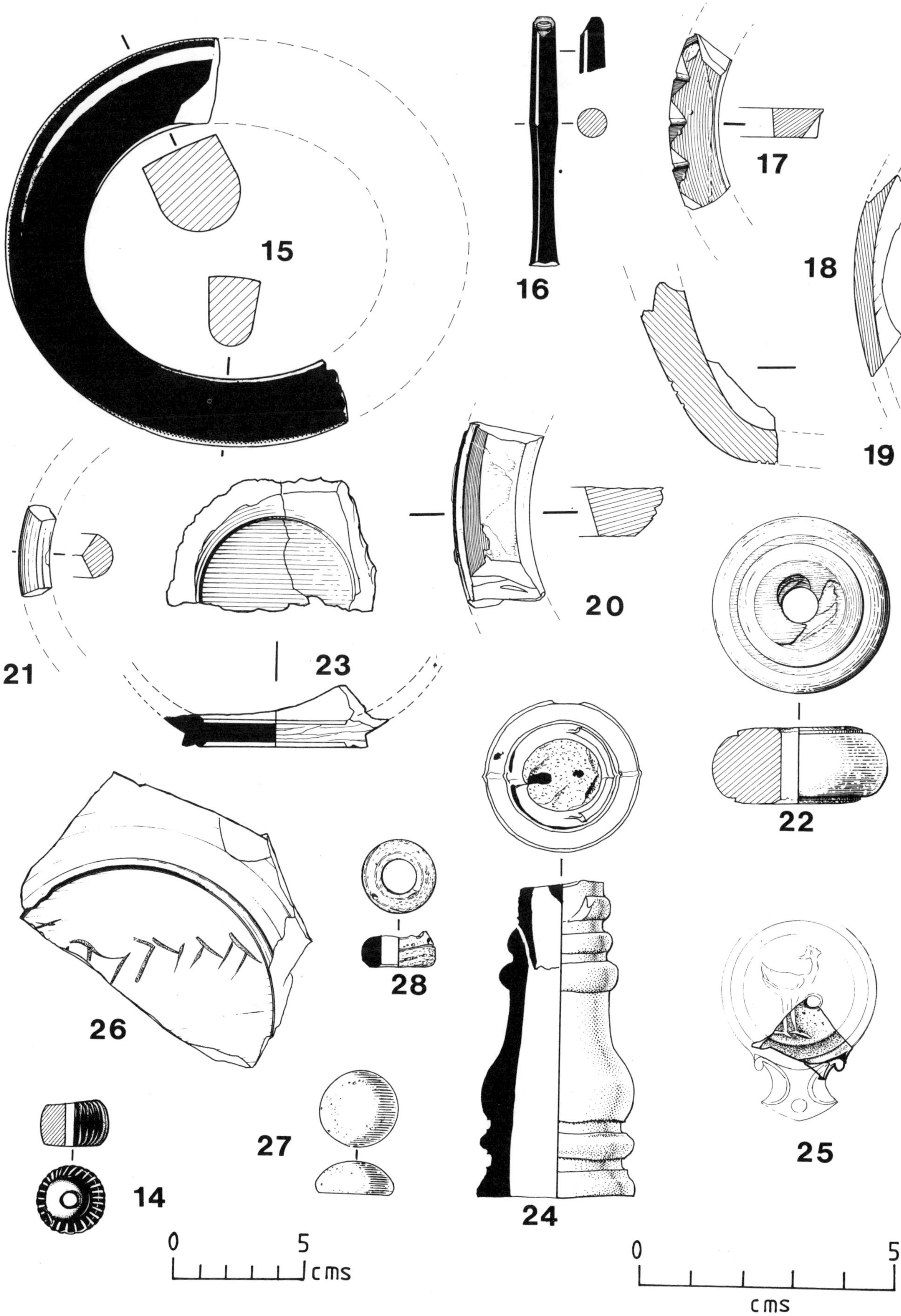

Fig. 8.25. Small finds from Chapel Street. Jet, shale, pottery and glass. Nos. 23 & 25 (½), remainder ($\frac{1}{1}$)

Fig. 8.25

Objects of shale.

18. (301), Fragment of bowl. (X 89).
19. (743). Fragment of bowl. (P 2),
20. (188). ? Bangle, or rim of bowl. (X 80).
21. (564). Bangle. (X 194).
22. (612). Spindle whorl. (P 2).
23. (754). Base of a bowl. (Pit P.28d).

Fig. 8.25

Objects of pottery.

24. (594). Pipeclay pedastal. (X 1).
25. (431). Fragment of moulded pottery lamp. (X 155).
26. (599). Base of imitation T.N. jar with graffito scratched on base after firing. (Pit X 97), *c.* Flavian.

Fig. 8.25

Objects of glass.

27. (543). White glass gaming counter. (X 157).
28. (476). Blue bead. (X 148).

Figs. 8.26 and 8.27

Objects of bone.

29. (676). Pin. (Pit P.28b).
30. (213). Hairpin. (X 3b).
31. (392). Hairpin. (X 136).
32. (559). Hairpin. (Pit X 159b).
33. (574). Hairpin. (X 106).
34. (106). Hairpin. (X 61).
35. (681). Hairpin. (Pit P.28b).
36. (693). Hairpin. (P.18).
37. (544). Toilet instrument. (Pit X 159).
38. (502). Gaming counter. (X 147).
39. (498). Part of a dice box. (X 167).
40. (331). ? Whistle, or possibly some form of container as it is rebated at one end to take a disc. (X 110).
41. (595). Part of a bone box. The exterior is polished and the interior left rough, but this might be because it broke before being finished on the lathe. However, it has been rebated at both ends for closure. (X 102).
42. (425). Bone handle of an iron scoop. (X 148).
43. (661). Fragment of a ? balance arm. (Pit P.28b).
44. (748). Bone knife handle (probably post medieval). (P.2).
45. (251). Bone handle. (Pit X 41).
46. (534). Bone handle. (X 187).

Fig. 8.27

Object of wood.

47. (646). Hairpin. (Pit P.28b).

Fig. 8.27

Objects of lead.

48. (312). Lead bung, probably used to repair an iron tank. (Pit X 127).
49. (208). Fragment of a handle. (X 92).

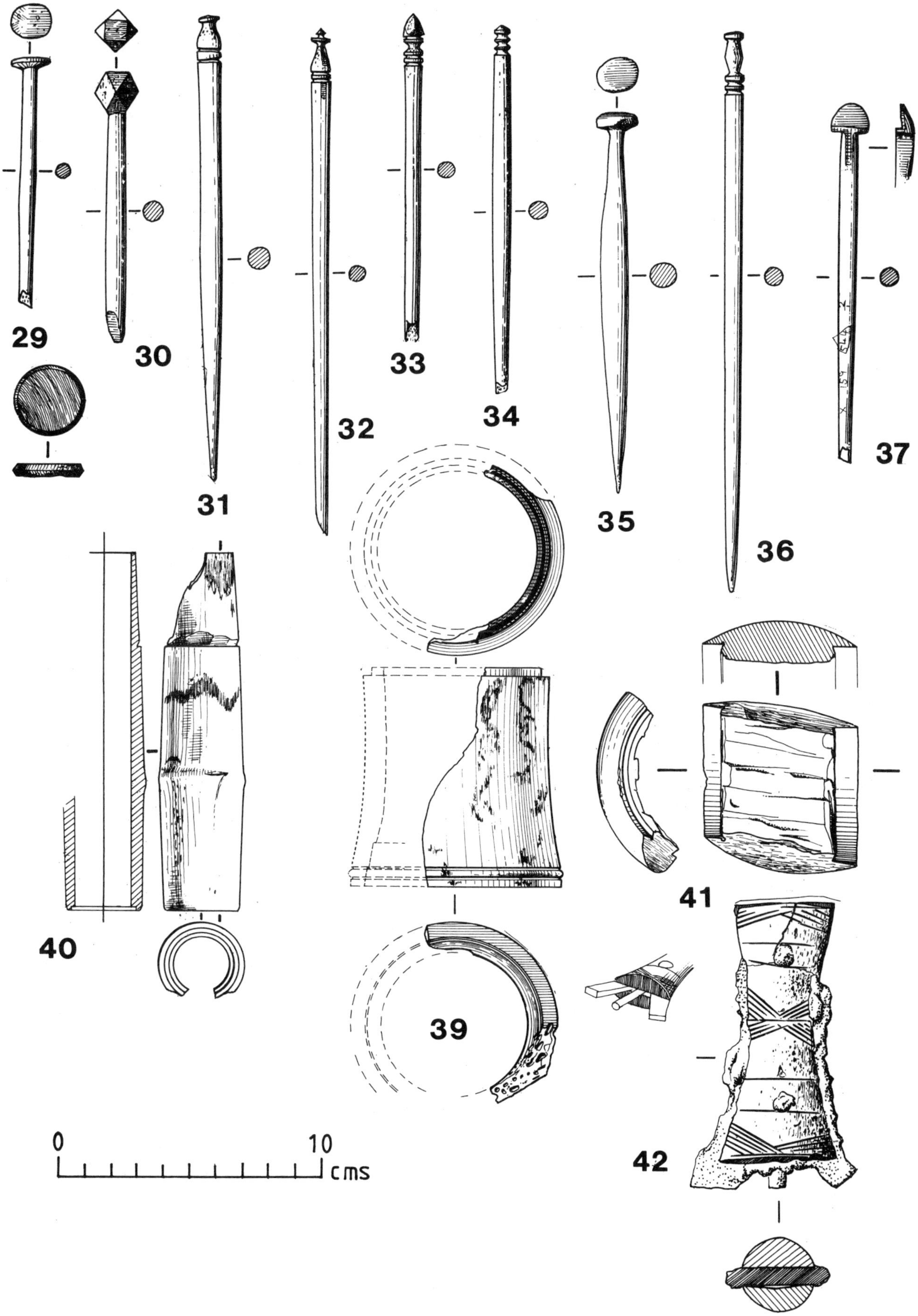

Fig. 8.26. Small finds from Chapel Street. Bone. ($\frac{1}{1}$)

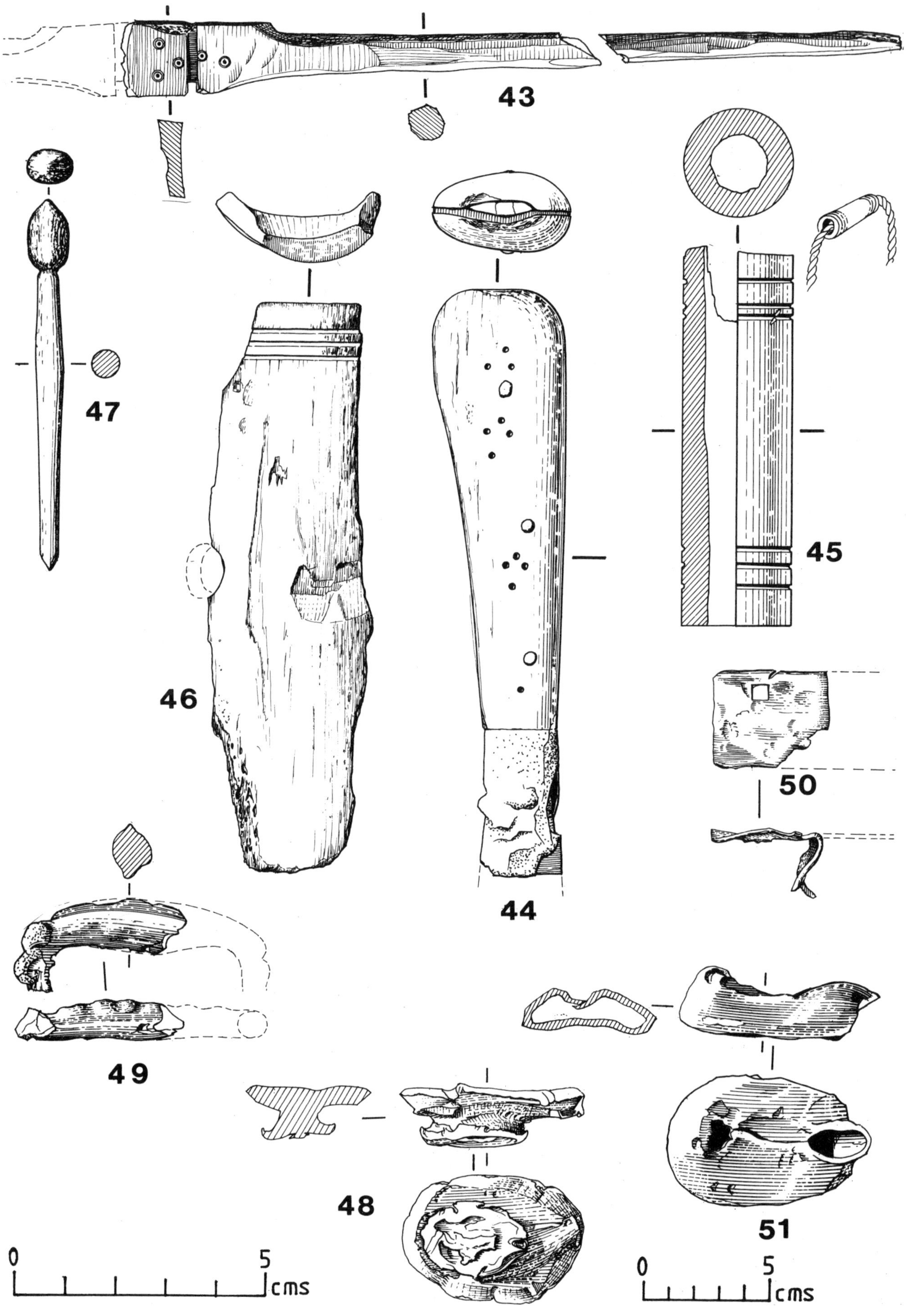

Fig. 8.27. Small finds from Chapel Street. Bone, Nos. 43-45 ($\frac{1}{1}$), Lead, Nos. 48-51 (½).

50. (401). Part of a strip, chisel cut, with a square punched hole. (X 95).
51. (377). Receptacle, probably intended for use as an oil lamp.

Figs. 8.28 and 8.29

Objects of Iron

(a) Military or probably so

1. Gladius: (see report by Dr. Webster, below).
2. (536). Neck segment from the *lorica* (X 184).
3. (435). Iron sheet pierced with a slot to take a transverse iron member, and with square punched holes at one end. (X 155).
4. (110). Fragment of iron plate, *c.* 3.5 mm thick, which has been folded over. The folded-over fragment has been cut away, and this, plus the width of the fragment (60 mm), makes it the right size and shape to be from the left shoulder-piece of the *lorica.* (Pit X 90).

(b) Other iron finds

5. (678). Iron object, possibly the base of a vessel, or perhaps a boss. (Pit P.28).
6. (660). Two fragments of an arangement of iron studs all fused together by corrosion and probably driven through a leather sheet covering a wooden chest. These are two of the largest of many fragments found in Pit P.28.
7. (659). Iron wire with looped end and rivet rusted to it. (Pit P.28).
8. (645). Possibly a farrier's tool. (Pit P.28).
9. (658). Square-sectioned rod with ball-headed end. (Pit P.28).
10. (519). Fragment of flat iron with two rounded corners and wedge-shaped in section. (X 183).
11. (335). Fragment of iron strap, pierced for a rivet. (Slot X 18).
12. (160). Fragment of iron strap pierced for rivets. Possibly from a cart or perhaps a large door hinge. (X 57).
13. (145). Fragment of iron plate with a square punched hole. (X 137).
14. (176). Fragment from a key. (X 57).
15. (460). Tang end of a ? sickle. (X 162).
16. (494). Chisel. (X 167).
17. (513). Section of elliptical pipe with one end peened over with a hammer. Possibly the shoe for a wooden staff. (X 144).
18. (732). ? Ferrule for a wooden staff. (Pit P.60).
19. (582). Fragment of iron sheet. (X 184).
20. (369). Iron knife handle (cf. *Chichester Excavations 4*; Fig. 48, 26).
21. (577). Stylus. (X 139).
22. (475). Stylus. (X 148).
23. (596). Lashing cleat, probably from the side of a wagon. (X 157).
24. (405). Part of a bucket handle. (X 117).

(c) Post-Roman

25. (41). Tip of a knife blade, probably late Saxon. (Pit X 50).
26. (751). Horseshoe, late or post-medieval. (P.15).
27. (688). Belt buckle; medieval or post-medieval (P.15).
28. (752). Part of a gun rest ? 18th–19th century. (Pit P.3).

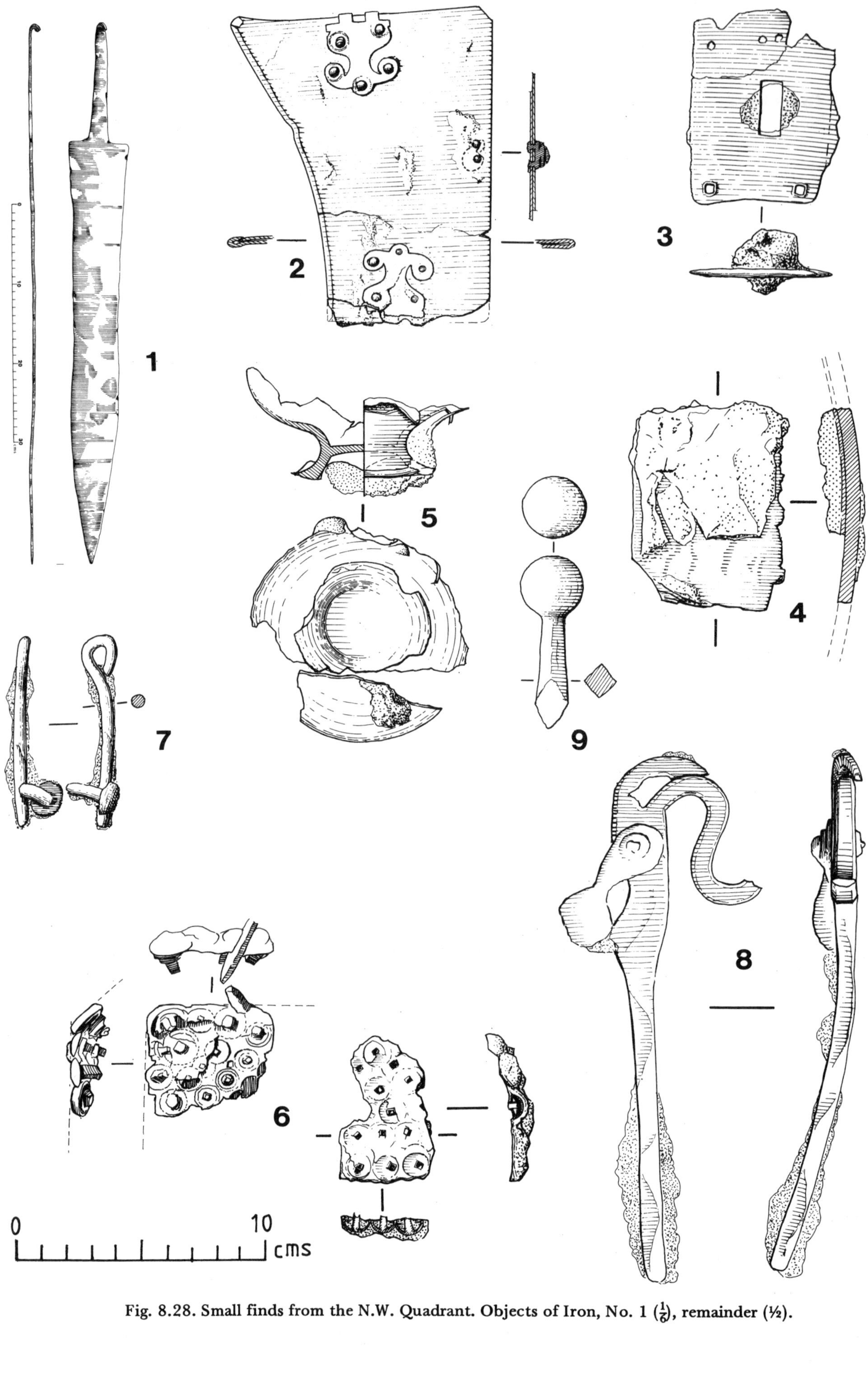

Fig. 8.28. Small finds from the N.W. Quadrant. Objects of Iron, No. 1 (1/6), remainder (½).

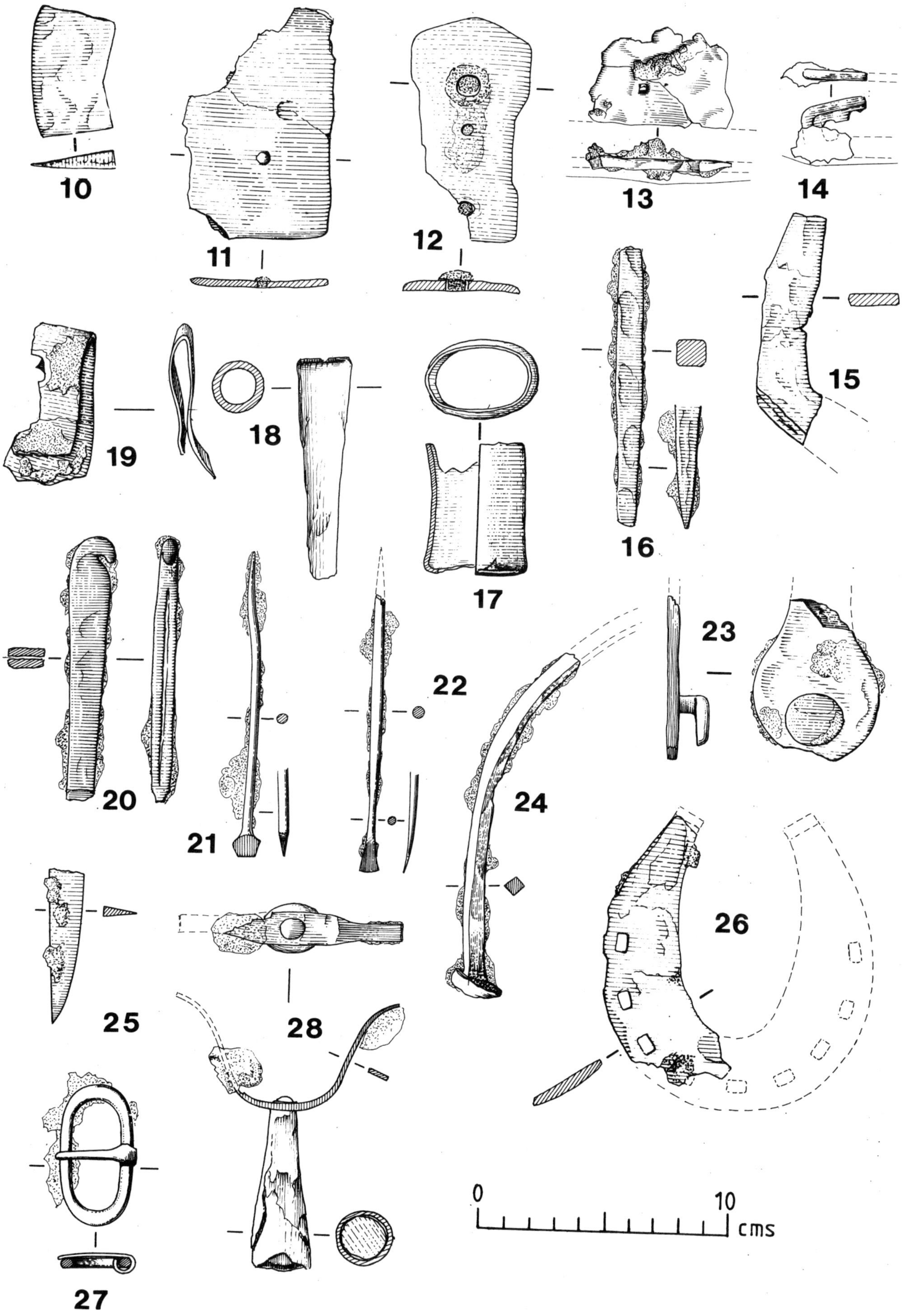

Fig. 8.29. Small finds from the N. W. Quadrant. Objects of iron. Nos. 10-24; Roman, Nos. 25-28; post-Roman (½).

Objects of Bronze

(a) Military

1. Belt plate from the *cingulum* embossed with the wolf and twins motif. There is a parallel from Ritstissen now in the Wurttenbergisches Landesmuseum, Stuttgart (cf. *Ulbert* 1970, Taf. 1.1). (X 1).
2. (419). Two sections of a hinged plate with rivet holes, possibly military (X 153).
3. (451). Belt strap with niello inlay. (X 155).
4. (359). Hinged buckle from the *lorica*. (X 129).
5. (366). Ornamental boss, either from the helmet or the *lorica* (cf. *Robinson* 1975, p. 48, Fig. 83) for similar examples. (Pit X 133).
6. (525). Embossed and tinned decorative strip, probably military, possibly a helmet fitting (cf. *Robinson* 1975, p. 48, Fig. 82). (Pit X 156).
7. (566). Fragment of curved bronze sheet, possibly scabbard edging. (X 200).
8. (490). Swaged bronze strip, possibly military. (X 153).
9. (426). Part of the binding from the scabbard of a gladius (cf. *Chichester Excavations 3*, Fig. 10.31, 22). (X 155).
10. (298). Decorative stud. (X 110).
11. (503). Rivet and washer with the remains of a thin iron sheet between. (X 105).
12. (355). Fragment of a bronze plate from the *cingulum*. (X 125). Not illustrated.

(b) Other Roman finds

13. (77). Bronze decorative plate with millefiore enamel. There are no signs of fixing rivets at the back, which is smooth except for several excresences which appear to be due to corrosion. It may well have been a panel set into the side or lid of a small wooden casket.

    The plate was examined and conserved by the Ancient Monuments Laboratory of the Department of the Environment, to whom thanks are due, and a report by Justine Bayley is filed with the Level 3 archive.

    The four main panels each contains 12 smaller panels incorporating two basic designs which are displayed alternately. Panel A (see Fig. 8.31), is a simple checkerboard panel with alternate blue and white squares, while Panel B comprises three lines of alternate blue and white segments set in a border which now appears black, but which Miss Bayley advises was probably red originally. It is difficult to be sure as the glass is very decayed. The pair of long thin fields at either end of the plate also contained enamel, but here it has decayed completely. The object cannot be dated closely as it was residual in a late Saxon pit.
14. (181). Surgical knife, of which only the bronze spatula handle remains (Pit X 83).
15. (389). Bronze terminal, possibly from a hairpin or a toilet instrument. (X 146).
16. (30). Cosmetic scoop. (Posthole X 9).

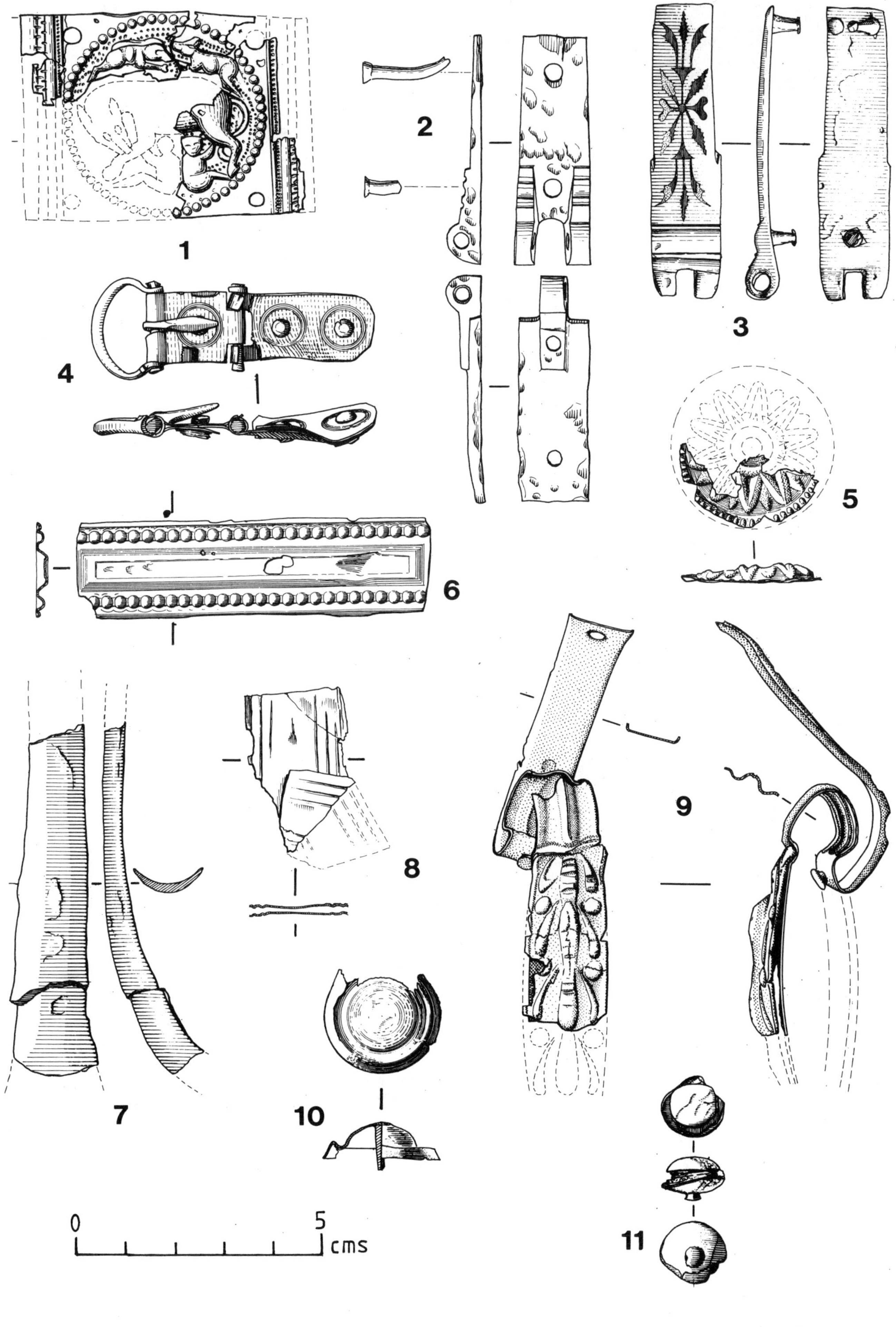

Fig. 8.30. Small finds from the N.W. Quadrant. Bronze; Nos. 1-11, Roman military equipment. ($\frac{1}{1}$)

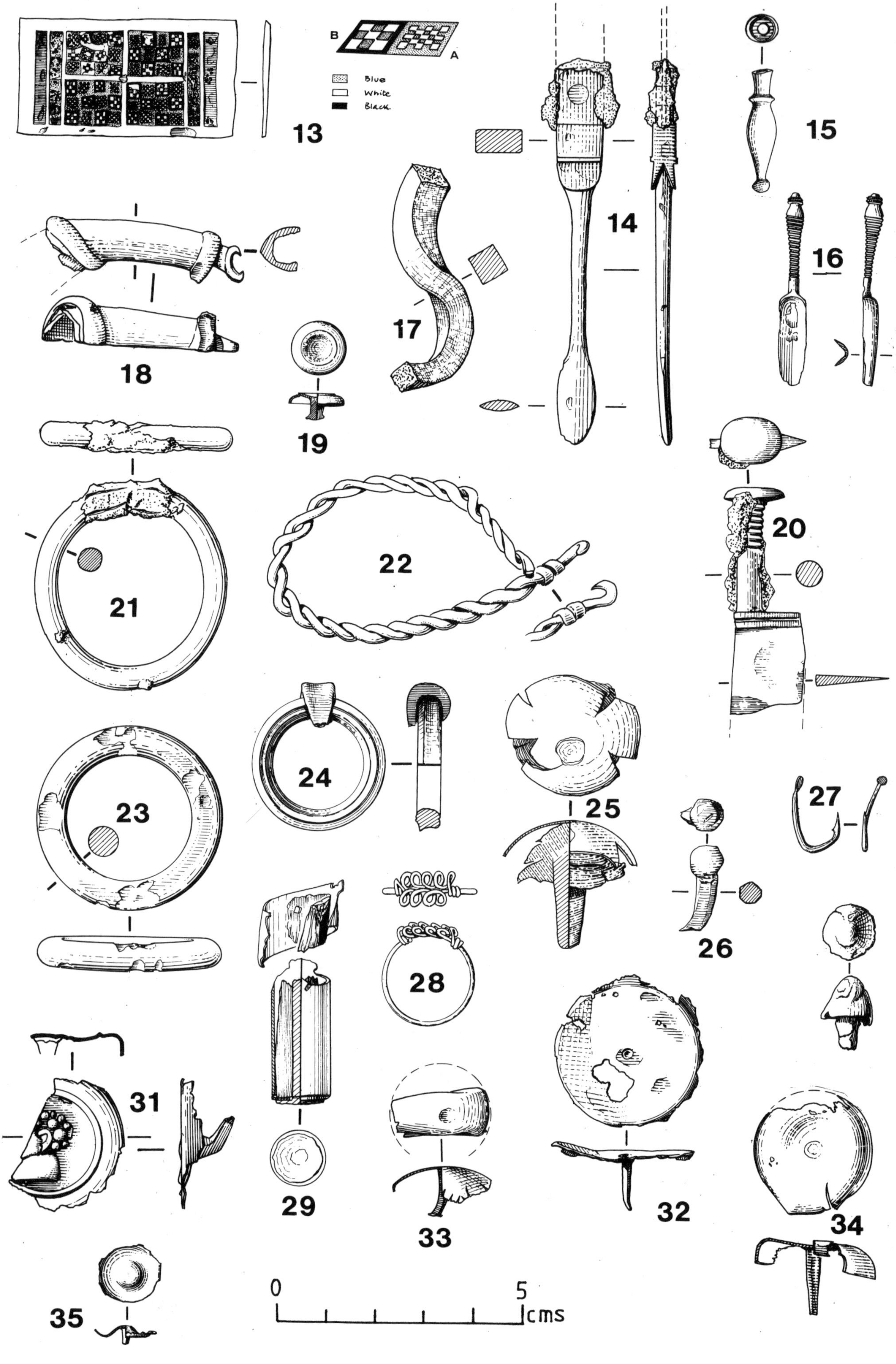

Fig. 8.31. Small finds from the N.W. Quadrant. Bronze; No. 31 ($\frac{2}{1}$); remainder ($\frac{1}{1}$). Roman.

17. (583). Square-sectioned cast bronze bar which has been twisted to form a hook. (X 184).
18. (205). Part of a cast bronze object, function unknown. (Posthole X 114).
19. (501). Decorative stud for leather. (X 132).
20. (541). Part of a bronze-handled, iron-bladed knife. (X 184).
21. (738). Harness ring. (P.19b).
22. (640). Twisted wire bangle. (Pit P. 28).
23. (719). Cast bronze harness ring. (Pit P.41b).
24. (382). Cast bronze ring attached to an iron shank used to fix it into wood. Probably for a cabinet drawer. (X 131).
25. (706). Large iron stud with bronze sheet covering the head. Probably from a door or chest. (P.11).
26. (573). Head of cast bronze pin. (X 19).
27. (219). Fish hook (X 3c).
28. (488). Twisted bronze wire ring. (X 148).
29. (563). Bronze ferrule secured to a wooden rod, part of which has survived. (Slot X 47).
30. (352). Stud. (X 131).
31. (187). Part of a decorative stud head, possibly an upholstery stud. (X 80).
32. (537). Upholstery tack. (X 165).
33. (444). Decorative stud. (X 133).
34. (699). Decorative stud. (P.21).
35. (524). Decorative stud. (X 144).
36. (731). Curved bronze plate. (Posthole P.60).
37. (170). Cast bronze hinge. (X 57).
38. (35). Small ring with rivet attachment. (X 12).
39. (496). Bell. (X 147).
40. (514). Fragment of plate with two pierced holes and cutaways, ? for attachment to leather. (X 144).
41. (497). Decorative fitting in the form of a lozenge, with a lead reinforcement. (X 167).
42. (330). Chain, manufactured from bronze sheet, punched, cut and folded into links. One fragment of a total length of *c.* 35 cm illustrated here. (X 110).
43. (692). Decorative bronze wire, ? part of a bangle. (P.18).
44. (468). Terminal from a snake's head bangle. (X 163).
45. (424). Shaft of a toilet instrument. (X 148).
46. (222). Unguent scoop. (X 19).
47. (273). Hairpin. (X 65).
48. (134). Hairpin with cast silver decorative head which is slotted, presumably for the attachment of a carved gemstone.
49. (380). Cast bronze terminal with the remnants of a square sectioned iron shank. Possibly a handle for a drawer. (X 139).
50. (289). Cast bronze ring. It might be a bangle, but there are no terminals. (X 39).
51. (548). Tube. (X 167).
52. (528). Part of a strap which has been rivetted to leather. (Pit X 159).
53. (72). Decorative strip, probably originally part of a bracelet. (Pit X 57).

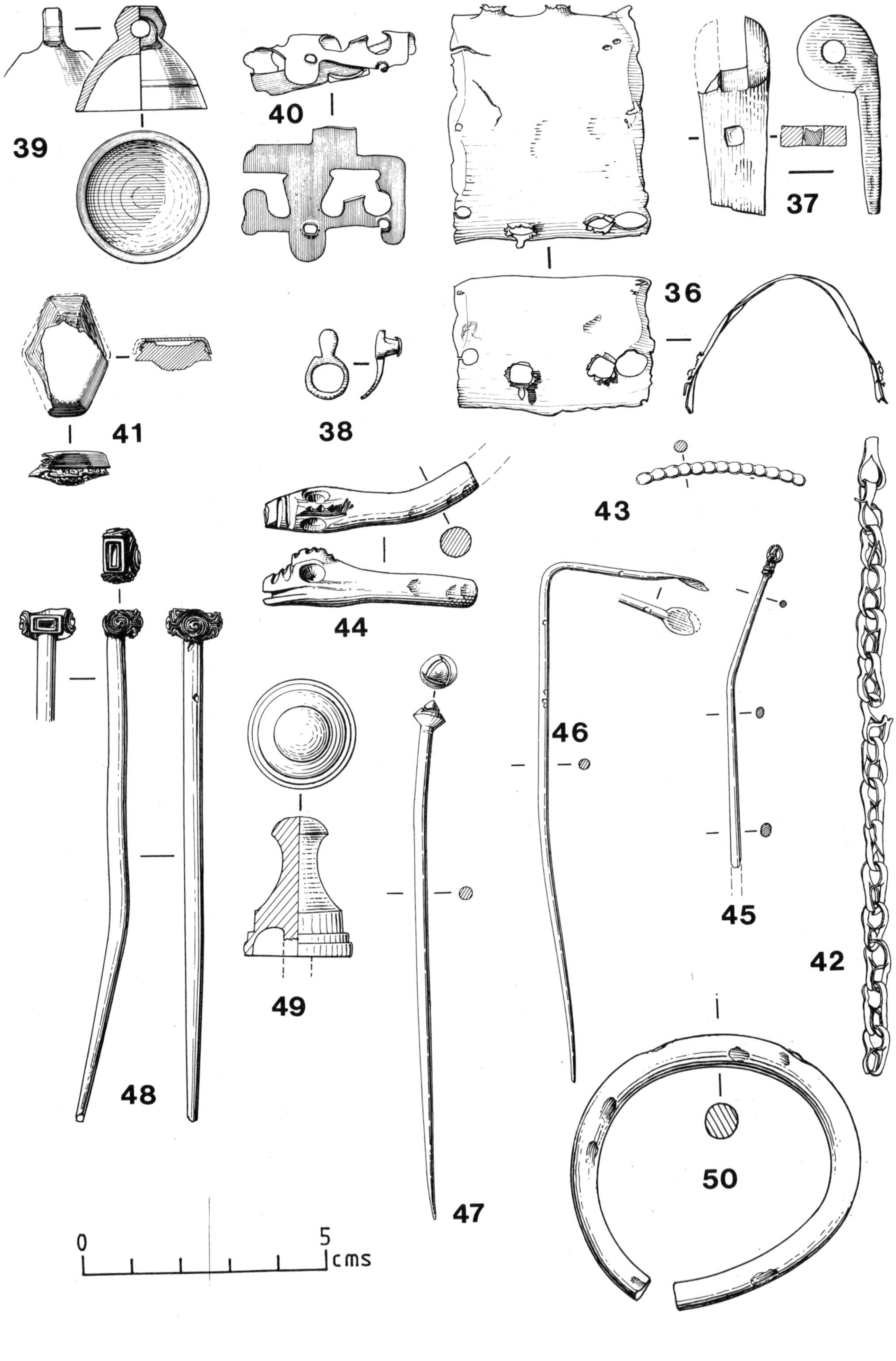

Fig. 8.32. Small finds from the N.W. Quadrant. Bronze, Nos. 36-50, ($\frac{1}{1}$). Roman.

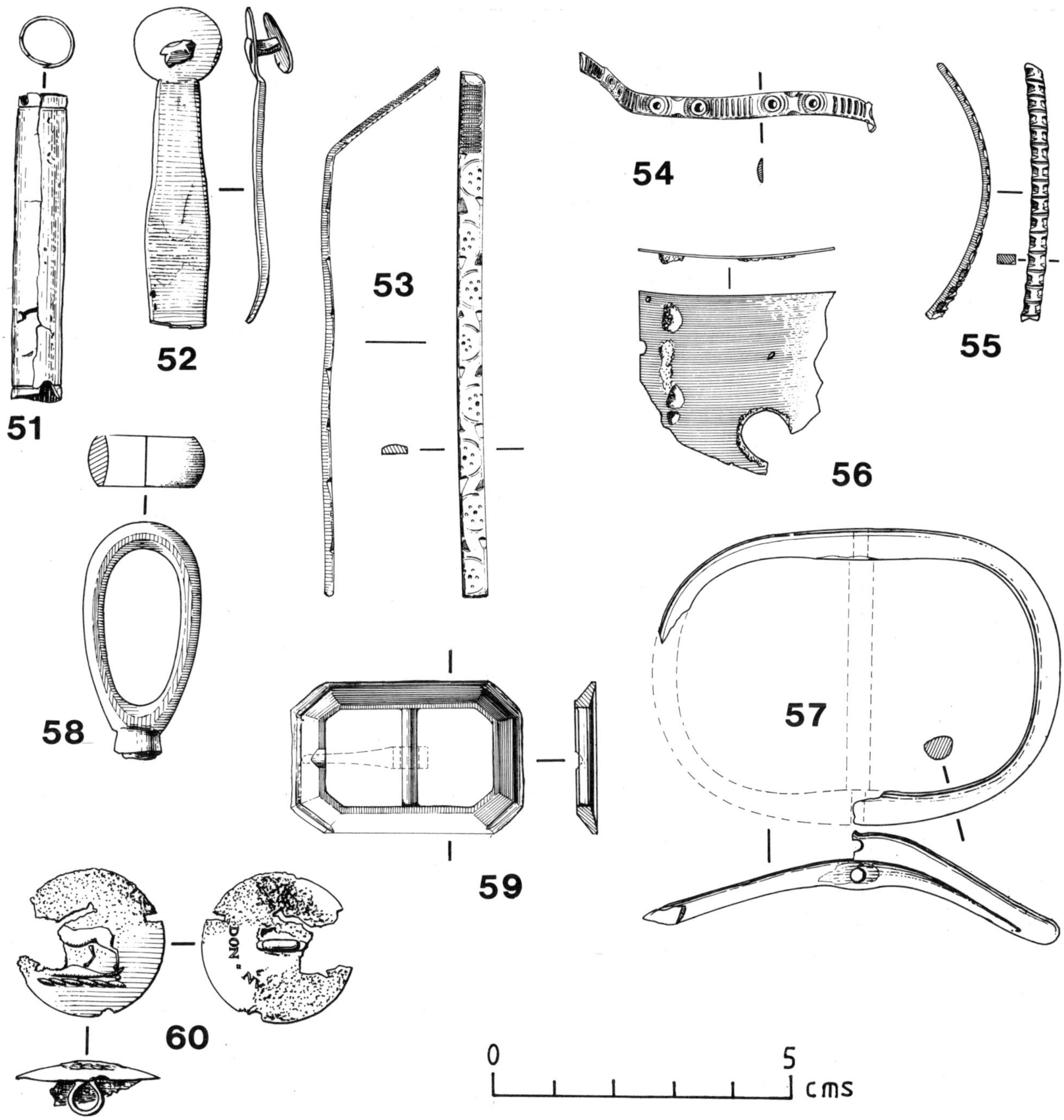

Fig. 8.33. Small finds from the N.W. Quadrant. Bronze; Nos. 51-56, Roman, Nos. 57-60, post medieval. All $(\frac{1}{1})$

54. (268). Part of a bangle (unstratified).
55. (246). Bangle. (X 69).
56. (527). Fragment of a rectangular bronze tinned mirror. (X 151).

(c) Post-medieval finds

57. (745). Shoe buckle, ? 17th century. (P.2).
58. (609). Cast bronze loop end, probably from a pair of tongs. (P.2).
59. (620). Cast bronze belt buckle. (Pit P.11).
60. (6). Bronze button with the design of a stag or horse upon it and the makers mark DON. NV on reverse. (X 1). Probably 18th or 19th century.

References

CHICHESTER 1 — Down, A. and Rule, M., *Chichester Excavations* 1; 1971.

CHICHESTER 3 — Down, A., *Chichester Excavations 3*, 1978.

CHICHESTER 4 — Down, A., *Chichester Excavations 4,* 1979.

FISHBOURNE II — Cunliffe, B. W., *Excavations at Fishbourne*; Vol. II, The Finds. Society of Antiquaries Research Report, No. XXVII, 1971.

ROBINSON 1975 — Robinson, H. Russell, *The Armour of Imperial Rome*; London, 1975.

ULBERT 1970. — Ulbert, Gunter; *Das Romische Donai-Kastell Ritstissen*, Teil 1, Stuttgart, 1970.

A Gladius from Chichester (Fig. 8.28, No. 1)

by Graham Webster

This sword, a *gladius* used normally by the legionaries of the early Imperial Roman army, was found at Chichester in the Chapel Street excavations of 1977. It came from the early military occupation which in this area takes the form of timber buildings on almost a north-south axis. It now seems evident from excavations in other parts of the town that there was a large military establishment here in the first period of the Roman conquest, and this could have been a legionary fortress in the Plautian phase (i.e., A.D. 43-48), before the westward advance under Ostorius Scapula, when the legion was presumably moved to Exeter.

The sword, in excellent condition when lost, is slightly waisted, the maximum width being 60 mm, and 55 mm at the waist; the blade is 520 mm long and the tang 15.4 mm, the tip being bent over. In his classic paper on the *gladii* from Pompeii,[1] Professor Ulbert lists two main types:

1. The Pompeian;
2. The Mainz.

The differences between these two types is basically in their shape, the Mainz type having a much longer point, giving it the appearance of a large dagger and well exemplified by one from Rheingonheim[2] with a 590 mm long blade and a shape like a very elongated triangle. The blades of the Pompeian types on the other hand are rectangular with short triangle points. This may not be a valid classification, since so much depends on the grinding and sharpening during the life of the sword, and which would tend to re-shape this blade and the point. On the other hand, there are hardly two identical blades which also throws some doubt on these basic divisions.

To the twenty-three swords listed by Ulbert, must be added the fine example of type 2 found at Mainz in 1971-72,[3] the blade of which is 620 mm long and the tang 15 mm and totally lacks a waist. The British examples are two from Newstead[4] both of the Pompaeian type and one from the Thames at Fulham of the Mainz type[5] which has the same blade length as the Chichester example, is slightly waisted but has a larger point.

The Chichester sword is finely proportioned and its long point would classify it as a Mainz type. There is no indication of the presence of a scabbard or hilt and it has the appearance of being an unused blade, perhaps lost when removing or transferring stores.

Unfortunately, not enough of the plan of the timber structure with which it was associated was uncovered to make a positive identification of its function. It seems to have been in the south-east corner of a large building, rather than a normal barrack block.

Notes

1. *Germania* 47 (1969), 97–128.
2. Günter Ulbert, *Das Frühromische Kastell Rheingönheim; Limesforschungen*, 9, 1969, Taf. 32.
3. von Helmut Schoppa. "Ein Gladius von Typus Pompeji", *Germania* 52 (1974), 102–108.
4. J. Curle, *A Roman Frontier Post and its People*, 1911, Pl. XXXI, Nos. 11 and 13.
5. *Antiquities of Roman Britain*, 1951, Fig. 36, No. 5.

The Chapel Street Intaglio (Plate 19 a & b)

by Martin Henig

The new intaglio, convex, oval, 17 mm by 13 mm by 3 mm, superior in style to most others yet unearthed in Britain, is cut on green chalcedony (plasma). Only sixteen other gems from the province are composed of this attractive but somewhat scarce stone, and of these, three (*Henig* 1978, Nos. 33, 96, 103), were certainly engraved in the third century A.D. The remainder are earlier and in fact none of them is likely to have been lost after the Antonine age. Sena Chiesa (1966, 54) dates her "Officina dei Prasii" to the beginning of the first century A.D., but the present author (*Henig* 1978, 33) has supported a Flavian attribution for many plasmas, and he seems to be followed in his views by Maaskant-Kleibrink (1978, 196–8). Nevertheless, it is plain that plasma was extensively used in the Augustan period, and at least two of the British intagli, a bust of the Moon-goddess (*Henig* 1978, No. App. 64), and the Chichester gem (No. App. 108), may be assigned to the end of the first century B.C.

It was noted by*Fossing* (1929, 24), that gem-cutters liked to use plasma when they were engraving subjects of a classicising nature such as representations of statues. Many of our examples from Britain fall into this category. Thus we have a Diana Venatrix (*Henig* 1978, No. 254), a Victory holding a wreath and palm (No. 295), a Nemesis with her wheel (No. App. 144), two representations of Methe, the personification of drunkeness (Nos. 343 and 345), Meleager with his hound (No. 453) and Leda seated on a throne (No. App. 146). In addition there are two cupids, one putting on a greave (no. 115), and the other shooting a bow (No. 135), both loosely related to sculptural types. The remaining stones show a lion seated beneath a tree (No. App. 220), certainly classicising in the power and dignity of its composition, a dolphin and trident (No. 649) and a little bird (No. 671). The last is of some interest to us as it was found in an early level at Fishbourne.

Perhaps plasma was chosen as a suitable material for intagli of high quality because it was used as a substitute for the emerald (*smaragdus*) to which Pliny assigns a place immediately after diamond and pearl (*Pliny N H* XXXVII, 62 ff), because "of all colours, green is the most pleasing to the eye". However, he goes on to say that by general consent emeralds themselves are not cut as intagli but preserved in their natural state.

The plasma (*prasius*) is much commoner, but although Pliny mentions its green colour, presumably a strong point in its favour, he does not provide any further discussion (*Pliny N H* XXXVII, 113). The implication is that it was a gem which would, as a matter of course, be cut as a seal.

The device is a satyr, distinguished as such by his equine tail, seated on a low projection, probably a stone. His body is in profile (to the right on an impression) but his head is turned as though to confront the spectator. Apart from his fawn-skin (*nebris*) draped over his left shoulder on the far side of his body, the satyr is nude. In front of him are two flutes leaning against a high rock: each is carefully detailed, an ovoid bulb or holmos being shown below its mouth-piece and five projections, possibly side-tubes as Angela Wardle (1978, 377) suggests, branch from its side. These pipes could be played either singly, as by the satyr portrayed on a rock-crystal plaque in Detroit (*Ross* 1947, 110, No. 535, Pl. lxxiii) or as a pair (*Henig* 1978, No. 179).

As pointed out in my *Antiquaries Journal* note (*Henig* 1978 a[1]), the detailed and careful representation is close to that of some of the gems cut by Augustan court gem engravers, and I singled out the work of Sostratos and Dioskourides in particular; furthermore the type can be related to the resting satyr on rare denarii struck by the moneyer P. Petronius Turpilianus in about 19 B.C. The art of the Augustan age was to a large degree dependent on earlier Greek works of the late fifth and of the fourth centuries and it is perhaps to the beginning of the Hellenistic period that we should look for the conception of our gem and especially to the work of Lysippos. Certainly, as Martin Robertson says (1975, 473) "a figure seated informally on stool or rock, as against the four-square enthroned figure of earlier times, becomes a favourite in this period". That there was such a prototype is virtually proved by the existence of a late Etruscan scarab, dated to the end of the fourth-century which also shows a seated satyr (*Zažoff* 1968, 108, III, Pl. xl).

Although the satyr on the Chichester gem is clean-shaven, I have suggested that, like the figure on the Sostratos cameo, the subject is Marsyas after his defeat in a musical contest with Apollo (*Henig* 1978a, 376). An intaglio in the Georgian State Museum at Tbilisi (*Lordkipanidze* 1967, 86, No. 21) shows the same bearded Silenus with his double flutes as appears on the cameo and in front of him for good measure is shown the tree on which the unfortunate creature will be suspended and flayed. There is no denying the fact that when this gem is compared with the one from Chichester the poses of the figures, their turned heads and worried expressions are the same. In each case the flutes have been laid aside as useless. For the owners of our intaglio the myth could have suggested a variety of morals ranging from the avoidance of *hubris* to a love of liberty which is prepared, in the last resort, to challenge overwhelming and inexorable forces. We must not, of course, forget that although it was cut some decades before the invasion, its final resting place was in a late Roman context. Nevertheless, I believe that it probably came to Chichester in the middle decades of the first century A.D. Incidentally, another intaglio which I have recently recognised as a masterpiece from a metropolitan studio—a cornelian showing cupid holding a bow—was excavated in a residual context at Winchester, another early urban centre of Romanisation in Britain (information M. Biddle). I would like to thank Alec Down, Aidan Cooper (the finder), Alison Macaulay, Tania Tinkoff-Utechin and Robert Wilkins for assistance in various ways. while working on this intaglio.

1. The black jasper, formerly in the Marlborough Collection, referred to here may not be antique and certainly the inscription seems to be spurious (Zwierlein-Diehl 1979, 33, No. 624).

References

FOSSING, P. — *The Thorvaldsen Museum. Catalogue of the Antique Engraved Gems and Cameos,* Copenhagen 1929.

HENIG, M. 1978 — *A Corpus of Roman Engraved Gemstones from British Sites,* BAR 8—second edn. 1978.

HENIG, M. 1978a — "A Roman intaglio from Chichester", *Antiq. Journ.* LVIII, 1978, 374, 376f.
LORDKIPANIDZE, M. N. — *Gemmy Gosudarstvennogo Muzeia Gruzii, IV, Katalog* - Gems of the Georgian State Museum, IV, Catalogue, Tbilisi 1967.
MAASKANT-KLEIBRINK, M. — *Catalogue of the Engraved Gems in the Royal Coin Cabinet, The Hague, The Greek, Etruscan and Roman Collections*, The Hague 1978.
ROBERTSON, M. — *A History of Greek Art*, Cambridge 1975.
ROSS, M. C. — *Early Christian and Byzantine Art. An Exhibition held at the Baltimore Museum of Art*, Baltimore 1947.
SENA CHIESA, G. — *Gemme del Museo Nazionale di Aquileia*, Padua 1966.
WARDLE, A. — "A note on the tibiae" in *Henig* 1978a.
ZAZOFF, P. — *Etruskische Skarabäen*, Mainz 1968.
ZWIERLEIN-DIEHL, E. — *Die Antiken Gemmen Des Kunsthistorischen in Wien II*, Munich 1979.

Pottery from the North-West Quadrant

Fig. 8.34

Atrebatic and "overlap" wares

1. Rim of small bowl; sandy fabric with a few small grits. (Slot P. 13).
2. Lid; similar fabric to 1 but no grits (from P.38, the earliest occupation layer in Area 9).
3. Jar; handmade and finished on a slow wheel. Lumpy exterior finish with a burnished zone over and below rim. Probably earlier than 1 and 2, *c.* late 1st century B.C. (X 155).

Miscellaneous Roman wares

4. Rusticated beaker in an oxidised fine red fabric with a white slip coating over the body below the shoulder, which is left red. This is a product of the Chapel Street kilns and is a larger and more complete example of the one previously published (cf. *Chichester Excavations 3*; Fig. 10.3, 21 and Fig. 10.6, 1). (Pit X 171).
5. Rouletted bowl in a fine grey fabric oxidised red. Possibly a product of the Chapel Street kilns (X 78).
6. Neck of a large flagon or bottle in a hard grey ware with a metallic grey slip over the neck and rim (X 35).
7. Rim of a small cup in a fine pinky cream ware with an exterior buff slip (X 36).
8. Flat rimmed bowl in fine grey fabric (X 190);
9. Bowl in a very fine pale grey micaceous fabric, burnished surfaces reduced black (Pit X 133).
10. Bowl in a fine sandy fabric (X 155).
11. Body sherd from a storage jar in a very fine pink/buff ware.

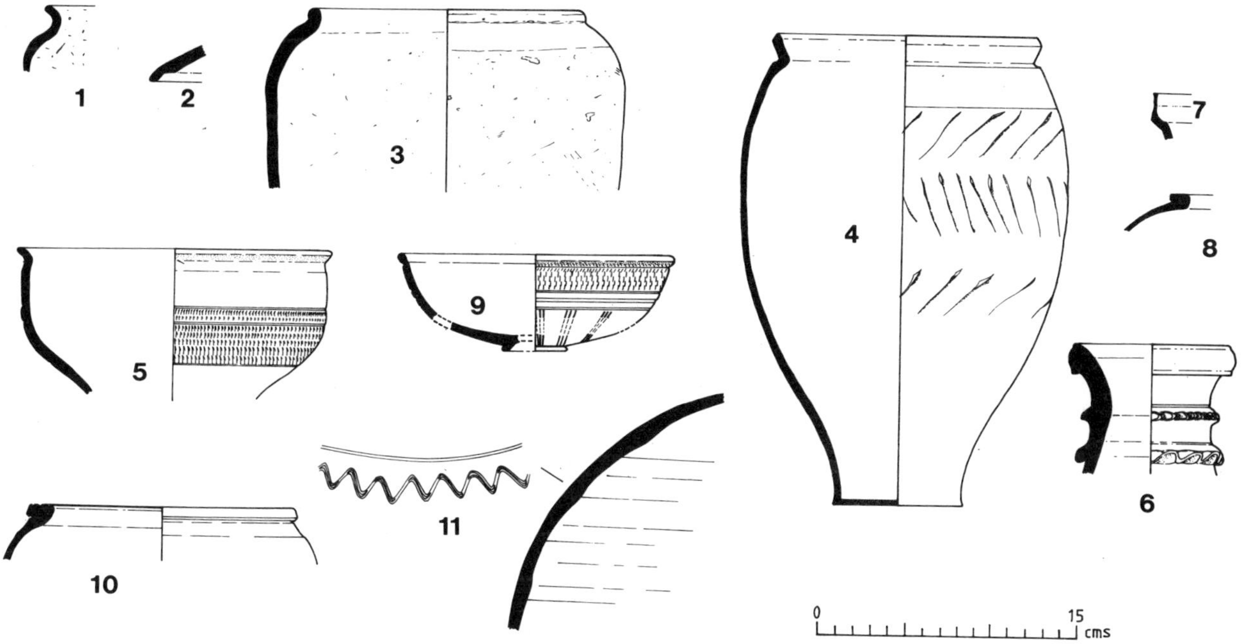

Fig. 8.34. Pottery from the N.W. Quadrant. Nos. 1-3; Atrebatic overlap wares, Nos. 4-11; Miscellaneous Roman wares. (¼)

Fig. 8.35

The pottery from Pit P.28

Note. This pit was a late Roman timber-lined well, and a representative selection of the coarse and fine wares is published here.

1. Flanged bowl, handmade and finished on a slow wheel. The fabric is hard, poorly levigated and reduced to a pale grey. The interior and exterior surfaces are lumpy and have been roughly burnished with the fingers.
2. Flanged bowl; fine grey sandy ware with black metallic slip inside and over rim.
3. Flanged bowl; similar fabric to 1.
4. Flanged bowl, very over fired black fabric.
5. Flanged bowl in hard grey ware.
6. Dish with handle; fine light-grey sandy ware, interior and exterior surfaces reduced black and burnished.
7. Small dish with handles; coarse sandy fabric reduced black. Interior roughly polished.
8. Shallow dish; similar fabric to 1.
9. Lid; hard sandy fabric reduced black.
10. Jar, coarse sandy ware reduced black; burnished above lattice decoration.
11. Necked jar with flattened cordon; similar fabric to 10; burnished on neck and shoulder.

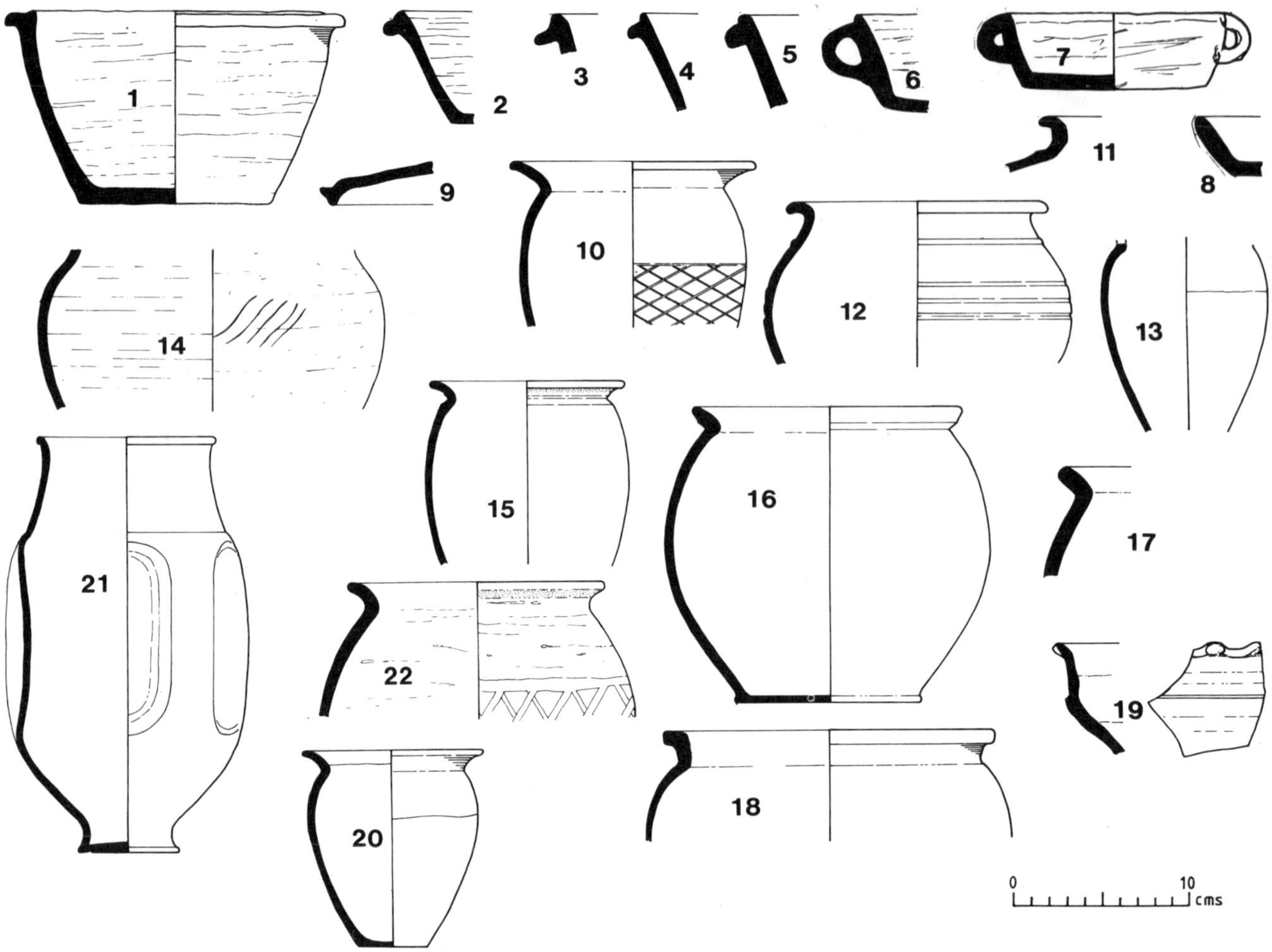

Fig. 8.35. Pottery from the N.W. Quadrant; Nos. 1-22; Pit P.28, Roman grey wares. (¼)

12. Cordoned jar in a very fine grey ware.
13. Beaker with burnished shoulder; fine sandy fabric.
14. Body sherd from a large jar with traces of rusticated decoration. The fabric is burnt black.
15. Jar in fine sandy ware.
16. Cooking pot in fine grey sandy fabric.
17. Cooking pot in similar fabric to 16.
18. Necked jar in a fine white fabric with a white slip coating over the rim and exterior surface.
19. Rim of a tazza in fine cream ware (cf. *Chichester Excavations 1*; Fig. 5.19, 14 G).
20. Complete beaker in fine grey ware with a glossy black slip on shoulder and over rim.
21. Large indented beaker in a fine sandy fabric.
22. Jar in a sandy grey ware.

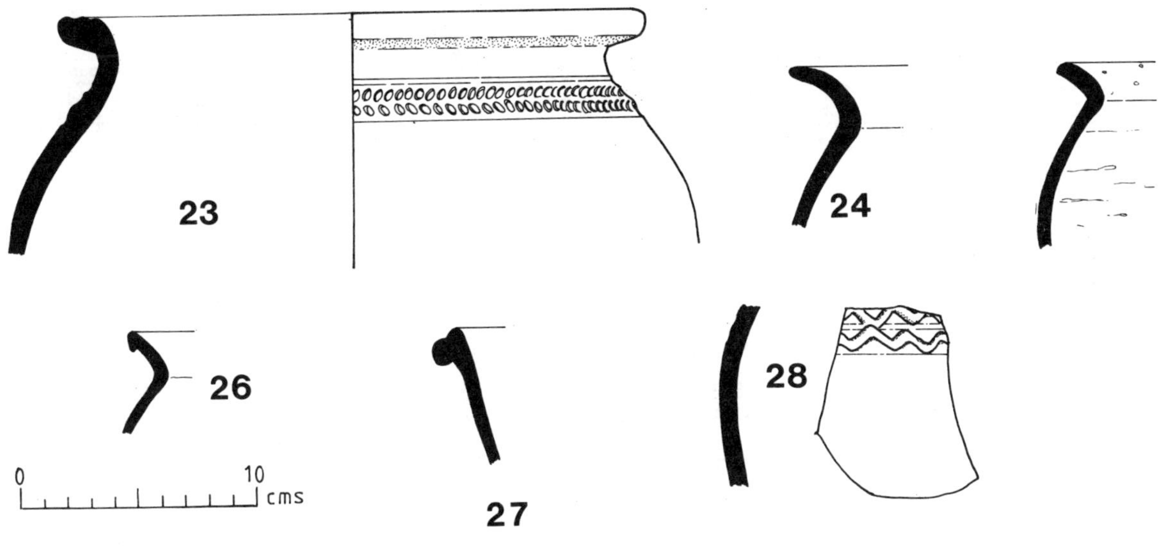

Fig. 8.36. Pottery from the N.W. Quadrant; Nos. 23-28, Pit X 49, Roman grey wares, (app. ¼)

Summary of other wares and finds

(i) *Colour-coated wares.* See Dr. Young's report below (p. 286).

(ii) *Samian (all residual).* A total of 22 vessels represented, the latest being late Antonine.

(iii) *Other finds.* The small finds from the pit totalled 47 of which the majority were objects of iron (see Fig. 8.28). There were 14 coins, the latest being of Valens (see pp. 180-183).

Fig. 8.36

The pottery from Pit X 49

23. Storage jar with pecked cordon, hard sandy grey fabric.
24. Rim of large cooking pot, dark grey fabric tempered with coarse sand; reduced slate grey.
25. Cooking pot with a hard sandy fabric.
26. Jar with a hooked rim; fine grey sandy ware.
27. Flanged bowl, burnished and white-slipped over rim and interior surface. Fine grey sandy ware.
28. Body sherd from a jar in fine sandy grey ware; white-slipped surface below a zone of wavy line decoration.

Summary of other wares

(i) *Samian.* Eight vessels represented, none later than late 1st–2nd century. All residual.

(ii) *Colour coated wares.* See Dr. Young's report below. The latest dated of these is post A.D. 270.

(iii) *Coarse wares.* In addition to those illustrated, 20 other vessels were represented. Of these, 10 were in fine grey ware and 6 in a coarse sandy fabric burnt black. Two of these were also grogged with small lumps of chalk.

THE ROMAN COINS FROM THE NORTH-WEST QUADRANT—compiled by Roger Lintott

Find No.	Denomination	Emperor and date	Reverse type	Mint mark	Date of coin	Ref. No.	Notes
493	Ae Ses.	Agrippia	S C		A.D. 23–32	RIC (Tib)32	Layer X167
409	Ae As	Agrippina Senr w. of Germanicvs	Memoriae Agrippinae		A.D. 37–41	RIC (Cal)42	Layer X117
421	Ae As	Germanicvs	S C		A.D. 37–41	RIC (Cal)42	Layer X155
579	Ae Dup.	Germanicvs	Signus recept Divictis Germ.		A.D. 37–41	RIC (Cal) p119	Layer X167
556	Ae Ses.	Claudius A.D. 41–54	Spes Augusta	Rome	A.D. 41–54	RIC 64	Layer X151
287	Ae As, copy	Claudius A.D. 41–54	Minerva type				Layer X65 contemporary forgery
423	Ae As, copy	Claudius A.D. 41–54	Minerva type				Layer X148 contemporary forgery
447	Ae As, copy	Claudius A.D. 41–54	Minerva type				Layer X148 contemporary forgery
568	Ae As copy	Nero A.D. 54–68	S C		A.D. 54–68		Layer X136
696	Ae Dup	Nero A.D. 54–68			A.D. 54–68		Layer P8
603	Ae As	Vespasian A.D. 69–79	Provident	Lugdunum	A.D. 77–78	RIC 763	Layer P2
247	Ae Dup or As	Vespasian A.D. 69–79			A.D. 69–79		Layer X19
358	Ae Ses	Domitian A.D. 81–96	S C	Rome	A.D. 86	RIC 318	Layer X129
166	Ae As or Dup	Domitian A.D. 81–96			A.D. 86		Slot X10
155	Ae As	Domitian A.D. 81–96	Virtuti Augusti	Rome	A.D. 87	RIC 351	Slot X4
279	Ae As	Domitian A.D. 81–96	Virtuti Augusti	Rome	A.D. 92–96	RIC 409	Layer X65
26	Ae As	Trajan A.D. 98–117			A.D. 98–117		Pit X46
121	Ae Ses	Hadrian A.D. 117–138			A.D. 117–138		Layer X3
341	Ae Ses	Hadrian A.D. 117–138			A.D. 117–138		Layer X43
600	Ae Ses	Hadrian A.D. 117–138			A.D. 117–138		Layer P1
351	Ar Den.	Hadrian A.D. 117–138	Fortuna	Rome	A.D. 134–138	RIC 244	Layer X72
263	Ae Dup	Faustina Senr	Aeternitas		*c.* A.D. 141	RIC 1155	Layer X69
104	Ae Dup or As	Antoninus Pius A.D. 138–161	Security		A.D. 138–161		Layer X9
248	Ae Dup or As	Faustina Junr, w of M. Aurelius			A.D. 138–161		Struck under Ant. Pius. Layer X19
112	Ae Dup or As	Faustina Junr, w. of M. Aurelius			A.D. 138–161		Struck under Ant. Pius. Layer X1
96B	Ae Ses	Marcus Aurelius A.D. 161–180			A.D. 161–180		Pit X56A
210	Ar Den.	Julia Soaemias	Venus Caelestis		A.D. 218–222	RIC 243	Struck under Elagabalus. Layer X1.
66	Ae As or Dup.	Philip I, A.D. 244–239			A.D. 244–249		Pit X29
22	Ae Ant.	Gallienus A.D. 253–268			A.D. 253–268		Layer X1
610	Ae Ant.	Gallienus A.D. 253–268			A.D. 253–268		Layer P2
203	Ae Br	Gallienus type			A.D. 253–268		Layer X1
81	Ae Ant.	Valerian I, A.D. 253–260	Sol	Lugdunum	A.D. 258–9	RIC 12	
27	Ae Ant.	Victorinus A.D. 268–270			A.D. 268–270		Layer X1
103	Ae Ant.	Tetricvs I A.D. 270–3	Hilaritas		A.D. 270–3		Pit X51
10	Ae Ant.	Tetricvs I A.D. 270–3	Pax		A.D. 270–3		X unstratified
40	Ae Ant.	Tetricvs I A.D. 270–3			A.D. 270–3		Pit X42
631	Ae Ant.	Tetricvs II A.D. 270–3	Spes		A.D. 270–3		Layer P13
80	Ae Ant.	Tetricvs II A.D. 270–3	Hilaritas		A.D. 220–31		Pit X56
115	Ae Ant.	Claudius II A.D. 268–270	Large altar type		A.D. 268–70		Pit X39
23	Ae Ant.	Claudius II A.D. 268–270	Large altar type		A.D. 268–70		
689	Barb. Rad.	Tetricvs I type			*c.* A.D. 270–3		Pit P34
90	Barb. Rad.	Tetricvs II type			*c.* A.D. 270–3		Pit X52
621	Barb. Rad.	Tetricvs II type			*c.* A.D. 270–3		Pit P21
626	Barb. Rad.	Tetricvs II type			*c.* A.D. 270–3		Pit P3
11	Barb. Rad.	Claudius II type	Large altar type		*c.* A.D. 270–3		Layer X1
200	Ae Ant.	Claudius II A.D. 268–270	Large altar type		A.D. 268–270		Layer X1

Find No.	Denomination	Emperor and date	Reverse type	Mint mark	Date of coin	Ref. No.	Notes
173	Ae Ant.	Claudius II A.D. 268–270	Large altar type		A.D. 268–270		Layer X57
134	Ae Ant.	Carausius A.D. 287–293	Pax		A.D. 287–293		Pit X48
650	Ae Ant.	Carausius A.D. 287–293	Moneta	S/C / Camulodunum	A.D. 290–293	RIC 469	Pit P28B
94	Ae Ant.	Carausius A.D. 287–293			A.D. 290–293	RIC 469	Pit X56A
440	Ae Ant.	Allectus A.D. 293–296	Laetita Aug	S/A / ? London	A.D. 293–296		Imp Allectus PF Aug. Not in RIC Layer X132
619	Ae 2	Constantine I A.D. 306–337	Sol	1 / PTR Trier	A.D. 310–311	RIC 900	Layer P2
89	Ae Follis	Constantine I A.D. 306–337	Sol	T/F / PTS Trier	A.D. 313–315	RIC 40	Layer X26
46	Ae 3	Constantine I A.D. 306–337	G.E. 2 std	1 / TRS Trier	A.D. 330–331	RIC 520	Layer X29
156	Ae 3	Constantine I A.D. 306–337	G.E. 2 std	1 / TRP Trier	A.D. 330–331	RIC 526	Layer X57
192	Ae 3	Constantine I A.D. 306–337	G.E. 2 std	1 / TRP Trier	A.D. 332–333	RIC 538	Large S in obv Legend. Unstratified
97	Ae 4	Constantine I A.D. 306–337	G.E. 1 std		A.D. 336–341		Layer X1
559C	Ae 3	Constantine II A.D. 317–340	G.E. 2 std.	1 / TRP Trier	A.D. 330–331	RIC 527	Layer X29
34	Ae 4	Constantine II A.D. 306–337	G.E. 1 std.		A.D. 336–341		Layer X23
38	Ae 3	Constans A.D. 333–350	G.E. 2 std	1 / RXP Rome	A.D. 335–336	RIC 367	Layer X35
99	Ae 4	Constans A.D. 333–350	G.E. 1 std.	1 / TRS Trier	A.D. 335–337	RIC 593	Layer X29
120	Ae 4	Constans A.D. 333–350	G.E. 1 std	1 / TRP Trier	A.D. 335–337	LRBC 90	Layer X19
48	Ae 3	Constans A.D. 333–350	2 Victories	Trier	A.D. 341–346	LBRC 158–160	Layer X35
64	Ae 3	Constans A.D. 333–350	2 Victories		A.D. 341–346		Layer X14
29	Ae 3	Constantius II A.D. 324–361	G.E. 1 std	G / PARL Arelate	A.D. 337–341	LBRC 442–3	Layer X1
101	Ae 4	Constantius II A.D. 324–361	G.E. 1 std		A.D. 336–341		Layer X9
701	Ae 4	Constantius II A.D. 324–361	G.E. 1 std.		A.D. 336–341		Layer P21
24	Ae Cent	Constantius II A.D. 324–361	Phoenix on globe	1 / TRS Trier	A.D. 346–350	LRBC 39	Unworn. Layer X1
37	Ae 4	House of Constantine	G.E. 1 std.		A.D. 336–341		Layer X9
87	Ae 3	House of Constantine	G.E. 1 std.		A.D. 336–341		Pit X43
169	Ae 4	House of Constantine	G.E. 1 std.		A.D. 336–341		Layer X57
326	Ae 4	House of Constantine	G.E. 1 std.		A.D. 336–341		Layer X110

THE ROMAN COINS FROM THE NORTH-WEST QUADRANT—*continued*

Find No.	Denomination	Emperor and date	Reverse type	Mint mark	Date of coin	Ref. No.	Notes
33	Ae 4	House of Constantine	2 victories		A.D. 341–346		Layer X22
117	Ae 3	House of Constantine	2 victories		A.D. 341–346		Layer X57
607	Ae 3	Urbs Roma	Wolf and twins	U / P Const Arles	A.D. 331	RIC 356	Layer P2
637	Ae 3	Urbs Roma	Wolf and twins	Trier	A.D. 333–334	RIC 561	Pit P28
158	Ae 4	Urbs Roma	Wolf and twins		A.D. 330–335		Layer X57
54	Ae 3	Urbs Roma	Wolf and twins		A.D. 330–335		Pit X45
21	Ae 4	Constantinopolis	Victory on prow	1 / PLG Lyons	A.D. 330–331	RIC 241	Layer X12
76	Ae 3	Constantinopolis	Victory on prow	1 / TRP Trier	A.D. 330–331	RIC 523	Pit X57
96A	Ae 3	Constantinopolis	Victory on prow	1 / TRP* Trier	A.D. 332–333	RIC 543	Pit X 56A
82	Ae 3	Constantinopolis	Victory on prow	Trier	A.D. 333–334	RIC 554	Pit X56
52	Ae 4	Constantinopolis	Victory on prow	1 / PLG Lugdunum	A.D. 335–337	LRBC 225	Pit X 29B
123	Ae 4	Constantinopolis	Victory on prow		A.D. 330–335		Pit X62
153	Ae 3	Constantinopolis	Victory on prow		A.D. 330–335		Layer X15
477	Ae 4	Constantinopolis	Victory on prow		A.D. 330–335		Layer X80
114	Ae 4	Helena, w. of Constantius	Pax Publica		A.D. 337–340		Layer X1
608	Ae 4	Helena, w. of Constantius	Pax Publica		A.D. 337–341		Layer P2
702	Ae 4	Helena, w. of Constantius	Pax Publica		A.D. 337–341		Layer P11
132	Ae 4	Theodora, 2nd w. of Constantius	Pietas Romana	1 / TRP Trier	A.D. 337–341	LRBC 113	Layer X26
79	Ae Cent.	Magnentius, A.D. 350–353	Felicitas Republicae	1 / TRS Trier	A.D. 350–351	LRBC 49	Pit X57
55	Ae Cent.	Magnentius, A.D. 350–353	2 victories	1 / TRP Trier	A.D. 351–353	LRBC 56	Pit X64
611	Ae Cent.	Magnentius, A.D. 350–353	2 victories	1 / AMB Amiens	A.D. 351–353	LRBC 5	Layer P2
105	Ae 18 mm. barb.	Magnentius, A.D. 350–353	2 victories		A.D. 351–353		Layer X20
102	Ae Cent.	Decentius, A.D. 351–353	2 victories	P / AMBU Amiens	A.D. 351–353	LRBC 14	Unworn. Pit X51
65	Minim	Fallen horseman type					Unstratified
148	Minim	Fallen horseman type					Layer X60
615	Minim	Fallen horseman type					Layer P2
638	Minim	Fallen horseman type					Pit P28a
147	Minim	Hut type					Layer X60
140	Ae 3	Valentinian I, A.D. 364–375	Salus Republicae		A.D. 364–375		Layer X1

THE ROMAN COINS FROM THE NORTH-WEST QUADRANT—*continued*

Find No.	Denomination	Emperor and date	Reverse type	Mint mark	Date of coin	Ref. No.	Notes
57	Ae 3	Valens, A.D. 364–378	S.R.	OF/11 / CON* Arelate	A.D. 367–375	RIC 173?	Pit X29
642	Ae 3	Valens, A.D. 364–378	S.R.	OF/11 / CO-- Arelate	A.D. 364–375		Pit P28B
694	Ae 3	Valens, A.D. 364–378	S.R.	OF/11 / CON- Arelate	A.D. 364–375		Layer P18
622	Ae 3	Gratian, A.D. 367–383	S.R.	OF/1 / LUG- Lugdunum	A.D. 367–375	RIC 21B	Pit P17
9	Ae 3	Gratian, A.D. 367–383	G.N.S.	1 / CON Arelate	A.D. 367–375		Pit X3A
126	Ae 3	Gratian, A.D. 367–383	VOT/XV/MULT/XX	1 / LUGP Lugdunum	A.D. 378–383	RIC 30A	Posthole X102
25	Ae 4	Valentinian II, A.D. 375–392	Salus Republicae	P1 / Aquileia	A.D. 388–393	RIC 58 A–D	

ABBREVIATIONS

Ae	Copper, bronze or orichalcum.	Fol	Follis.
Ae 1	coin diameter from 25 mm.	G.N.S.	Gloria Novi Saeculi.
Ae 2	coin diameter from 21 mm.	G.R.	Gloria Romanorum.
Ae 3	coin diameter from 17 mm.	G.E. (1 or 2 stds)	Gloria exercitvs, 1 or 2 standards.
Ae 4	Coin diameter under 17 mm.	LRBC	Late Roman Bronze coinage (Carson, Hill and Kent).
Ant.	Antonianianus,	Obv	Obverse.
Ae	silver.	Px or Rev	Reverse.
Barb. Rad.	barbarous radiate.	RIC	Roman Imperial Coinage (Mattingley, Sydenham, Sutherland and Carson).
C	Centenionalis.		
Den	Denarius.		
Dup	Dupondius.	S.R.	Securitas Republicae.

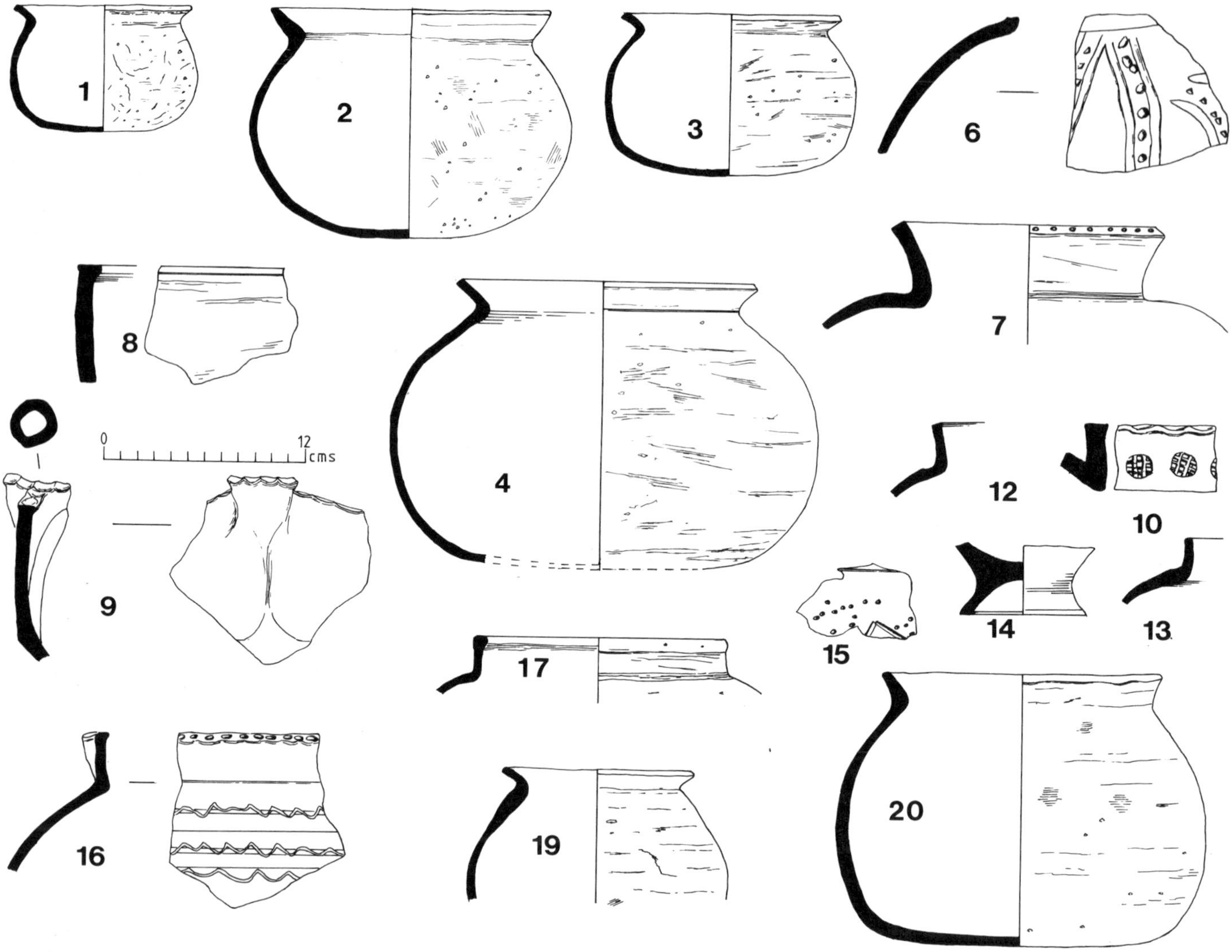

Fig. 8.37; Saxon pottery from Chapel Street, Nos. 1-20 (¼).

Middle to Late Saxon Wares from Chapel Street

Figs. 8.38-8.41

As in the earlier excavations in the north-west quadrant *(Chichester 3*, Figs. 11.1–11.5), large amounts of Anglo-Saxon wares were found, the majority being of late Saxon date (Groups 2 and 3, *Chichester 3*, 341–352), although a few Group 1 wares are present, usually as residual material in later pits. A selection is illustrated below:

Pit X 137

1. Small, handmade vessel, almost complete, heavily tempered with shell and small grits with some organic material (chaff or grass). Could be as early as 7th century. The ware is reduced to a dark grey; the rim is flattened.
2. Chalk and flint tempered; finished on a slow wheel; reduced grey.
3. Handmade; grogged with selected flints and some chalk, a good deal of which has leached out of the fabric. Finished on a slow wheel; reduced.
4. Similar fabric to 3 and also finished on a slow wheel.
5. Fragments of two loom weights, similar to those from Pit X 84 (Fig. 8.43). *Not illustrated.*

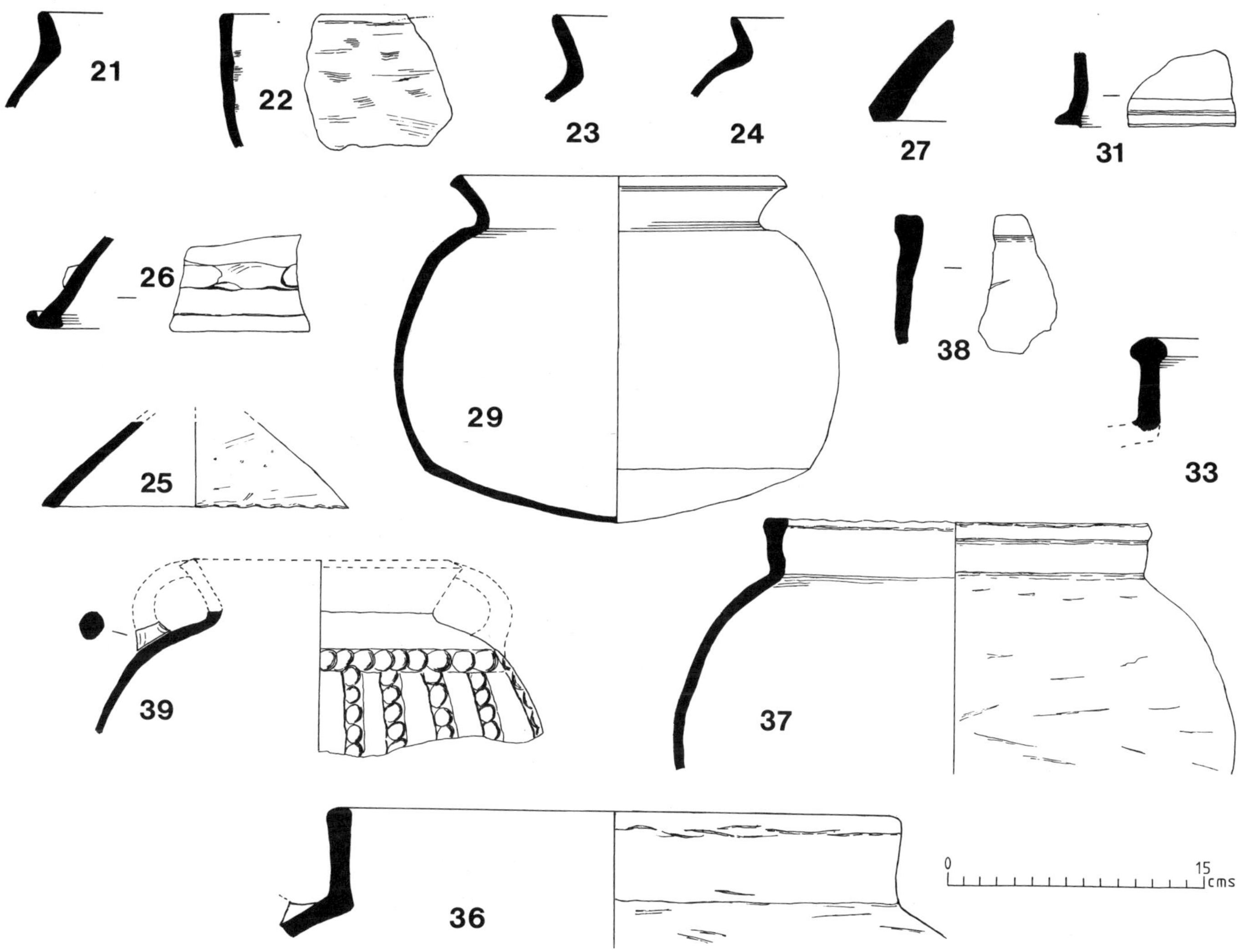

Fig. 8.38; Saxon pottery from Chapel Street, Nos. 21-39 (¼).

Pit X 57

6. One of four body sherds from a large storage jar. Grey fabric tempered with flint grits. Oxidised reddish-buff.
7. Large jar with upstanding rim. The fabric is soft, dark grey with small flint grits.
8. Flat-rimmed dish approximately 36 cm diameter. Dark grey fabric tempered with coarse sand.
9. Spouted bowl with finger-impressed rim and rounded base. Reduced grey fabric tempered with flint grits.
10. Rim sherd from a cooking pot with grid stamps inside the rim. Dark grey fabric with chalk and flint tempering, oxidised reddish-buff.

11. Rim sherd from the neck of a handled cooking pot (cf. *Chichester 3*, Fig. 11.3, 60). Grey fabric, oxidised reddish-buff with flint and some sand tempering. *Not illustrated.*
12. Cooking pot, oxidised reddish-buff, chalk tempered.
13. Cooking pot, reduced grey fabric tempered with flint grits and some chalk.

Pit X 41

14. Base of lamp. Grey ware, flint tempered, oxidised reddish-buff.
15. Body sherd from a storage jar. Similar ware to 14.
16. Spouted jar or pitcher. Black ware oxidised a dirty reddish-buff outside; coarse sand tempered with some translucent grits.
17. Cooking pot, black fabric, coarse sand and flint tempered.
18. Sherd from a spouted pitcher. Chalk tempered and oxidised reddish-buff. *Not illustrated.*

Pit X 60

19. Cooking pot, handmade with a lumpy exterior finish. The fabric is soft, black and tempered with small flint grits.
20. Cooking pot with flat base. Soft dark grey ware, flint tempered.
21. Similar handmade vessel to 20, but fabric is tempered with chalk and flint.

Pit P.10

22. Straight-sided bowl; soft black fabric, flint tempered. Handmade.
23. Rim of large cooking pot. Handmade; similar fabric to 22.
24. Similar fabric to 21.

Pit X 43

25. ? Lid with finger impressed rim, soft black fabric tempered with chalk and flint grits.
26. Rim of a curfew *c.* 46 cm diameter. Grey ware, chalk and flint tempered, oxidised reddish-buff outside.
27. Fragment of a large lid or perhaps a curfew in excess of 51 cm diameter. The fabric is grey, hard-fired and tempered with small flint grits and chalk.
28. Bowl with finger-impressed rim. Black fabric, flint and chalk tempered (cf. *Chichester 3*, Fig. 11.4, 68). *Not illustrated.*
29. Cooking pot, grey fabric oxidised a dirty brown, flint and chalk tempered. One of three examples found in this pit.
30. Cooking pot, hard fired grey ware oxidised pinky-buff. Flint and chalk tempered (cf. *Chichester 3*, Fig. 11.4, 72). *Not illustrated.*
31. Possibly a chimney vent, *c.* 12-15 cm diameter. The fabric is reduced dark grey and is tempered with flint grits.
32. Spouted bowl, similar to 9. Fabric is dark grey, oxidised reddish-buff and is tempered with flint grits and chalk. *Not illustrated.*
33. Rim fragment from a large storage jar. Hard grey ware, flint and chalk tempered.
34. (a) and (b) Two rim sherds from cooking pots, one with a heavily thumbed rim, the other with a grid stamp. In a similar fabric to 33 (cf. *Chichester 3*, Fig. 11.4, 64). *Not illustrated.*

X 14 (residual in a post-medieval layer)

35. Fragments, including two small pieces of everted rim, from a handmade vessel, soft and underfired, the fabric heavily packed with flint grits and chalk. *Not illustrated.*

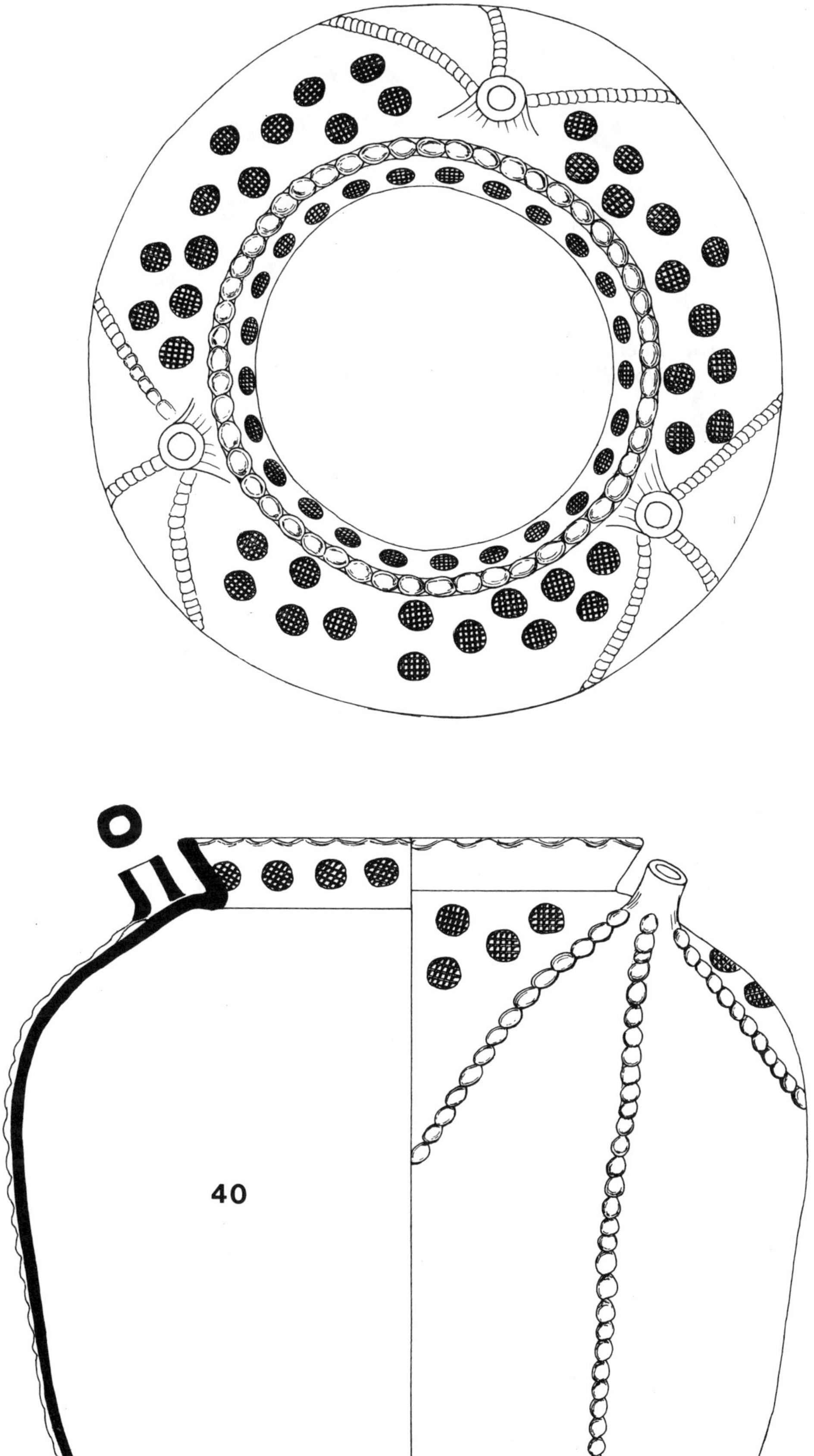

Fig. 8.39. Late Saxon triple-spouted vessl (¼).

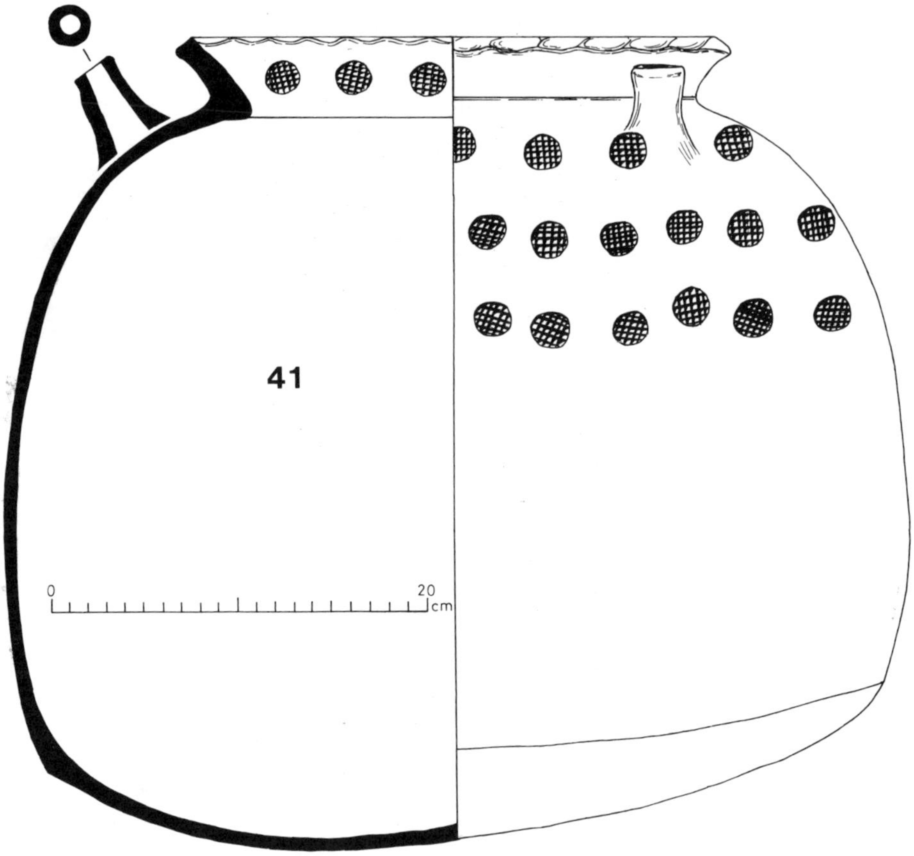

Fig. 8.40. Late Saxon triple-spouted vessel (¼).

Pit X 2

36. Rim of a large storage jar; hard grey fabric oxidised reddish-buff and tempered with flint grits.
37. Cooking pot with finger impressed rim. Hard grey fabric chalk and flint tempered. Saxo-Norman.

Pit X 1

38. Straight-walled vessel with flattened rim. Similar fabric to 36 but chalk and flint tempered.

Pit P.8

39. Saxo-Norman cooking pot, probably with three handles or lugs. Grey fabric, flint and chalk tempered, oxidised reddish-buff.

Fig. 8.39 & Plate 20(a)

Pit X 100

40. Triple-spouted vessel with finger impressed rim, grid stamps on shoulder and applied strip finger-impressed decoration. Grey fabric, chalk and flint tempered.

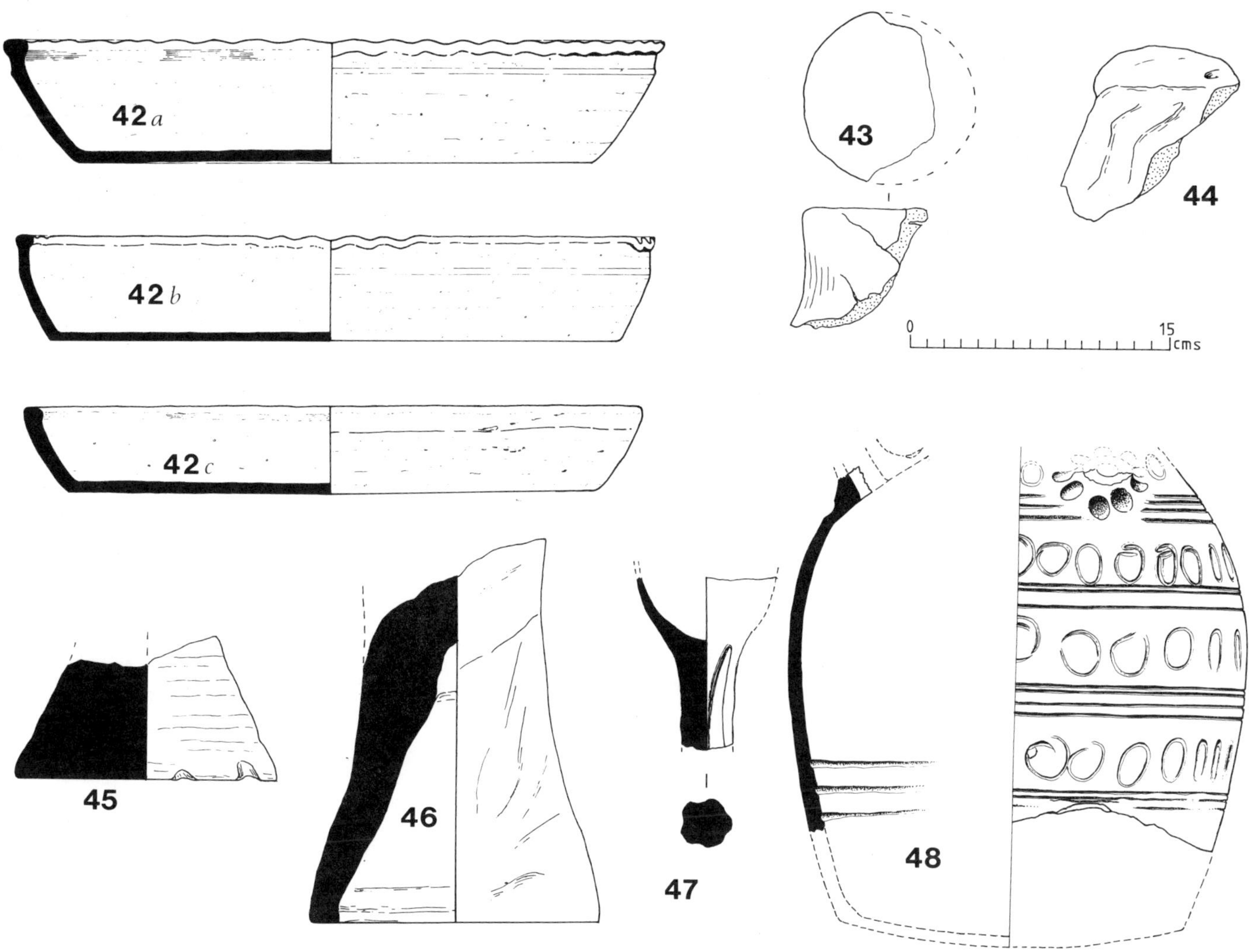

Fig. 8.41. Saxon pottery from Chapel Street. Nos. 42-48 (¼).

Fig. 8.40
& Plate 20(b)

41. Similar vessel to No. 40 but without applied strips and with a more pronounced sagging base.

Neither of these vessels can be paralleled in Chichester or elsewhere at present and their function can only be conjectured. The three "spouts" would not function as such and it might be that they are vents into which wooden plugs or spigots might be inserted. This would make the pots some kind of pressure vessel, perhaps for fermenting beer, with a cloth tied over the top.*

42. (a) Platter in similar fabric to 40 and 41, finger impressed decoration all around the rim.

42. (b) As 42(a), but the finger impressed decoration is in four groups of five impression evenly arranged around the circumference.

42. (c) As 42(a), but with a plain rim.

* I am indebted to Professor Cunliffe for this suggestion.

Pit X 56

43. Part of a pottery object which might be either the flat base and part of the side of a lamp, or alternatively perhaps the top of a chimney vent, although in this latter instance there would not have been a central hole through the top, which is approximately 10 cm in diameter. The fabric is soft and chalk tempered.
44. A crude "knob" of pottery, similar fabric to 43, function unknown.

X 34

45. Similar object to 43 and in the same fabric. Diameter approximately 15 cm.

Pit X 50

46. Chimney vent ? of unusual shape or part of a large pottery cresset. Fabric identical to Nos. 43–45.

X 68

47. Fluted stem and part of the bowl of a lamp, with traces of soot in the bowl. The fabric is underfired, heavily tempered with chalk and oxidised to a patchy buff. This lamp could equally post-date the late Saxon period, although the fabric suggests that it could be 10th–11th century. Residual in a late or post-medieval well pit.

Pit X 51

48. Spouted pitcher with sagging base in a hard fired grey fabric tempered with flint grits and chalk. The outside is reduced black. The body of the vessel is decorated with bands of roughly tooled circles between bands of horizontal grooving. This type of decoration on a late Saxon vessel is unique in Chichester.

Figs. 8.10 and 8.42

The Late Saxon Coarse Wares from the Clamps in Chapel Street

The clamps

Six were found; of these, one was in the north section and only a small area could be excavated. Of the other five, one, X 28 cut X 25. They were all cut into the foundations and destruction levels of the Roman house and the tops of the clamps had been levelled at some time after they went out of use and the land ploughed a number of times, so that the total undisturbed thickness remaining was in the region of 30 cm. In X 8, the remains of a wall was found on the south side (Fig. 8.12). The stones, which derived from the destroyed Roman house had been set in clay and both had been burnt red in the firing. The absence of any flues and the circular or oval shape suggests that these were simple clamps and not kilns.

The remains of a clamp or clamps, together with wasters were found nearby in 1974 when the site of the Roman baths was excavated in Tower Street (*Chichester 3*; 158), but there the clamps had been totally destroyed by the robbing of the bath house masonry. It is likely that the robbing post-dated the Norman Conquest and was for masonry to build the cathedral and the wares are contemporary with those from the Chapel Street clamps. The majority of the fragments from Chapel Street were small. All the wares appeared to be wheel made and most were oxidised, although there was a degree of patchy reduction

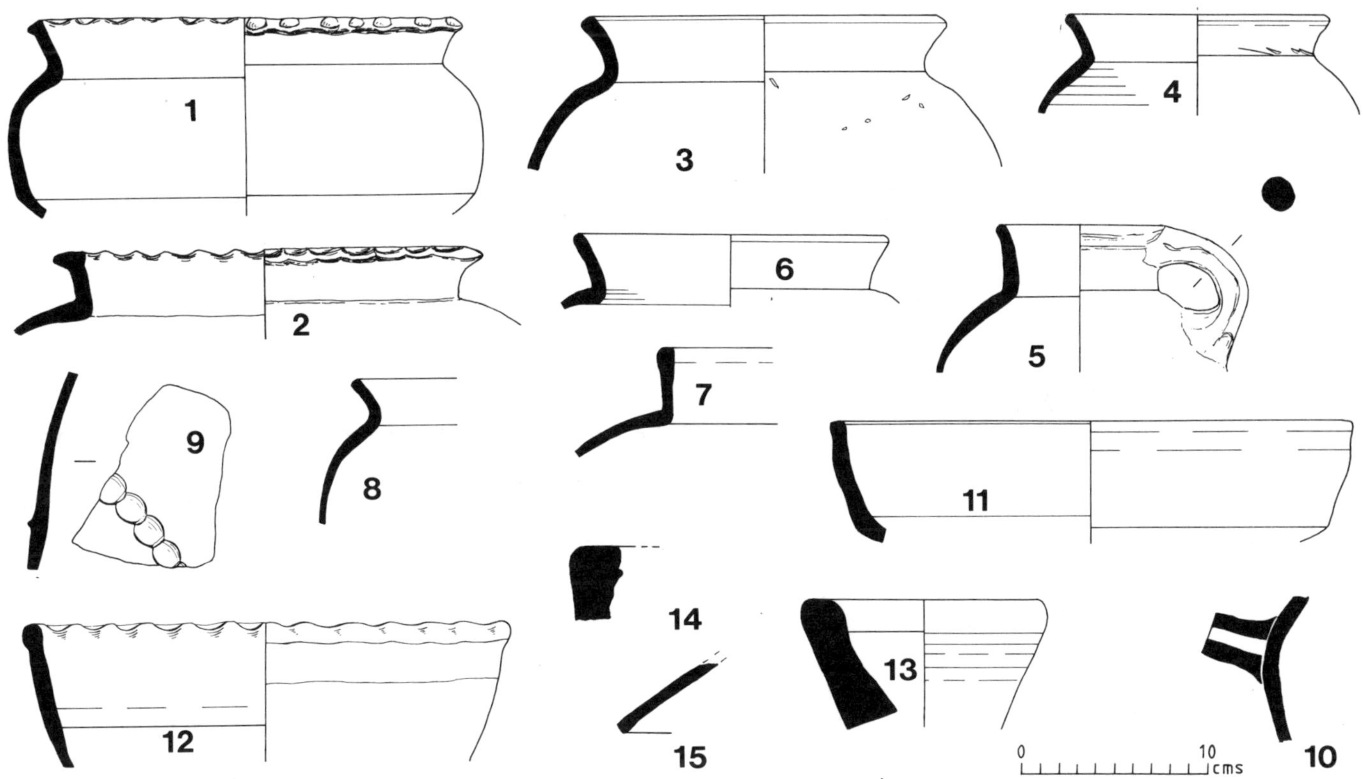

Fig. 8.42. Saxon pottery from the clamps in Chapel Street. Nos. 1-15 (¼).

on some sherds, which were mostly underfired and with a lumpy exterior finish. The number of clamps found within a relatively small area (six), suggests that production might have been on a commercial scale. The products are well attested in the cesspits nearby, and belong to the earlier end of the Group 3 range of wares (*Chichester 3*, Figs 11.3–11.5)

The variety of vessels produced must have been greater than those that could be identified within the fill of the clamps, where the range is restricted to cooking pots, pitchers with and without spouts, and shallow bowls. Only a few sherds from large storage vessels with applied strip decoration were noted which may be an indication that production was limited to domestic vessels for which the market was assured and which would be easier to make. The total weight of sherds was *c.* 86 kg, but as the overwhelming majority were featureless body sherds, it is unrealistic to attempt to quantify the wares by weight.

Samples were taken by the Ancient Monuments Laboratory of the Department of the Environment, for archaeomagnetic dating. These give a mean of 1050±50 A.D. for the operation of the clamps. The lower end of this bracket would fit quite well with what we know of the wares and a date of *c.* A.D. 1030–1050 is preferred by the writer. The lack of activity on the site after the Norman Conquest (*Chichester 3*, 86), suggests that the land may have changed hands with perhaps the occupants being evicted and the land becoming arable.

The Wares

1. Shallow cooking pot with finger impressed rim. Grey fabric grogged with small flint grits and some organic material which has burned out in the firing. Oxidised reddish-buff. (X 13).
2. As No. 1, but reduced to dark grey in patches. (X 13).
3. Vessel with upstanding rim, grogged with small to medium flint grits and some chalk lumps. Oxidised reddish-buff on exterior surface. (X 13).
4. As No. 3, but with rather more chalk tempering. (X 13).
5. Pitcher, fabric as No. 4, very soft. (X 13).
6. Fabric reduced to a dark grey, heavily flint gritted with some chalk inclusions. (X 25).
7. This vessel is remarkable for the large amount of chalk in the fabric, with lesser amounts of flint grits. Oxidised reddish buff. (X 13).
8. Chalk and flint grogged, oxidised reddish-buff. (X 13).
9. Body sherd from a large storage jar with applied finger-impressed strips. Fabric as No. 8. (X 13).
10. Sherd from a spouted pitcher. Fabric as No. 8. (X 13).
11. Shallow bowl with sagging base, very underfired and grogged with small flint grits and a little chalk. Reduced to a dark grey. (X 25).
12. Straight walled bowl with finger-impressed rim and lumpy exterior finish. Fabric as No. 12. (X 13).
13. Part of a ? lamp. Heavily flint gritted. (X 13).
14. Part of the base of a ? chimney vent or possibly a large lamp, grogged with flint grits and some chalk. (X 8).
15. ? Lid, flint tempered grey ware with some shell. Oxidised reddish buff. (X 8).

Fig. 8.43

The Saxon loomweights

A total of 44 weights were found in Trench X in Area 8. Of these, 39 were from Pit X 84 (B), and most were complete or nearly so. The weights varied between 1,080 gm for the heaviest, to 555 gm for the smallest complete example.

A detailed report on these loomweights has been compiled by Carol Edwards and is with the Level III material in archive. The majority of the loomweights fall into the category of Hursts' bun-shaped variety,[1] but there are a small number (see No. 2, Fig. 8.43), which are slightly flatter and might be said to resemble the "intermediate" type, although this may perhaps be attempting too great a refinement as they came from the same pit as the majority and are presumably contemporary.

Fabric

All were crudely made and most had large flint inclusions. A small number had been tempered with oat straw[2] (see Nos. 3 and 4).

1. Bun-shaped; weight 945 gm, diameter 125 mm, thickness 47 mm.
2. ?Intermediate; weight 690 gm, diameter 112 mm, thickness 45 mm.
3. Bun-shaped; weight 995 gm, diameter 139 mm, thickness 58 mm.
4. Bun-shaped; weight 1,080 gm; diameter 144 mm, thickness 61 mm.

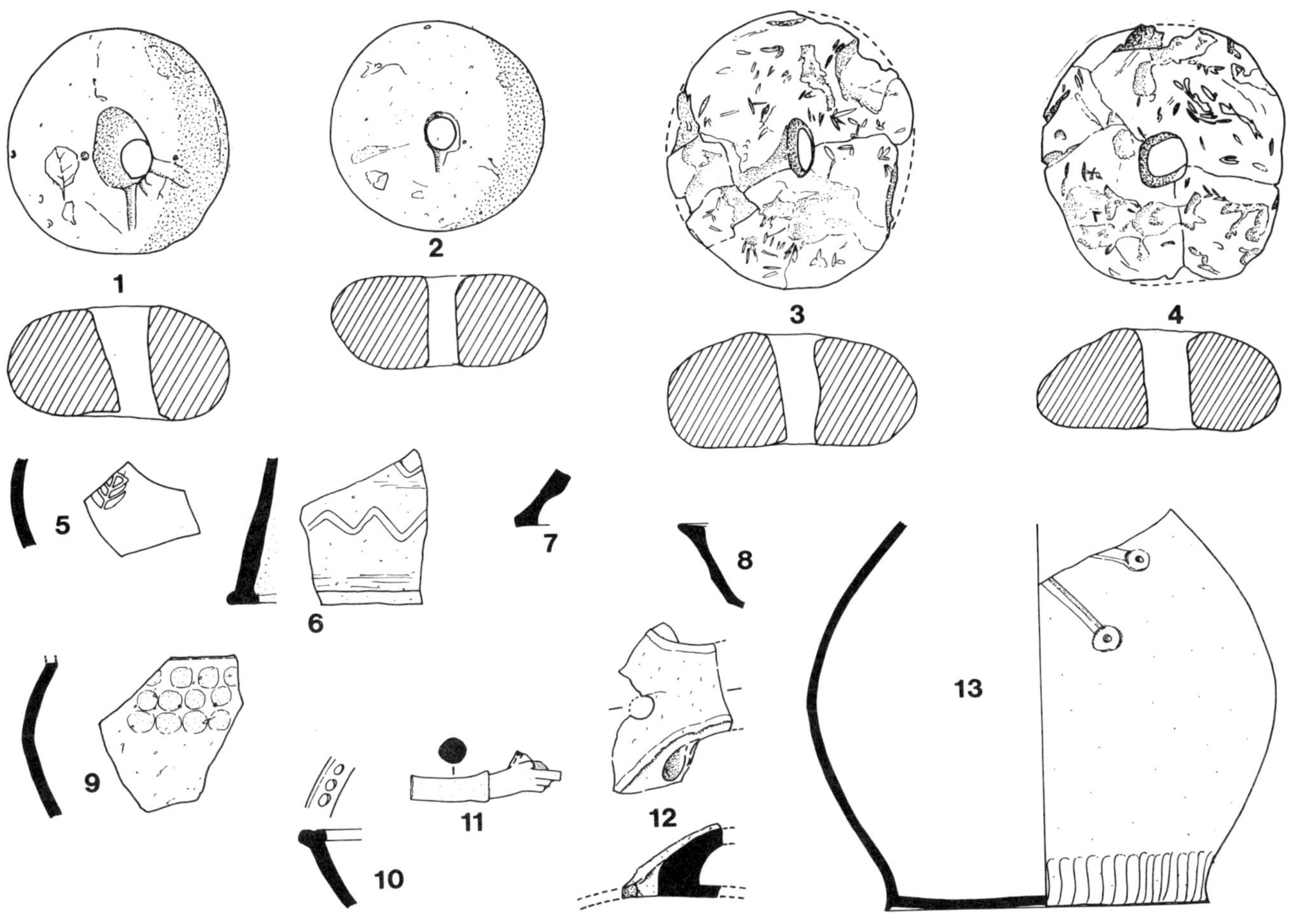

Fig. 8.43. Finds from the N.W. Quadrant. Nos. 1-4, Saxon loomweights; Nos. 5-13, medieval pottery (¼).

Fig. 8.43

Medieval pottery from Chapel Street

5. Sherd from a jug, green-glazed with part of a herringbone stamp decoration. Fabric is hard, mid-grey sandy ware, *c.* 13th–14th century. (Pit X 91).
6. Rim of a curfew. Grey, flint-gritted fabric, patchy green-yellow glaze inside. (Pit X 61).
7. Rim of a ? curfew, similar fabric to 6, smoke blackened inside. (Pit X 61).
8. Rim of a shallow bowl; hard-fired grey ware with sparse flint grits and traces of green glaze inside.
9. Body sherd from a vessel with finger-impressed dimples (cf. *Chichester 2*, p. 85 and Fig. 7.9, 18).
10. Rim of bowl with pecked rim and internal glaze. Dark-grey sandy ware, heavily burnt, *c.* 12th–13th century. (Pit P.27).

11. Arm from an anthropomorphic jug; *c.* late 13th–14th century.[3] Fine sandy grey ware, dark olive-green glaze. (Pit P.32).
12. Handle of a curfew with a vent hole at the point where it joins the body. Dirty-grey fabric with small flint grits. (Pit P.32).
13. Lower part of a jug with external green glaze and fine, light-grey fabric, *c.* late 14th century. (Pit P.5).

Notes

1. G. C. Dunning, J. G. Hurst, J. N. L. Myers and F. Tischler "Anglo-Saxon pottery; a Symposium", *Med. Arch.*, Vol. 3 (1959), pp. 23–5. See also E. W. Holden, "Excavations at Old Erringham, Shoreham; Part 1; A Saxon Weaving Hut"; *S.A.C.* 114 (1976), 308–321).
2. I am grateful to Miss P. Paradine for examining the loomweights and identifying the seed impressions and to Dr. Maureen Girling for her assistance in arranging this. A detailed report is with the Level III archive, but it can be said here that the seed impressions were *Avena Sp.*, probably *A. Sativa.* Caryopsis, florets and straw from oats.
3. See G. C. Dunning in G. Beresford: "The Moated House at Wintringham, Huntingdonshire", pp. 253–255 and Figs. 36 a and b; *Arch. J.*, Vol. 134, 1977, for a possible parallel.

The Medieval Coins

by Marion Archibald

1. (19). France; Charles the Bald, A.D. 840–877; Denier, Orleans mint.
Obverse: +G(RATIA)D¯I REX
Karolus monogram
Reverse: +AVRELIANI(S CIVITA)S
Cross pattée within inner circle.
Weight: 0.38 g = 5.9 gr (large fragment only).
Carolingian deniers are rarely found as isolated site-finds in England, although they have been included in hoards. Among the considerable number in the Cuerdale hoard, buried *c* A.D. 903, were several of this reign and mint. (See *British Museum Sylloge of Carolingian coins.* London 1966, Nos. 151–2). Carolingian coins, which are a recurring feature of hoards buried during the period of Viking raids and the lifetime of the Danelaw in the 9th and very early 10th centuries, virtually disappear from those concealed in England after the reunification of the country under the strong line of 10th century kings before Aethelred II. Carolingian coins are, of course, likely to turn up in a trading centre like Chichester regardless of the political situation.
While it is difficult to put a very precise date on the deposition of this coin, it looks as if it had seen some circulation and so it is likely to have been lost some time within the period *c.* A.D. 875–920.

2. (221). Edward II, 1307–27; Farthing, London mint, Fox group X.
Weight: 0.26 g = 4.0 gr (chipped).
This coin belongs to the later period of group X which was struck *c.* 1300–1310 and so can be ascribed to the first years of Edward II. The roughly rectangular appearance of the coin is a result of its having been struck on a blank of that shape and not of subse-

quent clipping. It was comparatively little worn when lost, which suggests a deposition date before 1350 at the latest, an earlier date within the possible bracket being preferable.

3. (15). Henry VI, 1422–61; Halfpenny, London mint, Annulet issue. Weight: 0.30 g = 4.6 gr (chipped).
The Annulet type was issued from 1422–27. This coin is not clipped, but has seen some circulation before deposition. It was almost certainly lost before the reduction in the standard weight of the coinage in 1464, with a deposit date in the middle of the possible bracket, say, *c.* 1430–50, being the most likely.

Post-medieval coins

4. (14). Copper farthing, Charles I, 1625–1649; Richmond round type.
5. (199). Halfpenny, George I, 1714–1727.
6. (602). Halfpenny, George II, 1727–1760.

Early Iron Age

7. (385). Half of a cast bronze coin of the Durotriges. These coins were still circulating possibly as late as *c.* A.D. 70. From Layer X 78. Residual in a Roman layer.

The Crane Street Kiln

The identification of this production source for some of the 17th century wares found in the City, coming so soon after the establishment of a research project to investigate the Graffham kilns where similar pottery was being produced, was a rare "bonus" which has made a significant contribution to our knowledge. Thanks are due to Ann Leyland who drew most of the pots illustrated below, to Caroline Scott who assisted in the classification of the wares and the preparation of the Report, to John Hurst and Felix Holling for help and advice, and to Anthony Streeten who reported on the fabric analysis. Acknowledgement should also be made of the considerable efforts made by the Documentary Research team and the West Sussex Record Office to identify the potter who must have operated at Crane Street.

While the location of the kiln or kilns is known within a few yards, it has not been possible to excavate it. It must lie either beneath the narrow two metre path left between our excavation and the west wall of No. 6 Crane Street, or beneath the house itself. In the latter instance, all traces will have been destroyed by the cellar below the house, but if it lies below the path or at the rear of the building, then there is a possibility that the future development of the Chapel Street-Crane Street sites for residential accommodation, planned for 1981–82 may yet reveal more of the industry.

The majority of the kiln products were in a fine grey fabric which oxidised red, but there was a small proportion (about 3.4% of the total weight), which were in a fine, white or off-white fabric and always with a pale yellow or light green glaze. Not all of these were wasters, although they were present in the same layers and it is not possible to be certain that they were all produced at Crane Street. Some may have been imported from elsewhere, e.g. Surrey or Graffham. Similar wares also formed a very small percentage of the fabrics collected by the late Miss P. A. M. Keef from the Graffham area *(Aldsworth* and *Down,* forthcoming).

All the wasters were collected from the site and weighed. The total weight was 111.0 Kg of which 40.5 Kg (36.49%) were unidentifiable by reason of distortion and/or size. In addition, 16 Kg of roof furniture, mainly peg tiles, but with a few pieces of ridge tile were found. Many of these were burnt and some were splashed with glaze but they are not likely to be evidence for roof tile production as there were no identifiable wasters. It seems more likely that they were present as surface debris and had been used by the potters as props for the wares. They are disregarded for statistical purposes, although their appearance suggests that they could be contemporary with the kiln.

Great difficulty was experienced in the identification of some of the wares and the percentage figures given, especially for skillets and cooking pots, should be treated with caution. Nevertheless, there are some interesting gaps in the production range by comparison with other kilns. No butter pots could be identified, although these are made at Graffham (*Aldsworth* and *Down,* forthcoming) and the number of chafing dishes, costrels and condiment vessels is negligible.

PERCENTAGE OF WARES BY WEIGHT

Type	Weight in Kg	Percentage of identifiable wares
Hollowares		
Pipkins	10.5	14.87
Skillets	2.8	3.97
Chamber pots	1.1	1.55
Bowls	13.6	19.20
? Cooking pots	6.4	9.00
? Saggars	3.7	5.24
Flatwares		
Plates	11.4	16.15
Pans	2.1	2.97
Cups pedestal	2.2	3.12
loop handle	0.8	1.13
Jugs brown glazed	1.5	2.12
other	12.8	18.13
Miscellaneous		
? Mugs Costrels Chafing dishes Condiments	1.7	2.55
Total	70.6	100.00

LAYERS CONTAINING KILN WASTERS

P.2—Brownish clayey soil with mortar and chalk lumps below the garden soil. A number of pits had been dug through it and there were large numbers of 18th and 19th century wares present which are reported on by Sheila Morgan (p. 217), the date range for which was *c.* A.D. 1750-1890. A large proportion of the finds were kiln wasters, with stoneware, clay pipes and glass roughly contemporary with the pottery.

P.5—The top layer of a pit dug through P.2.

P.6—A layer of well-levigated yellow clay, level with P.2 and partly in the east section (Fig. 8.23). It may well derive from a dump of clay prepared for the potters.

P.15—A consolidated layer of compacted chalk above an earlier pit (Pit P.34).

Pit P.3—A 19th-century pit cutting P.2.

Pit P.9—An earlier pit partly destroyed by Pit P.3.

Pit P.18—A pit cutting P.2, partly in the south section.

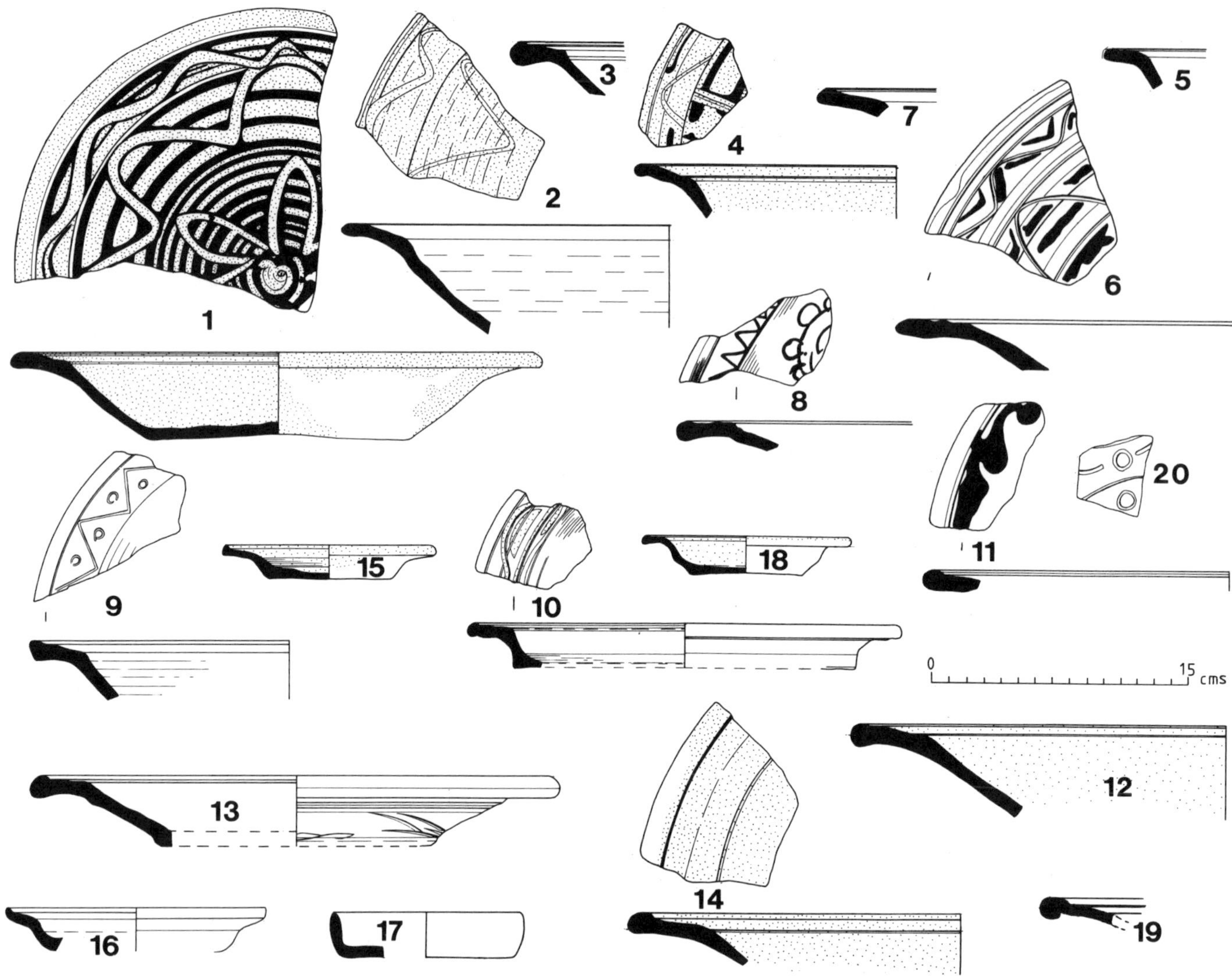

Fig. 8.44. 17th-century pottery from the Crane Street kiln.
Nos. 1-11; slip decorated flatwares, Nos. 12-20; plain glazed flatwares. All (¼).

LOCATION OF ILLUSTRATED KILN WARES

Context	*Vessel numbers*
P.2	1-5, 7, 14, 22-25, 29, 34-35, 37, 43, 45-48, 50-51, 55, 57, 63-64, 66, 70, 71, 74, 78-85, 87, 90, 95-99, 103, 105, 114-118, 121-122, 128
P.5	65
P.6	6, 11, 21, 27, 31-32, 36, 41, 56, 58, 62, 86, 92, 94, 106, 109, 124, 127
Pit P.3	8-9, 18-19, 33, 39, 42, 44, 49, 59, 68-69, 76-77, 107, 123
Pit P.9	89
Pit P.18	10, 13, 16-17, 20, 26, 28, 30, 38, 40, 52-54, 60-61, 67, 72-73, 75, 88, 91, 93, 100-102, 104, 108, 110-113, 119-120, 125, 126
Unstratified	12

THE WARES

Fig. 8.44

(a) *Slip-decorated flat-wares*

All in a fine red fabric unless otherwise stated.

1-5. Plates, brown glaze with applied white slip (cf. *Kelly*, 1973, p. 8, 38, for form description and date, also *Holling*, 1971, Fig. 2, A.1-3).

6-7. Plates as above, but with a green glaze below the white slip.

8-9. Light grey fabric, oxidized pinky red.

10. As 8 and 9, but press moulded.

11. Not a waster. Fine brick-red fabric, orange-brown glaze with applied trailed slip decoration. Might be later in date than Nos. 1-10.

Fig. 8.44

(b) *Plain glazed flatwares*

12. Plate in a coarser red fabric, with more sand. Internal olive-green glaze. 41 cm diameter.

13. Plate; similar fabric to 12. Light green interior glaze, overlapping the brown glaze on the rim in places. In some areas the green pigment is fugitive. The exterior is partially coated with a brown glaze which had dripped on it from another vessel during firing.

14. Plate in a fine off-white fabric. Internal mottled dark brown glaze. Not a waster.

15-16. Pink buff fabric. No. 15 has internal brown glaze with traces of green colouration. No. 16 has a darker, greenish-brown glaze inside and out.

17. Shallow dish or lid in a sandy orange fabric. Patchy internal green-brown glaze (cf. *Sheppard*, 1978, p. 106, 23).

18. Press-moulded vessel, white fabric with internal pale yellow glaze.

19. White fabric, internal pale yellow glaze.

20. Sherd from a plate; orange fabric, internal pale khaki glaze.

Note. The processes by which slip coating was applied to 17th century vessels is discussed in *Celoria* and *Kelly*, 1973, p. 15 and it is likely that the products listed above were treated in the same way. No. 1, for instance, was first coated with a brown "ground coat" and a coat of white slip applied above. The decoration was achieved by cutting back to the brown ground coat, with a final coat of transparent galena glaze being applied overall. Whether these processes involved more than one firing is uncertain.

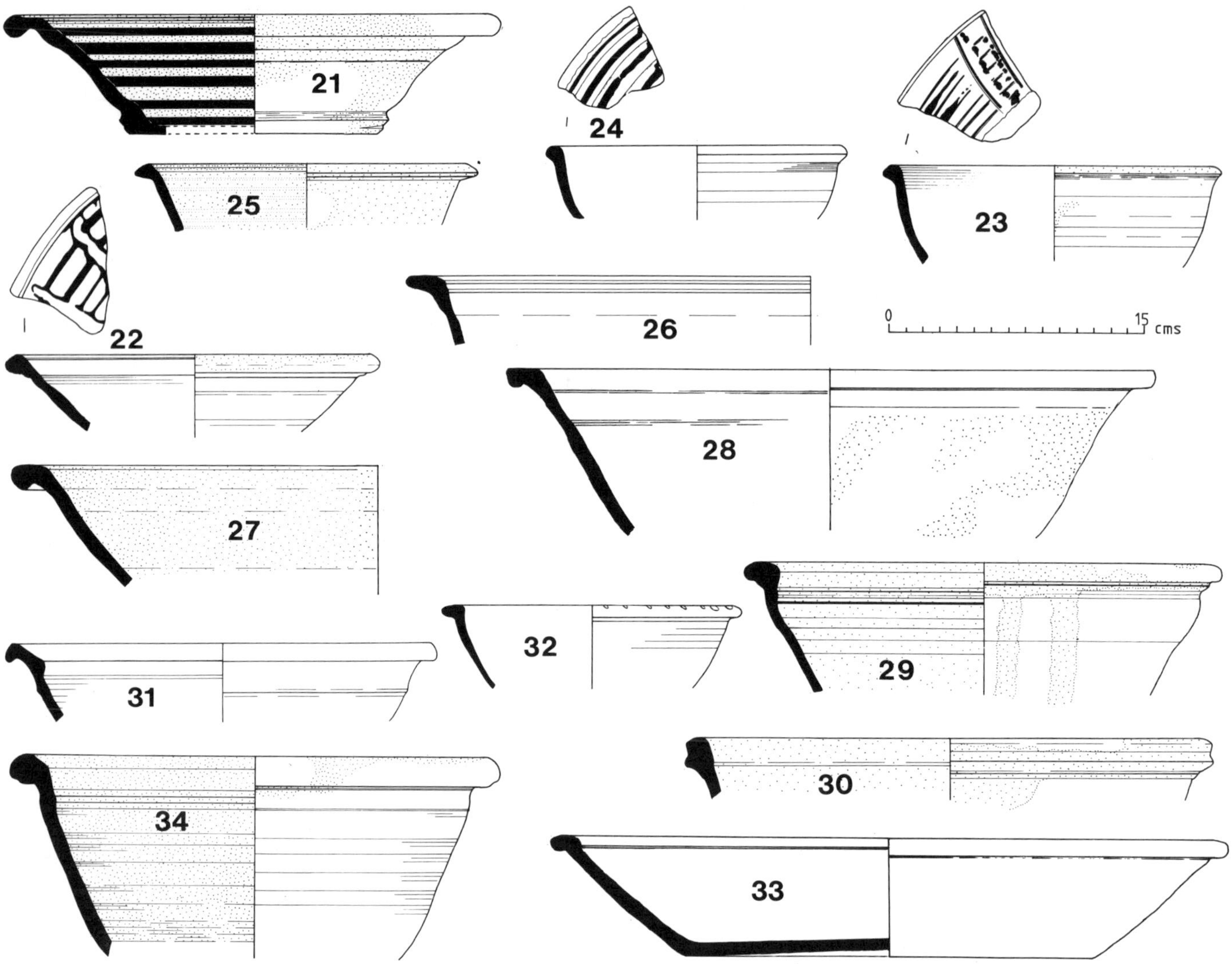

Fig. 8.45. 17th-century pottery from the Crane Street kiln.
Nos. 21-25; slip decorated bowls. Nos. 26-34; plain glazed bowls (¼).

(c) *Bowls: slip-decorated*

21. Interior olive-green glaze below a trailed white slip.

22–24. Interior greenish-brown glaze below a trailed white slip. No. 24 has patches of glazing on the outside.

25. Bowl, coated with a white slip which has fired a greeny-yellow.

Figs. 8.45 and 8.46

(d) *Plain glazed bowls*

26–30. Flat-rimmed bowls with greeny to orange-brown glaze, flecked with dark brown. All in a fine light grey fabric oxidised pinky red.

31. Bowl with thickened rim. Dark olive-green glaze inside (see *Sheppard* 1978, Fig. 119.2 for form and probable date).

32. Small bowl with pecked rim; internal green glaze.

33. Large bowl. The fabric has been grogged with small fragments of pottery ranging from 1–3 mm diameter. Light brown glaze inside with dark brown flecks. The rim is left unglazed to prevent sticking when stacked in the kiln.

34. Deep bowl with heavy rim, khaki-coloured glaze internally.

35. Small bowl with traces of brown glaze inside and out.

36. Pale buff fabric, remains of green glaze inside.

37. Rim of large bowl. Fine grey fabric, oxidised red; lustrous brown glaze inside and over rim. There is evidence that the second firing after the glaze was applied, was carried out in a reducing atmosphere. Not a waster. (cf. *Sheppard* 1978, p. 109, 5).

38. Bowl with thickened rim with a sparse interior brown glaze. Similar fabric to No. 50.

39. Bowl in a sandy red fabric. Orange-brown glaze with iron flecks inside and out. (cf. *Sheppard* 1978, p. 113, 12).

40. White sandy fabric with patchy internal khaki-coloured glaze.

41. Pinky-white fabric, light green glaze inside.

42. Bowl with wavy rim; sandy white fabric, "Tudor" green glaze inside. (cf. *Sheppard* 1978, p. 94, 3).

43–45. Hard white fabric, "Tudor" green glaze inside and over rim.

Miscellaneous: not wasters and probably post-dating the kiln.

46. Base of a large vessel. Dark red fabric with a black glaze inside and out.

47. Bowl in similar fabric to 46.

48–49. Sandy red fabric; orange glaze similar to 39 but without iron streaks.

50. Steep-walled bowl: red sandy fabric, internal reddish-brown glaze (cf. *Sheppard,* 113, No. 11, for similar form and glaze).

Figs. 8.47 and 8.48

(e) *Hollow-ware vessels*

51–52. Straight-walled vessels. No. 51 has traces of an olive-green glaze.

53. Straight-walled vessel: diameter *c.* 17 cm. Buff fabric; traces of a patchy glaze inside and out.

54. Large bowl, *c.* 44 cms diameter; orange-red fabric, internal olive-green glaze.

55. Skillet with internal yellow-green glaze (cf. *Holling* 1971, Fig. 4, F.2).

56–57. Skillet handles. No. 56 has a similar glaze to No. 55.

58. ? Skillet. Fine pale buff fabric; internal dark brown glaze, almost black.

59–61. Skillets. Fine pale grey fabric oxidised pinky-buff. Internal greeny-brown glaze. No. 61 has a stamp on the shoulder.

62. ? Pipkin. Fine pale-grey fabric oxidised pinky-buff. Internal olive-green glaze.

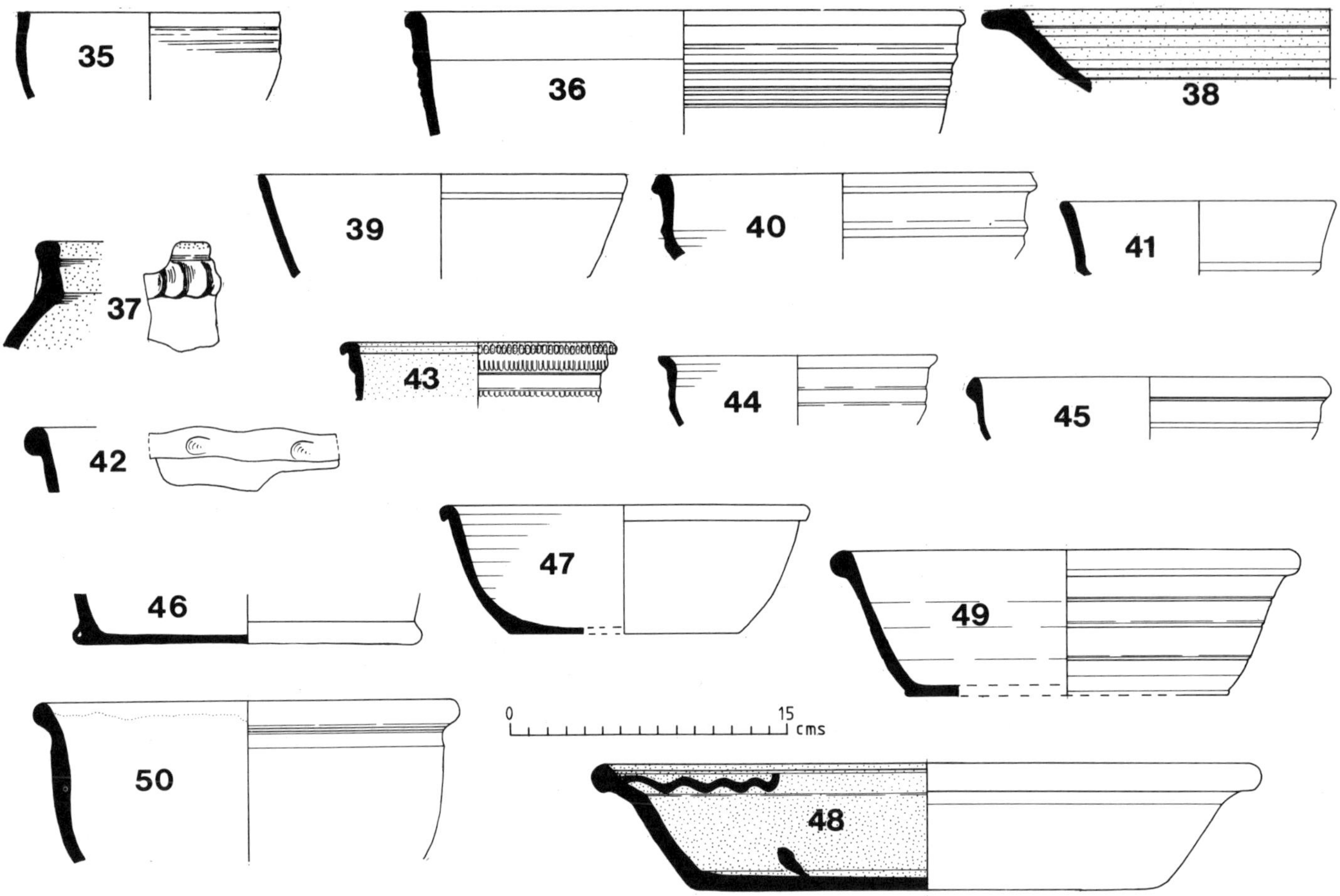

Fig. 8.46. 17th-century pottery from the Crane Street kiln.
Nos. 35-39; plain glazed bowls, Nos. 40-45; white fabrics, Nos. 46-50; miscellaneous. (¼)

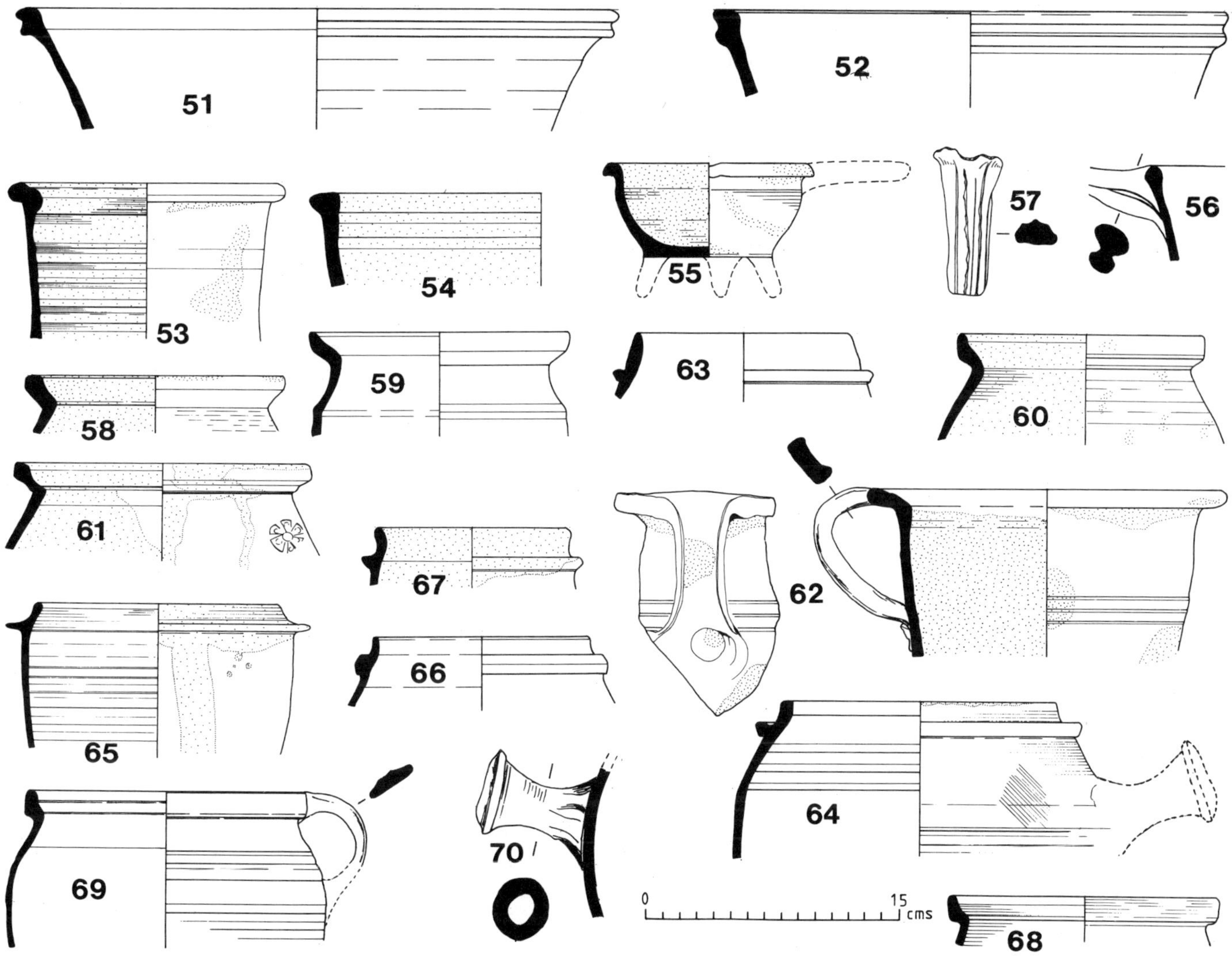

Fig. 8.47. 17th-century pottery from the Crane Street kiln. Nos. 51-70; Hollow ware vessels (¼).

63. Fine pale buff fabric; internal green glaze.
64. Similar fabric to 63; greeny-brown glaze.
65–67. Fine sandy orange fabric; internal brown glaze.
68–69. Pipkins; fine white fabric; internal yellow glaze.
70. Body sherd and handle from a pipkin; internal olive-green glaze. Fine grey fabric partially oxidised to a pinky-buff. Slate grey exterior.
71. Straight walled vessel, probably a saggar. Fine orange-buff fabric; 44 cm diameter.
72–73. Two fragments from saggars. Fine sandy fabric reduced grey (cf. *Kelly* 1975, Fig. 4.25, and *Kelly* 1973, pp. 23, 27).
74. Chamber-pot. Orange-buff fabric, internal green glaze.
75. Rim of chamber-pot. Creamy fabric, light green glaze inside and out.
76. Bowl in fine creamy fabric. Pale yellow glaze inside and over rim. Not a waster.
77. Two fragments from a ? stool pan. Fine white fabric, pale yellow glaze inside and over rim (cf. *Holling* 1971, Fig. 5, M.1).
78–79. Jars; orange fabric; 79 is brown glazed inside.
80. Narrow necked jar. Faint traces of brown glaze around neck and on rim. Pale orange fabric.
81. Jar, similar fabric to 80. Internal greenish-brown glaze.
82. Jar, similar fabric to 81 but reduced grey.
83. Narrow-necked vessel in red fabric; brown glaze inside and out. Not a waster; the glaze has been worn away from inside the rim and it may be a later piece.
84. Jar with an applied strip around the neck which has been thumb impressed. Orange fabric with a greeny-brown glaze inside and over the rim. Two examples found (cf. *Moorhouse* 1971. Fig. 1.14) for a similar style of thumb impressed collar, although there the date is early 16th century.
85. Rim of ? cooking pot. Pale orange fabric, two holes drilled in rim for suspension loop. Dribbles of brown glaze under flange.
86. Base in whitish-grey fabric; internal green glaze. Probably a jug, but might be a large tankard. Thumbed base of strap handle remaining.
87. Colander. Pale orange-buff fabric; internal dark brown glaze.

Fig. 8.48

(*f*) *Pans*

88. Handle and rim of a dripping pan. Dark green, almost black glaze inside and out. Heavily overfired. Orange fabric reduced to dark grey (cf. *Holling* 1971. Fig. 4, G.2).
89–90. Rim sherds from dripping pan. Both in orange fabric, with 89 having a patchy brownish-green glaze inside.

Fig. 8.49

(*g*) *Cups—(with loop handles)*

91. Thin-walled cup in buff fabric, dull green glaze inside and out.
92. Dark brown fabric, internal green glaze.
93. Orange fabric, greeny-brown glaze inside.
94. Similar fabric to 93; light brown glaze inside and out.
95. Pale orange fabric, internal patchy green glaze.
96. Orange fabric, faint traces of brown glaze inside.

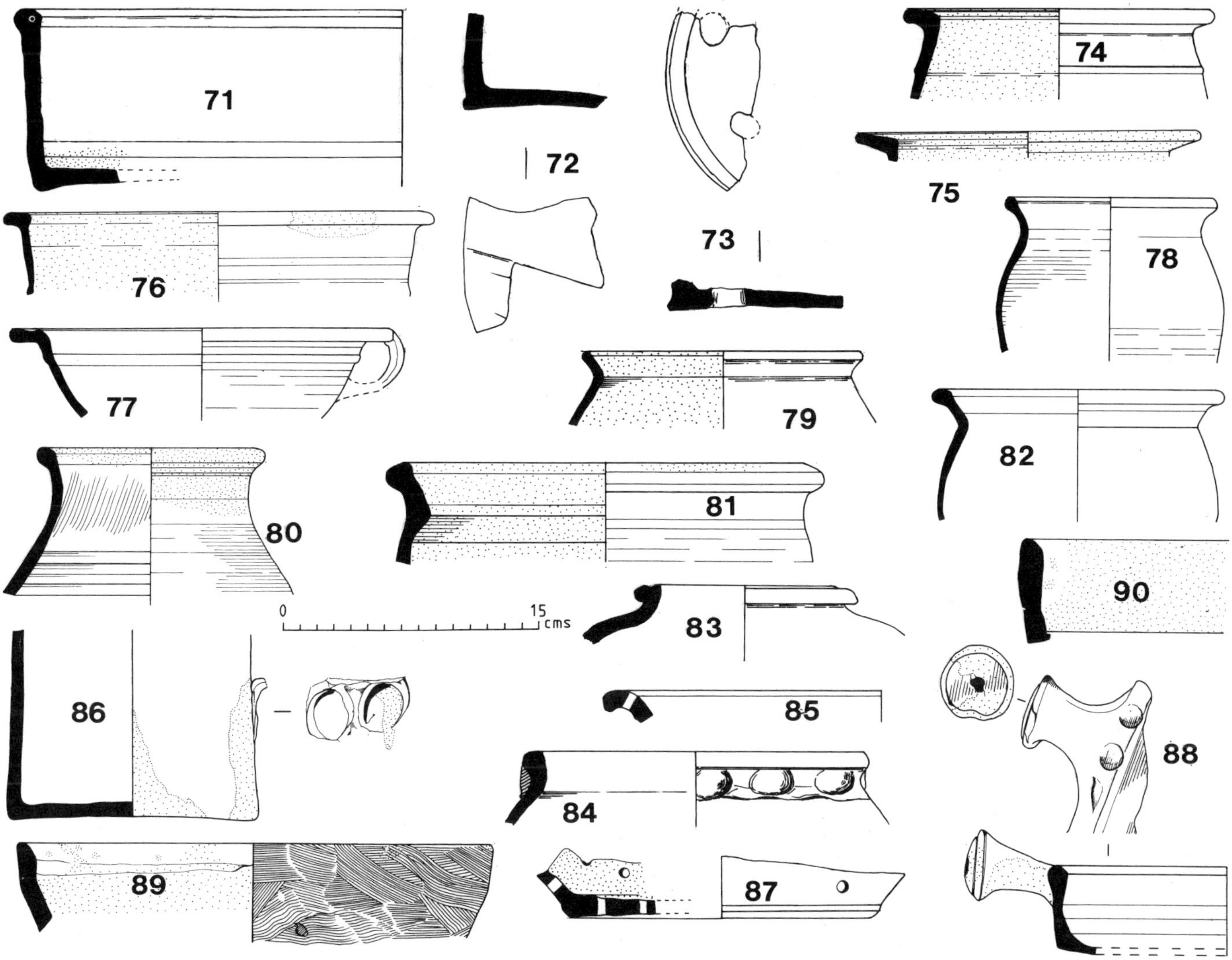

Fig. 8.48. 17th-century pottery from the Crane Street kiln. Nos. 71-90; Hollow ware vessels (¼).

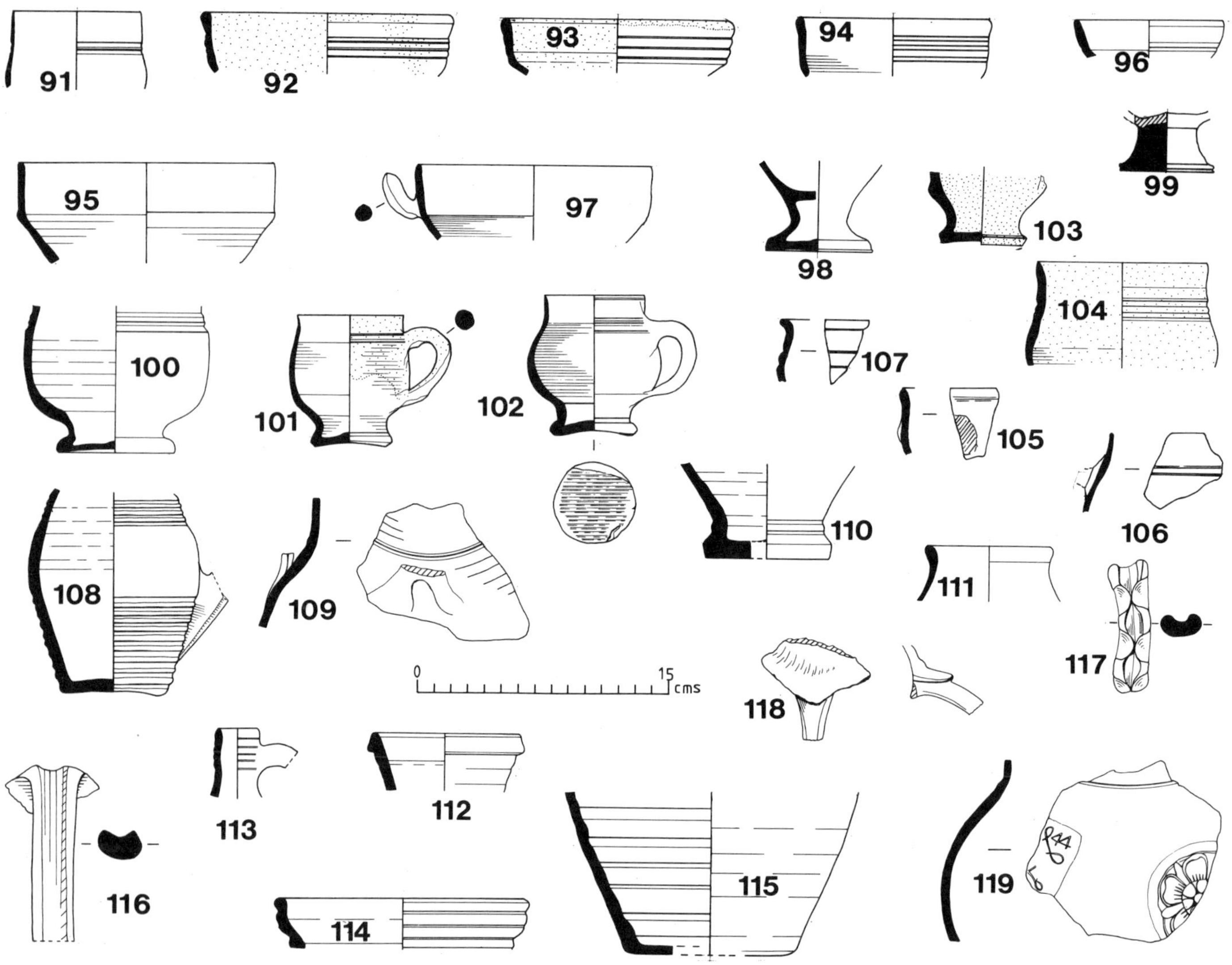

Fig. 8.49. 17th-century pottery from the Crane Street kiln.
Nos. 91-107; Cups, Nos. 108-119; Jugs (¼).

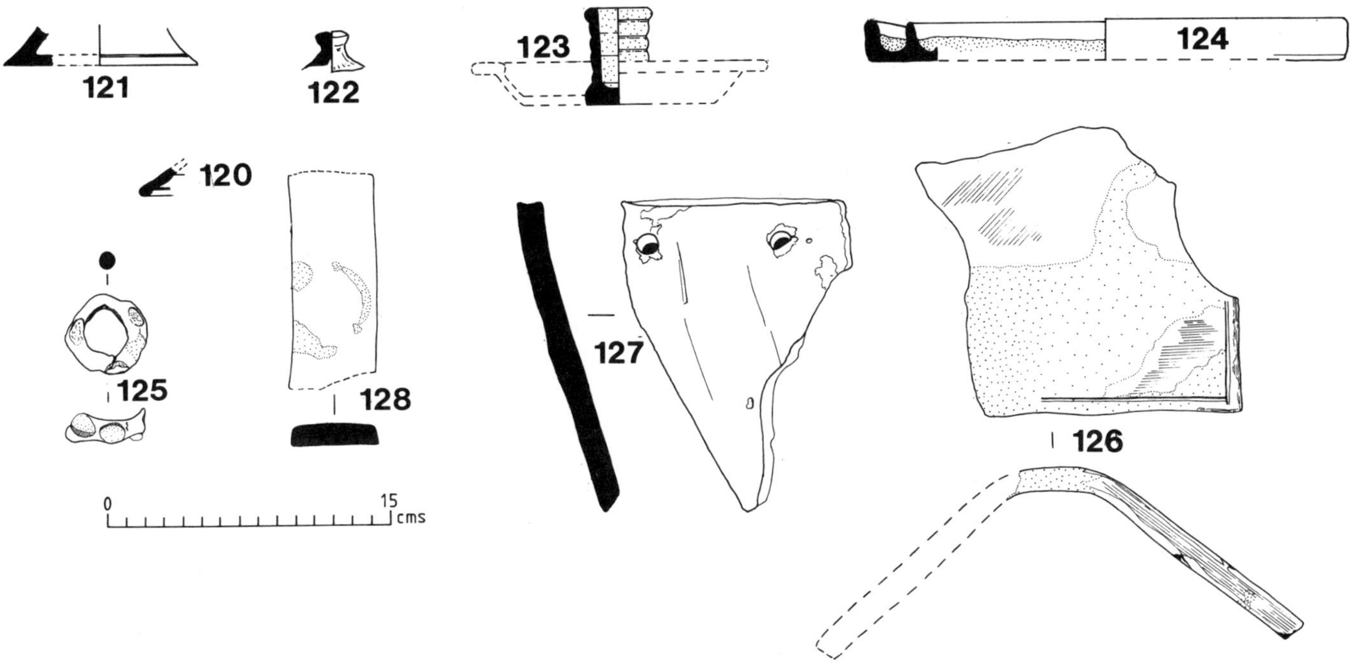

Fig. 8.50. 17th-century pottery from the Crane Street kiln.
Nos. 120-124; Miscellaneous, Nos. 125-128; kiln furniture (¼).

97. Orange fabric; remains of patchy brown glaze inside (cf. *Holling* 1971. Fig. 2, B.1, b–B.3) for similar examples.
vessels, ? cups; with pedestal base. (All glazed brown inside and out, except where otherwise stated).
98. Base of ? cup. Fine orange fabric; glazed inside only.
99. Pale orange fabric; slate grey exterior, possibly a salt.
100. Large cup, similar fabric to 99.
101–2. Similar fabric to 100.
103. Fine orange fabric; greeny-brown glaze.
104. Similar fabric to 103, brown iron flecked glaze.
105. ? Cup. Creamy-white fabric, pale greeny-yellow glaze. There is a scar where a handle has been, possibly a loop handle.
106. Rim sherd ? cup. Similar fabric to 105; apple-green glaze inside and out. Scar of handle on shoulder.
107. Rim of goblet-type cup. Similar fabric to 105; internal apple-green glaze (cf. *Holling* 1971, Fig. 2, B.1b).

Fig. 8.49

(h) Jugs
108. Dark brown ware oxidised red. Thick black glaze inside and out. May not be from Crane Street.
109. Fine reddish-buff ware. External black glaze with some patchy sparse glaze inside.
110. Base in fine orange fabric; dark brown glaze inside and out.
111. Rim of a ? jug. Very overfired waster reduced dark grey.
112. Rim of a ? jug. Fine pale orange ware.

113. Rim of a jug. Only one of this type noted although they were made in some quantity at Graffham (cf. *Aldsworth and Down*, forthcoming).
114. Rim of a ? jug. Fine reddish-buff ware reduced to grey.
115. Base of a ? jug. Fine reddish-buff ware with brown glaze inside.
116. Jug handle; fine grey ware with patches of dark green glaze.
117. Handle with thumbed decoration. Similar fabric to 116.
118. Handle in fine grey fabric, olive green glaze.
119. Body sherd from an imitation Bellarmine jug in a fine reddish fabric, with applied rosettes under an external mid-brown glaze. It carries a panel, of which just under half survives with the figures "44" on the right-hand side as viewed. The sherd is a waster and if, as seems almost certain, the figures are part of a date, then the date must be 1644 on analogy with the other wares from the kiln.

Brown glazed jugs with applied rosettes, but with a darker brown glaze were also made at Graffham. A vessel was published from Chapel Street (Area 2, Pit L.10) and then thought to be *c.* 19th century, but the remainder of the material published from this group shows a date bracket of late 17th to early 18th century in the light of present knowledge (*Chichester 3*, 1978, Fig. 11.12, No. 17).

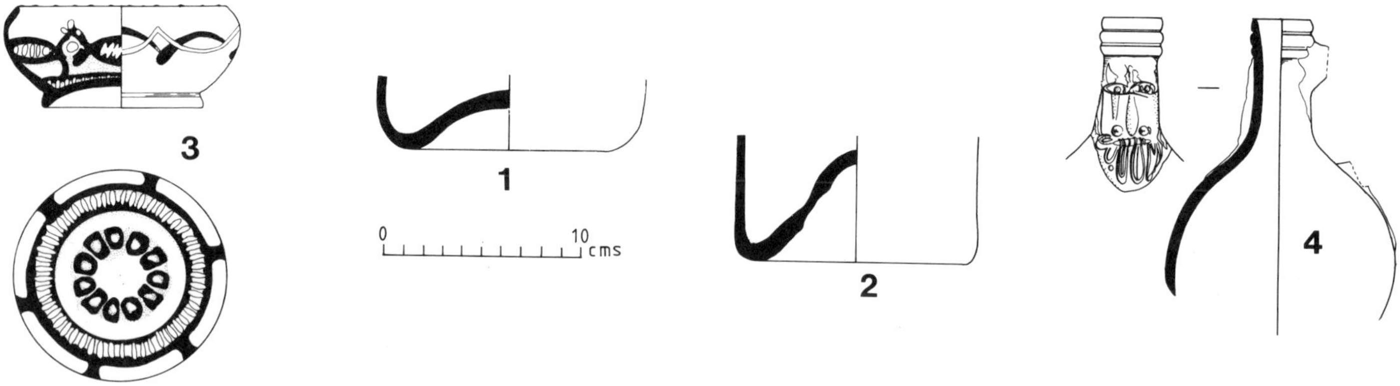

Fig. 8.51. Post-Medieval wares from Crane Street; Miscellaneous (¼).

Fig. 8.50

(*j*) *Miscellaneous*

120. Rim sherd from a lid. Similar fabric to 105. "Tudor" green glaze inside.
121. Base, probably from a chafing dish. Pale orange fabric, reduced to slate grey.
122. Knob from the rim of a chafing dish; external brown glaze.
123. Candlestick. Orange fabric, external brown glaze (cf. *Holling* 1971, Fig. 5, N.1). The example illustrated is not a waster and has been re-used after its base was broken.
124. Fragment from a ? chicken drinking pan in a hard white fabric with internal glazing. Numbers of these were also made at Graffham and similar objects in the Victoria and Albert and London Museums are described as chicken drinking pans (cf. *Sheppard* 1978, p. 114, No. 20).

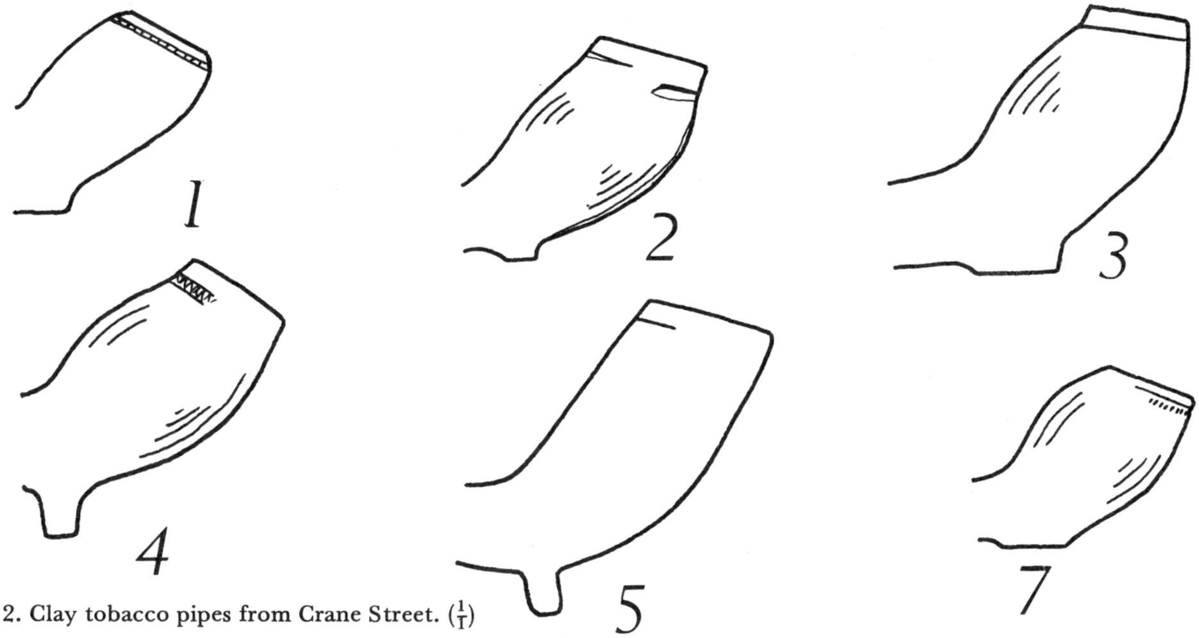

Fig. 8.52. Clay tobacco pipes from Crane Street. ($\frac{1}{1}$)

Fig. 8.50 *(k) Kiln furniture*

125. Spacer ring, one of a number found and identical to those used at Graffham.
126. Ridge tile used as a prop.
127. Peg tile, one of many used in the kiln. In a fine orange fabric which reduces to a pale grey.
128. Kiln support bar, one of a number found. Orange fabric.

Fig. 8.51 *MISCELLANEOUS POST-MEDIEVAL FINDS FROM CRANE STREET*

Most of the following finds came from Layer P.2 which contained the majority of the kiln wares and also later 18th and 19th century objects:

1. Base of a sack bottle with a high kicked base, probably as *Chichester 3*, Fig. 11.12, No. 6, late 17th or early 18th century.
2. Base of a sack bottle, *op. cit.*, Fig. 11.12, No. 7, late 17th or early 18th century.
3. Toft-ware bowl, hard white fabric, brown slip below a pale yellow glaze (cf. *Celoria* and *Kelly* 1973, Figs. 70 (144) and 79 (314)), for wares which, though not identical, were produced using similar techniques. A date of *c.* 1700 is proposed for the Hanley kiln but it should be emphasised that the bowl from Crane Street is not a product of the local kiln, but is likely to be slightly later in date and possibly early 18th century. (Pit P.3).
4. Bellarmine jug, 17th century (Pit P.3).

Fig. 8.52 *Clay tobacco pipes*

1. As *Atkinson,* Fig. 1 (1), *c.* A.D. 1620 (Pit P.3).
2. *Atkinson,* Fig. 1 (9), *c.* A.D. 1650 (Pit 2).
3. *Atkinson,* Fig. 2 (1), *c.* A.D. 1670 (P.2).
4. *Atkinson,* Fig. 1 (8), *c.* A.D. 1640 (P.2).
5. *Atkinson,* Fig. 2 (4), *c.* A.D. 1679–80 (P.2).
6. *Atkinson,* Fig. 1 (1), *c.* A.D. 1620 illegible stamp (P.2).

Discussion

As a result of the discovery of this kiln and of further work at Graffham, it is now possible to revise earlier conjectures about the post-medieval wares found in the City and published in Volumes 2 and 3 of *Chichester Excavations.* A re-examination of the "Surrey" type white wares previously identified in *Chichester 2*; Fig. 7.13, Nos. 28, 29 and 32, and Fig. 7.14, 48 A and B and 54, and *Chichester 3*; Fig. 11.12, Nos. 13 and 28; Fig. 11.13, No. 27, and Fig. 11.14, Nos. 44, 47, 62 and 64, suggests that they are probably from Crane Street or Graffham. The proportion of white wares from Crane Street is small (3.4% by weight of total), indicating that only small amounts of white firing clay were imported from time to time. Reading clay outcrops along the harbour, as it does along the Hampshire-Surrey border, where supplies of white firing clay were exploited by the medieval and post-medieval potters of that region (*Holling* 1971), and while the Reading clay seen by the writer is generally pink with white streaks it may well be that there are pockets of the whiter clay accessible locally and known to the 17th century Crane Street potters.

Other wares

The majority of the brown and green glazed wares of the 17th century date illustrated in *Chichester 2*; Figs. 7.13 and 7.14 and *Chichester 3*; Figs. 11.12, 11.13 and 11.14 are from Graffham or Crane Street. Two sherds can be specially mentioned here. *Chichester 3*; Fig. 11.12, No. 32 is from Graffham where this type of stamping on biscuit moulds is well attested (*Aldsworth* and *Down*, forthcoming), and No. 17 in the same illustration; a brown-glazed jug with applied rosettes. These jugs have now been found amongst the pottery collected from one of the Graffham sites by the late Miss P. A. M. Keef (see comments on No. 119, p. 208).

One of the most puzzling aspects of the site used for the kiln is its location, near to the centre of the town, where not only might there be a nuisance factor to neighbours, but where fuel certainly had to be brought in from some distance away. Some of the clay may have been dug on site. The local London clay is very suitable for potting as both the Roman and late Saxon occupants of the site have testified and the shallow pit (Pit 17/27) and the dump of waste clay found (Fig. 8.23 and *Streeten*, this volume, p. 213), both point to this possibility. It might well be that sea coal was used as the fuel. A number of small lumps of coal were found in pits which also contained wasters and certainly, potteries in the Stoke-on-Trent area were using open-cast coal local to their kilns (*Celoria* and *Kelly* 1973, 3) at a slightly later date than that proposed for the Crane Street kiln.

Newcastle was sending sea coals to Sussex during the 17th century and there are records of shipments to the Port of Chichester in 1667. A study of the coastal shipping trade at that time shows that Chichester was sending malt, wheat, hops and timber to London and also to ports further west (P.R.O. 8/58). It is likely that the person who owned the small pottery industry had other interests, mainly agricultural, and was probably a merchant doing sufficiently well to be able to ship in coal from one of the northern ports, possibly someone who was in the malting business, as part of the site was later recorded as a malthouse and the coal may have been used for malting as well as potting. The picture emerges of a

17th century entrepeneur, well diversified in his business activities, owning property in Crane Street and the area surrounding it and likely enough to be a man of substance in the community.

The port books for the 17th century are a useful source of information about the coastal trade between Chichester and other English ports and the names mentioned in the records of shipments are probably local merchants who combined the occupations of merchant and shipowner. Mr. Morgan of the Documentary Research Group has studied the names mentioned in the port books for 1666-1671 (there are no entries for the Civil War years), and points out that Thomas Miller, mentioned a number of times, had a large house in North Pallant and paid tax on two fire hearths or stoves in Crane Street in 1670. He was a merchant, was Mayor in 1668 and 1678, and M.P. for a number of years from 1688 and became a baronet in 1705. His father (Mark) lived in North Street and was Mayor in 1662. His grandfather (Thomas) was in North Street in 1621. This shows a connection with the Crane Street-North Street area over 80 years, and it might well be that the Millers operated an industrial complex which by 1670 involved a malthouse, pipe-making and the sale of tobacco. The latter activities are suggested by the presence in Crane Street of one Richard Trevatt, a tobacco cutter, who had a one-hearth house there, probably adjoining Miller's property, and by the fact that in the late 17th century tobacco pipe clay and tobacco were being imported (the clay from Dorset). Whether the kiln was functioning as late as 1670 is a matter for conjecture, but the date of 1644 on the imitation Bellarmine jug would perhaps indicate that it was Thomas Miller's father Mark, who was Mayor in 1662, who started the pottery industry.

No large waster spreads have been found like the ones at Norwood and Graffham, but it is possible that these might lie below the houses and gardens to the east of the site excavated. Alternatively, the kiln may have only had a short life before, perhaps, being moved elsewhere or the pottery manufacturing project being abandoned.

A comparison of the wares with those from Graffham shows that the Crane Street vessels are of a higher standard of competence, but that a more restricted range of wares was produced.

So far, no potters' names have been recorded for Chichester for this period. This might be because the activities were carried out under the control of a wealthy merchant, with the potters being employees, and thus not separately recorded. It might also serve to explain the apparent anomaly of a humble potter plying his trade in the centre of the town to the annoyance of others. The Millers were of sufficient standing in the City to do more or less what they liked on their own land.

References

ALDSWORTH and DOWN	Aldsworth, F. G. and Down, A., *The Medieval and post-Medieval pottery industry of the Graffham region* (forthcoming).
ATKINSON	Atkinson, D. R., *Sussex clay Tobacco Pipes and the pipemakers.*
CELORIA and KELLY 1973	Celoria, F. S. C. and Kelly, J. H., "A post-medieval pottery site with a kiln base, . . . Hanley"; *City of Stoke-on-Trent Museum Archaeological Society Report No. 4*, 1973.
CHICHESTER 2	Down, A., *Chichester Excavations* 2, 1974.
CHICHESTER 3	Down, A., *Chichester Excavations* 3, 1978.
HOLLING 1971	Holling, F. W., "A preliminary note on the Pottery Industry of the Hampshire-Surrey Borders", *Surrey Arch. Coll.* LXVIII, 1971.
KELLY 1973	Kelly, J. H., "A rescue excavation on the site of Swan Bank, Methodist Church Burslem, Stoke-on-Trent, Staffs"; *City of Stoke-on-Trent Museum Archaeological Society Report No. 5*, 1973.
KELLY 1975	*City of Stoke-on-Trent Museum Archaeological Report No. 5*, 1975.
MOORHOUSE 1971	Moorhouse, S., "Two late and post-Medieval pottery groups from Farnham Castle, Surrey", *Surrey Arch. Coll.* LXVIII, 1971.
SHEPPARD 1978	Sheppard, R. F., "Post-Medieval pottery" in R. Canham, *Brentford; 2,000 years*, 1978.

Characterisation of Post-medieval Wares in Chichester

by Anthony D. F. Streeten, B.A.

Variations in the style or manufacturing techniques of post-medieval ceramics are seldom sufficient to enable reliable distinction between the products of different kilns in the same region, in addition, the textural uniformity of earthenwares at this period hinders classification of the fabrics (*Mynard*, 1969, 43). The problems of identification must therefore be overcome before the distribution of marketed vessels can be examined. Medieval and early post-medieval wares from West Sussex have already been subjected to a programme of thin-section analysis (*Streeten*, forthcoming (a)), and the discovery of wasters in Chichester provides a welcome opportunity to apply the same techniques to material from a later period. Clearly, it would be valuable to establish an objective means of distinguishing products of the Crane Street kiln from vessels manufactured at Graffham or those made by potters working further afield in the Hampshire and Surrey border area.

The clays of south-east England do not contain diagnostic inclusions capable of linking locally produced ceramics with the source of their raw materials, and quartz is frequently the only mineral visible in thin-section. On the other hand, the size frequency of the quartz grains, which reflects both the character of the clay itself and any sand temper added by the potter, does offer a means of characterising the products of different kilns. *Peacock* (1971), used the techniques and formulae devised by sedimentologists to demonstrate that a group of Romano-British coarse-wares came from the same source of manufacture, and a simplified method, based on the same principles, has been applied to the Crane Street samples.

Detailed discussion of this modified technique, already outlined elsewhere (*Streeten*, forthcoming (b)), is intended to form the subject of a separate paper. In summary, however, a standard sample of measured grains is plotted on a graph showing size against frequency, thereby producing a curve which can be compared with the results from other thin-sections. In an attempt to establish the variation in grain-size frequency between different vessels from the same source of production, five sherds have been analysed from each kiln, and the data is plotted to show mean frequency ± one standard deviation for each grain-size group (Fig. 8.53, graph A).

The products of different post-medieval kilns are not so easily distinguished as those of the medieval period, and the fine-textured fabric is represented by a high proportion of small quartz grains seen in thin-section. Comparison of the precise position of the peak on the graphs does, however, enable the products of the Crane Street kiln to be distinguished from wasters found at Graffham (Fig. 1, graphs A and B), and it has been possible to demonstrate that certain vessels found elsewhere in Chichester did not come from the local kiln, but were made at Graffham (Fig. 8.53, graph C). The Crane Street fabric is also different from the red ware wasters from kilns at Cove, Hants. (*Haslam*, 1975), and Ash, Surrey (*Holling*, 1969 (Fig. 1, graph D)). No attempt has so far been made to establish whether these red wares of the Hampshire and Surrey border "industry" follow the same widespread distribution as the better-known white wares. Many doubtless pass unnoticed amongst assemblages of local red fabrics. Only time-consuming analysis would be able to provide an answer, but the results from Chichester demonstrate that differentiation is feasible.

The source of the clay used in manufacture of the Crane Street vessels is not known, but an artificial heap of clay, which had probably been prepared for use in potting, was found on the site (see p. 197). Samples have been examined, and, although the available techniques of analysis do not permit identification of the source, the clay samples provide a useful standard against which both the colour and the quartz grain-size frequency of the wasters can be compared.

Colour alone is not a generally reliable criterion for classification, but vessels from Crane Street are slightly more pink than those from Graffham. Munsell colour readings (*Munsell*, 1975), have been taken from sherds selected for thin-section analysis. Readings made on the margin of a dry fracture show that the oxidised Crane Street samples fall within a narrow range of colour (either 10R 6/6 or 2.5YR 6/6). One slightly reduced vessel has a grey margin (10R 2/6).

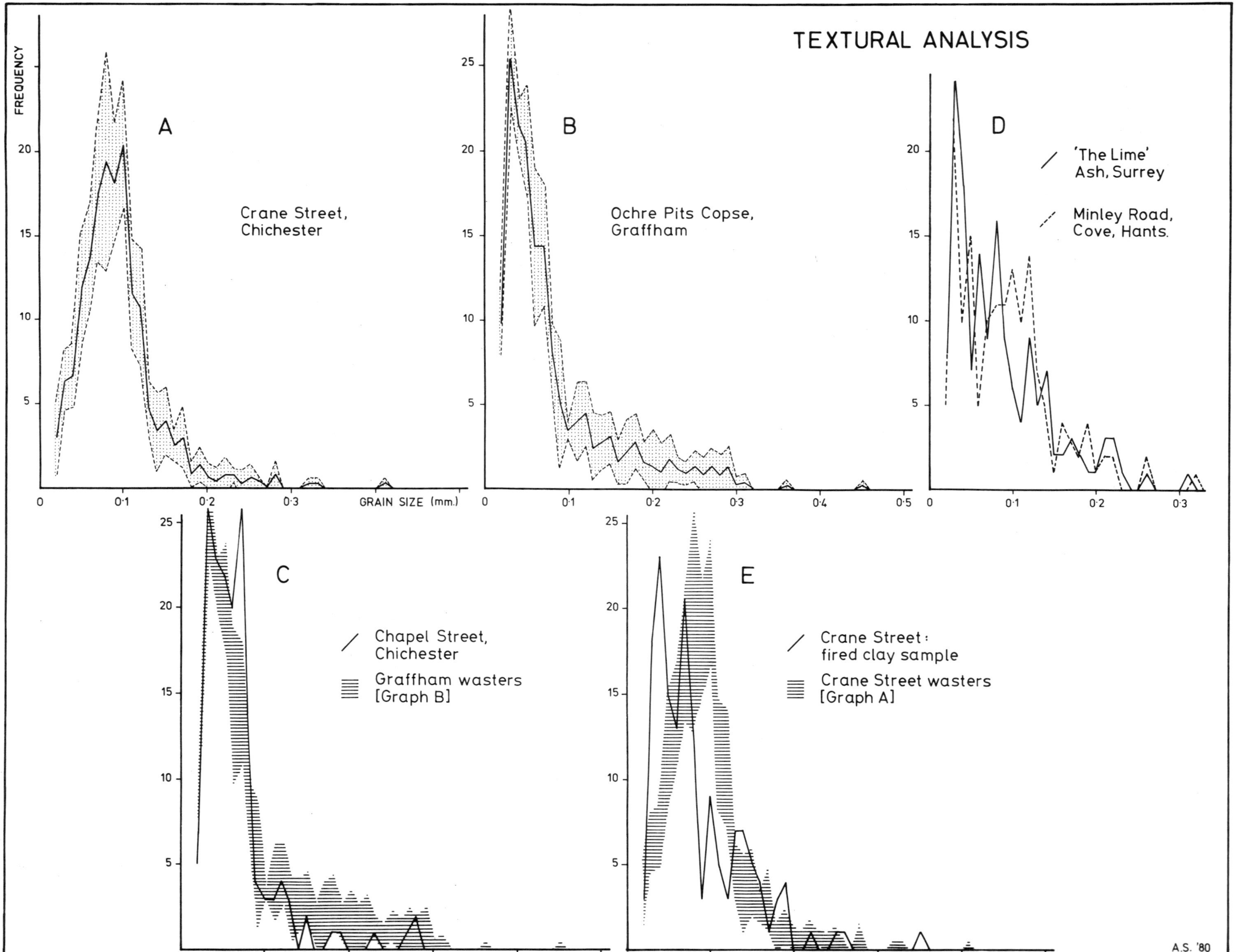
TEXTURAL ANALYSIS
FREQUENCY
GRAIN SIZE (mm.)
A
Crane Street, Chichester
B
Ochre Pits Copse, Graffham
D
'The Lime' Ash, Surrey
Minley Road, Cove, Hants.
C
Chapel Street, Chichester
Graffham wasters [Graph B]
E
Crane Street: fired clay sample
Crane Street wasters [Graph A]
A.S. '80

Comparison with the Chichester products shows that similar readings from wasters at Ochre Pits Copse, Graffham, have a brighter red colour (2.5YR 5/8), whereas medieval wasters from another Chichester kiln at Orchard Street (*Down* and *Rule*, 1971, 153–64) are generally similar to those from Crane Street (either 10R 6/6 or 2.5YR 6/6). One sample is slightly brighter in colour (10R 6/8). In this instance, therefore, colour does appear to distinguish the use of different clays in post-medieval ceramics, although the range of colours in a larger assemblage may well overlap. It would not be possible to attribute vessels to a particular clay source on the basis of colour, but it can be inferred from the medieval wasters that the same clays were used for locally produced ceramics in Chichester during both the medieval and later periods.

Samples of clay from the heap at Crane Street were made into small "bricks", dried, and then fired in an electric (oxidising) kiln to a variety of temperatures. The dry clay is a yellow-brown colour, but fired samples correspond closely with the wasters; nevertheless, the highest temperature appears to exceed that normally attained in the post-medieval kiln. Munsell readings from the samples fired at Southampton University are as follows:

CS 17 i	Unfired	10YR 6/4
CS 17 ii	650 deg. C	2.5YR 6/6
CS 17 iii	850 deg. C	10R 6/6
CS 17 iv	950 deg. C	10R 6/6
CS 17 v	1050 deg. C	10R 5/6

It is not possible to estimate the firing temperature from this evidence alone, but similarity between the wasters and sample "bricks" is sufficient to indicate that this clay was used, as suspected, for manufacture of the Crane Street products.

The quartz grain-size frequency of fired clay samples is not always precisely the same as that observed in pottery thought to have been made from the same material. At Parrock, Hartfield, Sussex, for example, samples from a dump of clay adjacent to the kiln showed a much higher proportion of fine quartz than was found in the fabric of the wasters (*Streeten*, 1979, 13 114–6). A similar pattern emerges at Crane Street, where, although the range of grain-size distribution is similar, the number of medium and large grains in the clay sample is lower than in the pottery. This increases the proportion of the groundmass which appears in the sample of measured grains (Fig. 8.53, graph E). Extensive comparative studies have not been made, but the implication appears to be that final preparation of the clay involved the addition of more sand (represented by the medium and large grains seen in thin-section). The heap of clay at both Parrock and Crane Street had already been brought to the working area near the kiln, and the extra sand must therefore have been added only shortly before forming the vessels.

Conclusion

Textural analysis not only gives insight into the potter's technology, but it also provides a means of identifying the products of known kilns. If, however, we are correct in the assumption that the Crane Street potter(s) were active for only a limited period (see p. 211), then the likelihood of selecting one of these vessels for analysis from among the wealth of post-medieval material in Chichester is remote. We can, however, be confident that Crane Street products were in competition with the widespread market for contemporary Graffham wares which are found over large areas of West Sussex and the Hampshire border (*Streeten*, forthcoming (a)). Unfortunately, reliable quantification of this trade is frustrated by the problems of visual classification. When the fabrics are so very similar, objective identification of sample sherds is not sufficient to measure the proportion of different sources represented in a large assemblage. The identification of Crane Street products outside the city would help to plot crude geographical limits to the distribution, and might perhaps give some insight into the hinterland of Chichester at this period, but practical difficulties of visual classification are likely to remain a barrier to reliable quantification.

References

CHICHESTER 1	Down, A. and Rule, M., *Chichester Excavations 1*, 1971.
HASLAM 1975	Haslam, J., 'A 17th-century pottery at Cove, E. Hampshire', *Post-Med. Archaeol.* 9, 164-187 (1975).
HOLLING 1969	Holling, F., '17th-century pottery from Ash, Surrey', *Post-Med. Archaeol.* 3, 18-30 (1969).
MUNSELL 1975	Munsell, *Munsell Soil Color Chart*, Baltimore, U.S.A. (1975).
MYNARD 1969	Mynard, D. C., 'A group of post-medieval pottery from Dover Castle', *Post-Med. Archaeol.* 3, 31-46 (1975).
PEACOCK 1971	Peacock, D. P. S., 'Petrography of certain coarse pottery', in Cunliffe, B., *Excavations at Fishbourne*, Society of Antiquaries Res. Rep., xxvii, London, 255-9 (1971).
STREETEN 1980 a	Streeten, A. D. F., 'Potters, kilns and markets in medieval Sussex: a preliminary study', in Freke, D. (Ed.), *The Archaeology of Sussex Pottery, S.A.C.* 118 (1980).
STREETEN 1979 b	Streeten, A. D. F., 'Fabric analysis and distribution', in Freke, D., 'The excavation of an early 16th-century pottery kiln at Lower Parrocks, Hartfield, E. Sussex, 1977', *Post-Med. Archael.* (1979).

Chapel Street, 1978
Post-medieval Wares from Layers P.1, P.2 and Pit P3

by Sheila Morgan

The largest proportion of the sherds from this excavation are, as one would expect, the underglaze blue transfer printed wares. The earliest identifiable pattern is No. 28, *c.* 1809–20, although the printing and design of No. 38. while not attributable to a factory, suggests a turn of the century date. Grey and black printing is represented in products of the 1860's (Nos. 32 and 35), when blue printing was not so fashionable and its quality deteriorated. Pit P.3 provides an example of blue printing of the highest quality, No. 62, Spode's "Lucano" pattern introduced *c.* 1819. This Pit also shows us that potters in the 19th century were ready to take advantage of royal occasions to market their wares as do their counterparts today: No. 67, a plate issued to commemorate Queen Victoria's coronation in 1837. This plate is also an educational aid with letters of the alphabet moulded round the rim, a reminder that the majority of the population could not afford to send their children to school.

Nos. 40 and 41 are typical examples of hand-painted decoration before the widespread use of transfer printing.

Another form of decoration was lustre, imitating silver and gold, introduced in the early 1800's. No. 5 is a tiny fragment of a rare background colour—yellow—with a silver lustre lining on the rim.

No. 59 is an example of a pearlware stand or plate, moulded with a basket weave pattern and pierced rim with touches of blue enamel. A very popular produce of *c.* 1800–10.

There is nothing distinctive about the creamware fragments and the absence of bone china in any quantity reflects its value as a luxury item.

Some of the earliest sherds are the tin-glazed wares, only found in P.2 and No. 9 is the most interesting fragment: part of a tile printed in Liverpool, one of a well known series of famous actors of the period (1770–80), representing characters from plays in which they appeared. These tiles would be used to decorate the surrounds of fireplaces.

Even earlier are the white saltglaze stoneware fragments. No. 14, *c.* 1750, is a good example of the skill of the early Staffordshire potters in throwing and finishing a teapot with such a thin profile.

Date range:	P.1	1820–1860
	P.2	*c.* 1750–1890
	Pit P.3	*c.* 1800–1840

None of the wares are illustrated but all have been placed with the excavation archive in the Chichester District Museum.

CH/78/CS P.1

Earthenwares

1. Part of tureen cover and flat ware, printed in underglaze blue with Wild Rose pattern—Coysh No. 62.
2. Fragments of hollow and flat ware printed in underglaze blue with standard willow pattern.
3. Fragment of soap dish transfer printed in brown.
4. Fragment of mocha decorated ware.
5. Fragment of hollow ware rim, bright yellow with silver lustre decoration inside and outside edge of rim, *c.* 1820.
6. Fragment of flatware rim, moulded with stylised daisies and line of pink lustre round the edge, *c.* 1830.
7. Fragment of flatware rim, moulded decoration of five-petalled flower (? primrose), *c.* 1840.

Other sherds of underglaze blue printed wares too fragmentary to identify.

Bone china

8. Fragment of saucer with applied blue motifs.

CH/78/CS P.2

Tin-glazed earthenware

9. Fragment of wall tile printed in black "Mr. Shuter". One of a series of

theatrical tiles dated *c.* 1770–80. See Anthony Ray "Liverpool Printed Tiles" in *English Ceramic Circle Transactions*, Volume 9, pt. 1, 1973. "Mr. Shuter in the character of Lovegold".

10. Fragments of rim, base and handle of bowl, diameter 18 cm.
11. Fragment of rim with stilt mark on underside, painted with blue leaf and lines.
12. Fragments of two footrims.
13. Body sherd with wide blue line decoration.

White salt-glazed stoneware

14. Fragment of shoulder and gallery of circular teapot.
15. Fragments of rim and base of plate. Moulded decoration on rim.

Cream coloured earthenware

16. Fragment of thick rim with wide brown enamelled line on outer edge and narrow brown line where rim joins well of plate.
17. Fragment of plate rim with dark blue enamelled edge.
18. Fragment of shaped rim.
19. Fragments of flat and round rims of bowls and basins.
20. Fragments of bases of three bowls and one mug.
21. Two large and one small handles.
22. Bases of two plates.
23. Fragments of a mug.
24. Fragment of a straight-sided circular teapot with remains of handle near the shoulder. Grey-coloured body, line moulding beneath the shoulder coloured green.
25. Fragments of hollow ware rims with brown and green underglaze painting.
26. Fragment of hollow ware with brown, cream and green banding.

Transfer printed earthenware (all printed in blue unless stated otherwise)

27. Fragments of two plates with indented rims, two plates with plain rims, a strainer and bowl, all decorated with the traditional willow pattern. Backstamp printed under one plain rim "STAFFORDSHIRE Stone China" within an oblong bordered with pseudo-Chinese characters, similar to No. 2618 in Godden, attributed to Chas. Meigh and successors, 1840's onwards.
28. Fragment of hollow ware decorated with Tendril pattern and brown enamelled rim. Illustrated in Coysh, No. 3, where the design is attributed to Benjamin Adams, 1809–20.
29. Fragment of dinner plate. The border matches that of "Eton College", see Coysh, No. 69. Pattern manufactured by George Phillips of Longport, *c.* 1834–48.
30. Fragment of plate with Wild Rose pattern. Illustrated in Coysh, No. 62.
31. Fragment of drainer decorated with "Filigree" pattern. Illustrated in Whiter, No. 47. *c.* 1823. Spode.
32. Fragment of plate rim decorated with concentric lines, flower sprays and scrolls, printed in grey. Illustrated in Lockett, No. 34. Davenport, *c.* 1865.
33. Fragment of bowl rim decorated with border stimilar to No. 52 in Whiter. Spode's "British Flowers" pattern, *c.* 1828.
34. Fragment of base of plate, with printed backstamp "P.B. & Co." within an oval frame. "Armitage" presumably name ARMITA.. of pattern. See Godden, No. 3038. Pinder Bourne & Co., Burslem, 1862–82.

35. Base and part of cup printed in black with stylised flower design. Backstamp: A beehive with "Florentine China" in ribbon below and "STANTON" above. Probably mark of Burgess Leigh, 1867–89. See Godden No. 715.
36. Fragment of London shape cup. Design: man in a wide brimmed hat leaning on a cow and facing a man in a frock coat sitting under a tree. River and castle with flag flying in the background, *c.* 1820.
37. Tureen cover handle in the form of a flower, and another in the form of a stylised leaf.
38. Fragment of cup, chinoiserie design of figure with pennant standing on top of a three-arched bridge, *c.* 1800.
39. Fragment of cheese dish printed in green with trees and flowers.

The remainder of the sherds are too fragmentary to identify, but are typical of the designs and printing of the first half of the 19th century.

Other earthenwares

40. Base of tea bowl painted in underglaze blue, *c.* 1790.
41. Fragment of saucer painted in underglaze blue, *c.*1780.
42. Rims of two pearlware plates, shell edge moulding painted in blue.
43. Fragment of London shape bowl painted with a broad band round outside of rim and alternating dots and leaf shapes below, in blue.
44. Fragments of hollow ware with mocha decoration in brown and black.
45. Fragments of deep cream kitchen ware with blue and white banding.
46. Fragments of neck and spout of moulded jug, with brown glaze round the neck.
47. Fragments of bowl—grey body with blue painted lines around the middle.
48. Fragments of lead-glazed hollow ware, rims, handles, etc.

Bone china

49. Fragments of two saucers printed with chinoiserie pattern in pale blue.
50. Fragments of cup and saucer with applied blue motifs (similar to No. 8).
51. Fragments of flat and hollow ware painted on glaze in polychrome, *c.* 1810.

CH/78/CS Pit P.3

Cream-coloured earthenware

52. Nearly complete small oval pie dish, length 19 cm, height 3.5 cm.
53. Fragments of rims of two bowls, one with small bead rim.
54. Fragments of rims of two plates, one a large serving plate.
55. Bases of two dishes, no footrims.
56. Footrims of two bowls.
57. One plain loop handle.
58. Fragment of plate rim, painted in underglaze blue with two lines separated by a line of dots.

Pearlware

59. Fragmentary 22 cm diameter plate, moulded in basket weave pattern, with pierced rim. No footrim. Touches of blue enamel round central medallion and on edge of rim.

Transfer printed earthenware (all printed in blue unless stated otherwise)

60. Nearly complete plate, 26 cm diameter. Wild Rose pattern, Coysh No. 62, impressed with * on base. Double footrim.
61. Nearly complete plate, 17 cm diameter. Pattern as above, but printed in a grey/blue shade.
62. Fragments of two plates, 22 cm diameter, no footrim. "Lucano" pattern. Spode. Illustrated in Whiter, No. 68. *c.* 1819.
63. Side of oval dish, printed with large flowers and leaves.
64. Base of cup. Imitation Chinese seal mark backstamp.
65. Fragments of flatware decorated with standard willow pattern, and Wild Rose pattern.
66. Fragment of hollow ware, "British Flowers" pattern. Spode. No. 52, Whiter. *c.* 1828.
67. Fragment of nursery plate, printed in brown with picture of young Queen Victoria and words "Born 25th May 1819 Proclaimed 20 . . .". Letters of the alphabet moulded around the rim. Possibly a Coronation commemorative plate of 1837.
68. Fragment of base of bowl printed in brown.
69. Tea-cup handle with green printing.

References

COYSH, J. W. *Blue Printed Earthenware 1800–50.* David & Charles, 1972.

GODDEN, G. A. *Encyclopaedia of British Pottery and Porcelain Marks*, Herbert Jenkins, 1964.

LOCKETT, T. A. *Davenport Pottery and Porcelain 1794–1887.* David & Charles, 1972.

RAY, ANTHONY *English Ceramic Circle Transactions, 1973.*

WHITER, L. *Spode.* Barrie & Jenkins, 1970.

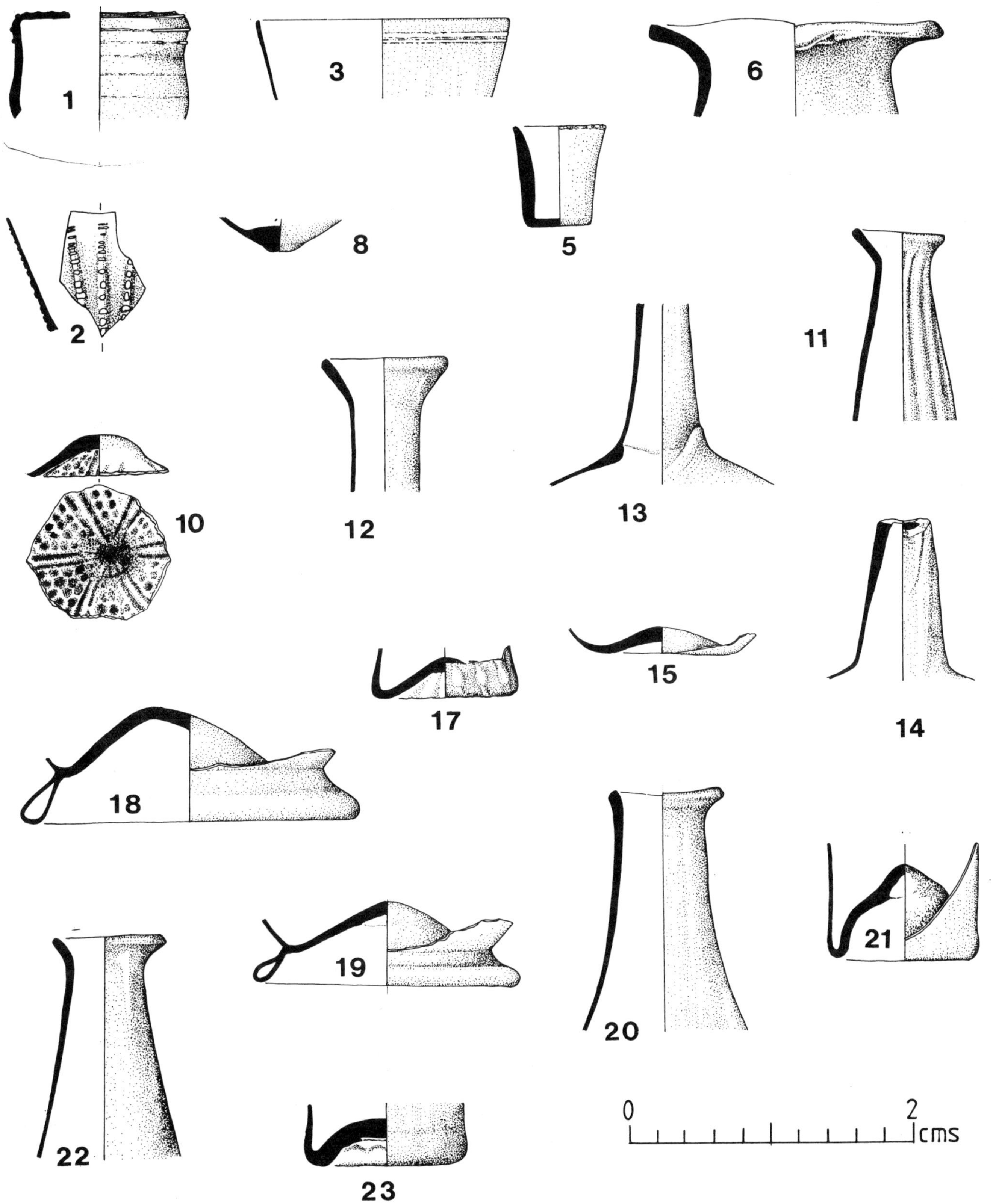

Fig. 8.54. Medieval and post-Medieval glass from the N.W. Quadrant, Nos. 1-23 (½).

Medieval and Post-medieval Glass from the North-West Quadrant
by Robert J. Charleston

Introduction (Figs. 8.54-8.55)

As on most sites with a concentration of 16th-century finds, the Chichester material contains a preponderance of English-made green glass, with a small minority of fragments of imported colourless glass made in Venice or elsewhere in the "*fason de Venise*". One curious fragment (No. 1), without obvious parallels, appears to have most affinity with a family of more or less colourless glasses decorated with blue threading, of 13th–14th-century date and probably Italian origin; it is not possible at present to say just where in Italy they were produced. Another (No. 5), of heavy colourless crystal-glass, is thickly made and bears all the signs of being a product of the second half of the 17th century, when a robuster type of glass found favour at the expense of the thinner Venetian *cristallo*.

Green glass, made mainly in woodland furnaces which also produced the potash flux which characterises its composition, was produced for utility purposes. This consideration, however, by no means always deprived of attractiveness the vessels made from it. It may be taken as axiomatic that such glasses would be obtained from the nearest accessible furnace, and since throughout the period covered by the Chichester finds the Weald of Surrey/Sussex was the most important glass-manufacturing area in the country, it may reasonably be assumed that the Chichester green glasses were made there. *Note.*—Figures in brackets indicate find numbers.

More or less colourless (cristallo) glass

(i) (?) *Italian: 13th–14th century*

1. Fragments from the shoulder or base-angle of a flask or beaker
H. 3.5 cm. Max. D. approx. 6 cm. Perhaps Italian; 13th–14th century.
Bubbly pale-green glass with enclosures of "stone", decorated with an applied spiral of thin blue threading, which has become detached, or become so thin as to lose its colour, on the wall of the vessel.
Note.—Blue-threaded vessels, usually of fine colourless body-glass, have been found on numerous English sites (for a discussion, see Charleston in *Bulletin* of the International Association for the History of Glass, Liege—1981, pp. 66–7). Occasionally a finely-decorated medieval piece of this general character is made of pale-green glass—*cf.* a jug decorated with sealing-wax red trailing, found at Southampton (*Charleston* [1975], p. 216. No. 1489—*cf. ibid.*, p. 218, No. 1521.) (*Chapel Street, Area 4,* [1106]).

(ii) *Venetian and "fason de Venise" glass; 16th–17th century*

2. Fragment of a crystal-glass goblet.
H. 4.3 cm. Max. D. approx. 9 cm. Venetian; first half of 16th century.
Almost colourless "cristallo" glass, decorated with "broken threading" of opaque-white glass over mould-blown ribbing. Probably from a biconical goblet.
Note.—These glasses, of which a number of fragments have been found in English excavations, were apparently made by blowing the paraison into a vertically-ribbed mould, then laying a spiral trail of opaque-white thread over the ribbing; further inflation then broke the trail, so that white dots or dashes remained on the high-points of the ribs. Examples have been found at, e.g., Winchester (*Charleston* [1964], p. 149, No. 7; and unpublished) and Southampton (*Charleston* [1975], pp. 207 and 221, No. 1552). (*Tower Street, Area 7,* E.11 [201]).
3. Rim-fragments of a crystal-glass goblet.
H. 3 cm. D. approx 11.5 cm. Venetian; first half of 16th century.
Almost colourless "cristallo" glass, decorated with two turns of opaque-white threading below the lip. Probably from a biconical goblet.
Note.—Threading is one of the oldest and commonest types of applied decoration. An example of a similarly threaded crystal-glass rim-fragment, but with more turns, was found at Southampton in a garderobe pit containing much fine Venetian glass of late 15th–16th-century date (Bugle Street site, unpublished). (*Chapel Street, Area 1.*)

4. Bottle-base of colourless or greenish glass with strongly iridescent weathering.
H. 2.2 cm. max. D. approx, 5 cm. Perhaps Venetian, or "*fason de Venise*"; 16th–17th century.

Pushed-in "kick" of a medium-sized flask, with ring-pontil underneath just below the apex of the kick. It is not possible to judge the shape of the flask from this fragment. (*Chapel Street, Area 5,* Pit 0.27 [2022]). *Not illustrated.*

5. Bird-feeder or ink-well, clear colourless glass.
H. 3.4 cm. Max. D. 3.3 cm. Perhaps English; third quarter of 17th century.

Flat-based container of slightly spreading cylindrical shape, broken at the top, the rim apparently "grozed" level. The flat base shows all the signs of being mould-blown, and since there is no pontil-mark, it must be concluded that the container was knocked off the blow-pipe, suggesting that the vessel did not require to be carefully finished.

Note.—No exact parallel is known to the author. In a genre painting by Frans van Mieris, however, dated 1663 (Mauritshuis, The Hague), a bird-cage is shown with a container of which the lower half is shaped like the present glass; it widens to a rim which presumably secures the feeder when slipped into the ring fixed to the side of the cage. The container in the picture is coloured red, however, and is clearly intended to represent pottery. The late date is consonant with the character of the glass-material of the Chichester container, and its considerable wall-thickness (*c.* 2 mm.). (*Tower Street, Area 7,* A2 [24]).

Green glass

(i) 13th–14th century

6. Rim-fragment of urinal or flask, thick pale yellowish-green glass, with heavy black weathering and brown surface incrustation.
H. approx. 3 cm. D. approx. 10 cm. (not completely circular). English; perhaps 13th–14th century.

Thick horizontal rim of a neck with internal diameter of about 6.5 cm. Not enough remains to establish the profile of the neck.

Note.—Examples of similar glasses have been found in Southampton (*Charleston* [1975], p. 216, No. 1506, from a 14th-century context); at Bramber Castle, Sussex (unpublished; in Barbican House Museum, Lewes); and at Denny Abbey (unpublished). A comparable neck-fragment was found in a drain on a site in Göttingen, Germany, which was dated by accompanying material to the late 14th or first half of the 15th century (*Schütte* [1976], pp. 107, 109, Abb. 7, 2). This piece is also identified as a urinal, but the thickness of these glasses must raise some question as to their suitability for this purpose. On the other hand, there is considerable variety in the forms shown in 15th-century woodcuts and earlier carved reliefs, etc., and these wide-necked containers fall well within this range.

This fragment appears to fit No. 7, found on another part of the site (*Tower Street, Area 7,* Pit B40.)

7. Rim-fragment of urinal or flask, thick (presumably green) glass with heavy black weathering, much distorted, but probably part of the same vessel as No. 6. *Not illustrated.*
H. 3.2 cm. D. approx. 10 cm. (not completely circular). See No. 6. (*Tower Street, Area 7,* Pit B.6 [A]. [35]).

(ii) *Late medieval–17th century*

(a) *Urinals*

8. Base-fragment of urinal, originally probably green glass, now completely covered with black incrustation.
W. 4 cm. English; late-medieval or 16th century.

Note.—The fragment shows the characteristic thickened base with pontil-mark on the convex surface, the glass tapering rapidly towards the edges of the fragment. Examples are found on most late-medieval sites and up to the 17th century—e.g., at Winchester (*Charleston,* forthcoming, Nos. 11–15, probably of 14th century date) and at Nonsuch (unpublished, with throw-away date between *c.* 1540 and 1680). (*Chapel Street, Area 6,* R.16 [1180]).

(b) *Bottles and flasks*

9. Base-fragment of bottle, pale yellowish-green glass with heavy black weathering and sandy incrustation.
W. 8.5 cm. English; late-medieval or 16th century.
The base has a low rounded "kick", the sides beginning to curve upward to give a rounded body. There are traces of a pontil-mark on the underside, in the apex of the "kick".
Note.—This bottle was probably of the characteristic form, usually with ribbed neck and slightly spreading lip, which survived from the late-medieval period (*Hume* [1957], Nos. 5–6, dated to the late 15th century) into the 17th century (Nonsuch, unpublished). (*Tower Street, Area 7,* Pit. C.8 [390]). *Not illustrated.*

10. Base-fragment of bottle, pale yellowish-green glass with heavy black weathering and sandy incrustation on the underside.
W. 5 cm. English; late medieval or 16th century.
The base has a low rounded "kick", the highest point slightly off-centre. The underside slows the traces of mould-blowing in a design of radiating paired lines with honeycomb patterning between.
Note.—Occasionally late-medieval bottles were decorated with mould-blown patterns, usually vertical ribbing, but no survey has yet been made of the designs represented. See note on No. 9. The present bottle was probably of considerably smaller size. (*Tower Street, Area 7,* C.1, [81]).

11. Neck- and rim-fragment of a bottle, pale green glass with brown incrustation.
H. 6.3 cm. D. of rim. approx. 3.2 cm. (not completely circular). English; late-medieval or 16th century.
Neck of a medium-sized bottle, the slightly spreading rim cut off aslant; decorated with vertical mould-blown ribbing (18 ribs).
Note.—cf. a London example (*Hume* [1957], p. 107, No. 3, dated to the late 15th century). (*Chapel Street, Area 3,* Pit W.2.)

12. Rim-fragment of a bottle, pale green glass with patchy black weathering and sandy incrustation.
H. 5 cm. D. approx. 4.5 cm. (not completely circular). English; late medieval or 16th century.
Spreading rim cut off slightly aslant and thickened at the edge. (*Chapel Street, Area 3,* Pit. W.14.)

13. Neck- and shoulder-fragment of a bottle, or possibly body and stem-fragment of a lamp, pale green glass with patchy brown/black weathering and sandy incrustation.
H. 5.5 cm. D. of broken-off neck (or stem) 2 cm. English; late-medieval or 16th century.
Tapering neck or stem, considerably thicker at the broken extremity, spreading to an almost horizontal shoulder. (*Chapel Street, Area 3,* Pit W.14.)

14. Neck- and shoulder-fragment of a bottle, pale green glass with patchy brown/black weathering and sandy incrustation.
H. 5 cm. D. of broken-off neck 2.2 cm. English; late-medieval or 16th century.
Fragmentary neck sloping out to an almost horizontal curved shoulder. Faint "wrythen" mould-blown ribbing on a "second gather." (*Chapel Street, Area 3,* Pit W.14.)

15. Base-fragment of a bottle, pale green glass with patchy brown/black weathering and slight sandy incrustation.
W. 6 cm. English; late-medieval or 16th century.
Low domed "kick" from a small bottle (*Chapel Street, Area 3,* Pit W.14.)

16. Base-fragment of a bottle, pale yellowish-green glass with patchy brown weathering.
W. 6.5 cm. English; late-medieval or 16th century.
Fragment of the irregular domed "kick" of a medium-sized bottle, with traces of pontil-mark visible on the under-surface. (*Chapel Street, Area 3,* W.1.) *Not illustrated.*

17. Base-fragment of beaker or flask, pale green glass with beige enamel-like weathering.
D. 5 cm. H. 2 cm. Probably English; 16th century.
Circular base of a beaker or flask with slightly constricted sides, decorated with mould-blown vertical ribbing; low domed "kick" with pontil-mark in the apex.

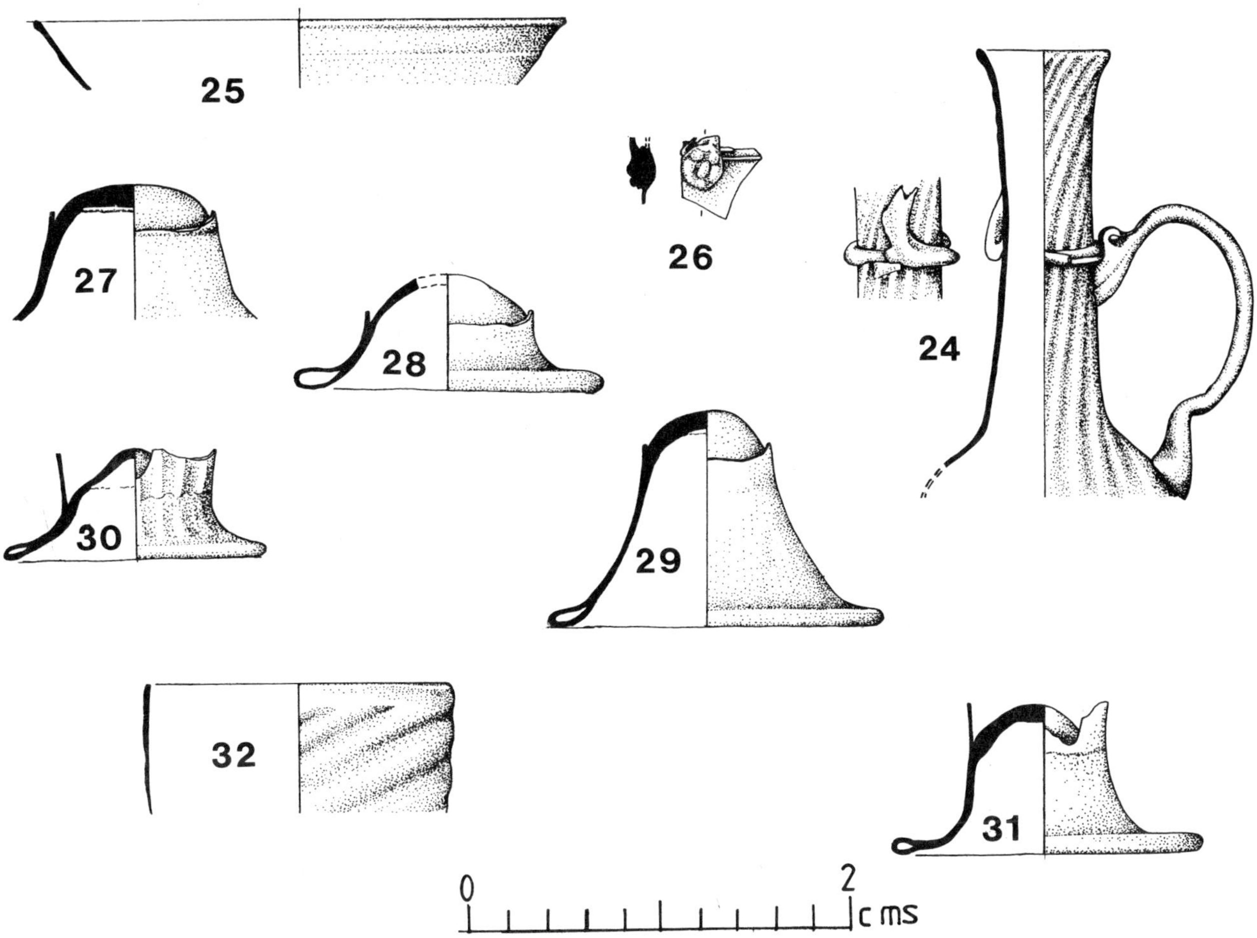

Fig. 8.55. Medieval and post-Medieval glass from the N.W. Quadrant, Nos. 24-32 (½).

Note.—A fragment from the Buttermarket, Ipswich, shows that the shape is drawn in to a point about 2 cm. above the base-rim, and then spreads slightly, the vertical mould-blown ribbing taking a sharp slant to the right at the narrowest point; unfortunately, the upper part of the flask is missing. A second example from an unspecified site in Ipswich shows only the same amount of the base as the Chichester fragment; it is decorated with vertical ribbing (both fragments in the Ipswich Museum, unstratified). The quality of the glass suggests a date in the second half of the 16th century. (*Tower Street, Area 7,* B.2.)

18. Base of a bottle or jug, pale green glass with patchy brown/black weathering.
D. 11.5 cm. H. 4 cm. English; 16th century.
Broad foot made by a fold in the original paraison, giving a low, roughly conical "kick" with traces of a ring-pontil on the underside.
Note.—Both piriform flasks and jugs with tubular spouts are found in Germany with bases made in this way. The bottles are dated to the late 15th-early-16th century, and the jugs to the first quarter of the 16th century; these dates receive support from representations in contemporary pictures, etc. (see *Rademacher* (1933), pp. 70ff., Pls. 14–15, 17 c-d). (*Chapel Street, Area 3,* Pit W.2.)

19. Base of a bottle or jug, pale green glass with patchy brown weathering, and sandy incrustation.
D. 9.5 cm. H. 2 cm. English; 16th century.
See observations on No. 18. (*Chapel Street, Area 3,* W.1.)

20. Neck-fragment of a bottle, pale green glass with sandy incrustation.
H. 10 cm. D. of rim 3.7 cm. (not completely circular). English; probably 16th century.
Short tapering neck with out-turned irregular rim. (*Chapel Street, Area 3,* W.1.)

21. Base-fragment of cylindrical bottle, pale green glass with iridescent weathering and internal incrustation.
H. 4 cm. D. 5.5 cm. English; 16th century.
Cylindrical base with highish irregular conical "kick", partially distorted by the pressure of a disc-pontil which survives on the underside as a perforated diaphragm.
See observations on No. 23. (*Chapel Street, Area 3,* W.1.)

22. Neck-fragment of a bottle, pale green glass with slight sandy incrustation.
H. 7.5 am. D. of rim approx. 3.8 cm. (not completely circular). English; probably late 16th century.
Short tapering neck with spreading, slightly irregular rim. (*Chapel Street, Area 3,* W.1.)

23. Base-fragment of cylindrical bottle, pale green glass with some black weathering and sandy incrustation.
D. 5.8 cm. H. 2.3 cm. English; probably 16th or early 17th century.
Cylindrical base with low rounded "kick" and remains of a disc-like pontil-mark on the underside.
Note.—The cylindrical or polygonal bottle seems to be mainly a development of the 16th century and perhaps the latter part of it (see *Hume* [1956], pp. 100–101. Nos. 4, etc.). (*Tower Street, Area 7,* Pit E.34[B] [204]).

(c) *Jugs or cruets*

24. Neck and handle of a jug or large cruet, pale green glass with slight enamel-like weathering.
H. of neck 11 cm.; of handle 7.5 cm. D. of orifice 3.5 cm. English; probably late 16th century.
Cylindrical neck with slightly spreading rim, mould-blown with faintly "wrythen" vertical ribbing. At half-height a thick trail has been laid round the neck to provide anchorage for the ear-shaped handle, which is of flattened half-round section, and thickens towards the lower sticking-part.
Note.—Other examples of this neck-type have been found in London (*Hume* [1956], p. 98, No. 1 found with material dating to *c.* 1580), and at Basing House Hants., which was destroyed in 1645 (*Moorhouse* [1971], p. 64, No. 16). This type of cruet probably had a globular body, the tall curving spout rising from it (see Moorhouse, *l.c.*). (*Chapel Street, Area 3,* Pit W.2.)

(d) *Lamps*

25. Rim-fragment, perhaps from a lamp, greenish glass with black weathering.
D. approx. 11.5 cm. H. 2.2 cm. English; late-medieval or 16th century.
The fragment has a thickened edge and appears to slope inward from the rim.
Note.—This fragment perhaps comes from the rim of a cup-topped lamp such as was common in the Middle Ages (*cf.* the complete specimen found in Winchester (*Harden* [1969], Fig. 4). The general type continues into the 16th century, but the one surviving specimen is in a blue-green glass of better quality than the Chichester fragment (*Oakley* [1979], p. 298, No. G53). See also No. 3. (*Tower Street, Area 7,* Pit C.8. [385]);

(e) *Beakers*

26. Beaker fragment of pale green glass, with slight iridescent weathering.
W. 2.2 cm. H. 2 cm. English; late 16th-early-17th century. The thin wall of a cylindrical beaker has been decorated with two applied self-coloured horizontal trails, over which has been applied a pad of glass stamped to give a "raspberry prunt".
Note.—This type of decoration occurs at two glass-making sites in England: Woodchester, in Gloucestershire (*Daniels* [1950], p. 12, Figs. 11, 43), and Hutton, in Yorkshire (*Crossley and Aberg* [1972], Fig. 67, 115). The Woodchester furnace was probably run by Lorrainers towards the end of the 16th century, and the Hutton glasshouse has been dated to the last quarter of that century (*Chapel Street, Area 3,* Pit W.2 [2103]).

27. Base-fragment of a beaker, pale green glass with patchy brown weathering and some sandy incrustation.
H. approx. 3 cm. English; probably second half of 16th century.
Folded foot of a cylindrical beaker, made from a single paraison.
Note.—This type of beaker was made by pushing in the bottom of the paraison and working the two layers of glass together to give a double thickness except at the rim of the foot, where the enclosure of air keeps the two layers apart. These tall cylindrical beer-glasses were made at a number of English glass-making sites (e.g., Woodchester, Rosedale, Hutton, and a number of Wealden sites—see Charleston, *Bulletin,* of the International Association for the History of Glass, Liège, 1981 (pp. 87-9); the Weald of Sussex suggests itself as the source of these Chichester finds). These beakers probably date from the second half of the 16th century and a little later. For rim-fragments, see No. 32 below. (*Chapel Street, Area 3,* Pit W.2.)

28. Base-fragment of a beaker, pale greyish-green glass with overall iridescent weathering.
H. approx. 2.8 cm. D. approx. 7.5 cm. English; probably second half of the 16th century.
Folded foot of a cylindrical beaker, made from a single paraison, with almost half the foot-rim preserved.
See observations on No. 27 above. (*Chapel Street, Area 3,* Pit W.2.)

29. Base-fragment of a beaker, greenish-colourless glass with patchy brown and iridescent weathering.
H. approx. 6 cm. D. of foot 8.8 cm.; of beaker at base approx. 3.5 cm. English; probably second half of 16th century.
Folded foot of a cylindrical beaker, made from a single paraison. Pontil-mark visible on under-surface of the dome of the foot.
See observations on No. 27 above (*Chapel Street, Area 3,* W.1.)

30. Base-fragment of a beaker, pale green glass with patchy brown weathering and some sandy incrustation.
H. approx. 3 cm. D. of foot 6.7 cm.; of beaker at base approx 4 cm. English; probably second half of 16th century.
Folded foot of a cylindrical beaker, made from a single paraison. The base of the beaker-wall shows traces of light mould-blown ribbing.
See observations on No. 27 above. Mould-blown ribbing is not infrequently found on these beakers—e.g., at Woodchester (*Daniels,* [1950], Figs. 49, 53, 56); Rosedale (*Crossley and Aberg* [1972], Fig. 60, 17), etc.
See also the rib-moulded rim- and wall-fragments Nos. 32 and 33 below. (*Chapel Street, Area 3,* W.1.)

31. Base-fragment of a beaker, greenish-colourless glass, with some grey enamel-like and overall iridescent weathering.
D. 8.2 cm. H. 3.5 cm. English; probably second half of 16th century.
Folded foot of a cylindrical beaker, made from a single paraison.
See observations on No. 27 above. (*Chapel Street, Area 3,* W.1.)

32. Rim-fragment of a beaker, pale greyish-green glass with patchy black and iridescent weathering.
D. approx. 9 cm. H. 4 cm. English; probably second half of 16th century.
The fragment comes from the rim of a tall cylindrical beaker (beer-glass), which has been decorated with mould-blown vertical ribbing "wrythen" after delivery from the mould. (*Chapel Street, Area 3,* Pit W.2.)

33. Wall-fragment of a beaker, pale greyish-green glass with patchy black and iridescent weathering.
D. approx. 6.5 cm. H. 4.5 cm. English; probably second half of 16th century.
The fragment comes from a tall cylindrical beaker (beer-glass), which has been decorated with mould-blown vertical ribbing "wrythen" after delivery from the mould. *Not illustrated.*
See observations on No. 30 above. (*Chapel Street, Area 3,* W.1.)

(f) *Window-glass*

34. Fragment of window-glass, pale green glass with overall iridescent weathering. L. 2.5 cm. H. 1.8 cm. English; late-medieval–16th century.

The fragment has a line of sealing-wax red embedded in its thickness (*Tower Street, Area 7,* C11. [427]). *Not illustrated.*

35. Fragment of window-glass, green glass with patchy iridescent weathering. L. 2.5 cm. H. 2.6 cm. English; late-medieval–16th century.

The fragment has a thicker band of sealing-wax red embedded in the surface and several thinner lines in the substance of the glass (*Tower Street, Area 7.* [503]). *Not illustrated.*

References

CHARLESTON 1964	Charleston, R. J., Medieval and Later Glass, in Barry Cunliffe, *Winchester Excavations 1949/60,* City of Winchester Museum and Libraries Committee, Winchester, 1964, 1, 145–151.
CHARLESTON 1975	Charleston, R. J., The Glass, in Colin Platt and R. Coleman-Smith, *Excavations in Medieval Southampton,* 1953–69. 2. *The Finds,* Leicester, 1975, 204–26.
CHARLESTON (forthcoming)	Charleston, R. J., Vessel Glass of the late Medieval to Modern Periods, in Martin Biddle and Suzanne Keene, *The Crafts and Industries of Medieval Winchester,* Part II, *Crafts and Industries other than Ceramics, Winchester Studies,* Oxford, 7.
CROSSLEY and ABERG 1972	Crossley, D. W. and Aberg, F. A., Sixteenth Century Glass-making in Yorkshire: Excavations at Furnaces at Hutton and Rosedale, North Riding, 1968/71, *Post-Medieval Archaeology* (1972), 6, 107–59.
DANIELS 1950	Daniels, J. S., *The Woodchester Glass House,* Gloucester, 1950.
HARDEN 1969	Harden, D. B., Medieval Glass in the West, *Proceedings VIIIth International Congress on Glass, 1968,* Society of Glass Technology, Sheffield, 1968, 97–111.
HUME 1956	Hume, I. Noel, A Century of London Glass Bottles, *The Connoisseur Year Book,* London, 1956, 98–103.
HUME 1957	Hume, I. Noel, Medieval Bottles from London, *The Connoisseur* (March 1957), 104–8.
HUME 1962	Hume, I. Noel, Tudor and early Stuart glasses found in London, *The Connoisseur* (August 1962), 269–273.
KENYON 1967	Kenyon G. H. *The Glass Industry of the Weald,* Leicester, 1967.
MOORHOUSE 1971	Moorhouse, S., Finds from Basting House, Hampshire (*c.* 1540–1645): Part II, *Post-Medieval Archaeology* (1971), 5, 35–76.
OAKLEY and HUNTER	Oakley, G. E. and Hunter, J., "The Glass", in John H. Williams, *St. Peter's Street, Northampton Excavations, 1973–76.* Northampton (1979), pp. 295–302.
RADEMACHER 1933	Rademacher, F. (1933). Die deutschen Gläser des mittelalters, Berlin, 1933.
SCHÜTTE	Schütte, S., "Mittelalterliches Glas aus Göttingen", *Zeitschrift für Archälogie des Mittelalters,* 4 1967), pp. 101–117.

1. St. Andrew Oxmarket; Memorial stone of Thomas Gounter.

8. North Street, looking [illegible] Roman masonry wall in front of No. 82

3. Chichester, East Street; Stylobate in front of Midland Bank (looking west).

4. Stylobate block removed.

5. East Street; Roman wall in front of Lloyds Bank.

6. Fragment of the gutter found alongside east-west stylobate in front of the Dolphin & Anchor, West Street. Scale: 1 metre.

7. Southgate; Trench A, looking south. Period 1? Roman ditch with Period 2 postholes cut into silt.

8. Southgate; Trench F, looking south. Period 1 ? Roman ditch cut by east-west post-medieval Ditch 2.

9. Eastgate Needlemakers; Half-section across military ditch.

10. Eastgate Needlemakers; Late Roman burials.

11. Eastgate Needlemakers; Late-post medieval drainage ditch.

12. Eastgate Needlemakers; Trench A. Re-cut postholes of post-medieval house.

13. Eastgate Needlemakers; Inscription.

14. N. W. Quadrant; Area 8, Trench X. Ranging rods mark position of Period 1, Claudian structures below Period 3 Flavian house.

15. N. W. Quadrant, Area 8, Trench X. Roman gladius lying upon the Period 1 horizon.

16. N. W. Quadrant, Area 8, Trench X, looking north. Slots belonging to the Period 3 Flavian house.

17. N. W. Quadrant, Trench X. Late Saxon pottery clamp, *c.* mid-11th century.

18. N. W. Quadrant, Area 9, Trench P. Period 3 timber slots and drains below Roman street at the south end of the site. Edge of street seen in west section, cut by medieval pit.

19 a & b. Roman intaglio from Trench X. a) seal; b) impression.

20 a & b. N. W. Quadrant, Trench X. Late Saxon triple-spouted pitchers (a & b).

21. N. W. Quadrant, Chapel Street, 1977.

9

Medieval Carpentry in Chichester:

13th-Century Roofs of the Cathedral and Bishop's Palace

by Julian Munby

Summary

The crown-post roof of the Cathedral and the recently-discovered king-strut roof of the Bishop's Chapel are described, and considered in relation to the structural phases of the stonework on which they stand. The stylistic and documentary evidence for the date of the Cathedral and Chapel is discussed, and the roofs are dated to the second half of the 13th century. Related roofs at Maubuisson (Seine-et-Oise, France) and Bishops Waltham (Hants.) are considered. The development of English roof types is discussed, and the place of the Chichester roofs in it, especially in relation to the introduction of purlins and the varieties of early crown-post roofs.

ACKNOWLEDGEMENTS

Access to the roofs would have been impossible without the permission of the Bishop of Chichester and the Dean and Chapter, and the co-operation of the Surveyor to the Fabric, the Cathedral Works Organisation, the Bishop's Chaplains, and in particular the Cathedral Verger and his staff. I am most grateful to Dr. John Fletcher whose interest led to the making of this survey. Its completion was only possible with the assistance of others. Philip Morris joined in the major part of the measuring work, and Michael Coker directed the photography, with the aid of lighting provided by the A.V.C. Department of Bishop Otter College. Further visits were aided by Alison Macaulay and Bridget Sands. The forbearance of the staff of the West Sussex Record Office in the face of constant demands has made work there a pleasure. The text has benefited from the comments of Eric Mercer and John Smith, and I am grateful to Walter Horn's generosity in making his work available. The views expressed here remain the author's responsibility.

Introduction

There survives in Chichester a remarkable group of timber constructions dating to the 13th century. Deservedly the best known, St. Mary's Hospital, is an aisled timber hall with adjacent stone chapel, surviving virtually as built, *c.* 1290. Of equal importance, but less visited, is the near-contemporary Kitchen of the Bishop's Palace, where massive hammer-beams raise the pyramidal roof clear above the 32ft.-square floor. It is a roof that rivals those of the few later medieval kitchens which still exist. Above the vaulting of the Cathedral the principal medieval roofs stand intact, though barely noticed until examined by Cecil Hewett, who first appreciated their significance and described them as "among the least spoiled and most important surviving roofs in the kingdom".[1] In following up Hewett's work, a companion roof has come to light, that over the Chapel of the Bishop's Palace, which is of similar date and interest to those of the Cathedral.[2]

This study is the record of an investigation into the roofs of the Cathedral and Bishop's Chapel. The timberwork is described together with its archaeological relationship to the stonework on which it stands. The roofs are provisionally dated from a consideration of the structural and stylistic dating of the stonework, and the meagre documentary history of the Cathedral and Palace. Finally, their place in the development of roof types in England is discussed.

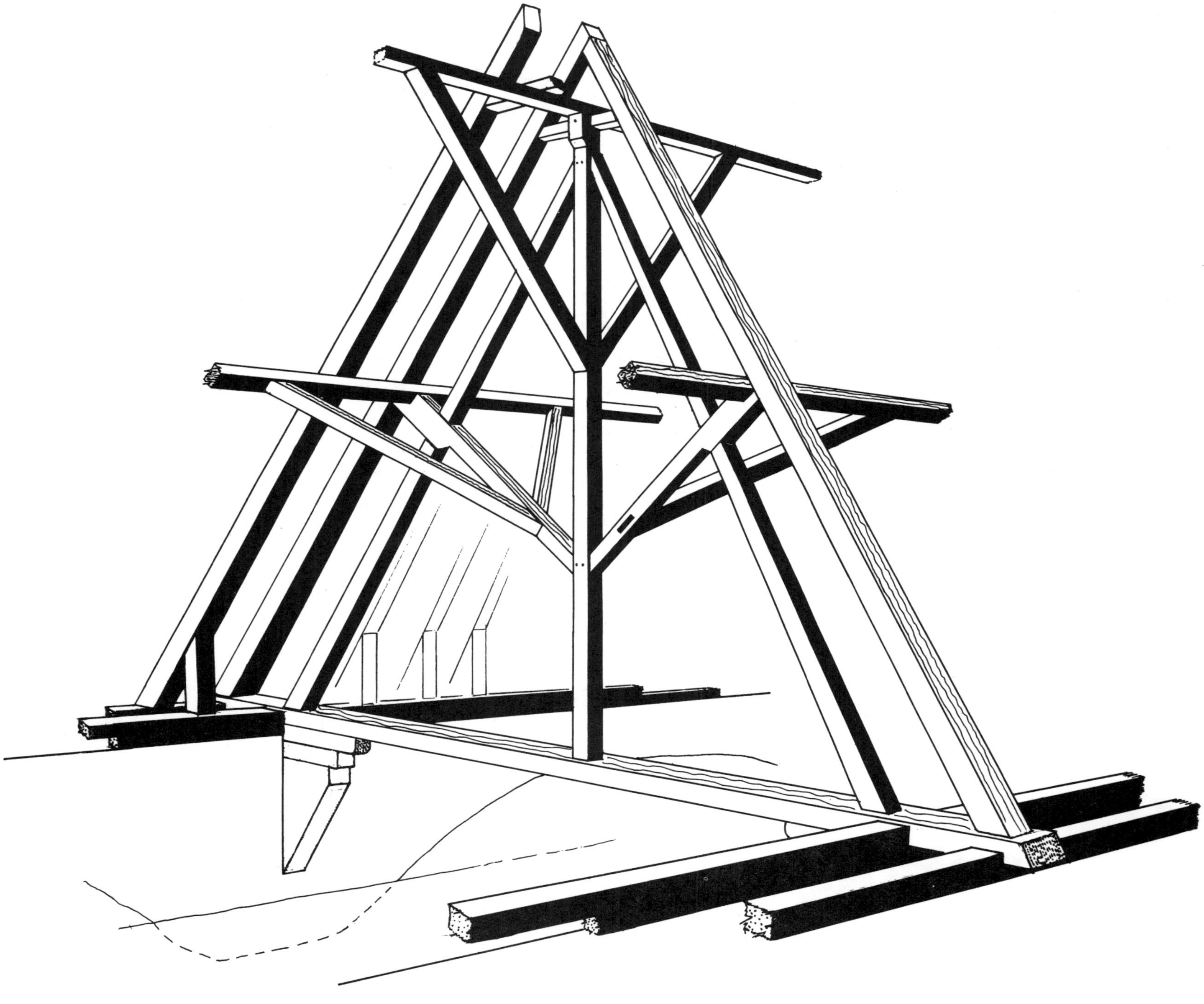

Fig. 9.1. Perspective view of nave roof of Chichester Cathedral.

Cathedral roof

Ancient roofing survives for the entire length of the Cathedral from east to west, interrupted only by repairs made after the fall of the spire in 1861. Only the Lady Chapel and Transepts have lost their roofs, appearing on early views with low-pitched roofs, but in the 19th century built up again to their medieval pitch. Both Choir and Nave have similar roofs, apart from minor differences in detail and the special arrangements made between the towers of the west front. Principal dimensions are given in the following Table:

	Internal length	Internal width	Number of trusses	Spacing of trusses	Rafters per bay	Pitch
CHOIR	29.9m. (98ft.)	8.45m. (27ft. 9in.)	5 (+ 1)	5.71m. (18ft. 9in.)	9	54deg.
NAVE	48.4m. (159ft.)	8.05m. (26ft. 5in.)	6 (+ 3)*	5.59m. (18ft. 4in.)	9 (5)*	54deg.

* Nave west end.

General description (Figs. 9.1-9.2)

The roof consists of pairs of trussed rafters of approximately uniform scantling, provided with longitudinal support by collar- and side-purlins that are held in position by principal trusses. These principals have tie-beams resting on wall-plates (two interior and one exterior) and sustained from below by timber pads on large projecting stone corbels. A tall crown-post

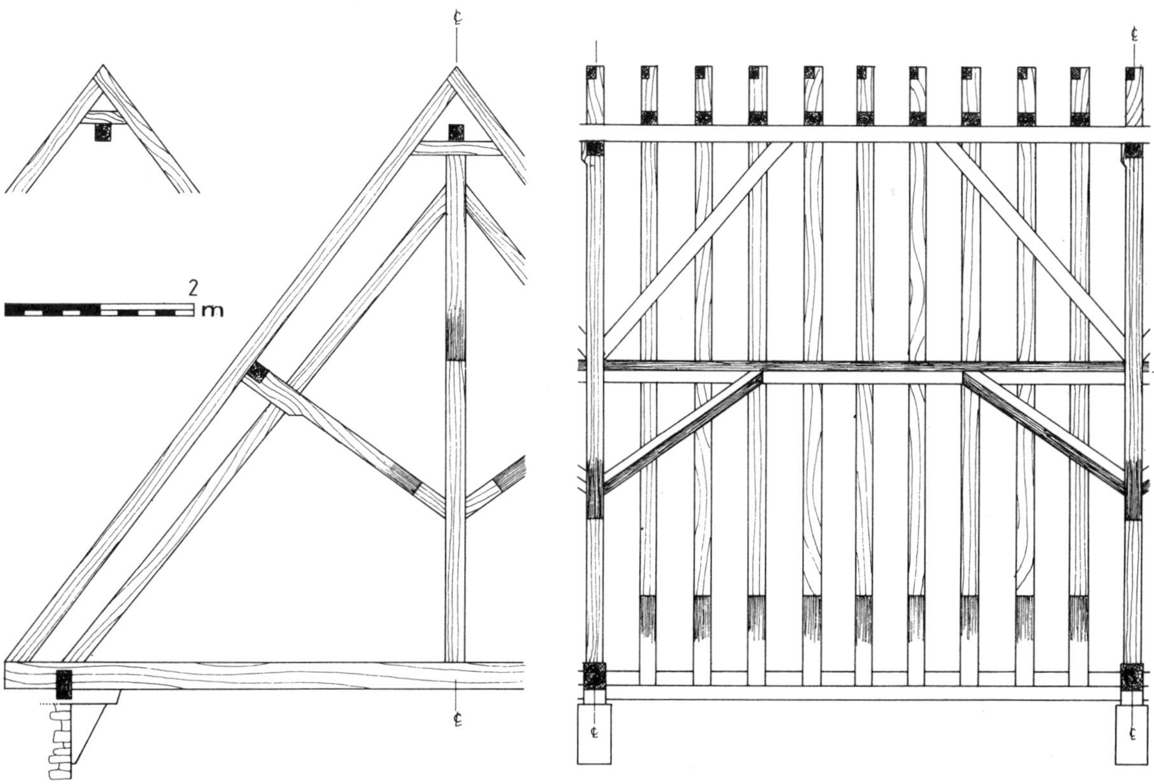

Fig. 9.2. Section of principal truss and longitudinal section of bay in nave roof of Chichester Cathedral. (P. Morris)

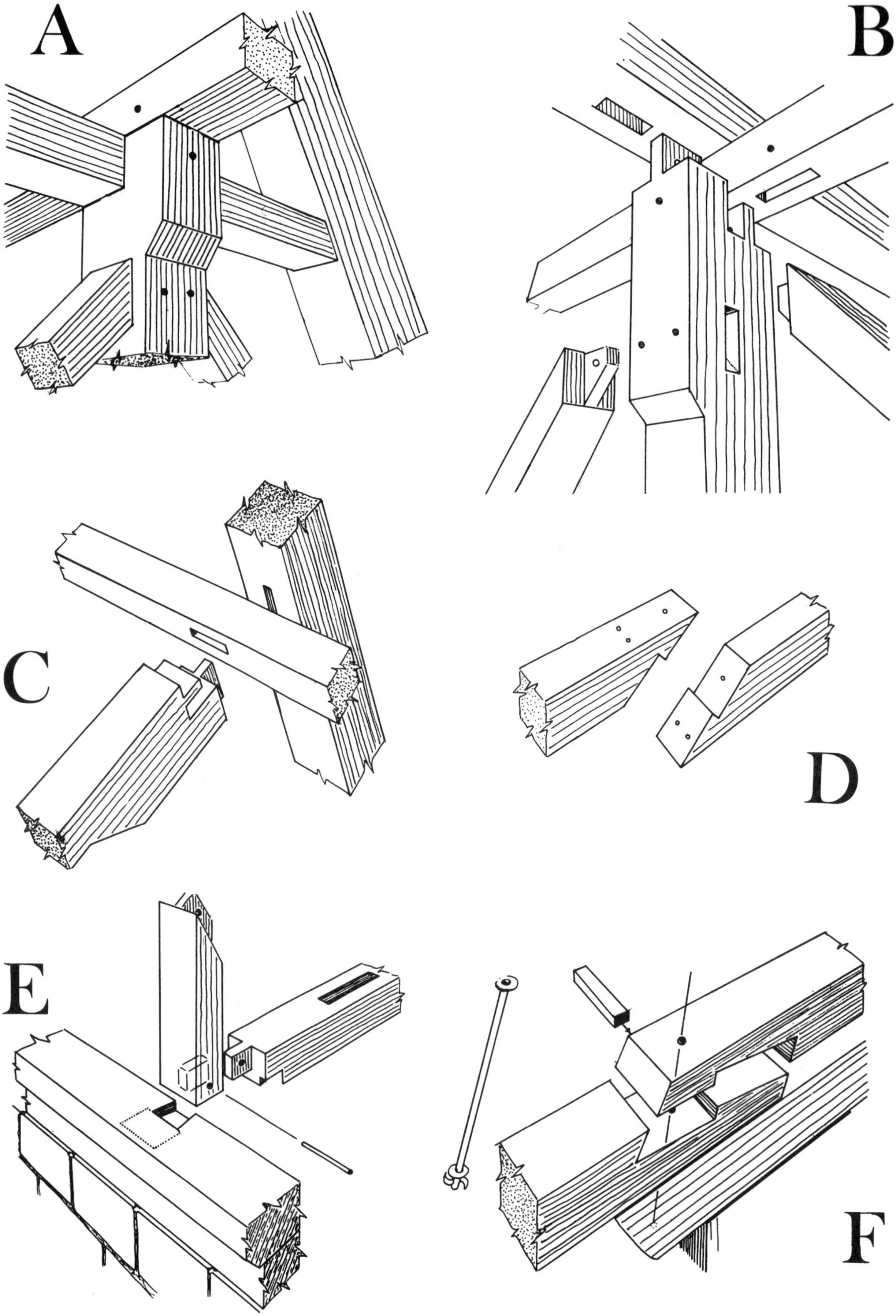

Fig. 9.3. Construction details of roof of Chichester Cathedral.
A — Nave crown post, jowl
B — Choir crown-post, jowl
C — Side-strut jowl to purlin and rafter
D — Trait-de-Juppiter scarf in side-purlin
E — Base triangle, relationship of ashlar and sole-piece to wall plates
F — Scarf repair to nave tie-beam

in the centre of the tie rises to a high collar-beam, round which it is jowled to reach the collar-purlin above. The purlin is further stabilised by steeply-pitched longitudinal braces rising from half way up the crown-post. From below that point two lateral braces (or raking struts) rise from the outer faces of the crown-post to meet the side-purlins which are inclined in the plane of the roof. As at the top of the crown-post, the further ends of the raking struts broaden to a jowl, passing beneath the purlin to tenon into the rafter. Although these raking struts are secured at either end by mortice-and-tenon joints, they are given additional support by long braces parallel to the rafters which run in two lengths: from near the top of the crown-post to the upper face of the struts, and from the soffit of the struts down to the tie-beams. In this way the purlins are firmly clasped in position at the point where they pass the principal truss; but they are also stabilised on either side of it by long braces which are splayed out from the raking struts and mortised into the purlin. These braces minimise any sagging of the purlin in the middle of each bay. Such an arrangement at the sides of the roof exactly conforms with that at the centre, where the braces from the crown-post prevent the collar-purlin from sagging.

The common trusses are pairs of rafters tenoned together at the top and joined by a high collar which (unlike those of the principals) is above the collar-purlin. At the base of the rafters is a triangle made up of a sole-piece dovetailed over the wall-plates, and an upright ashlar. Exceptions to the general rule of nine trusses per bay are to be found at the east end, where there is a small three-truss bay (which accommodates the corner turrets) followed by a bay with six trusses only, and also at the west end of the nave, now to be described.

The west end

In the two western bays of the nave the internal walls of the towers rise flush with the internal face of the main nave walls, thus precluding the continuation of the wall-plates to the west end. However, the height and pitch of the roof are unbroken, and the side-purlins continue without interruption to the west wall; the accommodation for the narrower width is made at the base of the roof. After the first six normal trusses in the nave roof, the next bay has only six common trusses and then, at the end of the wall-plates against the tower, a common truss with the addition of a tie-beam. The last three principal trusses have tie-beams at a higher level, now resting on stone corbels. Modern repairs have obscured the original arrangement for receiving the feet of common rafters, but they seem to have stood on a plate running along the face of the wall (this is discussed further below). There are five trusses in each bay. The crown-posts on the principals are shorter, but the struts are as in the rest of the nave. The westernmost of the three principals differs from the other two in that the lower length of the crown-post have been replaced by two splayed supports, as shown in the forefront of Hewett's drawing.[3] This construction is jointed with pegged mortice-and-tenons and a distinct system of carpenter's marks (the number XIII); the timber is partly re-used and is weathered, and all stained red; it is very probably a post-medieval repair.

Details of construction (Fig. 9.3)

There are few exceptional features employed in the construction of the roof. Most of the joints are of pegged mortice-and-tenon type. The jowling of the crown-posts and raking struts has been mentioned, and is illustrated here, showing the slight difference between those used in the choir and nave. Also shown is the junction of wall-plate, ashlar and sole-piece. The wall-plates are in bay lengths, the inner ones tenoned into the tie-beams and pad-timbers; the outer plates have mostly been removed in the recent works involving the insertion of a concrete ring-beam along the top of the walls. The purlins are each scarfed at some point in each bay, usually near the middle; their lengths are connected with a splayed and tabled joint (commonly known as the trait-de-Jupiter) across the face-soffit and held by edge pegs, four each in the choir roof and three in the nave. In the first three (east), bays of the nave the rafters are pegged to the purlins, perhaps to make up for the absence of a principal truss next to the tower.

Many of the nave tie-beams have added lengths scarfed on to them at their outer ends, though it seems probable that these are later repairs. All have iron bolts with forelocks. Those at the south ends have simple edge-halved scarfs, but on the north (from the fourth truss westwards) they are "stop splayed with under-squinted, square butts and transverse keys". This joint was in use at an early period in Essex, but is not necessarily a primary feature in this context.[4] The question of the nave repairs is discussed further below.

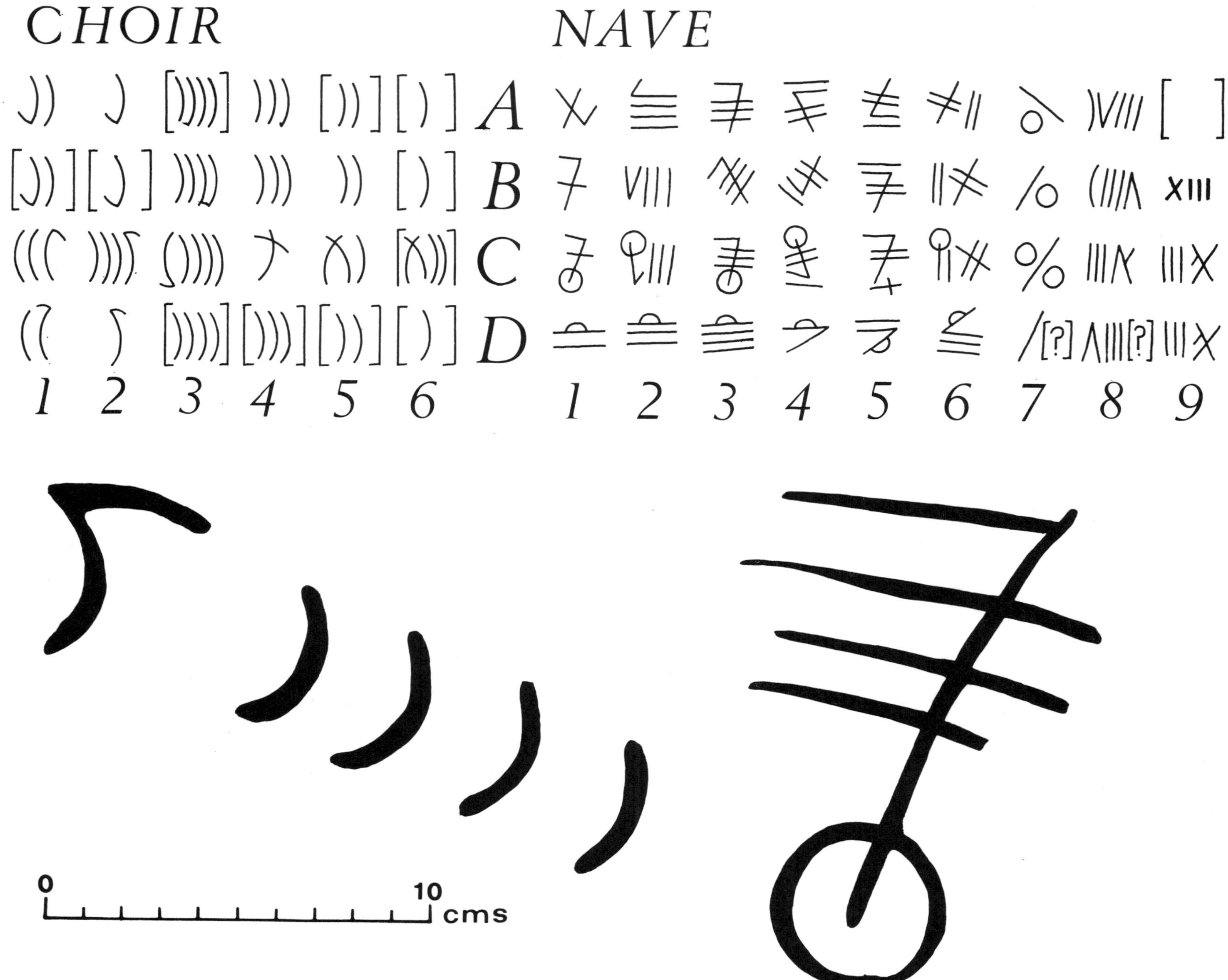

Fig. 9.4. Representative carpenters' marks in choir and nave of Chichester Cathedral. Trusses are numbered from east to west. Location of marks: A – tie beam and foot of crown-post; B – Crown-post and foot of side-struts; C – soffit of side-struts and braces (north side): D – As last (south side).

Carpenters' marks (Fig. 9.4)

The original carpenters' marks survive on many of the timbers. The principal choir trusses appear to have had a Roman system of numeration cut with regular curved lines. At the junctions of tie to crown-post and post to side struts these run from II to VI (west to east). On the outer strut to brace junction they would have run from II to VI on the south side (west to east) and from VII to XI on the north side (east to west). If the interpolated numbers are correct, and if there was a sixth truss next to the central tower (and such is implied by a comment in Willis,[5] then the series would have run I to VI and VII to XII, and been complete. It would then be apparent that the trusses were marked for erection in that particular order.

In the nave, the principal trusses have marks that are hard to interpret as a system of serial numeration, but distinghish between trusses (in one case only by inverting the sign). The marks are cut in longer and straighter lines than those of the choir, and employ a combination of V or 7 with straight lines cut across it or next to it. As in the choir, similar marks are used at the two lower junctions on the crown-post, but the junctions on the struts and braces have in addition a circle (on the north side) and a semi-circle (on the south side). This only applies to the first six regular trusses in the nave; the last three have quite a distinct system, but again one which relates the timbers in a single truss and does not denote their order.

The common rafters also have marks on them, in both nave and choir.

Pegs

Stout wooden pegs are fixed to the outer sides of most of the crown-posts in the nave and choir, in a manner that suggests they were intended for climbing up into the top of the roof. Similar ones appear in a photograph of one of the shoring posts added to the roof of Westminster Abbey.[6] Pegs which can hardly have had the same funtion also occur in the nave, where they are attached to the east or west sides of rafters, usually just below the level of the side-purlin, but not all at the same level, nor in pairs. Their purpose is obscure.

Timber

Most of the timbers are regular and square-cut, and always with a flat surface where necessary, as on the outer side of purlins and rafters. However, many waney edges are present, though it is difficult to determine what fractions of the tree were being used. The tie-beams were probably whole trees, and several other members may have been whole trees or branches. End sections are rarely visible for the rings to be counted, but a dismantled truss lying at the east end of the nave has rafters cut from oaks of about forty years growth; the larger pad-timber at the north end of nave truss 3 was from a tree over fifty years old (and there is apparently some sapwood still on it). When roofs are examined in a dismantled state, much can be discovered about the use of timber in their construction, as in the recent case of the Blackfriars' church at Gloucester.[7] Happily there is no threat of this extreme measure at Chichester; the roof is in excellent condition and shows little signs of decay or of movement out of true. The timbers have been limewashed at some point in their history. Some of the nave rafters are blackened, as if from burning, though it is not clear why this is so. Although Professor Willis reported molten lead in a mortice of one of the dismantled trusses examined after the collapse of the tower,[8] it would be hard to connect this with the fire of 1187, as the roof must be of a much later date, as will be shown below.

Repairs

Substantial additions have been made in the choir, where, apart from the rebuilt western bay next to the tower, the south wall has also been reconstructed in brick, and large softwood trusses have been interposed in the middle of each bay. These have queen-struts and collars and are secured with screwed iron bolts. Similar ironwork has been applied to the ancient trusses, with bands round the bases of the principals, and rods passing from the outside of principal rafters through the tie-beam and emerging on the inner end of the pad timber with screwed bolts. Associated with these rods are short timber struts inclined inwards and downwards from the outer rafter to the inner parallel brace (as shown on Hewett's drawing).[9] All these works, with the exception of some of the ironwork, seem to post-date the fall of the tower, as none are shown on the drawings made then.[10]

The scarfing of the nave tie-beams has been referred to above. There is no evidence which conclusively proves that this is secondary work, though it seems unlikely that it is all original. As the wall-plates are tenoned into the tie-beams and pads, replacing the ends of ties would have involved a major operation. The lack of chamfers on the southern wall-plates, in contrast

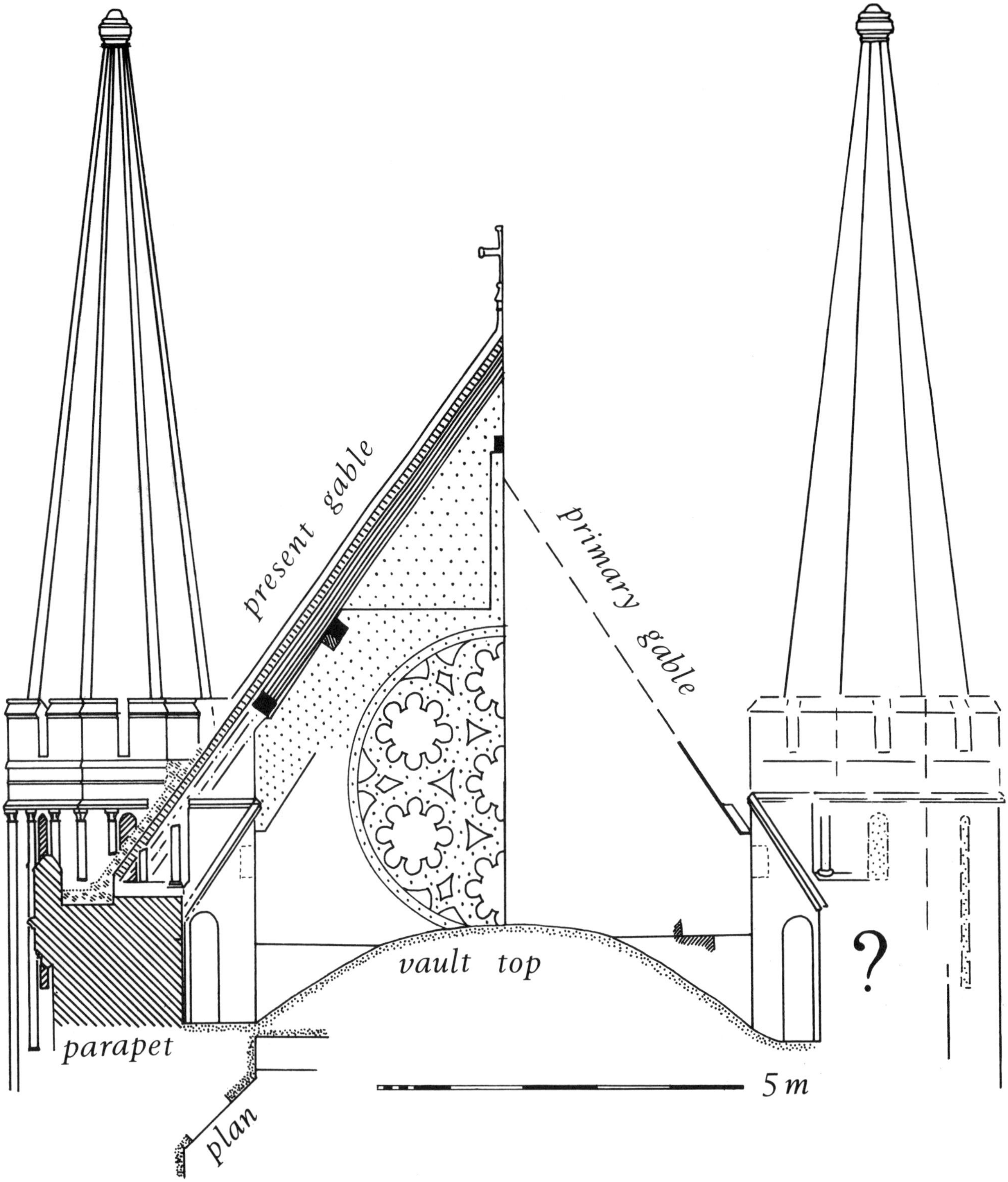

Fig. 9.5. Internal elevation of east wall of Chichester Cathedral, showing relationship of primary gable line to later roof and parapet.

with those opposite, may indicate that the simpler scarfs used there may have been part of an extensive repair which included replacing the wall-plates. There are certainly some new rafters in the nave, beyond what was necessary to be done in repairing the bay next to the tower. On the north side of the nave, whilst the complex scarfs could be original, if there had been insufficient timber to make up the required lengths (as was the case with the rafters of the Angel Choir at Lincoln),[11] there is one feature which could suggest that they are secondary. The scarfed ties all have pad timbers with their ends cut diagonally in a straight line, but those without scarfs (e.g., the third and fourth ones) have gently-curved ends to the pad timbers, and these are undoubtedly original. That the central lengths of the tie-beams are original is not in question, as they all carry the carpenters' assembly marks. The only further point that can usefully be made in relation to this problem is that although the forelocked bolts need not be contemporary with the scarf joints, they are likely to pre-date the introduction of screwed nuts and bolts in the post-medieval period.[12]

Earlier Roofs

Masonry of the choir (Fig. 9.5)

Evidently the present roof is not the first that was built over the Cathedral when it was re-fitted and extended after the fire of 1187. That it does post-date the fire is shown by its continuation without break over the old work in the choir as well as the new extension to the east. The main evidence for the roof not being primary is in the east wall of the choir, where both inside and out the partial outline of an earlier and lower gable can be seen. At its full height this earlier gable could have accommodated neither the present roof nor the rose window. Internally the restored stonework of the window has obscured the evidence for its insertion, but of the earlier gable there is visible the sloping top of the primary phase of ashlar on the north, and on the south the first coping stone is still *in situ*. The eastern corner turrets are only bonded into the east wall below the line of the first gable. They are octagonal and contain spiral stairs giving access to the roof space through round-headed doors. A drip-course passes across the internal diagonal face of the turrets just above the doors; it would have been outside the original roof line. The west faces of the turrets, visible partly inside and mostly outside the present roof, have remnants of the (blocked) windows and detached shafts which occur on the other external elevations. As Willis demonstrated, and is apparent from the foregoing, the choir parapets and to some extent the corbel table impinge on the primary arrangement of the corner turrets.[13] Thus the raising of the parapets and gable, the insertion of the rose window, and the building of the roofs as they are now, were all subsequent to the primary design of the east end. Although it cannot be proved, it is likely that these alterations were contemporary.

Evidence for the primary roof is hard to find in the choir. The surviving stonework on the north wall of the choir provides no consistent indication of any earlier and lower level (it is even hard to see evidence for the addition of the two eastern bays). From the outline of the early gable in the east wall, it can be deduced that the side walls must have been some 50 cm. below their present level. The height of the vaulting (which rises towards the east end) comes to within 1 m. of the top of the wall at the sides of the eastern bay. The north wall is in two stages; the lower of coursed rubble, finished irregularly (from 110 cm. to 140 cm. below the top) but levelled up with ashlar courses to make the upper stage on which the wall-plates rest. The rubble is too low and uneven to have provided the original roof line, and no consistent level can be discerned in the ashlar above at an appropriate height. There must have been a considerable amount of rebuilding here when the walls were raised and the new roof put in.

What sort of external arrangement went with the primary roof is not clear. Willis seems to have over-estimated the amount of heightening on the outside (as he certainly did in the nave), and it is possible that the corbels themselves belong to the primary phase. On the analogy of Boxgrove, the corbels may have been immediately below the dripline of the eaves, and have been left in place when the parapet was built and the walls raised.

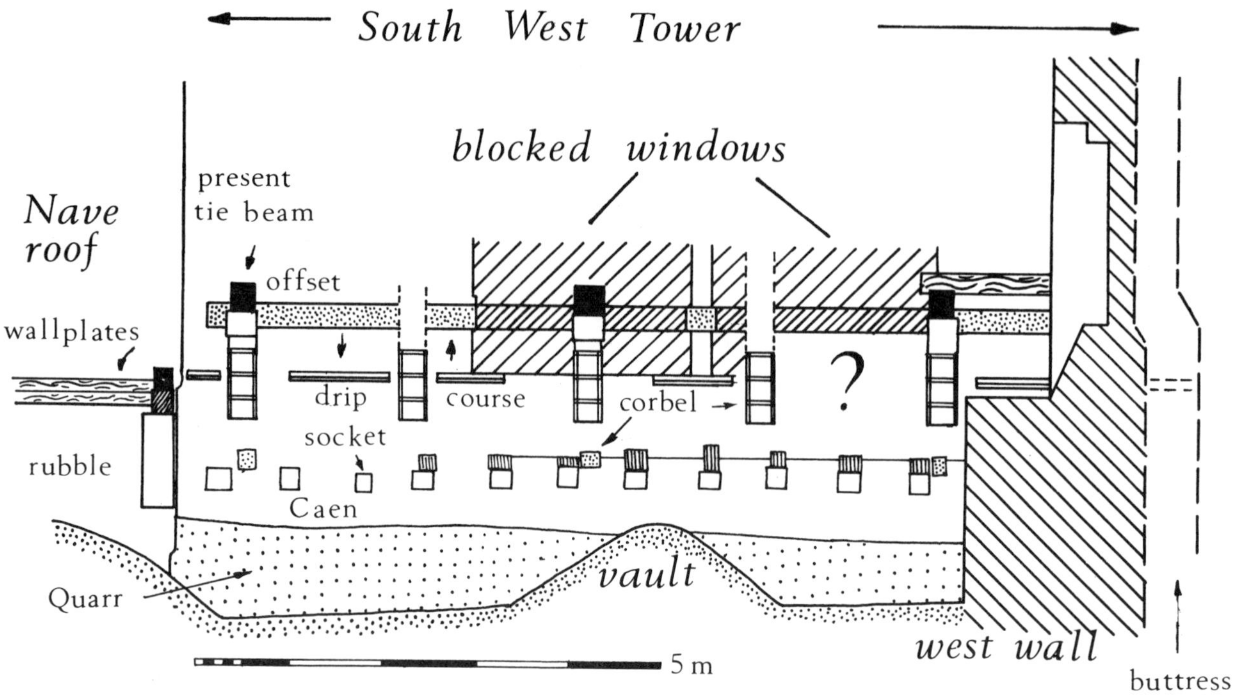

Fig. 9.6. Internal elevation of south-west tower of Chichester Cathedral, looking south. The windows, drip course and rafter sockets on the rebuilt tower shown in relation to corbels and offset for the present roof.

Masonry of the nave (Fig. 9.6)

In the nave there is less evidence to go on. The tower and east bay are all post-1861; the west wall is apparently all of one build (and thus perhaps contemporary with the roof). The side walls of the nave, which are about 30 cm. lower than those of the choir, are all of rubble except for one top course of ashlar which was probably inserted to provide a level surface for the wall-plates. Willis suggested that the elaborate provisions to counter the leaning of the nave walls to the south was contemporary with the raising of the parapets and rebuilding of the roof.[14] But the corbelling out of the north wall and reduction inwards of the south wall occur at a level below the top of the crown of the vault. As there is no internal evidence of the walls having moved significantly since the vault was built, it is more likely that these provisions were made at the time the vault was constructed. It would certainly have been very hard to have based any roof on the walls at this primary stage unless this correction had already been made.

Between the west towers can be found clear indications that the present roof is higher than the primary one. Whilst the rebuilding of the north-west tower in 1901 has reduced the reliability of its stonework for our purposes, the south-west tower preserves some traces of its former state. The arrangement of timberwork in the two western bays has already been described. Their trusses rest on large stone corbels which cut through a drip-course on the tower that must have been an external feature (it can be seen on the buttress outside). Above the top of the corbels a course of ashlar has been chipped back to provide a ledge (which may have carried a wall-plate to take the rafter feet). Two parts of this ledge are not cut out of existing ashlar, but are lined at the back with tooled ashlar. These parts coincide with straight joints passing up the wall above the level of the drip-course. They are the outer splays of the two blocked windows that are visible from ground level inside the (open) south-west tower. In the earlier roof arrangement these windows must have been open to the north above the roof line; when provision for the new roof was made at a higher level, the windows were blocked.

The towers were part of the first Norman cathedral, and are unlikely to have received much damage from the fire. But the south-west tower was evidently rebuilt in the 13th century, probably after the fall of towers recorded in 1210 (see below). Typical Norman ashlar of

Quarr stone can be seen lower down in the wall being described (in the vault wells) but above all is of Caen stone. Cut into the Caen ashlar below the bottom of the main corbels for the present roof is a series of 11 rectangular recesses, of irregular dimension and height, but fairly evenly spaced. Several of these have been filled, or used to support a series of rough corbel blocks, which seem to be secondary and in some cases support timber struts to the roof above. The holes which have not been filled have sloping backs. The height and spacing of these holes is not inconsistent with their having been sockets for rafter-feet of the primary roof. If this were so, the roof may have been of regular trussed-rafter type, with no principal trusses or bay divisions.

Two further features are probably associated, not with the roof, but the building campaign on the tower itself. At about the level of the sockets there is a change from diagonal tooling on the stones below to vertical tooling on the stones above. There is also a small offset on the western half of the wall, just above the sockets, putting the tower on a slightly different alignment.

As to the arrangements for the present roof, it should be observed that there are two intermediate corbels, as well as the three supporting the trusses. Though all the corbels now have additional stone blocks placed on top of them, the most satisfactory explanation of the original layout is that the corbels all gave direct support to a wall-plate lying in the recess, as described above. At the very west end is a short length of plate lying, by contrast with that just described, above the final tie-beam, and receiving the feet of the western rafters. A similar plate, of unknown age, is in use along the opposite wall of the north-west tower. The remaining rafters against the south-west tower can give no help in determining the conflict of evidence as to their original footing; they are all truncated and rest on a modern plate.

The main series of corbels in the nave and choir are presumably contemporary with the addition of the present roofs. Those in the choir are composite, with rubble and mortar, whilst those in the nave are of large, chamfered blocks, often topped with single stones of varied sizes, probably chosen to make a perfect fit beneath the pad-timbers.

The roofs and the tower

According to Sir Gilbert Scott's account of the reconstruction of the central tower after its collapse his 'only deviation from the design of the old steeple' was to add 'five or six feet to its height', to restore the original relationship between tower and roofs.

> "The four arms of the cross had been (probably in the 14th century) raised some five or six feet in height, and thus had buried a part of what had originally been the clear height of the tower, and with it an ornamental arcading running round it. I lifted out the tower from this encroachment . . ."[15]

It is possible to see in pre-1861 views of the Cathedral how the roof-line impinged on the design of the tower, and the apex of the gable actually seems to have risen above the sill of the main belfry windows. Thus if the tower was designed with a lower roof in mind, the present roof must be subsequent to the building of the tower, though it is probably not as late as Scott believed.

The date of the roof

To summarise the archaeological evidence for the roof in relation to the structural sequence of the Cathedral: it cannot be the primary post-fire roof, it must follow the rebuilding and use of the south-west tower as that was first planned, and it was subsequent to the building of the central tower. Most probably its construction was associated with the raising of the east gable, the reconstruction of the parapets, and the insertion of the rose window.

The probable date for the roof, short of scientific investigation, can only be determined by considering the stylistic and documentary evidence for building works on the Cathedral in the 13th century. Discussion of this will be postponed until the very similar roof of the Bishop's Chapel has been described.

The Bishop's Chapel (Fig. 9.7)

The Bishop's Chapel stands opposite the south-west tower of the Cathedral at the east end of the principal range of buildings which forms the Palace. Once separated from the Hall to its west by a single-storey lobby, the range is now roofed continuously. The 14th-century roof above the hall has previously been described and illustrated,[16] and the roof over the connecting section is of no great age, but it has only recently been noted that the chapel roof is ancient,

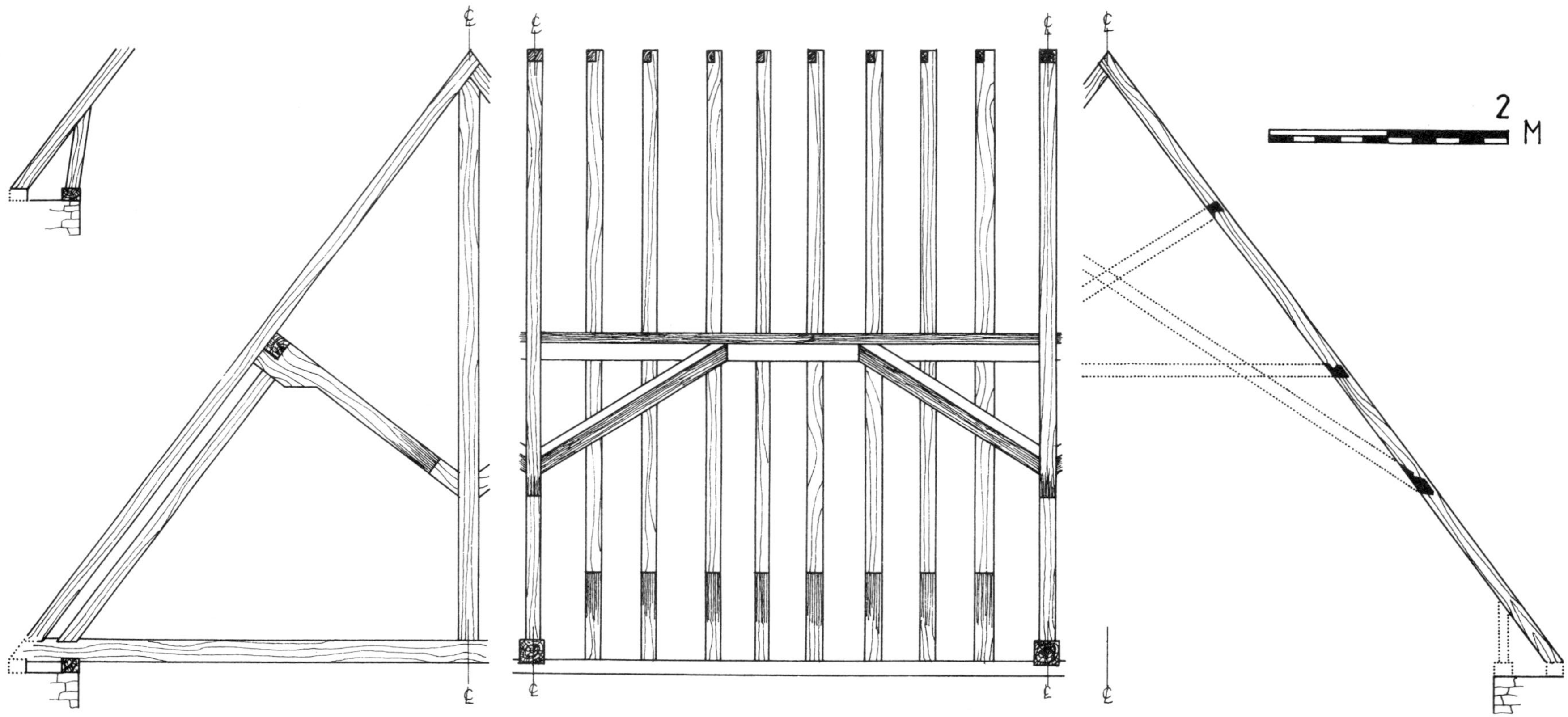

Fig. 9.7. Section of principal truss and longitudinal section of bay in roof of Bishop's Chapel, Chichester. Conjectural reconstruction of earlier roof, derived from mortices in re-used rafters, shown on right. (P. Morris)

and must in part be original. It is in three bays: the eastern one open above the vault, the middle one cut through by a modern corridor and partly visible in a store cupboard, the western one only to be seen above a bedroom ceiling. The internal dimensions are 6.5 m. by 13 m. The construction of the chapel is as hard to date as the main body of the Cathedral, but belongs in the first half of the 13th century. The vaulting may be an insertion subsequent to the first building (its crown is built flush with the north wall, but stands 35 cm. clear of the south wall, on an offset). The walls are of rubble, topped with double wall-plates. The outer plate on the north has been removed in repairs. At the south-east corner the walls and inner plate are cut away for a small brick door which at one time was probably the only entry to the roof. Adjacent to this a spacing piece can be seen tenoned into each of the plates; it is probably original. The mortices for ashlar posts on the inner wall plate are not fully utilised by the present ashlars, so it would seem that the plates belong to a previous phase.

The first roof

In the present roof the rafter couples are supported by side-purlins and king-post trusses, but as most of the rafters are re-used this cannot be the primary arrangement. Mortices in the rafters for lap- and notch-lap joints are consistent with there having been scissor-brace trusses originally. These mortices are all visible in the east bay, at the foot of the north side in the middle bay (along the passage), and at the top in the west bay. The primary roof was presumably based on the existing wall-plates, with *c.* 27 pairs of rafters (each square in section and tapered towards the top), ashlars, pairs of scissor-braces and collars. All the internal members were lap-jointed to the rafters with the same notched joint, varied according to the angle between the timbers with the two extreme forms appearing at the foot and top of the scissor brace. All the rafters have empty peg-holes just above their base. For some unknown reason, a few of the trusses received the foot of the scissor-brace below the top of the ashlar piece rather than in the usual place above it. As the scissors in these trusses would have been longer, and would probably have crossed each other below the collar instead of above it, it is conceivable that the intention was to clear space above the collars, perhaps for a bell. As the distribution of the odd rafters shows, they are not now paired as originally, and indeed many of the rafters are lying on their side, with their mortices turned outwards. When the roof was reconstructed they were perhaps re-aligned to present their straightest edge to the exterior.

The second roof

Most likely the replacement of the roof was necessitated by longitudinal racking of the unsupported trusses. In many roofs which lacked lengthways stiffening, particularly if of relatively small size as this, movement could be countered by the insertion of crown posts and collar purlin, as appears to have been done at Boxgrove. But no doubt with the re-roofing of the Cathedral in mind, it was decided to replace in a grander style. Principal trusses were inserted at the ends and at two places in the length of the roof. Three are visible, the fourth at the west end was probably removed for the insertion of a chimney stack. Constructed on tie-beams laid across the wall-plates, they have a central king-post rising to the apex where new principal rafters (no larger than the common ones) meet it. Raking struts rise from the king-post and are jowled to meet the purlins and rafters at right-angles, in exactly the same way as in the Cathedral roof. Braces parallel to the rafters support the struts—they are probably, but not necessarily, original, having unpegged mortice-and-tenon joints at each end. From the struts longitudinal braces rise to give additional support to the purlins. The purlins, square and inclined in the plane of the roof (54deg.), are in two lengths, scarfed in the central bay with the Trait-de-Jupiter. There are eight common rafter pairs in each bay. Ashlars, probably ancient (but smaller than the regularly-cut mortices into which they are roughly tenoned), are nailed to the face of the rafters. The timbers are in general cut straight, especially the purlins and raking struts. The latter appear from their jowls to have been cut from large, slow-grown trees. The rafters, longitudinal braces and king-posts have waney edges, and the tie-beams are probably whole trees.

The date of the roof

Subject to the general problems of dating discussed below, the scissor-braced roof was probably the original roof of the chapel, dating from early in the 13th century, though the lack of plaster on the walls would suggest that it was contemporary with the vaulting. The alteration of the roof to make it a smaller version of the Cathedral roof must have been contemporary with or subsequent to the changes there. The renewal of the chapel windows in the early 14th century, perhaps by Bishop John Langton (1305–1337) need not have affected any other part of the structure.[17] Dating can best be considered in relation to the problematic sequence of work on the main Cathedral roof.

The stylistic sequence

It is necessary to look briefly at the stylistic sequence of post-fire works in the Cathedral and Chapel before considering the historical evidence for them. Although Chichester is fortunate in having been the subject of one of Willis's monographs, and has been described in detail by Godfrey and Bloe in 1935[18] and then by Nairn and Pevsner in 1965,[19] there is still more to be learnt of the relationship between the Cathedral and the local group of large churches (Portsmouth Cathedral, New Shoreham, and Boxgrove). There are few firm dates for any of these buildings, and in any case the written evidence is strictly separate from the story of development that derives from analysis of the stonework. The sequence of construction has to be built up from a comparison of such relatively minor details as the carving of capitals, roof bosses, and vault ribs. The masons' marks and even the tooling of stone can be significant. At certain places structural sequence can be demonstrated from the relationship between adjacent features, but these can only provide relative dating evidence. In the case of Chichester there is still much that remains to be done in working out the order of building, and the dates of the work. According to which criteria are relied upon it is possible to produce alternative versions of the sequence, as can be seen by comparing the account of Godfrey and Bloe with that of Nairn and Pevsner.

At its simplest, the Normal Cathedral was re-structured after the fire of 1187, then altered and extended in a long campaign which was largely finished perhaps by *c.* 1270. Whilst the roofs in their present form must belong at the end of this period, the primary roofs must have been constructed somewhere near the beginning of it. For our purposes, it is important to note that work on the principal vault of the choir and nave, and particularly the eastwards extension of the choir, may have continued well into the second quarter of the 13th century. The sculpture in the east arcade of the retrochoir, supposed by Nairn to have been inserted, could be of 1230–40.[20] The primary roof must have been erected, or at least extended, when this east end was built. Apart from the main body of the church, other work included the south and north porches, the transept chapels and sacristy, the north-east nave chapel, and the south nave chapels. All these were added in something like that order, before the building of the north nave chapels in the second half of the century. The rebuilding of the south-west tower and the construction of the central tower fit somewhere in this series, whilst the west porch, west door and perhaps the whole of the upper part of the west wall are probably later.

Features related to roofs

The features likely to be associated with the roofs: the rose window, corbel table and parapets do not admit of any very close dating. The type of corbel table employed in the primary phase after the fire was perhaps like that still to be seen at Boxgrove, where corbels support a flat stone table immediately below the eaves.[21] The choir aisles of the Cathedral have a similar flat table below the (? later) parapet, whilst in their east chapels the eaves simply overshoot the wall, perhaps the only fragment remaining as first built. The high walls of choir and nave have corbels supporting trefoiled arches for the table. Immediately above these arches is a drip course, then ashlar courses making up the parapet wall. The Lady Chapel has similar arcading, but no drip course, and only layer of ashlar for the parapet wall. The type of corbel used at Chichester is not dissimilar from that discussed by Professor Horn in connection with the barn at Great Coxwell, Berks.[22] He showed that they were widely used in the 13th century (though, in fact, the barn has now been shown to be of slightly later date than hitherto supposed).[23] Trefoiled arcading appears on the south-east corner turret at Chichester, though the north-east one has only a flat table, and the arcading might be a later repair rather than primary work. However, trefoiled arcades of more elaborate form at Salisbury, or used in a simpler manner at Netley Abbey were certainly not out of place in the second half of the 13th century.[24] The Chichester Lady Chapel (*c.* 1300), with a corbel table resembling that of the choir, was probably made to conform with it. There is no need to suppose that the corbel tables and parapets of nave and choir are contemporary with the Lady Chapel, or are additions of the 14th century, as proposed by Willis and accepted by later authorities.[25] If the restored detail can be trusted, the gable of the south transept which is certainly of 14th-century date, has a different form of arcading.

The same applies to the rose window at the east end, which is of earlier type than that in the south transept. Although it has been completely restored (i.e., replaced), its form of six circles surrounding a seventh is "exactly the pattern of the east window of the Angel Choir at Lincoln, which was completed in 1280".[26] The dogtooth surround of the window is also shown by Nairn to be a sign of late date at Chichester.[27]

The Bishop's Chapel

The Chapel poses the same problem as parts of the Cathedral when it comes to dating. In particular it is similar to the south ("St. Richard's") porch in having an indeterminate mixture of early and late features. Thus the Chapel door, vault ribs and south windows are held to be of likely early 13th-century date, whilst some details which should be contemporary (the corbels supporting the vault, and roof bosses) look more of the 1240s.[28] So the scissor-braced roof could be of almost any date in the first half of the century. As has already been stated, the date of the re-structured roof must depend on the date of its companion in the Cathedral.

Documentary evidence

In the absence of extensive records surviving for the medieval church of Chichester, the written history of the buildings has to be put together from chance mentions in a variety of records. The nearest thing to a narrative source is the "Catalogue of Bishops", compiled by or for Bishop William Reed (1369–1385), which mentions the most notable building activities of his predecessors[29] (and was later used to supply the captions beneath the portraits of bishops in the Cathedral). There is a danger in telling the story too much from the point of view of what individual bishops did, and thus ignoring the continuing work and responsibility of the Dean and Chapter.[30] Bishops were able to be a focus of activity and no doubt on occasions initiated works; but how often the limited income from one of the poorest sees was likely to be diverted towards the fabric, except posthumously, one does not know.

Chronicles record the consecration of 1184, the fire of 1187, and re-dedication of 1199.[31] Bishop Seffrid II (1180–1204) is said to have "rebuilt the church of Chichester after a second fire and the palace" (*et domos suas in palatio*).[32] That refitting was not completed by Seffrid is suggested by his successor, Simon fitz Robert (1204–1207) obtaining a licence to bring Purbeck marble by sea to Chichester.[33] No doubt these works received a setback during the eight years after his death during which the see was kept vacant by King John (it was also the period of the Interdict, which certainly disrupted work elsewhere, e.g., at Wells).[34] In 1210 a great storm brought down "two towers" at Chichester;[35] it is probable that this refers to the south-west tower and possibly the central one also.

It is not until the episcopate of Ralph Neville that there is evidence of renewed activity, though this is largely through his position as the royal Chancellor, and is revealed by the remarkable survival of some of his personal correspondence in the national records.[36] Thus we hear of lead for the roof of the church being speeded on its way by the king in 1224.[37] In the lively correspondence from Chichester to the absent Bishop (most of it unfortunately not closely datable) the Dean reports the loss of the Cathedral carpenter who is going on crusade,[38] and the Bishop's steward asks for timber to be found for building the Cathedral belfry.[39] Twelve acres of timber were purchased in the Broyle, sawn, and carried "to your court" (in Chichester).[40] The newly-received land in the Broyle, just north of Chichester, was being developed as the Bishop's home farm after disafforestation; much of the land here came from the Crown.[41] A new 100-foot ox-shed there was doubtless a recipient of some of the timber.[42] Royal grants of oak included 60 trees for "timber, shingles and lathes" for the bishop's houses (? in Chichester or London), 100 trees for the fabric of the Cathedral in 1232, and similarly 50 trees in 1234.[43] The king granted a special licence for removing the timber, and Neville made indulgences in 1234 for contributions to repairs and the carting of timber.[44] To his episcopate belong capitular statutes of 1232 which devoted one-twentieth of the common fund to much-needed work on the fabric;[45] there is also a document of great interest, a contract of 1239 with a glazier to make and repair windows in the Cathedral.[46] Neville, who died in 1244, is credited in the *Catalogue* with building campaigns on his London house (in the eponymous Chancery Lane), the chancel of Amberley church, and the chapel of St. Michael outside the east gate of Chichester.[47] It is only a statement by his executors which refers to the money he left to the fabric being put towards the speedy completion of the stone belfry begun by him. It had stood for a long time unfinished, and was almost despaired of.[48]

His successor, Richard of Wych (1244/46–1253, later canonised) seems to have organised quite a fund-raising campaign with a series of indulgences for visits and almsgiving to the Cathedral. Circular letters were sent out by other bishops, and the total of days of remission rose to 400.[49] Through statutes chance windfalls of money were directed to the fabric, like the revenue of deceased canons' prebends, down-payments from new residentiaries, and even sums improperly willed by clerks to their concubines.[50] Richard died in 1253, leaving £40 to the fabric,[51] and brought even greater benefits to the church when the exertions of his successors had resulted in his canonisation and his body was eventually translated to the new shrine in 1279.

It has been supposed that parts of the Cathedral could be associated with records of the foundation of chantries and altars. An altar of St. Anne, founded by Dean Walter of Gloucester (1254–75) "which I had built in the high church of Chichester" was endowed for his chantry.[52] The Dean and Chapter established a chantry for Bishop John Climping in the Cathedral "at the altar of SS. Catherine, Margaret and Agatha in the north part" (of the church) in 1269.[53] The latter has been taken to prove that the north nave chapels were completed by 1269; it is equally possible that this refers to the area of the north transept, and that the former foundation of Dean Walter was in the nave chapels. There is little certainty about the site of altars in the church, and modern plans show them in different positions.[54]

After the time of Bishop Richard there are few records of work on the Cathedral, beyond the entries in the *Catalogue*. John Climping (1254–62) was chiefly remembered for endowing the bishopric with a new manor at Drungewick.[55] Stephen Bersted (1262–87) is said by the author of the *Catalogue* to have spent more than £1,000 on the translation of St. Richard, and was active in other fields, as is shown by his foundation of the New Haven at Wardur in Sidlesham.[56] Gilbert of St. Leofard (1288–1305) is said to have built the Lady Chapel *a fundamentis* and have left 1,250 marks (£416 13s. 4d.) to the fabric; he also directed sums to the fabric in his statutes.[57] His successor, John Langton (1305–1347) spent £310 on "a certain wall and window built from the ground to the top in the Chapter House, on the south side" (presumably the south transept window and gable); he also left £100 to the fabric.[58]

In conclusion, apart from the general impression of building activity provided by these diverse references, it might be said that the only firm dates provided by records are for the fire of 1187, the building of the Lady Chapel, and the window in the south transept; that is the initial date of the work of reconstruction, and the final phases after which little was to be done on the Cathedral.

The date of the roofs

Although it seems most unlikely that Seffrid completed the refitting of the church, there is no doubt that re-roofing after the fire would have been of immediate importance. From structural evidence it would appear that there is virtually no trace left of this first roof. It may have remained in place during the progress of work undertaken in Neville's time, when the "belfry" (presumably the central tower) was begun, the south-west tower was probably rebuilt and the first nave chapels were perhaps added. Unless Neville was carrying out major works it is hard to see how the 150 oaks could have been used, as they were unlikely to be used for scaffolding. Some were perhaps directed to the roofs of the nave chapels; the scissor-braced roof of the Bishop's Chapel could belong to Neville's time. Richard of Wych was clearly active in completing Neville's campaign, and may have initiated works of his own, perhaps the first of the north nave chapels which received the dedication to St. Edmund Rich (whose friend he had been). The other north chapels might have been added under Climping or Bersted. These two bishops spanned the time taken in building the Angel Choir at Lincoln, which provides the parallel for the one feature at Chichester most able to date the insertion of the roofs. What the connection between the Lincoln and Chichester use of this rose window motif is likely to have been is hard to say; perhaps the best use of the link is merely to provide a probable date range, the Angel Choir being conceived in *c.* 1255 and consecrated in 1280.[59] By the time that Langton built the rose window in the south transept "say about 1330",[60] a completely different style was employed, so the east rose window is unlikely to be of his time, or even perhaps of his predecessor.

The re-roofing of the church could have marked the end of the main phase of rebuilding, with the towers and chapels complete. It incorporated in the parapet walks, buttress channels and gargoyles a systematic provision for the removal of water, and this may have been a relevant factor in deciding to replace the roofs, especially after the completion of the nave chapels.[61] It is possible that the new roof was of lead, replacing a tiled one with overshot eaves (as still remains at Boxgrove). In this case there would have been the additional benefit from the new arrangement of easy access to the roofs for maintenance. It is, of course, not impossible that the new roof was part of the fitting-out of the church for the costly translation of St. Richard, or, indeed, that offerings made at the shrine were sufficient to pay for new work on the church. But apart from this possibility, the roof cannot really be placed with any certainty at any one point within the second half of the 13th century. This is quite an acceptable date from the point of view of the roof's typology, which will be discussed next. In the absence of any evidence to the contrary, I assume that the Bishop's Chapel roof is so similar to the Cathedral one that it is contemporary, or nearly so. It might perhaps be possible to obtain more evidence for the date of the timberwork with a combination of dendrochronology and carbon-14 determination; however, unless a large (and expensive) programme were carried out, the results could be as vague and imprecise as any of the forms of evidence discussed above.[62]

Discussion of the roof type

The Chichester roofs belong to the class of rafter roofs, with members of roughly equal dimensions (scantling). They are "double-framed" in that the principal trusses with their system of purlins form an inner structure on which the outer rafters are carried. Trusses have a central crown-post in the Cathedral roof, or in the case of the Chapel a king-post (though this might more properly be termed a king-strut as it does not carry a ridge-purlin). The raking side-struts (or twin angle struts) are common to both roofs. It is the ensemble of central posts and side-struts that is initially something of a surprise in the context of English roof carpentry of the medieval period, though it was common enough in quite ordinary buildings of the 18th and 19th centuries, when it became almost a vernacular type. This was probably as a result of the reintroduction of the type into England in the 17th century in buildings based on classical and renaissance prototypes. It was first used by Inigo Jones, and then regularly by Christopher Wren, for example in the virtuoso roof over the *Sheldonian* theatre in Oxford (1663–9), and at St. Paul's Cathedral (1675–1711).[63] The western end of Winchester Cathedral was repaired with such a roof after the fire of 1698.[64] The immediate source of knowledge for the type was Italian textbooks on classical architecture, from whence it passed to builders' manuals.[65] For not only was the king-post roof with side-struts and purlins commonly used in medieval and renaissance Italy (albeit in roofs of lower pitch), but it also seems to have been a survival of a classical type. Vitruvius's description of "broader span" roofs was apparently of this sort, while ancient evidence is provided by Syrian churches of *c.* 400 A.D., and the surviving 6th-century roof of St. Catherine's Monastery on Mount Sinai.[66]

French roofs

Quite apart from the reappearance of this roof type into northern Europe in the Renaissance, it had already come into use for French purlin roofs of the 13th century, and it is not necessary to seek a classical source for Chichester. For as Cecil Hewett observed, the Cathedral roof can be exactly paralleled with that of a barn belonging to the Cistercian monastery of Maubuisson, near Pontoise (Seine-et-Oise), in France.[67] The roof has been illustrated by Walter Horn and carbon-dated by Rainer Berger; the abbey was founded in 1236, and the carbon-14 date, although short of the historical date, confirms that the barn was built early in the 13th century.[68] The Maubuisson roof is over a stone-aisled barn; unlike either of the Chichester roofs, it has a ridge-purlin lying on top of the king-posts, and the side-struts are not jowled, but are simply tenoned into the long braces running parallel to the rafter (and the purlins are supported by short spacing blocks). Apart from these features, the roofs are strikingly similar, with the long splayed braces to each of the purlins. The barn at Maubuisson represents one solution to the problem of providing support for a rafter roof. In the first phase of rafter roofs, where the separate individual trusses relied only on the external roof covering to hold them in place, there was always the likelihood of lengthways movement (racking). To combat this various forms of strengthening were tried out in the experimental era of roof-construction at the beginning of the 13th century that marked one of the great leaps forward in medieval carpentry technology.[69] In the roofs of the larger French churches a wide variety of assemblages was devised, often of considerable complexity, but generally employing multiple purlins and tall posts with long braces (either at the centre or at the sides, or both). For the most part the French carpentry tradition was later to retain the central king-post or king-strut rising to the apex of the roof, and maintain these forms in a surprisingly conservative manner for many centuries.[70]

English parallels

In England, where the same experimental phase took place, the appearance of new forms was slower, and the resulting tradition of crown-post roofs was to flourish for a shorter period until further developments supplanted it. Before this is discussed, it is necessary to consider some other buildings which demonstrate the particular characteristics of the Chichester and Maubuisson roofs. There stood until 1968 in Bishops Waltham, Hants., a building with a roof similar to that of the Chichester Bishop's Chapel.[71] In modern times it was used as a stable, but its original function is unknown. Excavations, which have indicated a late–13th century date, suggest that the building was aisled on one side and probably used for domestic purposes.[72] Demolished in a road-widening scheme, to preserve the ditch of the Bishop of Winchester's Palace, the true age and significance of the building were not appreciated when this took place. One truss survives at the Palace, and fragments were taken to the Weald and Downland Museum at Singleton. The roof spanned about 6 metres (20 feet), with common rafter couples supported by side-purlins and a ridge-purlin below the apex. These axial members were held up by king-posts mounted on tie-beams and by raking struts to the purlins and rafters (jowled as in the Chichester roofs). Apart from the ridge-purlin, this and the roof of the Bishop's Chapel are virtually identical. Whilst it is hard to find other roofs that are so similar, there are further examples of south-eastern roofs which employ the king-strut, that is a member rising to the apex and with the principal rafters tenoned into it. The motif appears as an element in the special arrangement used for the apsidal ending of the choir roof at Westminster Abbey (1245–59).[73] In Canterbury, the Abbot's Guest Hall at St. Augustine's Abbey, perhaps dating to the third quarter of the 13th century, has a three-bay roof which appears to be of crown-post type (internal span: 8.4 m.; 27 ft. 6 ins.).[74] However, the collar-purlins are merely tenoned into the "crown-post" which, in fact, continues up to the apex as a king-strut. A very similar five-bay roof exists over the sole surviving building at Robertsbridge Abbey in East Sussex (span: 7 m.; 23 ft.).[75] The vicarage of All Saints church, Maidstone (demolished in 1964) had an irregular five-bay roof with plain, unbraced crown-posts continuing upwards as king-struts (span: 5.9 m.; 19 ft. 4 ins.).[76] These three buildings are all of stone and probably belong to the second half of the 13th century. An aisled timber hall of about the same age, Ratling Court, Aylesham, Kent (three bays; span: 5 m.; 16 ft. 6 ins.), has one proper crown-post over the screens, but the central hall truss and the end trusses have crown-posts continued to the apex as king-struts.[77] These examples, none of which can be closely dated, form a group with a distribution in south-east England and can perhaps be seen as variant forms constructed at a time when the standard type of crown-post had yet to be established. This will be discussed further below. One feature which did persist until later and with a wider distribution was the king-strut in the end truss, which appears in crown-post roofs in Essex, Middlesex and Hertfordshire.[78]

All the examples described here can be distinguished from the later medieval king-post roofs found in the north of England (and occasionally in the south), often of low-pitch, with stout king-posts, ridge-pieces, and purlins carried on the outside of principal rafters.[79] The origins of the "northern school" of roof-carpentry are debatable and may or may not be related to the antecedents of the group under consideration. To be sure, the Bishops Waltham roof had a ridge-purlin, and so does the barn at Great Coxwell (supported on short king-posts above the upper collars).[80] As demonstrated by Eric Mercer, there are king-post roofs in southern England that resemble the northern type, and one might add to his examples the barn of Syon Abbey at Charlton Court, near Steyning in Sussex.[81] Its roof has king-posts braced to the ridge-purlin, with the unusual feature of side-purlins supported on the back of large curved braces descending from the king-post to the tie-beam in an ogival or serpentine pattern. The barn is likely to be late-medieval.

Development of English roofs

Before assessing the significance of the Chichester roofs and the linked group of roofs with king-strut variants of the crown-post, it might be useful to reconsider the outlines of development in major English roofs during the 13th century. Since the publication of initial accounts by Smith,[82] and then by Fletcher and Spokes,[83] the material available for consideration has been increased, particularly by Hewett's work on cathedral roofs, and various refinements of the argument have been proposed by Smith[84] and by Mercer.[85] What is now clear is that most major roofs of the first half of the 13th century lacked integral methods of axial support. Thus in the principal roofs of Ely Cathedral,[86] in a large barn like Cressing Temple Barley Barn (Essex),[87] and in the local example of the choir of Boxgrove Priory (West Sussex),[88] only the external fittings for the roof gave lengthways strengthening. In some cases diagonal bracing was applied, running across rafter couples, either internally as at Gloucester Blackfriars,[89] or externally as in the north transept of Westminster Abbey.[90] The most common form of lateral stabilisation was provided by scissor-bracing and in the case of framed timber buildings often by the passing brace—the latter arguably providing some measure of support against axial movement.[91] Purlins may have made their first appearance *above* the collar beams, as in the nave of Lincoln Cathedral.[92] About the middle of the century side-purlins occur, lying on the horizontal plane (on the collars at Siddington, Gloucestershire, and Cressing Temple Wheat Barn)[93] or doubling as plates in raised-aisle construction (as at the Ely Sextry Barn).[94] The true side-purlin, lying on the inclined plane of the roof, was perhaps first used in lean-to roofs, as in the north triforium at Wells (pre-1209)[95] and in the north triforium at Salisbury (1225-37).[96] In these roofs their main function would have been to alleviate the potential sagging of rafters at one or more points down their length, though the very fact of contact between the members would also have tended to prevent racking. An early appearance in main span roofing was in the north choir transept of Salisbury (1225-37),[97] though here the purlins rest on inward-canting posts and are not completely parallel with the rafters. By the second half of the century integrally planned side-purlins were in regular use, either clasped to the rafters by a collar, or resting on a short strut between the rafter and a bracing member. At Middle Littleton (Worcs., *c.* 1250), they are clasped in the upper triangle of the roof and strutted in the aisles below.[98] The later series of roofs at Wells Cathedral probably belong to an unrecorded re-roofing between the initial completion of the church (1229) and the rebuilding of the parapet (*c.* 1301 ?). Those over the choir began with an upper pair of side-purlins clasped by the top collar then continued with the addition of a lower pair of side-purlins, supported on short struts; in the south transept only the lower, strutted pair were employed.[99] Similar forms were used at Exeter Cathedral in the east end (1290-1300) and the west end (*c.* 1325+).[100] If the roof of the great barn at Frocester (Gloucs.) retains any elements of its late-13th-century build in its late medieval rebuilding, then its clasped side-purlins and inclined main plates (clasped both by tie-beam and ashlar posts) may be considered here.[101] Another major barn, at Great Coxwell (Berks., *c.* 1305) has both clasped and strutted purlins.[102] All these roofs have side-purlins as a means of axial support for the whole roof, or as lateral support for long rafters. None have the particular arrangement found at Chichester, and the nearest parallel to the raking struts of our roof is to be found in the long struts used in various lean-to roofs, as in the north choir triforium at Salisbury.[103] Jowled struts which support both purlin and rafter can only be found at Carlisle, in the north triforium (? *c.* 1290)[104] and York Minster (apparently 14th century).[105]

The only one of these roofs which has a crown-post is the later roof at Exeter (after *c.* 1325).[106] This is consistent with the argument propounded by Mercer that crown-post roofs were not initially used in large-scale constructions over churches and barns which were not necessarily built to be seen or admired.[107] Whatever their date of introduction, crown-post roofs seem to have been built for display, and they became common in open domestic roofs of the later 13th century. Setting aside the nave roof at Harwell church,[108] it may be that the hall of the Old Deanery at Salisbury (probably in existence by *c.* 1274) is one of the earliest occurrences.[109] The use of a crown-post in the 1290s at St. Mary's Hospital, Chichester, was quite in keeping with this development.[110]

By contrast with the general progress of English roof carpentry was that of France, which saw a greater diversity of experimentation almost a generation ahead of similar developments in England. Moreover, the appearance of king- and crown-posts in France seems to have been quite unrelated to the "visibility factor" deemed to be at work when they appeared on a wide scale in England, for many of the great French roofs were above vaulting.[111]

Conclusions

How do the Chichester roofs relate to all this? It seems fair, despite the danger of arguing on the basis of a very small sample, to suppose some sort of link between the roof of the Cathedral and the barn at Maubuisson, though it would be fruitless to speculate on the circumstances which led to the construction of two such similar roofs on either side of the Channel. Given the wide date-range of the second half of the 13th century for the Cathedral roof, the ensemble found there, although understandable in the English context of experimentation with side-purlins in large roofs, seems to belong more directly to French traditions. The same could apply to the Bishop's Chapel, and the roof at Bishops Waltham, they could all be seen as exotic creations outside the mainstream of evolution of English roof types. But the linked group of roofs with crown-posts and king-struts suggests another aspect. It is possible that at the initial stage when new ideas were being tried out (doubtless under some influence from across the Channel), the king-strut and crown-post were both experimented with, and it was only secondarily that the crown-post (also increasingly more decorative) became *de rigeur* for display roofs. Future developments were to be affected by not only the "visibility factor", but also the size of the roof involved, and the steepness of pitch. The Chichester roofs provide a unique illustration of the modifications to a single concept of roof form made necessary by differences in scale. Many of the experiments with side-purlins so vital for devising a strengthened roof of large span were quite inappropriate for smaller roofs. Similarly, the suitability of crown-post roofs to relatively small roofs of steeper pitch can be observed, just as the later king-post roofs were found to be compatible with a lower pitch. These variables add to the complexity of the evidence, which is in any case affected by a random and low rate of survival, and further confused by a general lack of reliable dates. Despite these difficulties, the Chichester roofs are able to throw light on one of the most interesting phases in the development of roof carpentry, and once again demonstrate the significance of Continental practice to the evolution of English techniques.

Appendix

A Boxgrove Priory

The choir of the Priory church appears to preserve much of its original roof, dating perhaps to *c.* 1220.[112] This deserves further study, but it may be worth printing a few notes based on one visit.[113]

The crown of the vault is level with the top of the walls. The roof is of plain trussed rafters, with two collars, ashlars and braces from rafters to collars, making the standard seven-cant profile. Subsequent to its first building, the roof was given bay divisions with inserted tie-beams. On these were placed crown-posts, braced down to the ties and up to an irregular collar-purlin (which is not pegged to the collars). This must all be a repair, doubtless to prevent longitudinal racking of the primary trusses; it might well date to within 100 years of the first build. At the west end, there are four bays with post-medieval additions. New principal rafters support a side-purlin (they are diminished above it). Raking side-struts from the tie-beam support these purlins. The primary roof is a valuable indication of what Chichester might have been like, had there not been a wholesale replacement of the roofs in the Cathedral.

B St. Mary's Hospital, Chichester[114]

This is a building that could have an entire monograph written on it, and still calls for careful examination at close quarters. Most published illustrations are derived from F. T. Dollman's survey of 1857.[115] The timber aisled hall with its crown-post roof, and the chapel are likely to post-date 1290, when a lane crossing the site was allowed to be closed.[116] The chapel is comparable with the Lady Chapel of the Cathedral in the tracery of its windows.[117] Hewett has illustrated the probable form of one of the scarfs in the main plate.[118] A magnificent series of drawings had been published by Walter Horn and Ernest Born in their study of *The Plan of St. Gall.*[119]

C Other roofs in the Cathedral and Bishop's Palace

On the triforium roofs, the doors and cloisters, I have made no further investigation, and can add nothing to what has been illustrated by Hewett. The Bishop's Palace, and particularly its kitchen, is to be the subject of another paper.[120]

References

Anc. Corr.	Public Record Office, Ancient Correspondence. Calendared in *List and Index Soc. XV* (new ed., 1968); Neville is mostly in Vol. 6.
BERGER 1970	R. Berger, ed., *Scientific Methods in Medieval Archaeology*, Univ. of California.
BoE	I. Nairn and N. Pevsner, *The Buildings of England: Sussex*, Penguin, 1965.
C.C.	W. D. Peckham, *The Chartulary of the High Church of Chichester*, Sussex Record Soc., 46, 1946. (MSS. in W.S.R.O.)
CORLETTE 1901	H. C. Corlette, *The Cathedral Church of Chichester*, Bells Cathedral Series.
DENEUX 1927	H. Deneux "Evolution des charpentes du XIe au XVIIIe siècle", *L'Architecte*, 49–53, etc., to 89.
FLETCHER and SPOKES	J. M. Fletcher and P. S. Spokes, "The Origin and Development of Crown-Post Roofs", *Med. Arch.*, viii, 152–83.
HEWETT 1967	C. A. Hewett, "The Barns at Cressing Temple . . .", *Jnl. Soc. Archit. Hist. (Amer.)*, xxvi, 48ff.
HEWETT 1969	*The Development of Carpentry*, 1200–1700.
HEWETT 1974	*English Cathedral Carpentry.*
HEWETT 1980	*English Historic Carpentry.*
HORN and BORN 1979	W. Horn and E. Born, *The Barns of the Abbey of Beaulieu . . .*, Univ. of California.
HORN and BORN 1979	*The Plan of St. Gall*, Univ. of California.
McDOWELL, *et. al.*, 1966	R. W. McDowall, J. T. Smith, and C. F. Stell, "Westminster Abbey The Timber Roofs . . ..' *Archaeologia*, 100, 155–74.
MERCER 1975	E. Mercer, *English Vernacular Houses.*
OSTENDORF 1908	F. Ostendorf, *Die Geschichte des Dachwerks*, Leipzig and Berlin.
RACKHAM, *et al.*, 1978	O. Rackman, W. J. Blair and J. T. Munby, "The Thirteenth-century Roofs and Floor of the Blackfriars Priory at Gloucester", *Med. Arch.*, xxii, 1978, 105ff.
SMITH 1958	J. T. Smith, "Medieval Roofs: A Classification", *Arch. Jnl.*, 115, 111–49.
SMITH 1970	"The Reliability of Typological Dating of Medieval English Roofs", in Berger, 1970, 239–69.
SMITH 1974	"The Early Development of Timber Buildings . . .", *Arch. Jnl.*, 131, 238–63.
SWAINSON	C. A. Swainson, *The History and Constitution of a Cathedral of the Old Foundation*, London and Chichester, 1880.
V.C.H.	*Victoria County History, Sussex*, iii, 1935.
WALCOTT	M. E. C. Walcott, "The Early Statutes of the Cathedral Church of the Holy Trinity, Chichester . . .", *Archaeologia*, 45, 1877, 143–234.
WILLIS 1861	R. Willis, *The Architectural History of Chichester Cathedral* (Repr. 1972).
W.S.R.O.	West Sussex Record Office, Chichester.

Notes

1. Hewett, 1974, 28–9, Fig. 16; Willis, 1861, 30 thought the roofs "quite modern" (!). The roof was sketched at the beginning of the century by Ostendorf, 1908, 87.
2. I am most grateful to Dr. John Fletcher whose visit to Chichester resulted in the discovery of this roof (May 1978).
3. Hewett, 1974, Fig. 16.
4. Hewett, 1969, 174.
5. Willis, 1861, note 'o' on p. x.
6. McDowall, *et al.*, 1966, Pl. LXII.
7. Rackham, *et al.*, 1978
8. See Note 5 above.
9. Hewett, 1974, Fig. 16.

10. W.S.R.O., Add. MSS. 1850–1861 (esp. 1851 and 1858).
11. Hewett, 1974, 33–4, Fig. 19.
12. Hewett, 1974, 47, and Hewett, 1980, 241.
13. Willis, 1861, 30.
14. Willis, 1861, 29–30, Pl. 3 (opp. p. 1).
15. V.C.H., 126 (without source): Corlette, 1901, 48, quoting Scott's *Recollections.*
16. I. C. Hannah, "Bishop's Palace, Chichester", *Sx. Arch. Coll.,* 52, 1909, 1–23, esp. 8–11, V.C.H., 148 and note 43.
17. V.C.H., 148; BoE, 164.
18. V.C.H., 105ff.
19. BoE, 128ff.
20. BoE, 147–8, 151; V.C.H., 117 and Plate.
21. BoE, Pl. 23a.
22. Horn and Born, 1965, 26–30, and Figs.
23. Siebenlist-Kerner, Schove and Fletcher, "The Barn at Great Coxwell, Berkshire", in John Fletcher, ed., *Dendrochronology in Europe,* British Archaeol. Reports Internat. Ser., 51, 1978, 295–302; also *Vernac. Archit.,* 11, 1980, 34; (date now thought to be *c.* 1305).
24. Horn and Born, 1965, 26–30; F. Bond, *Gothic Architecture in England,* 1905 edition, Chap. xxv.
25. Willis, 1861, 30; Corlette, 1901, 57; V.C.H., 110; BoE, 134: "probably late C13".
26. BoE, 138.
27. BoE, 152.
28. BoE, 164; C. J. P., Cave, *Roof Bosses in Medieval Churches,* 1948, 78 and 187; *see also Sx. Arch. Coll.,* 71, 1930, 1–9.
29. C.C., 275ff. (903); Liber. E, f. 169–72 (W.S.R.O.). For Reed's lives of the Archbishops of Canterbury, see A. B. Emden, *Biographical Register of the University of Oxford,* 1957–9, 1556, 1560.
30. H. Mayr-Harting, *The Acta of the Bishops of Chichester, 1075–1207,* Cant. and York Soc., 1964, 47–8. In general, see K. Edwards, *The English Secular Cathedrals in the Middle Ages,* 1949, esp. 233–8, and C. R. Cheney, "Church-building in the Middle Ages", reprinted in *Medieval Texts and Studies,* 1973, 346–63.
31. Walcott, 156, note a; V.C.H., 106–7.
32. C.C. (903, No. 29).
33. *Rot Litt. Pat.* (Rec. Comm.), i, 65; *ducendi marmor suum per mare a Purbic usque Cicestr' ad reparationem ecclesie suae de Cicestr'.*
34. Hewett, 1974, 15–17; L. S. Colchester and J. H. Harvey, "Wells Cathedral", *Arch. Jnl.,* 131, 1974, 200ff., esp. 203.
35. Walcott, 157 note c; *Annales Monastici* (Rolls Ser. 36), iii, 32; *impetu venti ceciderunt . . . duae turres Cicestriae.*
36. M. B. Fradin, "Ralph Neville, Bishop of Chichester . . ." (unpublished Oxon. thesis), Bodleian MS., B. Litt., d. 38; J. Boussard, "Ralph Neville Évêque de Chichester . . .", *Revue Historique,* 176, 1935, 217–33; Letters in W. W. Shirley, *Royal Letters, Henry III* (Rolls Ser. 27, 1862 and 1866), and W. H. Blaauw, "Letters to Ralph de Nevill", *Sx. Arch. Coll.,* 3, 1850, 35–76; these are selective, but all the letters are calendared in *Anc. Corr.*
37. *Rot. Litt. Claus.* (Rec. Comm.), i, 615a, 640: *plumbum ad ecclesiam Cicestr' cooperiendam.*
38. *Anc. Corr.,* 6, No. 102 ("1226–30"); *Sx. Arch. Coll.,* 3, 75.
39. *Anc. Corr.,* 6, No. 153: *ad faciend' Berfrej in ecclesie Cicestr'.*
40. *Anc. Corr.,* 6, Nos. 132–3; *Sx. Arch. Coll.,* 3, 63–5.
41. V.C.H., 81; C.C. (137) and (853–857); *Cal. Chart. R.,* i, 86, 107; *Sx. Arch. Coll.,* 3, 53ff.; W. D. Peckham, *Sussex Custumals,* Sx. Rec. Soc., 31, 1925, 128.
42. *Anc. Corr.,* 6, No. 145; *Sx. Arch. Coll.,* 3, 55–8.
43. *Cal. Close. R. (1231–4),* 34: *meremium . . . ad reparationem domorum suarum episcopatus sui; ibid.,* 81: *ad fabricam ecclesie sue; ibid.,* 461, 506: *ad operationem predicte ecclesie Cycestrensis.*

44. C.C. (75); Liber Y, f. 80v. (W.S.R.O.): *qui ad reparacionem ecclesie nostre elimosinas conferre et ad meremium predictum cariandum.*
45. Walcott, 161; Swainson, 13 (40): *in usus fabrice eiusdem ecclesie que multiplici reparatione indigere dinoscitur.*
46. C.C. (404); Swainson, 19 (59).
47. C.C. (903, No. 33).
48. C.C. (37), dated 1247; Swainson, 20 (61). I assume the *opus Berfridi* is the same as the *opus cuisdam turris lapidee.* This document is the only one which mentions the *custos et procurator fabricae,* one Walkelin de Cycestria.
49. In 1247–8: C.C. (76–90); Swainson, 31 (67). See E. F. Jacob, "St. Richard of Chichester", *Jnl. Eccl. Hist.*, vii, 1956, 174–88, esp. 183-4.
50. C.C. (36), and Swainson 32 (68); *ibid.*, 37 (74); for Richard's Synodal Statutes of 1245–1252, see F. M. Powicke and C. R. Cheney, *Councils and Synods II, 1205–1313,* 1964, 451ff., 463 (59).
51. C.C. (903, No. 34). For his will (Liber E, f. 165/42—W.S.R.O), see *Sx. Arch. Coll.*, 1, 164–92.
52. C.C. (68) and (65–9); also (657).
53. C.C. (656).
54. Walcott, at p. 234; Corlette, 1901, at end; V.C.H., at p. 112.
55. C.C. (903, No. 35).
56. C.C. (903, No. 36); C.C. (971), Liber P., f. 167v. (W.S.R.O.).
57. C.C. (903, No. 37); *Councils and Synods,* 1082–1090 for Gilbert's Synodal Statutes of 1289: caps. (7) and (35).
58. C.C. (903, No. 38).
59. BoE *Lincolnshire,* ed. N. Pevsner and J. Harris, 1964, 105.
60. BoE, 135.
61. Bond, *op. cit.*, note 24, 393–4.
62. Berger, 1970, Chaps. i–v.
63. See Jones design in J. Harris, S. Orgel and R. Strong, *The King's Arcadia: Inigo Jones and the Stuart Court,* 1973. Cat. No. 195. Theatre roof illustrated in R. Plot, *The Natural History of Oxford-shire* (1677), 1705, Tab. xiiii; also H. M. Colvin, *The Sheldonian Theatre and the Divinity School,* 1964. St. Paul's: Hewett, 1974, 47–8, Fig. 36; see Tewkesbury, Fig. 35. See also Hewett, 1980, Chapter 8.
64. Simon Jervis, *Woodwork of Winchester Cathedral,* 1976, 6; Hewett, 1974, 159, Fig. 154. The remaining roof at Beaulieu St. Leonard's, Hants., is perhaps more likely to be post-medieval in date rather than being a reused portion of the original medieval roof as was suggested by F. W. B. Charles, in Berger, 1970, 225, Figs. 18–22. It has butt-purlins and the side-struts spring from offsets on the king-posts, as in some post-medieval roofs.
65. Serlio's seventh book deals with roofs: *Tutte L'Opere D'Architettura et Prospetura di Sebastiano Serlio,* Venice, 1619, vii, caps. 73–5, pp. 196–201 (repr. Gregg Press, 1965; first edn. was 1575); Andrea Palladio, *I Quattro Libri dell'Architettura,* 1570, etc., English edition of I. Ware, *The Four Books of Palladio's Architecture,* 1738, shows several roofs in sections. Manuals: J. Moxon, *Mechanick Exercises: or the Doctrine of Handy works (III) Applied to the Art of House-Carpentry,* 1677, etc., Pl. 11 of Part III; James Smith, *The Carpenter's Companion,* 1733, various Pls.; B. and T. Langley, *The Builder's Jewel,* 1741 (and later edns.), Pls. 88–99.
66. See discussion of the roof of St. Gall in Horn and Born, 1979, i, 173–6, Figs. 126–9, citing Vitruvius, *De Architectura,* Lib. IV, cap. 2 and G. H. Forsyth, *et al.*, *The Monastery of St. Catherine at Mount Sinai,* Ann Arbor, 1973. See also Ostendorf, 1908, 1.
67. Hewett, 1974, 29.
68. W. Horn in Berger, 1970, 28–30, Fig. 6; Ostendorf, 1908, 161, Fig. 249.
69. Deneux, 1927; *Charpentes,* Vols. 1–3 (Centre de Recherches sur les Monuments Historiques), *c.* 1960 and 1972, *passim.* M. David Roy, "Les Granges Monastiques en France aux XII et XIII siècles", *Archeologia: Tresors des Ages,* 58, Mai 1973 (Maubuisson, p. 59), 52–65; Pere Anselme Dimier, "Les Belles Granges Cisterciennes du departement de L'Oise", *ibid.*, 85. Aout, 1975, 49–61. (These last références were kindly brought to my attention by Anthony King.) See also G. I. Meirion-Jones, "The Roof-Carpentry of Brittany", *Vernac. Archit.*, 9, 1978, 17ff; Ostendorf, 1908; Fletcher and Spokes, 1964,

and Smith, 1974.
70. Deneux, 1927, 81ff.; see the French market halls in Berger, 1970, 31–41, built on a similar pattern from the 15th to the 17th centuries.
71. Mercer, 1975, 163 (160), Fig. 117.
72. *Med. Arch.*, xiii, 1969, 249–50; R.C.H.M. files and ex inf. E. Lewis.
73. McDowall, 1966, Figs. 1 and 3.
74. Ex inf. Tim Tatton-Brown; *BoE NE. and E. Kent*, ed. J. Newman, 1969, 227.
75. Ex inf. David Martin and Tim Tatton-Brown.
76. Mercer, 1975, 176 (224) after E. W. Parkin, "The Old Vicarage, Maidstone", *Arch. Cant.*, 80, 1965, 205–14.
77. E. W. Parkin, "Ratling Court, Aylesham", *Arch. Cant.*, 92, 1976, 53–64.
78. Essex: Hewett, 1969, e.g., Figs. 51, 59b and 60; Herts.: ex inf. J. T. Smith; Middlesex: Mercer, 1975, 188 (296), Pl. 58.
79. Smith, 1958, 128–30; Smith, 1970, 267–8; Mercer, 1975, 109–111.
80. Horn and Born, 1965, Figs. 5, 18 and 19.
81. Mercer, 1975, 109–111; Tim Hudson of V.C.H. Sussex directed me to this most interesting barn. See *V.C.H. Sussex*, vi(i), 227.
82. Smith, 1958.
83. Fletcher and Spokes, 1964.
84. Smith, 1970 and 1974.
85. Mercer, 1975, Chap. vi.
86. J. Fletcher, "Medieval Timberwork at Ely", in *Medieval Art and Architecture at Ely Cathedral*, Brit. Arch. Assoc., 1979, 58ff.
87. Hewett, 1967, 49ff; Hewett, 1969, 22ff; Hewett, 1980, 59ff.
88. Not published: see appendix above.
89. Rackham, *et al.*, 1978, and Hewett, 1974, Fig. 12.
90. McDowall, *et al.*, 1966, 164 and Fig. 4; Hewett, 1980, 112.
91. Smith, 1974, 250–2.
92. Hewett, 1974, 20–1, Fig. 9; Hewett, 1980, 79.
93. C. A. Hewett, "The Tithe Barn at Siddington, Gloucestershire", *Arch. Jnl.*, 129, 1972, 145–7, Fig. 1; Hewett, 1967, 59ff; Hewett, 1969, 40ff; Hewett, 1980, 87–8 and 102–5.
94. Fletcher and Spokes, 1964, Fig. 51b; *op. cit.* in note 86, Fig. 4; Smith, 1970, Fig. 3 and 1974, Fig. 1A; after R. Willis, "The Sextry Barn at Ely", *Cambr. Antiq. Soc. Proc.*, 4to Ser. I (1840–6), item vii, 1843, 8pp. 4 Pls.
95. Hewett, 1974, 51–2, Fig. 40; Hewett, 1980, 65–6.
96. Hewett, 1974, 52–4, Fig. 42, and 149–50, Fig. 137; Hewett, 1980, 92–3.
97. Hewett, 1974, 29–30, Fig. 17; Hewett, 1980, 91.
98. W. Horn and F. W. B. Charles, "The Cruck-built Barn at Middle Littleton in Worcestershire, England", *Jnl. Soc. Archit. Hist. (Amer.)*, xxv, 1966, 221–39, esp. Figs. 8, 13 and 14.
99. East end: Hewett, 1974, 36–7, Fig. 23; Transept: *ibid.*, 21–2, Fig. 10.
100. *Ibid.*, 24–8, 108, Figs. 13–15; it is perhaps unlikely that much of the timberwork is as early as *c.* 1190–1200; see Hewett, 1980, 149–51.
101. S. E. Rigold, "Frocester Court Tithe Barn", *Arch. Jnl.*, 122, 1965, 209–11, Fig. 10, Pl. xxxvi; W. Horn in Berger, 1970, 46–8, Fig. 19; Note on its date in *Arch Jnl.*, 134, 1977, 329.
102. Horn and Born, 1965, Figs. 5, 8, etc.; for the date see note 23 above.
103. As note 96 above.
104. Hewett, 1974, 125–6, Fig. 106.
105. *Ibid.*, 57, Fig. 46 (over masonry of *c.* 1230); Hewett, 1980, 181.
106. Hewett, 1974, 25-7, Fig. 14; Hewett, 1980, 150.
107. Mercer, 1975, 85–7.
108. Dr. Fletcher does not now believe that this roof is necessarily as old as was claimed in Fletcher and Spokes, 1964, 169–72.
109. Thus Smith, 1970, 259; see N. Drinkwater, "The Old Deanery, Salisbury", *Antiq. Jnl.*, xliv, 1964, 41–59, and illus.
110. See appendix above.

111. As note 69 above.
112. BoE, 114ff.
113. Examined on 12 December 1978, through the kindness of the vicar.
114. See V.C.H., 78–9 and Pls.; *V.C.H. Sussex ii*, 101; Plan in *Arch. Jnl.*, 92, 1935, 394; Canon A. C. Powell, *The Hospital of the Blessed Mary, Chichester* (var. dates) is the current guide.
115. *Antient Domestick Architecture,* 1858, Pls. 21–3; also in Dollman and Jobbins *An Analysis of Ancient Domestic Architecture,* 1861-3, and Ostendorf, 1908, 100.
116. Licence granted after an Inquisition *ad quod damnum: Cal. Pat. R. (1281–92),* 356.
117. BoE, 173–4.
118. C. A. Hewett, "Scarf Jointing during the Later Thirteenth and Fourteenth Centuries . . .", *Arch. Jnl.,* 134, 1977, 287–96: 289, Fig. 2.
119. Horn and Born, 1979, ii, 91–5, Figs. 341–3 (page proofs kindly supplied by Prof. Horn in advance of publication).
120. Hannah, *op. cit.,* in note 16; Ostendorf, 1908, 184; Smith, 1970, Fig. 9; Horn and Born, 1979, i, 276, Fig. 224 C.

10

The Roman Brooches

by D. F. Mackreth and S. A. Butcher

All brooches are made from a copper alloy.

Figs. 10.1-10.2

Colchesters

1. *c.* 90 mm. long. Of the hook and spring, only the stubs remain. The wings are relatively short and plain. The bow is also plain and may have been facetted behind. The catch-plate is largely missing, but shows that at least two rectangular piercings had been created by using a punch. The junction of the catch-plate with the bow also shows the deep marks made by the tool used in forging the catch-plate from the short stub on the casting (*Stead,* 1975). For discussion, see after 2. (*Chapel Street, X3 [g], below street 1*), (231).
2. *c.* 56 mm. long. Half the spring with the pin is missing. The hook is long and, in profile, a hollow can be seen just in front of the chord. The bow is thin, facetted behind and under the head shows signs of cold-working; the bead-row was also formed by cold-working and a mis-strike of the tool used can be seen on the upper part of the bow. Nearly all of the catch-plate is missing, however, sufficient is left for the remains of one rectangular piercing, formed by using a punch, to be seen. Part of a line of rocker-arm ornament can be seen along the top of the catch-plate (*Chapel Street, X105*), (323).

The large size of 1 should be a sufficient guarantee that it was made before the Conquest. On the other hand, the relatively crude piercings in the catch-plate may mean that it is not early in the life of the type. In default of well-dated examples which demonstrate clearly the development of the type, it is not possible to do more than suggest that the brooch belongs to the period *c.* 20–40 A.D. As for 2, the smaller size, the shaping of the profile of the bow and the bead-row down the centre of the bow all betoken a late Colchester. Attention was drawn in the previous report to the signs that late Colchesters showed of the stylistic traits which characterise a large number of its progeny (*Chichester 3,* 277). In the present case, bead-rows can be found on two more from Chichester (*Hildyard,* 1955, 104, frontispiece 54; *Chichester 2,* 52, Figs. 5, 6, 18), one from Cirencester (Cirencester Excavations Committee, forthcoming), and one from Colchester which was described as being a Continental form (*Hawkes* and *Hull,* 1947, 310, Pl. XCI, 35). The broad short hook of the last, along with its very thin bow, suggest that this is so, and the same might apply to the one from Cirencester, but for the others, especially the present example, a British origin is likely. None of these specimens is closely dated, but it may be suggested none is likely to have been made later than 50 A.D., if as late as that.

Colchester derivative

3. The pin was hinged and each wing is short and has a moulding at the end. On the head is a pedestal, with a moulding across the top, for a loop whose broken ends were filed down in antiquity. The bow is divided into three parts. The top division has two longitudinal recesses, each retaining traces of at least two differently-coloured enamels, a blue and, possibly, a red. The next section is marked off from the top and bottom parts by divided lenticular bosses, the bottom ones being placed diagonally. Both the lower and middle parts are plain with a rounded front. The elaborate foot consists of a sunken cross-moulding above a lower projecting moulding each end of which has another divided boss. (*Eastgate, C.103*), (65).

Four very close parallels come from Nor'Nour in the Isles of Scilly, but there are sufficient differences to show that they were not made from the same master (*Dudley,* (1967, 32, Figs. 11–2, 12–5); two do not have pedestals for the loop, all the Nor'Nour ones have an arris down the bow beneath the enamelled part, and three have more elaborate mouldings at the ends of the wings. To those listed by Hull (*ibid.*) can be added one from Stockton, Wilts. (*Mackreth,* 1973, 17, 9), and another, with three square recesses for enamel, from Worcester (excavations, M. O. H. Carver, to be published).

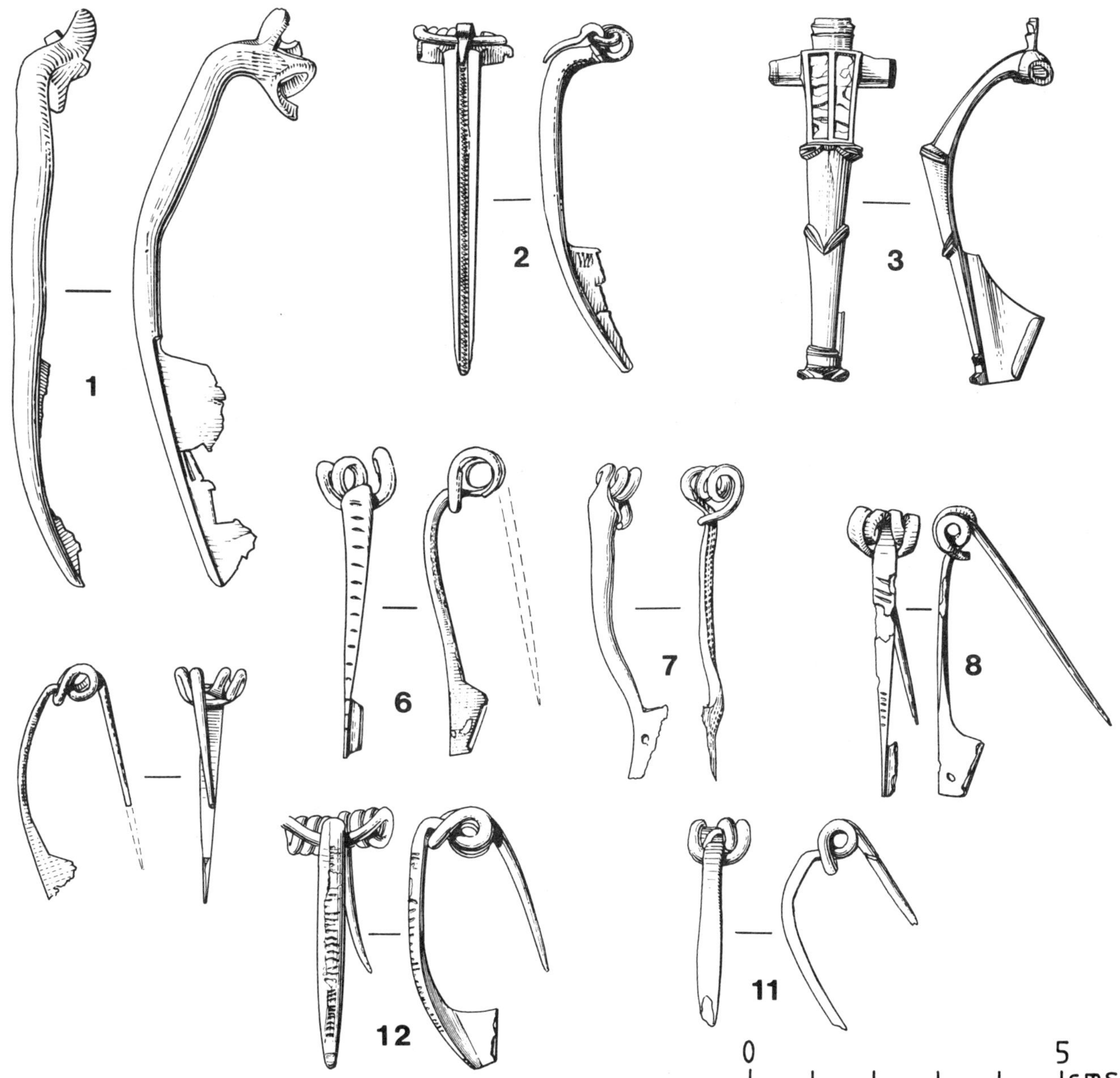

Fig. 10.1. Roman brooches, Nos. 1-12 ($\frac{1}{1}$).

All these brooches are elaborations of a more simple design (*cf. Dudley*, 1967, 34, Figs. 12–3, 16–32), and the variety of ornament suggests that the type was popular and made in more than one centre for some time. That the latter may be true is shown by some examples which have the Polden Hill spring arrangement instead of a hinged pin; the Stockton brooch is an example of the elaborate type, and one from Wroxeter (*Atkinson*, 1942, 205, Fig. 36, H40) is a simple one. A brooch from Croft Ambrey shows the influence derived from another type which habitually had a Polden Hill spring arrangement and which is commonly found in the West Midlands (*Stanford*, 1974, 144, Fig. 67, 4; *ibid.*, Fig. 67, 1–2) and which flourishes in the later 1st century and the early second. For the present type in both simple and complex forms there is very little dating evidence and not enough for a trend to be discerned. In the case of the present specimen, the use of a hinged pin might indicate a date after the time when the Polden Hill spring fixing arrangement had passed out of use, perhaps the middle of the 2nd century, but it may only be that the type abandoned the use of sprung pins early and that the use of a hinged pin as opposed to a sprung one is no criterion, in which case a date range from the later 1st century to the middle of the second may be suggested.

Nauheim derivatives

For discussion, see after 13.

4. Very corroded, the basic shape is a broader version of three from other sites in Chichester (*Chichester 3*, 280, Figs. 10.26, 10.27). There is no sign of ornament visible under the accreted corrosion. The catch-plate is missing (*Chapel Street, X103*), (36). *Not illustrated.*
5. A small fragment of a smaller brooch than the last, but of the same type. (*Chapel Street, X110*), (319). *Not illustrated.*
6. Complete, except for the pin and one coil of the spring, the bow tapers to a pointed foot and has a series of cross-cuts down it to the top of the catch-plate. (*Chapel Street, unstratified*), (364).
7. As the last brooch, except that the half spring which survives shows that it once had six coils, and the cross-cuts down the bow are closer set (*Chapel Street, X3[g]*), (229).
8. Complete, although the bow had been straightened in antiquity. The bow has the same form as the previous two, but has cross-cuts forming Vs at the top of the bow and a short row of cross-cuts just above the start of the catch-plate. (*Chapel Street, P24*) (709).
9. Part of the bow and catch-plate most probably from a Nauheim derivative. There are three or four cross-cuts on the bow where the upper part of the catch-plate occurs. (*Eastgate, Pit A29*), (44). *Not illustrated.*
10. Complete except for part of the pin and catch-plate, the bow has a thin rectangular section bow and tapers to a pointed foot. (*Chapel Street, X117*), (418).
11. As the last, except for the pin and catch-plate which are missing, and the section of the bow is less firmly rectangular. (*Chapel Street, Slot X24*), (466).
12. The spring has eight coils and the chord is tucked under a very sharp angle at the head of the bow which has a swelled front and a bead-row down it. The foot is slightly rounded and the catch-plate is short. (*Eastgate, Pit C19*), (25).
13. The four-coil spring and part of the pin from a Nauheim derivative. (*Chapel Street, X169*), (538). *Not illustrated.*

There is little to add to the remarks made about this type of brooch in the last report on brooches from Chichester (*Chichester 3*, 280–2). Nos. 4 and 5 are two more examples of a bow design which is well represented at Chichester and which seems seldom to occur north of the Thames, beyond Gloucestershire. Similarly, 6 and 7 display a kind of ornament which is also relatively restricted in its distributional area which is largely that ascribed to the Atrebates.

No. 11 is unusual not only in having so many coils, but also in the way in which the lower bow is not reduced to the thickness of the catch-plate; 7 is only exceptional in the number of coils in its spring. Although the standard brooch of the Nauheim and its later derivative sequence is one in which the spring has four coils, exceptions to the norm are, perhaps, less rare than might be thought. In Britain the main deviation is three coils (*cf. Atkinson*, 1916, 33, Pl. VII, 13), the spring curling over and passing under the bow without completing a coil first. Thus, examples with broken springs are relatively easy to identify. Concentrations of the examples noted by the writer lie in two areas, one centred on Wiltshire and the other in Kent. There is also a possibility that there is another, largely pre-Conquest, group in Essex. Brooches with more than four coils are rarer, but, to some extent, the small number known have only been identified because of the survival of more than two coils on one side. One with six coils from London may be noted (*B.M. Guide*, 64, Fig. 24.5), it has ornament down the bow consisting of incised circles between punched dots. An iron example with six coils and another of five coils come from Old Winteringham (*Stead*, 1976, 198–9, Fig. 100. 21 and Fig. 101.24), the first having a Neronian-early Flavian context.

Aucissa-Hod Hill

For discussion, see after 20.

14. The head is missing and so is the foot-knob. The bow is distorted and has the typical section of the inscribed Aucissa; a swelled front, with a sunken bead-row down the centre, rising between a ridge on each side. This part of the bow is finished off with a flat area which steps down to the foot section which also appears to be flat (*Southgate*, F.6), (9). *Not illustrated.*
15. The head and part of the upper bow is missing. The surviving part of the upper bow is flat with a very pronounced but thin ridge with a beaded top on each side. At the bottom is a waist with a marked cross-moulding above and below. The lower bow is a flat surface tapering to a two-part foot-knob. There are traces of tinning or silvering. (*Chapel Street, X65*), (290). *Not illustrated.*
16. The brooch is very corroded and all the detail may not be visible. The upper bow has three vertical mouldings separated by flutes. On one side at the lower end of the upper bow is a wing with a boss at the end. Across the bottom of the upper bow is a step from which the lower bow re-curves and tapers to a two-part foot-knob. (*Chapel Street, X117*), (402).
17. The upper bow has a cross-moulding at top and bottom and five vertical mouldings, alternating narrow and wide, between; the central one has diagonal beading. The lower bow is flat, wide at the top, with a cross-moulding, an incised line down each side, and tapers to a well-formed two-part foot-knob. There are traces of tinning or silvering. On the catch-plate and to either side on the back of the lower bow are toolmarks suggesting that the catch-plate had been cold-forged. (*Chapel Street, Pit X29*), (60).
18. An elaborate brooch with a strong cross-moulding above a panel of three vertical mouldings, the outer ones may have been beaded. On either side of the panel at the top is a wing with two more vertical mouldings. Below the panel is a short horizontal section with beaded mouldings on either side of a raised wavy line formed by cold-working. Next comes a cross-moulding and then a flat triangular plate with its tip cut off by the top of four cross-mouldings, the outer ones beaded, and with the flutes between having cut-outs at each end. Below this part are two more, but shorter, cross-mouldings the lower of which tapers away to the top of the two-part foot-knob. The catch-plate also shows signs of cold-working. (*Chapel Street, X196*), (569).
19. Another elaborate brooch which has the head and part of the top panel missing. The rest of the upper panel has three vertical flutes, the central one beaded and the outer ones each with a groove. The next section of the bow has two wide flutes each with a cross-moulding to top and bottom and separated one from another by a single cross-moulding. The bow is finished off by a two-part foot-knob. (*Chapel Street, X79*), (439). *Not illustrated.*
20. Only the upper bow and part of the lower survives. There are five vertical ridges on the top panel alternating narrow and wide, the latter being beaded. There is a wing to either side at the bottom with a two-part moulding at the head. Beneath the panel is a cross-flute with a cross-moulding at the bottom. What survives of the lower bow suggests that it was flat and re-curved into the upper part. (*Chapel Street, Pit P41 [B]*), (724).

There is little to add to what was said in *Chichester 3* (283–5). There is only the one Aucissa, 14, and there are no early Hod Hills (*cf. Chichester 3*, 282, Fig. 10.27, 36). No. 15 may have derived from a main variety of the Aucissa type in which there is a deep central flute instead of the swelled front (*cf. Chichester 3*, 282, Fig. 10.27, 33; *Hawkes* and *Hull*, 1947, 322, Pl. XCVI, 125–6; *Frere*, 1954, 140, Fig. 23-1). The floruit of the Hod Hill hardly runs beyond 60 A.D., and there were very few in use at *c.* 70 A.D.

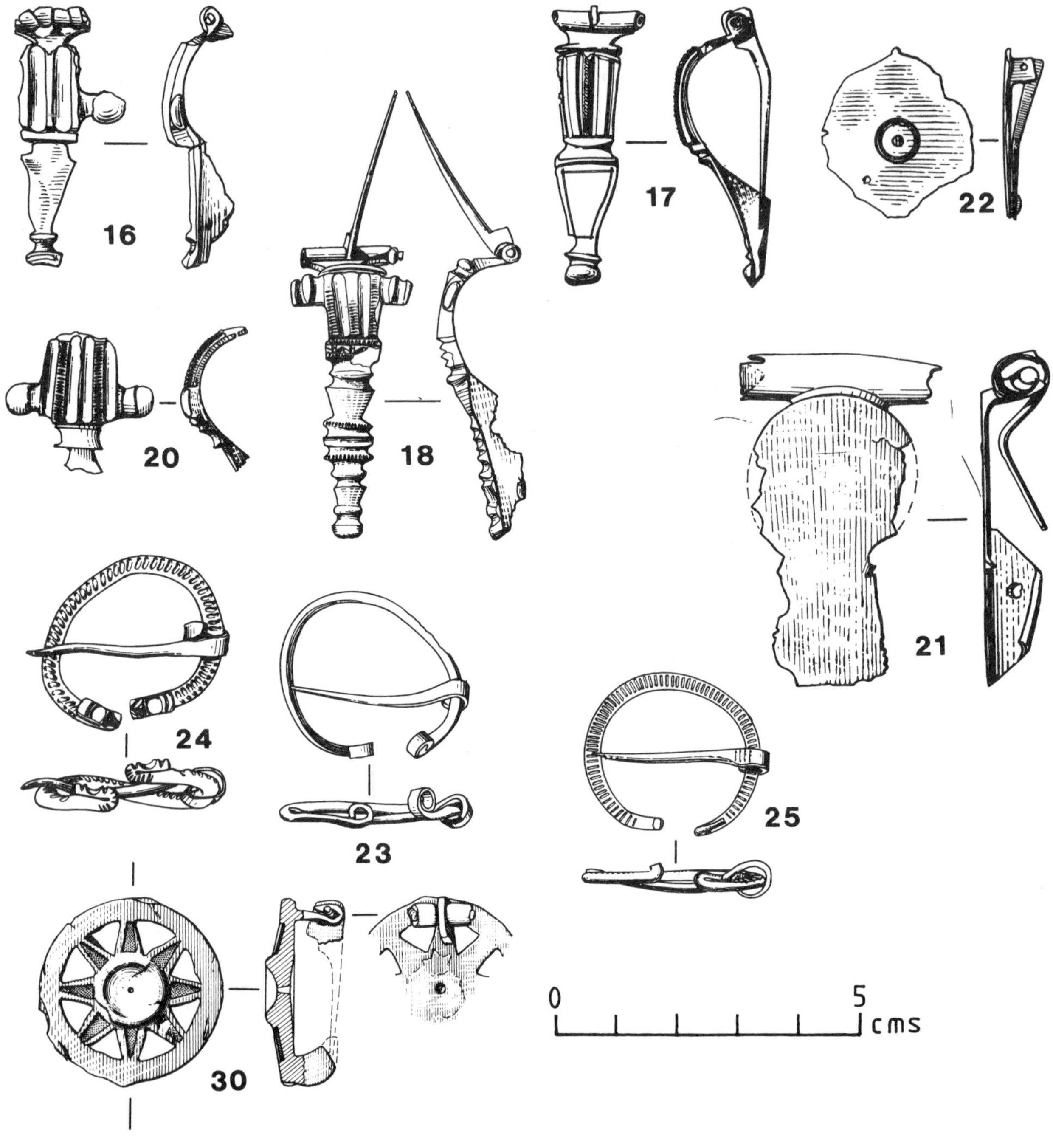

Fig. 10.2. Roman brooches, Nos. 16-30 ($\frac{1}{1}$).

Rosette

21. Two flaps cast along the head of the brooch were closed round the separately-made spring leaving a slot for the pin. The bow is set off from the spring-case by a step and consists of a flat plate formed into a roundel above and a fantail foot below.

The brooch has been stripped in conservation. There is no trace of ornament on the spring-case and no sign of an applied repoussee plate. The front of the brooch almost certainly had an applied plate, possibly not with a rosette (*cf. Westell* and *Hull*, 1935, 350, Fig. 2) as there is no hole for an enamel stud and the design may have been a variation of the gladiator or warrior and beast design (*cf. Thill*, 1969, 150, abb. 8, 81). At-Augst the bulk of this general type of rosette was being lost or discarded in Claudian times. The *floruit* should therefore start earlier and one of the Augst specimens comes from a late Augustan-Tiberian context (*Riha*, 1979, 106, taf. 21, 550–70). (*Eastgate, C11*), *(30)*.

Plate

22. A flat circular plate which, before conservation, had six equally-spaced projections around the periphery. In the centre is a circular recess with a hole in the middle and two mouldings near the outer edge. The pin is hinged. (*Chapel Street, X138*), (371).

A close parallel comes from Colchester and from a context dating to before *c.* 48 A.D. (*Hawkes* and *Hull*, 1947, 326, Pl. XCVIII, 179), and one other specimen has been recorded from Chichester (*Hildyard*, 1955, 111, frontispiece 61). I am grateful to Lady Pauline Richmond-Brown for kindly allowing me to examine the brooch. It is possible that this brooch comes from a single workshop producing a wide range of plate brooches which have a small range of decorative traits. There are two main distinguishing features, the first is the use of bifurcated terminals, and the second is the invariable presence of the central recess and a hole for an enamelled stud (*cf. Hawkes* and *Hull*, 1947, 325, Pl. XCVIII, 165). The chief forms for the plate are a lozenge with concave sides and the bifurcated terminals on the long axis; an equal-armed cross with similar sides and four divided ends (*Bushe-Fox*, 1949, 109, Pl. XXV, 6); and a simple and complex peltas (*Clifford*, 1961, 184, Fig. 36, 6. *Hawkes* and *Hull*, 1947, 325, Pl. XCVIII, 170). Circular brooches employ the recess alone as there is no real opportunity of using the terminal, there can be open forms (*Ward-Perkins*, 1938, 352, Fig. 2.2) or closed as in the present instance. The dating is consistently Claudian with a drift into Neronian times, but it would seem that the workshop was in being before Claudius assumed the purple (*Riha*, 1979, 182, taf. 58, 1535).

Penannulars

For discussion, see after 25.

23. Complete with a slightly distorted ring of plain circular section, each terminal is coiled up at right-angles to the plane of the ring, but each coil is simple, i.e., not completing more than one spiral. (*Eastgate, Pit B10*), (177).

24. Complete, but slightly distorted, the ring has an oval section with a beaded effect around the upper surface created by a punch. The terminals are returned along the surface of the ring and each has a fluted waist with a cross-moulding on each side. The inner end of each has diagonal grooves. On each side of the inner ends are a series of nicks. (*Chapel Street, X110*), (311).

25. The ring has been severely stripped during conservation and the details are no longer clear. The ring has a flat rectangular section with a series of cross-cuts along the upper surface. One terminal survives, but it appears to be plain and returned along the surface of the ring. (*Eastgate, Pit B10 [E]*), (225).

No. 23 belongs to Fowler's type C. (*Fowler*, 1960, 151-2) and is given the date range of 1st century B.C. into Saxon times (*ibid.*, 175). However, the examples occurring in Saxon graves should be regarded as being out of their correct horizon, which is essentially before the 2nd century A.D.

No. 24 belongs either to Fowler's type D4 or is covered by her category D6 (*ibid.*, 151–3). The date range given is the 1st and 2nd centuries for D4, and 1st to 3rd centuries A.D. for D6 (*ibid.*, 176).

Little can be said about 25 as it is not clear whether or not the terminal was as plain as it appears to be now.

Fragments (not illustrated)

26. The complete pin from a hinged pin brooch. The short length suggests that it might have come from a plate brooch. (*Chapel Street P4*), (705).
27. Most of the pin from a similar kind of brooch. (*Eastgate, Pit C27*), (32).
28. The corroded remains of a spring and pin most likely from a Colchester or one of its derivatives. (*Chapel Street, X111*), (304).
29. A length of copper alloy of uneven section and curved in a manner which suggests the bow of a brooch. There are no diagnostic features. (*Chapel Street, X1*), (201).

Enamelled disc brooch from Chichester by S. A. Butcher

30. Within a plain circular border an eight-pointed star in open-work surrounds a central disc. The rays of the star contain translucent olive green enamel (Miss J. Bayley identified this as the original colour, now obscured). The centre is recessed, possibly for enamel, but a central hole may once have held the rivet for a separate decorative plate. In profile the centre is seen to be slightly raised. The lug on the underside which holds the hinged pin is unusually long and broad. Diameter 30 mm.

    This is an unusual brooch for which I can quote no close parallel. However, in general design it resembles a well-known type of British umbonate disc-brooch with concentric rings of enamelled triangles. Examples of these have been found throughout the province from Richborough (*Bushe-Fox,* 1926, Pl. XII, 7, p. 43) to Newstead (*Curle,* 1911, Pl. LXXXIX, 20, p. 331) on both military and native sites. One from Wroxeter was in a deposit dated *c.* A.D. 100 (*Bushe-Fox,* 1913, Fig. 10.9). The long catch-plate and lug are the only features which might suggest a later date for the present variant. (*Chapel Street, P8*), (695).

References

ATKINSON 1916 — Atkinson, D., *The Romano-British site on Lowbury Hill in Berkshire,* Reading, 1916.

ATKINSON 1942 — Atkinson, D., *Report on Excavations at Wroxeter (The Roman City of Viroconium) in the County of Salop,* 1923, Oxford, 1942.

B. M. GUIDE 1958 — *Guide to the Antiquities of Roman Britain,* The Trustees of the British Museum, London, 1958.

BUSH-FOX 1913 — Bushe-Fox, J. P., *First Report on the Excavations on the Site of the Roman Town at Wroxeter, Shropshire,* 1912 (London, 1913).

BUSHE-FOX 1926 — Bushe-Fox, J. P., *First Report on the Excavations of the Roman Fort at Richborough, Kent,* London 1926.

BUSHE-FOX 1949 — Bushe-Fox, J.P., *Fourth Report on the Excavations of the Roman Fort at Richborough, Kent.* Reports of the Research Committee of the Society of Antiquaries of London, No. XVI, Oxford, 1949.

CHICHESTER 2 — Down, A., *Chichester Excavations 2,* 1974.

CHICHESTER 3 — Down, A., *Chichester Excavations 3,* 1978.

CLIFFORD 1961 — Clifford, Elsie M., *Bagendon: A Belgic Oppidum, A record of the excavations of 1954–56,* Cambridge, 1961.

CURLE 1911 — Curle, J., *A Roman Frontier Post and its People. The Fort of Newstead in the Parish of Melrose,* Glasgow 1911.

DUDLEY 1967 — Dudley, Dorothy, Excavations on Nor'Nour in the Isles of Scilly, 1962–6, *The Archaeolgical Journal,* CXXXIV, 1967, 1–64.

FOWLER 1960 — Fowler, Elizabeth, The Origins and Development of the Penannular Brooch in Europe, *Proceedings of the* Pre-historic *Society,* XXVI, 1960, 147–177.

FRERE 1954 — Frere, S. S., Canterbury Excavations, Summer, 1946, The Rose Lane sites, *Archaeologia Cantiana,* LXVIII, 1954, 101–143.

HAWKES and HULL 1947 — Hawkes, C. F. C. and Hull, M. R., Camulodunum, *First Report on the Excavations at Colchester,* 1930–1939; Report of the Research Committee of the Society of Antiquaries of London, No. XIV, Oxford, 1947.

HILDYARD 1955 — Hildyard, E. J. W., Roman fibulae from Chichester, *Sussex Notes and Queries,* XIV, 1955, 7 and 8, 109–12, and frontispiece.

MACKRETH 1973 — Mackreth, D., *Roman Brooches*, Salisbury, 1973.

RIHA 1979 — Riha, Emile, *Die Römischen Fibeln aus Augst und Kaiseraugst*, Forschungen in Augst, Band 3, August, 1979.

STANFORD 1974 — Stanford, S. C., *Croft Ambrey*, Hereford, 1974.

STEAD 1975 — Stead, I. M., A Roman Pottery theatrical face-mask and a bronze brooch-blank from Baldock, Herts, *The Antiquaries Journal*, LV, 1975, 397–8.

STEAD 1976 — Stead, I. M., *Excavations at Winterton Roman Villa, and other Roman sites in north Lincolnshire*, 1958–69. Department of the Environment Archaeological Report 9, London, 1976.

THILL 1969 — Thill, Gerard, Fibeln vom Titelberg aus der Beständen des Luxemburger Museums, *Trierer Zeitschrift*, 32, 1969, 133–171.

WARD-PERKINS 1938 — Ward-Perkins, J. B., The Roman Villa at Lockleys, Welwyn, *The Antiquaries Journal*, XVIII, 1938, 339–376.

WESTELL and HULL 1935 — Westell, W. P., and Hull, M. R., Bronze objects found in Hertfordshire, *The Antiquaries Journal*, XV, 1935, 349–51.

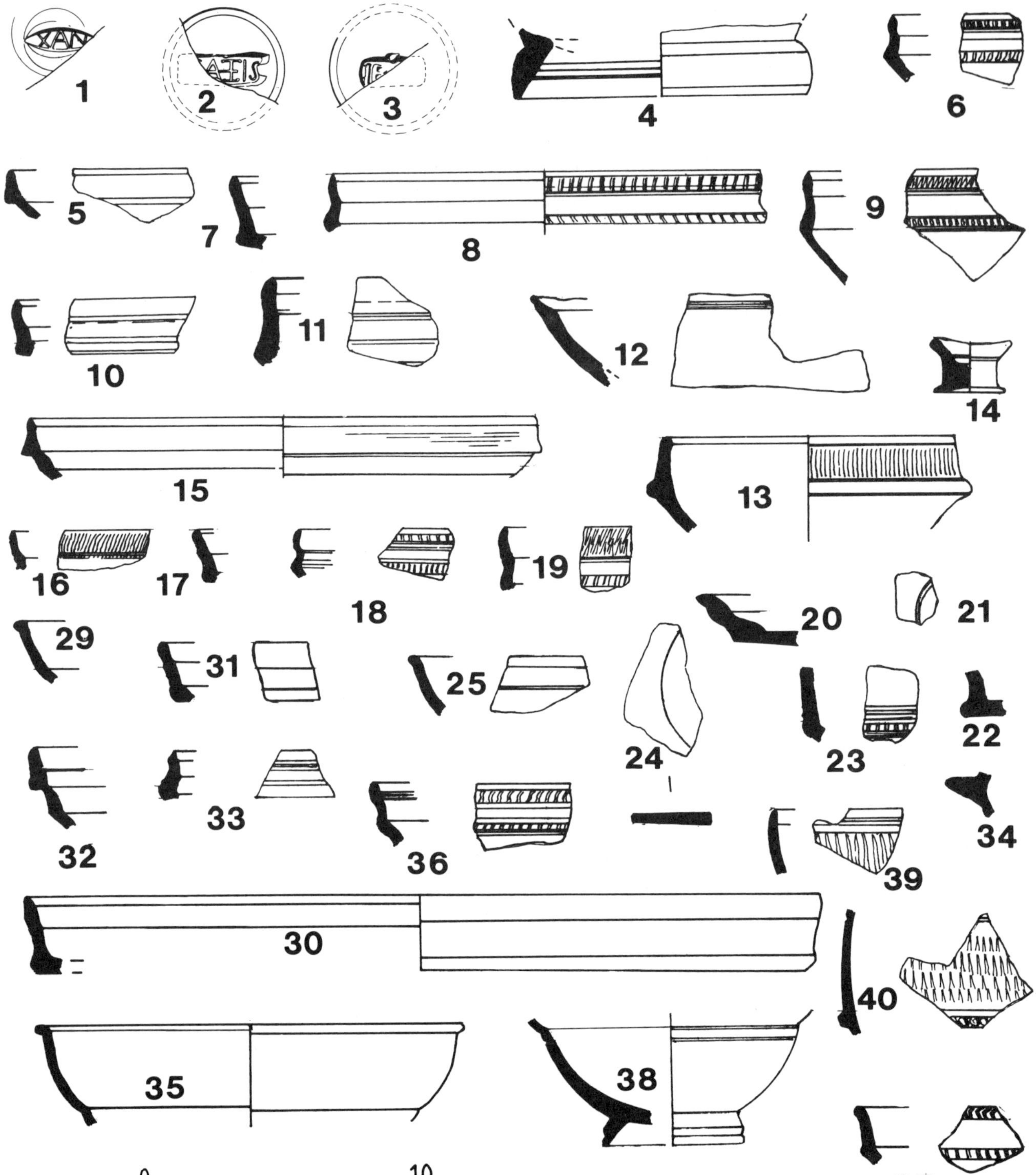

Fig. 11.1. Samian plain forms from Chapel Street and Eastgate.
Nos. 1-3, Arretine stamps; Nos. 13, 20, 25 & 29, Lezoux; No. 21, South Gaulish, remainder Arretine (½).

11a

The Samian Ware

by G. B. Dannell

Note.—Numbers in brackets are the site and layer numbers.

The group is too small for meaningful statistical comparisons to be made. As before, the importation of samian begins in the Augustan period, with material from Arezzo, including stamps of MAHES and XANTHUS, both of whom worked in the ATEIVS shops. Tiberian activity includes some pieces which David Williams[1] thinks are possibly Lyons products, together with the earlier products of La Graufesenque. It is noteworthy that the latter are in plain ware, and it is clear that the decorated vessels of the period *c.* A.D. 25–40, which are frequently found at Camulodunum, do not, in general, appear in the Chichester collections.[2] Indeed, even early Claudian vessels like the f.29s with rouletted central mouldings, which are found at Richborough and Valkenburg, do not feature strongly here. One unusual platter of the earlier period is a f.16 from Lezoux (20).

During the main period of importation, there is nothing to distinguish the collections from others in southern Britain. The strong showing of the Trajanic potters of Les Martres-de-Veyre is to be expected by virtue of the geographical position. It is interesting that the group does not close with a material quantity of Rhenish samian, again some geographical selectivity may be at work. One slightly disturbing point is the appearance of a number of pieces for which origins cannot be ascribed. Chichester has always had a persistently small quantity of "strays", many of which are in a smooth, well-finished, hard-fired fabric, which is quite orange-red. What looked to be a late-Flavian or early 2nd-century f.18 or 18/31 was sent to David Williams, who commented that the thin section obtained was indistinguishable from Arretine ware, so fine is the body. Other vessels in this fabric have included f.27 and f.35. We must await a stamp in the hope that it will shed some light on the matter.

1. Dr. Williams's work on the fabrics is gratefully acknowledged.
2. *cf.* No. 46 for example

Fig. 11.1

THE ARRETINE STAMPS

1. (CS. 551). Cup, stamped XAN [in ellipse, *cf. CVA.*, 177.331. Augustan, Arretine.
2. (CS. 437). Plate; stamped M] AEIS. *cf. CVA.*, 169.35, etc. Augustan/Tiberian? Provincial Arretine?
3. (CS. X133); Plate; stamped] l, illegible – Augustan; Arretine.

Fig. 11.1

THE PLAIN FORMS. (L = Loeschke, Dr = Dragendorff).

4. (CS. X132). L8, Augustan; Arretine.
5. (CS. X80). L1. Augustan; Arretine.
6. (CS. Pit X123). L1, Augustan; Arretine.
7. (CS. X148). L2, Augustan-Tiberian; Arretine.
8. (CS. X167). L8 Ab; Augustan; Arretine.
9. (CS. X183). L8 Ab; Augustan; Arretine.
10. (CS. X183). L2A; Augustan; Arretine.
11. (CS. X130). L2B; Augustan; Arretine?
12. (CS. P18 and 19). L8; Augustan; Arretine.
13. (CS. Pit X41). Dr 24/5; Claudian, Lezoux.
14. (CS. X121). Pedestal; Augustan-Tiberian; Arretine.
15. (CS. Pit X156). L1A; Augustan; Arretine.
16. (CS. X105). L8B; Augustan; Arretine.
17. (CS. Pit X66). L2A; Augustan; Arretine.
18. (CS. X68). L8A; Augustan; Arretine.
19. (CS. X129). L8Ab; Augustan; Arretine.
20. (CS. X138). Dr 16; Tiberian; Lezoux.
21. (CS. X144). L8, South Gaulish.

22. (CS. X147). L2B; Augustan; Arretine.
23. (CS. X157). L8Ab; Augustan; Arretine.
24. (CS. X124). Plate; Augustan; Arretine.
25. (CS. X136). Dr 18; Claudius-Nero; Lezoux.
26. (CS. Slot X43). Plate; Augustan; Arretine. *Not illustrated.*
27. (CS. X78). Plate; Augustan; Arretine. *Not illustrated.*
28. (CS. Slot X12). Plate; Augustan: Arretine. *Not illustrated.*
29. (E.G. A53). Dr 18; Claudian; Lezoux.

The group from Pit X 165(D).

30. Dr 17. Large platter of the Colchester S4B type, *cf. Hawkes & Hull,* 1947. Fig. 42.12 and Pl. XXXIX. South Gaulish.
31. Dr 15/17. Small platter of the Colchester 6A type, *cf. Hawkes & Hull, op. cit.* Fig. 42.19. South Gaulish.
32. Dr 15/17. A simplified version of 31, the reduced height of the wall abbreviating the mouldings. South Gaulish.
33. L3. The moulding here is more complicated, *cf. Hawkes & Hull, op. cit.* Fig. 42.20. Arretine?
34. Ritt. 12. This flanged bowl is common on sites of the Conquest period. It probably began life in the later Tiberian period, and there is no Arretine progenitor, *cf. Hawkes & Hull, op. cit.*, p. 188–9 (Table). South Gaulish.
35. Dr 27. This flat-topped, bead-rimmed variety is a clear inter-face between the Arretine form and that of South Gaul. The small plain band immediately below the external constriction is Arretine in tradition, *cf. Hawkes & Hull, op. cit.*, Fig. 43.7, a "provincial" piece which should be compared with 8; the rim and plain change of internal angle are Gaulish. South Gaulish.
36. L8. This version is slightly splayed in the rim and represents the later Arretine production. Arretine.
37. L8. An even more stylised type than 36. The internal and external mouldings have been simplified to the point of extinction. Arretine.

38/39. L11. The classic Arretine type, *cf. Hawkes & Hull,* Fig. 43.7. The rouletting is not as fine as on the earlier examples. Arretine.

40. L12. There is too little to be diagnostic. Arretine.

This group contains plain wares of both Italian and Gaulish origin. Both of the fabrics are homogenous within themselves, apparently coming from two factory sites. The Italian ware shows late stylistic traits, particularly in the simplification of mouldings, coarseness of rouletting and thickness of wall; the Gaulish vessels appear to be late Tiberio-Claudian, and earlier than one finds on invasion sites without pre-Roman, native occupation. It would be most convenient to see this group dated so that both of its constituents were contemporary, since there are no overt signs of differential ageing, or other condition. To do this would imply a range of *c.* A.D. 25–40, with the weight of the evidence on the Gaulish side being towards the middle of the range. This would push the Arretine on a little in conventional terms, but not out of keeping with the problems already raised at Camulodunum, *cf. Hawkes & Hull, op. cit.*, p. 179, and Fishbourne, *cf. Dannell,* 1978, pp. 225–6.

However, the group itself is residual within the context in which it was found. The pit is dated by the excavator to Period 2, *c.* Claudius-Nero, on the evidence of a T.N. stamp (Rigby, this volume, p. 281, GB.29), with a date range of *c.* A.D. 50-85, and by the presence of wares from the Chapel Street kilns, which were not established until Period 2 (*Chichester 3*, p. 56). Some of the residual coarse wares in the same context may be Abtrebatic "overlap" wares.

The figured wares (Figs. 11.2-11.3)

41. (CS. X169). Form 30. Winding scroll with seven-lobed leaves and two birds, a goose, O. 2244 type, and an O. 2262 type. The leaf appears on a f.30 from Rottweil, *cf. Knorr,* 1912, Taf. XVI.1, *c.* A.D. 70–90 SG.
42. (CS. X169). Form 37. Kneeling stag O. 1699 above an S motif wreath. Similar to a bowl by MERCATO, *Bushe-Fox,* 1928, XVII.11, and *cf. Knorr,* 1919, Taf. 74C by SECVNDVS, *c.* A.D. 75–95 SG.

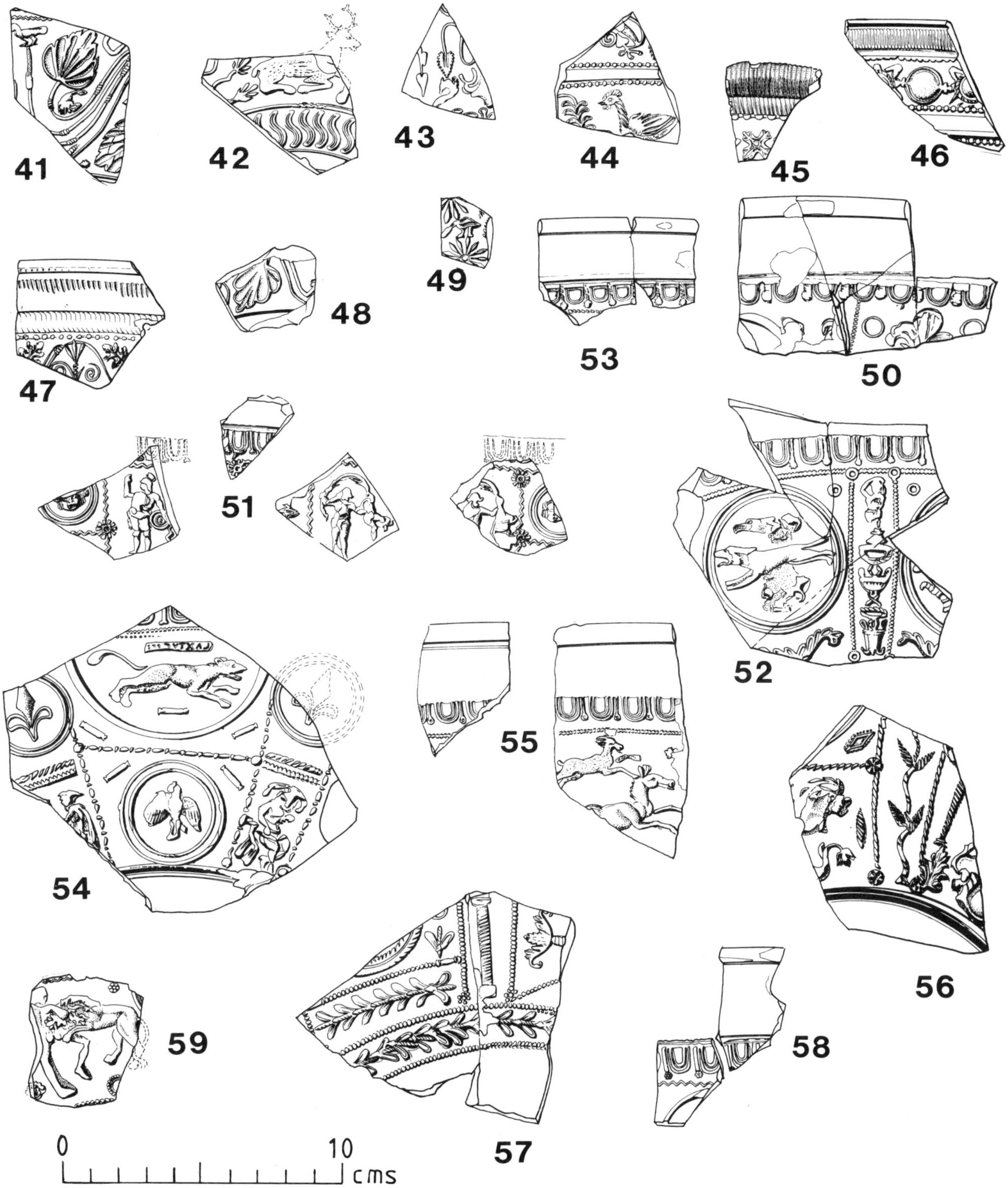

Fig. 11.2. Figured samian, Nos. 41-59 (½).

43. (CS. X202). Form 30 CALVS style; his ovolo and leaf, *cf. Knorr,* 1919, Taf. 16.13, L15, *c.* A.D. 45-60 SG.
44. (CS. X129). Form 29. AQVITANVS style; his cock O. 2349, and bud, *cf. Mary,* 1967, Taf. 11.16. The wreath is on a f.29 fromValkenburg (*Glasbergen,* 1940-44, Afb. 58.3), *c.* A.D. 45-60 SG.
45. (CS. X148). Form 29. Rosette similar to that used by LICINVS, *cf. Knorr,* 1919, Taf. 46D & E. This vessel has the pale paste of the early Claudian wares, *c.* A.D. 35-50 SG.
46. (CS. Pit X.165). Form 29. An early piece with a slightly purplish cast to the brown slip. It belongs to the first group of South Gaulish potters to export in quantity, like AVE VALE, *cf. Knorr,* 1952, Taf. 72C for an early f.29 from Bregenz and generally the preliminary study of Vernhet (96e Congress national des Sociétes savantes. Toulouse, 1971 archaélogie, t.1, pp. 175-90), *c.* A.D. 20-40 SG.
47. (E.G., A122). Form 29. Small leaf used by the OFFICINA LICINIANA, *cf. Knorr,* 1919, Taf. 47F, *c.* A.D. 45-60 SG.
48. (CS. X32). Form 29. Large seven-lobed leaf, *cf. Knorr,* 1919, Taf. 32 by FIRMO; light coloured paste, *c.* A.D. 35-50 SG.
49. (CS. X129). Form 29. Style of BASSVS & COELVS and SENO. Their rosette, *cf. Knorr,* 1952. Taf. 58, and tips of the leaf wreath shown there. The goose is a variant of O. 2286, *c.* A.D. 55-70 SG.
50. (CS. X159). Form 37. Double-bordered ovolo with corded tongue to left ending in a hollow rosette. Rogers does not show a clear example. It is similar to, but different from his B6—note the slightly asymmetric egg, and that the rosette does not come below the egg as he shows. However, they are very close. The potter involved, LALVS (?. = P 11), also used the small trifid, corded, leaf motif G.37, and the large acanthus leaf J 11. The smaller leaf, K 11, was used by Rogers' potters P 10 and P 17. A bowl in a similar style with the same ovolo is shown, *cf. S & S,* Pl. 74.12, *c.* A.D. 100-120 M-de-V.
51. (CS. 138). Form 37. Style of G. I. VIBIVS, his ovolo Rogers's B 76. The figures are warrior O. 163 and Danseuse O. 363. The face-mask is a variant of O. 1294, *c.* A.D. 120-140 Lezoux.
52. (SG. F9). Form 37. DIVIXTVS style; his ovolo as *S & S,* Pl. 116.17, which looks like Rogers's B 52. The present example shows more detail, note that the egg slopes up to the right and there is a suggestion that the tongue is really corded. The acanthus leaf, Rogers's K 2 is a linking detail to *S & S,* Pl. 116.16 and 17. The large compound ornament (note the extra detail), Rogers's Q 10 also appears with this motif, together with the torso of the caryatid. The medallion contains a dog (not shown by Oswald in his Index), in the style of animals used by CRICIRO, *cf. S & S,* Pl. 117.1, which has upward curving front legs, *c.* A.D. 140-170, Lezoux.
53. (E.G. A68 = A75). Form 37, Rogers's ovolo B 28 type—but note the asymmetric egg, as used by Potter X-3, *c.* A.D. 125-140?. Lezoux.
54. (CS. Slot X10). Form 37. Stamped LAXTVCIS F; his ovolo, *cf. S & S,* Fig. 27.1; leaf 2 and astragalus 3. The bead-row is Rogers's A 10, while the opposed dogs-tooth ornament can be seen, *cf. S & S,* Pl. 98.13. The figures are a seated man O, 913, a lioness O. 1511, and an eagle O. 2183. Part of an erotic group shows to the left, *cf. S & S,* Pl. 102 by CENSORINVS, *c.* A.D. 140-160, Lezoux.
55. (CS. X151). Form 37. PATERNVS style; his ovolo, Rogers's B 206. The goat is O. 1840, *c.* A.D. 160-190, Lezoux.
56. (E.G. Pit C11). Form 37. A bowl in the style attributed to PATERNVS 1, *cf. S & S,* Pl. 105. Note the undercutting at the base of the decoration like that on the earlier f.29. The colour is red-brown matte on a light biscuit paste. The decorative detail is shared with IVSTVS, *cf. S & S,* Fig. 31.11, for the beaded lozenge and the column 5; Fig. 30.16 gives the striated rod (this time a clear impression) and detail 30, the leaf. The rosette is as *S & S,* Pl. 108.37. The dolphins are O. 2384 and 2392, *c.* A.D. 140-170 Lezoux.
57. (CS. Slot X41). Form 37. DONNAVCVS style; his leaf, *cf. S & S,* Fig. 11.15, medallion 23, column, Pl. 49.581 and basal wreath Pl. 42.487. The small leaf of the basal wreath is close to Rogers's G 172, *c.* A.D. 100-120, M-de-V.
58. (CS. X138). Form 37. Style of IGOCATVS: his ovolo, *cf. S & S,* Fig. 6.1, *c.* A.D, 100-120, M-de-V.

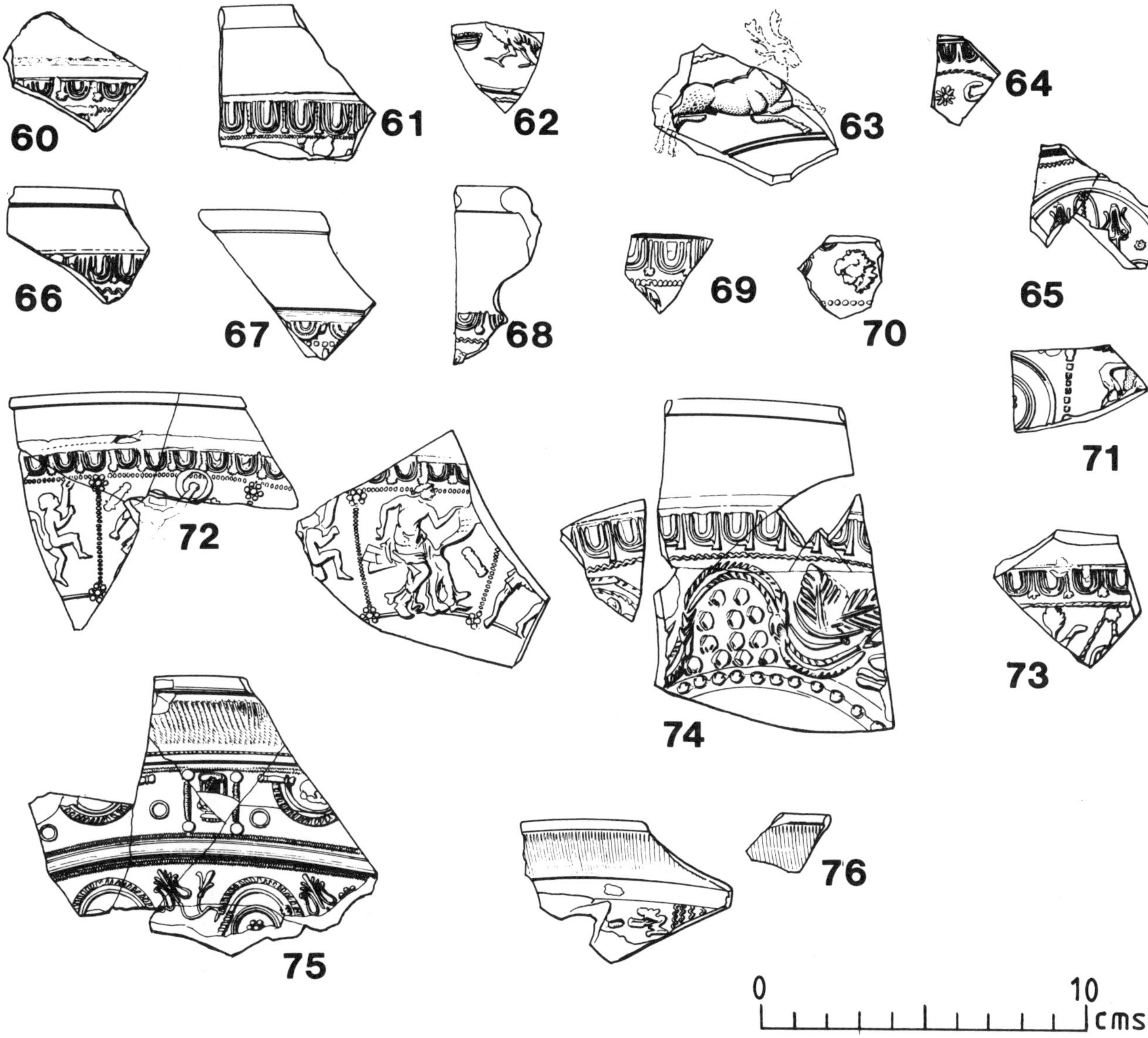

Fig. 11.3. Figured samian, Nos. 60-76 (½).

59. (CS. X18). Form 37. Hercules and lion, D. 624? on a burnt sherd. The figures are much smaller than those normally seen, *cf. S & S*, Pl. 74.11, and for the Trajanic prototype, Pl. 40.468, *c.* A.D. 125–145?, Lezoux.
60. (CS. X110). Form 37. SACER style, his ovolo, Rogers's B 14, previously used by DONNAVCVS, *c.* A.D. 125–145, Lezoux.
61. (CS. p h X155). Form 37. Rogers's ovolo B 108 on a vessel with very fine bead rows, *c.* A.D. 125–145, Lezoux.
62. (CS. X118). Form 37. DONNAVCVS style; his cup and cockerel, *cf. S & S*, Pl. 43.491, *c.* A.D. 100–120, M-de-V.
63. (CS. X158). Form 37. Torso of stag, O. 1720, Antonine, Lezoux.
64. (CS. Pit P41A). Form 30. Fine, small, double-bordered ovolo with a straight tongue to the left, which is very lightly impressed. The shape is similar to that shown from La Graufesenque in the style of LICINVS, *cf. Hermet*, 1930, Pl. 69.6, *c.* A.D. 40–55 SG.
65. (CS. X129). Form 30. Small lanceolate bud used by CRESTIO and DARIBITVS, *c.* A.D. 45–60 SG.
66. (CS. X137). Form 37. BVTRIO style, his ovolo, *cf. S & S*, Fig. 13.2, *c.* A.D. 120–145, Lezoux.
67. (SG. A14). Form 37. The ovolo shown for CARATILLVS, *cf. S & S*, Pl. 96.1. This is not the ovolo given for him as a type, *cf. ibid.*, Fig. 26.1, *c.* A.D. 125–145, Lezoux.
68. (CS. X146). Form 37. Ovolo of potter X-6, *cf. S & S*, Fig. 18.2, *c.* A.D. 125-145, Lezoux.
69. (CS. X89). Form 37. Double-bordered ovolo with straight tongue starting slightly below the level of the egg, ending below it in a six-pointed rosette. Rogers's does not show this type, and there is confusion in *S & S*, presumably because of the impression. For BVTRIO, the ovolo is drawn with the tongue to the right, *cf.* Fig. 13.2, the rosette tip is blurred. Their references to Pl. 57.653 and Pl. 58.656 do not really help, because they have centrally-placed tongues. Antonine?, Lezoux.
70. (CS. X106). Form 37. Face-mask, O. 1218 type. In this version it is reversible, facing left as a bald-headed, bearded man, and to the right as a wild-haired pugilistic native, or more probably, a negro, *c.* A.D. 125–150, Lezoux.
71. (CS. X113). Form 37. DIVIXTVS style; his circles and caryatid, *cf. S & S*, Pl. 116.15, *c.* A.D. 160–190, Lezoux.
72. (E.G. A76). Form 37. DONNAVCVS style; the ovolo is the one sometimes used by SACER and DIVIXTVS at Lezoux, Rogers's B 12. The figures are putti, O. 395, Abundance, O. 802 and the restored hunter, *cf. S & S*, Pl. 47.555, *c.* A.D. 100–120, M-de-V.
73. (E.G. A91). Form 37. MERCATO ovolo; his leaf motif, *cf. Knorr*, 1919, Taf. 57.10 and 19, *c.* A.D. 75–95 SG.
74. (E.G. A91). Form 37. A bowl from Montans in the style of CHRESIMVS and his associates. The ovolo is Simpson's No. 3 (*Brittania*, 1976, pp. 244–73), which looks as if it is applied by a roulette, as opposed to the similar one used by her "bird-stamp" potter, *cf. ibid*, p. 257 and Fig. 5.15 with p. 262 and Fig. 6.22–24, which is singly impressed. The closest parallel is the mould signed by SABINVS, which has an identical motif used as a demi-medallion to that used to form the scroll here (*ibid*, No. 29). The leaf-tips are shown on No. 23, but the hare and large leaf are not shown, unless the latter is Rossignol's Pl. 124.2. (*Simpson*, No. 27), *c.* A.D. 110–145, Montans. (Thanks are due to Dr. Simpson for her generous help with this sherd.)
75. (CS. Pit X41). Form 29. DONNAVCVS style; he made F.29s, *cf. S & S*, Pl. 44 for details. Note that the stand, Rogers's Q 65, contains a pine cone and not a twisted rod, *c.* A.D. 100–120, M-de-V.
76. (E.G. A25). Form 29. Upper zone; two small opposed hares flanked by a panel of wavy lines. Probably Nero-Vespasian, Lezoux.

Abbreviations

CVA	Oxé, A., and Comfort, H., *Corpvs Vasorvm Arretinorvm*, Bonn, 1968.
D	Déchelette, J., *Les vases céramiques ornés de la Gaule Romaine*, Paris 1904.
O	Oswald, F., *Index of Figure-Types on Terra Sigillata*, Liverpool 1937.
S & S	Stanfield, J. A., and Simpson, G., *Central Gaulish Potters*, London 1958.

References

BUSHE-FOX 1928	Bushe-Fox, J. P. *Report on the Excavations of the Roman Fort at Richborough, Kent*, Oxford 1928.
BUSHE-FOX 1949	Bushe-Fox, J. P., *Report on the Excavations of the Roman Fort at Richborough, Kent*, Oxford 1949.
CUNLIFFE 1971	Cunliffe, B., *Excavations at Fishbourne*, Leeds 1971.
DANNELL 1978	Dannell, G. B., "The samian pottery" in *Chichester Excavations 3*, 1978.
GLASBERGEN 1940	Glasbergen, W., *Jaaverslag van de Vereeniging voor Terpenonderzoek*, 25/28, Groningen 1940–44.
HERMET 1930	Hermet, F., *La Graufesenque*, Paris 1930.
KNORR 1912	Knorr, R., *Südallische Terra Sigillata Gefässe von Rottweil*, Stuttgart 1912.
KNORR 1919	Knorr, R., *Topfer und Fabriken verzierter Terra-Sigillata des ersten Jahrhunderts*, Stuttgart 1919.
KNORR 1952	Knorr, R., *Terra-Sigillata Gefässe des ersten Jahrhunderts mit Töpfernamen*, Stuttgart 1952.
MARY 1967	Mary, G. T., *Novaesium 1 (Die südgallische Terra Sigillata aus Neuss)*, Limesforschungen Band 6 1967.
RICKEN-LUDOWICI 1948	Ricken, H., and Ludowici, W., *Katalog II, Die Bilderschüsseln der römischen Töpfer von Rheinzabern*, Speyer 1948.
ROGERS	Rogers, G., *Poteries Sigilleés de la Gaule Centrale*, XXVIIIe supplément a "Gallia", paris 1974.
TERRISSE 1968	Terrisse, J. R., *Les céramiques sigilliés gallo-romaines*, des Martres-de-Veyre, Paris 1978.

11b

The Samian Stamps

by B. R. Hartley and Brenda Dickinson

See Fig. 11.4 for interpretation

1. *76 S Area 4, Pit A2*. Acurio uncertain 1 18/31 or 31 Lezoux.[2] On present evidence Acurio seems to be the only Central Gaulish potter to whom this stamp could belong. He worked at Lezoux in the Antonine period, making forms 18/31, 18/31R, 27, 38, 79 and 80. *c*. A.D. 150–180.
2. *76 S Area 2, 20*. Aestivus la 31 Lezoux.[2] One of Aestivus's less common stamps, for which there is no site dating. His wares occur at Birrens, Castle Cary and Pudding Pan Rock. His forms include 27 (rarely), 31R, 79 and Ludowici Tx. *c*. A.D. 155–190.
3. *77 CS X75 211B*. Aestivus 2a 79 or Ludowici Tg Lezoux.[2] Several examples of this stamp have been recorded in the Pudding Pan Rock wreck. *c*. A.D. 165–190.
4. *77 CS X105 314*. Amabilis i 2a 27g La Graufesenque.[3] A minor South Gaulish potter, who made forms 24 and Ritt. 9 and, with this particular stamp, Ritt. 8. One of his stamps is in Period 1 at Valkenburg, ZH. *c*. A.D. 40–60.
5. *77 CS Pit X158 522*. Anaillus 6a 27 Lezoux.[1] Most of the recorded examples of this stamp are on form 27. His work in general is common in the Rhineland. *c*. A.D. 120-145.

6. *77 CS X148.* Arcanus cursive 37 (from a mould signed below the decoration). Signed bowls of Arcanus occur at Lezoux and in the Rhineland. Their decoration has stylistic links with Geminus iii, and clearly belongs to the Hadrianic–Antonine period. His plain forms include 18/31, 18/31R and 27. *c.* A.D. 125–145.

7. *77 CS Pit 119.* Ardacus 12a (possibly this) la Graufesenque.[2] This stamp appears on forms 24, 29 (with decoration of the Claudio-Neronian period) and Ritt. 9. He also made forms 16 and Ritt. 1. *c.* A.D. 45–60, if correctly identified, but, in any case, pre-Flavian.

8. *76 E Pit A33 94.* Aricus la 33 (slightly burnt) Lezoux.[1] Aricus's dating rests on his forms, which include 31 and 38. Antonine.

9. *78 CS Pit P19 627.* Bellicus ii 2a 80 or Ludowici TX Lezoux.[3] This stamp appears at Risingham and has been recorded on forms 18/31, 31 and 38. One of his fabrics closely resembles an unusually pale one associated chiefly with the Quintilianus i group of potters. *c.* A.D. 140–180.

10. *77 CS X19 224.* Burdo 3b 18/31 or 31 Lezoux.[2] There is no dating evidence for this particular stamp, but Burdo's work appears in early- and mid-Antonine contexts at Castleford and Alcester, respectively. His forms include 15/31R, 27, 38, 42 and 80. *c.* A.D. 135–170.

11. *77 CS X89 227.* Calvus i 5m 15/17 or 18 La Graufesenque.[1] The dating evidence for this stamp is mainly Flavian, and includes Castleford, the Red House site at Corbridge and the Nijmegen fortress and Ulpia Noviomagus. It occurs on form 29. *c.* A.D. 65–85.

12. *78 E B2 4 124.* Cinnamus ii 5b 37 retrograde Lezoux.[1] This stamp occurs on both the Antonine Wall and Hadrian's Wall, but is much less common on the latter. *c.* A.D. 150–180.

13. *77 CS X119 334.* Cintusmus i 5a 31R Lezoux.[1] This is one of his latest stamps. Most of the recorded examples come from the Pudding Pan Rock cargo. Some of his other stamps appear on the rims of decorated bowls by Advocisus and Cinnamus ii. His main activity was in the mid- to late-Antonine period, but he occasionally made form 27. *c.* A.D. 165–190.

14. *76 E Pit C11 16.* Corisillus 3a 33 Lezoux,[2] Lubié-la Palisse,[2] Vichy, Terre-Franche.[2] A minor Central Gaulish potter, working on a small scale. The distribution of this stamp suggests that he used it at Lezoux. It appears on forms 38 and Ludowici Tg. He also made form 79/80 at Lezoux, and 80 at Lubie and Vichy. There is no evidence for the sequence of migration. *c.* A.D. 150–180.

15. *77 CS Pit X68.* Co(sius?) Iucundus la 18 La Graufesenque.[3] The evidence for this potter points to Flavian or early-Trajanic date. This particular stamp occurs at Newstead. *c.* A.D. 80–110.

16. *77 CS X84 191.* Cracuna i 2a 33 Lezoux.[1] This stamp occurs in early-and mid-Antonine contexts, at Castleford and Alcester, respectively. It has also been recorded at Binchester and South Shields. The forms are mainly 18/31 and 27. *c.* A.D. 130–155.

17. *77 CS X78 256.* Diogenes la cup retrograde Les Martres-de-Veyre.[1] Diogenes's forms and his stamping under the base, after moulding, of form 37 demonstrate Trajanic date. *c.* A.D. 100–120.

18. *77 CS X151 589.* Donnaucus 5a 27 (?) Les Martres-de-Veyre.[1] This stamp is in the material from the London Second Fire. It was used on forms 15/17 and 15/17R, which at Les Martres were confined to the Trajanic period. *c.* A.D. 100–120.

19. *77 CS X148 487.* Felix i 47a 24 La Graufesenque.[2] This stamp nearly always occurs on form 24. It has previously been recorded in a Claudian pit-group at Chichester (*Chichester Excavations 2* [1974], p. 5. *c.* A.D. 40-60.

20. *77 CS X19.* Felix ii 2a 31 Lezoux.[3] This stamp is in the material from a pottery shop of the 140s at Castleford, and was used on forms 18/31 and 27. He also made form 80 and one of his stamps occurs at Carzield. *c.* A.D. 140-170.

21. *77 CS Pit X165 540.* Firmo i 4a Ritt. 8 La Graufesenque.[2] Firmo's forms include 16, 17 and Ritt. 5 and 9, so he will have started work under Tiberius. *c.* A.D. 35–60.

22. *77 CS X81 189.* Geminus v 5a 31 Lezoux.[3] Geminus's work appears in the Rhineland and in an early-Antonine context at Castleford. His forms include 15/31R and 27. This particular stamp occurs in Antonine Scotland. *c.* A.D. 140–170.

23. *76 E A17 14.* Germanus i 28i 18 La Graufesenque.[2] One of his less-common stamps, noted at the fort at Newton Kyme. *c.* A.D. 65–85.

24. *77 CS Pit X97 216 and 131.* Habilis la 31 Lezoux.[1] The site evidence for this stamp includes Chester-le-Street and Chesters. It appears on forms 27, 31R, 38 and 80. *c.* A.D. 150–180.

25. *77 CS X20 593.* Habilis 5b 18/31R or 31R Lezoux.[1] This stamp occurs in the material from the Antonine fire at Verulamium, and on forms 27, 38 and 80 *c.* A.D. 150–180.

26. *77 CS X78.* Laxtucissa 5a 37 (from a mould stamped in the decoration) CISF retrograde Lezoux.[1] There are two decorated bowls with this stamp in a pit-group of the 150s at Alcester. It also occurs at Halton Chesters and Ilkley, and was used on form 27 and on an early version of form 79. *c.* A.D. 150–180.

27. *77 CS X105 321.* Licinus 7b 15/17 or 18 La Graufesenque.[2] There is no dating evidence for this particular stamp, but the occurrence of his other stamps at Waddon Hill, in a Claudio-Neronian depot at Narbonne and in the Boudiccan burning at Colchester and his use of form Ritt. 1 suggests a date *c.* A.D. 45–65.

28. *77 CS X144 592.* Masc(u)lus i 5b 33a (?) La Graufesenque.[2] This stamp occurs in the Colchester pottery shop of A.D. 60 *c.* A.D. 50–70.

29. *77 CS X84 193.* Maternus iii 1c 18/31R or 31R Lezoux.[3] A stamp of the earlier Central Gaulish Maternus, used on forms 18/31, 18/31R and 27, and occurring in the Rhineland. *c.* A.D. 125–150.

30. *North Street 1979 +.* Mercussa i 4a 33 Lezoux.[1] This stamp occurs at Chester-le-Street (after *c.* A.D. 160), but was used on forms 18/31R and 27. He also made forms 79 and 80. *c.* A.D. 150–180.

31. *77 CS Pit X159(B) 584.* Moxius ii la 33. This stamp has been recorded at Les Martres-de-Veyre, though not necessarily from the kiln-site. However, the forms and fabrics suggest origin there. Moxius must have been one of the later potters at Les Martres, since this stamp occurs at Carzield, in the forum destruction at Wroxeter and on form 38 or 44. *c.* A.D. 130–160.

32. *76 E Pit A33 126.* Namilianus incomplete 2 31 Lezoux.[2] A mid- to late-Antonine potter, whose stamps occur in the Pudding Pan Rock cargo and on Hadrian's Wall and its hinterland forts. *c.* A.D. 160–200.

33. *77 CS X124 511.* Niger ii 4a 15/17 or 18 La Graufesenque.[1] This stamp has been recorded from the Cirencester fort ditch and on forms Ritt. 1 and 8. *c.* A.D. 55–65.

34. *78 E Pit B 10(E) 226.* Patricius i 17é 27g La Graufesenque.[2] This stamp is common at Flavian foundations. It occurs at Corbridge and in Period IIA at Verulamium (after A.D. 75). *c.* A.D. 70-100.

35. *77 CS X65 288.* Primus iii 12g 15/17 or 18 La Graufesenque.[2] One of Primus's latest stamps, recorded several times at Vespasianic foundations. *c.* A.D. 60–70.

36. *77 CS Slot X12 362.* Priscianus la 80 or Ludowici Tx Lezoux.[1] This stamp has been recorded on a bowl of form 37 with mid- to late-Antonine decoration. It also appears on forms 31R, 79 and 80. *c.* A.D. 150–190.

37. *77 CS X79.* Priscinus 3a (almost certainly this) 18/31 or 31 Lezoux.[1] This stamp occurs in Period IID at Verulamium (after A.D. 150) and on forms 18/31, 27 and 81. One of his others is in a group of burnt samian of *c.* A.D. 170 at Tác. *c.* A.D. 145–175 if correctly identified, but Antonine, in any case.

38. *78 CS Pit 17 623.* Quintus iv 2a 33 Lezoux.[1] A stamp of the earlier Lezoux Quintus, whose work occurs in Antonine Scotland and in the material from the Worcester Fire. It has been recorded at Newstead and on form 27. *c.* A.D. 140–170.

39. *78 CS Pit 28 634.* Reburrus ii 14c 33 Lezoux (14c). The original die for this stamp, with ansate ends, was used on form 15/31. Stamps from the reduced die (14c′, without *ansae*) have not been noted in dated contexts, but as Reburrus's work occurs on both the Antonine Wall and Hadrian's Wall and on forms 27 and 79, a range *c.* A.D. 140–170 is likely.

40. *78 CS Pit 41(C) 725.* Regenus 5a on a thin, flat rouletted base, with a double circle round the rouletting, La Graufesenque.[2] This stamp has not been recorded before. Regenus's work occurs in a Tiberio-Claudian grave at Bregenz (*Bonner Jahrbücher*, 140/1 [1936], p. 342, in a Claudian group at Chichester (*Chichester Excavations 2* [1974], p. 50, and at Velsen (*Glasbergen* and *van Lith*, 1977, Nos. 70-75; probably before A.D. 47). His forms include 17. *c.* A.D. 35-55.

1	ACV[	22	[GE]MINIM[A]	43	[RVFIN]I·MA
2	AES[TIVIMA]	23	GERMANI	44	RVFVS·F◂
3	[AIIS]TIVI:M	24	HABILISM	45	SABINI·MA
4	AMABI	25	HAB[ILISF]	46	SACROTICI
5	ANAIL	26	[LAXTV]CISF	47	SAT[VRNINI]
6	ARCANV[	27	IICINIANAO	48	SECVNDINI
7	[ARDA]CI	28	OFMASC[I]	49	SEVERVS
8	ARICIM	29	[MA]TERNI·M	50	OF·SE[VERP] OR [VER+]
9	BIILLICCIM	30	MERCVSSEM	51	SILVANI
10	BVRDONIOF	31	MOXIVS·F	52	SVLPICI
11	OFCA[LVI]	32	NAM[	53	TIB[ERI·M]
12	[CINN]AMI	33	[OFN]IGR	54	VERE[CV]
13	CIN[TVSM]	34	⟨P⟩ATRI⟨C⟩	55	[OF.VIIR]ILI
14	CORISILLI	35	[O]FPRIMI	56	[OFVI]RTVTIS
15	[OFC]O·IVC	36	PRISCIANIM	57	VITALISF
16	CRACVN[A·F]	37	P[RISCINVSFC]	58	VIT[AL]
17	[DI]DCIIN[CIS]	38	QVINTI	59	AN[
18	[DO]NNAV[C·F]	39	ЯEBVЯB	60	]SSI
19	FELIXF	40	REGENVS·F	61	]MAII
20	[·KFEL]IXF[K·]	41	[REGIN]VS·F	62	DO[
21	OFI·FIRM	42	OF.RV[FNI]	63	]F
				64	]FE
				65	]VS

Fig. 11.4. Interpretation of samian stamps, Nos. 1-65.

41. *77 CS X43.* Reginus ii 2a 18/31 Les Martres-de-Veyre.[1] This stamp occurs at Malton and in the London Second Fire. One of his others has been noted twice at Mumrills, however, so he does not belong to the earlier group of potters at Les Martres. A range *c.* A.D. 115–145 is likely.

42. *76 E A68 121(T).* Rufinus ii 3a 15/17 or 18 La Graufesenque.[2] This stamp seems to have been used mainly in the Flavian period. Dated contexts include Cardiff, Hayton and Valkenburg, ZH (Period 3). *c.* A.D. 65–85.

43. *77 CS X147 (T).* Rufinus ii 15a 15/17 or 18 La Graufesenque.[2] This stamp has been noted at Caerleon and the Nijmegen fortress, but the decoration on the one form 29 on which it appears looks pre-Flavian. A range *c.* A.D. 65–85 is likely.

44. *77 CS X20 108.* Rufus iv la 33 Lezoux.[3] There is no site-dating for this potter but the high kick on one of his dishes suggests mid- to late-Antonine date.

45. *76 E Pit A33 93.* Sabinus viii 7b 33 Lezoux.[1] This stamp occurs at Piercebridge and on forms 31, 79/80(?) and 80. He also made forms 31 R and 79R. *c.* A.D. 155-185.

46. *77 CS X136 391.* Sacroticus 2b 27 Lezoux.[3] This stamp occurs in the Rhineland, at Birdoswald and on forms 18/31, 18/31R, 27 and 46. His work appears in an early-Antonine context at Castleford. *c.* A.D. 125-150.

47. *76 E A122 122.* Saturninus ii 8a 33 (burnt) Lezoux.[1] The site record for this stamp includes Bainbridge, Catterick and Pudding Pan Rock. The forms include 31R, 79R and 80. *c.* A.D. 160-200.

48. *77 CS X95 343.* Secundinus iii 5a 38 or 44 Lezoux.[2] One of the less-common stamps of a potter whose work includes forms 18/31, 18/31R, 27, and decorated bowls of the Hadrianic-Antonine period. One of his stamps comes from the Saalburg Erdkastell. *c.* A.D. 125-150.

49. *77 S Pit X98 462.* Severus i 25a 15/17 or 18 La Graufesenque.[2] There is no dating evidence for this stamp, but Severus worked in the Neronian-Flavian period, producing both forms 29 and 37. His stamps are relatively common at Domitianic foundations. *c.* A.D. 65-90.

50. *77 CS Pit X162 531.* Severus i-Pud(ens) 3a or a 15/17 or 18. The lettering of this stamp shows that the well-known South Gaulish Severus is involved (see No. 49). A longer stamp of this partnership or association gives the second name as Pud . . ., presumably Pudens, for whom the date would fit. Examples from the broken die (3a) occur at Carmarthen and Corbridge. *c.* A.D. 70-90.

51. *77 CU U/S 581.* Silvanus ii 3c 18/31R (top of letters only) Lezoux.[2] Silvanus's work appears in Antonine Scotland and the Rhineland. This particular stamp occurs mainly on forms 18/31 and 27. He also made forms 18/31R and 80. *c.* A.D. 135-160.

52. *77 CS X151 430.* Sulpicius 8f 27(?) La Graufesenque.[1] Sulpicius's stamps have been noted several times at Domitianic foundations. This particular one comes from Corbridge. Another (at Wilderspool) is on form 37, with decoration typical of the period *c.* 85-110.

53. *77 CS Pit X97.* Tiberius ii 1B 18/31 or 31 Lezoux.[2] This stamp occurs at Benwell and on forms 18/31R, 31R and 38. He also made forms 27, 42 and 80. *c.*A.D. 140-165.

54. *78 CS Pit P17 624.* Verecundus ii 8a 27g La Graufesenque.[2] Apart from one example on form 29, this stamp has only been recorded on form 27. It has been noted at Caerleon and Segontium. He must have begun work under Nero, since he made form 24, but this stamp is probably Flavian. *c.* A.D. 70-90.

55. *78 CS P24.* Virilis i 6c 15/17 or 18 La Graufesenque.[2] The dating evidence for this stamp is entirely Flavian or later. It includes Corbridge and the Saalburg. *c.* A.D. 80-110.

56. *77 CS Pit X159(A) 586.* Virtus i la 29 (without surviving decoration) La Graufesenque.[2] This stamp was reserved mainly for form 29. The decoration of the bowls and the contexts in which they appear are predominantly Flavian, but Virtus also worked in the Neronian period, and possibly earlier. However, for this particular stamp, a range *c.* A.D. 70-80 is likely.

57. *78 E B2 Pit B10(D) 222.* Vitalis ii 24a 27g La Graufesenque.[1] This stamp has been noted at the Nijmegen fortress and (once) on form 24. Vitalis's range is *c.* A.D. 65-90.

58. *76 E A15 120.* Vitalis ii 27d 33 La Graufesenque.[2] The site record includes Chester, the Nijmegen fortress and Rottweil. *c.* A.D. 65-90.

Unidentified

59. *77 CS X151 591.* On a dish, South Gaulish. The letter after the N seems to have a diagonal stroke (X?). The fabric suggests a Claudio-Neronian potter, probably Anextiatus.
60. *76 E A76.* On Form 18, South Gaulish. Probably a stamp of Bassus i. Neronian.
61. *78 CS Pit 20.* On form 27 (?), South Gaulish. The stamp is very unclear, and is probably illiterate. Flavian or Flavian-Trajanic.
62. *77 CS X19 233.* On form 18/31 or 31, in the fabric of Les Martres-de-Veyre. The form suggests Hadrianic or early-Antonine date.
63. *77 CS X151.* On form 33, Central Gaulish. Antonine.
64. *77 CS X43 340.* Retrograde (?) on form 33, Central Gaulish. Antonine.
65. *77 E C35.* On form 31, Central Gaulish. Mid- to late-Antonine.

Reference

GLASBERGEN and van LITH 1977 — Glasbergen, W., und van Lith, S. M. E., "Italische und frühe südgallische Terra Sigillata aus Velsen (Provinz Nord-Holland)", *Rei Cretariae Romanae Fautorum Acta*, XVII/XVIII (1977), pp. 5-21.

12

Gallo-Belgic and Imported Roman Fine Wares (Figs. 12.1-12.2)

by Valery Rigby

The classification of the vessel forms and for terra rubra fabrics are based on those published in *Camulodunum*, p. 202, and Nijmegen (*Holwerda*, 1941) where necessary, and has been used in previous volumes. The fabric classification of terra nigra is specifically for the material in this volume, and was used to save space.

TN 1. – sandy, rather coarse-grained texture; light in colour, white to light blue-grey; darker, blue-grey surfaces with polished finish on upper visible surfaces. Generally used for platters of medium to large diameter. Imported.

TN 2. – fine-grained matrix, occasional grog and iron grits; pale grey to brown in colour; dark blue-grey surfaces; polished finish. Imported.

TN 3. – fine-grained dense matrix; white to pale blue-grey or brown in colour; blue-grey surfaces, with a marked tendency to flake and laminate, so little or no surface finish survives. A fabric particularly associated with the stamps of Benio, who appears to have worked in the Vesle valley potteries, in and around Rheims.

TN 4 – fine-grained sandy matrix; white; very dark metallic blue-grey surfaces; highly polished finish. Imported.

Note.—The wares are published by site and context. Where the date of the layer is reasonably certain it is included. Figures in brackets, e.g. (426) are sherd identification numbers given to assist students to locate these wares in the Chichester District Museum. Only those sherds which have a number against them in the margin are illustrated.

Chapel Street. Trench X

X27. (420). Sherd; platter; TN 2, worn. Residual.
X37. (389). Locally-made platter. Nero-Flavian. Residual.
X49. (434). Base; small platter; TN 4. Residual.
X65. (431). Rim: platter, Cam. 5 variant with no top facet; TN 1, Claudian. Import.
(426). Sherd: platter, Cam. 16: TN 1: *c.* A.D. 50–85. Import.

Fine wares

(430). Sherd from a lamp, probably a volute lamp as *Camulodunum*, Pl. XLIV, 3; cream ware, thin brown slip; South Gaul. Pre-Flavian.

(427). Base; small beaker, possibly Cam. 94; light orange matrix, darker orange slip, fine sand rough-casting inside and out; possibly Colchester. Nero-Flavian. Context is mid-late 2nd century.

X72. (435). Two rim sherds; platter, Cam. 2; TN 2, worn. Claudian at the latest. Import.
(436). Rim; large platter, Cam. 5; TR 1(C)—orange ware, darker slip on upper surface. Pre-Claudian. Import (joins X78). Residual.
X84. (437). Base; small platter with footring. TN 1. Residual.
X 97. Ten + joining sherds; large platter, Cam. 5; TN 1. Below Roman street.
X98. Base sherd; platter TN 1. Import. Neronian at the latest. Residual.

Fig. 12.1

X105. *Gallo-Belgic imports*

1. (379). Rim sherd; platter, Cam. 9 in TR 1(C). Import, Tiberian-Neronian, possibly from Trier. Joins (397) in X117. Residual.

2. (336). Rim sherd; platter of Cam. 16, in fine-grained white ware with no trace of a surface colour and finish. Possibly imported. Nero-Flavian. Residual.

Fine and colour-coated ware

3. Rim and base sherds; globular beaker with moulded footring; grog rough-casting outside; cream ware; orange-brown slip. Possibly Central Gaul. Flavian.

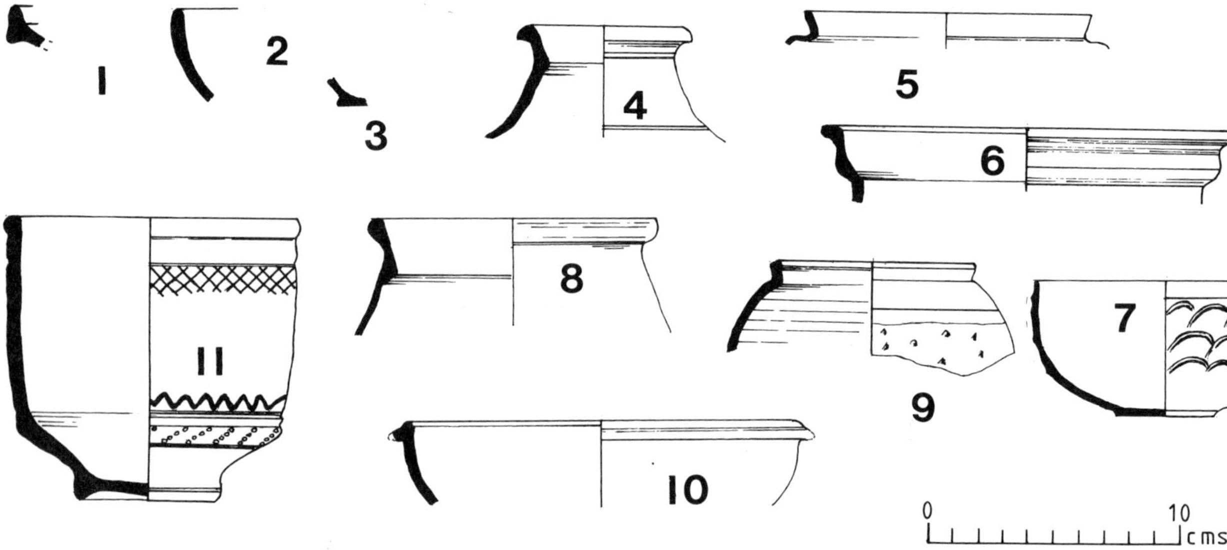

Fig. 12.1. Gallo-Belgic; imported and local fine wares ($\frac{1}{3}$).

Shoulder sherd from a second example.

Body sherd from a beaker decorated with barbotine "hairpins"; cream ware, metallic brown slip. Central Gaul, *c.* A.D. 85–150. (*Chichester 3,* Fig. 10.2, 6.)

Body sherd from a bag-shaped beaker, with cream grog rough-casting on the outside; cream ware, metallic dark brown slip. Imported from Central Gaul or the Rhineland. Trajanic-Hadrianic.

Body sherd, bag-shaped beaker with fine grog rough-casting outside; orange ware, metallic brown slip. Second century.

X106. (367). Base and three joining sherds; small barrel-shaped beaker; fabric closely resembles that of TN (see X128 [410], and [414]).

Colour-coated wares

(378). Rim sherd; beaker with cornice rim, *cf.* Gilliam 86; orange-brown matrix, dark brown matt slip; no evidence for the type of decoration. Possibly Colchester. Second century A.D.

X110. *Gallo-Belgic imports*

(388). Rim sherd; platter, Cam. 2; TN 1. Pre-Flavian import, Residual.

Fine ware

(387). Base; beaker, Cam. 94, sand rough-casting.

X117. *Gallo-Belgic wares*

(397). Joins (379) in X.105. Tiberio-Claudian.

(395) + (396). Rim and base sherds from the same platter, Cam. 16, as (160), X136.

Fine wares

(394). Sherd from a volute lamp like *Camulodunum*, Pl. XLIV, 3; South Gaulish. Pre-Flavian (possibly the same lamp as [430]).

(393). Base and body sherds; beaker, Cam. 94; South Gaulish; sand rough-casting confined to exterior, metallic bronze slip. Pre-Flavian.

(391). Sherd from a second example as (393).

(392). Sherd. beaker, Cam. 94, sand rough-casting; not obviously from the usual sources: South or Central Gaul—possibly Camulodunum.

White wares

Two sherds from imported white pipeclay ware flagons. Tiberio-Claudian, (*Chichester 3*, Fig. 10.2, 16.)

Fig. 12.1 4. X121. (390). Rim sherd. Butt beaker, *cf.* Cam. 113, with slight internal offset; orange cream ware, from a local source. (*Chichester 3*, Fig. 10.3, 1.1.)

Sherds from various flagons produced locally (see *Chichester 1–3*.)

X128. *Gallo-Belgic ware*

(417). Sherd; platter TN 1. Import.

Fine wares

(416). Rim; butt beaker, Cam. 113; typical white ware, probably from Camulodunum. Not later than A.D. 60.

(415). Rim; bowl, Cam. 62; typical ware with fine sand rough-casting inside and out. South Gaulish. Pre-Flavian.

(414). Base; barrel-shaped jar; the fabric closely resembles TN. See (367).

X133. *Gallo-Belgic*

(400). Sherds; large platter, Cam. 5; TN 2. A late variant: *c.* 50–60 A.D. Import, possibly from Trier.

—Base; large platter with footring; TN 1. Pre-Flavian. Import.

(399). Three sherds; butt-beaker, Cam. 112; TR 3: orange ware, decorated with coarse rouletting. Claudian.

Butt beakers

(389). Rim; butt beaker, Cam. 113; typical creamy white ware; rim details identical to those from Camulodunum region. Pre-Flavian. Context is Nero-Flavian.

X136. *Gallo-Belgic imports*

(160). Rim sherd; platter, Cam. 16 in TN 1. Import, *c.* A.D. 50–85.

5. (419). Rim sherd; globular beaker, *cf.* Cam. 95; orange-brown sandy matrix, with mica gilt slip on outside; decoration-undefined bosses. Nero-Vespasian. Import.

There is a similar beaker with undefined bosses from the filling of one of the ditches of the Leaholme Fort, Cirencester, which was filled *c.* A.D. 70.

6. (418). Rim and body sherds; carinated bowl, *cf.* Drag. 29; fine-grained cream ware, with light orange slip. Flavian, possibly local. Context is 2nd century.

A sherd; platter, Cam. 15; TN 1. *c.* A.D. 50–85.

Flagons

A sherd; flagon, in typical white pipe-clay ware. Pre-Flavian.

Fine wares

7. Approximately half of a bowl with applied scale decoration, Cam. 62 Ad; fine sand rough-casting inside. South Gaulish, pre-Flavian.

A rim; bowl with sand rough-casting inside and out, Cam. 62 Ae. Pre-Flavian.

Two sherds; bowl with sand rough-casting inside, possibly with applied scale decoration outside, Cam. 62 Ad. South Gaulish. Pre-Flavian.

X146. Base sherd; platter, possibly Cam. 14; TN 1. Import. Claudio-Neronian.

Flagons

Sherds from two locally-made flagons in white ware with some red grog grits. Context is early 2nd century.

X147. *Gallo-Belgic*

(403). Base; small platter with footring and bordered rouletted wreath; TN 3—badly flaked and laminated, possibly a Benios product. Claudio-Neronian. ? Sept-Saulx, Marne.

(402). Base; large platter with footring; TN 1. Pre-Flavian.

(401). Base; small platter with footring; TN, heavily burnt. Pre-Flavian. Import.

(440). Sherd; pedestalled beaker, any one of Cam. forms 72–9; TR 1(A)—creamy pink matrix, coral red slip on outside. Late Augustan–Claudian. Import.

(438). Sherd; beaker, Cam. 82, 84 or 112; TR 3—light orange, Tibero-Claudian. Import.

Fine wares

(439). Sherd; small beaker, *cf.* Cam. 95; orange-brown sandy ware with mica gilt slip on exterior; decoration—undefined bosses below a shoulder groove. Possibly local. Flavian–Trajanic. Base and rim sherds from two flagons in white pipeclay ware. Import. Pre-Flavian.

X148. *Gallo-Belgic imports*

(377). Base sherd; large platter with footring in TR 1(C); heavily burnt and discoloured. Import. Probably pre-Claudian, Claudian at the latest.

(376). Base and body sherds from a beaker in TR 3, light orange ware. Import; pre-Flavian.

(375). Rim sherd; beaker, Cam. 114 in cream fine-grained ware, with a mica gilt slip on the rim and shoulder. An import, probably from Central Gaul. Pre-Flavian.

Butt beakers

(374). Body sherd; butt beaker, Cam. 113 in typical white ware, with greyish exterior. Probably from the Camulodunum region. Pre-Flavian.

(373). Two rims; butt beakers, *cf.* Cam. 113; cream ware with a darker slip, burnished lip and matt neck; probably from the same local pottery which provided whitish ware flagons in the later 1st century A.D. (See *Chichester 1–3.*)

Other wares

(372). Two base sherds from a flask or beaker with a moulded footring; possibly Holwerda types 25, 26 or 27 in fine-grained dense micaceous grey ware with dark grey-black surfaces, exterior smoothly polished. Probably imported; possibly from Bavay. Neronian-Flavian.

(371). Body sherd; carinated beaker, Holwerda type 26 in the same ware as (372); almost certainly from the same vessel.

(370). Rim sherd; flasks of Holwerda 25 in the same ware as (371) and (372).

Flagons

(369). Rim sherd; flagon with undercut collar produced by the Chichester kilns (*Chichester 3,* type 10.1). In addition, there are body sherds from two others. Context is early 2nd century.

X153. *Gallo-Belgic wares*

(425). Rim; platter, Cam. 2; TN 2, very worn. Claudian. Import.

(424). Base; either girth or butt beaker, Cam. 82, 84 or 112; TR 3, light orange fine-grained ware, burnished finish.

Fine wares

(423). Rim; butt beaker, Cam. 113; white ware, with smoky edge to lip and grey core; from the same source as the Camulodunum beakers, probably Camulodunum. Not later than A.D. 60. (? joins X201.)

(422). Sherd; beaker with barbotine decoration. A local Chichester product, see *Chichester 3,* K.2. Pre-Flavian. Context is 1st century.

X155. *Fine wares*

(448). Base; small bowl, possibly Cam. 62; buff matrix, worn brown slip, fine sand rough-cast inside, none survives outside. Possibly South Gaulish; pre-Flavian.

(447). Rim, beaker, Cam. 94; buff matrix, bronze slip, sand rough-casting outside only. Possibly South Gaulish.

(446). Sherd; beaker, Cam. 94; sand rough-casting outside, possibly South Gaulish. Claudian—early Flavian.

X157. *Gallo-Belgic wares*
(454). Base; small platter, possibly Cam. 16; TN 2. *c.* 50–85 A.D. Import.
(453). Sherd; large platter with footring; TN 4. Pre-Flavian. Import.
(452). Sherd; cup, Cam. 56, large version; TR 1(C), orange matrix, darker slip on inside. Claudian at the latest. Import.
(451). Four sherds; butt beaker, Cam. 112; TR 3—light orange matrix, smoky haze on exterior; decoration—upper zone, incised cross hatching, lower zone, rouletted. Tiberio-Claudian. Import. Context is early 2nd century.

X159. (466). Base; platter, probably Cam. 16; TN—dark grey matrix, dark blue-grey surfaces. *c.* A.D. 50–85. Import.

X161. *Gallo-Belgic imports*
Tiny sherd from a pedestalled beaker; typical TR 1(A), pre-Claudian.

Local ware
Sherd from a flagon made by the Chichester kilns (see *Chichester 3*, Type K.10).

X165. (444). Rim; platter, Cam. 5; TR 2—orange matrix, with self-coloured highly polished finish. Claudian at the latest. Import.
(443). Base; small platter, domed at the centre; TN—badly flaked and laminated like the typical products of Benios, who worked at Sept-Saulx, Marne. Claudian.
(442). Rim; Cam. 13. TN 1—flaked and laminated. Pre-Flavian. Import.
(441). Base; platter or dish with an unusually tall footring; TN 1—badly flaked and laminated, grey surfaces.
(479). Base; beaker, Cam. 82, 84 or 112; TR 3—red ware with smoky grey exterior finish. Tiberio-Claudian. Import.
(475). Two sherds; butt beaker Cam. 112; TR 3—apricot matrix, smoky grey surface. Tiberio-Claudian. Import.

Fine wares
(472). Sherd; beaker, Cam. 94; typical ware, with sand rough-casting inside and out. ? Colchester. Claudian—early Flavian.
(471). Rim, base and body sherds; butt beaker, Cam. 113; typical white ware. From the same source as beakers at Camulodunum, probably Camulodunum itself. Not later than A.D. 60.

Local copies
(470). Rim, platter, similar to Cam. 16; local copy. Claudian-Flavian.
(473). Base; platter with footring; local ware. Claudian-Flavian.

X167. (445). Sherds making up into an almost complete bowl; Cam. 64; black eggshell ware. Possibly from Italy. Neronian? Besides Camulodunum, identical examples occur at Exeter and Cirencester, in the vicinity of military establishments pre-dating *c.* A.D. 70. Context is pre-Flavian and probably Claudian.

X185. (455). Sherd; platter; TR 4. Neronian at the latest. Import.

X190. (449). Rim; platter, Cam. 16; TN 1, with very dark surfaces. Nero-Flavian. Contest is ? Flavian.

X192. *Gallo-Belgic wares*
(421). Rim; platter, Cam. 5—joins (431) in X65.
(460). Rim; platter, Cam. 5; TN 4, very worn. Claudian at the latest. Import.
(459). Base; platter with footring; TN 4. Claudio-Neronian. Import.

Fine wares
(458). Sherd; small beaker, probably Cam. 94; cream matrix, metallic bronze slip, sand rough-casting outside only. Probably South Gaul. Claudio-Neronian.

Note.—This layer and X193 below, rested on the original turf line on the site and represent the earliest occupation.

X193. (381). Rim; platter, Cam. 14—with marked offset and slighly convex exterior profile; TN 2—with traces of highly polished black finish. Claudio-Neronian. Import.

X201. *Gallo-Belgic imports*

(383). Sherd; pedestalled beaker; typical TR 1(A), very worn. Pre-Claudian.

Butt beakers

Fig. 12.1 8. (385). Two rims and body sherds; butt beaker Cam. 113; typical fine cream ware. Probably from Camulodunum.

(384). Base sherds from a second example.

Local products

9. (382). A "waster". Context is mid-1st century.

X202. Sherds from locally-made flagons in orange and white wares. Local version of Drag. 37 in orange ware with rouletted decoration. After A.D. 75. Context is mid-late 1st century.

Slot X15. (413). Joins (397) and (379) from X117 and 105.

Slot X22. (412). Sherd; beaker, Cam. 82, 84 or 112; TR 3—orange, very worn.

(410). Sherd; butt beaker; grey surfaces (possibly joins [414] in X128).

Slot X31. (407). Rim. Globular beaker, Cam. 91; TR 3—red ware, very worn. Claudio-Neronian. Import

Slot X32. *Gallo-Belgic*

(408). Lower body sherd; girth beaker, Cam. 84, TR 3—light orange ware, with smoky grey polished exterior. Tiberio-Claudian. Import.

(406). Base; beaker, Cam. 82, 84 or 112; TR 3—orange-red. Tiberio-Claudian. Import.

Fine wares

(404). Sherds; beaker with barbotine decoration. A local Chichester product, see *Chichester 3*. Pre-Flavian.

Slot X34. (405). Sherd; bowl, Cam. 62; typical ware, with sand rough-casting inside and out. South Gaulish. Pre-Flavian.

Slot X37. Ribbed handle; flagon; white pipeclay ware. Pre-Flavian. Import.

Slot X51. (465). Base; platter, Cam. 16; TN 1, *c.* A.D. 50–85. Import.

Unstratified. (409). Base; beaker, Cam. 82, 84 or 112; TR 3—light orange.

TRENCH P

P19C. (469). Two base sherds; platter, Cam. 16 in TN 4, with a matt band between the concentric grooves on the upper surface of the base.

(514). (Examined by Mr. G. Marsh.) Marbled sherd. A small body sherd, possibly from a bowl. Cream, fine-grained even textured ware; bright orange marbled slip inside and out. Similar to examples found in London (Marsh, 1978, p. 119), which may be the source. Early 2nd century A.D.

P32. (498). Rim sherd; platter, Cam. 14 in TN 1. Pre-Flavian. Import.

P33. (518). A rim; platter, Cam. 14 in TN 1. Import. Pre-Flavian.

P39. (469). A sherd; girth beaker, Cam. 84 in TR 3—apricot ware with pearly-grey polished finish. Tiberio-Claudian.

P41/44. (467). Rim sherd; platter, Cam. 16 in TN 4—facetted exterior finish, very dark blue-black metallic surfaces.

EASTGATE NEEDLEMAKERS

Fig. 12.1 10. A19. (463). Three rims and body sherd; bowl with flanged rim in very worn TN. Possibly the type of bowl which has a totally useless footring applied about half an inch above the maximum depth, as at Exeter and Winchester (Bidwell, 1979, No. 247; Winnal Housing Estate, excavated by Dr. J. Collis, forthcoming).

11. Pit A29/A76. (497). A complete cylindrical pedestal beaker, or bowl, similar to Drag. 30. Fine-grained orange slightly micaceous ware with a darker orange-red slip on the exterior and extending approximately one inch into the inside; facetted

burnished exterior decorated with diagonal comb impressions on the carination, a narrow band of burnished lattice below the rim and a burnished scroll on the lower body on a matt ground. At the end of the firing a small amount smoke contaminated the kiln, either accidentally or by design, resulting in contrasting areas of blue-grey colour over the orange-red ground where burnishing occurred, at the base and rim, and also picking out the lattice and scroll patterns. Probably a local product. No close parallels have been identified, but similar deep bowls were in use during the period A.D. 80–180.

POTTERS STAMPS ON TERRA NIGRA

GB 28. A[CVTII] ; (559), Pit X103G.

A radial stamp abutting a double incised circle, on a large platter with an applied footring, 10 mm. wide. TN—pale blueish-white paste with occasional grey iron grits; light blue-grey surfaces, with an even but rather matt finish.

Acuto Die 3B2. Radial stamps from a similar die, 3B1, have been found at Camulodunum, Period I-III and Verulamium, both on T.N. platters, and a central stamp on a TN Platter, Cam. 8, at Nijmegen (*Hawkes* and *Hull*, 1947; Pl. XLV, 4; excavations by Prof. S. S. Frere, forthcoming; *Holwerda* 1941; Pl. XIX, 3c).

According to Koethe, stamps from Die 3B1 occur at Trier on comparatively late pieces, which could support the Claudian date of the Camulodunum find (*Koethe*, 1938; p. 91). *Not illustrated.*

GB 29. [IOV] AXV; (558), Pit X165.

A central stamp within a single incised circle, on the upper surface of a cup, Cam. form 58. TN—blueish-white ware with some grey iron and grog grits; pale dove-grey polished upper surface, darker blue-grey matt lower surface.

UX Die 141. A badly-impressed and distorted stamp from the same die as examples on the TN cups Cam. forms 56 and 58, from Camulodunum No. 162(7), Old Winteringham, South Humberside (*Rigby*, 1976, Fig. 61.12) and Bavay (Nord), and, on a small TN platter from Leicester (*Hull*, 1948, p. 221–2). The kiln site has not been identified, but the fabric suggests Bavay. A.D. 50–85.

Fig. 12.2. Potters stamps on coarse wares ($\frac{1}{1}$).

30

31

Fig. 12.2

POTTERS STAMPS ON COARSE WARES

XCH30. CH/76/E; (119), A79

A central mark on the upper surface of a platter, probably with a moulded footring. Dense fine-grained micaceous ware, with a highly burnished grey upper surface. The stamp is from the same die as examples foundat Wigginholt (1), Hardham (7), and Elstead (1), (*Rigby*, 1974; Fig. 9.21; *Winbolt*, 1927; Pl. II, 5; Pl. IV. 1–2; excavations by M. Millett [forthcoming]). The concentration of finds in Sussex strongly supports a local source. (*c.* A.D. 60–90).

XCH31. Ch/77/CS; (590), X202.

A central mark overstamping a combed circle, on the upper surface of a platter, possibly with a footring. There are also traces of another combed circle towards the edge of the base and a third on the underside, at the centre. Brown fine-grained highly micaceous ware, with very dark grey-black evenly burnished surfaces.

The stamp is from the same die as an example found in Sussex, during excavations at Frost Hill (D. Rudling, publication forthcoming). The fringed border can be paralleled at Fishbourne, Chichester—on white ware, and Southwark. (*Cunliffe,* 1971; Fig. 80.9; *Chichester 3,* Fig. 10.1, 24; *Rigby,* 1978; p. 280, G.5). The Period 1 provenance for the Fishbourne find gives a date of earlier than A.D. 75 for the introduction of fringed borders on coarseware stamps. The use of a fringe suggests a connection with the production of mortaria. However, the stamps found to date are from dies which appear too small for use on mortaria.

The source would appear to be local and a tentative date for its manufacture is *c.* A.D. 60–90.

References

CHICHESTER 1 — Down, A. and Rule M., *Chichester Excavations 1.* 1971.

CHICHESTER 2 — Down A., *Chichester Excavations 2.* 1974.

CHICHESTER 3 — Down A., *Chichester Excavations 3.* 1978.

CUNLIFFE 1971 — Cunliffe, B., *Excavations at Fishbourne*; Vol. 2. The Finds, 1971. Society of Antiquaries Research Report XXVII.

HAWKES and HULL 1947 — Hawkes, C. F. C. and Hull, M. R., *Camulodunum; First Report on the Excavations at Colchester,* 1930–1939. Report of the Research Committee of the Society of Antiquaries, No. XIV.

HULL 1948 — Hull, M. R., in Kenyon, K. M., *Excavations at Jewry Wall Site, Leicester.* Society of Antiquaries Research Report XV.

HOLWERDA 1941 — Holwerda, J., *De Belgische Waar in Nijmegen,* 1941.

KOETHE 1938 — Koethe, H, Zur gestempelten belgischen Keramik aus trier, *Festschrift für August Oxè,* ed. von Petrokovits, 1938.

RIGBY 1974 — Rigby, V., in Evans, K. Jane, "Excavations on the Romano-British Site, Wiggonholt", 1964, *SAC* 112, 1974.

RIGBY 1975 — Rigby, V., in Jarvis, K. and Maxfield, V, "The excavation of a first century Roman farmstead and a late Neolithic settlement, Topsham, Devon". *Proc. Devon. Arch. Soc.* 33, 1975.

RIGBY 1976 — Rigby, V., in Stead, I. M., *Excavations at Winterton Roman Villa and other sites in North Lincolnshire.* D.o.E. Arch. Report No. 3.

RIGBY 1978 — Rigby, V., in Sheldon H. L., *Southwark* Excavations, 1972–4. Joint publication No. 1, London and Middlesex Arch. Society and Surrey Arch. Society. 1978.

WINBOLT 1927 — Winbolt, S. E., "Excavations at Hardham Camp, Pulborough", *SAC* 68, 1927.

13

The Amphorae from the Sites

All the amphorae from the sites were submitted to Dr. D. P. S. Peacock at Southampton University for identification and comment, and his observations are contained in the following Table:

CHAPEL STREET 1977 and 1978

No.	Drawn	Context	Form	Fabric	Origin	Contents	Remarks
1	–	X106	Dressel 20	–	S. Spain	Oil	1st–3rd cent.
2	–	X64	Dressel 20	–	S. Spain	Oil	1st–3rd cent.
3	–	ph.X203	Dressel 20	–	S. Spain	Oil	1st–3rd cent.
4	–	X113	Dressel 20	–	S. Spain	Oil	1st–3rd cent.
5	–	P11	Dressel 20	–	S. Spain	Oil	1st–3rd cent.
6	–	Pit X169	Dressel 20	–	S. Spain	Oil	1st–3rd cent.
7	–	P22	Dressel 20	–	S. Spain	Oil	1st–3rd cent.
8	–	Pit X165	Uncertain	–	–	–	–
9	–	X94	Dressel 20	–	S. Spain	Oil	1st–3rd cent.
10	–	X77	Dressel 20	–	S. Spain	Oil	1st–3rd cent.
11	–	P4	Uncertain	–	N. Africa	–	Very late 4th cent.
12	–	Pit X172	Cam. 185B	–	S. Spain	–	1st–mid-2nd cent.
13	–	X94	Dressel 20	–	? Cadiz S. Spain	Oil	1st–2nd cent.
14	–	X65	Dressel 20	–	S. Spain	Oil	1st–2nd cent.
15	–	P4	Dressel 20	–	S. Spain	Oil	1st–2nd cent.
16	–	Pit X33	Uncertain	–	N. Africa	–	3rd–4th cent.
17	–	X65	Cam. 185B	–	? Cadiz S. Spain	–	1st–mid-2nd cent.
18	–	P10	Dressel 20	–	S. Spain	–	1st–3rd cent.
19	–	X105	Dressel 20	–	S. Spain	Oil	1st–3rd cent.
20	Fig. 13.1	X1	Dressel 20	–	S. Spain	Oil	1st–3rd cent.
21	Fig. 13.1	Pit X165	–	Peacock Fabric 2	Rhodian	Wine	1st cent.
22	–	X105	Dressel 20	–	S. Spain	Oil	1st–3rd cent.
23	–	X65	Dressel 40	–	S. Gaul	Wine	1st–3rd cent.
24	–	X65	Dressel 20	–	S. Spain	Oil	1st–3rd cent.
25	–	X50	Dressel 20	–	S. Spain	Oil	1st–3rd cent.
26	–	X20	Dressel 20	–	S. Spain	Oil	1st–3rd cent.
27	–	Pit X154	Dressel 20	–	S. Spain	Oil	1st–3rd cent.
28	–	X169	Dressel 20	–	S. Spain	Oil	1st–3rd cent.
29	–	X185	Cam. 186	–	Cadiz S. Spain	–	Up to mid-2nd cent.
30	–	X39	Dressel 20	–	S. Spain	Oil	1st–3rd cent.
31	–	X65	Dressel 20	–	S. Spain	Oil	1st–3rd cent.
SOUTHGATE							
32	–	A16	Dressel 20	–	S. Spain	Oil	1st–3rd cent.
33	–	Pit A2	Dressel 20	–	S. Spain	Oil	1st–3rd cent.
34	–	F9	Dressel 20	–	S. Spain	Oil	1st–3rd cent.
EASTGATE							
35	–	Pit A33	Dressel 20	–	S. Spain	Oil	1st–3rd cent.
36	–	A116	Dressel 20	–	S. Spain	Oil	1st–3rd cent.
37	–	C35	Dressel 20	–	S. Spain	Oil	1st–3rd cent.
38	–	Pit B11	Cam. 186	–	Cadiz S. Spain	–	Up to mid-2nd cent.
39	–	A91	Cam. 186	–	Cadiz Spain	–	Up to mid-2nd cent.

No.	Drawn	Context	Form	Fabric	Origin	Contents	Remarks
40	–	Pit A33	Dressel 20	–	S. Spain	Oil	1st–3rd cent.
41	–	Pit A33	Dressel 20	–	S. Spain	Oil	1st–3rd cent.
42	–	A19	Dressel 20	–	S. Spain	Oil	1st–3rd cent.
43	–	Pit A33	Dressel 20	–	S. Spain	Oil	1st–3rd cent.
44	–	A78	Dressel 20	–	S. Spain	Oil	1st–3rd cent.
45	–	A45	Dressel 20	–	S. Spain	Oil	1st–3rd cent.
46	–	Pit A33	? Dressel 20	Red	?	?	1st–3rd cent.
47	–	Pit A33	Dressel 20	–	S. Spain	Oil	1st–3rd cent.
48	–	Pit A33	? Dressel 20	–	–	–	–
49	–	A19	Dressel 2–4	–	Campania	Wine	1st to mid-2nd cent.
50	–	Pit A33	Dressel 20	–	S. Spain	Oil	1st–3rd cent.
51	–	B2.16	Dressel 20	–	S. Spain	Oil	1st–3rd cent.
52	–	Pit A33	Dressel 20	–	S. Spain	Oil	1st–3rd cent.
53	–	A19	Dressel 20	–	S. Spain	Oil	1st–3rd cent.
54	–	A19	Dressel 20	–	S. Spain	Oil	1st–3rd cent.
55	–	Pit A33	Dressel 20	–	S. Spain	Oil	1st–3rd cent.
56	–	Pit A33	? Dressel 20	Red	S. Spain	–	1st–3rd cent.
57	–	Pit A33	Dressel 20	Red	S. Spain	–	1st–3rd cent.
58	–	Pit A33	Uncertain	–	–	–	–
59	–	A19	Dressel 20	–	S. Spain	Oil	1st–3rd cent.
60	–	Pit A33	Dressel 20	–	S. Spain	Oil	1st–3rd cent.
61	–	Pit A33	Dressel 20	–	S. Spain	Oil	1st–3rd cent.
62	–	Pit A29	Dressel 20	–	S. Spain	Oil	1st–3rd cent.
63	Fig. 13.1	Pit A33	*Callender Form 18 stamped ACIRGI F or E)	–	S. Spain	–	A.D. 90–140

*Reference. M. H. Callender, *Roman Amphorae,* London, 1965, Fig. 3.9

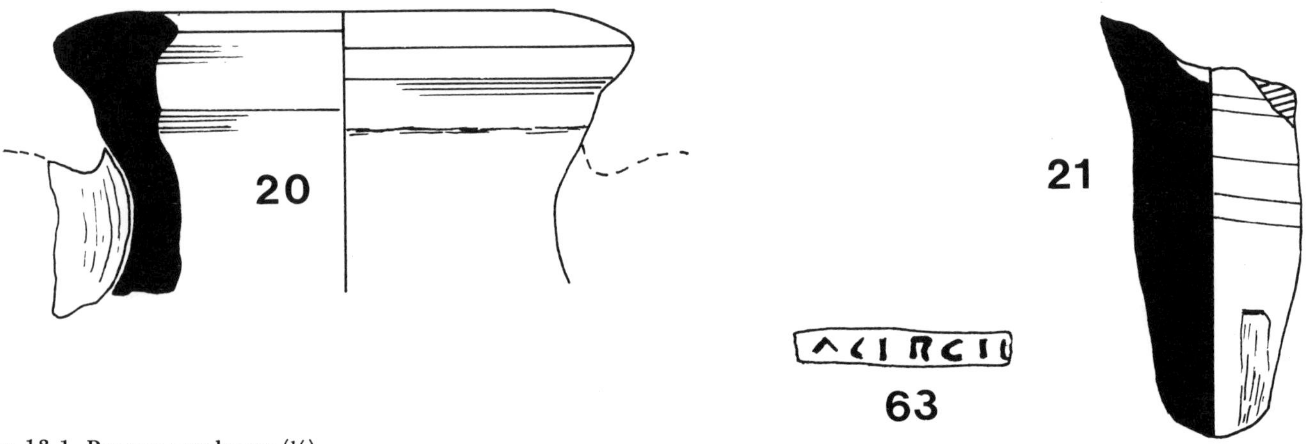

Fig. 13.1. Roman amphorae (½).

14

Post-Flavian Roman Fine Wares

by C. J. Young

This report discusses the Roman fine wares from sites described in this volume of *Chichester Excavations*, excluding pre-Flavian fine wares, Samian and mortaria (except those of the New Forest and Oxfordshire which have been included to present a full picture of the wares supplied by those industries).

As is usual, the pottery has been classified by fabric and form according to context and has been quantified by weight, sherd count and vessel equivalent. Some 1,100 sherds, weighing nearly 18 kg. have been examined.

The full record is deposited in the site archive and this published report summarises the evidence, listing first of all fabrics and forms present. This is followed by a discussion of their significance. For ease and convenience the fabrics have been divided into early (*c.* A.D. 70–250) and late (post *c.* A.D. 250) groups since there is a very clear break in sources of supply and patterns of use in the early third century. In this level 4 report, only the sherd count has been quoted, since this seems the most useful method of quantification for wares which frequently occur only in small quantities in many different contexts.

CATALOGUE OF FABRICS AND VESSEL TYPES

In this catalogue the fabrics have been divided into two main groups—those dating before *c.* 250 and those that are later. Since many of the wares are from unknown sources and seldom occur in usefully dated contexts, this division has in many cases had to be done on typological grounds alone. In such cases it is not possible to date the ware more closely than the broad divisions into pre- and post-250. In a few cases no typologically useful sherds were found, and these wares are listed in a third section. Known, easily recognisable fabrics have been called by their normal common-ware names. Others were numbered as they were identified and these numbers are used here as identifiers. Certain fabrics (Nos. 1, 3, 8, 19, 14, 17) were subsequently recognised as being minor variants of well-known ones and have been subsumed therein. Fabric 18 is modern.

Full stratigraphic information is contained in the archive. Accounts of the fine ware present in important groups are contained in the main pottery report. This catalogue merely summarises the information in the archive. For each ware, the fabric is described macroscopically or reference is made to a published description, and the occurrence on the three sites (Eastgate Needlemakers, North-West Quadrant and Southgate) are summarised.

Pre-c. A.D. 250 (Fig. 14.1)

1. *Lezoux white ware*—hard white ware with brown colour-coat, decorated with clay-pellet roughcasting or barbotine "hairpin" motifs (*Greene*, 1978, 17), dated *c.* 70–150. All sherds were from beakers, and all but one were decorated with barbotine "hairpins".

   Eastgate—2; N.W. Quadrant—2; Southgate—2.

2. *Rhenish white ware*—fine, hard white ware made in the lower Rhineland from the pre-Flavian period through to the early third century, but not exported to Britain after *c.* 160/170 (see *Anderson*, 1980, 14–20, lower Rhineland fabric 1).

   All the Chichester sherds are from beakers and the bulk of them are roughcast. The only recognisable form is the cornice-rim bag beaker and all sherds probably date *c.* 70–160/170.

   Eastgate—2 rims, 18 body sherds (13 roughcast); N.W. Quadrant—1 rim, 9 body sherds (5 roughcast).

3–5. *Central Gaulish "Rhenish" ware*—fine hard pink-red ware with glossy black colour-coat, probably dating *c.* A.D. 150–200 (*Greene*, 1978, 18–19). The principal forms are the bag or bulbous beaker, with or without indentation, sometimes with barbotine decoration, and the small hemispherical bowl (*Greene*, 1978, Figs. 2.3, 4–9).

The present group of pottery contains one beaker with barbotine decoration, some indented beakers and 2 hemispherical bowls.

	Eastgate	N.W. Quadrant	Southgate
As Fig. 14.1, 3	—	1	—
indented beaker	—	4	—
other beaker sherds	5	14	1
bowls Fig. 14.1, 4-5	2	—	—

6–7. *Trier "Rhenish" ware.* Ware similar in appearance to last, but normally has a grey core, and is used for bag or bulbous beakers sometimes decorated with indentations or white barbotine patterns; normally dated late 2nd–mid-3rd century (*Greene*, 1978, 18–19). All the Chichester examples come from bulbous beakers.

	Eastgate	N.W. Quadrant	Southgate
barbotine beaker (Fig. 14.1, 6, 7)	1	7	—
indented beaker	2	13	—
other beaker	7	40	1

? Colchester—hard, red-brown fabric, normally with brownish colour-coat, dating probably from the mid-2nd to early 3rd centuries (*Anderson*, 1980, 35). Apart from one "castor box" lid, all the sherds found were from enclosed vessels, including three rouletted and one with white barbotine.

Eastgate—5; N.W. Quadrant—4.

Nene Valley—hard, white ware, with visible inclusions of iron ore, with colour-coat varying from red to black (*Anderson*, 1980, 38–40). Nene valley colour-coat wares were produced from the mid-2nd century to the end of Roman Britain, but none of the Chichester examples are likely to date later than the mid-3rd century. Apart from one "castor-box" lid, all sherds found were from beakers. Decoration included barbotine and paint.

Eastgate—7; N.W. Quadrant—11; Southgate—1.

8. *Fabric 2*—hard, pink ware, containing some flecks of mica, black specks (? iron ore), occasional red or white lumps; matt red-brown colour-coat. Only four sherds were found, all from enclosed vessels. The only identifiable rim is probably from a squat globular beaker, more likely to be early than late.

Eastgate—2; N.W. Quadrant—2.

9. *Fabric 4*—hard, reddish ware with dark grey skin, dark grey core in thick parts of the vessel, containing bright red inclusions and some white lumps: matt black colour-coat. Apart from its colour-coat the ware is similar to Trier "Rhenish" ware. Only seven sherds have been identified, all from enclosed vessels. One body sherd is indented and roughcast. The only rim sherd is from a cornice-rim beaker (Fig. 14.1, 9). Origin and dating are unknown, but probably it dates well before *c.* 250, as roughcasting is not normal later than *c.* 200.

Eastgate—1; N.W. Quadrant—6.

10–11. *Fabric 5*—fine hard white ware, no visible inclusions, with fine sand roughcasting, occasional rouletting, and a matt black colour-coat. The fabric is very similar to, and may be the same as, the Lower Rhineland Fabric discussed above.

All sherds found came from enclosed vessels. The only identifiable forms are a straight-sided beaker (Fig. 14.1, 10), and a cornice-rimmed bag-beaker (Fig. 14.1, 11), with rough-casting. The dating and origin of the ware are uncertain.

Eastgate—1; N.W. Quadrant—17.

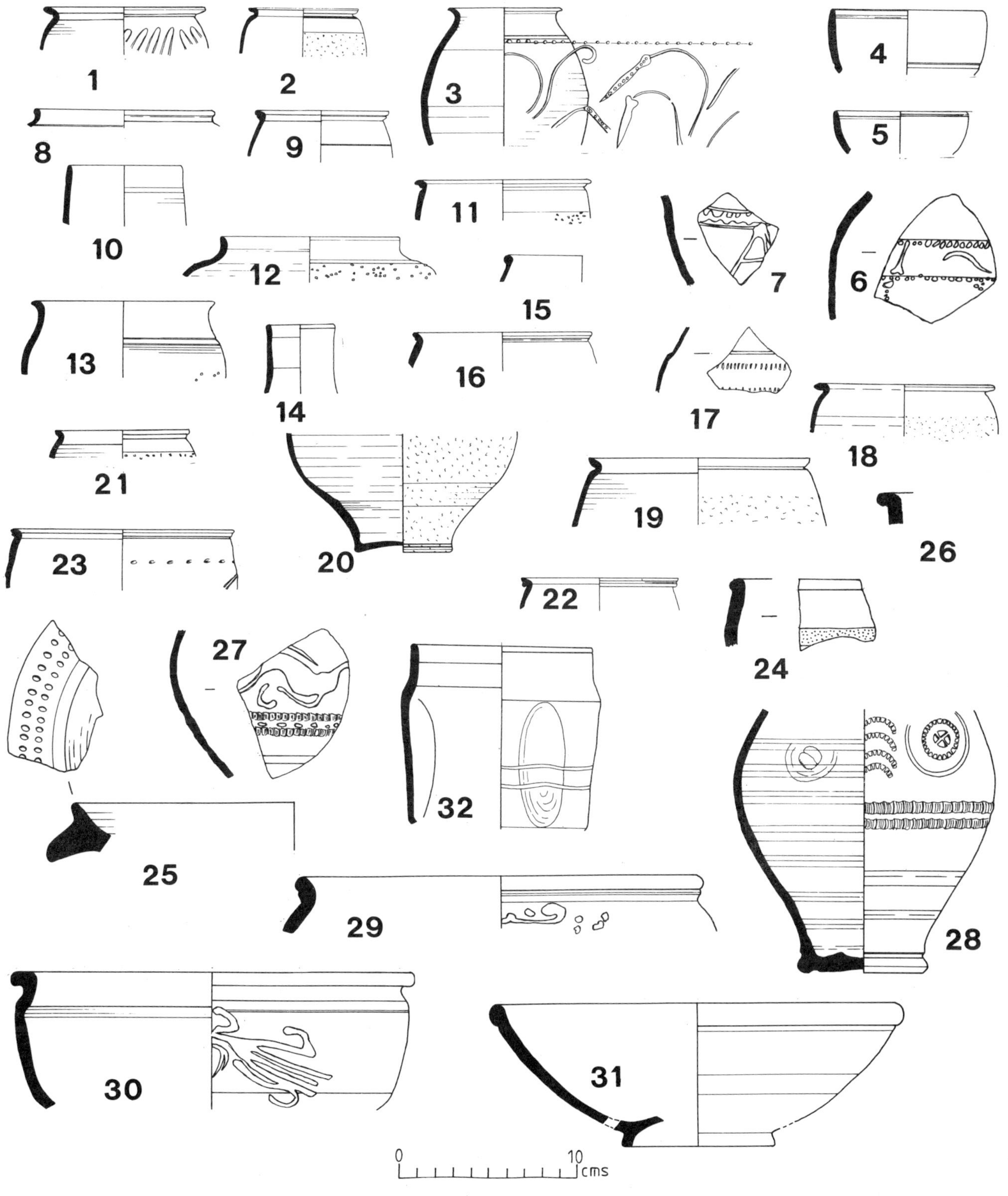

Fig. 14.1. Post Flavian Roman Fine Wares. Nos. 1-23, pre-A.D. 250; Nos. 24-32, post-A.D. 250. ($\frac{1}{3}$)

12–13. *Fabric 6*—fine reddish-brown ware; dark-brown colour-coat. The ware is not common. All five sherds come from a maximum of three vessels, all enclosed. The two drawable vessels are both globular, roughcast beakers with upstanding rims. The origin and dating of the ware are uncertain.

Eastgate—3; N.W. Quadrant—2.

Fabric 7—light pink ware with visible plates of mica on the surface, and some white inclusions, and a "varnishy" dark-brown colour-coat. Two sherds only were found. Dr. Fulford suggests they might be Central Gaulish.

Eastgate—2.

Fabric 11—very hard, sandy dark-grey core with pink skin, some white inclusions and sand roughcasting; glossy black colour-coat. Only six sherds were found, all from enclosed vessels.

N.W. Quadrant—6.

14–17. *Fabric 12*—hard, fine, brick-red ware, some voids, occasional matt white inclusions; matt-black colour-coat, with clay pellet roughcasting. Forms include a narrow, indented beaker (Fig. 14.1, 14), plain and cornice-rimmed bag-beakers (Fig. 14.1, 15, 16) and a bulbous beaker with rouletted bands (Fig. 14.1, 17). Dating and origin are uncertain.

N.W. Quadrant—11.

18–20. *Fabric 19*—fine, hard, pink-red ware with thin grey core and white inclusions; colour-coat matt-red on interior, black-purple on exterior, roughcast with clay pellets. The only form found is a bag beaker with a simple everted rim. The origin and dating of this ware are uncertain.

N.W. Quadrant—24.

21–22. *Fabric 20*—fine, pink ware, some black inclusions; colour-coat matt, dark-grey inside, shiny black outside. There is some roughcasting. The only forms recognised are plain and grooved-cornice rim bag-beakers. The origin and dating of this ware are uncertain.

N.W. Quadrant—26.

23. *Fabric 21*—hard, sandy, pale pink ware, with red inclusions; colour-coat matt purple-black inside, shiny black outside. Two sherds only were found. One vessel has barbotine decoration (Fig. 14.1, 23), the other sherd is roughcast with clay pellets. The only form recognised is a bag-beaker with cornice rim.

N.W. Quadrant—2.

Post c. A.D. 250

Argonne ware—see *Fulford*, 1977, 39, for description of fabric. One sherd only, of the standard bowl form (*Chenet*, 1941, Pl. 14, type 320), was found.

N.W. Quadrant—1.

24–26. *New Forest wares*—see *Fulford*, 1975 for definition of the various wares and forms, and their dating (number of sherds in brackets).

New Forest 1A:

Eastgate: Types 11(1), 27(44), 30(1), 30/41(2), 44/52(1), 52(1), 47(1), 57(1); flagon handle (1); enclosed body sherds (34).
N.W. Quadrant: Types 1/10.3(2), 8(2), 27(80), 30(8), 33(2), 39(2), 42(5), 44(4); flagon body (1); enclosed body sherds (139).
Southgate: Types 1(1), 27(9), 30(1); enclosed body sherds (10).

New Forest 1B:

Eastgate: Types 59(2), 63(1), 67(2), 72.3(1), 73(7), 74(1), 77(5); bowl body sherds (15); enclosed body sherds (1).

N.W. Quadrant: Types 63(11); flagon handle (1); enclosed body sherds (2); bowl body sherds (22); mortaria bodys (2), 73(1).
Southgate: Types 63(1); bowl body sherd (4).

New Forest 2A:

Eastgate: Types 88 variant (1 only: Fig. 14.1, 24), 88(1).
N.W. Quadrant: Types 60(1), 89(4), 103 (1 only, stabbed decoration on flange: (Fig. 14.1, 25).
Southgate: Types 89(1); body sherds (1).

New Forest 2B:

Eastgate: Types 88 variant (1 only: Fig. 14.1, 26), 88(3), 90(1); bowl body sherds (1); 104(1).
N.W. Quadrant: Type 88(1).

27-28. *Oxford wares*—see *Young*, 1977 for definitions of fabrics, forms and dating (numbers of sherds given in brackets).

Oxford parchment ware:

N.W. Quadrant: Types P1/4(1), P24(1).
Southgate: Type P24(1).

Oxford white-ware mortaria:

N.W. Quadrant: Types M18(1), ? M22(1); body sherds (2).

Oxford white colour-coat ware:

N.W. Quadrant: mortarium body sherd (1).
Southgate: Type WC7(1).

Oxford red colour-coat ware:

Eastgate: Types C22(1), C23(6), C25 (one only, illustrated to show possible "hunt-cup" decoration: Fig. 00, 27); enclosed body sherds (20), C48(1), C50(5), C47/50(4), C51(14), C52(1), C55(1), C68(2), C70(3), C71(4), C75(5), C78(2), C83(2); bowl body sherds (17, C97(5), C100(2); mortaria body sherds (3).
N.W. Quadrant: Types C8(1), C16(1), C22(4), C23(6), C26(1), C27(10), C28(3); enclosed body sherds (62), C45(1), C46(1), C50(2), C51(2), C55(1), C68(3), C69(1), C71(1), C74(1), C75(10), C77(1), C78(1), C80(1), C83(1), C84.12-14(1); bowl-body sherds (34), C97(11), C100(4); mortaria body sherds (5).
Southgate: Types C22(1), C29(1); enclosed body sherd (9), C44(1), C45(1), C50(1), C47/50(2). C51(4), C68(1), C75(1), C80(1); bowl body sherds (14), C97(1), mortaria body sherds (1).

? Oxford red colour-coat ware

Eastgate—C22(2), C23(1), C30 (1: Fig. 14.1, 28); enclosed body sherds (4); bowl body sherd (1).

29-30. *Pevensey ware*—see *Fulford,* 1973, for description of fabric, and *Bird and Young,* 1981 for forms. In this catalogue forms are defined by the type numbers of their Oxford counterparts. Pevensey ware probably dates predominantly to the second half of the 4th century.

Eastgate—as Oxford C70(1); bowl body (2).
N.W. Quadrant—As Oxford C68(1), as Oxford C69 (1: Fig. 14.1, 29), as Oxford C75(1), as Oxford C77 (1: Fig. 14.1, 30).

31. *Local red-slip ware*—sandy red ware, with small black and red inclusions, sometimes with a grey core. Most sherds have a red slip. It has been recognised previously at Chichester (*Fulford and Young,* 1976, 257), and at Chilgrove (*Young,* 1979, 196). Forms identified to date include copies of Dr.31, Dr.38, deep hemispherical bowls, dog dishes, and flange-rimmed straight-sided bowls. Only one sherd has been found in the present series of excavations, copying Dr.31 (Fig. 14.1, 31).

N.W. Quadrant—1.

Fabric 13—orange-pink sandy ware, containing much mica, and many white flecks on the inner surface; matt red colour-coat. A similar ware has been found at Chilgrove (*Young*, 1979, 196), where the form was a late one.

N.W. Quadrant—5 bowl body sherds.

Fabric 15—light orange sandy ware with faint, pale grey core, red and grey inclusions; dark brown colour-coat. The ware is undated, but the forms and decorations are close to those of the Oxford industry, and it is presumably late Roman.

N.W. Quadrant: as Oxford C22(1), as Oxford C27(1), two body sherds from an indented beaker, 10 body sherds rouletted overall from a bulbous beaker (*cf.* Oxford type C23).

32. *Fabric 22*—hard, sandy pink ware, with red inclusions; brown-red colour-coat. This fabric is otherwise unknown, and all the sherds from Chichester probably came from one vessel only (Fig. 14.1, 32). In form this indented beaker is closest to the products of the New Forest (*cf. Fulford*, 1975, type 27), so it is presumably late Roman.

N.W. Quadrant—6.

Fabrics of uncertain date

Fabric 9—soft, orange ware, heavily tempered with red inclusions (? grog); matt red-brown colour-coat. One sherd only from an indented beaker.

Southgate—1.

Fabric 16—hard, pink ware, light grey core, red and grey inclusions; dark brown colour-coat. One sherd only.

N.W. Quadrant—1.

Discussion

Since so little of the pottery discussed here comes from usefully dated contexts, it is very difficult to detect changing patterns of supply through time, except for the broad contrast between the period before and after the mid-3rd century. Direct comparison with the fine wares published in *Chichester 3* is complicated by the fact that there they were quantified by weight not by sherd count (*Fulford and Young*, 1978).

Any discussion of supply before *c.* 250 is bedevilled by the fact that so many of the fabrics come from unknown sources and by the relatively small size of the sample. The known sources suggest that the main sources of supply were Continental. The information summarised on Table I shows that over a third of the fine wares are "Rhenish" ware either from Central Gaul or from Trier, and that the only other ware to form more than 10 per cent. of the sample came also from the Rhineland. Known British sources (Colchester and Nene Valley) jointly account for only 10 per cent. of the sample.

This contrasts strongly with the proportions reported from the earlier North-West Quadrant excavations (Colchester, 45 per cent.; "Rhenish" wares, 33 per cent; Nene Valley, 21 per cent. by weight). This may be accounted for partly by the different quantification method used, but probably more by insufficient sub-division of the fabrics. Alternatively it may represent a genuine difference in supply. Further work is required to clarify this point.

Table II gives a summary of the fine wares dated after *c.* 250 and demonstrates, as is usual in this area, that the main sources of supply in this period were the New Forest and Oxford industries. The proportions from the various sources are similar to those published in *Chichester 3* (*Fulford and Young*, 1978), despite the different method of quantification used, and reflect general patterns of supply in this part of southern England. Also to be expected are the small amounts from what must be local sources (e.g., local red-slip wares, fabrics 13 and 15).

TABLE I—Summary of Post-Flavian Wares to *c.* A.D. 250 (total No. of Sherds, 266)

FABRIC	No. of Sherds	%	FABRIC	No. of Sherds	%
Lezoux	6	2	5	18	7
Rhenish white ..	30	11	6	5	2
C G "Rhenish" ..	27	10	7	2	—
Trier "Rhenish" ..	70	26	11	6	2
Colchester	9	3	12	11	4
Nene Valley ..	19	7	19	24	9
2	4	2	20	26	10
4	7	3	21	2	—

TABLE II—Summary of Roman Fine Ware, post *c.* A.D. 250 (total No. of Sherds, 762)

FABRIC	No. of Sherds	%	FABRIC	No of Sherds	%
Argonne	1	—	Oxford p.w.	3	—
New Forest 1A ..	353	46	Oxford white ware mortaria	4	—
New Forest 1B ..	79	10	Oxford white colour-coat	2	—
New Forest 2A ..	10	1	Oxford red colour-coat	271	36
New Forest 2B ..	8	1	Pevensey	7	1
Local red slip ..	1	—	13	5	—
15	12	2	22	6	1

EASTGATE NEEDLEMAKERS, WELL 2

(For conventions used and fabric descriptions, see pp. 285-290).

Rhenish White Ware—body sherd (1).

New Forest Wares (*cf. Fulford,* 1975).

New Forest Fabric 1A: Types 27(11), 30(1), 30/41(2), 57(1); enclosed body sherds (15).

New Forest Fabric 1B: Types 57(1), 59(1), 63(1), 67(2), 72.3(1), 73(7), 74(1), 77(5); enclosed body sherds (2); enclosed bowl sherds (17).

New Forest Fabric 2A: Types 88(1), 88 variant (1: Fig. 14.1, 24); bowl body sherd (1).

New Forest Fabric 2B: Types 88(1), 88 variant (1: Fig. 14.1, 26), 89(1), 90(1), bowl body sherd (1), 104(1).

Oxford Wares (*cf. Young,* 1977).

Oxford white ware mortaria: M22(1).

Oxford red colour-coat ware: C25 (1: Fig. 14.1, 27); enclosed body sherds (20), C48(1), C50(5), C48/50(3), C51(12), C52(1), C55(1), C68(2), C70(2), C71(4), C75(1), C78(2), C83(2), bowl body sherds (21).

? Oxford red colour-coat ware: C22(2), C23(1), C30(1); enclosed body sherds (3); bowl body sherd (1).

Pevensey Ware

as C70(1); bowl body sherds (2).

The presence of the Oxford stamped wares (C78, C83), show clearly that the fill of this pit was deposited later than 350.

References

ANDERSON 1980 — Anderson, A. C., *A Guide to Roman Fine Wares* (Vorda Research Series I), Highworth (1980).

BIRD and YOUNG 1981 — Bird, J. M., and Young, C. J., 'Late Roman migrant potters—the Oxford connection', in Anderson, A. C., and Anderson, A. S.

CHENET 1941 — Chenet, G., *La Ceramique gallo-romaine d'Argonne du IVe siecle et la terre sigillee decoree a la molette*, Macon (1941).

FULFORD 1973 — Fulford, M. G., 'A fourth-century colour-coated fabric and its types in South-East England', *S.A.C.*, 111, 41-4.

FULFORD 1975 — Fulford, M. G., *New Forest Roman Pottery*, B.A.R. 17, Oxford.

FULFORD 1977 — Fulford, M. G., 'Pottery and Britain's Foreign Trade in the later Roman Period', in D. P. S. Peacock (ed.), *Pottery and early commerce*, London (1977).

FULFORD and YOUNG 1978 — Fulford, M. G., and Young, C. J., 'A discussion of the later Roman Fine Wares', in *Chichester Excavations 3*, 256-7 (1978).

GREENE 1978 — Greene, K., 'Imported fine wares in Britain to A.D. 250, a guide to identification', in Arthur, P., and Marsh, G., *Early Fine wares in Roman Britain*, B.A.R. 57, Oxford (1978).

YOUNG 1977 — Young, C. J., *The Roman Pottery Industry of the Oxford Region*, B.A.R. 43, Oxford (1977).

YOUNG 1979 — Young, C. J., 'The Roman Fine Wares', in *Chichester Excavations 4* (1979).

15

The Roman Glass

by Dorothy Charlesworth

Figs. 15.1-15.2

VESSEL GLASS

The report cannot give a balanced picture of the glass for the excavations. The bulk of material is unidentifiable fragments of natural green glass from a wide range of utilitarian vessels for storage or table-ware. which are not worth individual mention. On the other hand the comparatively small quantity of good quality coloured glass is all recorded, merely because it is less common. The numbers in brackets are the catalogue numbers.

A. *Coloured fragments*

1. (295). Fragment of abraded millefiori, green with opaque yellow and red streaks. Mid 1st century.
2. (261). Fragment of thick emerald green glass. Mid 1st century?
3. (265). Two small fragments of deep blue glass with opaque white marvered blobs. Mid 1st century. *Not illustrated.*
4. (278). Three fragments of blue grass with parallel white marvered lines. Probably mid 1st century.
5. (293). Fragment of light blue with an unmarvered white trail.
6. (302). Colourless fragment partially covered with a casing of blue glass. Mid 1st century.

   None of the above types of decorated glass has been recorded in previous reports.
7. (262). Fragment of a dark brown pillar-moulded bowl, from near the base, with two internal cut lines. For other examples of pillar-moulded bowls see *Chichester 2,* p. 133, and *Chichester 3,* p. 267, includes one in amber-coloured glass.
8. (288). Two fragments of a small ribbed bowl in greenish glass with a white marvered trail, knocked off, unworked rim, some flaking iridescence. Mid 1st century.

   Another example of this type is discussed in *Chichester 3,* p. 267, No. 13. The technique there suggested of pre-moulding the ribbing has been reconsidered. It could equally well be created by trailing and marvering, indeed the fact that there is no hollow on the inside suggests that added trails rather than mould-blowing is likely to be the method adopted, but mould-blowing does not necessarily leave a hollow inside to correspond with a rib or boss outside.
9. (273). Rounded, thickened rim with white marvered trails.

B. *Colourless glass*

10. (263). Rim in good quality colourless glass from a bowl or beaker, knocked off and ground, with ground moulding below. Abraded, cloudy weathering; presumably residual. Late 1st–2nd century.
11. (277). Ribbed fragment, iridescent, from bowl or jar. 1st–3rd century.
12. (282). Good quality colourless fragment, slight S-curve, ground rim, faint cut lines immediately under the rim and deeper line at the top of the row of facets.

    Two certain, and one possible, facet cut beakers were published in *Chichester Excavations 2,* p. 134, Fig. 8.13, Nos. 11-13. They differ from this example in having horizontal ribs where this has cut lines. This resembles more closely an example from Corbridge (*Charlesworth,* 1959, 42, Fig. 3.7) than the earlier Chichester finds and the examples there quoted illustrated in *Masterpieces of Glass in the British Museum,* Nos. 101. 102, Isings form 21.
13. (266). Rim fragment of large 3rd/4th-century flagon, outsplayed, rounded at the tip, trail below it, flaking iridescence. The glass has a greenish tinge but the obvious intention was to produce a colourless glass.

    This is a common rim type on many bulbous and cylindrical-bodied vessels with or without a handle. It is thought to be from a handled pouring vessel (flagon) because of the apparent size of the vessel. Isings forms 120b, 123 are possible, 102 has the same rim. (*Isings,* 1957; *Charlesworth,* 1959, 37, 33–58).

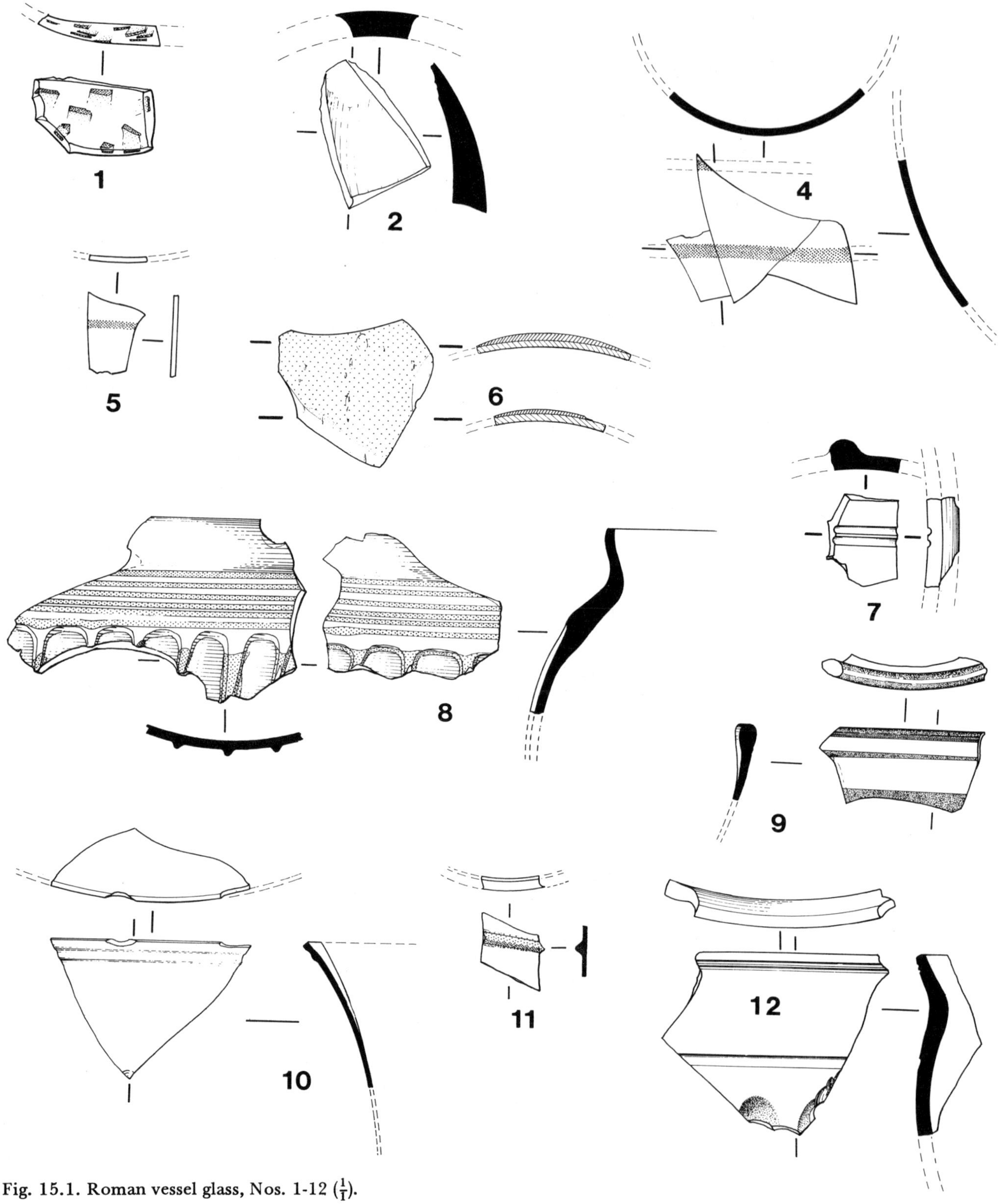

Fig. 15.1. Roman vessel glass, Nos. 1-12 ($\frac{1}{1}$).

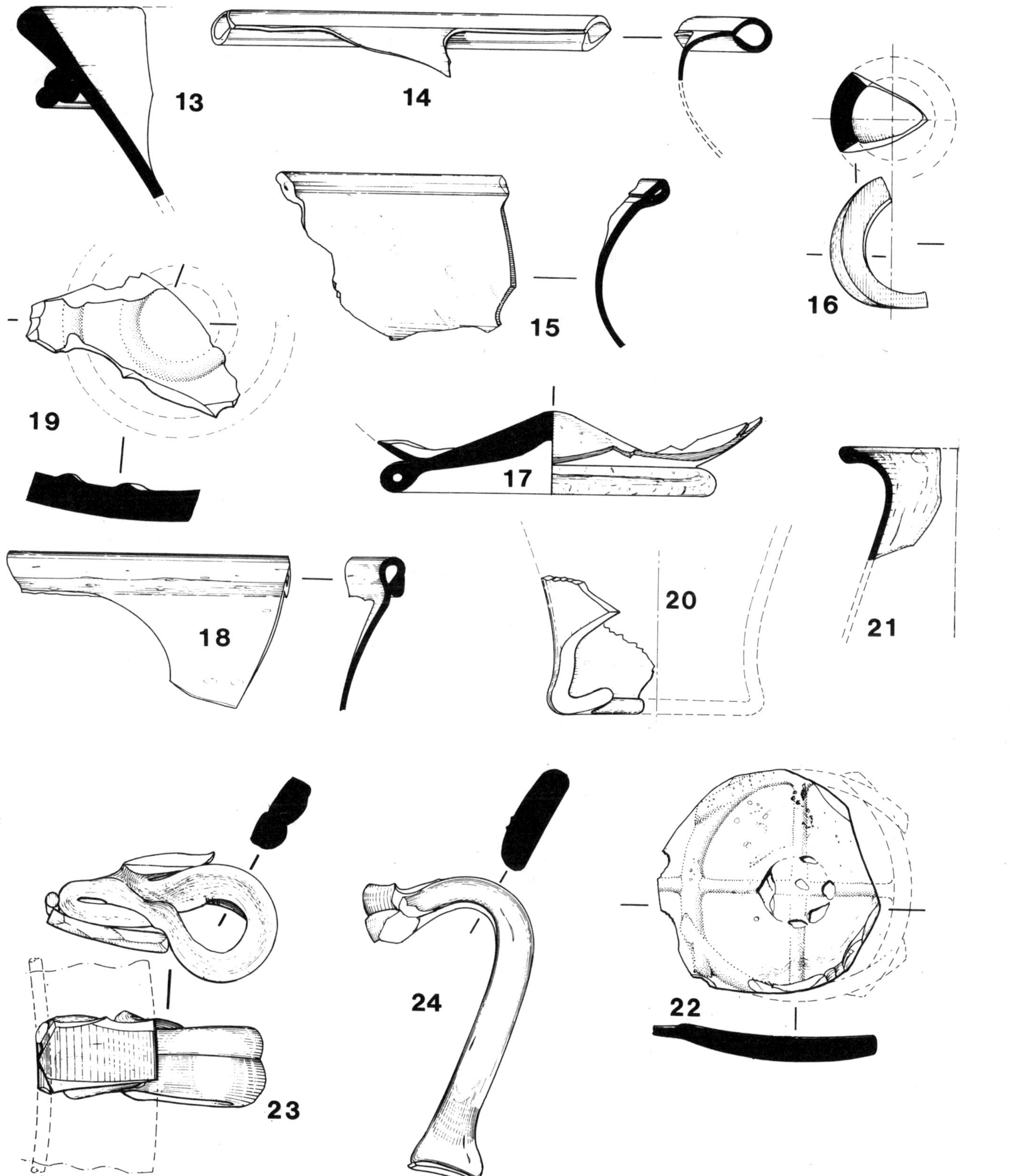

Fig. 15.2. Roman vessel glass, Nos. 13-24 ($\frac{1}{1}$).

C. *Natural green glass*

14. (267). Fragments of a jar rim, folded outwards.
15. (271). Similar rim, but folded inwards.
16. (287). Part of the base of a small unguent flask. Isings form 26. !st–early 2nd century.
17. (289). Complete base with a ring and concave centre with a pontil mark. 2nd–3rd century, from a beaker or flask.
18. (300). Fragment of a hollow tubular rim of a bowl with part of a straight side. Late 1st–2nd century.
    A ribbed example of a similar bowl is published in *Chichester 3*, p. 267, No. 14.
19. (294). Fragment of a square bottle base with two concentric circles. Other examples are in *Chichester 2*, p. 134 and *Chichester 3*, p. 267, 5 and 6.
20. (276). Base and part of side of tall vessel, beaker or flask. 2nd–3rd century.
21. (280). Outsplayed rim, rounded at the tip, from a flask. 1st–3rd century.
22. (297). Broken base, apparently trimmed for re-use, faint moulded marks.
23. (296). Upper sticking part of a handle with a decorative loop, from a flagon. For possible type of vessel see *Masterpieces*, 109, 119, 123.
24. (268). Flat strap handle in greenish glass with elongated bubbles, from a single or two handled flask. 2nd–3rd century.

Fig. 15.3

THE OBJECTS

D. *Bangle*

25. (301). Fragment of natural green glass plano-convex section with a twisted white and blue trail along the outer surface *Kilbride-Jones* (1938), type 2.
    Glass bangles are common finds on 1st- and 2nd-century sites in northern Britain, but seldom recorded in the south. Two important fragments of this type from dated contexts at Fishbourne (*Harden* and *Price*, 1971, 366–7), *c.* A.D. 50/5–75, and Valkenburg (*Van Lith*, 1977), A.D. 47-69 show that they are manufactured earlier than was formerly supposed, but the fragment in the sewer at Church Street, York (*MacGregor*, 1976) cannot have been lost earlier than the Trajanic period. There are two other fragments from York, Bishophill and Skeldergate (*MacGregor*, 1978). The most recent discussion of glass bangles is by R. B. K. Stevenson in *Glasgow Archaeological Journal 4* (1976), 45–54.

E. *Beads*

26. (281). Annular bead, pinkish-colourless with unevenly distributed opaque yellow round the perforation, Guido class 5. This bead has a limited distribution and is found mainly in Iron—Age contexts, but is recorded in possibly early Roman contexts at Maumbury Rings and Non'Nour. (*Guido*, 1978, 51–2;)
27. (272). 28. (290); 29. (303). Melon-shaped beads in turquoise frit.
30. (270). Drawn bead more-or-less square section, blue glass, *Guido*, 1978, 96.
31. (274). Poor quality opaque blue, twisted segmented bead, *Guido*, 1978, 91–3.
32. (283). Annular blue bead, *Guido*, 1978, 67–8.
33. (298). Small globular green bead, *Guido*, 1978, 70.
34. (299). Globular blue bead, *Guido*, 1978, 70.
35. (304). Small globular blue bead, *Guido*, 1978, 70.

F. *Stirring rod*

36. (291). Fragment of twisted blue-green glass rod with part of a stud-shaped top. These are a common find on Roman sites, but this seems to be the first example to be recorded from Chichester. They could be used in the long-necked flasks which are thought to have held unguents and cosmetics.

G. *Gaming counters*

37. (279). Dark glass plano-convex section, brown?
38, 39. (284, 5). Two blue glass plano-convex section.
40. (292). Dark glass, plano-convex section, green? This is larger than average.

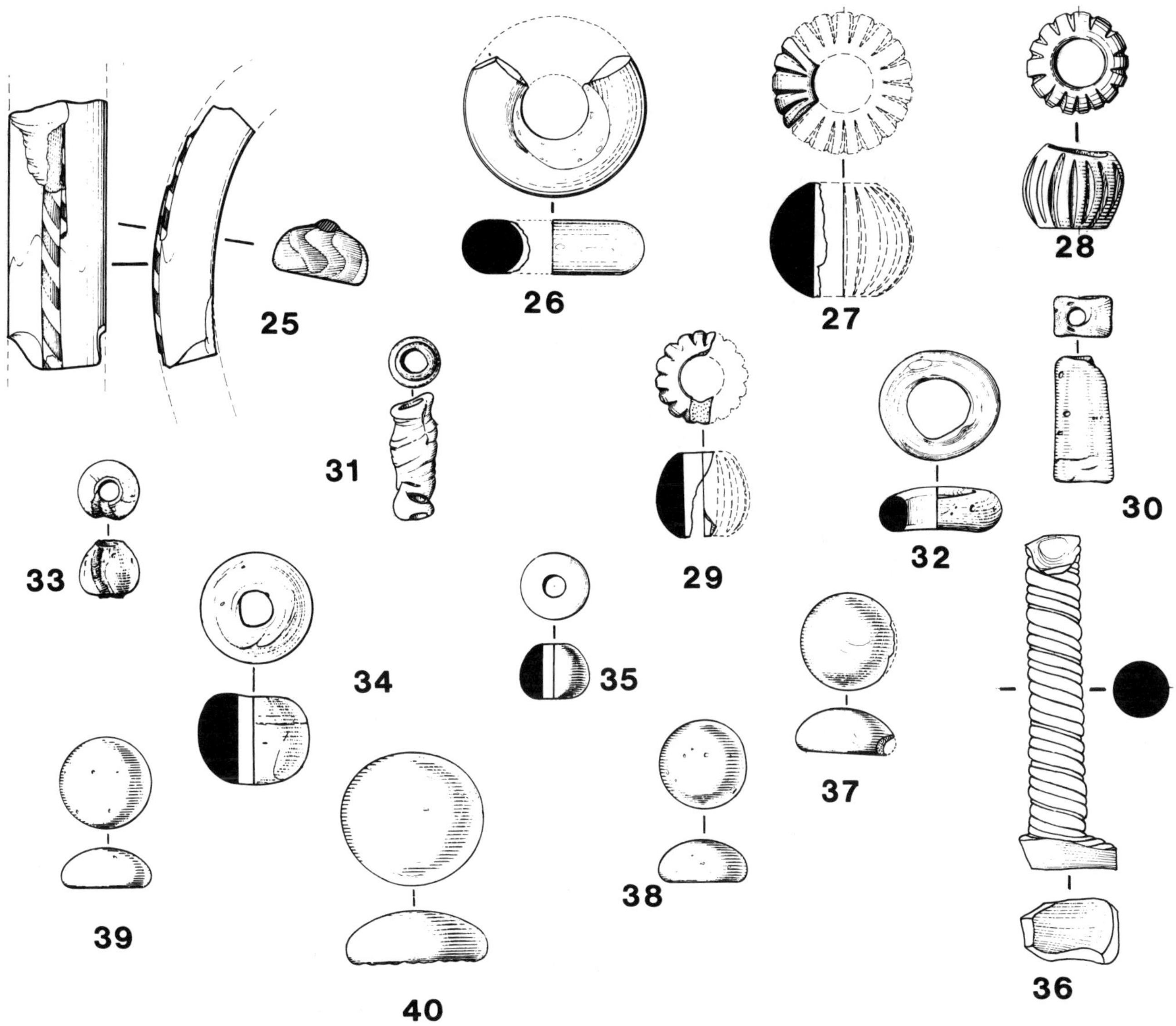

Fig. 15.3. Roman glass objects; Nos. 30, 31, 33 & 35, ($\frac{2}{1}$), Remainder ($\frac{1}{1}$).

CONTEXT

1. *Chapel Street, X130,* 2nd century or later.
2. *Chapel Street, X115,* ? 2nd century.
3. *Chapel Street, X65,* 2nd century or later.
4. *Chapel Street, X115,* pre-Flavian.
5. *Chapel Street, X84,* 2nd century.
6. *Chapel Street, X105,* ? late 1st century.
7. *Chapel Street, X159,* pre-Flavian.
8. *Chapel Street, X148/X167,* pre-Flavian.
9. *Chapel Street, X100,* 2nd century.

10. *Chapel Street, X127*, 2nd century.
11. *Chapel Street, X128*, pre-Flavian.
12. *Chapel Street, Pit X159(B)*, 2nd century or later
13. *Chapel Street, Pit X29(B)*, late Roman.
14. *Chapel Street, X31*, late Roman.
15. *Chapel Street, X65*, 2nd century or later.
16. *Chapel Street, Pit X173*, ? 4th century.
17. *Chapel Street, X174.*
18. *Chapel Street, X43*, 4th century.
19. *Chapel Street, X77*, Antonine or later.
20. *Chapel Street, X148*, 2nd century.
21. *Chapel Street, X151*, late 2nd century.
22. *Chapel Street, X131*, ? late 3rd century.
23. *Chapel Street, Slot X4*, post-Roman robber trench.
24. *Chapel Street, Pit X97*, late or post Roman.
25. *Chapel Street, X105*, ? late 1st century.
26. *Chapel Street, P32*, ? mid 1st century.
27. *Chapel Street, X98*, late 2nd century or later.
28. *Chapel Street, X117*, ? Flavian.
29. *Eastgate, A25*, Antonine.
30. *Chapel Street, Pit X56*, post Roman.
31. *Southgate, Pit G.3*, late Roman.
32. *Chapel Street, X117*, ? Flavian.
33. *Chapel Street X105*, ? late 1st century.
34. *Chapel Street, X110*, 2nd century.
35. *Eastgate, B2.3.*
36. *Chapel Street, Oven 7*, 2nd century or later.
37. *Chapel Street, X155*, pre-Flavian.
38. *Chapel Street, Slot X45*, mid 1st century.
39. *Chapel Street, X106*, 2nd century or later.
40. *Chapel Street, Pit X114*, post Roman.

References

CHARLESWORTH 1959	Charlesworth, D. "Roman glass in Northern Britain", *Archaeologa Aeliana* (4).
CHICHESTER 2	Down, A., *Chichester Excavations 2*, 1974.
CHICHESTER 3	Down A., *Chichester Excavations 3*, 1978.
GUIDO 1978	Guido, M., "Prehistoric and Roman glass beads in Britain and Ireland", *Society of Antiquaries Research Report*, 35, 1978.
HARDEN and PRICE 1971	Harden, D. B. and Price, J., "The Glass", in Cunliffe B., *The Roman Palace at Fishbourne*, 1961-9, Vol. 2, 317-370.
ISINGS 1957	Isings, C., "Roman glass from Dated finds" (*Groningen/Djakarta*).
KILBRIDE-JONES 1938	Kilbridge-Jones, H. E., "Glass Armlets in Britain", *Proc. Soc. Ant. of Scotland*, 82 (1937-8), 366-95.
MASTERPIECES 1968	Harden, D. B., *et al Masterpieces of Glass*, British Museum, 1968.
MacGREGOR 1976	MacGregor, A., "Finds from the Roman Sewer system in Church St.".
MacGREGOR 1978	MacGregor, A., "Roman Finds from Skeldergate and Bishophill".
VAN LITH 1977	Van Lith, S. M. E., "A Romano-British bangle from Valkenburg ZH, Ex Horreo, Albert Egges van Giffen Institute voor Prae-en Protohistoric, Cingula IV 1977. 130-4.

List of Subscribers

Mrs. Ann Adams
Major J. F. Ainsworth
Mr. J. E. Andrews
J. C. Armstone
Ashmolean Library, Oxford
J. G. Ayling
John E. Ayto

Dr. Rodney M. Baguley, B.A., Ph.D., D.Litt., F.S.A.Scot.
Dr. Martin Bell
Alec Barr-Hamilton
Dr. and Mrs. D. G. Bird
Brighton Museum
W. G. Budden
C. G. Busbridge
Dr. N. F. H. Butcher, M.A., F.R.I.C.

Chichester Cathedral Library
Geoffrey Claridge, R.I.B.A.
Elizabeth Clarke
Gillian Clegg
Michael Coker
John L. Cole
John Collis
Miss D. M. Cox
E. A. Crossland, I.S.O.

A. P. Detsicas
J. C. Dove
P. J. Drury

Dr. P. W. Edbury
Mrs. C. Edwards
Mr. J. E. Eschbaecher

Mr. and Mrs. H. R. Fawcett
Fishbourne Roman Palace
Frederick E. Ford, A.R.I.B.A.
Professor S. S. Frere
Dr. M. G. Fulford, F.S.A.

Roger Goodburn
Mr. T. K. Green
F. W. Greenaway
Miss M. L. Grenfell

Dr. Roger C. Hammond
Dorothy Howell-Thomas
Dr. R. F. Hunnisett
Rev. J. Hurd

W. T. Jones, F.S.A.

Mr. M. J. Karn

Mrs. Pat Laing
Mr. and Mrs. A. W. Lane
Kim C. Leslie
Ch. Leva, c/o Cira-I.C.L. 291, av. Brugmann, B1180 Brussels (Belgium)
K. G. Lintott

Mrs. Alison McCann
F. M. Markwick
Ron Maskelyne
Dorothy Mellor
Ralph Merrifield
A. G. Eric Millington
Martin Morris
Julian Munby
Dr. K. M. E. Murray, F.S.A.

National Museum of Wales, Cardiff

J. J. O'Hea

Keith Parfitt, B.A.
Molly K. Pears
Miss J. G. Pilmer
John Piper
Michael W. Pitts
J. E. Pratt

Richard Reece
Reflex 1946
Dr. Warwick Rodwell, F.S.A.
D. R. Rudling

Anne Scicluna
Alan G. Scott
Mr. and Mrs. D. Screen
C. G. Searle
Mr. W. Shannon
James L. Shields
Louis Smith
Maurice J. Smith
Mr. Graham Soffe
Miss K. M. Stanford
S. G. Stow
Michael L. Stuart
Vivien G. Swan, F.S.A.
Mr. M. B. Swatridge

Tim Tatton-Brown
Mr. J. C. H. Templer
H. L. Tewkesbury

Miss W. Underhay

Mollie Vernon
J. S. Wacher
C. M. Walker, Esq.
Dr. Graham Webster
Basil Wedmore
M. G. Welch
P. V. Webster
West London Archaeological Field Group
Ken Whale
John Wildman